THE COOKBOOK THAT BECAME A CLASSIC

This is America's bestselling basic cookbook of all-time—the one indispensable cookbook that includes a complete range of recipes in every category: every-day, classic, foreign, and de luxe. Everything needed for the success of a recipe is clearly explained and illustrated, and recipes within a recipe are cross-referenced at the point of use by volume and/or page number. For example, in this volume a recipe to be found in Volume 2, Page 194 will be cross-referenced as (II, 194).

JOY OF COOKING, now being published in two convenient-to-use volumes, has added over 1,200 new recipes, new menus, and new chapters on ingredients and entertaining to the trusted, well-loved material that has made it first among the basic cook-books for more than a quarter of a century.

JOY OF COOKING

The encyclopedia of cooking know-how

"A masterpiece of clarity."

—*Craig Claiborne*, author, NEW YORK TIMES COOKBOOK

"As essential as the kitchen range."

—*Clementine Paddleford*, THIS WEEK Food Editor

VOLUME I

MAIN COURSE DISHES

IRMA S. ROMBAUER

MARION ROMBAUER BECKER

ILLUSTRATED BY

Ginnie Hoffmann

AND

Beverly Warner

A SIGNET BOOK

SIGNET
Published by the Penguin Group
Penguin Books USA Inc., 375 Hudson Street,
New York, New York 10014, U.S.A.
Penguin Books Ltd, 27 Wrights Lane,
London W8 5TZ, England
Penguin Books Australia Ltd, Ringwood,
Victoria, Australia
Penguin Books Canada Ltd, 2801 John Street,
Markham, Ontario, Canada L3R 1B4
Penguin Books (N.Z.) Ltd, 182–190 Wairau Road,
Auckland 10, New Zealand

Penguin Books Ltd, Registered Offices:
Harmondsworth, Middlesex, England

Published by arrangement with the Bobbs-Merrill Company, Inc.

First Signet Printing, May, 1974
30 29 28 27 26 25 24 23 22

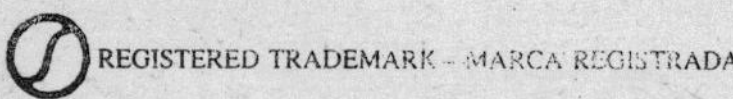

Printed in the United States of America

CONTENTS

DEDICATION

In revising and reorganizing "The Joy of Cooking" we have missed the help of my mother, Irma S. Rombauer. How grateful I am for her buoyant example, for the strong feeling of roots she gave me, for her conviction that, well-grounded, you can make the most of life, no matter what it brings! In an earlier away-from-home kitchen I acted as tester and production manager for the privately printed first edition of "The Joy." Working with Mother on its development has been for my husband, John, and for me the culmination of a very happy personal relationship. John has always contributed verve to this undertaking, but during the past ten years he has, through his constant support and crisp creative editing, become an integral part of the book. We look forward to a time when our two boys—and their wives—will continue to keep "The Joy" a family affair, as well as an enterprise in which the authors owe no obligation to anyone but themselves—and you.

MARION ROMBAUER BECKER

"That which thy fathers have bequeathed to thee,
earn it anew if thou wouldst possess it."

GOETHE: *Faust*

FOREWORD AND GUIDE

"The cook," said Saki, "was a good cook, as cooks go; and as cooks go, she went." Indeed she did go, leaving us, whether in charge of established or of fledgling families, to fend for ourselves. We are confident that after you have used this book steadily for a few months, paying due attention to our symbols ❋, ▲, ( ), ⊗, ⅄, ⊟, ★, and especially to our "pointers to success" ◆—as identified at the end of the Foreword—you will master the skills the cook walked off with. What is more, we believe that you will go on to unexpected triumphs, based on the sound principles which underlie our recipes, and actually revel in a sense of new-found freedom. You will eat at the hour of your choice. The food will be cooked and seasoned to your discriminating taste. And you will regain the priceless private joy of family living, dining and sharing.

For a number of years, manuscript in hand, I have lunched with friends to whom the preparation and presentation of food is a major interest. At these meetings this text, as it grew, came in for lively critical evaluation. I wish you could have been part of the proceedings, as the chefs, food chemists, processors and artists piled in on the problems which arose, searching for the simplest, the most practical and the most comprehensive approaches to this fresh version of "The Joy," and pored over our new illustrations.

The nucleus of this group included Chef James E. Gregory, American-trained and French-finished, with his flair for making food as appetizing to look at as it is delicious, and Chef Pierre Adrian, at whose restaurant we gathered. Pierre grew up in the Vosges, and has a down-to-earth understanding of food as it comes from the land, coupled with a mastery of the *haute cuisine.*

Other "regulars" were Lolita Harper who, as chief home economist for Cincinnati's utility company, has made a career of rescuing frantic housewives from one dilemma after another; and Luella Schierland, a well-traveled, knowledgeable and skilled hostess. Always present through their handiwork, and sometimes in person, were Ginnie Hofmann and Beverly Warner, whose sensitive response to our layouts resulted in the spirited drawings which make our cooking techniques come alive.

What fun we have had talking out and resolving culinary questions—which I brought back for further scrutiny to the staff at home: to Jane Brueggeman who headed it, and whose unerring common sense and devotion have been invaluable; to Dorothy Wartenberg, our consultant for the English edition; and to Odessa Whitehead, who kept the stove warm and the kitchen bright.

As you can guess, we are also indebted to uncounted friends and "fans" of "The Joy," and to any number of technical consultants, both private and governmental, who have given generously of their time, experience and special competence. Of course, any expression of indebtedness does not discharge us from responsibility for the entire contents of the book—a responsibility which rests with Mother and me as its sole authors.

We have assumed that in buying this book you intend to use it daily. For this reason every effort has been made, space permitting, to provide information at the point of use. Whenever emphasis is needed, when an important principle is involved, we have inserted a "pointer." "Pointers" are vital, friendly reminders which guide you through more exacting processes—beating egg whites, heating delicate food over—not in—hot water, the proper temperatures for holding and storage.

There are also the seven other graphic symbols mentioned in the first paragraph. Among these we have retained from the previous edition the parentheses to indicate that an ingredient is optional: its use may enhance, but its omission will not prejudice, the success of a recipe.

You will notice too that we have attached to certain words, phrases and categories special meanings. For example, any meat, fish, or cereal, unless otherwise specified, is *raw*, not cooked. Again, eggs are the 2-ounce size; milk means fresh whole milk; butter means sweet, unsalted butter; chocolate means bitter baking chocolate; flour denotes the all-purpose variety; spices are ground, not whole; condensed canned soup or milk is to be used undiluted. Recipes which have the word "BLENDER" in their title are only successful when an electric blender is used. Many dishes made with cooked, canned and frozen cooked food are grouped in the chapter BRUNCH, LUNCH AND SUPPER DISHES.

Also, for greater clarity, we define culinary terms for which there are no generally accepted meanings: see the Index for "parboil," "simmer," and "casserole." Finally, in response to many requests from users of "The Joy" who ask "What are your favorites?", we have added to some of our recipes the word "Cockaigne," which signified in medieval times "a mythical land of peace and plenty," and also happens to be the name of our country home.

There are two other parts of the book with which we hope you will quickly acquaint yourself: KNOW YOUR INGREDIENTS, and THE FOODS WE HEAT. Both are brand new. INGREDIENTS will tell you in detail about the properties of the materials you commonly combine in cooking, how and why they react as they do and, when feasible, how to substitute for them. To us, the chapter on HEAT is one of the most important. When you become familiar with its contents you will understand why we assign a high priority to it. And do read the ABOUTS for special information.

We have tried to correlate the entire text so that you can readily find your way around in it. But, as in the past, we have kept in mind the tremendous importance of a detailed Index. Not the least of its virtues is the stimulus it gives to the cook's aspiring eye.

New, too, in this edition is a far more conscious emphasis on interpreting the classic cuisine—those dishes whose circulation is worldwide, and whose traditional language, like that of love and diplomacy, is French. We propose clearing up once and for all the distinctions between terms like *printanière*, *bonne femme*, *bordelaise*, *allemande*, and *polonaise*, while giving at the same time authentic descriptions of such national culinary enthusiasms as *couscous*, Devonshire cream, *strudel*, *zabaglione* and *rijsttafel*. Actually, the experienced cook will recognize many of these exotics as intimates whom she has known for years in her own kitchen under other names.

Ever since the last revision, a decade ago, we have been refashioning "The Joy" into a handbook which will more faithfully and flexibly meet your needs. How do we know these needs? From the hundreds and hundreds of heart-warming letters which have set out in detail your own experiences with our book, and reflected new tastes and trends in American living. Many of your messages reflected not only the revolution in transport which has made available distant and previously unobtainable foods, but showed a reawakened interest in the cookery of far-off lands.

Most important to us are all of you, both at home and abroad, who are preoccupied every day with that old yet ever-new question, "What shall we have for dinner?" This revision, we hope, is the inclusive and effective answer.

WATCH FOR THESE SYMBOLS

 POINTERS TO SUCCESS

 FROZEN FOODS

 OPTIONAL

 PRESSURE COOKING

 BLENDER

 OUTDOOR COOKING

 CHRISTMAS

 ALTITUDE COOKING

THE FOODS WE EAT

We enjoy the cynical story of the old-fashioned doctor who insisted first on going straight to the kitchen of the afflicted household. Not until he had effusively thanked the cook for giving him a new patient did he dash upstairs to see how he could relieve the cook's victim. The fact is that everyone who runs a kitchen can, in the choice and preparation of food, decisively influence family health and happiness.

Nutrition is concerned not with food as such but with the substances that food contains. To present these essential nutrients in the very best state for the body's absorption is the cook's first and foremost job. Usually taste, flavor and color, at their best, reflect a job well done. Read The Foods We Heat, and follow our pointers ⧫ for effective ways to preserve nutrients during cooking.

To live we must eat. To live in health we must eat intelligently. By whose intelligence? How directed? The intuitions and impulses of the present generation seem, alas, not to be the kind that led our forebears to search for greens each spring. The sensational press releases which follow the discovery of fascinating fresh bits and pieces about human nutrition confuse the layman. And the oversimplified and frequently ill-founded dicta of food faddists can lure us into downright harm.

On the positive, scientific side we may turn to the helpful information contained in the United States Handbook on the Composition of Foods. For further guidance we print later in this book the daily allowances recommended by the Food and Nutrition Board of the National Research Council as well as calorie values based on the edible portion of common foods. All three are extremely helpful in alerting us to the source-material of a sound dietary. But no one chart or group of charts is the definitive answer for most of us, who are simply not equipped to evaluate the complex relationships of these elements, or to adapt them to the practicalities of daily living. Such studies are built up as averages, and thus have greater value in presenting an overall picture than in solving the nutrition problem of the individual.

Nevertheless, by applying plain common sense to available mass data, we, as well as the experts, are inclined to agree that most Americans are privileged to enjoy superabundance ⧫ and that our nutritional difficulties have to do generally not with under- but overeating. Statistics on consumption also bear out other trends: first, that we eat too much of certain kinds of food; and, second, that many of of us overconsume drugs as well as foods. Medication, often a lifesaver, may, when used habitually, induce an adverse effect on the body's ability to profit fully from even the best dietary intake.

We must consider, too, that while great strides have been made in the keeping of foods (II, 527), many of today's additives and preserving processes have a devitalizing effect on them. ➧ If fresh foods are available, and in their prime, start with fresh foods every time. For the relative nutritive values in frozen, canned and dried vegetables, see page 251.

ABOUT CALORIES

With these thoughts in mind, let's review other changing attitudes that underlie today's thinking about nutrition. A too naive theory used to prevail for explaining regeneration through food. The human system was thought of as an engine, and you kept it stoked with foods to produce energy. Food can be and still is measured in units of heat, or calories, a Calorie being the amount of heat needed to raise one kilogram of water one degree Centigrade. Thus translated into food values, each gram of protein—egg, milk, meat, fish—is worth four calories; each gram of carbohydrate—starches and sugars—four calories; and each gram of fat—butters, vegetable oils, drippings, etc.—about nine. The mere stoking of the body's engine with energy-producing foods may keep life going in emergencies. But food, to maintain health, must also have, besides its energy values, the proper proportions of biologic values. Proteins, vitamins, enzymes, hormones, minerals and their regulatory functions are still too complicated to be fully understood. But fortunately for us the body is able to respond to them intuitively and instantly.

What we really possess, then, is not just a simple stoking mechanism, but a computing setup far more elaborate and knowledgeable than anything that man has been able to devise. The body sorts and routes nutrients on their way as soon as they are ingested. Our job is to help it along as much as possible neither stinting it nor overloading it. Depending on age, weight and activity the following is a rough guide to the favorable division of daily caloric intake: about 15% for proteins, under 25% for fats and about 60% for carbohydrates.

ABOUT PROTEINS

A greater and greater emphasis has been placed in recent years on the need for protein at all ages—for proteins contain a great many of the essential elements the body must have to rebuild itself. Proteins are complexly constructed of amino acids, some of which the body can and some of which it cannot manufacture from other substances. So to make food really useful to the body we must include in every meal or snack some of those protein foods that have the non-manufacturable amino acids already built into them. These are present in the most favorable proportions in eggs, milk, meat and fish. They are also present in nuts, seeds, whole grains and legumes. But in such vegetable foods some of the essential aminos are either lacking entirely or are not available in satisfactory proportions. This is why pork is often served with beans, and why pastas are reenforced with cheese, meat or fish—to provide those essential aminos in which the vegetable content of the dish is deficient. Again, complete reliance on grain protein combinations is not nearly as satisfactory as one based on eggs, milk, meat and fish; partly because such large quantities of the grain must be consumed to amass enough proteins whose biologic values approach animal-derived proteins in strength. Climate and age also change protein requirements. The colder the climate the greater the need. ➧ And no matter what the climate, growing children, pregnant women and nursing mothers need a larger proportion of protein than the average adult.

The need in everyone, from birth to death, to establish a kind of "endless chain" of protein intake persists. ➧ Since the vegetable proteins are incomplete, it is wise to draw two-thirds of the daily protein intake from animal sources. Meats should preferably be fresh, not pickled, salted or highly processed. Protein foods should also be very carefully cooked at not too high heat, so that their values are not impaired. Familiar danger signals are curdling in milk, "stringiness" in cheese, dryness in meat and fish.

ABOUT FATS

While fats have fallen into disrepute of late, we must not forget how essential they are. As parts of our body fabric ➧ they act as fuel and insulation against cold, as cushioning for the internal organs, and as lubricants. Without fats there is no way to utilize fat-soluble vitamins. Furthermore the fats we eat which are of vegetable origin contain unsaturated fatty acids which harbor necessary growth factors, and help with the digestion of other fats. For more about the character of fats and their use, see (II, 170).

➧ We suggest, again, the consumption of a variety of fats from animal and vegetable sources; but remind you that the fat consumption of the United States has climbed in twenty years from the recommended minimum of 20 per cent to over 40 per cent today. Check your diet for the percentage you are getting, taking into account that ➧ there are hidden fats in food—as discussed in greater detail on (II, 170).

All fats are sensitive to high temperatures, light and air. For best nutritive values store them carefully; and when cooking with them be sure that you do not let them reach the smoking point. If properly handled they have no adverse effect on normal digestion. Favorable temperatures are indicated in individual recipes. Fats are popular for their flavor, and for the fact that, being slow to leave the stomach, they give a feeling of satiety.

ABOUT CARBOHYDRATES

Vegetables and fruits are included in the carbohydrate category, as well as flour, cereals and sugars. The caloric value of fruits and vegetables is frequently lower than that of cereals; while that of all concentrated sweets is high. It is possible for children and athletes to consume larger amounts of sugars and starches with less harm than more inactive people; but most of us tend to eat a greater amount of carbohydrates than we can handle. Our consumption of sweet and starchy foods, to say nothing of highly sweetened beverages, is frequently excessive. The imbalance that results is acknowledged to be one of the major causes of malnutrition, for the demands excess carbohydrates make on the system may cause a deficiency in its supply of the vitamin B complex.

ABOUT ACCESSORY FACTORS IN FOOD

There are some forty-odd important known minerals, vitamins, enzymes, hormones and other accessory factors which the body needs from the diet. A few it can store; but many must constantly be replaced. These latter, like vitamin C, often occur in those fragile food constituents that are lost through indifferent handling, excessive processing, and poor cooking. To retain as many of them as possible please follow the cooking suggestions given in the chapters on vegetables, meats, fish, eggs and cereals.

While we have printed below the average daily caloric needs, and we have discussed their approximate distribution, we have still to assure ourselves a practical way of including optimal amounts of accessory factors. If you check prime sources of minerals and vitamins you will find that foods rich in one vitamin or mineral may also be rich in others. It happens too that some foods heavily weighted with biologic values yield the best quality proteins. Many of the foods rich in accessory values also have bulk, a factor to be considered in planning the daily intake so as to include more high- than low-residue foods. A few accessory factors the body can store—such as the fat soluble vitamins A, D, E and K. Some, like the water-soluble C and B-complex, must be replenished constantly.

Here is a shopping guide for accessory factors. ➧ Fill your market basket so that it holds a minimum of 2 fruits and 3 vegetables daily. Concentrate on salad materials, especially the lively green ones, and on green and yellow vegetables. Cultivate the cabbage family, root vegetables, potatoes and especially sweet potatoes, tomatoes, peppers and avocados. Include in the fruits apricots, peaches and melons, as well as plenty of citrus types. Be on your guard in distinguishing genuine fruit juices from the so-called "juice drinks," for many of the latter are higher in carbohydrate values than anything else, and their C-vitamin values are frequently low. Prime choices in the protein budget are milk, cheese and eggs, fish and fish roe, organ meats such as liver, kidneys, heart and brains, lean-muscle cuts of beef, pork and lamb, dried peas and beans, especially soybeans and peanuts. See triple-rich Cornell Flour Formula (II, 243). Include also 1 tablespoon daily of butter or fortified fat or oil, and 1 pint of milk or equivalent milk products. Bake with whole grains and flavor with brown sugar, molasses, wheat germ and butter. Don't forget the cheapest of all accessory factors, outdoor exercise, to whet your appetite, tone your muscles and get you out where you absorb the sunlight vitamin D.

Other incidentals to bear in mind are to drink seven or eight glasses of fluid a day, see About Water (II, 147), and to use iodized salt, see About Salt (II, 195), if you live in a region that calls for it.

The schedule outlined above is not necessarily a costly one. It is nearly always possible to substitute cheaper but equally nutritious items from the same food groups. Vegetables of similar accessory value, for example, may be differently priced. Seasonal foods, which automatically give us menu variations, are usually higher in food value and lower in cost. Whole-grain cereals are no more costly than highly processed ones. Fresh fruits are frequently less expensive than canned fruits loaded with sugar.

If you are willing to cut down on refined starch and sugar items, especially fancy baked goods, bottled drinks and candies, a higher percentage of the diet dollar will be released for dairy products, vegetables and fruits. Do not buy more perishable foods than you can properly store. Use leftovers cold, preferably. To reheat them with minimal loss, see page 98.

Summing up, our fundamental effort always must be to provide this highly versatile body of ours with those elements it needs for efficient functioning, and to provide them in such proportions as to subject it to the least possible strain.

Well-grown minimally processed foods are usually our best sources for complete nourishment; and a well-considered choice of them should in most cases meet our needs without the use of synthetic vitamin preparations.

You will find in this book, along with the classic recipes, a number which remain interesting and palatable although they lack some usual ingredient, like eggs, flour or fat, and which may be used by those who may be allergic. But we do not prescribe corrective diets, feeling that such situations demand special procedures in consultation with one's physician. As to the all-too-prevalent condition of overweight, it is now generally recognized that the on and off use of crash reducing diets is dangerous, and that re-education in moderate eating habits is the only safe and permanent solution to this problem.

We stress again that the housewife who has the responsibility for supplying her family with food will do well to keep alert to advances in the field of nutrition and to the individual needs of herself and her family.

CALORIE VALUES

"Personal size and mental sorrow have certainly no necessary proportions. A large, bulky figure has as good a right to be in deep affliction as the most graceful set of limbs in the world. But, fair or not fair, there are unbecoming conjunctions, which reason will patronize in vain—which taste cannot tolerate—which ridicule will seize." —Jane Austen.

The following calorie list is given hopefully to offset those "unbecoming conjunctions." We have tried, from data furnished by the U.S. Department of Agriculture and other authoritative sources, to give you as accurate a calorie count as possible for an average individual serving of food as it comes to you at table. In each instance, the number of calories is based on the total edible portion. These are not diet portions. Smaller servings of the foods mentioned will mean a proportionate reduction in their calorie count. Our soup figures are for canned soups diluted with the same amount of water—or whole milk, in the case of cream soups—unless we specify them as home-made. A cup is the standard 8 oz. measure, and a tablespoon or teaspoon is always a level one. Since we do not expect you to weigh your food at table, this chart should give you a fairly accurate guide for normal servings to a healthy adult. Remember, however, that two martinis before dinner count as much as a generous slice of pie for dessert and, if you are trying to keep your weight constant, second thoughts are better than second helpings. In addition,

"Let your contours be your guide."

Food	Calories
Almonds, 12 to 14 shelled	100
Apple, 1 medium-sized, baked with 2 tablespoons sugar	200
Apple, 1 large fresh, 3" diam.	117
Apple butter, 1 tablespoon	37
Apple dumpling, 1 medium-sized	235
Apple juice, 1 cup	126
Apple pie, ⅙ of 9" pie	377
Applesauce, sweetened, ½ cup	92
Applesauce, unsweetened, ½ cup	50
Apricots, canned, sweetened, 4 halves, 2 tablespoons juice	80
Apricots, dried, stewed, sweetened, 4 halves, 2 tablespoons juice	123
Apricots, 3 whole fresh	60
Artichoke, globe, 1 large, cooked	51
Artichoke, Jerusalem, 4 small	70
Asparagus, 8 stalks	25
Asparagus soup, cream of, 1 cup	160
Avocado, ½ medium-sized	275
Bacon, 1 crisp 6" strip	48
Banana, 1 medium-sized	130
Banana cream pie, ⅙ of 9" pie	300
Batter cakes, 2	150
Beans, baked, canned, ½ cup	162
Beans, green or snap, ½ cup cooked	13
Beans, kidney, ½ cup cooked	115
Beans, Lima, ½ cup cooked or canned	80
Beans, navy pea, ½ cup cooked	118
Bean soup, 1 cup, homemade	260
Bean sprouts, Mung, ½ cup cooked	13

Food	Calories
Bean sprouts, ½ cup raw	10
Beef, corned, 3 oz., 3 slices 3" x 2½" x ¼"	216
Beef, corned, hash, ½ cup	145
Beef, dried, 2 thin slices 4" x 5"	61
Beef, 1 filet mignon, 4 oz.	400
Beef, hamburger, 1 large patty	300
Beef heart, 3 oz.	118
Beef loaf, 1 slice 2½" x 2¼" x ⅝"	115
Beef, rib roast, 3" x 2½" x ¼" slice	96
Beef soup, 1 cup	113
Beefsteak, sirloin, 3 oz.	300
Beef stew, 1 cup	260
Beef tongue, 3 slices, 3" x 2" x ⅛"	160
Beer, 12 oz. can or bottle	173
Beer, 1 glass, 8 oz.	115
Beet greens, ½ cup cooked	30
Beets, ½ cup	40
Berry pies, ⅙ of 9" pie, average	365
Biscuit, baking powder, 2½" diam.	130
Blackberries, fresh, ¾ cup	62
Blueberries, fresh, ¾ cup	64
Bologna sausage, 1 slice, 4½" diam. x ⅛"	66
Bouillon, 1 cup	32
Bouillon cube, 1	2
Brazil nut, 1 shelled	50
Bread, commercial, rye, 1 slice, ½" thick	55
Bread, commercial, white, 1 slice, ½" thick	60–65
Bread, commercial, whole wheat, 1 slice, ½" thick	55
Bread, gluten, 1 slice, 4" x 4" x ⅜"	64
Bread pudding, ½ cup	200
Broccoli, 1 large stalk or ⅔ cup, cooked	29
Brown Betty, ½ cup	254
Brussels sprouts, ½ cup, approx. 5	30
Butter, 1 square, ¼" thick	50
Butter, 1 tablespoon	100
Buttermilk, 1 glass, 8 oz.	85

Food	Calories
Cabbage, ½ cup chopped, raw	10
Cabbage, ½ cup, cooked	20
Cake, angel, plain, 3″ slice	150
Cake, cheese, 2″ wedge	250
Cake, chocolate layer, 2″ square	356
Cake, coffee, 1 piece 3″ x 2½″ x 2″	133
Cake, cup, 1 medium-sized, frosted	229
Cake, fruit, dark, 1 small slice ½″ thick	142
Cake, sponge, 2″ slice	145
Cantaloupe, ½ of a 4½″ melon	30
Caramels, 1 medium	42
Carbonated water	0
Carrots, ½ cup cooked	30
Carrot, 1 whole raw, small	20
Cashew nuts, 6 to 8	88
Catsup, 1 tablespoon	17
Cauliflower, cooked, 1 cup	30
Caviar, granular sturgeon, 1 tablespoon	66
Celeriac, 1 medium-sized	40
Celery, raw, 3 small inner stalks	9
Charlotte Russe, 1 serving	265
Cheese, American, 1″ cube	79
Cheese, Camembert, 2″ wedge	220
Cheese, cottage, ½ cup	100
Cheese, cream, ½ 3 oz. cake	159
Cheese, Edam, 1″ cube	51
Cheese, Liederkranz, 1 oz.	85
Cheese, Parmesan, 1 tablespoon, grated	20
Cheese, Roquefort, 1″ cube	39
Cheese, Swiss, 1 oz.	105
Cheese soufflé, 1 cup	238
Cheese straws, 3	100
Chef salad without dressing, ¾ cup	90
Cherries, canned, sweetened, ½ cup	100
Cherries, fresh, sweet, 15 large	61
Chicken, broiler, ½ medium	125
Chicken, canned, ½ cup boned meat	200
Chicken, fried, ½ breast	232
Chicken, fried, drumstick	64
Chicken livers, 1 medium-large liver	74
Chicken pie, 1 individual pie 3¾″ diameter	460
Chicken, roasted,	
Chicken, roasted, 4″ x 4″ x ¾″ slice, dark meat	170
Chicken, roasted, 4″ x 4″ x ¾″ slice, light meat	166
Chicken salad, ½ cup	200
Chicory, or Curly Endive, 15 to 20 inner leaves	10
Chocolate, 1 cup made with milk	277
Chocolate bar, milk, 1 oz.	154
Chocolate creams, 1 small	51
Chocolate éclair, custard filling, 1 average-size	316
Chocolate fudge, 1″ square	100
Chocolate ice cream, ½ cup	180
Chocolate malted milk, made with 8 oz. milk	502
Chocolate milk shake, made with 8 oz. milk	421
Chocolate soda	255
Cinnamon bun, 1 average	200
Clam chowder, Manhattan, 1 cup	87
Cocoa, made with milk and water, 1 cup	150
Cocoa, made with whole milk, 1 cup	232
Coconut, shredded, dried, 2 tablespoons	83
Coconut custard pie, ⅙ of 9″ pie	311
Codfish, creamed, ½ cup	200
Codfish balls, 2 of 2″ diameter	200
Cod liver oil, 1 tablespoon	100
Coffee, clear, 1 cup	0
Coffee, with 1 tablespoon cream, 1 cup	30
Coffee with 1 lump sugar, 1 cup	27
Cola beverages, 1 glass, 8 oz.	105
Consommé, canned, 1 cup	35
Cookies, sugar, 1 3″ diameter	64

Food	Calories
Corn bread, 1 square 2" x 2" x 1"	139
Corn, canned, ½ cup drained solids	70
Corn flakes, ¾ cup	62
Corn meal, cooked, ⅔ cup	80
Corn on cob, 1 medium	92
Corn sirup, 1 tablespoon	57
Corn soup, cream, ½ cup	100
Cornstarch blancmange, ½ cup	152
Crab meat, canned, ½ cup	91
Crab meat fresh, ½ cup	54
Cracker, graham, 1 2½" square	14
Crackers, oyster, 12 1"	50
Cracker, saltine, 1 2" square	17
Cracker, soda, 1 #2 ½" square	24
Cracker, butter, 1	16
Cranberry jelly, 2 tablespoons	47
Cream, coffee, 18.5% fat, 2 tablespoons	60
Cream, cultured, sour, 1 tablespoon	45
Cream soups, canned	250
Cream, whipping, 36%–40% fat, 2 tablespoons	98
Cream of wheat, cooked ¾ cup	100
Cream sauce, white, ¼ cup	180
Cucumber, 12 slices	10
Custard, ½ cup	164
Custard pie, ⅙ of 9" pie	266
Daiquiri cocktail, 3 oz.	130
Dates, 3 or 4	85
Divinity, 1½" cube	102
Doughnut, cake type, plain, 1	135
Doughnut, sugared, 1	151
Doughnut, yeast, plain, 1	121
Duck, roast, 1 medium piece	300
Dumpling, 1 small	100
Egg, 1 fried with 1 teaspoon butter	105
Egg, 1 scrambled with 2 tablespoons milk and 1 teaspoon butter	130
Egg, 1 whole, boiled or poached	75
Eggnog, ½ cup	196
Eggplant, 2 slices ½" thick, breaded and fried	210
Egg yolk, 1 raw	61
Farina, ¾ cup cooked	100
Fig, 1 large dried	55
Figs, 3 small fresh	79
Flounder, baked, average serving	204
Frankfurters, 1	125
French dressing, commercial, 1 tablespoon	59
French dressing, homemade, no sugar, 1 tablespoon	86
French toast, 1 piece	170
Frog legs, 2 large, fried	140
Fruit cocktail, fresh, ½ cup	50
Fruit cocktail, canned, drained, ½ cup	50
Fruit cocktail, fresh, with 1 tablespoon dressing	150
Gelatin, dry, 1 tablespoon	34
Gelatin dessert, ½ cup	103
Gin, 1 oz.	70
Ginger ale, 1 cup	80
Gingerbread, 1 2" square	200
Ginger snap, 1	20
Goose, roast, 3½ oz. serving	354
Gooseberries, cooked, sweetened, ½ cup	100
Grapefruit, ½ medium	70
Grapefruit juice, unsweetened, 1 cup	92
Grape juice, 1 glass, 8 oz.	178
Grapes, green seedless, 60	66
Grapes, Malaga or Tokay, 22	66
Gravy, thick, 3 tablespoons	180
Green pepper, 1 whole	20
Griddle cakes, 2 of 4" diam.	150
Grits, hominy, cooked, ¾ cup	90
Guavas, 1 medium	70
Gum drop, 1 large	35

Food	Calories
Haddock, 1 fillet 3″ x 3″ x ½″, fried	214
Halibut steak, 3″ x ½″ x 1″, sautéed	125
Ham, baked, medium fat, 4¼″ x 4″ x ½″ slice	400
Ham, boiled, 4¼″ x 4″ x ¼″ slice	200
Hamburger—see Beef	
Hard Sauce, 1 tablespoon	50
Herring, fresh, 3 oz.	128
Herring, pickled Bismarck, 3½″ x 1½″ x 1¼″	218
Herring, smoked, 3 oz.	200
Hickory nuts, about 12	100
Hollandaise sauce, 1 tablespoon	65
Honey, 1 tablespoon	62
Honeydew melon, ¼ medium-sized	32
Horseradish, grated, 1 tablespoon	12
Ice cream, commercial, plain, ½ cup	100–150
Jam or jelly, 1 tablespoon	60
Kale, 1 cup, cooked	50
Kidneys, beef, braised, 3 ½ oz.	159
Kohlrabi, ½ cup, cooked	23
Kumquats, 3	35
Lady fingers, 1	37
Lamb, roast leg, 2 slices 3″ x 3¼″ x ⅛″	206
Lamb chop, broiled, 1 ¾″ thick	175
Lamb stew with vegetables, 1 cup	250
Lard, 1 tablespoon	126
Leek, 1	10
Lemon, 1 medium-sized	30
Lemonade, 1 cup	100
Lemon gelatin, ½ cup	100
Lemon ice, ½ cup	116
Lemon juice, 1 tablespoon	4
Lemon meringue pie, ⅙ of 9″ pie	280
Lentil soup, 1 cup, home-made	606

Food	Calories
Lettuce, iceberg, ¼ large head	18
Lettuce, 6 large leaves	18
Lime juice, 1 tablespoon	4
Liver, beef, fried, 2 slices 3″ x 2¼″ x ⅜″	175
Liver, calf, fried, 2 slices 3″ x 2¼″ x ⅜″	147
Liverwurst or liver sausage, 2 slices 3″ diam. x ¼″	160
Lobster, canned, 1 cup	108
Lobster, fresh, 1 cup	105
Lobster, whole, small, baked or broiled with 2 tablespoons butter	308
Loganberries, canned, ½ cup	55
Macaroni, cooked, plain, ½ cup	110
Macaroni and cheese, ½ cup	300
Mackerel, broiled, 3 oz.	200
Malted milk, 8 oz.	270
Mangoes, tropical, 1 large	85
Manhattan cocktail, 3 oz.	160
Maple sirup, 1 tablespoon	50
Margarine, 1 tablespoon	100
Marmalade, 2 tablespoons	120
Marshmallows, 5	125
Martini cocktail, 3 oz. 3:1	145
Mayonnaise, 1 tablespoon	109
Meat loaf, beef and pork, 1 slice 4″ x 3″ x ⅜″	264
Melba toast, 1 slice 4″ x 4″	39
Milk, condensed, sweetened, ½ cup	490
Milk, evaporated, ½ cup	173
Milk, half and half, ½ cup	165
Milk, powdered, skim, 1 tablespoon	28
Milk, powdered, whole, 1 tablespoon	40
Milk, skimmed, 1 cup	88
Milk, whole fresh, 1 cup	166
Mincemeat pie, ⅙ of 9″ pie	398
Mints, chocolate cream, 3 small	100
Molasses, 1 tablespoon	55
Muffin, 2″ diameter	120
Muffin, English, 1 large	280
Mushrooms, canned, ½ cup	14
Mushrooms, fresh, 10 small	16

Food	Calories
Mushrooms, sautéed, 7 small	78
Mustard greens, cooked, 1 cup	60
Mutton—see Lamb	
Nectarine, 1	40
Noodles, egg, cooked, ½ cup	100
Oatmeal, cooked, ½ cup	75
Okra, 10 pods	38
Old-fashioned cocktail, 1 glass	185
Olive oil, 1 tablespoon	124
Olives, green, 2 small or 1 large	20
Olives, ripe, 2 small or 1 large	25
Onion soup, 1 cup	100
Onions, 4 small	100
Onions, creamed, ⅓ cup	100
Onions, raw green, 5 medium	23
Orange, 1 average-sized	75
Orange ice, ½ cup	110
Orange juice, 1 cup	110
Oxtail soup, 1 cup	100
Oysters, raw, 6 medium	75
Oyster stew, with milk, 1 cup	275
Pancake, 1 4″ dia.	75
Papaya, ½ medium	72
Parsley, chopped, 2 tablespoons	2
Parsnips, cooked, ½ cup	65
Peaches, canned, 2 halves with 2 tablespoons juice	85
Peach, fresh, 1 large	50
Peanut butter, 2 tablespoons	180
Peanuts, 20 to 24 nuts	100
Pears, canned, 2 halves with 2 tablespoons juice	85
Pear, fresh, 1 medium-sized	60
Peas, canned, ½ cup	73
Peas, dried, cooked, ½ cup	103
Peas, fresh, cooked, ½ cup	56
Pea soup, cream, 1 cup	270
Pecans, 6 halves or 2 tablespoons chopped	52

Food	Calories
Pepper, green, 1 medium-sized	25
Perch, breaded and fried, 3 oz.	195
Persimmons, 1 medium-sized	78
Pickles, cucumber, 1 large dill	15
Pickles, cucumber, 1 sweet-sour	20
Pigs' feet, pickled, ½ foot	125
Pineapple, canned, 1 slice with juice	78
Pineapple, fresh, ½ cup sliced	52
Pineapple ice, ½ cup	120
Pineapple juice, 1 cup	120
Plums, fresh, 3 or 4	100
Plums, canned, 3 or 4 with juice	150
Pimiento, canned, 1 medium	10
Popcorn, 1½ cups, no butter	100
Popover, 1	100
Pork chop, rib, broiled, 3″ x 5″ x 1″	290
Pork roast, 4 oz.	450
Pork tenderloin, 2 oz.	200
Potato, baked, 1 medium-sized	90
Potato, boiled, 1 medium-sized	90
Potato chips, 8 to 10 large	100
Potato salad, ½ cup	167
Potato, sweet, baked, 1 medium-sized	155
Potatoes, French-fried, 10 pieces	155
Potatoes, mashed, 1 cup, milk and butter added	230
Praline, 1	300
Preserves, 1 tablespoon	75
Pretzels, 5 small sticks	20
Prune juice, 1 cup	170
Prunes, dried, 1 large	25
Prunes, stewed, 4 medium with 2 tablespoons juice	120
Pumpkin, 1 cup	76
Pumpkin pie, ⅙ of 9″ pie	300
Rabbit, baked, 3½ oz.	177
Radishes, 5 medium	10

Food	Calories
Raisins, seedless, ¼ cup	107
Raspberries, red, fresh, ½ cup	42
Raspberries, red, frozen, sweetened, ½ cup	120
Red snapper, baked, 3″ x ½″ x 4″	183
Rhubarb, fresh, 1 cup diced	20
Rhubarb, stewed, sweetened, ½ cup	137
Rice, brown, cooked, ½ cup	100
Rice, white, cooked, ½ cup	100
Rice, wild, cooked, ⅔ cup	103
Roll, hard, white, 1 average-sized	95
Roll, Parker House, 1	81
Rum, 1 oz.	73
Rutabagas, cooked, ½ cup	25
Salmon, canned, ½ cup	206
Salmon, fresh, poached, 3½ oz.	200
Sardines, canned, 4 large	100
Sauerkraut, ⅔ cup	27
Sauerkraut juice, ½ cup	4
Sausage, pork link, 3″ x ½″	94
Scallops, fried, 5 to 6 medium-sized pieces	427
Shad roe, sautéed, average serving	175
Sherbets, ½ cup	135
Sherry, dry, 3 oz.	110
Sherry, sweet, 3 oz.	150
Shortcake with ½ cup berries and cream, 1 medium-sized biscuit	350
Shredded wheat biscuit, 1 large	100
Shrimp, boiled, 5 large	70
Shrimp, fried, 4 large	259
Shrimp cocktail with sauce, ½ cup	100
Sirup, corn, 1 tablespoon	57
Smelts, baked or broiled, 4 or 5 medium-sized	91
Smelts, fried, 4 to 5 medium-sized	448
Snow pudding, ⅔ cup	114
Sole, Dover, fried, 3½ oz.	241

Food	Calories
Sole, Dover, steamed, 3½ oz.	84
Sole, fillet—see Flounder	
Soybeans, dried, cooked, ½ cup	120
Spaghetti, plain, cooked, 1 cup	218
Spareribs, meat from 6 average-sized ribs	246
Spinach, cooked and chopped, ½ cup	23
Spinach soup, cream, 1 cup	240
Split pea soup, 1 cup	268
Squab, 1 whole, unstuffed, 2½ oz. meat	149
Squash, Hubbard or winter, cooked, ½ cup	50
Squash, summer, cooked, ½ cup	19
Starch, cornstarch, etc., 1 tablespoon	29
Strawberries, fresh, ½ cup	30
Strawberries, frozen, sweetened, ½ cup	120
Strawberry shortcake with cream, average serving	350
Succotash, canned, ½ cup	85
Sugar, brown, 1 tablespoon	50
Sugar, confectioners', 1 tablespoon	42
Sugar, granulated, 1 tablespoon	50
Sweetbreads, broiled, ½ pair medium	185
Swordfish, average serving	180
Tangerine, 1	35
Tangerine juice, ½ cup	50
Tapioca pudding, ½ cup	133
Tartar sauce, 1 tablespoon	100
Tea, clear, unsweetened, 1 cup	0
Tomatoes, canned, 1 cup	50
Tomato catsup, 1 tablespoon	17
Tomato, fresh, 1 medium-sized	25
Tomato juice, 1 cup	50
Tomato purée, 1 tablespoon	6
Tomato soup, clear, 1 cup	100

Food	Calories
Tomato soup, cream, home-made, 1 cup	250
Tripe, cooked in milk, average serving	150
Trout, brook, broiled, 3 oz.	216
Trout, lake, broiled, 3 oz.	290
Tuna fish, canned, water packed, ½ cup	165
Tuna fish, canned in oil, ½ cup	300
Turkey, roast, dark meat, 4″ x 4″ x ¾″	205
Turkey, roast, light meat, 4″ x 4″ x ¾″	183
Turnip greens, cooked, 1 cup	45
Turnips, cooked, 1 cup	40
Veal chop, loin, fried, 1 medium-sized	186
Veal cutlet, breaded, average serving	217
Veal roast, 2 slices 3″ x 2″ x ⅛″	186
Veal stew, 1 cup	242
Vegetable cooking fats, 1 tablespoon	110
Vegetable juice, 1 cup	48
Vegetable soup, 1 cup	100

Food	Calories
Venison, baked, 3 slices 3½″ x 2½″ x ¼″	200
Waffles, 1, 5½″ diameter	232
Waldorf salad, average serving	137
Walnuts, English, 4 to 8 halves	50
Water cress, 1 bunch	20
Watermelon, 1 slice, ¾″ thick, 6″ diameter	90
Welsh rarebit, 4 tablespoons on 1 slice toast	200
Whisky, bourbon, 1 oz.	83
Whisky, Scotch, 1 oz.	73
Whitefish, average serving	100
White sauce, ¼ cup	106
Wines, dry, 3 oz.	65–95
Wines, sweet or fortified, 3 oz.	120–160
Yams—see Potatoes, sweet	
Yeast, brewers, 2 teaspoons	18
Yeast, compressed, 1 cake	10
Yogurt, whole milk, ½ cup	83
Zucchini, cooked, 1 cup	40
Zwieback, 1 slice	35

RECOMMENDED DAILY DIETARY ALLOWANCES (ABRIDGED)[1]

[DESIGNED FOR THE MAINTENANCE OF GOOD NUTRITION OF HEALTHY PERSONS IN THE U.S.A.]

Persons				Food energy	Protein	Calcium	Iron	Vitamin A	Thiamin	Riboflavin	Niacin equivalent[2]	Ascorbic acid
	Age in years[3] *From up to*	*Weight in pounds*	*Height in inches*	*Calories*	*Grams*	*Grams*	*Milligrams*	*International units*	*Milligrams*	*Milligrams*	*Milligrams*	*Milligrams*
Infants	0–⅙	9	22	lb. x 54.5	lb. x 1.0	0.4	6	1,500	0.2	0.4	5	35
	⅙–½	15	25	lb. x 50.0	lb. x .9	0.5	10	1,500	0.4	0.5	7	35
	½–1	20	28	lb. x 45.5	lb. x .8	0.6	15	1,500	0.5	0.6	8	35
Children	1–2	26	32	1,100	25	0.7	15	2,000	0.6	0.6	8	40
	2–3	31	36	1,250	25	0.8	15	2,000	0.6	0.7	8	40
	3–4	35	39	1,400	30	0.8	10	2,500	0.7	0.8	9	40
	4–6	42	43	1,600	30	0.8	10	2,500	0.8	0.9	11	40
	6–8	51	48	2,000	35	0.9	10	3,500	1.0	1.1	13	40
	8–10	62	52	2,200	40	1.0	10	3,500	1.1	1.2	15	40
	10–12	77	55	2,500	45	1.2	10	4,500	1.3	1.3	17	40
	12–14	95	59	2,700	50	1.4	18	5,000	1.4	1.4	18	45
Boys	14–18	130	67	3,000	60	1.4	18	5,000	1.5	1.5	20	55
	18–22	147	69	2,800	60	0.8	10	5,000	1.4	1.6	18	60
	22–35	154	69	2,800	65	0.8	10	5,000	1.4	1.7	18	60
	35–55	154	68	2,600	65	0.8	10	5,000	1.3	1.7	17	60
Men	55–75+	154	67	2,400	65	0.8	10	5,000	1.2	1.7	14	60
	10–12	77	56	2,250	50	1.2	18	4,500	1.1	1.3	15	40
	12–14	97	61	2,300	50	1.3	18	5,000	1.2	1.4	15	45
	14–16	114	62	2,400	55	1.3	18	5,000	1.2	1.4	16	50
Girls	16–18	119	63	2.300	55	1.3	18	5,000	1.2	1.5	15	50
Women	18–22	128	64	2,000	55	0.8	18	5,000	1.0	1.5	13	55
	22–35	128	64	2,000	55	0.8	18	5,000	1.0	1.5	13	55
	35–55	128	63	1,850	55	0.8	18	5,000	1.0	1.5	13	55
	55–75+	128	62	1,700	55	0.8	10	5,000	1.0	1.5	13	55
Pregnant	....	......	......	+200	65	+0.4	18	6,000	+0.1	1.8	15	60
Lactating	....	......	......	+1,000	75	+0.5	18	8,000	+0.5	2.0	20	60

[1] Source: Adapted from Recommended Dietary Allowances, Seventh Edition 1968, Publication 1694, 169 pages. Published by National Academy of Sciences—National Research Council, Washington D.C. 20418. Also available in libraries. This publication includes discussion of allowances, eight additional nutrients, and adjustments needed for age, body size, and physical activity.

[2] Niacin equivalents include dietary sources of the vitamin itself plus 1 milligram equivalent for each 60 milligrams of dietary tryptophan.

[3] Entries for age range 22 to 35 years represent the reference man and woman at age 22. All other entries represent allowances for the midpoint of the specified age group.

NOTE.—The Recommended Daily Dietary Allowances should not be confused with Minimum Daily Requirements. The Recommended Dietary Allowances are amounts of nutrients recommended by the Food and Nutrition Board of National Research Council and are considered adequate for maintenance of good nutrition in healthy persons in the United States. The allowances are revised from time to time in accordance with newer knowledge of nutritional needs.

The Minimum Daily Requirements are the amounts of selected nutrients that have been established by the Food and Drug Administration as standards for labeling purposes of foods and pharmaceutical preparations for special dietary uses. These are the amounts regarded as necessary in the diet for the prevention of deficiency diseases and generally are less than the Recommended Dietary Allowances.

BEVERAGES

As our friend, Edgar Anderson, points out in his stimulating book, "Plants, Man and Life," primitive man located the only sources of caffeine known to this day: in tea, coffee, cola, cocoa and yerba maté and its relatives. Other less brisk brews have been made from leaves, roots, bark, blossoms and seeds. In France, for example, the tisane mentioned so lovingly by Colette is frequently served as a comforting after-dinner drink, page 20. If you don't grow and dry your own herbs, the drugstore will do very well as a source.

The recipes in this chapter, except for a few variations under Coffee and Tea, are nonalcoholic. For alcoholic liquors of all kinds, their preparation and use, see **Drinks** (II, 25). Remember that, in any beverage you may brew, the quality of the water greatly affects results.

ABOUT COFFEE

Coffee has always thrived on adversity—just as people in adversity have thrived on it. When this beverage began its highly successful career, the Mohammedan priesthood identified it with wine—a new kind of wine which was all the more offensive to Koranic teaching because it did not merely loosen men's tongues, but sharpened their critical faculties.

Thanks especially to vacuum-packed cans, making good coffee at home has become a surefire delight. Of the several ways of preparing this beverage, we prefer the drip method. Vacuum preparation and the percolator have their advocates, too; but we regard them as, respectively, more troublesome and less apt to produce fresh flavor. The steeped-coffee recipe which follows is suggested for campers or others who happen to lack any equipment more specialized than a saucepan. Illustrated are two devices for making filtered coffee: the first employs a metal filter, the second, which is made of chemical glass, uses a paper filter folded into conical shape.

The latter gives a pure essence, with no sediment—which a coffee connoisseur demands in a perfect brew. Also sketched is the proper equipment for Caffè Espresso and Turkish coffee.

Whatever device you choose ➧ follow the directions of its manufacturer carefully, especially as to the grind recommended—regular, drip or fine. In each case, to assure a full-bodied brew, ➧ use not less than 2 level tablespoons of coffee to each ¾ cup of freshly drawn water. Other things to remember are: use soft, not softened or hard, water; when brewing coffee keep the coffeemaker almost full; time your method consistently; keep the coffeemaker scrupulously clean, rinsing it with water in which a few teaspoons of baking soda have been dissolved and always scalding it before re-use. If cloth filters are required, do not allow them to become dry, but keep them immersed in cold water. ➧ Never boil coffee, since boiling brings out the tannic acid in the bean and makes for a bitter as well as a cloudy brew. Remember that any moisture activates coffee and that water between 200°–205° is ideal for extracting flavor without drawing acids. Never, of course, re-use coffee grounds.

If coffee is ground in the household, it should be done in small quantities, in a meticulously clean grinder. Open only one can at a time. Store ground coffee in a tightly closed jar in the refrigerator.

For those who love coffee but are highly sensitive to caffeine or in whom it induces insomnia, we suggest the use of a decaffeinized product rather than a coffee substitute. It may be helpful to remember also, that certain varieties of coffee—such as those grown in Puerto Rico—have a substantially lower caffeine content than the typical Brazilian or Colombian bean.

For those who hanker after coffee such as the kind their German grandmother used to make or a brew which reminds them of that little brasserie on the Left Bank, the answer may be to add an ounce of ground chicory to a cup of ground coffee before brewing. ➧ When cream is used in coffee, allow it to reach room temperature beforehand, so as to cool the drink as little as possible. For coffee-chocolate combinations, see About Chocolate, page 20, and Brazilian Chocolate, page 21.

DRIP COFFEE OR CAFÉ FILTRÉ

Place finely ground coffee in drip filter.

Allow:

2 tablespoons coffee for each ¾ to 1 cup water

Pour freshly boiled water over the coffee. When the dripping process is complete, serve coffee at once. Dripping coffee more than once, contrary to popular belief, does not strengthen the brew.

Serve with a:

Twist of lemon peel

VACUUM-METHOD COFFEE

Allow:

2 tablespoons regular or fine-ground coffee for every

¾ to 1 cup water

Measure water into lower bowl. Place on heat. Place a wet filter in upper bowl and add the ground coffee. Insert upper bowl into lower one with a light twist to insure a tight seal. Insert it at this time or not, depending on your equipment. If your equipment has a vented stem, you may place it on the heat already assembled. If it does not have this small hole on the side of the tube above the hot-water line, wait until the water is actively boiling before putting the upper bowl in place. When nearly all the water has risen into the upper bowl—some of it will always remain below—stir the water and coffee thoroughly. In 1 to 3 minutes, the shorter time for the finer grinds, remove from heat.

PERCOLATED COFFEE

Place in the percolator:

¾ to 1 cup cold water for every 2 tablespoons coffee you have measured into the percolator basket

When water boils, remove percolator from heat. Put in the basket. Cover percolator, return to heat and allow to percolate slowly 6 to 8 minutes. Remove the coffee basket and serve. ➧ Over-percolating does not make coffee stronger. It impairs its flavor.

STEEPED COFFEE

Place in a pot:

2 tablespoons regular or fine grind coffee to each ¾ to 1 cup freshly boiling water

Stir the coffee for at least ½ minute. Let it stand covered in a pan of boiling water from 5 to 10 minutes, depending on the grind and the strength of brew desired. Pour the coffee off the grounds through a strainer; or, if preferred, settle the grounds by stirring into the pot before draining:

(1 slightly beaten egg)

The egg merely serves to clarify the coffee. If anything, it detracts from rather than adds to its flavor.

COFFEE IN QUANTITY [40 to 50]

Put in a cheesecloth bag large enough to allow for double expansion:

1 lb. medium-grind coffee

Shortly before serving, have ready a kettle holding:

5 to 7 quarts water

Bring the water to a boil. Place the coffee-filled bag in it. Permit to stand in a warm place from 7 to 10 minutes. Agitate the bag several times during this period. Remove bag, cover kettle, serve at once.

INSTANT COFFEE

The polls are against us, but we really can't yet regard the jiffy product as in any way comparable to the one that takes a few minutes longer to prepare. If you insist, use for each serving:

1 teaspoon instant coffee
5½ oz. boiling water

For 6 servings:

6 teaspoons instant coffee
1 quart boiling water

Add the water to the instant coffee to avoid foaming. A better flavor is obtained by simmering gently for about 2 minutes.

ESPRESSO COFFEE

This Italian specialty, which, of course, is called Caffè Espresso on its home grounds, must be carefully distinguished from any brew made by filtering, no matter how concentrated. The Espresso machine works by an entirely different "steam pressure" principle, uses a very dark, very powdery grind identified as "Espresso" on the package and delivers a powerful drink with the consistency of light cream. Use the recipe for Espresso which comes with your equipment and serve it after dinner, in a demitasse or Espresso glass, with or without lemon peel. Vary the brew with a dash of Tía Maria or a dash of Strega and a dollop of whipped cream.

COFFEE CAPUCCINO

Combine equal parts of:

Espresso Coffee
Hot Milk
Dash of Cinnamon or
Grating of Nutmeg

TURKISH COFFEE

As Turkish coffee settles very rapidly, it is made at the table, over an alcohol lamp. The average content of the long-handled metal pot is about 10 ounces of liquid, and it should never be filled to more than ⅔ capacity. The pot is narrowed before it flares at the top, to allow the swishing and swinging of its contents between "frothings"—a procedure which keeps the very finely divided grains in suspension, until the liquid is sipped from tiny stemmed cups holding about a tablespoon of fluid. In the Near East it is not considered polite to drink more than three of these—although more may be served in the United States. The glass of ice water and the Rahat Loukoum candy (II, 519) served on the side for "non-habitués" are often welcome additions. The connoisseur adds no sweetening to the brew itself. Serve the coffee so that a little of the lighter frothy top goes into each cup first and is followed on the next round by some of the heavier liquid on the bottom. No commercial grind available in America proves fine enough for Turkish coffee; so take the finest you can get and pulverize it further in an electric blender. For each serving, bring to a boil in a Turkish coffeemaker:

⅓ cup water
1 teaspoon to 1 tablespoon finely pulverized coffee
(2 teaspoons sugar)

Place the pot over heat and allow the coffee to rise. Remove pot from heat, momentarily. Repeat this process a second and third time. ➧ Never allow the coffee to boil. Serve it at once, as described above.

CAFÉ AU LAIT

The famous milk coffee of France.
Combine equal parts of:

Strong coffee
Hot milk
(Sugar to taste)

CAFÉ BRÛLOT, DIABLE OR ROYAL [8]

This festive coffee bowl requires a darkened room. Prepare:

1 small orange

by studding it with:

20 whole cloves

Place in a deep silver bowl the thinly sliced:

Peel of 1 orange
Peel of 1 lemon and
2 sticks cinnamon
10 small cubes sugar

Heat ➧ do not boil, and pour over these ingredients:

¾ cup brandy or ¼ cup Cointreau

Place bowl on a tray and bring bowl, orange and a ladle to the table. Ignite the brandy and ladle the mixture repeatedly over the spices until the sugar melts. Pour into the bowl:

4 cups freshly made coffee

Now fill the ladle with:

¼ cup warm brandy or ¼ cup Cointreau

Tip the orange carefully into it, ignite liquid, and lower the flaming ladle into the bowl, floating the orange. Ladle the café brûlot into demitasse cups.
Here are 2 easier versions:
For individual servings put a

small cube of sugar in a coffee spoon, saturate it with brandy, ignite. When sugar is melted, lower spoon into a partially filled demitasse of hot coffee. Add a lemon twist, 1 or 2 cloves and stir mixture with a cinnamon stick. Also, you may simply stir a teaspoonful of warmed light rum or whisky into a small cup of hot coffee—adding a twist of lemon peel and sweetening to taste.

IRISH COFFEE

[Individual Serving]
Some people hold that Irish coffee can only be made "proper" with Demarara sugar (II, 166). It does make a difference. Try it sometime.
Heat ➧ but do not boil and place in a prewarmed 7-ounce goblet or coffee cup:

1 jigger Irish whisky
1 or 2 teaspoons sugar

Fill to within ½ inch of top with:

Freshly made hot coffee

Stir until sugar is dissolved. Float on top of liquid:

Chilled whipped cream

ICED COFFEE

Prepare any way you wish, using:

2½ to 3 tablespoons to ¾ cup water, Coffee, page 15

Chill it or pour it hot over cubed ice in tall glasses. You may sweeten the drink with:

(Sugar or Sugar Sirup to taste)

Stir in:

(Cream)

or top with:

(Whipped Cream or Vanilla Ice Cream)

ICED COFFEE VIENNOISE

[Individual Serving]
Prepare:

Iced Coffee

in a tall glass. Add:

1 small jigger light rum

Top with:

Whipped cream

⅄ BLENDER FROZEN COFFEE

Place in electric blender for each drink:

¼ cup coffee

prepared as for Iced Coffee, above.

1 tablespoon sugar
1/16 teaspoon ground cloves
(1 small jigger medium rum)

Add not less than:

2 cups crushed ice

Blend thoroughly and serve in chilled, tall glasses.

ABOUT TEA

In one of Lin Yutang's books, he tells of the infinite care with which a certain sage living in the second or Classical period of Chinese teamaking procured from a famous spring, in just the proper sort of earthen pot, sufficient water for a brew with which he intended regaling an honored guest; how, on a clear, calm evening, taking pains to keep the water undisturbed, he sailed with it cautiously across an arm of the sea to his home; and how, before steeping the choice leaves, he brought the water to precisely the critical boil. There were other refinements, too, most of them equally unthinkable in our less leisurely age.

However, no matter how we abridge the teamaking ritual today, it is well to keep in mind the importance of the water we use and its temperature. It should be freshly drawn, soft—not softened and not hard—and heated, if possible, in a glass or enameled vessel. When the leaves are dropped into it, the water should only just have arrived at a brisk rolling boil—so the tea will not have a flat flavor and the leaves will describe a deep wheel-like movement, each one opening up for fullest infusion. If you doubt the effectiveness of this step, test it for yourself, adding tea leaves to underboiled, just boiling and overboiled water. Then watch the difference.

Tea brewers who do not wish to trouble with a strainer and are willing to compromise may use a tea ball. In any case ➧ stirring the brew just before serving in a scalded, preheated pot is imperative, since it circulates through the liquid the essential oils which contribute so much to tea's characteristic flavor.

There is only one tea plant; but there are many commercial varieties of tea, depending upon soil, locality, age of leaf, manufacture, grading, blending and the addition of blossoms, zests or spices. The two chief basic types are green and black. The former is dried immediately after plucking, the latter—by all odds the more favored—is allowed to ferment before further processing. Oolong, a semi-fermented leaf, is in a class by itself.

Chinese teas which, less than a century ago, dominated the world market, have now largely yielded to the more robustly aromatic varieties of India, Ceylon and Southeastern Asia. Unfortunately, tea producers have not yet followed the example of coffee manufacturers, by putting up tea in vacuum packages. Therefore, when it reaches your kitchen, we suggest you place it at once into a tightly sealed jar.

TEA

Place tea leaves in a preheated pot. Allow:

1 teaspoon tea leaves

for each:

5 to 6 oz. water

Proceed as indicated above, permitting the leaves to steep not less than 3 and not more than 5 minutes. Serve the tea promptly, stirring and straining. Sugar or lemon? Yes, if you wish—the earliest teamakers, curiously enough, added salt! On a chilly afternoon we sometimes like to put a small decanter of rum or brandy on the tea tray for the cup that cheers. But we draw the line at tea bags and cream. The bag container or the fat in the cream will adulterate the flavor of this subtle beverage. Milk, of course, is frequently added in England. Never steep tea leaves more than once.

SPICED TEA [8]

Prepare an infusion by bringing to a boil:

½ cup water
¾ cup sugar

Remove from heat and add:

¼ cup strained orange juice
½ cup strained lemon juice
6 cloves
1 stick cinnamon

Meanwhile, prepare:

Tea, above

Use, in all, 10 teaspoons tea and 5 cups water—in a regular measuring cup. Put the hot, spiced infusion in a heavy crystal bowl.

Pour the steeped tea over the mixture and serve at once in punch or tea cups.

ICED TEA

We swell with patriotic pride when we recall that this beverage originated in our native town, St. Louis—even though the inventor was actually an Englishman who arrived at the concoction as an act of desperation. The year was 1904; the place, the St. Louis World's Fair; the provocation, the indifference of the general public, in the sweltering midwestern heat, to Richard Blechynden's tea concession. In brewing iced tea, avoid China teas—they lack the requisite "body." Hard water produces murky iced tea due to a precipitate.

Prepare:

Tea, page 19

Use twice the quantity of leaves indicated for making the hot beverage. Stir, strain and pour over cubed ice. Serve with:

Lemon slices
(Sprigs of mint)
(Sugar to taste)

FLAVORINGS FOR ICED TEA

I. Pour hot, steeped tea over:

Bruised mint leaves
Lemon rind

Chill the tea. Remove leaves and rind. Pour the tea into tall glasses. Add ice cubes and:

(Sprigs of mint)
Sugar to taste

II. Add to each serving of iced tea:

1 teaspoon rum

Garnish the glasses with:

Slices of lemon or lime
(Sprigs of lemon thyme)

ABOUT TISANES AND OTHER INFUSIONS

From time immemorial various plants, less stimulating than tea or coffee, have been used the world over as restoratives. They range all the way from such homely makings as rose hips and sassafras bark to that Paraguayan tea shrub, maté, the leaves of which are still commercially obtainable in some North American localities.

Some of the homegrown herbs which, singly or in combination, may become interesting beverages are the fresh or dried leaves of alfalfa, angelica, bergamot, hyssop, lemon verbena, mints, sages, thymes; the blossoms of camomile, clover, linden, orange, lemon, wintergreen and elderberry; also, the seeds of anise and fennel. There is a good general rule for quantity per cup of water in preparing these infusions.

For strong herbs, allow:

½ to 1 tablespoon fresh material
¼ to ½ teaspoon dried material

For mild herbs, allow:

Twice the above amounts

➧ Never use a metal pot. Steep for 3 to 10 minutes in water brought to a rolling boil before straining and serving. Serve with:

(Honey or lemon)

Habitués say "never use cream." Try one of the following dried herbs, allowing for each cup:

1 star anise cluster
6 camomile flowers
⅛ teaspoon powdered mint
¼ teaspoon powdered fennel
½ teaspoon linden blossom
½ teaspoon verbena

Steep for 5 minutes before serving.

ABOUT CHOCOLATE AND COCOA BEVERAGES

Chocolate, an Aztec drink, comes to us via Spain with the addition of sugar and spice. ➧ It really pains us to speak evil of so distinctively delicious a drink. But chocolate, with its high fat and sugar content, if habitually substituted for milk, may create an imbalance in the diet. In some places, unless you ask for French chocolate, the base will be water and the drink garnished with whipped cream. In France, you can count on a milk base and cream incorporated into the drink. In Vienna, they add a generous topping of whipped cream. In America, you may have to face a marshmallow or a piece of cinnamon-stick candy; in Russia and Brazil, coffee is added; and in modern Mexico, we find in it cinnamon and even orange rind and sherry. For more information about chocolates and cocoas, see (II, 191).

Cocoa does not always combine easily with liquid. To remove any lumps before cooking, combine it with the sugar or mix it in the blender with a small quantity of the water called for in the recipe. You may want to keep on hand homemade cocoa or chocolate sirups, see page 22. ➧ Both coco.. and chocolate scorch easily, so brew them over hot water as suggested below. In Mexico, a special wooden stirrer or whipper called molinillo is used to fluff chocolate drinks just before serving. This also inhibits the formation of the cream "skin" which often forms on top. If you want this aerated effect, try a wire whisk or a rotary beater. Serve the hot beverage in a deep narrow chocolate cup so as to retain the heat.

COCOA
[About 4 Servings]

Combine, stir and boil for 2 minutes—in the top of a double boiler over direct but low heat:

1 cup boiling water
¼ cup cocoa
⅛ teaspoon salt
2 to 4 tablespoons sugar

Then add:

½ teaspoon cinnamon
1/16 teaspoon cloves and/or nutmeg

Place the top of the boiler ➧ over boiling water. Add:

3 cups scalded milk

Stir and heat the cocoa. Cover and keep over hot water for 10 more minutes. Beat with a wire whisk before serving.

CHOCOLATE
[About 4 Servings]

Melt ➧ in the top of a double boiler:

1½ to 2 oz. chocolate

with:

1 cup boiling water

Now, over direct heat, bring this mixture in the top of the double boiler to the point where it begins to foam up. Quickly lift it from the heat. Let the liquid recede, then repeat the foaming and receding process 3 or 4 times in all. Scald:

3 cups milk

with:

1 vanilla bean

Dissolve in the hot milk:

¼ cup sugar
⅛ teaspoon salt

Remove the vanilla bean. Pour these ingredients while hot over the smooth chocolate mixture and beat well with a wire whisk. In each cup, place:

(A stick of whole cinnamon)

Before serving, fold into the mixture or top it with:

(¼ cup whipped cream at room temperature)

BRAZILIAN CHOCOLATE
[About 4 Servings]

Melt in a double boiler ➧ over hot water:

1 oz. chocolate
¼ cup sugar
⅛ teaspoon salt

Add and stir in:

1 cup boiling water

Continue to heat 3 to 5 minutes.
Add:

½ cup hot milk
½ cup hot cream
1½ cups freshly made hot coffee

Beat mixture well and add:

1 teaspoon vanilla
(A grating of cinnamon)

ICED CHOCOLATE

Prepare and then chill:

Chocolate, or
Brazilian Chocolate, above

Serve over crushed ice. Top with:

Whipped cream or coffee ice cream

Garnish with:

Grated sweet chocolate

CHOCOLATE OR CHOCOLATE MALT SHAKE SIRUP [20]

First, make the following sirup which you may keep on hand in the refrigerator about 10 days.
Melt in the top of a double boiler over hot water:

7 oz. chocolate

Stir slowly into the melted chocolate:

15 oz. sweetened condensed milk
1 cup boiling water

Stir in, until dissolved:

½ cup sugar

Cool the sirup.
To make up an individual shake, use:

2 tablespoons chocolate sirup
1 cup chilled milk

Beat the mixture well or blend it. For increased food value, add:

(½ cup milk solids or malt)
(2 teaspoons debittered brewers' yeast)

Serve at once blended with:

A dip of vanilla, chocolate, or mint ice cream

or over:

Cracked ice

COCOA SHAKE SIRUP

[About 8 Servings]
In the top of a double boiler make a lumpless paste of:

1 cup sugar
½ cup cocoa
¼ cup cold water
(½ cup malt)

Bring this mixture just to a boil over low direct heat, stirring constantly. Then continue to heat over hot water from 3 to 5 minutes. Cool mixture. You may store it covered and refrigerated for 2 to 3 weeks.

HANDY HOT CHOCOLATE OR COCOA

[About 1 Serving]
Prepare:

Chocolate Shake Sirup or Cocoa Shake Sirup, above

For each 8 oz. cup of cocoa desired, use:

2 tablespoons sirup

Stir in slowly:

¾ cup scalding milk

and heat thoroughly without boiling before serving.

MILK AND EGG BEVERAGES

Some of the formulas given in this section are nutritious enough to serve as complete meals for dieters or invalids.

MILK EGGNOG [4]

Combine in a shaker:

4 cups chilled milk
4 eggs

4 tablespoons confectioners' sugar or honey
1 teaspoon vanilla, grated orange or lemon rind
(½ cup orange juice)
½ cup cracked ice

Shake the eggnog well. Sprinkle the top with:

Freshly grated nutmeg

Of course, it will do no harm to add a jigger or two of whisky, cognac or rum.

FRUIT MILK SHAKE [4]

Combine in a shaker or blender:

1⅓ cups chilled sweetened apricot, prune, strawberry or raspberry juice
2⅔ cups cold milk

Serve over cracked ice.

ABOUT JUICES AND FRUIT BEVERAGES

Fresh herbs and fruits, when available, make attractive garnishes for cold fruit beverages. Try a sprig of common mint or velvety, frosty-looking apple mint. A few leaves of borage or its bright, starry blossoms are pretty additions or the wheel-like foliage of sweet woodruff—the German Waldmeister, see (II, 215). Use also garnishes of lemon balm, lemon thyme, pineapple sage and scented geranium.

Charming decorations for beverages are strawberries and cherries. So are pineapple slices or citrus fruits, cut into attractive shapes. For winter concoctions, put a few cloves into the citrus slices and use them to garnish the glasses, adding one or two thin twisted citrus rind shavings to the drink itself. Another way to heighten the charm of cold beverages is to spruce them up with decorative ice cubes. Fill a refrigerator tray with water. Place in each section one of the following: a maraschino cherry, a preserved strawberry, a piece of lemon or pineapple, a sprig of mint, etc.

You may flavor the cubes, before freezing, with sherry or whisky—using not more than 2 tablespoons per tray. The short recipes which immediately follow are designed mainly to whet the appetite. They are dedicated to two kinds of people—those who cannot take cocktails because of their alcoholic content and those who like to appear convivial but who are convinced that a stiff alcoholic drink before dinner blunts the flavor of good food. Their basic liquid ingredients may, of course, be served without our suggested modifiers.

To make rich vegetable juices, blend vegetables, but be sure to cook first any fibrous ones such as celery. Don't forget the convenience of frozen concentrates, especially for strongly flavored, quick-chilling drinks.

FRESH TOMATO JUICE [4]

Simmer for ½ hour:

12 medium-sized, raw, ripe tomatoes

with:

½ cup water
1 slice onion
2 ribs celery with leaves
½ bay leaf
3 sprigs parsley

Strain these ingredients. Season with:

1 teaspoon salt
¼ teaspoon paprika
¼ teaspoon sugar

Serve thoroughly chilled.

CANNED TOMATO JUICE [4]

Combine in shaker:

2½ cups tomato juice
½ teaspoon grated onion
1 teaspoon grated celery
½ teaspoon horseradish

1½ tablespoons lemon juice
A dash of Worcestershire or hot pepper sauce
⅛ teaspoon paprika
¾ teaspoon salt
¼ teaspoon sugar

This juice may be served hot or chilled. Curry powder, a few cloves, a stick of cinnamon, tarragon, parsley or some other herb may be steeped in the cocktail and strained out before it is served.

CHILLED TOMATO CREAM [4]

Combine in a shaker:

1½ cups chilled tomato juice
¾ cup chilled cream
1 teaspoon grated onion
⅛ teaspoon salt
⅛ teaspoon celery salt
A few drops hot pepper sauce
A few grains cayenne
¼ cup finely cracked ice

TOMATO AND CUCUMBER JUICE [4]

Combine in a shaker:

2 cups tomato juice
2 tablespoons salad oil
1 tablespoon vinegar
½ teaspoon salt
⅛ teaspoon paprika
(¼ teaspoon basil)

Peel, seed, grate and add:

1 cucumber
½ cup cracked ice

ORANGE AND TOMATO JUICE [4]

Combine in a shaker:

1½ cups tomato juice
1 cup orange juice
1 teaspoon sugar
1 tablespoon lemon or lime juice
½ teaspoon salt
½ cup crushed ice

SAUERKRAUT JUICE [4]

This is also called Lumpensuppe and is recommended by some people for a hangover.

I. Combine:

1 teaspoon lemon juice
⅛ teaspoon paprika
2 cups sauerkraut juice

II. Chill, then combine:

1 cup sauerkraut juice
1 cup tomato juice
(½ teaspoon prepared horseradish)

CLAM JUICE [4]

Combine:

2 tablespoons lemon juice
1½ tablespoons tomato catsup
2 cups clam juice
A drop hot pepper sauce
Salt if needed
(½ teaspoon grated onion)
¼ teaspoon celery salt

Chill these ingredients. Strain before serving. This is a good combination, but there are many others. Horseradish may be added, so may Worcestershire sauce. The cocktail may be part clam juice and part tomato juice. Serve sprinkled with:

Freshly ground pepper

ORANGE AND LIME JUICE [4]

Combine in a shaker:

2 cups orange juice
1 tablespoon lime juice or 2 tablespoons lemon juice
⅛ teaspoon salt
½ cup cracked ice

FRESH PINEAPPLE JUICE

[About 1½ Cups of Juice]

A very refreshing drink.

Peel a:

Pineapple

Cut it into cubes. Extract the juice by putting the pineapple through a food grinder or a ⅄ blender. There will be very little pulp. Strain the juice and serve it iced with:

Sprigs of mint

PINEAPPLE AND TOMATO JUICE [4]

Combine in a shaker:

1 cup pineapple juice
1 cup tomato juice
¼ teaspoon salt
½ cup crushed ice

PINEAPPLE AND GRAPEFRUIT JUICE [4]

Boil for 3 minutes:

⅓ cup sugar
⅓ cup water

Chill the sirup. Add:

1¼ cups grapefruit juice
⅔ cup pineapple juice
¼ cup lemon juice

Serve chilled.

FRUIT SHRUBS OR VINEGARS

These are most refreshing in hot weather. Try adding rum in the winter.

Prepare:

Fruit juice

Depending on the sweetness of the juice, simmer until the sugar is dissolved:

1 cup juice
1 to 1½ cups sugar

For every cup of juice, add:

¼ cup white wine vinegar

Bottle in sterile jars. Serve the shrub over shaved ice.

CITRUS-FRUIT JUICE MEDLEY [4]

Combine in a shaker:

¾ cup grapefruit juice
¼ cup lemon juice
½ cup orange juice
⅓ to ½ cup sugar
1 cup cracked ice

Pour into glasses and serve garnished with:

Sprigs of mint

★ HOT OR MULLED CIDER

Good on a cold night, with canapés or sandwiches. Heat well, but do not boil:

Apple cider
A few cloves
A stick of cinnamon

CRANBERRY JUICE [4]

Cook until skins pop open, about 5 minutes:

1 pint cranberries
2 cups water

Strain through cheesecloth. Bring the juice to a boil and add:

¼ to ⅓ cup sugar
(3 cloves)

Cook for 2 minutes. Cool. Add:

¼ cup orange juice or
1 tablespoon lemon juice

Serve thoroughly chilled. Garnish with:

A slice of lime

FRUIT JUICE TWOSOMES

Good combinations are equal parts of:

Orange juice and pineapple juice

or:

Loganberry juice and pineapple juice

or:

White grape juice and orange juice

or:

Cranberry juice and sweetened lime juice

or:

Grapefruit juice and cranberry juice

★ HOT CRANBERRY JUICE

Heat well, but do not boil:

Cranberry juice
A thinly sliced lemon
A few cloves
A cracked nutmeg
(Honey to taste)

Serve in mugs, with cinnamon stick stirrers.

⅄ ABOUT BLENDED JUICES

The blender transforms many kinds of fruit and vegetables

into rich and delicious liquid food. The only trouble in using it is that the enthusiast often gets drunk with power and whirls up more and more weird and intricate combinations—some of them quite undrinkable. Resist the temptation to become a sorcerer's apprentice.

Sometimes too, a gray color results. If so, gradually stir in lemon juice, a little at a time. Serve immediately after adding the lemon juice, as the clear color may not last long. A few suggestions follow. Each recipe yields about 3 cups.

I. Combine in blender:
- **1½ cups chilled, seeded orange pulp**
- **1 cup chilled melon meat (cantaloupe or honeydew)**
- **2 tablespoons lemon juice**
- **⅛ teaspoon salt**
- **½ cup finely crushed ice**

II. This is almost like a sherbet. Combine in blender:
- **1½ cups chilled apricot or peach pulp**
- **½ cup milk**
- **½ cup cream**
- **2 tablespoons sugar**
- **½ cup finely crushed ice**
- **(1 tablespoon lemon juice)**

III. Combine in blender:
- **1 cup chilled, unsweetened pineapple juice**
- **1 cup peeled, seeded, chilled cucumber**
- **½ cup water cress**
- **2 sprigs parsley**
- **½ cup finely crushed ice**

IV. Combine in a blender:
- **1½ cups chilled, unsweetened pineapple juice**
- **1 ripe banana**
- **2 teaspoons honey**
- **Juice of ½ lime**
- **½ cup finely crushed ice**
- **(4 maraschino cherries)**

Garnish with:
(Sprigs of mint)

PINEAPPLE OR ORANGE EGGNOG [4]

Combine in a shaker or blender:
- **2 cups chilled pineapple or orange juice**
- **1 tablespoon confectioners' sugar or honey**
- **1½ tablespoons lemon juice**
- **1 egg or 2 egg yolks**
- **A pinch of salt**
- **¼ cup cracked ice**

Shake or blend well.

ABOUT PARTY BEVERAGES

As with Party Drinks, each of the following recipes, unless otherwise indicated, will yield about 5 quarts and accommodate approximately 20 people. For "ice-bowl" containers and other suggestions for attractively serving large groups of people, see Party Drinks (II, 43).

GALA TOMATO PUNCH

For a summer brunch in a shady corner of the veranda.
Combine:
- **4 quarts tomato juice (II, 537)**
- **1 quart canned beef consommé**

Season to taste with:
Garlic salt
(A chiffonade of herbs)

Chill, pour into bowl and decorate with:
Decorative ice ring (II, 43)

in which has been set:
An herb bouquet

LEMONADE

For each cup of water, add:
- **1½ tablespoons lemon juice**
- **3 to 4 tablespoons sugar**
- **⅛ teaspoon salt**

The sugar and water need not be boiled, but the quality of the lemonade is improved if they

are. Boil the sugar and water for 2 minutes. Chill the sirup and add the lemon juice. Orange, pineapple, raspberry, loganberry, white grape juice and other fruit juices may be combined with lemonade. Chilled tea, added to these fruit combinations, about ⅓ cup for every cup of juice, gives lemonades an invigorating lift.

LEMONADE FOR 100 PEOPLE

Boil for 10 minutes:
- 4 cups water
- 8 cups sugar

Cool the sirup. Add:
- 7½ cups lemon juice

Stir in the contents of:
- 2 No. 2½ cans crushed pineapple or 6 to 8 cans frozen juice concentrate

Add:
- 8 sliced seeded oranges
- 4 gallons water

Chill. Serve over ice.

LEMONADE SIRUP

[About 4½ cups]

I. Boil for 5 minutes:
- 2 cups sugar
- 1 cup water
- Rind of 2 lemons, cut into thin strips
- ⅛ teaspoon salt

Cool and add:
- Juices of 6 lemons

Strain the sirup. Store in a covered jar.

Add:
- 2 tablespoons sirup

to:
- 1 glass ice water or carbonated water

II. Add:
- 1 tablespoon sirup
- 2 tablespoons orange, apricot or pineapple juice

to:
- 1 glass ice water or carbonated water

ORANGEADE

Serve undiluted:
- Orange juice

over:
- Crushed ice

or add to the orange juice, to taste:
- (Water, lemon juice and sugar)

PINEAPPLE PUNCH

Place in a large bowl:
- 2 cups strong tea

Add and stir well:
- ¾ cup lemon juice
- 2 cups orange juice
- 2 tablespoons lime juice
- 1 cup sugar
- Leaves from 12 sprigs mint

Place these ingredients on ice for 2 hours. Shortly before serving, strain the punch and add:
- 8 slices pineapple and juice from can
- 5 pints chilled ginger ale
- 4 pints chilled carbonated water
- Crushed ice

FRUIT PUNCH

Boil for 10 minutes:
- 1¼ cups sugar
- 1¼ cups water

Add:
- 2½ cups strong, hot tea

Cool the mixture. Add:
- 1 cup crushed pineapple
- 2½ cups strawberry juice or other fruit juice

Juice of 6 lemons
Juice of 7 oranges

Chill these ingredients for 1 hour. Add sufficient water to make 4 quarts of liquid. Immediately before serving, add:

1 cup maraschino cherries
1 quart carbonated water

Pour over large pieces of ice in punch bowl.

FRUIT PUNCH FOR 50 PEOPLE

Make a sirup, by boiling for 10 minutes:

1¼ cups water
2½ cups sugar

Reserve ½ cup of this. Add to the remainder, stir, cover and permit to stand for 30 minutes or more:

1 cup lemon juice
2 cups orange juice
1 cup strong tea
2 cups white grape juice, grapefruit juice, pineapple juice or crushed pineapple
1 cup maraschino cherries with juice
2 cups fruit sirup

The fruit sirup, we find, is the main ingredient. Your punch is apt to be just as good as this touch. Strawberry jam may be diluted, canned raspberry or loganberry juice may be sweetened and boiled until heavy. Strain these ingredients. Add ice water to make about 1½ gallons of liquid.

Add at the last minute:

1 quart carbonated water

If you find the punch lacking in sugar, add part or all of the reserved sugar sirup.

STRAWBERRY FRUIT PUNCH

Boil for 5 minutes:

4 cups water
4 cups sugar

Cool the sirup. Combine:

2 quarts hulled strawberries
1 cup sliced canned or fresh pineapple
1 cup mixed fruit juice—pineapple, apricot, raspberry, etc.
Juice of 5 large oranges
Juice of 5 large lemons
(3 sliced bananas)

Add the chilled sirup or as much of it as is palatable. Chill these ingredients. Immediately before serving, add:

2 quarts carbonated water
3 cups or more crushed ice

This is a strong punch. It is purposely prepared this way, as the ice will thin it. Water also may be added if desired.

MOCHA PUNCH

Prepare, then chill well:

7 cups freshly made coffee

Whip until stiff:

2 cups whipping cream

You may whip an additional ½ cup heavy cream and then reserve about a cup to garnish the tops. Have in readiness:

2 quarts chocolate ice cream

Pour the chilled coffee into a large chilled bowl. Add ½ the ice cream. Beat until the cream is partly melted. Add:

¼ cup rum or 1 teaspoon almond extract
¼ teaspoon salt

Fold in the remainder of the ice cream and all but a cup of the whipped cream. Pour the punch into tall glasses. Garnish the tops with the reserved cream. Sprinkle with:

Freshly grated nutmeg or grated sweet chocolate

SALADS

We remember the final scene of a Maeterlinck play. The stage is strewn with personages dead and dying. The sweet young heroine whimpers, "I am not happy here." Then the head of the house—or what remains of it—an ancient noble, asks quaveringly, "Will there be a salad for supper?"

The primal craving for fresh greens can urge you out, seasonally, trowel in hand, to dig along the roadside and in the wild; or, like Willa Cather's Archbishop —no matter how torrid the climate, how dry the soil—to tend carefully a small patch of succulent leafage or herbs.

There is an ever-increasing demand for salads of all kinds, and a greater and greater appreciation of their contribution to our gastronomical enjoyment and our improved health. Salads figure prominently in reducing diets, too, for they are low in calories. But to achieve your goal, be sure to serve them with only a sprinkling of lemon juice, a touch of spiced vinegar or a low-calorie dressing, page 345.

When to serve the salad? It used to appear almost invariably after the main entrée but has taken, these days, to gadding about. In California, where people have a habit of doing things their own way, you may expect it on the table ready to eat when you sit down. In restaurants, if the service is leisurely, this priority is a lifesaver. At informal luncheons, salads often accompany the entrée or may even be the main dish. Don't neglect the possibility of using salads like Celeri-Rave Remoulade, page 43, as an hors d'oeuvre and, vice versa, appetizers like Vegetables à la Grecque, page 257, as a salad.

Originally, salads were the edible parts of various herbs or plants dressed only with salt—from which the word salad comes. But they now include a wide variety of ingredients, cooked and uncooked. Aside from fruits, vegetables and herbs, all kinds of meat, cheese and fish abound in salads—all served with some sort of moist dressing. The danger in this embarrassment of richness is that, in some carelessly planned meals, the salad tends to outshine the main entrée and plays the part of a "satisfier," rather than that of a stimulator.

➧ Keep the rest of the menu well in mind when preparing your salad and its dressing. A rich, heavy entrée demands a tart green salad. Slaws go well with casual meals, cookouts and impromptu suppers—at which hearty, uncomplicated foods are served. Elaborate salads, beautifully arranged and garnished, brilliant aspics and decorative chaud-froids, all look well on formal buffet tables or at special summer luncheons. In some cases, these are made as individual servings rather than as a grand "pièce de résistance."

➧ Always use your common sense and good taste in the matter of dressings. We have suggested suitable dressings for the individual salads in this chapter and want you to try some of the variations listed. Don't go overboard, however, in experimenting: a heavy dressing, undiluted, will make any lettuce, except iceberg, collapse just when you want to keep it crisp. Your dressing should enhance the salad by summoning forth its special flavor and texture and adding a delicate piquency.

ABOUT CULTIVATED SALAD GREENS

➧ Do experiment with some of the greens sketched on the next page. On successive rows reading left to right are on the bottom row: Bibb lettuce, escarole, corn salad or mâche and oak leaf lettuce; on the second row: Boston and water cress; on the top row, iceberg and Chinese or celery cabbage, Belgian, French or Witloof endive, romaine or Cos and curly endive.

ICEBERG OR CRISP HEAD LETTUCE:

Large, firm head, with crisp, brittle, tightly packed leaves. The outer leaves are medium green and fringed, the inner ones are pale green and tightly folded. Can be torn, shredded or sliced like cabbage for a salad. Adds "crunch" to it and does not wilt.

ROMAINE OR COS LETTUCE:

Elongated head, with long stiff leaves which are usually medium dark to dark green on the outside and become greenish-white near the center. Its more pungent flavor adds a tang to tossed salad.

BOSTON OR BUTTERHEAD LETTUCE:

Smaller, softer head than iceberg. Delicate leaves, of which the outer are green, the inner light yellow with a buttery feeling.

BIBB LETTUCE:

The aristocrat of all lettuce. Dark, succulent green leaves, loosely held together; tender and mild.

LEAF LETTUCE:

Crisp and, unless very young, a somewhat tough, non-heading type. The loose leaves branch from a single stalk and are light or dark green. Frequently used as an undergarnish for molded salads, aspic or arrangements of salad vegetables and fruits.

OAKLEAF LETTUCE:

A type of leaf lettuce resembling its name. There are two types: one green, one bronze.

LAMB'S LETTUCE, MACHE, OR FIELD OR CORN SALAD:

Although found wild here, lamb's lettuce or mâche is cultivated extensively and in a number of varieties in France and Italy. It is an excellent winter salad and can be grown outside without protection. Small smooth green leaves, loosely formed into a head. Good for tossed salad and sometimes used as cooked greens.

CURLY ENDIVE OR CHICORY:

Curly fringed tendrils, coming from a yellow-white stem. It adds a bitter flavor and rather prickly texture to a tossed salad. Also used as a garnish.

ESCAROLE OR CHICORY ESCAROLE:

Also known as Batavian endive. The leaves are broader and less curly than endive, also a paler green. The taste is less bitter.

BELGIAN OR FRENCH ENDIVE OR WITLOOF:

These 6- to 8-inch, elongated, crisp yellow-white leaves look like a young unshucked corncob. The bitter flavor complements blander lettuces in a tossed salad or a bland filling for an hors d'oeuvre.

CHINESE OR CELERY CABBAGE:

About the size of a bunch of celery, its closely packed, whitish-green leaves are crisp and firm and, as the name implies, the flavor is between that of cabbage and celery.

WHITE MUSTARD:

A European annual, with small tender green leaves, usually cut about a week after the seeds have been sown and used with garden cress in salads or for garnish.

GARDEN CRESS:

Do not confuse with water cress. Has very tiny leaves, picked 14 days after sowing. It is frequently combined in sandwiches, hors d'oeuvre, etc., with mustard greens.

WATER CRESS:

Dime-size dark green glossy leaves, on sprigged stems. The leaves and tender part of stems are spicy and peppery additions to the tossed salad.

Water cress in France is the invariable accompaniment to a roast chicken. In America, it is one of our most interesting greens, frequently available in the wild. Its consumption, however, is often discouraged by the fact that it may be growing in ➧ polluted water. To settle any doubts you may have, soak the cress first in 2 quarts of water in which 1 tablet of water purifier has been dissolved. Then rinse the cress in clear water. Dry and chill before serving.

➧ To keep water cress, cut off ½ inch of the stems. Loosen the tie and set in a container which does not press it on the sides or top. Fill the container with 1 inch of cold water, cover and set in the refrigerator. Wash thoroughly when ready to use. Cut off the tough ends before tossing.

SEA KALE:

A native of most seacoasts of Western Europe, sea kale is cultivated for its leafstalks, but the curly leaves can be used uncooked in salad, either alone or with lettuce.

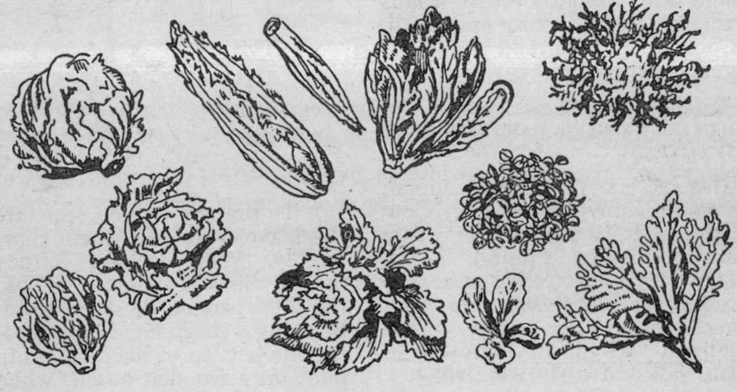

CELERY AND SPINACH:

Both these stables lend color variation to salads.

ABOUT WILD GREENS

These can add a different flavor and texture to your mixed green salads. Be absolutely sure, however, that you know the ones you are using and wash them very carefully. Here are some of the more common edible varieties, which can be identified fairly easily:

DANDELION, TARAXACUM OFFICINALE:

Abundant in lawns, fields, meadows and roadsides. It is easiest to handle and wash if it is cut off at the root crown, so that the cluster of leaves holds together. Its slightly acrid taste goes well with beetroot. After flowering, the plants become tough and rather bitter.

SORREL, RUMEX ACETOSELLA OR RUMEX ACETOSA:

There are many edible varieties of sorrel. Both grow in cultivated and recently filled soil, neglected fields and old grasslands. The leaves have a sour or acid taste and are best for salads when gathered young and small. Cooked and puréed sorrel is good with fish.

WINTER CRESS OR BARBAREA VULGARIS:

This cress has dark-green, smooth, shiny leaves and yellow flowers. It is common in waste and cultivated ground, fields, roadsides and streams. Use the rosette of root leaves for salad and gather the early spring growth and the new growth in late fall and early winter.

ABOUT TOSSED SALADS

We hesitate to admit how often we follow the injunction, "Serve with a tossed salad." A tossed salad arouses the appetite, complements a rich entrée and, incidentally, provides us with valuable vitamins and minerals.

The resigned acceptance of ready-made salad dressing has deprived many of us of a treasured prerogative—the making of French dressing at table. Presiding over cruets, seasonings and greens was, not so long ago, a ceremonial privilege of host or hostess. If the host officiated, it was apt to have a markedly meticulous and conversational quality. Methods of mixing the dressing varied with individual taste, but there was no question of the importance of the moment or of its dignity.

➧ Salad ingredients prepared long in advance suffer a loss of nutritive value, and arrive at the table looking discouragingly limp. To serve one of the choicest treats of the table, take care ➧ to have salad ingredients fresh. ➧ In washing greens, be sure not to bruise them. ➧ Be sure, too, that they are well chilled, crisp and, especially, dry.

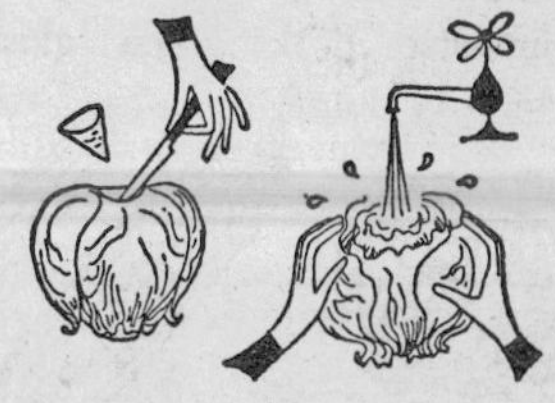

➧ To prepare lettuce, separate the leaves and wash them thoroughly. With iceberg lettuce this is difficult unless you core the solid part of the stem, either by using a sharp knife or pounding the bottom of the head quite hard on a wooden board, when the core will simply fall out. Hold the head upside down under running water. Water pressure pushes the leaves apart without bruising them. Boston and field lettuces must be inspected carefully for grit and sand. Try some of the wild as well as the cultivated salad greens previously listed, for their texture and flavors distinctively differ.

➧ Dry greens by letting them drip in a colander, wrapping them lightly in a soft absorbent towel until dry and chilling in the refrigerator until crisp and ready to use. Whirling greens in a wire salad basket is often recommended, but a Breton friend, observes that, at home, this kind of treatment is contemptuously referred to as "a ride in the jail wagon," because it manhandles the occupants. If you like to whirl, try doing it in a tea towel. To dry lettuces such as Bibb, that may be cleaned while still in head form, invert to drain, then place in the refrigerator on a turkish towel, cover with another plain towel and chill for several hours. Gravity and capillary action make them dry and crisp.

ABOUT MAKING A TOSSED SALAD

It is usual to tear rather than cut greens, except iceberg lettuce, which, if you desire smaller pieces, can be sliced or shredded. Place them in an ample bowl and give them a preliminary light coating of oil. About 1 tablespoon of salad oil will suffice for a medium-sized head of lettuce. Toss repeatedly by lifting the leaves gently with a large fork and spoon until each leaf is completely coated. This improves the salad from the standpoint of nutrition as well as that of gastronomy. Follow up with more oil, vinegar, and further tossing. If the salad is mixed on this principle, it will stay crisp, although it is usually eaten too rapidly to prove it.

Since vinegar and salt release juices and impair vitamin content, add them as close to serving time as possible. A good way to "toss" salad for a picnic is to have prepared, washed and drained greens in a large plastic bag. Take the dressing along in a separate container. Just before serving, pour the dressing into the bag and gently work it until the salad greens are coated. Serve from the bag or turn out into a large bowl.

The choice of salad oil is important. First in order of excellence is virgin-press olive oil, light in color and with a faint aroma. French and Italian groceries sell a very acceptable blend of olive, peanut and cotton seed oils which is more economical and has a greater degree of polyunsaturated fats (II, 170). You will also encounter an occasional gourmet who uses nothing but sesame oil or a cholesterol-conscious person who will eat only oil of safflower. An economical and effective substitute for straight safflower oil is a mixture of 20% safflower and 80% of another poly-unsaturated oil. If you find the taste of olive oil too strong, try combining it with one of the bland, more highly-polyunsaturated salad oils. Your choice of a sour ingredient will depend on your own taste, but a good wine vinegar or lemon juice is the usual accompaniment to oil. Various kinds of herb vinegars are frequently chosen, but you may prefer to add these herbs separately later when you add the other seasonings. For a discussion of vinegars, see (II, 150). Remember the old admonition: "Be a spendthrift with oil, and a miser with vinegar." The classic proportions are 3 to 1.

Additional dressings, condiments and trimmings may be added after oil and vinegar to produce that infinite variety in flavor which is one of the chief charms of a tossed salad. Garlic is perhaps the most essential. There are two ways of giving to a salad a delicate touch of this pungent herb. Split a clove of garlic and rub the inside of the salad bowl with it, or rub a rather dry crust of bread on all sides with a split clove of garlic. This is called a "chapon." Place the bread in the bowl with the salad ingredients. Add the dressing and toss the salad lightly to distribute the flavor. Remove the chapon and serve the salad at once. If you wish to have a slightly stronger flavor of garlic, you may mash it at the bottom of your salad bowl with other seasonings before adding oil and vinegar. This seems to modify its heavy pungency. ▶ Never leave a whole clove of garlic in any food brought to the table. Withhold salt until all other ingredients have been incorporated. Salting your salad may be unnecessary. If, after a cautious taste-test, you decide that it will improve your mix, sprinkle it on very sparingly and give the salad a final thorough tossing.

▶ Additions to tossed salads may include sliced hard-cooked eggs, radishes, chopped olives, nut meats, pimiento or green peppers, sardines, anchovy, slivered cheese, julienned ham, chicken, tongue, grated carrots, cubed celery, onions—pickled, grated or as juice—and horseradish. Even a bit of cream or catsup may transfigure an otherwise lackluster mayonnaise, French or boiled dressing. ▶ In particular, the use of fresh herbs (II, 204) may make a salad the high point of a meal.

▶ It is unwise to add cut-up tomatoes to a tossed salad, as their juices thin the dressing. Dress them separately and use them for garnishing the salad bowl. The French cut tomatoes in vertical slices, see page 49, since they bleed less this way. Another nice last-minute addition is small, hot Croutons, page 390, sprinkled over a tossed salad just before serving.

Well-seasoned wooden salad bowls have acquired a sort of sacred untouchability with some gourmets—which we think is misplaced. If the surface of a wooden salad bowl is protected by a varnish, as many are nowadays, the flavors of the oil, vinegar and herbs will not penetrate it, and you might just as well wash it in the usual way. An untreated wooden surface will certainly absorb some of the dressing used, but the residue left after wiping the bowl tends to become rancid, since we house our utensils in quarters warmer than they are abroad. This rancidity can noticeably affect the flavor of the salad. We prefer a bowl made of glass, of pottery with a glazed surface or of hard, dense, grease-proof plastic.

DRESSINGS FOR TOSSED SALADS

French Dressing, page 341
French Dressing with Cream Cheese

Roquefort or Bleu French Dressing, page 343
Water Cress Dressing, page 343
Blender Cress Dressing, page 343
Chiffonade Dressing, page 344
Half and Half Dressing, page 350
Lorenzo Dressing, page 342
Thousand Island Dressing, page 349
Anchovy Dressing, page 342
Anchovy and Beet Dressing, page 342
Low Calorie Dressing, page 345

CAESAR SALAD [4]

For this famous recipe from California, leave:

1 clove garlic, peeled and sliced

in:

½ cup olive oil: none other

for 24 hours. Sauté:

1 cup cubed French bread

in 2 tablespoons of the garlic oil, above. Break up into 2-inch lengths:

2 heads romaine

Wash and dry well. Place the romaine in a salad bowl. Sprinkle over it:

1½ teaspoons salt
¼ teaspoon dry mustard
A generous grating of black pepper
(5 fillets of anchovy, cut up small or mashed to a paste, see (II, 218)
(A few drops of Worcestershire sauce)

Add:

3 tablespoons wine vinegar

and the remaining 6 tablespoons garlic oil. Cook gently in simmering water for 1 to 1½ minutes, or use raw:

1 egg

Drop the egg from the shell onto the ingredients in the bowl. Squeeze over the egg:

The juice of 1 lemon

Add the croutons, and:

2 to 3 tablespoons Parmesan cheese

Toss the salad well. Serve it at once.

WESTERN SALAD [4]

Prepare:

Caesar Salad, above

omitting the anchovies and adding:

2 tablespoons crumbled Blue cheese

WILTED GREENS [4]

Sauté until crisp:

4 or 5 slices bacon

Remove from the pan, drain on absorbent paper and cut or crumble in small pieces. Heat:

2 tablespoons melted butter, bacon drippings or oil

Add:

¼ cup mild vinegar
(1 teaspoon chopped fresh herbs (II, 204))

Add the bacon and also, at this time, if you choose:

(1 teaspoon grated onion)
(1 teaspoon sugar)

Pour the dressing, while hot, over:

1 head lettuce, separated, shredded cabbage, dandelion, young spinach leaves or other greens

Serve it at once from a warm bowl onto warm plates, garnished with:

Hard-cooked sliced eggs

CHICORY AND BEETROOT SALAD [4]

This is a favorite winter salad in France. Cut in ½-inch slices, into a salad bowl:

6 heads Belgian or French endive

Add:

2 cups sliced canned or cooked beets

Toss in:

French Dressing, page 341, or Water Cress Dressing, page 343

ORIENTAL BEAN SPROUT SALAD [6]

Place in a salad bowl:

- 4 cups crisp salad greens
- 1 cup drained bean sprouts
- ½ cup thinly sliced water chestnuts
- ¼ cup toasted, slivered almonds

Toss, just before serving, in:

¼ to ⅓ cup Oriental Dip (II, 84)

thinned with:

2 tablespoons cream

COLE SLAW [6]

Red cabbage may be used. Very finely shredded red and white cabbage may also be combined with good effect. Pared and diced pineapple or apple may be added.

Remove the outer leaves and the core from:

A small head of cabbage

Shred or chop the remainder, cutting only as much as is needed for immediate use. Formerly, the chopped cabbage was soaked in ice water for 1 hour. If soaked, drain well, dry between towels and chill. Immediately before serving, moisten with:

French Dressing, page 341, or Boiled Dressing, page 350, Sour Cream Dressing, page 351, or equal parts mayonnaise and chili sauce, or thick cream, sweet or cultured sour

If you choose the cream, be sure to use a little vinegar, salt and sugar. You may add to any of these dressings:

(Chopped anchovies)
(Dill, caraway or celery seed)
(Chopped parsley, chives or other herbs)

COLE SLAW DE LUXE [8]

Shortly before serving time, remove the core of:

A small head of cabbage

Cut into the thinnest shreds possible. Place in a deep bowl. Add:

1 to 2 tablespoons lemon juice
(Fresh herbs: chopped parsley, chives, etc.)

Beat until stiff:

¾ cup whipping cream

Fold in:

- ½ teaspoon celery seed
- ½ teaspoon sugar
- ¾ teaspoon salt
- ¼ teaspoon freshly ground white pepper
- 1 cup seedless green grapes
- ½ cup finely shredded blanched almonds

Pour it over the cabbage. Toss quickly until well coated. Serve at once with:

Tomatoes or in an Aspic Ring, page 58

ROQUEFORT COLE SLAW [4]

This is based on a recipe from Herman Smith. His splendid books, "Stina" and "Kitchens Near and Far," should appeal to all lovers of good eating and reading.

Shred finely:

1½ cups red or green young cabbage

Peel and cut into long, narrow strips:

1 cup apples

In order to keep them from discoloring, sprinkle them with:

Lemon juice

Toss salad lightly with:

Roquefort Sour Cream

Dressing
Serve at once, garnished with:
Parsley

▤ COLE SLAW FOR BARBECUE [6]

The tangy dressing in this slaw goes well with meat broiled or barbecued outdoors. If you are cooking farther from home than your own backyard or patio, try the plastic bag method of "tossing" the slaw, described on page 33.

Combine.
1 cup mayonnaise, page 345
4 chopped scallions
1 tablespoon tomato catsup
2 teaspoons vinegar
⅛ teaspoon Worcestershire sauce
¼ teaspoon salt
⅛ teaspoon pepper
¼ teaspoon sugar

Add this mixture to:
3 cups shredded cabbage
3 cups salad greens
1 thinly-sliced carrot
½ green pepper, cut in strips

Toss salad lightly and serve.

HOT SLAW WITH APPLE [6]

Place in a skillet:
½ lb. finely diced salt pork

Render it slowly, then remove the crisp, browned pieces, drain them on absorbent paper and reserve. Add to the rendered fat in the skillet:
3 tablespoons vinegar
2 tablespoons water
1 tablespoon sugar
1 teaspoon caraway or celery seed
1 teaspoon salt

Cook and stir these ingredients over quick heat until they boil. ➧ Reduce the heat to a simmer. Stir in:
3 cups shredded cabbage
1 large peeled, grated apple

Simmer the slaw for about one minute longer and serve garnished with the tiny browned cubes of salt pork. You may also use the recipe for Wilted Greens, page 35, using the crumbled bacon as a garnish instead of hard-cooked eggs.

⅄ BLENDER SLAW [4]

This can only be made satisfactorily in a 2-speed blender with a chopping action.

Quarter and core:
1 small head of cabbage

Core, seed and remove membrane of:
½ green pepper

Peel:
½ medium onion
1 carrot

Chop these vegetables coarsely into the blender container, until it is half filled. Add to within 1 inch of the top:
Cold water

➧ Cover and blend for 2 seconds, no longer, using the chopping speed. Empty the vegetables into a sieve to drain and repeat the process until all the vegetables are shredded. Place them in a salad bowl and sprinkle with:
(1 teaspoon caraway seeds)

Toss lightly in:
Mayonnaise, page 345, or Sour Cream Dressing, page 351

thinned with:
2 tablespoons lemon juice

GINGHAM SALAD WITH COTTAGE CHEESE [4]

Place in a mixing bowl and toss:
1½ cups coarsely chopped young spinach leaves
2 cups shredded red cabbage
⅓ teaspoon salt
¼ teaspoon celery seed
3 tablespoons chopped olives or chives

1 cup cottage cheese

Place these ingredients on:

4 large lettuce leaves

Serve the salad with:

Mayonnaise, page 345, Sour Cream Dressing, page 351, or Green Mayonnaise, page 348

ABOUT TOSSED COMBINATION SALADS

Serve combination salads as a luncheon main dish, accompanied by Toasted Cheese Rolls, (II, 59) or savory sandwiches, page 240. Practically every restaurant serves some kind of combination salad, often named after its own inventive chef, but each has the chief distinction of containing some form of protein such as meat, chicken or cheese, in addition to the greens and vegetables. Here are variations:

COMBINATION SALADS

I. Rub a salad bowl with:

Garlic

Place in it:

Lettuce or spinach leaves
Cut-up anchovies
Chopped, pitted, ripe olives
Sliced radishes
Sliced hard-cooked eggs
Shredded Swiss cheese

Toss the salad with:

French Dressing, page 341

Garnish it with:

Peeled and quartered tomatoes

II. Combine:

Lettuce
Endive
Romaine
Water cress

Cut into narrow strips:

Salami
Sautéed bacon
Anchovies
Swiss cheese

Dice and add:

Raw cauliflower
Cooked string beans

Marinate these ingredients for ½ hour in:

French Dressing, page 341

Serve the salad half wilted.

GARNISHES FOR SALADS

To garnish salads, use the following:

Tomato slices, dipped in finely chopped parsley or chives
Parsley or water cress in bunches or chopped
Lettuce leaves, cress, endive, romaine, etc.
Heads of lettuce, cut into slices or wedges
Lemon slices with pinked edges, dipped in chopped parsley
Shredded olives or sliced stuffed olives
Cooked beets, cut into shapes or sticks
Carrots, cut into shapes
Pearl onions
Pickles
Capers
Pomegranate seeds
Fennel slices
Cucumbers or Cucumber Slices, page 43
Green and red peppers, shredded
Pepper slices
Mayonnaise or soft cream cheese, forced through a tube

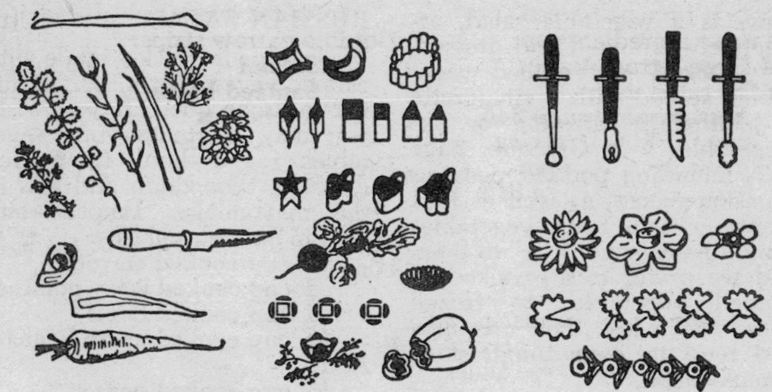

Aspic jellies in small molds or chopped aspic
Eggs—hard-cooked, sliced, riced or stuffed
Dwarf tomatoes, stuffed with cottage cheese
Cherry tomatoes
Fresh herbs, sprigs or chopped
Mint leaves
Nasturtium leaves
Nut meats
Chopped truffles
Shaped truffles

ABOUT CUTTING VEGETABLE GARNISHES AND CASES

Use vegetables as cases for piquant sauces, as sketched below. A pepper hollowed out, which can be lidded with its handsomely fat stem portion; an onion sliced to produce rings which will hold vinaigretted asparagus upright on an hors d'oeuvre tray; onion cups made from raw or slightly blanched onions; a cucumber slashed and hollowed to hold olives or gherkins and a simpler scored cucumber cup. Citrus rind rings or green or red pepper rings can be used in the same manner to hold food upright.

Try your hand at carving vegetables and see what fun you can have and how attractive your trays can look with a little effort. Don't force effects. Use them sparingly. See illustration for some very simple suggestions. Begin on the left with carrots cut in scrolls, etc., radishes made into roses and pickles into fans. Make geometric accents with hors d'oeuvre cutters and scoops, shown at center and at the top on the right. Shape flowers and borders of olives, as shown on the lower right, also twists of cucumber. Make an ingenuous turnip or egg white and carrot daisy, gay for spinach dishes, or small daffodill blooms of carrots shown above. These can have chive stems and leaves if you like. Try for some asymmetric drawing-like effects, such as shrimps suggested by thin lines of red pepper. One of the loveliest decorations we ever saw were 2 small lobsters, cut in a modern feeling from red peppers and placed casually on the side and the top of a cream-covered mousse. Seaweed was indicated by fennel leaves and partially crowned the top. See also (II, 101), for varied lemon garnishes.

ABOUT VEGETABLES FOR SALADS

A welcome summertime alternative to the crisp green salads or slaws is a vegetable salad, attractively arranged and dressed. Try cooked and chilled vegetables, served with a vinaigrette or chiffonade dressing or use Vegetables à la Grecque, page 257, including podded peas, as occasion pieces, as well as in a whole salad. Your vegetables should have some "bite" to them and we prefer fresh, cooked or canned vegetables to frozen ones, which lose their crispness and tend to have tough skins when cooked.

COOKED VEGETABLE SALAD PLATTER

Cook separately a variety of:

Vegetables—cauliflower, carrots, snap beans, Lima beans, beets, soy beans, bean sprouts, etc.

Marinate them in separate bowls for several hours with:

French Dressing page 341

Use about ¼ cup of dressing to 2 cups of vegetables. Drain well. Arrange in some attractive way on a large platter. For example, place the cauliflower or the beets in the center and alternate the other vegetables according to color in mounds, about them, on:

Lettuce leaves

Garnish the platter with:

Curled celery, radishes, sliced or riced hard-cooked eggs or deviled eggs

or, place in the center of a platter, chilled:

Snap Bean Salad, page 42

Surround it with overlapping slices of skinned:

Tomatoes or cherry tomatoes filled with cottage cheese

Garnish the platter with:

Shredded lettuce or watercress
Deviled eggs or sardines

RUSSIAN SALAD [6]

This recipe is quickly made with canned vegetables, although it is not quite as good. If you wish, you may marinate your vegetables for 1 hour in French dressing, then drain and toss in the mayonnaise. Prepare and dice in ¼-inch cubes:

1 cup cooked carrots
1 cup cooked waxy potatoes
1 cup cooked beets
½ cup cooked green beans

Add:

½ cup cooked peas

Toss the vegetables in:

Mayonnaise, page 345

with:

(A few capers)
(Julienned strips of ham)

Serve in mounds, on lettuce leaves.

ITALIAN SALAD [6]

Prepare and dice:

1 cup cooked beets
1 cup cooked carrots

These proportions may be varied. Chill the vegetables. Combine them with:

1 cup chopped celery
½ cup cooked or canned green peas
(½ cup pared, seeded and diced cucumbers)

Moisten the vegetables with:

Boiled Salad Dressing, page 350, mayonnaise thinned with cream, or Sour Cream Dressing, page 351

Serve the salad in a bowl garnished with:

Lettuce

For more elegant occasions, mold the salad into a fish shape and cover with thin, overlapping slices of cucumber for scales.

STUFFED ARTICHOKE SALADS

I. With Sea Food

Cook:

Artichokes, page 259

Chill, and remove the inedible choke. Marinate:

Shrimp, crab meat, oysters or bay scallops

with:

French Dressing, page 341

Fill the artichokes with sea food and serve with:

Mayonnaise

on a bed of:

Shredded lettuce

II. With Caviar

Fill the artichokes with:

Cultured sour cream
Caviar

III. With Meat

Fill with:

Ham, veal, tuna or chicken salad or liver pâté, page 525

ARTICHOKE HEARTS SALAD

Cooked or canned, these are delicious in salad. They may be cut up and added to green salads or aspics or they may be used as a basis on which to build up an attractive individual salad plate.

ASPARAGUS SALAD

Cook:

Asparagus, page 260

Drain and chill. Cover the tips with:

Mayonnaise or Boiled Salad Dressing, page 350

Thin the dressing with a little:

Cultured sour cream

Add:

(Chopped tarragon)

If that is not available, add:

(chopped parsley or chives)

or serve asparagus salad with:

Vinaigrette Dressing, page 341

ASPARAGUS TIP SALAD

Drain the contents of a can of:

Asparagus tips

Place around 4 or 5 tips a ring of:

Red or green pepper or pimiento

Place the asparagus in the ring on:

Shredded lettuce

Serve the salad with:

French Dressing, page 341 or mayonnaise

ASPARAGUS AND EGG SALAD [6]

Chill in a dish:

2 cups cooked, well-drained asparagus, cut in pieces
3 sliced hard-cooked eggs
6 sliced stuffed olives

Wash, drain and place in refrigerator to crisp:

1 bunch water cress
1 small head lettuce

When ready to serve, combine:

½ cup cultured sour cream
2 teaspoons grated onion or chopped chives
2 tablespoons lemon juice, caper liquor or vinegar
1 teaspoon salt
¼ teaspoon paprika
1/16 teaspoon curry powder
(2 tablespoons capers)

Line a serving dish with the larger lettuce leaves. Break the rest into pieces. Add these to the asparagus mixture. Chop and add the water cress. Pour the dressing over these ingredients. Toss them lightly. Place them in the serving dish. Serve the salad at once, garnished with:

Parsley

DRIED BEAN SALAD [4 to 6]

Lentils, kidney, navy, Lima or miniature green soy beans, cooked or canned, are the basis of these "stick-to-the-ribs" salads. Drain well and chill:

2½ cups canned or cooked kidney or Lima beans

Combine with:
¼ cup French Dressing, page 341
(A pinch of curry powder or ¼ cup chopped gherkins or pearl onions)
Serve on:
Lettuce leaves
Sprinkle with:
Chopped parsley
Chopped chives or grated onion

SNAP BEAN SALAD [4 to 6]

This is a fine picnic salad.
Prepare:
3 cups cooked Snap Beans, page 262
Drain well and toss, while warm, in:
French Dressing, page 341, or Lorenzo Dressing, page 342
Chill thoroughly, then add:
Chopped or grated onion, chives or pearl onions
Serve on:
Lettuce leaves

HOT SNAP BEAN SALAD [6]

Prepare:
3 cups cooked Snap Beans, page 262
Drain them. Combine them with the dressing for:
Wilted Greens, page 35
Season as desired or with:
(Summer savory)
Serve from a warm bowl onto warm plates.

COLD BEET CUPS

Pressure cook:
Large Beets, page 270
and chill. Fill the beets with:
Marinated Cucumbers with cultured sour cream or Russian Salad, page 40
Cole Slaw, page 36 or
Deviled Eggs, page 195
Garnish with:
Curly Endive

PICKLED BEET SALAD

Drain:
2½ cups cooked or canned beets
Reserve the juice. Slice the beets. Place them in a fruit jar.
Boil:
½ cup sharp vinegar
½ cup beet juice
Add and heat to boiling:
2 tablespoons sugar
2 cloves
½ teaspoon salt
3 peppercorns
¼ bay leaf
(1 sliced green pepper)
(1 small sliced onion)
(½ teaspoon horseradish)
Pour these ingredients over the beets. Cover the jar. Serve the beets very cold.

CARROT SALAD WITH RAISINS AND NUTS [4]

Scrape well:
4 large carrots
Place them on ice for 1 hour. Grate them coarsely into a bowl.
Add and mix lightly:
½ cup seedless raisins
½ cup coarsely chopped pecans or peanuts
¾ teaspoon salt
Freshly ground black pepper
2 teaspoons grated lemon peel
1 tablespoon lemon juice
Place the salad in a bowl. Pour over it:
1 cup or more cultured sour cream
Toss the salad if you wish.

CELERY CABBAGE SALAD

Use celery cabbage in any recipe for hot or cold slaw, page 35, or in the colorful recipe below:
Wash well, then crisp:
1 stalk celery cabbage

Cut it crosswise into shreds. Serve it very cold with:

French Dressing, page 341

This cabbage combines superbly with:

Water cress

Use any convenient proportion. Garnish the salad with:

Pickled Beets, page 42

COOKED CELERY OR ENDIVE SALAD

I. Prepare:

Braised Celery or Endive, page 282

and serve cold on:

Lettuce leaves

II. Simmer until tender:

Trimmed, halved dwarf celery or endive heads

in a quantity of:

Veal or chicken stock

Drain. Reserve the juices for soup or sauces. Marinate the vegetable in:

French Dressing, page 341

to which you may add:

1 teaspoon anchovy paste

Chill and serve on:

Lettuce

CELERIAC OR CELERY ROOT SALAD

Prepare:

Celeriac, page 283

Chill it. Toss it in:

Mayonnaise, well seasoned with mustard

or, best of all, in:

French Dressing, page 341

to which you may add:

Minced shallots or chives

Serve it on:

Endive or water cress

CELERIAC OR CELERI-RAVE REMOULADE [5 to 6]

One of the more classic ways is as follows: Blanch for 1 to 2 minutes and chill:

½ lb. celeriac

Steep it in:

Cold Mustard Sauce I, page 344

for 2 to 3 hours. Serve chilled.

CUCUMBER SALAD

Be sure to select firm, hard, green cucumbers. The slightly flabby or yellowing ones are old and often pithy and the skin seems to toughen. Some people who are allergic to cucumber find they can eat it if the skin is left on. It should have a slight sheen, but if highly polished it is probably waxed and in such case the skin should not be used. If you wish to make the cucumbers more decorative, leave unpared and score with a fork, as sketched, before slicing.

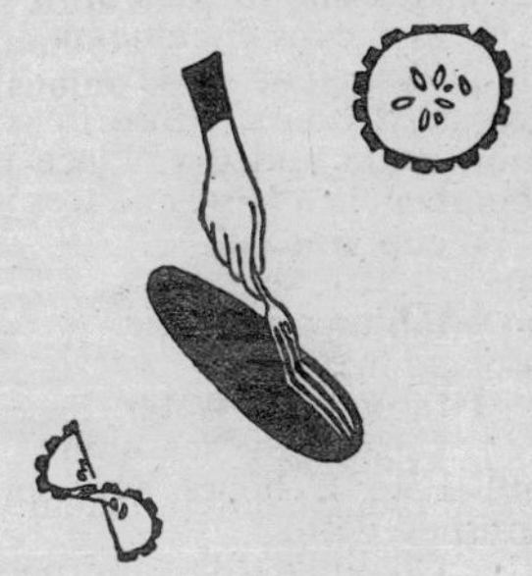

Chill, pare and slice:

Cucumbers

Combine them with:

French Dressing, page 341, or Sour Cream Dressing, page 351

to which you may add:

Finely minced parsley

Serve at once.

WILTED CUCUMBERS

Although nutrients are undoubtedly lost in soaking, this process gives cucumbers a quality that is cherished by many. It rids the cucumber of a slightly acrid taste and produces an appetizing texture. So, on occasion, try soaking them.

I.
Peel and slice very thin:

Cucumbers

A potato peeler does a fine job. Dispose them in layers in a bowl. Salt each layer and place a weight over the cucumbers. A plate with a heavy weight over all will do. Cover and refrigerate 3 to 6 hours. Drain and toss in:

Cultured sour cream

Garnish with:

Chopped dill, basil or tarragon

Serve chilled at once.

II. [3]
Slice, leaving the skins on, if very young and unwaxed:

1½ to 2 cups cucumbers

Salt and weight as above. Refrigerate 2 hours. Rinse in cold water, drain and dry. Place the cucumbers in a bowl and toss in:

¼ cup vinegar

also:

1 tablespoon sugar

dissolved in:

1 tablespoon water
Correct the seasoning

Chill 1 to 2 hours and serve garnished with:

Chopped dill or burnet or very thinly sliced Bermuda onion rings

COLD STUFFED CUCUMBERS

Good for a luncheon plate or as hors d'oeuvre.
Chill:

Small, shapely cucumbers

Pare them. Cut them in halves lengthwise or cut off a slice lengthwise and remove the seeds. The cucumber boats may be wrapped in waxed paper and chilled. Fill them with:

Chicken Salad, page 51 or a Fish Salad, pages 50–51

or anything suitable that you can think of, such as:

Celery, nut meats, green grapes, olives, etc.

These ingredients may be moistened with or served with:

Mayonnaise, Beet and Anchovy Dressing, page 342, Chutney Dressing, page 344, etc.

Serve the cucumbers on:

Shredded lettuce or water cress

LOTUS ROOT SALAD

Peel and slice thin, crosswise:

1 lb. lotus root

Soak for 10 minutes in:

Acidulated Water (II, 148)

Drain and dip slices in:

Fresh, boiling, acidulated water

Plunge quickly in:

Cold water

and drain again. Heat and mix:

2 tablespoons sesame oil
1 to 2 drops hot pepper sauce
1½ tablespoons sugar
2 tablespoons soy sauce

Pour this sauce over the drained lotus root and allow to stand about 1 hour. Serve chilled in the sauce.

OKRA SALAD

A fine hot-weather salad. The marinated pods are slightly reminiscent of oysters.
Prepare:

Stewed Okra, page 300

Place the drained okra in a dish and cover with:

Well-seasoned French Dressing, page 341 Horseradish Dressing, page 343, Mayonnaise, page 345

Chill. Serve very cold on:

Lettuce

HEARTS OF PALM SALAD

I. Cut into lengthwise strips:
Chilled canned hearts of palm
Serve on:
Romaine
garnished with:
Stuffed olive slices
Green pepper rings
Sprinkle with:
Chopped parsley
Paprika
Serve with:
French Dressing, page 341, or Mayonnaise, page 345

II. If you live in Florida, you can have fresh:
Hearts of palm
But be sure to eat them as soon as peeled, for they discolor quickly. Cut into dice, sprinkle with:
Lemon juice
and serve with:
French Dressing, page 341, made with lime juice
Another way to serve is to treat the hearts as for Cole Slaw, page 36.

PEPPER SLICES WITH FILLINGS

[8 to 10 slices]
These slices are highly decorative. They make a pretty salad and are good as canapés, on toast or crackers.
2 medium-size red or green peppers
Cut a piece from stem end and remove the seeds and membranes. Stuff the peppers with a Cream Cheese Spread (II, 58) or Ham Salad, page 52, and chill for 12 hours. Slice them with a sharp hot knife and replace them on ice. Serve the slices on:
Lettuce
with:
French Dressing, page 341, or Mayonnaise, page 345

★ FILLED PIMIENTOS OR CHRISTMAS SALAD [6]

A decorative and delicious salad, but do not expect the peppers to look like fresh ones. They are simply a casing for the soft filling:
Drain:
6 large canned pimientos
Dice:
2½ cups drained canned pineapple
Add to it:
1½ cups diced celery
1 tablespoon tiny pickled pearl onions
Whip until stiff:
¼ cup whipping cream
Combine it with:
1 cup mayonnaise
Fold into these ingredients the pineapple, celery and onions. Stuff the pimientos with the mixture. Chill. Bed on a nest of:
Shredded lettuce
Roll into small balls:
6 oz. soft cream cheese
Roll the balls in:
Chopped parsley
Place them around the pimientos or, if they are served individually, beside them.

POTATO SALAD

Potato salad is best made from potatoes cooked in their jackets and peeled and marinated while still warm. The small red waxy potatoes hold their shape and don't crumble when sliced or diced; furthermore, they do not absorb an excessive amount of dressing or become mushy. Do not try to make potato salad with yesterday's cold boiled potatoes—it is not good. For hot weather picnics, use an eggless dressing to avoid dangerous spoilage.

I. [4]
Prepare as above:
2 cups sliced, boiled, waxy potatoes

Marinate them in:
½ cup heated French Dressing, page 341
Mix in gently with a wooden spoon, just before serving:
1 tablespoon chopped parsley
1 tablespoon chopped chives or 1 tablespoon finely grated onion
(1 cup sliced cooked scallops)
Serve tepid.

II. [4]

Marinate the potatoes well with:
½ cup French Dressing, page 341, soup stock or canned bouillon
Chop or slice and add discreetly a mixture of any of the following:
Hard-cooked eggs, onions, olives, pickles, celery with leaves, cucumbers, capers
1 tablespoon salt
Paprika
A few grains cayenne
(2 teaspoons horseradish)
After one hour or more of refrigeration, add:
Mayonnaise, Boiled Salad Dressing, page 350, or cultured sour cream
Refrigerate about 1 hour longer. Shortly before serving, you may toss in:
(Coarsely chopped water cress)

POTATO AND HERRING SALAD [6]

Place in a large bowl and toss gently:
2 cups diced boiled potatoes
1¼ cups diced marinated or pickled herring fillets
¾ cup chopped celery with leaves
1 tablespoon minced parsley
1 tablespoon minced chives
6 tablespoons cultured sour cream
1½ tablespoons lemon juice
¾ teaspoon paprika
Serve the salad chilled in:
Lettuce cups

GERMAN HOT POTATO SALAD [6]

Cook in their jackets, in a covered saucepan, until tender:
6 medium-size waxy potatoes
Peel and slice while they are hot.
Heat in a skillet:
4 strips minced bacon or 2 tablespoons bacon drippings
Add and sauté until brown:
¼ cup chopped onion
¼ cup chopped celery
1 chopped dill pickle
Heat to the boiling point:
¼ cup water or stock
½ cup vinegar
½ teaspoon sugar
½ teaspoon salt
⅛ teaspoon paprika
(¼ teaspoon dry mustard)
Pour these ingredients into the skillet. Combine them with the potatoes and serve at once with chopped parsley or chives.

POTATO SALAD NIÇOISE [12]

Cook:
3 cups new potatoes
in water to which a clove of garlic has been added. Peel and slice and, while still warm, sprinkle with:
½ cup heated white wine or ¼ cup wine vinegar and ¼ cup stock
Let stand at 70° for 1 hour.
Have ready:
3 cups chilled cooked green beans
6 peeled quartered tomatoes
which have been marinating in:
French Dressing, page 341

To serve, mound the potatoes in a volcano in the center of a platter garnished with:

Salad greens

Garnish the potatoes with:

Capers
Small pitted black olives
1 dozen anchovy fillets

Alternate the tomato quarters and small heaps of the green beans around the potatoes. See the following Salad Niçoise for a version of this salad without potatoes, from the south of France.

SALAD NIÇOISE

Rub your salad bowl with garlic then place in it:

2 peeled and quartered tomatoes
1 peeled and finely cut cucumber
6 coarsely chopped fillets of anchovy
12 coarsely chopped pitted black olives
1 cup Bibb lettuce
1 cup romaine

Toss in:

French Dressing, page 341

RICE SALAD [4]

Prepare:

2 cups steamed rice

The grains must be dry and fluffy for the success of this salad. While the rice is warm, mix in:

¼ cup French Dressing, page 341 preferably made with tarragon vinegar and olive oil
A pinch of grated nutmeg
¼ cup coarsely chopped green pepper
¼ cup finely chopped celery
10 black olives, pitted and halved

Garnish with:

Peeled, quartered tomatoes

in a bowl lined with:

Leaf lettuce

This goes well with cold chicken or cold smoked tongue. Serve the salad tepid.

ABOUT TOMATOES FOR SALAD

Good flavor and texture are particularly important in tomatoes for salad. If you can get vine-ripened tomatoes, they are infinitely superior to those picked green and allowed to ripen on their way to the supermarket. The latter often become mealy and almost tasteless in spite of their deceptively ruddy complexion. Use them for Stuffed Tomatoes, page 48, where they can be spiced up with a peppy filling.

Always cut out the stem-end core. It is tough and often tastes bitter. If you are going to stuff the tomato in one of the ways suggested later in this chapter, turn it upside down so that the cored end rests on the plate. If you wish, you can fake a stem and leaves by making a tiny hole in the lid and inserting a sprig of mint, parsley or some other fresh herb. Keep your eyes open at market for the topepo, a hybrid between a tomato and red pepper which makes a good substitute for tomato.

FRENCH TOMATO SALAD

Cut into very thin vertical slices, page 49:

6 medium unpeeled tomatoes

Place them so that they overlap around a cold platter or across it. Pour over them a dressing made of:

French dressing
¼ cup minced parsley
2 minced shallots or green onions

CANNED TOMATO SALAD

Chill the contents of a can of:

Whole tomatoes

or use the firm part of any canned tomatoes. Place them in individual dishes. Sprinkle them with:

Celery salt
Salt
Lemon juice
Brown sugar

or anything you like. The main thing is to serve them very cold.

ABOUT COLD STUFFED TOMATOES

A bit of tomato skin was once as much out of place at a dinner table as a bowie knife. The discovery that tomato skins contain highly valued vitamins makes them "salon-fähig"—so whether to serve tomatoes skinned or unskinned rests with the hostess' sense of delicacy or her desire for health.

➧ To skin tomatoes, first wash them and then use one of the following methods: stroke the skin with the dull edge of a knife blade until the skin wrinkles and can be lifted off; or, dip the tomato in boiling water for 1 minute and then immediately in cold water, drain and skin; or, pierce the tomato with a fork and rotate it over a burner until the skin is tight and shiny, plunge into cold water and peel.

➧ To prepare tomato cases, first skin the tomatoes as described above, then hollow them. Invert the tomatoes to drain for 20 minutes. Chill them and fill the hollows with one of the fillings suggested below.

Tomatoes can be cut and filled in a variety of attractive ways and they provide a gay splash of color for buffet salads. If you do not wish to serve large portions, cut the tomatoes in halves or in slices. Place on each slice a ring of green pepper ½ inch or more thick. Fill the ring.

You can also cut them crosswise in zigzag fashion, fill them sandwich style and top with a mint leaf. Or slash into 6 sections, nearly to the base, and fill the center. Garnish with a stuffed olive.

Slice horizontally into quarters and fill as a club sandwich. Garnish with a slice of black olive or pimiento star or cover with a pepper lid as sketched.

FILLINGS

I. Pineapple and Nut Meats

Combine equal parts of:

Chopped celery
Fresh shredded pineapple
A few walnut meats
Mayonnaise

II. Eggs and Anchovies

Combine:

Chopped hard-cooked eggs
Chopped anchovies or anchovy paste
Onion juice or grated onion
Chopped parsley or other herb
Mayonnaise or thick cultured sour cream
Paprika and salt

III. Eggs and Ham

Combine:

2 chopped hard-cooked eggs

1 cup ground or minced ham
½ cup chopped celery
12 sliced olives
Fresh or dried savory
2 chopped sweet pickles
Sour Cream Dressing, page 351 or mayonnaise

IV. Deviled Eggs
Place in each tomato hollow:
½ Deviled Egg, page 195
Serve on:
Lettuce
with:
Anchovy Dressing, page 342

V. Aspic
For about 6 tomato cases prepare:
1½ cups aspic
This may be an Aspic Salad, page 58, to which chopped meat or fish and vegetables, etc., may be added. When the aspic is about to set, fill the tomato cases. Chill until firm. Garnish with:
Olives, parsley, etc.
and serve with:
Mayonnaise

VI. Some other good fillings are:
Wilted Cucumbers I, page 44
Crab Meat Salad, page 50, or A Fish Salad, pages 50–51
Chicken Salad, page 51
Guacamole I (II, 61)
Cole Slaw, page 36
Avocado chunks
Shrimp with mayonnaise
Cottage cheese or soft cream cheese mixed with mayonnaise and chopped chives

TOMATO AND ONION OR CUCUMBER SALAD

Skin and chill:
Medium-size tomatoes
Cut 5 or 6 crosswise gashes in the tomatoes, equal distances apart. Place in each gash, as shown below, a thin slice of:
Bermuda onion or cucumber
Serve the tomatoes on:
Lettuce or water cress
with:
French Dressing, page 341, or Sour Cream Dressing, page 351, etc.

MOLDED EGG AND CAVIAR SALAD

Also good as hors d'oeuvre.
Crush with a fork:
8 hard-cooked eggs
Stir into them:
3 tablespoons soft butter
⅓ teaspoon dry mustard
2 oz. caviar
3 tablespoons lemon juice
1 tablespoon Worcestershire sauce
Pack these ingredients into a tall, oiled glass. Chill. Unmold and cut into ½- to 1-inch slices.
Serve on:
Thick tomato slices
or use to decorate a salad platter.
Cover with a dab of:
Mayonnaise
(A rolled anchovy)

STUFFED LETTUCE ROLLS

Beat until smooth:
Cottage cheese
Add all or some of the following:
A sprinkling of chives or grated onion
Chopped boiled ham
Seedless raisins
Chopped celery

Chopped green peppers
Chopped nut meats

Spread a thick layer of the cheese mixture on:

Large lettuce leaves

Roll the leaves and secure with toothpicks. Chill. Allow 2 or 3 rolls to a person and serve with:

Mayonnaise or French Dressing, page 345

You may also use a fancy cut vegetable garnish, as sketched on page 39.

MACARONI OR SPAGHETTI SALAD OR CALICO SALAD [5]

Exact proportions are unimportant.

Prepare:

1 cup cooked elbow macaroni, page 170

Drain it. Beat well:

1½ tablespoons lemon juice or 2 tablespoons vinegar
1 tablespoon salad oil

Toss this into the cooked macaroni. There should be about 2 cups of it. Chill the salad for several hours. Toss into it:

1 teaspoon grated onion or 2 tablespoons chopped chives
1 cup diced celery with leaves
1 cup minced parsley
½ cup chopped stuffed olives
¾ teaspoon salt
Freshly ground black pepper
3 tablespoons cultured sour cream
2 tablespoons chopped pimiento

Serve on:

Lettuce

This makes an attractive filling for a tomato aspic ring.

CRAB MEAT OR LOBSTER SALAD

Combine:

1 cup crab meat or lobster
1 cup pared shredded apples
½ cup mayonnaise

CRAB LOUIS [4]

This salad is a product of the West Coast, where the magnificent Pacific crab is frequently served in this way. Arrange around the inside of a bowl:

Lettuce leaves

Place on the bottom:

¾ cup shredded lettuce leaves

Heap on these:

2 cups crab meat

Pour over the crab:

1 cup Pink Mayonnaise or Sauce Louis, page 350

Sometimes eggs are added to the salad. Slice:

(2 hard-cooked eggs)

Place them on top of the crab. Sprinkle over them:

Chopped chives

★ HERRING SALAD

[About 20 Servings]

Herring is a traditional dish for our family at Christmastime. Its rich color, thanks to the red beets, and elaborate garnishing make this dish an imposing sight.

Soak in water for 12 hours.

6 milter herring

Skin them, remove the milt and the bones. Rub the milt through a colander with:

1 cup dry red wine or vinegar

Cut into ¼-inch cubes the herring and:

1½ cups cold cooked veal
2 hard-cooked eggs
1½ cups Pickled Beet Salad, page 42
½ cup onions
½ cup pickles
2 stalks celery
½ cup cold boiled potatoes

Prepare and add:

3 cups diced apples

Blanch, shred and add:
1 cup almonds
Combine the milt mixture with:
1 cup sugar
2 tablespoons horseradish
2 tablespoons chopped parsley
Pour this over the other ingredients. Mix well. Shape the salad into a mound or place it in a bowl. Garnish it with:
Riced hard-cooked eggs
Pickles and olives
Sardelles and parsley

LOBSTER SALAD [4]

Dice:
1 cup canned or cooked lobster meat
Add:
(Grated onion)
Marinate with:
¼ cup French dressing
Chill for 1 hour. Combine with:
1 cup chopped celery
Place on:
Lettuce
Cover or combine with:
½ cup mayonnaise
to which you may add:
(2 tablespoons dry sherry)
Garnish with:
Lobster claws
Olives and radishes
Hard-cooked eggs
Capers and pickles
or prepare:
Tomato Aspic, page 65
Place it in a ring or in individual molds. Invert the aspic on:
Lettuce
Fill the ring or surround the molds with lobster salad.

SHRIMP OR LOBSTER MOLD [4]

This makes a lovely center for an hors d'oeuvre tray. Grind together:
1 lb. cooked shrimp or lobster
1 tablespoon capers
⅓ of a small onion

Add and mix well:
⅓ cup softened butter
3 tablespoons heavy cream
2 tablespoons Pernod
A dash of hot pepper sauce
1 teaspoon salt
1 teaspoon fresh tarragon
Pack into a mold. Refrigerate for 3 to 4 hours before serving. For a special occasion, mold the mixture flat in either individual molds or one large mold. Cover with a thin icing of:
Whipped cream
Cut large crescents from pieces of:
Red peppers
to suggest the tails, claws and feelers of lobster or shrimp. Apply them in these patterns. For an added touch of realism, garnish with seaweed made of:
Wisps of finocchio leaf
and a few:
Seedless green grapes

TUNA FISH, SHRIMP OR SHAD ROE SALAD [4]

Have ready:
1 cup canned fish
Flake it with a fork. Add:
½ to 1 cup diced celery or cucumber
Make a French dressing using:
2 tablespoons olive oil
2 tablespoons lemon juice
or use ¼ cup mayonnaise. Add:
(1 tablespoon chopped chives)
(1 tablespoon chopped parsley)
Serve very cold on:
Lettuce

CHICKEN SALAD [8]

A traditional "party" dish, chicken salad should taste of chicken, the other ingredients being present only to add variety of texture and to enhance the flavor. So always keep the proportions of at least twice as much chicken as the total of

your other ingredients. Since it is usually combined with mayonnaise, be careful to ♦ refrigerate it, particularly if you make it in advance.
Dice:

2 cups cooked chicken
1 cup celery
(¼ cup salted almonds)

Chill these ingredients. They may be marinated lightly with:

French Dressing, page 341

When ready to serve, combine with:

1 cup mayonnaise

Season the salad, as required, with:

Salt and paprika

Serve it on:

Lettuce

Garnish with:

Pimiento and olives
(Sliced hard-cooked eggs and capers)

Quantity note: Generous main dish servings for 50 will require:

1 gal. cooked cubed chicken

To obtain this amount, you need about 17 lbs. ready to cook chicken. If you substitute turkey, you need only a 12-pounder.

CHICKEN SALAD VARIATIONS

Follow the preceding recipe. You may substitute cooked duck, turkey or veal for the chicken, remembering to keep the proportions of 2 of meat or fowl to 1 of the other ingredients.

Chicken, celery and hard-cooked eggs
Chicken, bean sprouts and water chestnuts
Chicken, cucumber and English walnut meats
Chicken, Boiled Chestnuts, page 283, and celery—pimiento may be added
Chicken and parboiled oysters
Chicken and fruit such as seedless grapes, fresh chopped pineapple and pomegranate seeds

You may add to the mayonnaise:

(Strained chili sauce)

See also Chicken Mousse, page 60.

HOT CHICKEN SALAD [4]

Preheat oven to 350°.
Combine:

2 cups cubed cooked chicken
1 cup finely diced celery
½ teaspoon salt
½ teaspoon monosodium glutamate
¼ teaspoon tarragon
½ cup toasted almonds
1 tablespoon chopped chives
2 tablespoons lemon juice
½ cup mayonnaise
½ cup Béchamel Sauce, page 359

Bake in very shallow individual bakers for 10 to 15 minutes or until heated. Garnish with:

Parsley or small sprigs of lemon thyme

HAM, CORNED BEEF, VEAL OR BEEF SALAD

Let this be a matter of inspiration.
Dice:

Cooked ham, corned beef, veal or beef
Hard-cooked eggs
Celery with leaves
(Green peppers or pickles)

Combine these ingredients with:

Tart mayonnaise or French Dressing, page 341

Garnish with:

Chopped chives, parsley or other herbs

Surround the meat with tomatoes, sliced or whole.

ABOUT FRUIT SALADS

The purist frowns on fruit salads except for dessert and we ourselves have shuddered at the omnipresent peach half with cottage cheese and a blob of mayonnaise. Nevertheless, such a wide variety of fruit is available to us throughout the year, including many tropical ones, that we often delight in their color and taste in salad before or with the main entrée. Fruit salads offer great scope for the artist. A large arranged platter can substitute for flowers as a centerpiece on a buffet. With protein, such as chicken, meat, cheese, or fish, fruits make wonderful summer luncheon dishes. As a general rule, keep the dressings for pre-dessert fruit salads fairly tart, so that the appetite is not dulled. As a change from the usual base of salad greens, serve fruit salads, where suitable, in baskets, cups or cases made from fruit, as described on (II, 104). In preparing fruit salad in advance, ➧ store bananas, peaches and other easily discolored fruit covered with the acid dressing you plan on using, to avoid discoloration.

APPLE, PEAR, OR PEACH SALAD

Try this with an omelet, French bread and coffee.
Pare, core, slice and sprinkle with lemon juice to keep them from discoloring:

Well-flavored apples, pears, or peaches

Serve them on:

Lettuce

with:

Lemon and Sherry Dressing, page 352, or French Dressing

Garnish the salad with:

Cream cheese and nut balls or Roquefort cheese balls

The apples may be cut into rings and the cheese balls placed in the center.

WALDORF SALAD [6]

Prepare:

1 cup diced celery
1 cup diced apples
(1 cup Tokay grapes, halved and seeded)

Combine with:

½ cup walnut or pecan meats
¾ cup mayonnaise or Boiled Salad Dressing, page 350

ABOUT AVOCADO SALADS

Please read About Avocados (II, 96). To prepare avocado cups, cut the fruit in half lengthwise, place between the palms of the hands and gently twist the halves apart. Tap the large seed with the edge of a knife and lift or pry it out. ➧ To prevent the fruit from darkening after cutting, sprinkle with lemon juice. ➧ To store, spread with mayonnaise, soft butter or cream, allow the seed to remain in it and cover well with wax paper or plastic. Avocado has a soft, buttery texture and taste which combines best with citrus fruits or tomatoes and a sharp or tangy dressing. It also has an unexpected affinity with shrimp, crab or lobster. All of these combinations offer a pleasing contrast of color, as well as texture and taste—the hallmark of a delectable salad.

AVOCADO SLICES

These may be used as a garnish for meats and fish.
Chill:

Avocados

Pare and slice them. Marinate for about 5 minutes in chilled, highly seasoned:

French Dressing, page 341

You may also add:

(Hot pepper sauce, chili sauce, catsup, etc.)

Sprinkle with:

Chopped parsley or chopped mint

Try these avocado slices in:

(Tomato Aspic, page 65)

AVOCADO AND FRUIT SALAD

Pare:

Avocados

Slice them lengthwise and arrange them with skinned sections of:

Orange and grapefruit or pineapple slices

in wheel shape, on:

Lettuce

or, make a rounded salad by alternating the fruit with the green slices into an approximate half globe on the lettuce. Serve with:

French Dressing, page 341, or Lemon or Sherry Dressing, page 352

Prepare the dressing with lime juice in preference to lemon juice or vinegar.

AVOCADO SALAD CUPS

Cut into halves and remove the seeds from:

Chilled avocados

You may then fill the hollows with:

I. Chili sauce seasoned with horseradish

II. Marinated seedless grapes

Garnish with:

A sprig of parsley, mint or water cress

III. Dress up:

Crabmeat, chicken or fruit salad

with:

Mayonnaise

thinned with a little:

Lemon or lime juice

and fill the avocado cup.

IV. Fill with a Tomato Ice which can be made like:

Fruit Ice (II, 493)

only substitute tomato juice for the fruit juice.

V. Scoop the pulp out of the skin, instead of paring the avocado. Turn it into:

Guacamole (II, 61)

Put the mixture back in the half shell and garnish with:

A slice of stuffed olive

BANANA AND NUT SALAD

For each serving, peel and split lengthwise:

1 banana

Spread on the cut sides a thin coating of:

Peanut butter

Sprinkle with:

Chopped peanuts or chopped English walnuts

Serve on:

Lettuce

Garnish with:

Orange sections or red currant jelly

or sprinkle with:

Honey Dressing, page 352

CHERRY AND HAZELNUT SALAD

Drain and pit:

Canned white cherries

Insert in each cherry:

A hazelnut meat

Serve very cold with:

Cottage cheese
Mayonnaise

ABOUT GRAPE SALADS

Grapes are not only delicious as part of fruit and vegetable aspics but are superlative when served alone. Ever peel a grape? Well, it takes time, but what is more luxurious than a lovely mound of peeled, seeded grapes, lightly tossed in a mild olive oil and vinegar dressing, served in lettuce cups or as the center for a gelatin ring mold! You may also toss a few peeled, seeded grapes in a salad of tender lettuce. To make a baroque grape finish on a gelatin top, see (II, 185). See also Seedless Grape and Asparagus Aspic, page 64, or mix seedless grapes with cultured sour cream or yogurt as a fruit salad garnish.

GRAPE AND COTTAGE CHEESE SALAD

Place in an oiled ring mold or in individual ring molds:
Cottage cheese
Chill and invert onto:
Lettuce
Dust with:
Paprika
Serve filled with:
Seedless grapes
marinated in:
French Dressing, page 341

GRAPEFRUIT SALAD

Prepare:
Grapefruit segments (II, 100)
Serve them with:
French Dressing, page 341
Use grapefruit juice in place of vinegar and add a little:
Confectioners' sugar

MELON SALAD

Prepare:
Melon Baskets (II, 104), or Melon Rounds
Fill the baskets with:
Hulled berries
Diced pineapple or seedless grapes
Moisten with chilled:
French Dressing, page 341, or cultured sour cream

ORANGE AND ONION SALAD

Arrange:
Skinned orange sections or peeled, sliced oranges
Thin slices of Bermuda onion
(Pink grapefruit sections)
on:
Lettuce leaves, endive or escarole
Serve with:
French Dressing, page 341
An Italian version of this salad adds:
Pitted black olives

ORANGE AND GRAPEFRUIT SALAD

Prepare as directed (II, 100, 102):
Orange and grapefruit segments
Place them on individual plates on:
Lettuce or water cress
You may place between alternate segments of the fruit:
Long slivers of green pepper and pimiento
Serve with:
French Dressing, page 341

BLACK-EYED SUSAN SALAD

Skin unbroken whole or half sections of:
Orange or grapefruit
Arrange them on:
Lettuce
around a center of:
Chopped dates and nuts
Serve with:
French Dressing, page 341

ORANGE SALAD FCR GAME [4]

Peel and separate the skin from the sections of:
4 oranges
Arrange them on:
Water cress
Combine and pour over them:
2 tablespoons brandy
2 tablespoons olive oil

1 teaspoon sugar
¼ teaspoon salt
A few grains cayenne

Sprinkle the tops with:

Chopped tarragon

FRESH PEACH AND CHEESE SALAD [6]

Cut into 6 parts:

3 oz. cream cheese

Roll the cheese into balls, then in:

Chopped nut meats

Pare, cut into halves and pit:

6 peaches

Place a ball of cheese between 2 peach halves. Press the peach into shape. Roll it in lemon juice. If the peaches are not to be served at once, chill them in closed containers. Serve the peaches on:

Water cress

with:

French Dressing, page 341

A bit of cress, a stem and several leaves may be placed in the stem end of each peach. Decorative—though it may affront a horticulturist.

PEAR SALAD

Chill and pare:

Fresh pears or drained canned pears

Follow the preceding recipe for Peach Salad. Brush the side of each pear with:

Red coloring or paprika

Place in the blossom ends:

A clove

and in the stem ends:

A bit of water cress

Serve with:

French dressing

Garnish with:

Nut Creams (II, 73), or large black cherries, seeded and stuffed with cottage cheese

Or fill the hollows with cream cheese combined with chopped ginger.

PEAR AND GRAPE SALAD

Pare:

Fresh pears

or drain:

Canned pears

Place half a pear, cut side down, on a plate. Thin to spreading consistency:

Cream cheese

with:

Cream

Cover each pear half with a coating of cheese. Press into the cheese, close together to look like a bunch of grapes:

Stemmed seedless grapes

Add a leaf of some kind, preferably grape, but an ivy leaf and a bit of stem is a good substitute. Serve with:

Mayonnaise or French Dressing, pages 345, 341

JAPANESE PERSIMMON SALAD

This is an attractive-looking salad. If you wish to skin the fruit, rub it first with the blunt side of a knife and peel with the sharp edge.

Chill:

Ripe Japanese persimmons

Serve them whole or cut lengthwise almost to the base and insert in the slashes:

Slices of peeled orange, grapefruit and avocado

and serve with:

Boiled Salad Dressing III, page 350

PINEAPPLE SALAD

Drain:

Slices of canned pineapple

Serve them on:

Lettuce with French Dressing, page 341

Add to the French dressing:

A little confectioners' sugar

Or cover the slices with:

Riced soft cream cheese

Topped with:

A spoonful currant jelly

Serve the salad with:

French Dressing, page 341 or mayonnaise

ABOUT MOLDED SALADS

Any clever person can take a few desolate-looking refrigerator leftovers and glorify them into a tempting molded aspic salad or mousse. For utilizing leftovers, an aspic is second only to a soufflé. Well-combined scraps result in a dish that is sometimes as good as one composed of delicacies and with a further advantage to the busy housewife as it can be prepared a day in advance and chilled in the refrigerator until ready to serve. ➧ Do not freeze. Each of these salads depends on gelatin to hold its shape, so please read About Gelatin (II, 183). Molds may be filled when dry; but a jellied mixture is more readily removed when a mold has been moistened with water. If the mixture lightly brush the mold with oil. i. not a clarified one, you may Be sure to taste your salad before molding and correct the seasoning. ➧ Undersalt if it is to be held 24 hours.

Many of the recipes that follow can be made either in a large mold or in individual small ones. Ring molds can be used if you wish to fill the centers with some other kind of salad, such as chicken, Vegetables à la Grecque, page 257, fruit or cream cheese, dressed and garnished to your fancy. Fish-shaped molds can make a sea food aspic appear very professional. For large groups, you can even use small paper drinking cups for molding individual salads and tear off the cup when the salad is jellied and ready to serve. Or use large No. 2½ size cans and cut around the bottom of the can when ready to serve the salad. Push the salad out of the bottom of the can, slice and serve the rounds on lettuce.

➧ Aspics and other molded salads with a clear "body" lend themselves to highly decorative treatment, although their preparation can be time-consuming (II, 185). However, certain ingredients naturally come to rest either at the top or bottom of a jelling salad and you can achieve interesting layered effects by using "floaters" and "sinkers." See, on (II, 185), the list of ingredients which can be incorporated in your salad simultaneously.

ABOUT ASPICS

Nothing gives a cooler, lovelier effect on a hot summer night and nothing is easier to prepare than a brilliantly clear aspic. The problem, of course, is to keep the aspic properly chilled when serving. For small groups, chilled plates, individually served, will do, if you can control the timing. For large groups, if you want to use a quivery aspic, serve it molded in a crystal clear glass bowl set in another larger glass bowl with crushed ice between them or on a handsome, well-chilled platter, set on ice.

The most delicious aspics of all are reduced chicken and veal stocks, cooked down from the clarified gelatinous portions of these animals, page 58. Clarified strong meat, fish and fowl stocks with added gelatin are next in favor—but the average housewife seldom clarifies her own. She depends largely on canned bases for her jellies. ➧ Canned consommés, if over a year old, tend to lose some of their jelling power, so it is wise to refrigerate the can before using to test for texture. The consommé is still good to eat if it fails to jell just out of the can, but when used for aspic it will need about 1 teaspoon of gelatin per cup of consommé to firm it. To add gelatin, see (II, 184). If you save vegetable stocks (II, 138), you can add them to meat or fish stocks to modify and enrich the otherwise easily identifiable canned flavors. It is wise to choose a stock that has the same general base as the food to be molded: fish stock for fish, meat stock for meat.

➧ To make aspics, allow 1 tablespoon gelatin to 1¾ to 2 cups liquid. Use the lesser amount of liquid if the solids to be incorporated are juicy or watery. ➧ Never reduce aspic made with added gelatin, with the idea of thickening it. It only wastes your good stock and never thickens. If you run into trouble, start the gelatin process over again, judging the amount of fresh gelatin you should add.

➧ The addition of wine or liqueur to your aspics can make them something rather special. Don't add too much ➧ one or two tablespoons per cup of liquid is sufficient to heighten the flavor significantly. Substitute the wine for part of the liquid called for in the recipe ➧ and add it when the gelatin has been dissolved and is beginning to cool. Dry white wine or a dry sherry go well with savory aspics such as chicken and veal. Sweeter wines, such as sauterne, cognac or fruit-flavored liqueurs, are good for molded fruit salads.

Aspic should be clarified unless you want to serve up something that resembles a molded London fog. If you decide to skip this process, be sure to plan to mask your mold, see Mayonnaise Collée, page 387, or Sauce Chaud-froid, page 388.

➧ To clarify, see (II, 140). ➧ To make decorative molds, see (II, 185). Clear aspic jelly can make an attractive garnish for a meat or chicken aspic. Chill it in a refrigerator tray ➧ but do not freeze and, when ready to serve, cut in squares or fancy shapes or chop it rather fine and arrange it around the mold.

Many salads can become full-fledged luncheon dishes with the addition of various types of chopped meat, chicken or flaked fish. For other recipes including meat, fish and shellfish and Chicken Mousses see pages 60, 61.

A choice or a combination of the following ingredients may be included in a molded salad:

Cooked diced meat or poultry
Cooked flaked fish
Hard-cooked eggs
Cooked sweetbreads
Shredded cabbage
Diced celery
Diced cucumbers
Cooked celeriac
Sliced green peppers
Raw or cooked carrots
Cooked beets
Canned asparagus
Halved cranberries
Seedless grapes
Skinned grapefruit sections
Stuffed ripe or green olives
Pickles
Nut meats
Chopped parsley, chives or other herbs

BASIC ASPIC OR GELATIN SALAD [5]

Please read About Gelatin (II, 183).

Soak:

1 tablespoon gelatin

in:

¼ cup cold water

Dissolve it in:

¼ cup boiling stock

Add this to:

1½ cups cold stock or 1¼

cups stock plus ¼ cup tomato juice
2 tablespoons vinegar or 1½ tablespoons lemon juice
Salt and paprika
Celery salt
(1 tablespoon grated onion)

If the aspic is to cover unseasoned food, make the gelatin mixture "peppy." Chill it and when about to set combine it with:

1½ to 2 cups solid ingredients

Pour the aspic into a wet mold and chill until firm. Unmold. Surround with:

Lettuce leaves

Serve with or without:

Mayonnaise, Sour Cream Horseradish Dressing, page 351, etc.

ASPIC GARNISH

Prepare:

Basic Aspic Salad, above

When firm and just before serving, chop the aspic so the light catches its many facets, and use it to garnish salads or meats.

LUNCHEON ASPIC SALAD [8]

➧ Please read About Gelatin (II, 183).

Drain, reserving the juices:

2½ cups canned grapefruit sections
¼ cup green or white cooked asparagus
1 cup canned or cooked crab meat or shrimp

Cut the asparagus into pieces. Pick over the crab meat or remove the intestinal vein from the shrimp. Add to the juices, to make 2¾ cups of liquid:

Chicken broth, Stock, page 490, canned consommé or dissolved chicken bouillon cubes

Soak:

1½ tablespoons gelatin

in ½ cup of this liquid. Dissolve it in 1 cup hot liquid. Combine the gelatin and the remaining liquid. Season well with:

Juice of 1 or more lemons or with ¼ cup dry white wine

Add, if needed:

Salt

Add:

(3 or more tablespoons capers)

Chill the gelatin until it begins to thicken. Have ready a mold which has been rinsed in cold water. Pour part of the gelatin into it, sprinkle some grapefruit, crabmeat and asparagus over it, then alternate layers of gelatin and of the other ingredients. Wind up with gelatin on top. Chill the aspic until it is very cold. Serve on:

Lettuce

with:

Green Mayonnaise, page 348

JELLIED VEAL STOCK [4 to 6]

Sometimes it is fun to make an aspic without added gelatin.

Place in a soup kettle:

A knuckle of veal
¼ cup cut-up onion
½ carrot
6 ribs celery with leaves
1 teaspoon salt
¼ teaspoon pepper

Cover the veal with:

Boiling water

Simmer the meat until it is tender. Strain the liquid. Reserve it. Remove the veal. When cold, cut the meat into small cubes. Remove the fat from the stock. Heat the stock. Add the veal or reserve it for other dishes and use the stock after clarifying it (II, 140) to mold other ingredients.

Correct the seasoning

add:
(1 teaspoon dried herb—
basil, tarragon, etc.)
Rinse out a mold in cold water. Pour in the veal mixture. Cover and keep in a cold place to set. Unmold and slice.

CHICKEN ASPIC [6 to 8]

Soak:
1 tablespoon gelatin
in:
¼ cup cold water
Dissolve it in:
2 cups boiling chicken broth or stock
Add:
Seasoning, if needed
Chill and when the gelatin begins to set, rinse a mold in cold water and fill it with:
½ inch of the jelly
Build up layers of:
3 cups cooked, diced chicken
and the jelly. Ornament the layers with:
1 cup canned mushroom caps
2 hard-cooked eggs
12 sliced stuffed olives
Chill the jelly until firm. Unmold it and serve with or without:
Mayonnaise

JELLIED CHICKEN OR VEAL MOUSSE

I. [10]
Use the recipe for Jellied Ham Mousse, below. Use chicken stock. Substitute cooked ground chicken or veal for the ham or use part chicken and part ham.

II. [8]
Soak:
1½ tablespoons gelatin
in:
¼ cup Chicken Stock (II, 142)
Dissolve it in:
½ cup hot stock
Beat:
3 egg yolks
Add:
1½ cups milk
Cook these ingredients in a double boiler until they are smooth and fairly thick. Stir in the dissolved gelatin. When the mixture is cool, add:
2 cups cooked minced or ground chicken or veal
(½ cup diced seeded cucumber)
Season it with:
Salt, white pepper and paprika
Chill the jelly and when it is about to set fold in:
1 cup whipping cream
Place the mousse in a wet mold and chill it until it is firm. Unmold it.

JELLIED HAM MOUSSE [10]

Soak:
1 tablespoon gelatin
in:
¼ cup cold water
Dissolve it in:
1½ cups boiling Stock (II, 141)
Chill the jelly. When it is nearly set, combine it with:
3 cups cooked ground or chopped ham
¼ cup chopped celery
1 tablespoon grated onion
½ cup mayonnaise
¼ cup sour or sweet-sour chopped pickles
Add, if required:
Worcestershire sauce
Seasoning
Seasonal variation: Omit onion, olives and pickles and add:
(1 cup seedless green grapes)
Moisten a mold with cold water. If desired, decorate the sides and bottom with:
Stuffed olives and sliced hard-cooked eggs
Add the other ingredients. Chill the mousse until it is firm.

JELLIED CLAM JUICE RING [8]

◆ Please read About Gelatin (II, 183).
Dilute:

Clam juice or minced clams

with:

Water or vegetable juices

to make a palatable mixture. There should be 4 cups of liquid. Season this with:

Lemon juice and paprika
A few drops Worcestershire sauce

Soak:

2 tablespoons gelatin

in ½ cup of the liquid. Heat ◆ just to the boiling point 1 cup of the liquid. Dissolve the soaked gelatin in it. Return it to the remaining liquid with the minced clams if they were used. Pour in a wet 9-inch ring mold. Chill until firm. Invert the jelly onto a plate. Fill the center with:

Cottage cheese

Surround it with:

Tomato and cucumber slices

Serve with:

Mayonnaise

MADRILÈNE RING WITH SHAD ROE

A fine summer dish.
Fill a ring mold with:

Canned Madrilène aspic or well-seasoned meat stock aspic

Chill. Invert on:

Shredded lettuce

Place in the center:

Chilled canned shad roe

Garnish with:

Mayonnaise
Lemon wedges or parsley

If the Madrilène is of a wobbly type, serve it from a small dish, surrounded by pieces of roe on lettuce.

MOUSSELINE OF SHELLFISH [6]

Line a 1½-quart fish mold with half-set:

Fish or Chicken Aspic, page 60

Refrigerate it. Prepare:

2 cups Fish Velouté, page 362

to which has been added:

1 tablespoon gelatin

soaked in:

¼ cup cold stock or water

Combine the cooled sauce with:

1 lb. cooked chopped shellfish meat

Add:

½ cup partially whipped cream
Correct the seasoning

and pour into the fish mold over the aspic. Chill before unmolding onto a cold serving platter.

JELLIED SEAFOOD RING OR MOLD [6]

◆ Please read About Gelatin (II, 183).
Prepare:

Basic Aspic Jelly, page 58

using a fish fumet or light meat stock. Dice.

Celery

Pare, seed and dice:

Cucumbers or green peppers

Drain and flake:

Salmon, crab or tuna fish: 1½ cups fish and vegetables in all

Add:

(2 chopped hard-cooked eggs)
(Sliced stuffed olives)

When the jelly is nearly set, combine it with the solid ingredients. Pour it into a wet mold and chill until firm. Unmold and serve on:

Lettuce

with:

Mayonnaise or boiled dressing

MOLDED CREAMED FISH [6]

➧ Please read About Gelatin (II, 183).

Soak:

¾ tablespoon gelatin

in:

2 tablespoons water

Combine in a double boiler, then stir constantly ➧ over—not in—boiling water until thickened:

2 egg yolks
1½ tablespoons soft butter
½ tablespoon flour
1½ teaspoons salt
2 teaspoons sugar
1 teaspoon Worcestershire sauce, ¾ teaspoon curry or 1 teaspoon dry mustard
1 teaspoon grated onion
A few grains red pepper
¼ cup lemon juice
¾ cup milk or tomato juice

Add gelatin and stir until it is dissolved. Refrigerate. Prepare:

1½ cups seafood: cooked or canned shrimp, salmon, etc.

Or use part fish and part chopped celery. When the gelatin is nearly set, place part of it in the bottom of an oiled ring mold, add part of the fish, then more gelatin. Repeat this until all ingredients have been used, finishing with gelatin on top. Chill the salad until it is firm. Serve it on:

Water cress

Fill the ring with:

Marinated cucumbers

Surround it with:

Sliced tomatoes

SEAFOOD MOUSSE [6]

➧ Please read About Gelatin (II, 183).

Soak:

2 teaspoons gelatin

in:

¼ cup cold water

Dissolve it in:

¼ cup boiling water

Add it to:

¾ cup mayonnaise

Combine it with:

1 cup flaked crab meat or flaked tuna fish
½ cup chopped celery or carrots
2 tablespoons chopped parsley
½ cup chopped cucumber
2 tablespoons chopped stuffed olives
1 tablespoon or more lemon juice
Correct the seasoning

and place these ingredients in a wet mold. Chill them until they are firm. Unmold them on:

Cress or shredded lettuce

Serve with:

Cucumbers in Sour Cream

If you want a mousse based on whipped cream, see Lobster Mousse.

LOBSTER MOUSSE [6]

➧ Please read About Gelatin (II, 183).

This is an attractive salad, made in a 9-inch ring mold.

Soak:

1 tablespoon gelatin

in:

¼ cup water

Dissolve it over boiling water. Combine:

¾ cup minced celery
1½ cups canned or cooked lobster meat
(⅔ cup minced apple)

Season these ingredients with:

Salt and paprika

Stir the gelatin into:

¾ cup mayonnaise
3 tablespoons lemon juice
(1 teaspoon dry mustard)
(½ clove pressed garlic)
(A few drops hot pepper sauce)

Whip until stiff, then fold in:

⅓ cup whipping cream

Fold this mixture into the other ingredients. Place the mousse in a wet mold. Chill it thoroughly. Unmold it on a platter, garnished with:

Water cress
Marinated cucumbers

Serve it, if you like, filled with the following sauce. Simmer:

1 cup tomatoes

When reduced to ½ cup, chill the tomatoes. Add to them:

½ cup olive oil
½ teaspoon sugar
½ teaspoon salt
1 tablespoon chopped parsley
Freshly grated pepper
½ teaspoon Worcestershire sauce

EGGS IN ASPIC OR OEUFS EN GELÉE

Make one of the above:

Stock aspics, flavored with port and cognac

Have ready:

Poached eggs, page 184

Swish cold water in individual molds until they are cold and wet. Drain but do not dry. Coat the interior with the jelling aspic so that it adheres to the sides. Chill until congealed. Place an egg in the center of each mold and fill with more aspic. Chill. Serve masked with:

Mayonnaise Collée, page 387, or cold mayonnaise

EGGS IN ASPIC COCKAIGNE

Molded with one half egg this makes a pleasant hors d'oeuvre. With three halves, it makes enough for a luncheon salad. Prepare:

Eggs in Aspic, above

using rich chicken stock for the aspic base and replacing the poached eggs with:

Deviled Eggs, page 195

Place the molds on a bed of:

Water cress

Mask the eggs with a coating of:

Cultured sour cream

Garnish with:

Finely chopped chives, basil and chervil
Red caviar and tomato slices

MOLDED VEGETABLE GELATIN SALAD [6]

Dissolve the contents of:

1 package lime- or lemon-flavored gelatin

in:

2 cups hot water

Prepare and add, when the jelly is about to set:

1½ cups finely diced vegetables: cucumber, carrot, celery, unpeeled radishes, olive, pimiento
½ diced green pepper
2 teaspoons grated onion
¾ teaspoon salt
¼ teaspoon paprika

Place the salad in well-oiled individual ring molds. Chill thoroughly. Unmold on:

Lettuce or water cress

Fill the centers with:

Mayonnaise or Boiled Salad Dressing II, page 350

GOLDEN GLOW GELATIN SALAD [8 to 10]

Good in flavor and lovely in color.

Grate or grind:

2 cups raw carrots

Drain, reserving the juice:

1 cup canned crushed pineapple

Heat to the boiling point:

⅞ cup pineapple juice
⅞ cup water
½ teaspoon salt

Dissolve in the hot liquid:

1 package lemon-flavored gelatin

Chill and when the jelly is about to set, combine it with the carrots, the pineapple and:

(½ cup chopped pecans)

Place in a wet mold. Chill until firm. Unmold on:

Lettuce

Serve with:

Mayonnaise

SEEDLESS GRAPE AND ASPARAGUS ASPIC [10]

➧ Please read About Gelatin (II, 183).

A refreshing summer salad.

Drain the contents of:

2 cups canned asparagus tips

Reserve the liquor. The tips may be cut in two or they may be used whole as a garnish around the edges of the mold. Soak:

1 tablespoon gelatin

in:

3 tablespoons asparagus liquor

Heat the remaining asparagus liquor and dissolve the gelatin in it. Add to it to make 2 cups of liquor in all:

Chicken bouillon or canned bouillon

Season these ingredients with:

Salt and paprika

Chill them. When they are nearly set, combine them with:

2 cups seedless grapes
1 cup chopped celery

and the cut asparagus tips.

Chill the salad until firm. Unmold and serve with:

Mayonnaise

BEET GELATIN SALAD [8]

Wash well, then boil:

8 medium-size beets or use canned beets

Drain them. Reserve the beet juice. Peel the beets and dice them. There should be about 1 cup. Prepare:

¾ cup diced celery

Dissolve the contents of:

1 package lemon-flavored gelatin

in:

1 cup boiling water

Add to it:

¾ cup beet juice
3 tablespoons vinegar
½ teaspoon salt
2 teaspoons grated onion
1 tablespoon prepared horseradish

Chill these ingredients until they are about to set. Fold in the beets and the celery. Place the salad in a wet mold. Chill until firm. Unmold on:

Lettuce or endive

Serve with:

Mayonnaise, Boiled Salad Dressing, page 350, or cultured sour cream

CUCUMBER GELATIN ON TOMATO SLICES [8]

➧ Please read About Gelatin (II, 183).

Fine for a meat platter or a ring mold.

Pare and seed:

Cucumbers

Grate them. There should be 4 cups of pulp and juice. Soak:

2 tablespoons gelatin

in:

½ cup cold water or chicken stock

Dissolve it in:

¾ cup boiling water or chicken stock

Add:

6 tablespoons lemon juice
2 teaspoons grated onion

Add the gelatin mixture to the cucumber pulp with:

1 teaspoon sugar
Salt, as needed
¼ teaspoon paprika

Strain the jelly. Place it in small wet molds. When firm invert onto:

Thick slices skinned tomatoes

Garnish the slices with:

Water cress

Serve the salad with:

Mayonnaise

or, place in a 9-inch wet ring mold. Chill the jelly. When firm, invert onto a platter. Fill the center with:

Marinated shrimp

Garnish the edge with alternating:

Tomato slices
Cucumber slices

Serve the ring with:

Green Mayonnaise, page 348, or Water Cress Dressing, page 343

CUCUMBER MOUSSE [6]

➧ Please read About Gelatin (II, 183).

Soak:

2 teaspoons gelatin

in:

3 tablespoons cold water

Dissolve these ingredients over heat. Add:

2 teaspoons vinegar or lemon juice
1 teaspoon grated onion
¾ teaspoon salt
¼ teaspoon paprika

Chill until about to set. Drain well:

1 cup pared, seeded, chopped cucumbers

Whip until stiff:

1 cup whipping cream

Beat the gelatin mixture gradually into the cream. Fold in the cucumbers. Oil individual molds. Fill them with the mousse. When they are thoroughly chilled, invert the mousse onto a garnished platter.

CUCUMBER AND SOUR CREAM MOUSSE [6]

Dissolve:

1 package lime-flavored gelatin

in:

¾ cup hot water

Add:

¼ cup lemon juice
1 tablespoon grated onion

Chill until about to set, then stir in:

1 cup cultured sour cream
1 cup finely chopped unpared cucumber

Pour into 6 small oiled molds and chill until firm.

TOMATO ASPIC

[8 Servings, without the addition of solid ingredients]

➧ Please read About Gelatin (II, 183).

I. Simmer, for 30 minutes, then strain:

3½ cups tomatoes
1 teaspoon salt
½ teaspoon paprika
1½ teaspoons sugar
2 tablespoons lemon juice
3 tablespoons chopped onion
1 bay leaf
4 ribs celery with leaves
(1 teaspoon dried basil or tarragon)

Soak:

2 tablespoons gelatin

in:

½ cup cold water

Dissolve it in the strained hot juice. Add water to make 4 cups of liquid. Chill the aspic. When it is about to set add 1 or 2 cups of solid ingredients—a choice or a combination of:

Sliced olives
Chopped celery
Chopped green peppers
Grated or chopped carrots
Chopped meat
Flaked fish
Well-drained oysters
Sliced avocados, etc.

Chill the aspic until firm. Unmold and serve with:

Mayonnaise or Boiled Salad Dressing, page 350

II. If you prefer a ring, keep the aspic simple and fill the center with:

Cole slaw, marinated cucumbers or avocados, chicken or shrimp salad or cottage cheese and chives

Serve with a suitable dressing.

TOMATO ASPIC WITH TASTY CENTERS [8]

I. Prepare:

Tomato Aspic, page 65

When it is about to set, pour into wet individual molds or ice cube molds and fill them to ⅓ of their capacity. Combine and roll into balls:

1 package of soft cream cheese: 3 oz.
1 tablespoon anchovy paste
2 drops Worcestershire sauce

Drop a ball into each mold and cover it with aspic. Chill the aspic until firm. Unmold on lettuce leaves. Serve with:

Mayonnaise

II. Use for the filling:

Any small pieces of cooked meat, fowl or fish

CANNED TOMATO OR VEGETABLE JUICE ASPIC [8]

➧ Please read About Gelatin (II, 183).
Soak:

2 tablespoons gelatin

in:

½ cup cold canned tomato juice

Dissolve it in:

3½ cups hot tomato juice or canned tomato and vegetable juice

Tomato juice varies. It is wise to taste the aspic to see whether additional seasoning is required. Lemon juice is good, so is a teaspoon of chopped or dried herbs (II, 203), preferably basil. Add, if desired, 1 or 2 cups of solid ingredients. See Tomato Aspic, page 65. Mold, chill, unmold and serve the aspic as directed.

BASIC GELATIN FOR FRUIT SALADS [6]

➧ Please read About Gelatin (II, 183). It is well to know that fresh pineapple cannot be added to a gelatin salad without ruining it. This also applies to frozen pineapple juice, alone or combined with other frozen juices such as orange or grapefruit. The pineapple must be brought to ➧ a boil. Canned pineapple complies with this rule and may be used as is. The frozen juice is usable if boiled.
Soak:

1 tablespoon gelatin

in:

½ cup cold water

Dissolve it in:

1 cup boiling water or fruit juice

Add:

4 to 6 tablespoons sugar, less if sweetened fruit juice is used
⅛ teaspoon salt
¼ cup lemon juice

Chill the aspic and when it is about to set, combine it with:

1½ cups prepared drained fruit

Place it in a wet mold and chill until firm. Serve with:

Cream Mayonnaise, page 348

MINT GELATIN FOR FRUIT SALADS

Pour:

1 cup boiling water

over:

¼ cup crushed mint leaves

Allow to steep for 5 minutes. Drain this infusion. Add:

A few drops of green vegetable coloring

Prepare, by the recipe above:

Basic Fruit Salad Gelatin

substituting the mint infusion for the boiling water.

MOLDED AVOCADO SALAD [3 to 4]

Soak:

1 tablespoon gelatin

in:

2 tablespoons water

Dissolve it in:
1 cup boiling water
Add:
¼ cup lemon juice
1 cup mashed avocado
¼ teaspoon celery salt
1 teaspoon salt
½ teaspoon Worcestershire sauce
A few grains cayenne
¼ cup chopped pimiento
Mold and serve.

BLACK CHERRY AND ALMOND ASPIC [6]

Prepare:
Basic Fruit Salad Gelatin, above
Substitute for part of the boiling water:
Fruit juice
Cool the gelatin mixture. When it is about to set add:
1¼ cups pitted black cherries
⅓ cup blanched shredded almonds
These proportions may be varied. Place the aspic in a wet mold. Chill until firm. Unmold and serve with:
Mayonnaise

MOLDED CRANBERRY SALAD [6 to 8]

➧ Please read About Gelatin (II, 183).
Soak:
1 tablespoon gelatin
in:
3 tablespoons water
Cook until the skins pop:
2 cups cranberries
in:
1 cup boiling water or fruit juice
Use the cranberries strained or unstrained. If the former, strain them at this time. Add and cook 5 minutes:
½ cup sugar
¼ teaspoon salt
Add the soaked gelatin. Chill the jelly. When it is about to set, fold in:
⅔ cup diced celery
(½ cup chopped nut meats)
(1 cup canned, drained crushed pineapple)
Place in a wet mold and chill until firm. Serve with:
Mayonnaise

MOLDED CRANBERRY AND APPLE SALAD [8 to 10]

➧ Please read About Gelatin (II, 183).
Put through a food grinder:
1 lb. cranberries
Add:
The grated rind of 1 orange
½ cup orange juice
3½ tablespoons lemon juice
1½ cups sugar
Refrigerate overnight. Soak:
1 tablespoon gelatin
in:
3 tablespoons cold water
Dissolve:
1 package lemon-flavored gelatin: 3¼ oz.
in:
1 cup boiling water
Add the soaked gelatin. Stir until dissolved. Combine these ingredients with the cranberry mixture. Pare, then chop and add:
3 tart apples
Place the salad in a greased mold. When firm, unmold and serve on:
Water cress
with:
Cream Mayonnaise, page 348

GINGER ALE SALAD [10]

➧ Please read About Gelatin (II, 183).
This is about the best molded fruit salad given.
Soak:
2 tablespoons gelatin
in:
¼ cup cold water
Dissolve it in:
½ cup boiling fruit juice

Add:

½ cup sugar
⅛ teaspoon salt
2 cups ginger ale
Juice of 1 lemon

Chill these ingredients until the jelly is nearly set. Combine with:

½ lb. skinned, seeded Tokay grapes
1 skinned, sliced orange
1 grapefruit in skinned sections
6 slices canned pineapple, cut in pieces
3 teaspoons chopped preserved ginger

Place the salad in a wet mold. Chill and unmold on:

Lettuce

Serve with:

Cream Mayonnaise, page 348

GRAPEFRUIT JELLY WITH SHERRY [10]

➧ Please read About Gelatin (II, 183).

Soak:

2½ tablespoons gelatin

in:

½ cup cold water

Stir over heat until the sugar is dissolved:

½ cup water
1 cup sugar

Dissolve the gelatin in the hot sirup. Cool. Add:

2 cups and 6 tablespoons fresh grapefruit juice
3 tablespoons lemon juice
½ cup dry sherry
¼ teaspoon salt

Pour these ingredients into a well-oiled 9-inch ring mold. Chill the jelly until firm. Turn it out on a platter. Fill the center with:

Soft cream cheese balls, rolled in chopped nuts

Garnish the outer edge of the platter with:

Avocado slices

alternating with skinned:

Grapefruit or orange sections

on:

Water cress or shredded lettuce

Sprinkle with:

Pomegranate seeds

Serve the salad with:

Mayonnaise or French Dressing, pages 345, 342

MOLDED PEAR SALAD [6]

➧ Please read About Gelatin (II, 183).

Drain and reserve the juice from:

3½ cups canned Bartlett pears

Soak:

1 tablespoon gelatin

in:

¼ cup cold water

Add to the pear juice enough water to make 1¾ cups of liquid. Heat part of the liquid to the boiling point. Dissolve the soaked gelatin in it. Combine it with the rest of the liquid. Add:

3 tablespoons lemon juice
¼ teaspoon salt

Cool these ingredients. Moisten:

1 package of soft cream cheese or pimiento cheese

with a very little:

Cream

Use just enough to soften it. Add to the cheese:

¼ cup chopped nut meats
(¼ teaspoon salt)

Form the cheese into balls. Place one in the center of a half pear and cover with another half pear. If the pears are large, do not cover them. Place the stuffed pears in a ring mold or in cups. Pour the gelatin mixture over them. Add, if desired:

1 cup or more seedless grapes

Chill the gelatin until firm. Unmold on:

Crisp lettuce

Serve with:

Mayonnaise

This recipe may also be made with:

1 package lime or lemon gelatin
1 cup boiling water
1 cup pear juice
1½ tablespoons lemon juice
⅛ teaspoon ginger
¼ teaspoon salt

Substitute this for the gelatin mixture given in the recipe.

MOLDED STUFFED FRUITS [8]

➧ Please read About Gelatin (II, 183).

Soak:

2½ tablespoons gelatin

in:

½ cup water

Drain and reserve the juice from:

3½ cups canned peaches, apricots or pears

Combine and boil:

2 cups of the juice
1½ cups sugar

Dissolve the gelatin in it. Add these ingredients to the remaining juice with:

¾ cup lemon juice
3 tablespoons lime juice
¼ teaspoon ginger

Add water or other fruit juice to make up 4 cups of liquid in all. Chill the gelatin until it is about to set. Soften:

Cream cheese

with a little:

Mayonnaise

Roll it into balls. Roll the balls in:

Chopped nut meats

Stuff a cheese ball in each fruit, then place each fruit in an oiled individual mold. Chill well and invert onto:

Water cress

Serve with:

Mayonnaise

MOLDED PINEAPPLE RING [8]

➧ Please read About Gelatin (II, 183).

Soak:

2 tablespoons gelatin

in:

½ cup cold water

Strain and reserve the juice of:

2½ cups canned crushed pineapple

Add to the juice:

½ cup hot water

Bring these ingredients to the boiling point. Stir in the soaked gelatin until dissolved. Add:

⅝ cup sugar: ½ cup, plus 2 tablespoons

Cool the mixture. Add the pineapple and:

(2 cups grated cabbage)
The grated rind of 1 orange or lemon
¾ cup orange juice
5 tablespoons lemon juice

Pour these ingredients into a wet 9-inch ring mold. Chill the gelatin. Unmold on a bed of:

Lettuce or water cress

Fill the center with:

Cottage cheese, soft cream cheese balls rolled in chopped nut meats, chicken salad, etc.

Serve with or without:

Mayonnaise

SEEDLESS GRAPE AND CELERY RING [8 to 10]

Prepare:

Lemon Jelly or Orange Jelly, or Basic Fruit Gelatin, page 66

When it is about to set, add to it:

3 cups seedless grapes and diced celery, combined in any proportion

Place the jelly in a wet 9-inch mold and chill. Unmold on:

Lettuce

Fill the center with:

Cream Mayonnaise, page 348

FROSTED MELON OR PAPAYA SALAD [6]

You may use this as salad or dessert.

Pare:

1 large melon or papaya

leaving it whole. Cut off enough from one end so you can scrape out the seeds. Fill the cavity with water, pour it into a measuring cup; this is to guide you for the amount of gelatin you have to prepare. Stand the melon upside down to drain. Then fill, depending on the color of the melon flesh, with:

Fruit-flavored gelatin (Diced or small fruits)

Try a combination of:

Orange-flavored gelatin, canned crushed pineapple, canned mandarin oranges or sliced bananas

or try:

Raspberry gelatin with fresh raspberries

After the center is set, you may coat the melon with:

8 oz. cream cheese

softened with:

A little milk

and whipped until fluffy. Chill until ready to serve. Cut crosswise in 1-inch slices and serve on:

Lettuce

with:

French Dressing, page 341

SOUFFLÉ FRUIT SALAD [4]

Dissolve:

1 package lime gelatin

in:

1 cup hot water

Add:

½ cup cold water
½ cup mayonnaise
2 tablespoons lemon juice
¼ teaspoon salt

Whip with a rotary beater until well blended. Pour into a refrigerator tray and chill until firm at the edge but still soft in the center. Turn into a bowl and whip in the same manner until fluffy. Fold in:

1 cup peeled and diced apples
¼ cup chopped pecans
¾ cup seeded Tokay grapes

Pour into a mold and refrigerate until firm.

STRAWBERRY AND RHUBARB SALAD MOLDS [8 to 10]

Dissolve:

3 packages strawberry gelatin

in:

3 cups hot water

Drop in:

2 packages frozen rhubarb

Stir to separate the rhubarb. When the jelly begins to set, add:

1 quart sliced fresh strawberries

Pour into individual wet molds and chill until set. Unmold on:

Water cress

Garnish each with:

A fresh whole strawberry

Serve with:

Cream Mayonnaise, page 348, or Fruit Salad Mayonnaise, page 348

TWENTY-FOUR-HOUR FRUIT SALAD WITH CREAM [12 to 14]

Cook in a double boiler until thickened:

2 egg yolks
¼ cup sugar
¼ cup cream
Juice of 2 lemons
⅛ teaspoon salt

Stir these ingredients constantly. Chill them and add:

- **6 diced slices canned pineapple**
- **2 cups pitted Queen Anne cherries**
- **1 cup blanched, shredded almonds**
- **½ lb. marshmallows, cut in pieces**
- **1 cup heavy cream, whipped**
- **(½ lb. peeled, seeded grapes)**

Chill the salad for 24 hours. Serve on:

Lettuce

with:

Mayonnaise

or as a dessert, garnished with:

Whipped cream

THE FOODS WE HEAT

What do you think of when you think of cooking? Our own minds rush at once, with confidence, to a vision of food deliciously prepared, perfectly seasoned, beautifully presented —to, in short, the final product. But somewhere along the line, in perhaps ninety-nine out of a hundred kitchen sequences, heat has been applied—and its application is of crucial importance. From Charles Lamb's legendary Bobo—you will remember him from your high school English classes as the boy who couldn't make roast pig without burning down the house—to the bride of the moment, described by her maid of honor as incapable of boiling an egg, heating food has often turned into a frustrating, sometimes even a disastrous, experience.

It needn't be. We have tried throughout our book, but especially in this chapter, to identify and explain the various types of cooking heat; to tell you simply and clearly how these heats are initiated, controlled and arrested to ensure best flavor, nutritive value, texture and color. We have tried to indicate what processes, when followed, will bring cooked food to the table in that ideal state of readiness the French call "à point."

Asking a cook why he heats food at all is, of course, like asking an architect why men do not live in caves. The obvious answer is that it usually tastes better that way. There are other reasons, too. Some are prosaic. Cooking destroys unwanted and sometimes unfavorable microorganisms. Contrary to some remarkably persistent notions, it makes many categories of food more digestible and of more nutritive value and less—to toss in a stylish term—allergenic.

Cooking, again, can seal up in food most of those natural juices which nourish and delight us, instead of squandering them away on pan or oven. For some kinds of preparation—Stocks (II, 138), and soups are examples—the objective is just the reverse. It is true, also, that certain salted and variety meats, as well as a good many vegetables, profit by a precooking or blanching, page 88, which modifies texture or releases disagreeable odor and off-flavors.

Many cooks, like the rest of humankind, are born innovators, too. And they often introduce stimulating refinements in the heating of food, some of which —it must be said—emphasize taste at the expense of nutritional integrity.

▲ Cooking in mountainous country is an art all in itself. If high altitudes are new to you, watch for the high altitude cooking symbol ▲ which will give you formulas for adjusted ingredients or temperatures. Roasting procedure does not differ materially from that at sea level. But high altitudes do affect boiling considerably. In the following chart, we plot the difference in the boiling temperatures of water at sea level and at graduated elevations. Any process involving liquid will be proportionately lengthened as altitude increases.

	F.	C.
Sea level	212°	100°
2,000 ft.	208°	98°
5,000 ft.	203°	95°
7,500 ft.	198°	92°
10,000 ft.	194°	90°
15,000 ft.	185°	85°
30,000 ft.	158°	70°

Adjustments required in using sea-level baking recipes at high altitudes are indicated where necessary for each baking category. Basic cake recipes for high altitudes and their baking temperatures, marked ▲, may be found on (II, 381–385).

If these hints are not sufficiently specialized for your area, write the Home Economics Department of your State College or call your County Home Demonstration Agent for more information. And if you are doing any pressure cooking, the accuracy of the gauge is vital. These agencies can also tell you where to have gauges tested.

ABOUT HEATS

Let us consider first how heats are transferred to food, whether in air or in moisture, in fat or through a pan. Results in each case will be quite astonishingly different. Cooking heats are generally known as ➧ dry or moist. In the text following, we shall list types of each separately. Then, if a specific type of dry or moist heat involves more than one kind of food, a detailed description of it will follow. On the other hand, should the heat-process apply only to a single food category, like meat, you will find it elsewhere, under the cooking instructions for that particular food.

ABOUT DRY HEATS

➧ Truly dry heats are achieved in a number of ways. Grilling over coals is one, broiling or roasting in a ventilated oven another. When we say "barbecue," we may be referring to Pit-Cooking, page 90, in which case we refer to a moist heat process. Or we may mean skewer-cooking with its variants —spit, brochette or rotisseria— which is a dry one and itself a form of grilling. Parenthetically, the word "barbecue" has been traced back by some philologists to the Spanish "barbacoa," a raised platform for cooking; but we like to think of it, with other authorities, as originating among the French settlers in Florida, who roasted the native goats whole, "de barbe en queue"— from beard to tail. Some further remarks on barbecuing will be found farther along in this chapter, see Outdoor Cooking, page 89.

Baking is a dry heat process, too. In addition to the reflected and radiant heat of the oven, heat is transferred from the pan to the food and may be further diffused by the use of paper liners, temporary covers of foil or a dusting of flour between food and pan-bottom. Since, in baking, moisture is released from the food itself and, as warm vapor, continues to circulate in the closed oven chamber, this process is less dry than those previously mentioned.

Oddly enough, deep-fat frying is still another kind of dry heat cooking. Here the heat is not only transferred by the oil or grease used as a cooking medium, but by the moisture in the food itself—some of the steam from the food juices being forced into the fat and then out into the atmosphere. Among dry heat pan-processes, sautéing, page 253, uses the least fat. Pan-broiling and pan-frying are successive steps beyond sautéing and away from the driest heat.

In pan-broiling and pan-frying, the food develops a greater amount of rendered fat than in sautéing and it absorbs a larger share of it. In doing so, it gives up proportionately more of its juices. To keep both pan-frying and pan-broiling at their best, excess fat should be poured off during cooking.

While reducing—or concentrating—food through heat usually involves liquids, it also counts technically as a dry heat process since no additional moisture is introduced in accomplishing it.

Among dry heat processes which may be described as "partial" are planking and flambéing—or flaming. Either way, the food is heated beforehand and through them is given only its final finishing touch.

BROILING

The principle of broiling, whether on a grill or in a range, is identical. The heat is a radiant glow; and the process differs from roasting or baking in that only one side of the food at a time is exposed to the heating source.

However, all three of these types of dry heat depend, for their effectiveness, on proper ventilation. In the great majority of modern ranges, either gas or electric, you are given no selectivity in broiling temperatures. And individual variations in wattage—coil or burner area—and venting capacity make it necessary that you become familiar with the special requirements of your own equipment. Some ranges, for example, must be preheated before broiling can begin; in others, broiler heat is almost instantaneous. Likewise, in some electric ranges, broiling takes place with the oven door ajar; in others, the door may, or even must, be kept closed.

When the heat indicator on a household range is turned to a ▶ broil position, the temperature is normally 550° or slightly above. If you wonder why you cannot always match the results you admire in some restaurant meat and fish cookery, remember that commercial installations deliver temperatures up to between 700° and 1000° and that these are quite beyond the reach of home equipment.

Under the limitations of the household range ▶ as much temperature control in broiling is exerted by the placement of the oven rack as by any other means. It is usually adjusted so that there is a 3-inch space between the source of heat and the top of the food. ▶ To lower the broiling heat for browning fragile sauces or delicate dishes like sweetbreads or for cooking very thick meats—where the heat must have time to penetrate deeply without charring—lower the broiling rack to make a 4- to 6-inch interval between food and broiler. Place food on a cold rack to prevent sticking. If the rack is hot, grease it—or grease the food. For details of broiling Steaks, etc., see page 455, Fowl, page 575; Fish, page 399; Vegetables, page 254.

SKEWER COOKING

From a marshmallow impaled on a stick to the most delicate bay scallops, this type of grilled food never seems to lose its charm for young or old. A most important first step is to ▶ choose items that will cook at the same rate of speed or to make the proper adjustment if they do not. When the meat or fish selected is a quick-cooking one, see that the onions, peppers or other more resistant vegetables

which alternate with it are blanched in advance, so they will all be done at the same time. Should the meat need relatively longer cooking, skewer delicate alternates like tomatoes and mushrooms separately and mingle meat and vegetables in serving. Protect delicate meats —sweetbreads, liver, etc.—with breading or a wrapping of thinly sliced bacon. Choose skewers, whether metal or wood, that are either square or oval in section, so that, as the food softens in cooking, it will not slip while revolving.

If using a grill, grease it and cook the skewered food over medium heat. Turn the skewers often. Food grilled in this way may take anywhere from 6 to 12 minutes.

If cooking in a range, broil on a greased grill about 3 inches from the source of heat or adjusted on a pan, as shown on the illustration above. You may, of course, prefer to use the skewer element on your rotisserie. For more details about rotisserie or spit-cooking, see pages 93–94. Should you decide to precook any sort of skewered food, you may do so on the skewers themselves in a skillet, provided, of course, the skewers are no longer than the pan bottom. Sometimes partially precooked, skewered foods are coated with a sauce or with a bound breading and then cooked to completion in deep fat. When handled in this way, they are called atteraux. In flambéing skewered foods, page 80, provide some protection for your hand.

Attractive combinations for skewers or brochettes include the following: scallops, shrimps, or oysters with or wrapped in bacon, and firm miniature tomatoes; chicken livers or pieces of calf liver or kidney alternating with cocktail sausages and mushrooms; diced eggplant or squash, blanched small onions, firm small tomatoes and bacon; shrimp or diced lobster, diced cucumber and stuffed olives; pieces of fish, sections of blanched celery and bacon; pieces of sausage and pickled onions; bacon and pieces of unpeeled apple; scallops, bacon and blanched pieces of onion. In this sketch are some of the foods we have just mentioned as suitable for skewering and a decorative way to impale cocktail skewers in a potato or grapefruit, after they have had their turn at the grill.

DEEP-FAT FRYING

Deep-fat frying, like a number of other accomplishments in cooking, is an art in itself—an art in which experience is the best teacher. Even a novice, however, who follows our instructions to the letter, can succeed in turning out delicious dishes in this ever-popular category—and, what's more, food fried without excess fat absorption. A serving of French fried potatoes properly cooked may have a lower calorie count than a baked potato served with butter. Remember, too, that fat-absorption increases with the length of cooking time and with the amount of surface exposed to the fat.

We simply do not believe, as a cynic has remarked, at least in deep-fat frying, that "foresight is the last gift of the gods to man." While our directions may, at first glance, seem complicated, read them calmly and carefully and you will be rewarded with crisp, golden-brown fried foods every time.

➧ First, equipment need not be elaborate, for equally good French fried potatoes can come out of a black iron kettle as from the latest model electric fryer. This is not to underestimate the value of the fryer, which offers the convenience of a built-in thermostat and furnishes also a storage space for the fat—after straining—between fryings. Proper fat storage is of considerable importance, as fat must be kept covered and in a cool place if it is to remain in good condition for repeated use.

Any deep kettle or saucepan, preferably a heavy one, serves nicely for deep frying. Use in a 3- or 4-quart kettle about 3 pounds of fat. It isn't wise to try to skimp on the amount, for there must always be enough to cover the food and to permit it to move freely in the kettle. ➧ There must also be room in the kettle for the quick bubbling up of the fat which occurs naturally in frying potatoes, onions and other wet items. ➧ Never fill any container more than half full of fat. ➧ Remember, too, to heat the fat gradually, so that any moisture in it will have evaporated by the time it reaches the required temperature.

The kettle should have a flat bottom, so that it will set firmly on the burner. One without a long handle is desirable, to avoid the danger of accidentally overturning the hot fat and causing a small conflagration. In case fat should ever catch on fire, have a metal lid handy to drop over the kettle. You may also smother the flame with salt. ➧ Never, under any circumstances, use water, as this will only spread the fire.

For frying certain types of food such as doughnuts and fritters where bubbling is not a problem, a heavy skillet or electric fry-pan rather than a deep kettle is sometimes preferred, because of its wider surface, which permits frying more pieces at one time.

A wire basket is practically a necessity for successful results in frying any quantity of material such as potatoes, oysters, onions, eggplant, etc. The food is then raised and lowered more easily, and even browning is assured.

Helpful, too, in deep frying, is a slotted metal spoon and long-handled metal tongs. A supply of absorbent paper for draining the fried food is important for the final disposal of excess fat.

For judging the temperature of the fat, use a frying thermometer, no other. Have the thermometer ready in a bowl of hot water to lessen the chance of breakage; but ➧ never plunge it into the fat without wiping it very dry. Nothing is more important in frying than proper temperatures. As that wise old gourmet, Alexander Dumas, so aptly put it, the food must be "surprised" by the hot fat, to give it the crusty, golden coating so characteristic and so desirable. And the easiest way to assure this is by using a thermometer.

When no thermometer is

available, a simple test for temperature can be made with a small cube of bread about 1-inch square. When you think the fat is hot enough, drop in the bread cube and count slowly to sixty or use a timer for sixty seconds. If the cube browns in this time, the fat will be around 375°, satisfactory for frying most foods. A few—Soufflé Potatoes for instance, page 316—may require higher or lower temperatures, but these will always be noted in the specific recipes.

Above all, do not wait for the fat to smoke before adding the food. This is not only hard on the fat, since smoke indicates that it is breaking down and may be spoiled for re-use, but the crust that forms on the food is likely to be overbrowned before the product is cooked through; and the result will be burned on the surface and raw inside. On the other hand, food introduced into fat that isn't hot enough to crust immediately will tend to be grease-soaked.

Once the proper temperature is established, you are ready to add the food. ➧ Do not try to fry too much at a time. This will lower the temperature unduly and may also cause the fat to bubble up too fast and go over the top of the kettle. Naturally, the colder the food when added to the fat, the more the fat temperature will be reduced.

➧ Whenever possible, foods should be at room temperature when introduced into the kettle. ➧ Always immerse gently with long-handled tongs or a slotted spoon or in a frying basket. ➧ Always dip these utensils into the hot fat first, so that the food will release quickly from them without sticking. And have a pan ready in which to rest the utensils when they come dripping from the fat.

After frying one batch ➧ let the temperature come up again to the required heat, so that you may continue to "surprise" each additional one. ➧ Skim out bits of food or crumbs frequently—as they collect in the fat during frying. If allowed to remain, they induce foaming, discolor the fat and affect the flavor of the food.

At the end of frying, and after the fat has cooled somewhat, strain it to remove all leftover particles. Return it to the container and store for re-use. Adding some fresh fat for each new frying materially increases its length of life. When the fat becomes dark and thickish-looking, it will no longer be satisfactory for frying. At this stage, the smoking point has dropped too low; the flavor that it contributes

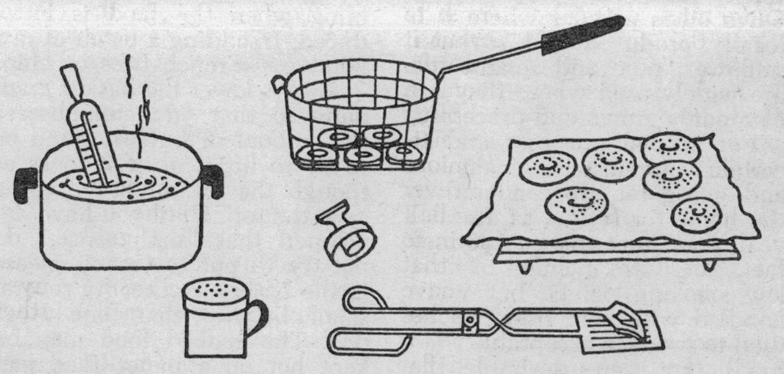

to the food will be unpleasant and absorption high. Discard it.

➧ The household cooking fat known as "all-purpose" or sometimes simply as "shortenings" are American favorites. These include the solid fats such as lard, the plastic and hydrogenated fats and the liquid oils, among which corn, cottonseed and peanut are most commonly available for household use. Except for lard, which has a characteristic odor and flavor, these fats are bland and very similar in appearance and composition. Most of them are 100% vegetable in origin. The oils, in particular, are so much alike that unless one knows the source or examines the label, it is practically impossible to tell which is made from peanuts and which from corn or cottonseed. They all have smoking points well above those needed for deep frying.

Butter and margarines, valuable as they are for other purposes, are not considered suitable for deep frying, because of their low smoking points. As has been mentioned earlier, smoking of fat during frying should not be tolerated. It is hard on the food, hard on the fat itself and unpleasant when wafted through the house.

Various other fats are sometimes used for deep frying. Olive oil is popular where it is locally produced and soybean, safflower, rape and sesame oils are widely used where they are commonly grown and processed.

For special purposes and in certain circumstances chicken and goose fat are rendered in the home for frying, as are also veal, pork, suet and beef kidney fats. These are inclined to have low smoking points, but when handled with care they can be used to produce acceptable fried foods. If it seems desirable, the smoking point of these animal fats can be brought up to the required limit by blending them with any one of the cooking oils.

➧ The best way to render animal fats in the home is to cut them into small pieces—after removing bits of membrane, skin, etc.—and heat in a double boiler until melted. This process can be hastened by pressing down on the fatty pieces occasionally with a fork or spoon. Strain through cheese cloth to remove solid particles and store the rendered fat in a covered container in a cool place. ➧ Do not use drippings or fats skimmed from soups or gravies.

➧ For good results, the food to be fried must be properly prepared. Pieces should be uniform in size, preferably not thicker than 2 inches, so that they will all cook in the same length of time. Small pieces, obviously, will cook through faster than large ones. It is difficult here to give advice about length of cooking. When in doubt, it is wise to remove one piece and try for doneness.

Raw foods, ➧ especially wet ones, should be patted between towels or absorbent paper before cooking to remove excess surface moisture. This not only helps to keep the fat temperature from dropping too low, but it reduces the amount of bubbling when the food is introduced. In adding a batch of raw potatoes—French fries or chips—always lower the basket gradually so that you can observe the amount of bubbling and be ready to lift it up if it looks as though the fat might be going over the top. Until you have developed that "sixth sense," do not try to put too many pieces in the basket—rather fry several small batches than one large one. The cooked food may be kept hot on a paper-lined pan in the oven, set at very low heat.

Certain types of food need special coating for proper browning and crust formation—croquettes, eggplant, fish, etc. For Breading, see (II, 160). The coating may be simply flour, cornmeal or finely crushed dry cereal. Or it may be a Fritter Batter (II, 125), an egg and crumb mixture or even a pastry envelope. Whatever it is, it should cover the surface evenly.

Foods to be coated with batter—shrimp, for instance, or pineapple slices—should be surface-dried before applying the batter. Doughnuts, fritters and other batter-foods need no extra coating, as the egg-starch mixture browns nicely by itself when lowered into the hot fat. Many cooks do not realize that the richer a dough or batter mixture, the more fat it will absorb during frying. By adding even a little too much shortening or sugar to the mix, a doughnut may become so rich that it will end up by being grease-soaked. Or a fritter may simply disintegrate in the hot fat or the batter may slide off onion rings altogether.

✻ Frozen foods designed for deep frying are usually completely prepared. All that remains to be done is defrosting, which is better accomplished outside the package. Otherwise moisture may form on the surface and interfere with proper browning and crusting. Frozen foods that have to be coated should be defrosted, dried on the surface, if necessary, and the coating applied as usual.

In deep-fat frying ▲ at high altitudes, you will find that the lower boiling point of the water inside moist foods will require lower fat temperatures. For instance, French fries, which call for 375° in their final frying period, might need only a 365° fat temperature at high altitudes.

SAUTÉING

"Sauter" literally means "to jump," and this is just what happens to the food you cook by this method. The cooking is done in an ➧ open pan, which is kept in motion. The process is rapid, the food usually thin or minced and the ➧ heat must be kept up from the moment cooking starts until the food is tender. Any reduction in heat will draw juices. There are other requirements. The ➧ small quantity of fat used must be hot enough, when the food is added, to sear it at once—again to prevent the loss of juices. ➧ This can only be accomplished if the food is 70° or more, cut to a uniform thickness and size and dry on the surface. If it is too cold it will lower the heat, and if it is wet it will not brown properly. Worst of all, steam will form and break the seal holding the juices. To ensure a dry surface, food is frequently floured or breaded, see (II, 160). ➧ Steam will also form if the pan is crowded. There must be space between the pieces of food you are sautéing.

For the best sauté, use a Clarified Butter, page 383, or a combination of 3 parts butter and 4 parts oil. When these fats reach the point of fragrance, the 70° food is added, but not so much at a time as to reduce the heat in the pan. To keep the food, which should be heated to at least 340°, from too quick browning agitate the pan constantly. Too much turning of the food delays the quickness of heating. But food with a Bound Breading (II, 160), especially if the coating has not been dried long enough before cooking, may steam. In this case, turning will help to release some of that steam more rapidly. Usually sautéed meat is browned or cooked on one side until the blood comes up to the surface of the exposed side, then turned and browned on the other side.

To serve sautéed food with a sauce, remove the food from the pan and keep it warm on a hot serving dish. Quickly deglaze the delicious brown residue in the sauté pan—unless you have been cooking a strongly flavored fish—with stock or wine. Reduce the sauce and pour it over the sautéed food. If you heat sautéed food in sauce, you steam it too much.

PAN-FRYING

Dredge the food with seasoned breading, flour, cornmeal or a Bound Breading, see (II, 160). Melt a small amount of fat in a heavy pan over moderate heat. For meat, use fat from the meat you are cooking. Brown the meat on one side. When juice begins to appear on the upper surface, turn the meat with tongs and brown it on the other side. Drain and serve at once. Proceed in the same way for fish; but the cooking time is apt to be less. Cook on one side until golden brown before turning. Drain on paper towels and serve at once.

REDUCING LIQUIDS

This process is used mainly to intensify flavor: a wine, a broth or a sauce is evaporated and condensed over lively heat. A so-called "double consommé" is made in this way, the final product being half the original in volume. Naturally, reducing applies only to sauces without egg. And those which have a flour base must be watched carefully and stirred often to avoid scorching.

PLANKING

Why bother about planking? One reason is the attractive appearance of a planked meat, surrounded with a decorative band of Duchess Potatoes, page 319, beautifully browned on their fluted edges and garnished with colorful vegetables, after it emerges from the oven. Another reason is the delicious flavor an oak slab can give to meat. Planks are of 1-inch-thick kiln-dried oak. An 18-inch oval usually serves four to six. They often have a tree design cut down their length to drain juices into a shallow depression toward one end.

If all the cooking is done on the plank, it will char rapidly. Usually steaks are broiled on an oven grille fully on one side and partially on the other before being planked. To season a new plank ➧ brush it with cooking oil and heat in a 225° oven for at least one hour before using. To protect it when cooking, oil well any exposed part or cover, as suggested above, with a decoration of mashed potatoes or other puréed vegetables.

FLAMBÉING

Flaming always comes at a dramatic moment in the meal, sometimes a tragi-comical one if you manage to get only a mere flicker. To avoid anticlimax, remember that ➧ food to be flamed should be warm and that the brandy or liqueur used in flambéing should also be warm —but well under the boiling point. For meat, do not attempt this process with less than one ounce of liquor per serving. For nonsweet food served from a chafing dish or electric skillet, pour the warmed liquor over the surface of the food and ignite by touching the edge of the pan with the flame of a match or taper. For hot desserts in similar appliances, sprinkle the top surface with granulated sugar, add the warm liqueur and ignite as above.

ABOUT MOIST HEATS

What a number of processes can be assigned to the moist heat category! There are complete ones like boiling, pressure cooking, scalding, simmering, poaching, stewing, fricasseeing, braising, casseroling, cooking in wraps, double boiler cookery and steaming. Also, just as with dry heats, there are partial moist heat processes, like those in blanching and fireless cookery. We may as well mention here and now—although not on the side of simplification—that certain classic terms for kinds of moist heat cookery are broadly interpreted, even by the most knowledgeable cooks. Also a number are neither moist nor dry, but a combination of both. Some stews, for example, may be begun in a pan by browning, while others, like the Irish variety, never see the inside of a skillet. Similarly, a braise, a fricassee and a "smother" may all, like a browned stew, have their origin in dry heat sautéing and then are finished by cooking in a little stock.

BOILING

Discussing this process tempts us to mention stews again, in connection with the old adage "A stew boiled is a stew spoiled." And we may point out that the same sentiment can be applied to almost every other kind of food. While recipes often call for foods to be brought to the boiling point or to be plunged into boiling water, they hardly ever demand boiling for a protracted period. Even "boiled" eggs, so-called, should be simmered.

Quick evaporation—seldom advisable—is one of the few justifications for keeping a food at boiling point. When evaporating, never boil covered, as steam condenses on the lid and falls back into the pot, reducing the amount of liquid very little, if at all.

Adding foods to boiling water will lower the boiling point, unless the quantity of water is at least three times as much as will cover the food—to offset its lower temperature. Such compensation is recommended in Blanching, page 88, and in the cooking of cereals and pasta. When the pores of food are to be sealed, it may be plunged into rapidly boiling liquid, after which the temperature is usually reduced to a simmer.

✪ PRESSURE COOKING

A sound approach to pressure cooking involves an appreciation of its advantages and a knowledge of its limitations.

No matter how high the heat source, boiling in water in the presence of air can never produce a temperature over 212°. But, because in pressure cooking the air in the pan is withdrawn first, heat as high as 250° can be maintained at 15 lbs. gauge-reading. Some home cookers are geared to a range of from 3¾ to 20 pounds, although 15 pounds is commonly used. Cooking time at 15 pounds pressure takes only about ⅓ the total time—from the lidding of the pressure cooker through the capping of the vent and the release of pressure—that it takes to cook food in conventional ways at boiling temperatures. In pressure cooking vegetables over short periods at these higher temperatures, more than time is saved. Nutrients and flavor are also well conserved, see Steam Pressuring of Vegetables, page 252.

➧ In the pressure cooking of meats and soups, however, the higher heats involved tend both to toughen the protein and affect flavor adversely. Therefore, we recommend this method only when time is more important to you than choice results.

➧ In the canning of all non-acid foods, the higher heat of pressure cooking is essential to kill unwanted organisms, see (II, 538).

➧ Pressure cooking of beans and cereals and dried or puréed fruits, which may sputter and clog the vent, is not recommended because of this danger.

A pressure cooker may be used also for sterilizing baby bottles. Allow 10 minutes at 10 lbs. pressure.

It is essential in any pressure cooking to know your equipment well. ➧ Follow manufacturer's directions to the letter, observing these general principles. ➧ Never fill a pressure cooker with more food than ½ its capacity if there is much liquid or ⅔ if the contents are mainly solids. ➧ Be sure the required amount of liquid has been put in the cooker. ➧ Season lightly, as there is less liquid to dilute the flavor than in more traditional types of cooking. Solid foods may be placed at once over high heat. If soup or foods requiring more than the usual amount of water are to be cooked, the heat is brought up slowly. ➧ Always be sure to exhaust the air in the cooker before capping the vent, as trapped air will cause cold pockets and uneven cooking. Allow the steam to come out in a solid column before capping. When the ➧ indicator shows that the desired degree of pressure has been reached or when the gauge or weight jiggles reduce the heat to just maintain desired pressures. ➧ Time from the moment of capping the vent. The pressure pan should show a mild form of activity by hissing occasionally during the cooking period.

If you have a stop clock, use it; if not, watch the time carefully as overcooking results very quickly. ➧ As soon as the time is up, to arrest further cooking and reduce the pressure in your cooker instantly, place it in cool water or let cool water run over the sides. Exceptions are steam puddings, preserves and soups, which should be allowed to cool gradually. When the temperature is brought down, exhaust the steam fully by removing the gauge.

➧ The cover must not be removed until all the steam is out of the pressure cooker. Here again, handle your particular type of appliance exactly as you are instructed. ➧ When the cover is difficult to remove, do not force it; there is still steam in the container which will be exhausted if you wait a few minutes.

If the amount of food to be cooked is increased, also increase the amount of liquid unless the units of the food are very small, when little or no additional liquid is necessary. But do not increase the amount of cooking time.

When cooking foods that require different periods of cooking, begin with the ingredient that requires the longest time. Always reduce the pressure, as directed in the manufacturer's booklet, before opening the lid to add the ingredient that requires the shorter period of cooking. Readjust the cover, place the cooker again over high heat and proceed as before.

When the desired degree of pressure has been reached, reduce the heat and begin to count the rest of the cooking time.

Or, when cooking together vegetables that require an unequal period of cooking, equalize them by cutting into small dice those that require the longer period: potatoes, turnips, etc.

▲ A general rule for pressure cooking at high altitudes, whether you are cooking at 10, 15 or 20 pounds pressure, is to ➧ maintain the same timing as at sea level, but to increase the pressure by ½ lb. for every rise of 1,000 feet.

For additional details about High Altitude pressure cooking, see Vegetables, page 254, Meat, page 457, Canning, page 748. To use a pressure cooker as a steamer, see Steam Puddings, page 703.

SCALDING

As the term is used in this book, scalding means cook at a temperature of about 185° or just below boiling. You will find this process discussed in relation to Milk (II, 137), the food for which it is most frequently used.

SIMMERING

This ranks as one of the most important moist heats. The temperatures range from about 135° to 160°. Simmering protects fragile foods and tenderizes tough ones. The French verb for it is "mijoter" and they engagingly refer to low simmers—between 130° and 135°—as "making the pot smile." When food is simmering, bubbles come gently to the surface and barely seem to break. It is the heat best used in cooking, uncovered, for soups and, covered, for stews, braises, pot-roasts, poêles, étouffés, page 493, and fricassees, page 577.

POACHING

This kind of moist heat cooking is one that most people associate only with eggs, but its range is much wider. The principle of poaching never varies. The heat source is a liquid just under the boiling point and a distinguishing feature of the process is the basting or self-basting which is constant during the cooking period.

➧ When an egg is properly poached, it is floated on simmering water and then either basted with this simmering liquid or covered with a lid, so that steam

accumulates to perform a self-basting action. Because the egg cooks in just a few minutes, the lid does not allow the formation of excess steam. In poaching meat or fish, where the cooking period is lengthened, entrapped steam may become too heavy. For these and delicate foods, therefore, a lid is not recommended. Instead, substitute a poaching paper, see sketch.

A poaching paper permits excess steam to escape through its small top vent and around the sides. The narrow vent also maintains better color in the food than when air is excluded altogether—as in other more tightly confined moist heat processes, such as casseroling. ➧ To make a poaching paper, take a piece of square parchment, the sides of which are a little larger than the diameter of the pan you wish to cover. Fold it in fourths and roll it diagonally: begin at the folded corner, as sketched. Hold it over the pan to determine the radius. Then snip off the part that projects beyond the edge of the pan. Cut a tiny tip off the pointed end to form a vent. When you unfold the paper you will have a circle just the area of your pan, with a perforation at its center. Place it over the food to form a self-baster. If the cooking process is a short one or if the food to be cooked is in small units, the liquid may be at simmering point when the food is added. If the food is chunky, like a whole chicken, the water it put on cold, the food added and the water brought to a simmer ➧ uncovered. The liquid may then be skimmed and the poaching paper applied. Should the liquid become too much reduced during the cooking process, it must be replenished. ➧ This type of poaching is often miscalled boiling or stewing.

CASSEROLING

The term casserole has been bandied about so carelessly that it is time we took stock of its meaning—or, rather, meanings. In correct parlance, a "casserole" is both a utensil—usually a lidded one—and the process used for cooking a raw food in that utensil. But it has also come to mean a favorite type of self-serve dish which graces so many American buffets, but is not in the least the real McCoy. This mock casserole is a mixture of several foods, one of which may be a pasta or rice in a sauce. The mixture is often precooked or consists of a combination of precooked and quick-cooking food; and it is served in the baker in which it was heated. ➧ Mock casseroles, if cooked covered, will develop too much steam and the sauce they are served in will break down. They often have a gratinéed top, page 389, to protect the food and absorb excess grease. ➧ It is wise to wipe "prefabricated" casserole dishes well before heating, so they will not show any browned spilled-over areas on the outside surface when served. Often, for large groups, a rather shallow dish is used, both to ensure its heating through quickly and the presence of plenty of gratinéed top for each serving. If topping with biscuit or corn pone, heat in a 375° to 400° oven.

Let's go back to the casserole as a utensil. The unglazed clay ware used in Europe today has not changed shape since very ancient times. It is squat, with bulging sides, easily grasped round handles and a slightly arched lid. ➧ To season unglazed casseroles and to prevent an "earthy" taste or the subsequent retention of unwanted flavors, rub them well, inside and out, with cut cloves of garlic. Then fill with water, add onion skins, celery and leek tops, put in a low oven, let the water come to a boil and simmer about 2 hours. Finally, discard the water, wash the dish and lid, after which the casserole is ready for use. ➧ To avoid cracking, never set clay casseroles on heating elements unless they have previously had butter, oil or other food put in them; and if your burner is not thermostatically controlled, it is wise to use an asbestos pad or wire trivet.

Today the word casserole is applied to any deepish pot in which cooking actually goes on, or even to pots more rightly called sauteuses or deep skillets. ➧ In true casseroling, as distinguished from "mock" casseroling, a tight lid is integral to the process. The very slow cooking goes on in about a 300° oven and develops a bare simmer. There is a continuous self-basting action, as steam condenses on the lid and falls back on the food. Inasmuch as only a small quantity of water has been used to begin with, the long, slow cooking condenses this and the food juices into a delicious residue. After the food is removed, the residue when degreased, if necessary, and then deglazed, forms the sauce for the dish. This form of closed cooking with only the barest escape of steam is also called cooking "à l'étouffée." Pot roasting of chicken or veal is sometimes carried on in a partially lidded casserole. This variant, because of greater evaporation, needs basting, and the meats should not be overcooked.

WRAP COOKERY

Food commonly needs heat; but we are forever inventing ways to protect it from drying out while cooking. Lids, as well as double boilers, are familiar to us all; but sometimes more interesting flavors and textures can be developed by other means. One of the most mouth-watering sights we ever saw was a movie of an Indonesian tribe on the march. When mealtime came, oldster to tot began devising cases for cooking their food in the coals: intricately folded leaves, large stoppered sections of bamboo, reed baskets. You knew at once that the cases all had enough moisture to withstand the heat of the coals they were buried in and that they would give special flavor and succulence to the food. Cooking in wraps may take other forms, too, and in less primitive company—from the clay enclosed meat pies of English kiln-workers to the "en croûte" cookery so esteemed in France, see page 458.

LEAF-WRAPPINGS

These make wonderful food cases. Choose only very fresh, unblemished green leaves. How to use them depends on the kind chosen.

➧ To prepare cabbage leaves: cut the stem from a head of cabbage deep enough to start a separation of the very outer leaves from the core. Dip the head in boiling water. This will loosen 3 or 4 leaves. Dip again and continue to remove the loosened leaves. Blanch, page 82, the leaves for 2 minutes, drain and plunge into cold water. To wrap meat in the leaves, see the illustration on the next page. Either tie the leaf-packet as shown or place it, if it is left untied, seam-side down. ➧ Cook the leaf-packets as follows.

I. Melt in casserole:

2 tablespoons butter

Add:

2 cups boiling water or stock

Put food in a single layer on bottom of casserole. Place a plate on top to give weight during cooking. If filling is uncooked, bake or simmer the packets, covered, 35 to 40 minutes—longer for pork. If filling is precooked, 10 minutes is enough to heat the food through.

II. If packets are tied, they may be dropped into simmering broth and cooked gently until done. See timing under I.

II. Or, as in Tamales, page 287, packets, see right above, may be steamed in a vegetable steamer. See timing under I.

➧ To prepare lettuce leaves: soak them very briefly in boiling water. Drain, dry and fill. Wrap as for cabbage leaves and cook as for I or III. They are not strong enough to cook as for II.

➧ To prepare fresh grape leaves for Dolmas, page 522, drop young pale-green leaves into boiling water and blanch till color darkens—about 4 to 5 minutes. Remove leaves. Drain them on a skimmer. Should you have to use large leaves, remove the tough part of the central rib. Place shiny side down on a board. Roll the filling in ¾-inch balls. If the filling is of rice, use not more than 2 teaspoons, as the rice will swell. Set one ball near the broad end of a leaf, fold over the left and right segments, as sketched. Then roll the leaf from beyond the filling ball toward its tip, just as though you were rolling a cigarette. Place it, loose end down, and cook as directed above.

➧ To prepare and separate canned grape leaves, place them briefly in hot water.

➧ To prepare papaya leaves, cover them with cold water. Bring ➧ just to the boiling point —uncovered. Drain. This will remove any bitterness. Plunge into boiling water to cover and ➧ simmer, uncovered, until tender.

➧ To prepare corn husks place them in boiling water, remove from heat and allow to stand 5 minutes before draining. To roll food in them, overlap two or three corn husks. Place the filling in an oblong shape centered on the leaves. Fold the leaves first from the sides and then from the ends, as shown, so they can be tied with one string.

FOIL COOKERY

Aluminum foil solves many kitchen problems, but if you cook food wrapped in foil, please consider the following. The foil is impervious to air and moisture from the outside. Therefore, it traps within its case all the moisture released from the food during the cooking period. So, even if the heat source is dry, like that of an oven, the result will always be a steamed food, never a roasted one. Since the foil also has high insulating qualities, foil-wrapped food will require longer cooking at 75° higher heat. You may be willing to pay for both the foil and the extra heat needed to have the convenience of an effortless Pot Roast, see page 498. If you are cooking out of doors, see Campfire Vegetables and the comments in Outdoor Cooking, pages 89–90.

COOKING EN PAPILLOTE

This is a delightful way to prepare delicate, quick-cooking, partially cooked or sauced foods. The dish, served in the parchment paper in which it was heated, retains the aromas until ready to be eaten. As the food cooks, some of the unwanted steam it generates evaporates through the paper. Just the same, the paper rises and puffs as heating progresses, putting considerable strain on the folded seam. So, note the following directions and sketches carefully.

To make a papillote: fold a parchment of appropriate size in half, crosswise. Cut from the folded edge to the open edge, a half heart shape, so that when the paper is opened, as shown, the full heart shape materializes.

Be generous in cutting—allowing almost twice again as much paper as the size of the object to be enclosed. Place the food near the fold—not too close to the seam. Turn the filled paper with the folded edge toward you. Holding the edges of the paper together, make a fold in a small section of the rim. Crease it with your fingers and fold it over again. Hold down this double fold with the fingers of one hand and with the other start a slightly overlapping and again another double overlapping fold. Each double fold overlaps the previous one. Repeat this folding, creasing and folding around the entire rim, finishing off at the point end of the heart with a tight twist of the parchment—locking the whole in place. Now butter the paper well. Place it in a buttered ovenproof dish in a 400° preheated oven for 5 to 6 minutes or until the paper puffs. In serving, snip about ¾ of the paper on the curved edge just next to the fold to reveal the lovely food and release the aroma.

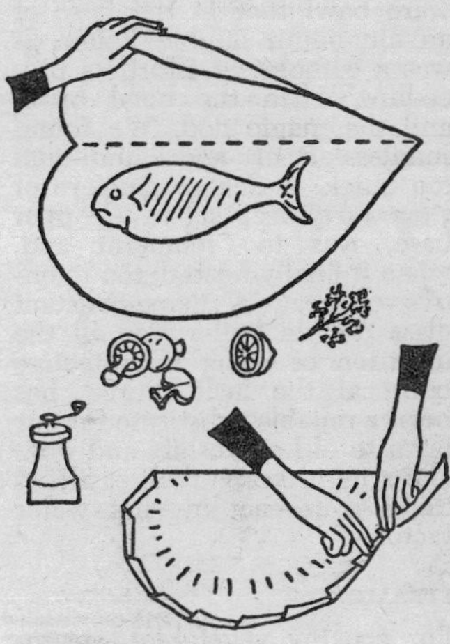

DOUBLE BOILER COOKING

For those foods which are quickly ruined beyond hope of resurrection if overheated, even for a short period—especially egg, cream or chocolate dishes—we recommend the use of a double boiler. It is a peaceful way to cook delicate sauces, particularly if you are obliged to make them at a time when preparing other dishes which need close surveillance.

Sometimes food is started over direct heat in the top of a double boiler and is finished ▶ over—not in—hot water. For sauces, we like a double boiler that is rather wide. Deep and narrow vessels tend to overheat the sauce at the bottom even when it is stirred—if it is held for any time at all. ▶ The material of which the upper portion of the double boiler is made is very important. When the material is too thin, it transmits heat too fast. If it is too thick, it absorbs and retains too much heat. For years, we made magnificent Hollandaise in a stoneware bowl that fit the base of an aluminum double boiler. It was a completely effortless procedure. Then the bowl broke and the magic fled. We found stainless steel and aluminum too quick. A deluxe saucière of stoneware, deep set in a copper base, was too reluctant and, when it finally heated, too retentive of heat. A flame-resistant glass double boiler, for all the irritation of using a protective trivet at the heat source, has been a reliable substitute for our favorite old makeshift and does allow us to keep track easily of the ▶ over—not in—hot water factor.

STEAMING

For cooking vegetables, steaming is an excellent process to use. On page 252, we describe two methods for this purpose: direct steaming over boiling water and pressure steaming at greater temperatures. Direct steaming is also a good way to plump raisins, to release salt from smoked birds and, more importantly, to cook fish, page 398.

BLANCHING AND PARBOILING

These terms are among the most carelessly used in a cook's vocabulary. To introduce some order into traditional confusion we describe and differentiate between four different types of blanching. Which type is required will, we believe, be clear from the context of our individual descriptions.

▶ BLANCHING I

This means pouring boiling water over food to remove outer coverings, as in loosening the brown hulls of almonds or making the skins of peaches and tomatoes easier to peel off. This process is also used to soften herbs and vegetables for more flexible and longer-lived decoration.

▶ BLANCHING II OR PARBLANCHING

This involves placing food to be blanched into ▶ a large quantity of cold water ▶ bringing it slowly to a boil ▶ uncovered, and continuing to ▶ simmer it for the length of time specified. Following this hot bath, the food is drained, plunged quickly into cold water to firm it and to arrest further hot water cooking and then finished, as directed in the recipe. This is the process used to leach excess salt from tongue, cured ham or salt pork and to remove excess blood or strong flavors from variety meats. The cold water plunge after blanching effectively firms the more fragile variety meats, like brains and sweetbreads.

▶ BLANCHING III OR PARBOILING

This means that food is plunged into ▶ a large quantity of rapidly boiling water a little at a time so as not to disturb the boiling and then cooked for the period indicated in the recipe. The purpose of this particular kind of blanching or parboiling may be to set color or—by partial dehydration—to help preserve nutrients and firm the tissues of vegetables. If further cooking follows immediately, the blanched food need not be chilled as above, but merely drained. Should an interval elapse before cooking and serving, use the cold water plunge, drain and store the food refrigerated. Blanching vegetables in this way preparatory to canning or freezing is described in greater detail on (II, 556). Small amounts of the vegetable are plunged into ➧ boiling water just long enough to retard enzymatic action and to shrink the product for more economical packaging. Then the vegetables are ➧ drained and quickly plunged into ➧ ice water, so that the cooking process is arrested at once.

➧ BLANCHING IV, STEAM BLANCHING OR PARSTEAMING

An alternate method for freezing and canning is also described on (II, 556).

FIRELESS COOKING

If fuel is scarce, and for food needing a long heating period, there is a possible advantage in using a fireless cooker. This appliance is enclosed on all sides by material that is a nonconductor of heat and is preheated to a desired temperature by an electric coil or by hot stones. Hot food set in it continues to cook without the addition of further heat.

OUTDOOR COOKING

Cooking out-of-doors may put to use all kinds of heat; but its enthusiasts do best when they stick to simple methods. As soon as

cookouts get complicated, the whole party—in our perhaps jaundiced opinion—will do well to move back into the kitchen, where equipment is handy, controls positive and effects less problematical. We never attend a patio barbecue featuring paper chef's hats, aprons with printed wise-cracks, striped asbestos gloves, an infra-red broiler on white-walled wheels and yards and yards of extension cord and culinary red tape, without anticipating a deservedly heavy thunderstorm.

For campers, al fresco cooking is a necessity—rather than a pleasant indulgence. On long trips or in emergencies, very primitive heat sources will do a surprisingly good job. This is true especially if the camper's cooking utensils can be largely confined to kettle, coffeepot and skillet. The illustration on page 89 foreground shows perhaps the easiest of all outdoor cooking set-ups. It is called ➧ a hunter's fire. Two fairly chunky green logs are set directly on the ground, open-V fashion, and oriented so that the prevailing wind enters at the wide end of the V. If big logs are not available, build the V of rocks. When the fire, which has been built inside, burns to embers, kettle, skillet and coffeepot can span the logs, as shown. ➧ Before bringing any sort of cooking container in close contact with a wood fire, remember to cover its under-surfaces with a film of soap or detergent. This precaution will greatly facilitate the removal of soot later, when the pan is cleaned.

Speaking of easy outdoor cooking devices, we once went on a picnic with some friends in a beech woods. Our host, toward supper-time, made criss-cross fires, just big enough for each individual steak. First, he set up log-cabin-like cribs about four layers high, with twigs approximately 1-inch thick. In these, he laid a handful of dry leaves and fine brush. On top of the cribs, he continued to build for about three inches an additional structure of pencil-like material. When, after firing, the wood had been reduced to a rectangular framework of glowing rods, he unlimbered some thin steaks from a hamper and, to our consternation, laid them calmly and directly on the embers. In a few moments he removed them with tongs, shook off whatever coals had adhered, turned the steaks over and repeated the process on the other side. They were delicious.

Another device for rough-and-ready outdoor cookery involves the principle of the crane. Two versions are illustrated, both for kettle cookery and both largely self-explanatory. A ring of rocks around a campfire will keep the flames from spreading and reflect the heat back into the cooking circle.

Pit-cooking is perhaps the most glamorous of all primitive types—glamorous because it is so largely associated with picturesque places, hearty group effort and holiday spirit. Pits may be small holes, of just sufficient depth and width to take a bean pot, a three-legged kettle or a true braizing pot with a depres-

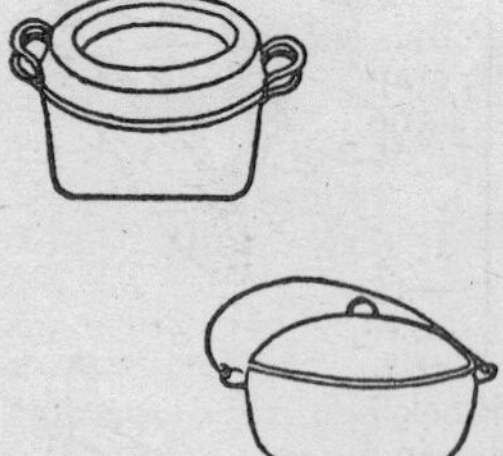

sion on top for coals, as sketched; or they may be big enough to accommodate a king-size luau, replete with suckling pigs. Sometimes hardwood embers are left in the pit. Then steel rods are put across it—held a few inches above the fire on the rocks or logs set around its periphery. The rods, in turn, support a wire mesh grid on which the food is cooked. A switch from direct pit-firing to fireless pit-cooking and a completely different range of culinary effects can be achieved by a variant of this procedure.

Fairly large scale cookery of the latter type will require digging a pit, to begin with, not less than 2 feet deep, 3 feet across, and 4 feet long. If pit-cooking is more than occasional and the locale does not vary, you may find it more convenient to build a pit in reverse, by constructing a hollow rectangle of concrete blocks, about the same height as a true pit is deep.

The next step is to line the bottom and sides of the pit with medium-size flat rocks ➧ never with shale, which may explode when heated. Toss in enough additional rock to approximate the area of the pit. Now spread over the rocks a substantial bonfire of hardwood deadfall or driftwood. Hickory, beech, maple or ironwood are prime for this purpose. And grape-vine cuttings lend grilled food special distinction. The French, incidentally, regard food broiled over grape-wood, or "sarments de vigne," as extraordinarily choice. When the fire has completely burned down—this should take not less than 2 hours—rake out the red embers and the top rocks. Now, sprinkle a quart or so of water over the hot rock bed remaining and add a two-inch layer of green leaves—grape, beech, pawpaw, sassafras, cornhusks or seaweed. If you have remembered to bring along some handfuls of aromatic herbs, add them too. ➧ Work quickly at this point, so that the rocks do not lose their stored heat. On the bed of packed foliage arrange the elements of your meal: fish, cuts of meat, green peppers, onions, corn in its husks, unpeeled potatoes, acorn squash. Pile over them a second layer of green leafage, then a second grouping of food and, finally, a third layer of green leafage. Cap the stratification off with the remaining hot rocks, a tarpaulin or canvas cover and four inches of earth or sand to weight things down and to keep heat and steam at work inside—cooking your meal. How long this will take depends, of course, on what's cooking—maximum time will probably be required for a small pig; it should test 190° when done and takes about 20 minutes per pound.

For shore dinners, with seaweed as filler, wire mesh is often placed over at least one layer to better support small crustaceans, clams and oysters. For details of a Clam Bake, see page 428. Such tidbits may also be steamed in closed ketttles—we have used a clean refuse can with a tight-fitting lid ➧ but be careful not to let such containers rest directly on the hot rocks or to cook any food that is very acid directly in them. Allow one live lobster or three softshell crabs per person.

In Hawaii, and in the East Indies generally, food cooked in pits is frequently wrapped in papaya leaves which not only protect but tenderize, see page 522. In the West Indies, petate mats are used for this purpose. ➧ Wrapping food before introducing it into direct heat is almost as old as cooking itself.

Primitive societies to this day surround pieces of food with a leaf and then with clay, to protect them from burning.

In France the technique has given rise to a branch of food preparation called "en croûte" cookery, page 458, in which the encasement is dough. Its principle is increasingly exploited in ➧ papillote, page 87. Both in the pastry and paper casings some steam escapes. But, in cookouts today, if ➧ wrapping the food in heavy duty aluminum foil, page 87, it must be remembered that the imperviousness of the foil makes for a truly steamed product and that texture and flavor are far removed from that of food typically cooked by direct heat. Indeed this is true of the closed-in type of pit-cookery., as described above, in general, but there the flavor of the charcoal and seaweed or leaves adds a delicious touch.

The whole pit-cookery operation, whether it is carried out on the beach or in the woods, has a distinctly adventurous character. And periodic tests for doneness performed on the foods closest to the edge of the pit are an essential part of the process.

In lifting the tarp and in removing it altogether when you are ready to serve, be extremely careful not to get food fouled up with sand or earth.

There are several ways to rig up simple stoves for camp cooking. One is made from a tin can of fairly large capacity—from a gallon on up, see the sketch at right, above. Its features are basic to stoves of any sort. The cylinder, or body, of the can shelters the fire from draft and supports the cooking pan; the fire below is kept supplied with oxygen by the bottom opening. The upper opening can be regulated to sustain the flow of heat and allows the release of smoke and hot gases. The holes punched in the top of the can steadily bring up a supply of heat to the pan. This can be fueled with canned heat or a small twig fire. ➧ You can cut a cooking utensil from a second can, but be sure to handle it with gloves!

Probably the most effective do-it-yourself device for smoking food is merely a modification of the tin-can stove—a can-on-can affair, with two hollow cylinders closely fitted together, as sketched. The fuel here is sawdust from nut or fruitwood, which is piled up to one-fourth the height of the lower can and which smolders

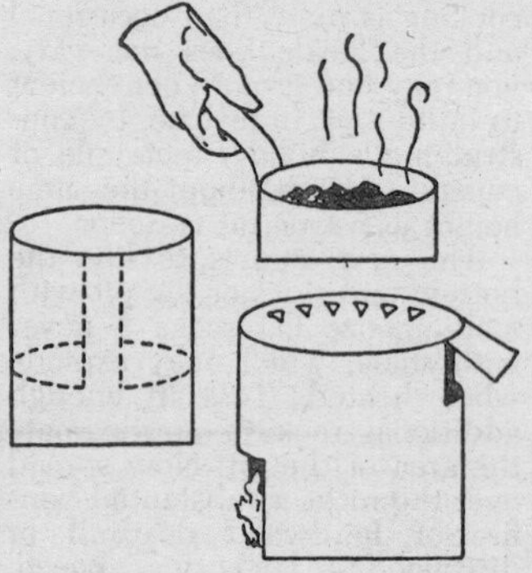

rather than burns, giving off, in so doing, the required abundance of smoke. The can should be preheated before the food is added. For smoking ham, meat, fowl or fish see (II, 543–546). The food to be treated is hung from a crossbar or bars inserted across the upper cylinder. ➧ To retain as much smoke as possible in the curing area, the upper can has only a single vent at the tops of the cans, some side-perforations at the bottom, and a 4-inch square base-vent.

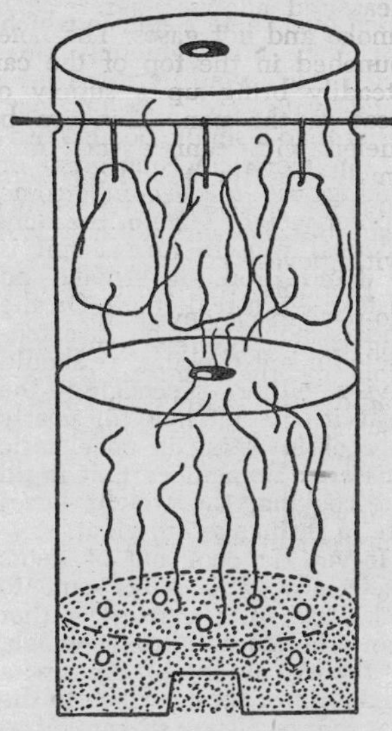

By projecting the device just described further, the Chinese, centuries ago, perfected a wholly distinctive type of food preparation, which is gaining popularity in this country today: smoke-cookery. A section through a typical smoke oven is L-shaped. The horizontal leg of the L contains the firebox; the vertical portion is fitted with horizontal bars or wire racks on which the food is placed. After igniting the fuel—generally fruitwood spiced with dried herbs—the box is closed and firing continued until the temperature of the stack reaches 400° to 500°, at which time the food to be smoke-cooked is introduced.

To return to the camper for a final word: There is no law, of course, against his availing himself of ready-made instead of improvised cooking gear; and as much of it as the traffic will bear. A gasoline or propane-fired stove is a great convenience and, if he expects to do any baking, a reflector oven a downright necessity. Shown on page 89 is a folding oven. If that is not available, use as a substitute a camp skillet, as sketched, braced either by a forked stick or rocks. There are even available, for the Davy Crocketts of the New Frontier, various solar heat cookers; but it is suggested that they be given home-side tryouts in advance.

We have described—at least briefly—the elements of camp and pit cookery. The disadvantages of the latter, as we have indicated, are several. The greatest, perhaps, is its relative inconvenience. That is one reason why the above-ground cookout—as distinguished from the subterranean type—is far and away the more popular. There, again, we most enjoy the simpler techniques and procedures: those which involve direct heat from reduced charcoal. Among them, we prefer, also, portable rather than built-in cookers; and here we seem to be following a definite trend. The rather formidable backyard fireplace is less and less favored. It had metal components which were hard to clean and rusted in the weather. These built-in features offered unintended hospitality to spiders, wasps and field-mice. And its homely architecture can hardly be said to have graced its surroundings. Now, the most popular cookout stove is the portable brazier-type, of which the hibachi is the Far-Eastern representative. To accommodate a main dish for groups of four or more, only the larger Westernized brazier offers an adequate cooking surface. A hibachi-type broiler or two will supplement this larger grill in the preparation of side dishes, such as hors d'oeuvre and vegetables. The circular grill (page 94) boasts some

improvements over the original prototype. It has, of course, fairly good-size wheels for easy transport, as well as a hood or collar to protect the grill surface against wind. The grill itself may be twirled, to expose food to the most active area of the heat and is equipped with a screw device which raises and lowers it for varied exposures. We also show another model with a bellows, which compensates for the small lower draft-port found on the hibachi. This

enables the cook to bring up quick high heat for searing and rewarming. Some braziers with horizontal grills have superimposed over them a spit, in which case they are commonly protected from wind by three bent metal walls and a metal roof, rather than a simple hood. Without an electrical connection or making use of a cumbersome counter-weight system, the only practical way to turn a spit is by hand; and this—make no mistake—is a real chore. On the whole, should you go in extensively for spit-cooking, we should advise either precooking the meat in the kitchen till nearly done or investing in an electric rotisserie. Remember that in all spit cooking, the weight losses due to shrinkage are great.

If you do cook out of doors electrically, you may want to make use of a vertical, rather than a horizontal, broiler which, in theory at least, exposes a maximum of food surface to the heat source. Newer still are infra-red broilers. But these, for what they are worth, we regard as strictly indoor appliances. Whatever equipment you use, pay close attention to the directions furnished with it by its manufacturer. Such brochures have become more and more informative and presently cover not only how to use the appliance itself, but how to cook a large number of typically outdoor dishes with it.

For cookout accessories, assuming a full scale operation, the following are recommended: a kettle for boiling water; a black iron pot for burgoos, stews or beans; a skillet or two; hinged wire basket grills with long handles—especially desirable for broiling fish and hamburgers; some sharp knives; a metal fork with an insulated handle; a spatula; tongs; a long pastry brush for glazing; a chopping block; skewers—these must be nonrusting ◆ square or oval, not round, in section and sharp-pointed; a roll of double-strength aluminum foil; a supply of potholders or a couple of pairs of asbestos mitts; individual serving trays; a pail of water and, with it, a flare-up quencher. For this last, an extra baster will do—or a water pistol. If you plan to roast a fowl or a joint, you will need, in addition, a baster, shown on page 457, and a meat thermometer.

► To prepare a brazier fire with charcoal, be sure that you build a big enough bed of coals to last out the cooking operation. We find prepared hardwood briquets most uniform and convenient. They should be put into the brazier approximately two deep—preferably over a layer of gravel—enough to level the bed out to the edge of the bowl.

A circle of aluminum foil, cut to size and put down over the gravel, will keep it from getting greasy and act as a heat reflector. Ignition may be helped along by pouring over the briquets a small amount of commercial lighter fluid ► before, not after, applying the match. Never use any strong-smelling substance as starter. To ready fuel for an extended firing period, arrange an extra circle of briquets around the edge of the brazier. As the center of your fire burns to embers, these may be pushed inward.

To ignite charcoal is often frustrating, especially if it is old and has been exposed to air—for it absorbs moisture so easily. A good way to avoid irritation is to keep a few briquettes soaking in lighter fluid ► in a tightly lidded metal container. You will find 1 or 2 of these saturated blocks is a great help.

Confect for yourself a 12- or 15-inch length of lightweight stove pipe, cut at the base every two inches with a tin snips to the depth of about 2½ inches to make a fluted edge—or punch holes in it about 1 inch up. Place it in the grill, put some paper near one of the fluted openings, place one or two of the saturated briquettes on the paper and then the other briquettes you are going to use on top. Light the paper. In about 5 to 10 minutes the briquettes will have become well ignited. Gently pull up the chimney with tongs and the briquettes will spread out so you can arrange them in whatever grilling pattern you plan to use—in one layer on one-half of the fire box of your circular twirl grill, as shown on page 94, or spaced at 1- to 2-inch intervals over the whole surface of the firebed or in a double ring around the edge for a spitted bird.

If you use any kind of smoked or flavored chips, soak them in water for several hours beforehand and then wait until a few minutes before the charcoal is completely reduced, which should take anywhere from a half hour to 45 minutes, before placing them on the coals. ► When the charcoal is covered with a fine white ash, you are ready to begin cooking. Flick off the ash, which acts as insulation.

Judging the heat of a brazier fire is strictly a matter of manual training. Hold your hand above the grill at about the same distance from the coals that the food will be while cooking, think of the name of a four-syllable state—"Massachusetts" or "Mississippi" will do nicely. If you can pronounce it once before snatching your hand away, your coals are delivering high heat; twice, medium heat; if three times, low heat.

Remember always that a number of factors influence the degree of heat transferred to food cooked on outdoor braziers; some of these being charcoals; their depth; distance between coals and grill; temperature of ingredients, which, if possible should be about 70°. You may also considerably influence heat transfer by your arrangement of coals: deepening them for concentration, spreading them apart for diffusion, etc. If you have the kind of brazier grill which twirls, heaping hot coals up on one side of the fire pot will make instantly available both very high and very moderate heat.

What food should be cooked out of doors? Just as we recommend simple cooking equipment in the open, so we now urge simple outdoor menus. The truth is that refined or fancy effects are—in the nature of things—all but impossible not to say inappropriate. Again, certain kinds of food respond unfavorably or indifferently to outdoor cooking techniques: yeast breads are a conspicuous example; some vegetables are another; and among the meats, veal and pork, except, of course, pork sausages and—just because they are so delicious on a sparkling autumn afternoon—spareribs. But spareribs should be at least parboiled beforehand, page 88, and only finished off and rebasted on spit or grill out of doors.

Build your cookout meal around one basic delicious grilled or roasted meat course, complemented by crisp bread and a crisp salad. Let side dishes be strictly side-issues. The dessert should be correspondingly uncomplicated and, if baked, prepared beforehand in the kitchen. ▶ Remember with Picnic Food (II, 23) to protect it always against insects.

Throughout this book you will find recipes which we regard as suitable for outdoor cookery marked with this grill-like symbol ⊟. While, obviously, pan-broiled and pan-cooked food may be prepared over a brazier out of doors, you will not find such recipes singled out by the distinctive outdoor cookery symbol. We have in large part, selected those in which the flavor is actually improved by the outdoor cooking medium.

Steaks and chops are extraordinarily well suited to flat-broiling on a brazier. ▶ Choose well-marbled meat—in other words, meat that is rather fatty in texture, page 450. But, by this, we definitely do not mean meat which has a rim or collar of fat. On the contrary, it is important ▶ to trim off all excess fat before broiling, to reduce the risk of flare-up. Also, cut through encircling sinew—being careful not to slice into the meat itself—so that the meat does not curl up under the high heat which initiates its cooking. ▶ Avoid excessively thick cuts: an inch and a half should be the limit for individual servings. Grease the grill first with some of the meat fat or with a vegetable oil. ▶ To sear the meat and seal in its juices, lower the grill close to the coals before laying the meat on it or use the bellows attachment if it is equipped with one.

Searing to seal is even more essential in flat-broil grilling than in pan or oven broiling, because the meat juices, once lost, are irrecoverable. After searing, raise the grill to about three inches from the fire and broil the meat until done. No specific time schedule for doneness can be set up because so much depends not only on the degree of heat itself, but on the age of the animal, how long the meat has been hung, the nature of the cut and, of course, individual preference.

Here are a few things to keep in mind: First, just as in indoor Timing, page 458, large cuts do not take weight for weight proportionately more cooking time. Second, to secure rareness in meat, turn it—but best practice is to turn as infrequently as possible. Third, if the cut is large, testing for doneness with a thermometer is safer than testing with a knife or fork. We would like to spare you the ordeal of an old friend of ours, whose enthusiasm for outdoor grilling is repeatedly dampened by his wife's low-voiced but grim injunction: "Remember, Orville, medium-burnt, not well-burnt."

➧ If you flat-broil chicken or other fowl, restrict the weight of the bird to two pounds or under. Split it in half, grease both sides with cooking oil, set the halves on the grill, cavity side down. The bony structure of the bird will transmit heat to the flesh above and at the same time provide insulation. Finish the cooking on the fleshy side; but ➧ to keep the skin from sticking, make sure to lower the heat before doing so.

Spit and rotisserie cooking are best for very small or large fowl; for joints, like leg of lamb, and for other chunky cuts of meat. Here again, consult the directions which come with your equipment to determine maximum weight, which will probably be in the neighborhood of ten pounds for roast meat and up to 15 for fowl. Smaller birds should be strung transversely on the spit, larger ones head to tail along the spit's axis, as illustrated.

For spareribs, get your butcher to cut them in half crosswise, forming two long strips; prebake or parboil them in the kitchen and then string them, in turn—like an accordion—on your outdoor spit, as shown. Fowl and certain other types of meat must be trussed before spitting. Especially if they are heavy or of irregular shape, it is necessary, while adjusting them to the skewer, to determine their approximate center of gravity.

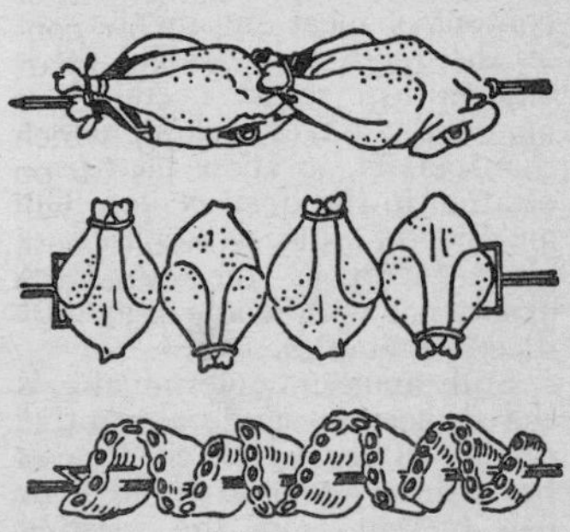

Fowl on a spit should be carefully coated in advance with melted butter or cooking oil. You may baste with butter or oil during the cooking period but ➧ do not apply any barbecue sauce until the last 15 to 20 minutes of cooking. For Barbecue Sauces, see page 374.

⊟ ➧ For cooking Vegetables, see page 253.

⊟ ➧ For Cooking on Skewers, see pages 75 and above.

TIMING IN COOKING

How long to heat food? There are many answers. They lie in the interaction of the heat source, the equipment and the cooking medium, air, liquid or fat.

Consider the following rates of heat transferral. A dough that either bakes at 400° or steams at 212° for 20 minutes will cook in deep fat heated to 400° in 3 minutes. A hard-cooked egg will cool off in five minutes if plunged into ice water, but will need 20 minutes to cool in 32° air. A vegetable that will cook in 20 minutes in water at 212° will need only 2 minutes steaming under 15 lbs. pressure at 250°.

A great deal in timing depends on the freshness of food—this is especially true of vegetables—on the aging and fat content of meat and on the size of the food unit. Large, thick objects like roasts need lower heat and a longer cooking period than cutlets, to allow heat penetration to the deep center. The amount of surface exposed is also a factor, as you know from experience with whole as against diced vegetables.

Still another determinant is the reflective and absorptive quality of the pan. Recent tests have shown that a whole hour can be cut from the roasting time of a ten- or twelve-pound turkey if it is cooked in one of those dark enamel pans which absorb heat rather than in a shiny metal one that reflects it. And we have discussed elsewhere, page 86, the insulative qualities of foil when used in wrap-cooking. Personal preference affects timing, of course, as well as the idiosyncrasies of equipment. Even placement in an oven, page 100, makes a difference and, last but not least, the temperature of food at the onset of heating. For all these reasons it is with some trepidation that we have indicated cooking periods in our individual recipes. And with some reluctance we have discarded the simple, safe admonition "cook until done." We know from our fan mail that cooking times are among the most worrisome of all problems for the beginning cook. Therefore, if our timing does not correspond to yours, we beg you to look for solutions in the facts we have set down above, before you take pen in hand.

HOLDING FOOD AT SERVING TEMPERATURES AND REHEATING FOOD

Everyone knows that food which is held hot or reheated is not as tasty or nutritious as that served immediately after preparation. Unfortunately, laggards and leftovers are a cook's frequent fate. Here are a few hints on the best procedures.

▶ There are 2 ways to reheat dishes which are apt to curdle when subjected to high, direct temperatures. These include au gratin, egg or creamed dishes or any other dish rich in fat. One way is to put them in the oven in a container of hot water—allowing the water to come up about two thirds of the way on the cooking pan. The other way is to place under the pan a cookie tin, with the shiny side down—so that the heat is deflected. The latter suggestion is particularly handy in reheating pies or cakes to avoid overbrowning.

▶ Reheat other cream and egg-sauced foods in a double boiler ▶ over—not in—hot water.

▶ To retain color in vegetables which are reheated in a double boiler, use a vented lid.

▶ If reheating whole roasts, bring them to room temperature and then heat through in a moderate oven.

▶ If reheating roasted meat, slice it paper thin and put it on hot plates just before pouring over it ▶ boiling hot gravy. Any other method of reheating will toughen it and make it taste second-hand.

▶ To reheat deep-fat fried foods, which tend to go limp if steam develops, spread them on racks ▶ uncovered, in a 250° oven.

▶ To hold pancakes, place them on and between cloth towels in a 200° oven.

➧ To reheat casseroles, bring to 70° then place in a 325° preheated oven.

➧ To hold delicate sauces, use a wide-mouthed vacuum bottle.

➧ To reheat creamed or clear soups or sauces, heat to boiling point and serve immediately.

Devices which also hold foods for short periods are electrically controlled trays, individual retractable infra-red lamps, the age-old chafing dish and the bain-marie or steam table. None of these should be used for a protracted period, however, if you hope to preserve real flavor. Holding temperatures should be at about 140°.

ABOUT COOKING EQUIPMENT

Certain cooking effects we have admired away from home and would like to bring back with us seem to defy domestication. Part of the difficulty may have to do with the way food is grown elsewhere or to the fact that it is sometimes impossible to buy ingredients of comparable freshness. But, just as often, the loss in translation may be traced to special techniques which simply cannot be duplicated in the average kitchen. This is true of the following: the quick, intense, short-lived fires and the huge pans which are essential to Chinese stir-frying; the very low, long-retained heat of the "étuve" in old French kitchens—so ideal for drying out meringues or for simmering foods in covered pots; and, for that matter, the open-air charcoal grilling in our own country, which imparts its distinctive aroma to a steak, or the seaweed-smother which gives that authentic touch to lobsters pit-cooked at the shore.

Conditions like these may be approximated in cooking on modern ranges, but never completely reproduced.

If you grew up using gas for cooking heat, you appreciate its dynamic flexibility of control. If your experience has been with electric ranges, you value the evenness of their broiling heat and the stored warmth of their surface units. The relatively new infra-red cooking appliances—including infra-red attachments for the conventional electric range—have attracted favorable attention because of their ability to reduce heating time to a fraction of its former length. Should you decide to invest in this type of equipment, be sure to read the manufacturer's booklet with care, making some mental reservations about the feasibility of "plate dinner" cooking.

Indeed, whatever your source of cooking heat, learn the characteristics of your range, thoroughly. Find out if the broiling elements need a preheating period; if broiling in the oven requires an open or a closed door; whether, when you turn the switch to "Bake," you do better leaving the top oven element in or taking it out.

In purchasing, consider the safety value of controls which are located along the front of a range instead of at the rear, where they may be obstructed by tall pans or cause injuries by bringing the hand and clothing into too near proximity to the burners. Pay particular attention, also, to the quality of oven insulation in the range you plan buying and to its venting characteristics.

In loading ovens, we make the following suggestions. ➧ Place oven racks where you want them before heating, not after. For soufflés, arrange racks to bring the dish below center, as on page 100. Often, in modern ovens, slight heat is provided by a top element, enough to harden the surface of a soufflé if set too close—keeping it from expanding. For cake-baking, the best position for the pan is just above center, as shown. Commercial ovens often feature devices for introducing moisture into an oven, as needed. In the home range, a practical substitute—should the recipe require it—consists of a shallow pan partially filled with water, as sketched on the right, below.

➧ Make sure that the pans or sheets you are using will fit the oven shelf comfortably and at the same time leave at least a 2-inch margin between them and all four walls of the oven. Overcrowding of pans must also be avoided, with none touching. If space for air circulation is not provided for, your baking will burn at the bottom. Never use 2 shelves if you can avoid doing so; but if you must, stagger the pans, as shown below. For a discussion of heat and pan-size relationships, see (II, 336).

In baking, set the oven control for the temperature indicated and ➧ preheat for not less than 5 minutes—in some cases, where noted, longer—before inserting the pans as quickly as possible. Try not to peek until the time is up; but if you have any doubts, wait until almost the end of the baking period.

If you use a thermostatically controlled gas or electric oven, don't think you are speeding things up by setting the thermostat higher than the recipe indicates. You will get better results at the stated temperature. And don't, incidentally, press a thermostatically controlled oven into service as a kitchen heater. This will throw the thermostat out of gear. Ovens vary, however, and thermostats, even under normal use, need frequent adjustment—at least once every 12 or 14 months.

Keep in mind always that a clean oven will maintain temperature and reflect heat more accurately than an untidy one.

As to the range top, here again, as with its interior, familiarity breeds assurance. Questions about its use are, almost without exception, answered fully in the booklet which comes with the equipment. But, if you are confronted with a range for which printed instructions are lacking or if special problems arise, call your local utility company. They maintain a staff of the most obliging and well-trained consultants, prepared to give you advice, free of charge. A most important discovery to make in electric ranges is whether your surface heating units—one or several—are thermostatically controlled to level off disconcertingly when you most need sustained heat for a sauté. Also, learn if they are so differentiated as to provide all the potentials of an electric skillet.

In using gas burners, watch not only the dial, if you have

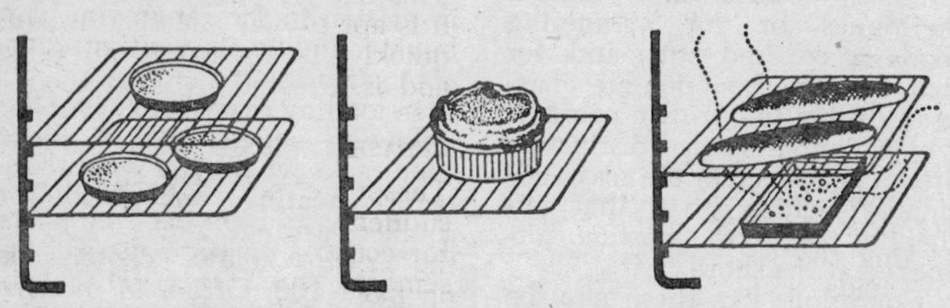

a dial set, but the relation of flame to pan. ➧ The flame should never extend farther than ½ inch inside the outer edge of the pan-bottom.

ABOUT UTENSILS

The material of which pots and pans are made, as well as their size and shape, can often spell success or failure. So, often in this book we not only caution about too high heat, but especially warn against the combination of high heat and thin cooking pans. We do so because when our mail brings distress signals—which are few—they are run up, as often as not, by users of "The Joy" who have neglected this warning. In addition to their other disadvantages, too-thin pans develop hot-spots, to which food will invariably stick. ➧ Choose a pan, then, of fairly heavy gauge, the bottom of which will diffuse heat evenly.

HEAVY ALUMINUM

This has good diffusion but it will pit—no matter how expensive. And it will tend not only to discolor but will affect the color of some foods adversely. Don't clean aluminum with harsh soaps, alkalis or abrasives. To remove discoloration, boil in aluminum pans a solution of 2 teaspoons cream of tartar to 1 quart of water for 5 to 10 minutes.

COPPER

This is best in heavier gauges. It gives a quick, even heat distribution if kept clean. But, unless well tinned, or lined with stainless steel on surfaces contacting the food—it is affected by acids and can prove poisonous.

STAINLESS STEEL

Of course, this is the easiest material of all to keep clean. Its poor heat-conductivity is usually offset by thinning down the gauge, so that hot spots develop and food cooked in it is apt to burn easily.

IRON

This also has low conductivity, rusts easily and discolors acid foods. To treat new iron skillets or Dutch ovens, grease well and place in a 450° oven for 30 minutes. Scour with steel wool before using.

TEMPERED GLASS AND PORCELAIN ENAMEL

Both are poor heat conductors. The glass is apt to crack and the enamel chips. Unless of best quality and treated to resist acid foods, the glaze of enamel ware is quickly affected by them. It also is marked by metal spoons and beaters, so only wooden utensils should be used with it.

EARTHENWARE

While a poor conductor of heat, glazed or unglazed earthenware holds heat well and doesn't discolor foods. But it is heavy and breaks easily with sudden temperature changes. To treat an earthenware casserole, see page 84.

TINWARE

This has good conductivity, but it is apt to mar and then it rusts quickly. It turns dark after use and is affected by acid foods.

GREASELESS PANS

These are a delight to people suddenly put on fat-free diets, for cooking in such utensils resembles pan frying. The soapstone griddle is the ancestor of greaseless pans. And then there are skillets with nonsticking silicone and fluoro-carbon resin surfaces. These need care in handling. Use a wooden paddle for turning or a wooden spoon for stirring—to avoid marring the surface which will melt off at 450°. Eggs, breaded fish and meat will need added water.

If you are on a fat-free diet and get tired of broiling or using greaseless utensils, remember that poaching in skim milk, fruit juice, stock or wine can flavor food without the addition of fat.

PLASTICS

There are plastics which can stand high heat. But many storage containers, funnels and other kitchen utensils cannot be washed in water over 140°. Others are ruined by oil and grease. The surfaces of all plastic utensils retain grease, so don't try to get egg whites to whip in a plastic bowl (II, 181).

You will wonder after reading these pros and cons what pan materials to choose. Fortunately there are on the market today a number of ➧ brands of cooking ware with good flat bottoms that combine metals to take advantage of the good diffusion of aluminum, the quick conductivity of copper and the noncorrosiveness of stainless steel. But while we are speaking of combinations of metal, let us say that ➧ copper, even when tin-lined, and iron pots must not be covered with aluminum foil if the food to be cooked is very acid, as the foil can be dissolved into it. In fact, it is usually best to avoid dissimilar metal pots and lids when cooking any very acid foods. In the final analysis, you may still prefer a heavy iron Dutch oven for stews, an earthenware casserole for fondues, a flameproof glass vessel for sauce-making. ➧ Don't invest in large pan sets of a single material, until you know what your preference really is.

When you cook, choose a pan that fits the size of the burner. This correlation gives better cooking results and is more economical of fuel. Be sure that the lid is tight-fitting if the process calls for one. In vegetable cookery, see that the pan is filled ½ to ⅔ full if you are using a small amount of water, so enough steam can develop to cook quickly. ➧ Be sure the cooking pan is appropriate in size to its contents. Especially in braising and baking is this vital, see pages 492 and (II, 337). Round pans will give you more even browning when baking. Square pans tend to brown too heavily at the corners. ➧ Note, too, that shiny metal baking pans deflect heat and that dark enamel or glass ones both catch and hold the heat more. Therefore, food cooked in glass or enameled pans needs at least a 25° reduction in the oven temperatures given in our recipes. While vitreous or dark metal materials may brown cookies too rapidly, they will insure better browning for pies and puff pastes. If cooking fuel is scarce, a great saving can be effected by the use of these heat-retaining pans.

In pan broiling or when using a griddle, utensils should be brought up slowly to cooking temperature. ➧ Do not make a habit of placing an unfilled pan on high heat unless it has grease or liquid in it.

➧ And should you scorch food by some unlucky chance, plunge the pan first into cold water before transferring the food to a clean container. This way the scorched taste is greatly lessened.

➧ To clean scorched pots, soak overnight with some detergent in the water. If that isn't enough, bring to boil with 1 teaspoon washing soda or cream of tartar for each quart of water.

➧ There is a certain pace in food preparation that an experienced cook learns to accept. This doesn't mean she scorns short cuts, but she comes to know when she has to take the long way 'round to get proper results. She senses, in short, not only the demands of her equipment but the reactions of her ingredients (II, 129).

A man once summed up his wife's life with the epitaph, "She died of things." It might have happened to any of us. We are constantly encouraged to buy the latest gadget that will absolutely and positively make kitchen life sublime. No kitchen can ever have enough space at convenient levels to take care of even a normal array of equipment. So think hard before you buy so much as an extra skewer.

➧ Get pans that nest well. And if you can't resist a bulky mold, see that it hangs on an out-of-the-way pegboard panel or make it a decorative feature for an odd, unused nook. Buy square rather than round canisters for economical storage—see (II, 337) for area comparisons. Keep them and your spices in alphabetical arrangement for quick identification. ➧ And place these close to the areas where you will be using them most.

Most kitchens today are fairly scientifically laid out. Everyone is aware that the big kitchen is a time and energy waster; and that ➧ the U-shape or a triangular relationship of sink, stove and refrigerator—with their accompanying work spaces—are step-savers. But it pays occasionally to think about your work habits. See if you can make them more efficient.

➧ Nonrusting well-designed hand tools save your towels and your temper. The following is a basic, reasonably comprehensive equipment list.

HOUSEHOLD NEEDS

FOR COOKING

2 saucepans with lids
2 frying pans—large and small —with lids
1 large stewing or soup kettle
1 Dutch oven
1 double boiler
1 mold for steaming
1 dessert mold
1 deep-fat fryer
3 strainers
1 steamer
1 colander
1 bean pot
Coffee maker
Tea kettle
China teapot
Candy thermometer
Deep fat frying thermometer

FOR THE OVEN

1 open roasting pan with rack
3 round 9-inch cake pans
2 square 9-inch cake pans
2 loaf or bread pans
2 cake racks for cooling
1 muffin tin
2 pie pans—tin or glass
2 cookie sheets
1 large casserole
6 custard cups
1 9-inch tube pan
1 shallow 9 x 12-inch pan
1 8-inch soufflé baker
Meat thermometer

FOR PREPARATION

1 set of mixing bowls
1 8-oz. dry measuring cup
1 8-oz. liquid measuring cup
1 set of measuring spoons
Serving spoons

1 wooden slotted spoon for cake mixing
3 wooden spoons
1 large fork
1 small fork
2 paring knives
1 bread knife and 1 meat knife
1 French chopping knife
Grapefruit knife
Cutting board
Spatula
1 egg beater and mixer
Ladle
A 4-sided and a rotary grater
1 meat grinder
1 sugar or flour scoop
Funnel
Tongs
Flour sifter
Potato ricer or food mill
Potato masher
Wooden chopping bowl and chopper
Salad bowl
Doughnut cutter
Biscuit cutter
Pastry blender
Pastry board
Pastry brush
Vegetable brush
Rolling pin
Pastry cloth and cover for rolling pin
Pancake turner
Apple corer
Vegetable slicer or parer
Rubber scraper
Weighing spoon or scales
Ice-cream freezer
Griddle
Citrus fruit juicer
Food mill or ricer
Electric mixer
Blender
Pressure cooker
Toaster
Waffle iron

KITCHEN ACCESSORIES

4 canisters
1 bread box and 1 cake carrier
1 dish drainer
1 garbage can
1 waste basket
1 vegetable bin
1 or more trays
Bottle opener
Corkscrew
Can opener
Pot holders
1 bucket
Kitchen shears
Toothpicks for testing cake
Nutcracker
Salt and pepper shakers
Knife sharpener
Set of refrigerator containers
Waxed paper
Plastic storage bags
Aluminum foil
Paper towels
Dishpan
Whisk broom
1 broom
1 dust mop
1 scrubbing brush
Dust pan and brush
12 dish towels
4 dish cloths
2 dust cloths
Plastic detergent dispenser with brush
Plastic sponges
Asbestos pad

ABOUT BURNS AND BURNING

In the foregoing pages we have supplied, among other information, enough facts to keep our readers from ever burning the food they heat. Now for a few safeguards against burning the cook—and what to do should such an emergency occur.

➧ Never throw water on a grease fire. Use salt, soda or, if the area is a small one, a metal lid.

➧ Choose a range, if you can find one, on which the burners are level with the surrounding platform area, so pots cannot tip.

➧ Use flat-bottomed, well-balanced pans that are steady when empty. Be sure handles are not too heavy for the pot so they will tip; or so long that they can be knocked against or catch a sleeve.

➧ When deep-fat frying, please note the precautions given on pages 75–79.

➧ Put boiling liquid to the back of the stove, out of reach of small children.

➧ In pan-frying, keep a colander handy to place over the pan should the fat begin to sputter.

➧ In pouring hot liquids into glass, be sure to put a metal spoon in the glass to absorb excess heat.

➧ Watch that your hands or the cloths you are using are not damp in touching or wiping electrical equipment.

➧ Have polarized attachments put on your electrical appliances to avoid shock.

➧ Should you receive extensive or painful burns, call a doctor, lie down until skilled help comes and keep quiet and warm to avoid subsequent shock. If someone is with you, let her remove any loose clothing near the burned area, but do not let her touch any material that is sticking to the burned flesh. If you are burned over a limited area, cover the burn with a sterile petrolatum salve and sterile gauze. Never use cotton on a burned area. If the burn is more extensive but light, apply strips of sterile bandage that have been dipped in a solution of 3 tablespoons soda or Epsom salts to 1 quart clear water. A new therapy for the treatment of small burns about the hands is to plunge the burned area into cold water as quickly as possible.

SOUPS

In the good old days, when a soup "bunch" cost a nickel and bones were lagniappe, pounds and pounds of meat trimmings and greenstuff were used in the household to concoct wonderful essences for everyday consumption. The best soups are still based on homemade stocks. ▶ Please read About Stocks (II, 138), and all the suggestions offered for the long slow cooking of meat stocks or the rapid cooking of fish fumets and vegetable stocks, which apply to soup making. Fish and vegetable stocks are especially important in "au maigre" or meatless cooking.

To minimize cooking time, use your ⅄ blender as a preliminary step for the processing of raw vegetables, your ⊗ pressure cooker for suitable meat scraps, fresh or leftover. See Quick Household Stock (II, 142). Because not everyone wants to bother with the painstaking methods often required to extract soup stock, and because soups are such an interesting addition to or base for meals, we suggest toward the end of this chapter a large number of time-saving prepared soup combinations. Have on hand a supply of canned, dried or frozen bases to bring quick and revivifying soups into the range of even the most casual cook. No one can afford to be without a varied store of these consistently good, and often excellent products. However, just because they are so convenient and constantly served, even as our spoons stir up their aroma, our palates weary of these prepared soup flavors.

Learn to use herbs and seasonings (II, 202–222). Keep your own economical stockpot (II, 138) to dilute concentrated soups, and to enrich them with added minerals and vitamins. Astound your friends with effortlessly made and unusually flavored soup sensations!

No matter by what method made, soup should complement or contrast with what is to follow; and however enticing its name, it will fit into one of the categories below:

Bouillon—concentrated brown stock ..... page 111

Consommé—clarified double-strength brown stock ..... page 109

Broths—clear liquors from fish, meat, fowl and vegetables (II, 143–145)

Jellied Soups—made from gelatinous knuckle bones, clarified and used as they are or with added gelatin .... page 113

Vegetable Soups—all vegetable or prepared with meat or fish stocks in which the vegetables predominate .. pages 116–117

Purée of Vegetables and Legumes—with or without cream added page 117 and page 118

Cream Soups—cream, butter, cereal or

egg-thickened soups, often on a vegetable base ....page 125
Bisques—shellfish based cream soups ......page 133
Chowders—thick fish, meat and vegetable soups, to which salt pork, milk, diced vegetables, even bread and crackers may be added ....pages 136–138

Some of the above are served hot, some cold, some either way, like bouillons, borsch and vichyssoise. ➧ To serve soups piping hot—use tureens, lidded bowls or well-heated cups. Especially if drinks and hors d'oeuvre have been offered before, a hot soup helps to recondition the palate.

➧ Cold soups should be very well chilled, and served in chilled dishes—especially jellied soups, which tend to break down more rapidly because they are relatively light in gelatin. Cold soups, when not jellied, may be prepared quickly by using a ⅄ blender and chilling in the freezer. On informal occasions, they may be chilled in a tall jug and served directly from it into chilled cups or bowls.

You should be able to count on about 6 servings from a quart of soup, unless it is being used as the mainstay for a lunch—as is so frequently the case with a potage, or a soup rich in solids. ➧ The quantities noted under the titles of individual recipes are consistently given in standard 8-ounce cups.

There are some classic dishes—Petite Marmite, New England Boiled Dinner or Goulash—that occupy middle ground between soups and stews.

▲ Above 2500 feet, soups need longer cooking periods than called for in the regular recipes, as the liquids boil at a a lower temperature.

ABOUT SEASONING SOUP

Soup is as flavorful as the stock on which it is based. See (II, 138), and the comments on seasoning (II, 140).

The addition of wine to soup frequently enhances its flavor, but ➧ do not oversalt soups to which wine is added, as the wine intensifies saltiness. Wines that blend well with bland soups, such as those made with chicken or veal, are a not too dry sherry or Madeira. Don't use more than ¼ cup wine to 1 quart soup. A strongly flavored soup, prepared with beef or oxtail, is improved by the addition of some dry red table wine—½ cup wine to 1 quart soup. A dry white table wine adds zest to a fish, crab or lobster bisque or chowder. Use ⅛ to ¼ cup wine to 1 quart soup. Wines should be added to the hot soup shortly before it is served. ➧ Do not boil the soup after adding the wine.

Beer adds a tang to bean, cabbage and vegetable soups. Use 1 cup for every 3 cups soup. Add the beer just before serving. Reheat the soup well, but ➧ do not boil.

ABOUT COLORING SOUP

If soups have been cooked with browned onions or onion skins, and if the amount of meat used has been substantial, they should have a good, rich color. Tomato skins also lend color interest. Caramelized Sugar II (II, 169) may be added if necessary. We prefer it to commercial soup coloring, which is apt to overwhelm a delicately flavored soup with its own pervasive and telltale aroma. About Vegetables for Soup, see (II, 144).

ABOUT CEREALS FOR THICKENING SOUPS

Precooked cereal garnishes, such as rice, noodles and dumplings, give an effect of body to a clear soup, but a very different one from the more integral raw thickeners suggested below. These make for intriguing texture and elegance of flavor.

To add any of the following, bring the soup to a boil and reduce the heat again to a simmer as soon as the addition has been made. Stir ➧ raw cereals into soup for the last hour of cooking. For a light thickening, allow to the original amount of water approximately:

> **1 teaspoon barley to 1 cup water**
> **1 teaspoon green kern to 1 cup water**
> **1 teaspoon rice to 1 cup water**
> **1 teaspoon oatmeal to 1 cup water**
> **2 tablespoons wheat germ flour to 1 cup water**
> **2 tablespoons peanut flour to 1 cup water**
> **2 tablespoons soya flour to 1 cup water**
> **½ teaspoon quick-cooking tapioca to 1 cup water**

If you wish to thicken cooked soup with flour, allow:

> **1½ teaspoons flour to 1 cup soup**

Make a paste of the flour with about:

> **Twice as much cold stock, milk or water**

Pour the paste slowly into the boiling soup, while stirring. Simmer and stir for 5 to 10 minutes. Or, as in cream sauce, make a Roux, see page 355, of:

> **1½ teaspoons butter**
> **1½ teaspoons flour**

Pour the soup over this mixture, stirring constantly until smooth and boiling. Or add:

> **Flour and butter**

to cooled soup in a ⅄ blender—then reheat the soup. Bring to a boil, lower heat and simmer for 5 minutes.

Additional thickenings for soup are dry, crustless French bread or Panades, page 123. Also, thick cream or a cream or Béchamel sauce, page 359, may be used.

ABOUT OTHER THICKENINGS FOR SOUPS

Egg yolks are one of the richest and best soup thickeners—but they must be added just before serving. ➧ Care must be taken, when this is done, that the soup is not too hot.

Allow for each cup of soup:

> **1 egg yolk, beaten with**
> **1 tablespoon cream or sherry**

To avoid curdling, it is wise to add to this beaten mixture a small quantity of the hot soup before incorporating it into the soup pot. ➧ When using egg or cream-based thickeners, it is always essential that the soup, after their addition, be kept below the boiling point. You may prefer riced hard-cooked eggs. Allow:

> **2 yolks for each cup of soup**

Add at the last minute and, of course, do not allow the soup to boil.

A good soup thickener, for those whose diet does not include flour, consists of:

> **3 tablespoons grated raw potato**

for each cup of soup. Grate the potato directly into the soup about 15 minutes before it has finished cooking. Then simmer until the potato is tender, when it will form a thickener.

Soups cooked with starchy vegetables, such as dried beans, peas or lentils, will separate and must be bound. To do this, allow:

1 tablespoon melted butter
1 tablespoon flour

Well blended with a small amount of:

Cold water, stock or milk

Stir this mixture into about:

3 cups strained boiling soup

and simmer at least 5 minutes before serving.

ABOUT REMOVING GREASE FROM SOUP

I. Chill the soup. The grease rises at once and will solidify when cold. It is then a simple matter to remove it.

II. Float a paper towel on the surface of the soup and when it has absorbed as much grease as it will hold discard it; or roll a paper towel and use one end to skim over the soup surface to remove the fat. When the ends become coated with grease, cut off the used part with scissors and repeat the process.

III. Use your meat baster with bulb as a suction device.

ABOUT SOUP MEAT

Any meat that is ➧ immersed in cold water and simmered for a long period is bound to give its best flavor to the cooking liquor. But some food values remain in the meat and it may be heightened in flavor by serving it, when removed from the soup, with one of the sauces below:

Horseradish Sauce, page 362
Mustard Sauce page 363
Tomato Sauce, page 376
Brown Onion Sauce, page 366

ABOUT CLEAR SOUPS

Because so much valuable material and expert time goes into the making of clear soups and because they taste so delicious, most of us assume that they have high nutritive value. It disappoints us to have to tell you that, while they are ➧ unsurpassed as appetite stimulators, the experts give them an indifferent rating as foods. If you have the time, do create these delicious broths by degreasing, clarifying and correcting the seasonings of stocks.

I. For chicken broth use:

Chicken Stock (II, 142)

II. For game broth use:

Fowl, Rabbit or Game Stock (II, 143)

III. For fish broth use:

Fumet or Fish Stock (II, 143)

IV. For vegetable broth use:

Vegetable Stock (II, 145)

➧ Be sure to see Garnishes for Soups, page 144.

CONSOMMÉ

Prep re:

Brown Stock I (II, 141)

and clarify it by the quick method (II, 140). This will give you a clear, thin consommé. For double strength, clarify the stock by the second method.

CONSOMMÉ BRUNOISE

[3 Cups]

Make a mixture of the following finely diced vegetables:

1 rib of celery
1 small carrot
½ small turnip
½ small onion

Sauté them gently in:

1 tablespoon heated butter

Enough time should be allowed to let the vegetables absorb the grease but ➧ do not let them brown. Add:

1 cup consommé

and continue cooking, covered, until the vegetables are tender. Pour into:

2 cups hot consommé

Degrease and

Correct the seasoning

Just before serving, add:

1 tablespoon finely chopped chervil
1 tablespoon cooked peas
1 tablespoon finely diced cooked green beans

CONSOMMÉ MADRILÈNE

[About 5 Cups]

Heat to the boiling point and strain:

2 cups tomato juice
½ teaspoon grated onion
2 cups Chicken Stock, page 109
A piece of lemon rind
Salt and pepper

Flavor with:

Lemon juice, dry sherry or Worcestershire sauce

Or garnish with:

Cultured sour cream

dotted with:

Red caviar

CHICKEN OR TURKEY BROTH

➧ See the many cream soups, page 125, and egg garnished soups, page 145, based on this simple broth.

Prepare:

Fowl, Rabbit or Game Stock (II, 143)

or use canned stock.

When it is boiling, remove from heat. You may add for each 4 cups:

½ cup cream

Reheat but ➧ do not boil. Serve with a chiffonade of herbs, page 151, with dumplings, page 146.

CHICKEN BROTH OR BOUILLON WITH EGG

[Individual Serving]

A good dish for an invalid, but not to be scorned by those in good health.

Degrease, clarify, and heat:

Chicken Broth, above
Correct the seasoning

For every cup added:

(1 teaspoon lemon juice)
(1 tablespoon chopped parsley)

When the soup is hot add:

An egg drop, page 145

allowing 1 egg per serving. Serve at once.

POT-AU-FEU, POULE-AU-POT OR PETITE MARMITE

[About 6 Cups Broth]

A marmite is an earthenware lidded pot, higher than it is wide. Its material accounts in part for the flavor of the soup. In pot-au-feu, another name for petite marmite, the major meat is beef, with an addition of chicken wings and gizzards. In making poule-au-pot, the beef is cooked with a juicy hen—the hen which Henry IV wanted for every pot. Marrow bones are usually included, tied in cheesecloth. The vegetables may be seasonally varied. Blanched cabbage is often added.

Put in a marmite:

2½ quarts cold water
2 lbs. shank or chuck beef, cut in chunks

Tie in cheesecloth and add:

(1 knucklebone)

Bring this mixture ➧ slowly to a boil and ➧ skim well. Cut Parisienne style, page 251, and add:

2 carrots

1 small turnip
3 leeks: white parts only
1 whole onion stuck with 1 clove
1 teaspoon salt
1 Bouquet Garni II (II, 220)

Bring these ingredients to a boil. ➧ Skim again. ➧ Cover and cook slowly for about 3 hours in a 350° oven. The bouillon should be clear and amber in color.

To serve, either start with the clear soup and offer the meat and vegetables on the side or reserve them for a second meal. Crusty thin slices of bread, which may be spread with Parmesan cheese, are delightful accompaniments to a pot-au-feu.

BOUILLON

Bouillon is an unsalted strong beef stock, not as sweet as consommé.

Clarify and reduce by ⅓:

Brown Soup Stock I or II (II, 141)

Correct the seasoning

Serve with:

A Garnish for Clear Soups, page 144

TOMATO BOUILLON

[About 3 Cups]

Bring to the boiling point and simmer for about 5 minutes:

3 cups strained tomato juice
½ small bay leaf
¼ cup cut up celery, with leaves
2 tablespoons chopped fennel
2 whole cloves
1 tablespoon fresh basil
(1 small skinned, chopped and sautéed onion)

Strain, and degrease if necessary.

Correct the seasoning

Serve hot or cold in cups, topped with a teaspoon of:

Whipped cream or cultured sour cream

BEEF TEA

[About ¾ Cup]

Grind twice:

1 lb. lean round steak or neck bone meat

Place in a quart mason jar and add:

1 cup cold water
½ teaspoon salt

Cover the jar lightly. Place the jar on a cloth in a pan containing as much cold water as possible without upsetting the jar. Bring the water slowly to a gentle boil and continue for about 1 hour. Remove the jar. Place on a cake rack to cool as rapidly as possible. Strain the juice. Store it in a covered container in the refrigerator until ready to heat and serve.

KREPLACH SOUP

[About 4 Cups]

Prepare:

Noodle Dough II, page 149

This will make about 20 pastries. Do not allow the dough to dry, however, before cutting it into 3-inch squares. Put about 1½ tablespoons of one of the following fillings in the center of each square.

I. Sauté in:

1 tablespoon cooking oil
½ cup minced onions
½ lb. ground beef

Add:

¾ teaspoon salt
¼ teaspoon pepper

II. Or combine:

1½ cups minced cooked chicken
¼ cup minced sautéed onion
1 egg yolk
¾ teaspoon salt
1 tablespoon chopped parsley

Fold the dough over into a triangular shape. Press the open edges carefully with a fork to seal them completely. Before cooking ◆ allow the kreplach to dry on a flour-dusted towel for 30 minutes on each side. Then drop them into:

About 1 gallon rapidly boiling broth or salted water

and ◆ simmer gently for 7 to 10 minutes. Drain well and serve in:

3 cups strong broth

WON TON SOUP

[About 4 Cups]
Prepare:

Noodle Dough II, page 149

The fillings may be:

Cooked pork, chicken, shrimp, crabmeat or Chicken Farce, page 564

Combine:

½ lb. cooked pork or veal, etc.
2 finely chopped green onions, white parts only
1 cup chopped spinach
1 beaten egg

There are many fancy wrappings for won ton, which in most cases produce a high proportion of paste to meat. If truly Chinese, won tons emerge with a rather loose shape and a fluttery outline. Cook by putting all the won ton at once into:

About 1 gallon rapidly boiling water

Lower the heat at once to medium. When the water again comes to a boil, add:

2 cups cold water

to temper the dough. About 10 minutes should elapse from the time the won tons are first added to the boiling water until they are ready to serve. Put 5 won tons for each serving into a soup bowl. Sprinkle them with:

(Soy sauce)

Have ready and pour over them:

3 cups hot, seasoned, clear chicken broth or bouillon

A few prettily cut Chinese vegetables or partially cooked spinach leaves with midstems removed, usually garnish the broth.

VEGETABLE BROTH

[About 3½ Cups]
Quickly made and very good. Serve strained or unstrained, hot or chilled.
Chop:

3 cups or more Vegetables for Soup (II, 145)

Sauté them gently and slowly for 5 minutes in:

3 tablespoons butter

◆ Do not let them brown. Add:

4 cups boiling water or part water and tomatoes or tomato juice

Simmer the soup, partially covered, for about 1 hour. Season and add:

(1 bouillon cube)

MUSHROOM BROTH

I. [About 6 Cups]
Prepare:

¾ lb. diced mature mushrooms
2 ribs celery, diced
½ skinned and diced carrot
¼ skinned and diced onion

Cover these vegetables with:

3 cups water

◆ Simmer partially covered for 45 minutes. Strain the broth. Add, to make 6 cups of liquid:

Chicken Stock (II, 142) or Beef Consommé, page 109

Add, if needed:

Salt and paprika

Serve very hot. Add to each cup:

1 tablespoon dry sherry

II. Blend or chop until fine:

¾ lb. mature mushrooms

Add them to:

6 cups Chicken Stock (II, 142), or consommé

Simmer, partially covered, for about 15 minutes or only 5 if you use the ⅄ blender. Strain if you like or thicken, page 108. Serve as for I, above.

ONION SOUP

[6 Cups]

Onion soup, with vegetable substituted for meat stock, is used for meals "au maigre," also see Fish Stock (II, 143).

Sauté until well browned, but not burned:

1½ cups thinly sliced onions

in:

3 tablespoons butter

Add:

6 cups beef or chicken broth
¼ teaspoon freshly ground black pepper

Cover and cook over low heat or in a 275° oven for 30 minutes. Either way, the soup is now put into a casserole, covered with:

6 slices toasted French bread

Sprinkle over the toast:

1 cup grated Parmesan cheese

Heat in the oven for about 10 minutes or until the cheese is melted. Add:

(A dash of cognac or dry sherry)

CLEAR WATER CRESS SOUP

[About 5 Cups]

Simmer together:

5 cups hot chicken broth
1½ cups chopped water cress

for 4 to 6 minutes or until water cress is just dark green—not an olive green. Serve at once.

COLD TOMATO SOUP OR GAZPACHO

[About 6 Cups]

A summer delight—chilled vegetable soup with fresh herbs.

Peel and seed:

2 large ripe tomatoes

Seed and remove membrane from:

1 large sweet pepper

Peel:

1 clove garlic

Wash:

½ cup or more fresh mixed herbs: chives, parsley, basil, chervil, tarragon

Place all ingredients in a wooden chopping bowl. Chop them. Stir in, gradually:

½ cup olive oil
3 tablespoons lemon or lime juice
3 cups chilled water or light stock

Add:

1 peeled, thinly sliced sweet Spanish onion
1 cup peeled, seeded, diced or grated cucumber
1½ teaspoons salt or more, if needed
½ teaspoon paprika

Some cooks prefer to use their ⅄ blender for the above vegetables. Chill the soup for 4 hours or more before serving.

To serve, place in each bowl:

2 ice cubes
1 tablespoon chopped parsley

Add the soup and sprinkle the tops with:

½ cup crumbled stale bread

JELLIED CLEAR SOUPS

These delicious warm weather soups may be more highly seasoned than hot soups, but ➧ watch their salt content. If you prepare them in advance, their saltiness is intensified.

Serve with:

A lemon and parsley garnish

You may add to the soup before jelling:

A few drops of Worcestershire sauce

Or allow per cup:

1 tablespoon sherry or
1 teaspoon lemon juice

If you add more lemon juice, be sure you have allowed sufficient gelatin. Stock made from veal knuckle and beef bone may jell enough naturally to be served without added gelatin. We have learned that if canned consommé is from a new pack, it, too, has enough gelatin in it to respond favorably to mere chilling. If the pack is as old as two years, it must be treated as though it had no gelatin. ➧ Do not freeze it, but try it out by refrigerating for at least 4 hours, to see how much additional thickening it will need. Keep in mind that, if too stiff, soup jellies are not very attractive. Allow, if necessary:

1½ teaspoons gelatin

to each:

2 cups consommé or broth

For rapid chilling, you may place clear soups in a bowl over cracked ice or give them a start by leaving them in the freezer for a few minutes ➧ but not longer, as intense cold, if continued, destroys the texture.

JELLIED TOMATO BOUILLON

[About 5 Cups]

Soak for 5 minutes:

2 tablespoons gelatin

in:

½ cup cold water

Heat to the boiling point and strain:

2 cups tomato juice
½ teaspoon grated onion
2 cups Light Soup Stock (II, 142)
A piece of lemon rind
Salt and pepper

Dissolve the gelatin in the hot stock. Cool. Flavor with:

Lemon juice, dry sherry or Worcestershire sauce

Pour stock into a wet mold. Chill. The bouillon may be beaten slightly before serving and garnished with:

Lemon slices, chopped chives, mint, small nasturtium leaves, chopped olives, hard-cooked riced eggs, relish, horseradish, parsley or watercress

JELLIED BEET CONSOMMÉ [4]

Combine and heat:

1 cup beet juice
1 cup consommé

Add:

1 tablespoon gelatin dissolved over hot water (II, 184)
Correct the seasoning

When about to jell add:

(1 tablespoon lemon juice)
1 cup minced cooked beets

Pour gelatin mixture into cups. In serving, garnish each cup with:

1 teaspoon caviar
A slice of lemon decorated with minced fresh tarragon or basil, or a dab of cultured sour cream

BROTH ON THE ROCKS

For the guest who shuns an alcoholic drink, offer a clear broth, such as:

Chicken broth or bouillon

combined with:

(Tomato and orange juice)

poured over ice cubes. ➧ Be sure the broth is not too rich in gelatin, for it may suddenly congeal.

FRUIT SOUPS

[4 Cups]

In Scandinavia, fruit soups are served as a dessert, but in Germany, they constitute a summertime chilled prelude to the entrée. Either dried or fresh fruits, cooked until they can be puréed easily, may be used. Cherries are the most popular. Prepare:

1 lb. stoned cherries

Place in an enamel pan and cover with:

2 cups water
1 cup red wine

Add:

¼ cup sugar
½ teaspoon grated orange rind

Cook until the fruit is soft, about 10 minutes. Blend or sieve the fruit and thicken the juice with:

1 teaspoon arrowroot

mixed with a little of the cooled sirup. Return the mixture to the soup and cook about 2 minutes. Serve hot or cold. Garnish with:

Unsweetened whipped cream or croutons or dumplings, page 146

ABOUT THICK SOUPS

Purée, cream, bisque, velouté, potage—to the connoisseur each of these is a quite distinctive embodiment of the indispensable thick soup.

If you like to attach a label to your creations, know that a purée is a soup which gets its major thickening from the vegetable or other food put through a sieve and has butter swirled into it at the very last moment. By omitting the butter or lessening the amount of it and adding cream and sometimes egg yolk, you get—guess what?—a cream soup! If that soup is on a shell fish base—and only if it is—you may call it a bisque. If you add both eggs and cream and a velouté sauce, see page 362, to a purée base, you achieve a velouté soup.

Potages, the most variable of soups, are likely to have the phrase "du jour" added, meaning that they are both the specialty of the day and, from the cook's point of view, seasonal and convenient to compose. Potages, which tend to be hefty, taste best when their vegetables are first braised in butter. For ways to thicken soups, see page 108.

Here are a few practical hints that will help you make the most of thickened soups. First, be sure to scrape the purée off the bottom of the strainer. ➧ If you use a ⅄ blender, first parblanch or cook any vegetables with strings, like celery, or hulls, like peas. After butter, cream or eggs are added ➧ never allow the soup to reach a boil. If you are not serving at once, heat it in a double boiler. To avoid a slight granular separation in legume soups, see page 108. Thick soups should not be served as the first course of a heavy meal. The wonderful thing about them is that they are nearly a meal by themselves. Balanced by a green salad or fruit, they make a complete luncheon.

BARLEY SOUP

I.

[About 9 to 10 Cups]

A favorite of French farmers. For the best flavor use stock from country cured hams, but not aged ones like Smithfield, Kentucky or Virginia.

Melt in a skillet:

2 tablespoons salt pork

Cook, until translucent, in the above:

3 tablespoons shallots or onions

Add:

½ cup barley

Agitate the pan to coat the barley well in the hot fat. After about 5 minutes, add:

1 quart hot stock from country cured ham

Cook the mixture, covered, until the barley is tender, about 30 minutes. Bind or not as you like, depending on how rich and thick you want the soup, with:

3 well-beaten egg yolks
1 cup cream

➧ Heat, but do not boil after adding the eggs and cream. Before serving, add as a garnish:

2 tablespoons finely chopped parsley
1 cup sautéed, coarsely chopped mushrooms

To keep the mushrooms white, add:

½ tablespoon lemon juice

II. Scotch Broth
[About 10 to 12 Cups]

Soak for 12 hours:

½ cup pearl barley

in:

2 cups water

If you use other barley, soak it for 1 hour. Add this to:

3 lbs. mutton or lamb with bones
10 cups water

Simmer, covered, for 2 hours or until the meat is tender. Add for the last ½ hour of cooking:

2 cups browned vegetables for soup (II, 145)
(A dash of curry)

Remove the meat from the soup. Dice it, return it to the soup. You may use a flour or egg thickener, page 108, to bind the soup.

Correct the seasoning

Serve garnished with:

Chopped parsley

GREEN KERN SOUP

[About 9 Cups]

If you are English, corn means wheat, if you are Scottish it means oats, but if you come from "down under" or are American, you know corn grows on a cob. Kern sounds as though it too might be somebody's word for corn, but it isn't. It's dried green wheat and makes a favorite European soup.

Soak for ½ hour:

½ to 1 cup green kern

in:

4 cups water

Drain, then cook, as for Barley II, above, replacing the lamb with beef.

VEGETABLE SOUP OR SOUP PAYSANNE

[5 Cups]

Place in a large kettle or pressure cooker:

2 tablespoons bacon fat or butter

Sauté briefly in the fat:

¼ cup diced carrots
½ cup diced onion
½ cup diced celery

Add:

3 cups hot water or stock
1 cup canned tomatoes
(½ cup peeled, diced potatoes)
(½ cup peeled, diced turnips)
1 tablespoon chopped parsley
½ teaspoon salt
⅛ teaspoon pepper

Cover and cook for about 35 minutes; then add:

(½ cup chopped cabbage, spinach or lettuce)

If using a ✪ pressure cooker, cook at 15 pounds pressure for 3 minutes. Remove from heat and let stand for 5 minutes, then reduce pressure instantly.

Correct seasoning

and serve with:

Melba Cheese Rounds, page 152

VEGETABLE CHOWDER

[About 6 Cups]

Cut the stems from:

1 quart okra

Slice the okra. Prepare:

2 cups diced celery

Seed and dice:

1 green pepper

Skin and chop:

1 small onion

Sauté the vegetables for 5 minutes in:

¼ cup butter or bacon drippings

Skin, chop and add:

2 large ripe tomatoes or 1 cup canned tomatoes
1 teaspoon brown sugar
¼ teaspoon paprika
4 cups boiling water

Stew the vegetables gently until they are tender, for about 1 hour. Add, if required:

Salt and paprika

Cooked chicken, meat, fish or crisp bacon may be diced and added to the chowder. Serve with:

Boiled Rice, page 158

⅄ BLENDER VEGETABLE SOUP

[About 4 Cups]
Blend in:

¼ cup stock
2 cups mixed, coarsely cut vegetables

If cucumbers, celery, asparagus or onions are used, blanch them first to soften seeds or fibers and to make the onion flavor more agreeable. Heat the blended vegetables until tender in:

3 cups boiling stock

Serve at once.

BEET SOUP OR BORSCH

[About 5 Cups]
There are probably as many versions of borsch as there are Russians. For good, quick versions, see page 140.
Peel and chop until very fine:

½ cup carrots
1 cup onions
2 cup beets

Barely cover these ingredients with boiling water. Simmer gently, covered, for about 20 minutes. Add and simmer for 15 minutes more:

1 tablespoon butter
2 cups beef or other stock
1 cup very finely shredded cabbage
1 tablespoon vinegar

Place the soup in bowls. Add to each serving:

1 tablespoon cultured sour cream

mixed with:

Grated cucumber

Correct the seasoning and serve hot or cold with:

Pumpernickel bread

Serve beer rather than wine with this dish.

CABBAGE SOUP

[About 6 Cups]
This superb cabbage soup, quick and inexpensive, is from Herman Smith's book, "Kitchens Near and Far." You will find it, as well as his incomparable "Stina," most rewarding.
Sauté gently in a saucepan until tender and yellow:

1 large minced onion
1½ tablespoons butter

Grate or shred and add:

1 small head green cabbage: about ¾ lb.

Bring to a boil:

4 cups Brown Stock I (II, 141)

Add the stock to the vegetables.
Season as needed with:

Salt and pepper

Simmer the soup for about 10 minutes. If you wish, use this delicious topping:

½ cup cultured sour cream
1 tablespoon minced parsley
(½ teaspoon caraway seeds)

Place a spoonful of the sour cream mixture on each plate of soup.

CHICKEN CURRY OR SENEGALESE SOUP

[About 2 Cups]
Melt:

1 tablespoon butter

Add to it:

¾ to 1 teaspoon curry powder

Stir in, until blended:

¾ tablespoon flour

Stir in slowly:

1½ cups chicken broth

When the soup is boiling, season it with:

Paprika

Reduce the heat. Beat:

1 egg yolk
¼ cup rich milk or cream

When the soup is no longer boiling, stir these ingredients into it. Stir over low heat until the egg has thickened slightly ◆ but do not boil. Add also, still not allowing the soup to boil:

¼ cup slivers of cooked white chicken meat
(2 tablespoons chutney)

Serve, hot or chilled, garnished with:

Chopped chives

CHICKEN GUMBO

[About 12 Cups]

Cut into pieces and dredge with flour:

1 stewing chicken

Brown it in:

¼ cup bacon grease

Pour over it:

4 cups boiling water

Simmer, uncovered, until the meat falls from the bones. Drain the stock and chop the meat. Place in the soup kettle and simmer, uncovered, until the vegetables are tender:

2 cups skinned tomatoes
½ cup green corn
1 cup sliced okra
(1 large green or 2 small red peppers)
½ teaspoon salt
¼ diced onion
¼ cup rice
5 cups water

Combine these ingredients with the chicken meat and stock.

Correct the seasoning

Add:

(1 to 2 teaspoons filé powder, moistened with a little water)

After adding the filé ◆ do not boil the soup, as it will become stringy.

BEEF GUMBO

[About 10 Cups]

Melt in a skillet:

2 tablespoons butter

Add and sauté until dark brown:

A soup bone with meat: 3 lbs.

Pour in:

12 cups water: 3 quarts

Simmer these ingredients, covered, for 2 hours. Add and simmer, covered, until the meat falls from the bone:

¼ cup chopped celery
¼ cup shredded parsley
¼ cup chopped onion
½ teaspoon salt
¼ teaspoon paprika

Strain, cool and skim the stock. Melt:

2 tablespoons butter

Add and sauté for 3 minutes:

½ cup chopped onion
½ cup fresh or canned sliced okra
1 cup chopped celery with leaves

Add:

2½ cups tomatoes
2 tablespoons quick-cooking tapioca
1 tablespoon sugar
The soup stock

Simmer the soup, covered, for 1 hour longer.

Correct the seasoning,

and serve.

ABOUT LEGUME SOUPS

Lentils, Beans, Peas

Some packaged, dried legumes do not require soaking. Follow directions on the label. Soak if required, using ham stock, other stock, a broken-up turkey or chicken carcass, to which you may add ½ cup tomato juice or purée, making in all about 10 cups of liquid. Add flavor with bacon or scraps of ham or fresh pork fat. Try them out (II, 174), then brown an onion in the fat. Reserve the cracklings to garnish the soup, or cook them in it. For vegetables and seasonings, see the following recipes.

For easy removal of fat, chill the soup, see page 109. Legume soups may be served unstrained, although they are usually more digestible if strained. They may be thinned with stock, tomato juice or milk. Navy bean soup always calls for milk.

Legume soups, whether made of fresh or dried materials, should be bound. To do this, melt 1 tablespoon butter, blend in 1 tablespoon flour and add a small amount of cold water, stock or milk. Stir this mixture into about 3 cups strained boiling soup and simmer at least 5 minutes before serving.

✪ We do not recommend the use of a pressure cooker for legume soups.

DRIED BEAN SOUP

[4 Cups]

If you use marrow beans and add the optional mashed potato, you will have come close to reproducing the famous United States Senate Bean Soup.

Soak, see above:

½ cup dried navy, kidney, Lima or marrow beans

Add:

A small piece of ham, a ham bone or ⅛ lb. salt pork
4 cups boiling water
½ bay leaf
3 or 4 peppercorns
3 whole cloves

Cook the soup slowly until the beans are soft, for about 2½ to 3 hours. For the last 30 minutes, add:

1 diced carrot
3 ribs celery with leaves, chopped
½ sliced onion
(1 minced clove garlic)
(⅛ teaspoon saffron)
(½ cup freshly cooked mashed potatoes)
(½ cup chopped sorrel)

Remove and mince the meat. Put the soup through a food mill, ⅄ blender or sieve. Thin the soup, if required, with boiling water or milk.

Correct the seasoning

Serve with the meat and:

Croutons, page 151
Chopped chives or parsley

BLACK BEAN SOUP

[About 9 or 10 Cups]

Follow the recipe for Split Pea Soup, page 120.

Substitute for the peas:

2 cups black beans

As this soup is drier, add:

3, instead of 2, tablespoons butter

Serve garnished with:

2 teaspoons deviled or Smithfield ham for each cup
Thin slices of lemon
Thin slices of hard-cooked eggs
(1 tablespoon dry sherry for each cup)

BEAN SOUP WITH VEGETABLES OR GARBURE

[About 10 Cups]

A highly variable soup. Perhaps the most famous version comes from Béarn. It includes preserved goose and is cooked in a glazed casserole. Exotic? It is made in season with freshly hulled haricot beans. Soak overnight:

1 cup dried haricot or navy or fava beans

You may blanch, page 88, or not, depending on its maturity:

2 lbs. green or white cabbage

Shred the cabbage finely the length of the leaf. Peel and slice:

1½ cups potatoes
1 cup carrots
1 cup white turnips

¼ cup leeks, using white portion only
½ cup onion
1 sprig thyme
(A ham bone)

Place all the above ingredients in a heavy pan and cover with:

Liquid

Use water if you plan to add salt pork; game stock (II, 143), with game.
Add:

1 lb. diced salt pork or boneless game or veal

➧ Simmer, partially covered, for 2½ hours or until the meat is tender.

Correct the seasoning

and serve the meat on the side. Pour the soup over:

Garlic buttered croutons, page 151

MINESTRONE

[About 8 Cups]

An Italian soup made with many kinds of vegetables, even zucchini blossoms. Sometimes elbow macaroni or other pasta and sometimes rice is added instead of dried beans. Sweet sausages and smoked spareribs may also be put in at the end. Simmer for about ¾ hour in a large soup kettle:

2 quarts stock
4 oz. diced fatty ham
1 cup chopped celery
½ cup fresh kidney beans
¾ cup fresh peas

Heat:

3 tablespoons olive oil

Sauté in it:

1 cup chopped spinach
1 small chopped vegetable marrow
¼ cup minced onion
1 diced carrot
1 cup chopped Savoy cabbage
1 cup diced tomatoes
1 diced leek

Pour the sautéed vegetables into the stock mixture and simmer about 25 minutes longer. Add:

1 tablespoon chopped parsley
1 tablespoon minced fresh sage
1 pressed garlic clove

Cook for 5 minutes more and

Correct the seasoning

Add:

½ cup Parmesan cheese

and serve with:

Italian Bread

LENTIL SOUP

[About 8 Cups]

Wash well and drain:

2 cups lentils

Add:

10 cups boiling water
¼ lb. salt pork or a piece of ham or a ham bone

➧ Simmer for about 4 hours. During the last hour, add:

1 large minced onion

which has been sautéed in:

3 tablespoons butter
Correct the seasoning

and serve puréed or not, as you prefer.

SPLIT PEA OR LENTIL SOUP

[About 8 Cups]

Try this on a cold winter day. Wash and soak, page 118.

2 cups split peas

Drain the peas, reserving the liquid. Add enough water to the reserved liquid to make 10 cups. Adding peas again, cook covered, for about 2½ to 3 hours with:

A turkey carcass, a ham bone or a 2-inch cube salt pork

Add and simmer, covered, for ½ hour longer until tender:

½ cup chopped onions
1 cup chopped celery with leaves
½ cup chopped carrots

Add:

(1 clove garlic)

(1 bay leaf)
(1 teaspoon sugar)
(A dash of cayenne or a pod of red pepper)
(1/4 teaspoon thyme)

Remove bones, carcass or salt pork. Put the soup through a sieve. Chill. Remove grease. Melt:

2 tablespoons butter or soup fat

Stir in it until blended:

2 tablespoons flour

Add a little of the soup mixture, slowly. Cook and stir until it boils, then stir it into the rest of the reheated soup.

Correct the seasoning

Serve with:

Croutons, or sour black bread and Pickled Pigs' Feet

⅄ BLENDER SPLIT PEA SOUP

[About 1 Quart]

Simmer about 45 minutes or until tender:

1/2 cup split peas

in:

2 1/2 cups water

When slightly cooled, pour into a blender and add:

1 cup chopped pork luncheon sausage
1 small sliced onion
1 diced stalk celery with leaves
1 clove garlic
1 teaspoon salt
2 teaspoons Worcestershire sauce
A pinch of rosemary
1/8 teaspoon pepper

Blend until smooth. Return the soup to saucepan to heat. Rinse the blender with:

1 cup water

Add this to the soup and simmer for about 10 minutes. Garnish with:

Pieces of crisp bacon
Cultured sour cream

SPLIT PEA SOUP AU MAIGRE

Use the recipe for Spit Pea Soup to make either a thick or thin soup. During the last 20 minutes of cooking, substitute for the fowl or ham bone any clean fish scraps—such as heads, tails and fins.

GREEN PEA SOUP OR POTAGE ST. GERMAIN

[About 6 Cups]

Do not attempt to make this soup with canned or frozen peas. ➧ If you do not have fresh peas, it is better to try the good Quick Pea Soup.

Hull:

3 lbs. green peas

There should be about 3 cups hulled peas. Shred:

1 head Boston lettuce
1 peeled onion
1/2 cup or more celery with leaves
2 sprigs parsley

Sauté the vegetables gently, until tender, in:

2 tablespoons butter

Add:

2 1/2 cups chicken stock
2 cups of the hulled peas
10 or 12 pea pods
(1/3 bay leaf)

Simmer these ingredients, covered, until the peas are very soft. Put the soup through a food mill or a potato ricer. Simmer until tender:

1 cup of the hulled peas

in:

1 1/2 cups chicken stock

Add them to the strained soup. To bind the soup, see About Legume Soups, page 118.

Correct the seasoning

You may color the soup with a drop or two of:

Green vegetable coloring

and serve it with:

Butter Dumplings, or Sponge Dumplings
(2 teaspoons chopped mint)

BOULA-BOULA [6]

➧ Simmer in boiling water until tender:

2 cups green peas

Purée them through a fine sieve. Reheat and add:

2 tablespoons sweet butter
Correct the seasoning

Add:

2 cups canned green turtle soup
1 cup dry sherry

Heat ➧ but do not boil the soup. Spoon soup into heated cups. Top each with:

2 tablespoons whipped cream

Place briefly under broiler. Serve at once.

MULLIGATAWNY SOUP

[About 4 Cups]

Sauté lightly, but do not brown:

½ cup diced onion
1 diced carrot
2 stalks celery, diced

in:

¼ cup butter or olive oil

Stir in:

1½ tablespoons flour
2 teaspoons curry powder

Stir and cook these ingredients for about 3 minutes. Pour in and simmer for 30 minutes:

4 cups chicken broth

Add and simmer for 15 minutes longer:

¼ cup diced tart apples
½ cup boiled rice
½ cup diced cooked chicken
1 teaspoon salt
¼ teaspoon pepper
⅛ teaspoon thyme

Immediately before serving, stir in:

½ cup hot cream

OXTAIL SOUP

I. [About 7 Cups]

Brown:

1 disjointed oxtail or 2 veal tails: about 2 lbs.
½ cup sliced onions

in:

2 tablespoons butter or fat

Add to the above and ➧ simmer, uncovered, for about 4½ hours:

8 cups water
1½ teaspoons salt
4 peppercorns

Add and simmer ½ hour longer or until the vegetables are tender:

¼ cup shredded parsley
½ cup diced carrots
1 cup diced celery
½ bay leaf
¼ cup barley
½ cup tomato pulp
1 teaspoon dried thyme, marjoram or basil

Strain, chill, degrease and reheat the stock. The meat and vegetables may be diced or blended and added to the soup later. Brown in a skillet:

1 tablespoon flour

Add and stir until blended:

2 tablespoons butter

Add the stock slowly and
Correct the seasoning

Shortly before serving you may pour in:

(¼ cup dry sherry or Madeira or ½ cup red wine)

Serve the soup with:

Fritter Garnish, or slices of lemon

II. ✪ [About 3 Cups]

Sear in a pressure cooker:

1 oxtail, joints separated
1 small diced onion

in:

3 tablespoons fat

Add:

4 cups hot water or ½ water, ½ tomato juice
1 teaspoon salt
2 peppercorns

Adjust cover. Cook at 15 pounds pressure for 15 minutes. Reduce pressure quickly. Remove the cover. Remove ox joints. Add to liquid in cooker:

1 diced carrot

4 ribs celery, diced

Readjust cover. Pressure cook the soup for 5 minutes longer. Degrease the soup after chilling it. Reheat and:

Correct the seasoning

You may add:

(2 tablespoons dry sherry or tomato catsup)

Separate meat from the joints. Add to soup. Serve with:

Chopped parsley

PANADES

[About 4 Cups]

These bread-thickened vegetable soups are practical and filling. They are a good way of utilizing leftover bread. Panades combine well with leeks, celery and sorrel; but watercress, spinach, lettuce, etc., may be substituted. Use:

1 cup finely chopped celery, leeks or onions

Cook the vegetables slowly until soft, but not brown, in:

1 tablespoon butter

Cover with a lid. If a leafy vegetable is used, add it to the butter, cover and cook slowly until wilted and reduced to about one fourth. Add:

2 cups hot water or milk
½ teaspoon salt
3 cups diced fresh or stale bread

Stir well and permit the mixture to boil. Simmer for ½ hour. Beat well until smooth with a wire whisk or in a ⅄ blender. Combine:

1 cup rich milk
1 large egg

Stir this slowly into the hot soup. Heat but ◆ do not permit the soup to boil. Serve it with:

Chopped parsley
Freshly grated nutmeg

PEPPER POT

[About 5 Cups]

Cut into small pieces and sauté in a heavy saucepan until clear:

4 slices of bacon

Add and simmer for about 5 minutes:

⅓ cup minced onion
½ cup minced celery
2 seeded, minced green peppers
(1 teaspoon marjoram or summer savory)

Wash and cut into fine shreds:

¾ lb. cooked honeycomb Tripe, page 548

Put into the saucepan with:

8 cups Brown Stock (II, 141)
1 bay leaf
½ teaspoon freshly ground pepper

Bring these ingredients to the boiling point. Add:

1 cup raw, peeled and diced potatoes

Gently simmer the soup, uncovered, until the potatoes are tender. Melt:

2 tablespoons butter

Stir in, until blended:

2 tablespoons flour

Add a little of the soup. Bring these ingredients to the boiling point, then pour them into the rest of the soup.

Correct the seasoning

Shortly before serving add:

½ cup warm cream

COCK-A-LEEKIE

[5 to 6 Cups]

Old recipes for this leek, chicken and cream soup start with a fowl or cock simmered in strong stock, and wind up with the addition of prunes. The following version is delicious, if not traditional.

Remove the dark green part of the tops and the roots from:

6 leeks

Wash them carefully—they may be sandy. Cut them in half lengthwise, then crosswise in ⅛-inch slices. There should be about 4 cups. Place in a pan with:

3 cups boiling water
1½ teaspoons salt

Simmer from 5 to 7 minutes or until tender but not mushy. Add and heat to a boil:

2 tablespoons chicken fat or butter
1½ cups well-seasoned strong chicken broth

Scald and stir in:

½ cup cream
Correct the seasoning

SAUERKRAUT SOUP

[About 7 Cups]
Sauté until golden brown:

½ cup chopped onion

in:

3 tablespoons bacon fat

Add:

½ clove minced garlic
½ lb. diced lean pork

Cover and cook over low heat for about 20 minutes. Add:

1 lb. chopped sauerkraut
6 cups stock

Cook until soft, about 45 minutes. Melt:

1½ tablespoons butter

Stir in:

1½ tablespoons flour

Stir in slowly a little of the hot soup, blend and return the mixture to kettle. Add:

(1 teaspoon sugar)
Correct the seasoning

and garnish with:

Diced salami or ham

SPINACH SOUP

[About 6½ Cups]
Pick over, wash, drain thoroughly, then chop fine or blend:

2 lbs. tender young spinach

You may use instead 4 cups cooked or two 14-ounce packages of frozen spinach, defrosted.
Melt in a saucepan:

¼ cup butter

Sauté in it until golden brown:

¼ cup minced onion

Add the spinach. Stir to coat it well with the butter. Cover, and cook gently till the spinach is just tender. ⅄ Blend or put the spinach through a food mill or sieve. Return to pan and add:

4 cups chicken stock
A grating of nutmeg
Salt or paprika

Bring the soup slowly to a boil and serve; or you may serve it cold, garnished with:

Diced, seeded cucumbers or chives and cultured sour cream

GREEN TURTLE SOUP

[About 8 Cups]
It is a timesaver to buy canned or frozen turtle meat. But if you can turn turtles, feel energetic and want to prepare your own, see page 447.
Place in a saucepan and bring to the boiling point:

1 lb. green turtle or terrapin meat cut into pieces
3 cups water
3 cups Brown Stock (II, 141)
1 bay leaf
1 sprig fresh thyme
2 cloves
¼ teaspoon ground allspice
Juice and thinly sliced peel of ½ lemon
A few grains cayenne
¼ teaspoon freshly ground black pepper
½ teaspoon salt
4 whole corianders

These pods will rise to the top by the end of the cooking period and can be skimmed out before serving.
Heat:

2 tablespoons cooking oil

Sauté in this for 2 minutes:

2 medium-sized chopped onions

Stir in:

1 tablespoon flour

Add:

1½ cups fresh skinned seeded tomatoes

Permit these ingredients to cook for 10 minutes. Combine them with the turtle mixture and:

1 tablespoon chopped parsley
2 cloves minced garlic

Simmer the soup until the meat is tender, at least 2 hours. You may add a few drops of caramel coloring. Add to each serving:

1 tablespoon dry sherry

Garnish the soup with:

2 chopped hard-cooked eggs
Lemon slices

MOCK TURTLE SOUP

[About 12 Cups]

This full-bodied, nourishing soup, served with crusty rolls, can be the main dish for any meal.

Cover:

5 lbs. veal bones

with:

14 cups water

Bring to the boiling point. Add and simmer for about 4 hours:

6 chopped celery ribs with leaves
5 coarsely cut carrots
1 cup chopped onion
2 cups canned tomatoes
1 small can Italian tomato paste
6 crushed peppercorns
1 tablespoon salt
2 teaspoons monosodium glutamate
6 whole cloves
2 bay leaves
½ teaspoon dried thyme

Degrease. Sauté for about 5 minutes in a greased skillet:

2 cloves minced garlic
2 lbs. ground beef
2 teaspoons salt

Add to the stock, with:

¼ teaspoon Worcestershire sauce
4 teaspoons sugar

Blend:

6 tablespoons browned flour (II, 153)
1 cup cooled stock

Stir this paste into the simmering soup. Permit it to simmer for 20 minutes more. Add:

2 thinly sliced lemons
1 set chopped, parboiled calf brains, page 540

Garnish the soup with:

3 sliced hard-cooked eggs

NEW YEAR'S SOUPS

Suggested below are traditional New Year's soups, served just before parties break up. They are also known as hangover soups, or Lumpensuppe, and are sometimes helpful for the morning after.

I. Onion Soup, page 113, with the addition of:

1 cup red wine

II. Lentil Soup with sour cream and sausage.

ABOUT CREAM SOUPS

These favored luncheon soups are also sometimes served at dinner. In this latter role, they satisfy what is, as often as not, a mechanical rather than a nutritional need. Like hors d'oeuvre, they act as a stabilizer for the cocktails which have just been drunk or as a buffer against the wines which are about to come.

For the richest of cream soups—the veloutés—first, sauté the vegetables in butter, purée them and combine the purée in equal parts with Velouté Sauce, page 362. Bind with egg yolk, allowing 2 to 4 yolks for each pint of soup. Simpler cream soups may be made on a Béchamel sauce base, page 359, or on this quick Béchamel: use 2 tablespoons butter to 1½ tablespoons flour, plus 2 cups cream and ¾ to 1 cup vegetable purée. Should you wish to thin these ingredients, use a little well-flavored stock.

For everyday cream soups, we find we can purée the tender vegetables raw or cook the more mature, fibrous ones and process them in a ⅄ blender. The soup is served without straining. ➧ If seafood or fowl is blended, it tends to be unpleasantly stringy and the entire soup will need straining before serving.

➧ All cream soups, whether bound with egg or not, are ruined by boiling, so be sure to heat just to the boiling point or cook them in the top of a double boiler ➧ over, not in, hot water. Reheat them this same way.

CREAM OF ASPARAGUS SOUP

[About 6 Cups]

Wash and remove the tips from:

1 lb. fresh green asparagus

Simmer the tips, covered, until they are tender in a small amount of:

Milk or water

Cut the stalks into pieces and place them in a saucepan. Add:

6 cups Veal or Chicken Stock (II, 142)
¼ cup chopped onion
½ cup chopped celery

Simmer these ingredients, covered, for about ½ hour. Rub them through a sieve. Melt:

3 tablespoons butter

Stir in, until blended:

3 tablespoons flour

Stir in slowly:

½ cup cream

Add the asparagus stock. Heat the soup well in a double boiler. Add the asparagus tips. Season the soup immediately before serving with:

Salt, paprika and white pepper

Garnish with:

A diced hard-cooked egg

CREAM OF CAULIFLOWER SOUP

[About 6 Cups]

Prepare:

1 large cauliflower, page 281

Drain it, reserving the water and about ⅓ of the florets. Put the remainder through a food mill, blender or sieve. Melt:

¼ cup butter

Sauté in it, until tender:

2 tablespoons chopped onion
3 celery ribs, minced

Stir in:

¼ cup flour

Stir in slowly and bring to the boiling point:

4 cups Veal or Chicken Stock (II, 142) and the reserved cauliflower water

Add the strained cauliflower and:

2 cups scalded rich milk or cream

Add the florets and:

A grating of nutmeg
Salt and paprika

Garnish with:

(Grated cheese)

CREAM OF CELERY SOUP

[About 4 Cups]

Melt:

1 tablespoon butter

Add and sauté for 2 minutes:

1 cup or more chopped celery with leaves
(⅓ cup sliced onion)

Pour in and simmer for about 10 minutes:

2 cups Veal or Chicken Stock

Strain the soup. Add and bring to the boiling point:

1½ cups milk

Dissolve:

1½ tablespoons cornstarch

in:

½ cup milk

Stir these ingredients gradually into the hot soup. Bring to the boiling point. Stir and cook for about 1 minute. You may add:

A grating of nutmeg

Serve with:

(2 tablespoons chopped parsley)

CHESTNUT SOUP

[About 3 Cups]

Prepare:

1 lb. chestnuts

Mash and beat them until smooth in:

2 cups milk

Melt:

¼ cup butter

Add and simmer until soft and golden:

1 minced onion

Sprinkle with:

1 tablespoon flour
1 teaspoon salt
⅛ teaspoon each nutmeg and pepper
½ cup chopped celery leaves

Stir and slowly add the chestnut and milk mixture. ➧ Simmer for about 10 minutes. Pour in:

1 cup cream

Heat ➧ but do not boil and serve immediately garnished with:

Parsley
Croutons, page 151

CREAM OF CHICKEN SOUP

[About 4½ Cups]

Simmer:

3 cups Chicken Stock (II, 142)
½ cup finely chopped celery

When the celery is tender, add and cook for 5 minutes:

½ cup cooked Rice, page 158

Add:

½ cup hot cream
1 tablespoon chopped parsley
Salt and paprika

➧ Do not boil the soup after adding the cream.

CREAM OF CORN SOUP

[About 5 Cups]

Put through a food mill or coarse sieve:

2½ cups cream style canned corn or 2½ cups corn, cut from the ear, simmered until tender in 1 cup milk

Melt:

3 tablespoons butter

Simmer in it until soft:

½ medium-sized sliced onion

Stir in:

3 tablespoons flour
1½ teaspoons salt
A few grains freshly ground pepper
(A grating of nutmeg)

Stir in the corn and:

3 cups milk or 2½ cups milk and ½ cup cream

Serve the soup sprinkled with:

3 tablespoons chopped parsley or chives

CORN CHOWDER

[About 6 Cups]

Sauté slowly until lightly browned:

½ cup chopped salt pork

Add and sauté until golden brown:

3 tablespoons chopped onion
½ cup chopped celery
3 tablespoons chopped green pepper

Add and simmer:

1 cup raw, peeled, diced potatoes
2 cups water
½ teaspoon salt
¼ teaspoon paprika
½ bay leaf

When the potatoes are tender, in about 45 minutes, combine until blended, bring to the boiling point, and add to the above:

3 tablespoons flour
½ cup milk

Add:

1½ cups hot milk
2 cups whole kernel corn

Heat but do not boil the soup. Serve it sprinkled with:

Chopped parsley

COLD BULGARIAN CUCUMBER SOUP

[About 3 Cups]

"Nazdrave" as the Bulgarians say for "Bon appétit."

Two to 6 hours before serving, refrigerate, covered:

1½ cups peeled, diced cucumbers

marinated in a mixture of:

1 teaspoon salt
¼ teaspoon pepper
¼ to 1 cup chopped walnuts
2 tablespoons olive oil
1 clove minced garlic
2 tablespoons chopped fresh dill

➧ The fresh dill is the essential touch. When ready to serve, add:

1 to 1½ cups thick yogurt or 1 cup cultured sour cream

Place 1 or 2 ice cubes in each soup bowl. Pour in the mixture. It should have the consistency of chilled borsch. If not thin enough, it can be thinned with a small amount of light stock. Serve at once.

CHILLED CREAM OF CUCUMBER HERB SOUP

[6 Cups]

Pare, seed and slice:

2 medium-sized cucumbers

Add to them:

1 cup water
2 slices onion
¼ teaspoon salt
⅛ teaspoon white pepper

Cook the cucumbers, covered, until very soft. Put them through a fine strainer or an ⅄ electric blender. Stir until smooth:

¼ cup flour
½ cup chicken stock

Stir into this flour paste:

1½ cups chicken stock

Add the cucumber purée and:

¼ bay leaf or 2 cloves

Stir the soup over low heat. Simmer for 2 minutes. Strain and chill in a covered jar. Stir into these ingredients:

¾ cup chilled cream or cultured sour cream or yogurt
1 tablespoon finely chopped dill, chives or other herb or grated lemon rind
Correct the seasoning

Serve the soup very cold.

CREAM OF MUSHROOM SOUP

[About 4½ Cups]

The flavor of mushrooms is more pronounced if they have begun to color. Prepare for cooking:

½ lb. mature mushrooms with stems

Sauté lightly in:

2 tablespoons butter

Add them to:

2 cups chicken stock or water
½ cup chopped tender celery
¼ cup sliced onion
⅛ cup shredded parsley

Simmer, covered, for 20 minutes. Drain the vegetables, reserving the stock. ⅄ Blend them or put them through a food chopper. Prepare:

Cream Sauce I, page 359

Pour the liquid slowly into the cream sauce, cook and stir until the soup just reaches a boil. Add the ground vegetables. Heat ➧ but do not boil. Season the soup with:

1¼ teaspoons salt
⅛ teaspoon paprika
(⅛ teaspoon nutmeg)
(3 tablespoons dry white wine)

Serve, topped with:

(Whipped cream)

Garnish with:

Paprika

Sprigs of parsley or chopped chives

CREAM OF NETTLE SOUP

[About 4 Cups]
Using rubber gloves, remove the central stem from:
1 quart young nettle tops
Have boiling:
5 cups stock
Blend in:
2 tablespoons cooked rice or oatmeal
Add the nettles and simmer for about 15 minutes.
Correct the seasoning
and serve.

CREAM OF ONION SOUP OR ONION VELOUTÉ

[About 4 Cups]
Melt:
3 tablespoons butter
Add and sauté till a golden brown:
1½ cups thinly sliced onions
Stir in:
1 tablespoon flour
½ teaspoon salt
Add:
4 cups milk or cream and Stock (II, 141)
Simmer, covered, until the onions are very tender. Add:
4 beaten egg yolks
Heat but ♦ do not boil. Season with:
Salt and paprika
Freshly grated nutmeg or (Worcestershire sauce)
Place in each cup:
1 teaspoon chopped parsley
Pour the hot soup over it.

POTATO SOUP

[About 3 Cups]
Peel and slice:
2 medium-sized potatoes
Skin and chop:
2 medium-sized onions
4 ribs celery
Sauté these ingredients in:
1½ tablespoons butter
Add:
Boiling water to cover
½ teaspoon salt
(½ bay leaf)
Boil the vegetables until the potatoes are tender or ⊗ pressure cook them for 3 minutes at 15 pounds pressure. Put them through a ricer or ⅄ blender. Beat into them:
2 tablespoons butter
Thin the soup to the desired consistency with:
Rich milk and/or Chicken Stock (II, 142)
Add if required:
Salt and paprika
A dash Worcestershire sauce
Serve with:
Chopped parsley, chives or watercress
1 cup sliced frankfurters, chopped, cooked shrimp or diced ham

POTATO SOUP WITH TOMATOES

[About 10–12 Cups]
A more sophisticated version of the previous recipe.
Prepare:
2 cups sliced onions
Sauté very gently until translucent in:
¼ cup butter
Add the onions to:
2 cups sliced potatoes
6 cups boiling water
Simmer for about ½ hour. Add and simmer, covered, for about 20 minutes:
5 cups sliced tomatoes or 3 cups canned tomatoes
2 teaspoons sugar
1 teaspoon salt
⅛ teaspoon paprika
A pinch of chervil
Put the soup through a fine strainer or ⅄ blender. Reheat and
Correct the seasoning
Scald and stir in:
1 cup cream

Heat ◆ but do not boil. Serve at once.

VICHYSSOISE OR LEEK POTATO SOUP

This leek soup may be served hot or very cold. Yes, the last "s" is pronounced. Most Americans shun it, in a "genteel" way, as though it were virtuous to ignore it. Be sure to serve the soup reduced to a velvety smoothness.

I. [About 6 Cups]
Mince the white part of:
 3 medium-sized leeks
 1 medium-sized onion
Stir and sauté them for 3 minutes in:
 2 tablespoons butter
Peel, slice very fine and add:
 4 medium-sized potatoes
Add:
 4 cups clarified Chicken Stock (II, 142)
Simmer the vegetables, covered, for 15 minutes or until tender. Put them through a very fine sieve, food mill or ⅄ blender. Add:
 1 to 2 cups cream
 (¼ teaspoon mace)
 Salt and white pepper
 Chopped watercress or chives

II. [About 2½ Cups]
Superlative! Less rich and made in about 20 minutes by using a ⅄ blender and ⊗ pressure cooker. Serve it hot or chill it quickly by placing it in a refrigerator tray or deep freeze.
Prepare as above:
 Vichyssoise
using ½ the amount of ingredients given. After adding the potatoes and stock, pressure cook the soup for 3 minutes at 15 pounds pressure. Cool. Add:
 1 cup peeled, seeded and diced cucumbers
Blend covered until smooth, about 1 minute. Place the soup in a jar. Chill it thoroughly. You may add the cream, but you will probably like the result just as well without it. Hot or cold, sprinkle the top with:
 Chopped chives

PUMPKIN SOUP

[About 4 Cups]
Place:
 3 cups canned or 2 lbs. cooked fresh pumpkin
in:
 3 cups scalded milk
Add:
 1 tablespoon butter
 1 tablespoon sugar or 2 tablespoons brown sugar
 Salt and pepper
 (Nutmeg and cinnamon)
 A very small pinch saffron
 ½ cup finely julienned ham
Heat ◆ but do not boil. Serve at once.

CREAM OF SORREL SOUP

[About 5 to 6 Cups]
Also known as Potage Germiny and a favorite combination with veal and fish dishes. Because of the oxalic acid in sorrel ◆ use a stainless steel or enamel pan.
Clean, shred from the mid rib and chop:
 2 cups sorrel leaves
Sauté them, until wilted, in:
 1 to 2 tablespoons butter
When they are sufficiently wilted, there will be only about 3 tablespoons of leaves. Add:
 5 cups Chicken Stock (II, 142)
 (1 tablespoon fresh pea purée)
Simmer for about 2 minutes. Remove from the heat and add:
 ½ cup cream
 3 beaten egg yolks
Heat until the soup thickens slightly ◆ but do not boil. Serve garnished with:
 Chopped chervil

CREAM OF SPINACH OR LETTUCE SOUP

[About 5 Cups]
Pick over and wash:
 1 lb. spinach or 1 lb. leaf lettuce
Or you may use:
 1 cup frozen spinach
Place it, while moist or frozen, in a covered saucepan. Cook for about 6 minutes. Drain. Put through a strainer or ⅄ blender. Melt in a saucepan:
 2 tablespoons butter
Add and sauté for 3 minutes:
 1 tablespoon grated onion or 1 slice of onion which can be removed easily
Stir in and cook until blended:
 2 tablespoons flour
Stir in gradually:
 4 cups milk and/or stock
Season with:
 ¾ teaspoon or more salt
 ¼ teaspoon paprika
 (A grating of nutmeg)
Add the spinach or lettuce. Heat the soup well. Serve sprinkled with:
 (Grated Parmesan cheese or sieved egg yolk)

CREAM OF TOMATO SOUP

[About 5½ Cups]
Simmer, covered, for about 15 minutes:
 2 cups canned or fresh, cut-up tomatoes
 ½ cup chopped celery
 ¼ cup chopped onion
 2 teaspoons white or brown sugar
Prepare:
 4 cups Cream Sauce I, page 359
Strain into this the tomato and vegetable stock.
 Correct the seasoning
and serve with:
 Croutons, page 151
 Chopped parsley, burnet or basil
If served chilled, garnish with:
 Chopped chives or whipped cream and paprika

CREAM OF WATER CRESS OR PURSLANE SOUP

I. [About 4 Cups]
Sauté:
 1 cup chopped cress or purslane
in:
 1 tablespoon butter
Add.
 Salt, white pepper and paprika
 ½ cup white wine
 4 cups cream
Heat but do not boil. Serve at once:

II. [About 5 Cups]
To:
 5 cups hot Cream of Chicken Soup, page 127
Add:
 1½ cups chopped or ⅄ blended water cress
Or, if you wish to try Gandhi's favorite vegetable, use an equal amount of:
 (Purslane)
Simmer the soup about 5 minutes. Add and stir a small quantity of the soup into:
 2 well-beaten eggs
Add this to the rest of the soup, stirring it in slowly. Heat the soup ♦ but do not boil. Serve at once.
An interesting taste variation results by adding:
 2 slices fresh ginger
which have been lightly sautéed in:
 Butter
 Salt
Remove ginger after reheating but before serving the soup.

MILK TOAST OR SOUP

[Individual Service]
While not exactly a soup, this dish can bring something like the same cozy comfort to the young or the ailing.

Toast lightly on both sides:

A slice of bread, ¾ inch thick

Spread it lightly with:

Butter

Sprinkle it with:

(Salt)

Place it in a bowl and pour over it:

1 cup hot milk

ABOUT FISH SOUPS

Making a good broth or fumet of fish is like making a stock of any kind of meat in that the process toughens the meat. It differs in that it takes a good deal less time. Extraction is limited to a ➧ 20 to 30 minute period ➧ over relatively high heat, instead of the slow simmering recommended for warm-blooded meat. ➧ As a consequence, most fish soups are quick soups. When fisherman's stews are served, the meat is often presented on the side; and in the preparation of delicate bisques based on shellfish, the shrimp or lobsters are often poached separately, then pounded in a mortar or minced before incorporation in a separate stock, cream and egg base.

The original stock may be used as a court bouillon for cooking other fish or reduced for use in "au maigre" or meatless sauces. Bisques, as well as oyster, clam and mussel soups and stews, need so little heat that the stock bases are warmed first and the shellfish then just heated through in them, preferably in a double boiler ➧ over, not in, hot water. Serve fish soups at once. If you must hold or reheat, be sure to do so again ➧ over, not in, hot water.

CLAM BROTH OR SOUP

[About 4 Cups]

Clams are of various types, see About Clams, page 427. The broth is delicious when fresh, but may be frozen until mushy and served in small glasses or on the shells with wedges of lemon. The meat of the clams themselves may be used in various sea-food dishes, see pages 229–234.

Wash and scrub well with a brush, then place in a kettle:

2 quarts clams in shells

Add:

1¾ cups water
3 cut up ribs celery with leaves
A pinch of cayenne

➧ Cover the kettle closely. You may double the quantity of this soup, even though the clam flavor will be lessened, by adding about 4 cups of water and minced vegetables which are suitable for soup, see Court Bouillon (II, 146). ➧ Steam the clams until the shells open, page 430. Strain the liquor through wet double cheesecloth to remove any sand. It may be heated and diluted with warm cream or rich milk. Add:

1 teaspoon butter
Correct the seasoning

and serve.

COQUINA BROTH

If you are lucky enough to be on a beach in Florida, collect in a sieve at ebb tide:

Coquinas

the little native periwinkle clams, in rainbow-hued shells.

Rinse them clean of sand, then barely cover with:

Water

Bring slowly to a boil and ➧ simmer for about 10 minutes. Pour the broth through a fine sieve. When you imbibe it, remember the advice of an old German who said, when serving a fine vintage, "Don't gullop it, zipp it!"

CRAWFISH BISQUE

[About 6 Cups]
Wash and scrub with a brush under running water:

3 dozen crawfish

Soak for 30 minutes in salted water, 1 tablespoon salt to 4 cups of water. Rinse thoroughly. Place the crawfish in a saucepan with:

6 cups boiling water
A few grains of cayenne
½ teaspoon salt

Bring to a boil, then ➧ simmer for 15 minutes. Drain, reserving the stock. Remove the heads and reserve 18 of them to be stuffed as a garnish for the bisque. Remove the meat from the heads. Devein the tails. Return all remaining shells to the stock. Bring to a boil. Add:

4 ribs chopped celery
2 tablespoons chopped parsley
½ diced carrot
⅛ teaspoon thyme or a sprig of fresh thyme

Simmer for 30 minutes. Strain. Meanwhile, prepare the stuffing for the heads. Mince the crawfish meat. Sauté until golden:

2 tablespoons minced onion

in:

2 tablespoons butter

Add and cook for 3 minutes:

2 tablespoons finely minced celery
1 tablespoon finely minced parsley

Remove from heat and add ½ the crawfish meat and:

½ cup bread crumbs

Beat and add:

1 egg
Salt and paprika as required

Stir lightly with a fork. Stuff the heads with this mixture. Place them on a greased shallow pan. Dot each head with butter. For 10 minutes, before serving the soup, bake the heads in a preheated 425° oven. Melt:

2 tablespoons butter

Sauté in it until delicately browned:

¼ cup minced onion

Add and stir until lightly browned:

2 tablespoons flour

Add the fish stock slowly, stirring until smooth. Add the remaining crawfish meat and

Correct the seasoning

➧ Simmer the bisque for about 5 minutes, stirring it often. To serve, place the heated heads in hot soup plates, then pour the bisque over them.

LOBSTER BISQUE

[About 6 Cups]
Remove the meat from:

2 medium-sized boiled lobsters

Dice the body meat and mince the tail and claw meat. Reserve it. Crush the shells. Add to them the tough end of the claws and:

2½ cups Chicken Stock (II, 142) or Fumet (II, 143)
1 sliced onion
4 ribs celery with leaves
2 whole cloves
1 bay leaf
6 peppercorns

Simmer these ingredients for ½ hour. Strain the stock. If there is coral roe, force it through a fine sieve, combine it with the butter in a mortar or bowl, add the flour and when well blended pour the heated milk slowly on it, stirring until the mixture is smooth.
Otherwise, melt:

¼ cup butter

Stir in:

¼ cup flour

Add gradually:

3 cups milk
¼ teaspoon nutmeg
Correct the seasoning

When the sauce is smooth and boiling, add the lobster and the stock. ➧ Simmer the bisque, covered, for 5 minutes. Turn off the heat. Stir in:

1 cup ♦ hot but not boiling cream

Serve at once with:

Minced parsley
Paprika
Dry sherry

MUSHROOM AND CLAM BISQUE

[About 3 Cups]

Sauté:

½ lb. chopped mushrooms

in:

2 tablespoons butter

Stir in:

2 tablespoons flour

Stir in slowly:

2½ cups clam broth

Simmer for 5 minutes. Remove from the heat. Heat ♦ but do not boil:

¾ cup cream

Add to the other ingredients.

Correct the seasoning

and serve with:

Chopped parsley or chives

SHRIMP BISQUE

[About 5 Cups]

Remove shells and intestines from:

1½ lbs. Poached Shrimp, page 442

Put the shrimp through a meat grinder or ⅄ blender. Cook, covered, in the top of a double boiler ♦ over, not in, hot water for 5 minutes:

6 tablespoons butter
2 tablespoons grated onion

Add the ground shrimp and:

3 cups warm milk

Cook for 2 minutes. Stir in slowly, heat ♦ but do not boil:

1 cup cream

Add:

Salt, if needed, and paprika or freshly ground white pepper
A grating of nutmeg
3 tablespoons sherry
2 tablespoons parsley or chives

Serve at once.

OYSTER STEWS AND BISQUES

Here are 2 good recipes which differ in nutritive value and effort of preparation. The first calls for milk and is unthickened; the second, a bisque, calls for milk, cream and egg yolks. To clean oysters, see page 422.

I. [About 4 Cups]

Our instructions are foolproof, as the use of a double boiler prevents overcooking of the oysters. Combine in the top of a double boiler over, not in, hot water:

2 to 4 tablespoons butter
½ teaspoon or more grated onion or leek, a sliver of garlic or ½ cup stewed celery

Sauté lightly and add:

1 to 1½ pints oysters with liquor
1½ cups milk
½ cup cream
½ teaspoon salt
⅛ teaspoon white pepper or paprika

Place the pan ♦ over, not in, boiling water. When the milk is hot and the oysters float, add:

2 tablespoons chopped parsley

II. [About 4 Cups]

This is a true oyster bisque. Prepare:

Oyster Stew I, above

Before adding the parsley, remove the soup from the heat and pour a small quantity over:

2 beaten egg yolks

After mixing, add them slowly to the hot bisque. Heat slowly for 1 minute but ♦ do not allow to boil; or hold over hot water in a double boiler until ready to serve.

MUSSEL STEW

Clean the mussels and remove the beard, page 426. Steam, strain and reserve the liquor. Use either recipe for Oyster Stew, above, substituting mussels for oysters.

LOBSTER STEW

[About 5 Cups]

Sauté for 3 or 4 minutes:

1 cup diced fresh lobster meat

in:

3 tablespoons butter

Add slowly:

4 cups scalded milk
2 teaspoons onion juice

A Maine correspondent writes that this stew is much improved by the addition, at this time, of ½ to 1 cup clam broth.

Correct the seasoning

and serve.

SHRIMP, CRAB AND OYSTER GUMBO

[About 8 Cups]

Melt:

1 tablespoon butter

Stir in and cook until golden:

¼ cup chopped onion

Stir in until blended:

2 tablespoons flour

Add and stir until smooth:

1½ cups strained tomatoes
4 cups Stock (II, 141) or Fumet (II, 143)
1 quart thinly sliced okra

Break into small pieces and add:

½ lb. raw, shelled, cleaned shrimp
½ lb. raw crab meat

➧ Simmer these ingredients until the okra is tender. Add:

16 shelled oysters

Correct the seasoning

and serve the gumbo as soon as the oysters are plump. Sprinkle with:

Chopped parsley

ABOUT BOUILLABAISSE AND OTHER FISHERMAN'S STEWS

Necessity is the mother of invention; and convenience gave birth to the can and the frozen package. Use frozen or canned fish, if you must, for fisherman's stews; but remember that ➧ their fragrant, distinctive and elusive charm can only be captured if the fish which go into them are themselves freshly caught. Curnonsky reminds us of the legend that bouillabaisse, the most celebrated of fisherman's stews, was first brought by angels to the Three Marys, when they were shipwrecked on the bleak shores of the Camargue.

Divinely inspired or not, it is true that bouillabaisse can only be approximated in this country, even if its ingredients are just off the hook. For its unique flavor depends on the use of fish which are native to the Mediterranean alone: a regional rock fish, high in gelatin content, for example, which gives a slightly cloudy but still thin texture to the soup, and numberless finny tidbits, too small for market. We offer a free translation of bouillabaisse into American—realizing fully that we have succeeded only in changing poetry to rich prose.

A similar accommodation has been made for matelote or freshwater fish stew, in which eel, carp, bream, tench and perch are combined with wine. A certain amount of freewheeling must be the rule, too, in concocting chowders and stews of both sea and fresh fish, which are milk-based and often have potatoes added. Whatever fish you use, see that it is as ➧ fresh as possible and experiment with combinations of those that are most quickly available.

BOUILLABAISSE

[8 Cups]
Have ready:

¼ cup finely chopped onion
4 finely julienned leeks: use the white portions only

Skin and squeeze the pulp out of and then dice:

4 medium-sized tomatoes

Combine:

5 cloves minced garlic
1 tablespoon finely chopped fresh fennel
½ to 1 teaspoon saffron
2 pulverized bay leaves
1 teaspoon grated orange rind
2 tablespoons tomato paste
⅛ teaspoon celery seed
3 tablespoons chopped parsley
1 teaspoon freshly ground pepper
2 tablespoons salt

Heat in a large casserole:

¼ to ½ cup olive oil

When the oil is hot, add the prepared ingredients above and cook until the vegetables are transparent. Meanwhile, cut into 1-inch dice and then add:

4 lbs. very fresh fish in combination: red snapper, halibut, pompano, sea perch, scallops; also 1-inch pieces of well-scrubbed lobster, whole shrimp, clams and mussels—all in the shell

You may prefer to leave the fish in 2-inch-thick slices and use some of the smaller fish whole. If so, add the thinner pieces or small scrubbed shellfish to the pot slightly later than the thicker ones ➧ but do not disturb the boiling. Cover the fish with:

2½ cups hot Fumet (II, 143) or water

➧ Keep the heat high and force the boiling, which should continue rapid for 15 to 20 minutes.

Correct the seasoning

To serve, have ready to arrange in the bottom of 8 hot bowls:

¾-inch slices of French bread

Dry the bread in the oven and brush with:

Garlic butter

When the bouillabaisse is ready, arrange attractively some of each kind of fish on and around the bread. You may remove the lobsters from the shell and remove the upper shells from the clams and mussels. Then pour the hot broth into the bowls and serve at once. Or, you may strain the broth onto the bread and serve the sea food on a separate platter. Plan the meal with a beverage other than wine.

MATELOTE

[8 Cups]
Depending upon the amount of wine used, this dish can be either a soup or a stew.
Cook separately and have ready to add as a garnish, just before serving the matelote:

12 small cooked onions, page 301
½ lb. sautéed mushrooms, page 296
½ lb. cooked shrimp, page 442

Now, clean and cut into 1-inch slices:

3 lbs. freshwater fish: eel, carp, tench, bream or perch

Cover first the fish that need the longest cooking with a combination of ½:

Good red wine

and ½:

Fish fumet or meat stock

Take note of the approximate amount needed, for this should be reduced by about one half later on. Add:

2 teaspoons chopped parsley

½ cup chopped celery
1 small bay leaf
2 cloves garlic
¼ teaspoon thyme
1 teaspoon salt

Bring the mixture to a boil, remove from heat and float on the surface:

2 tablespoons warm cognac

Ignite the cognac, and when the flame dies down, return the mixture to heat, add the remaining fish, cover the pan and simmer the soup for about 15 minutes. Now, remove the fish to a serving dish and strain the liquid into another pan. Thicken the soup with a beurre manié of:

3 tablespoons butter
2½ tablespoons flour

Add it a little at a time to the hot soup. Bring the soup just to a boil, stirring constantly. It should be creamy in texture, but will go thin if boiled.

Correct the seasoning

To serve, put the fish into soup bowls, cover first with the onions and mushrooms, then with the sauce; garnish the whole with the shrimp; and serve with:

Soup Croutons, page 151

MANHATTAN CLAM CHOWDER

[About 8 Cups]

Prepare:

1 quart quahog clams, page 428

Wash them in:

3 cups water

Drain through cheesecloth. Reserve liquid. Cut the hard part of the clams from the soft part. Chop finely:

The hard part of the clams
A 2-inch cube of salt pork or
3 slices of bacon
1 large onion

Sauté the salt pork very slowly. Remove and reserve the scraps. Add the minced onions and hard part of the clams to the grease. Stir and cook slowly for about 5 minutes. Sift over them and stir until blended:

3 tablespoons flour

Heat and stir in the reserved liquid. Peel, prepare and add:

2 cups raw diced potatoes
3 cups cooked or canned tomatoes
(½ cup diced green pepper)
(½ bay leaf)
(¼ cup catsup)

Cover the pan and simmer the chowder until the potatoes are done, but still firm. Add the pork scraps, the soft part of the clams and:

3 tablespoons butter

Simmer for 3 minutes more. Place the chowder in a hot tureen.

Correct the seasoning

Serve with:

Oyster crackers

You may substitute for the fresh clams:

2½ cups canned minced clams

Strain the juice. Add water to make 3 cups of liquid. Use this liquid in place of the water measurement given above.

Chowder should be allowed to ripen; it is always better the following day.

NEW ENGLAND CLAM CHOWDER

[About 8 Cups]

Most New Englanders consider the above recipe an illegitimate child. They omit the tomatoes, green peppers and catsup, but pour in:

4 cups hot ➧ not boiling, milk

after the pork scraps have been added. ➧ Do not let the mixture boil. Serve with large crackers.

CONCH CHOWDER

Prepare:

Manhattan Clam Chowder, above

using conch meat to replace the fish. ➧ To prepare conch in the shell, cover:

2 to 15 conchs or large whelks

with cold water and ➧ simmer 20 to 30 minutes. Remove from shell and beat the white body meat in a canvas bag until it begins to disintegrate. Marinate 2 hours in:

¼ cup lime juice

After adding the conch meat to the chowder, simmer about 3 to 5 minutes longer than directed for Manhattan Clam Chowder.

ABOUT QUICK SOUPS

When we were very young, we were more appalled than edified by "Struwwelpeter," a book of rhymed fables for children, which had been written in Germany by a Korpsbruder of our great grandfather. We remember the story of Suppenkaspar, a little boy who resolutely refused to eat his soup, wasted away for his stubbornness and was buried with a tureen as his headstone. Looking back and taking note of our wonderful present-day battery of canned, frozen and dried soups, we can see that Kaspar was born a century too soon and would, in this generation, have chosen, beyond a doubt, to live.

Know the comfort and reassurance of a larder well-stocked with processed soups. With them, you may in a jiffy lay the foundation of a good, square meal. If the unexpected guest prefers a clear soup, use a canned consommé or chicken broth with any one of several quickly confected egg-drops, page 145. If he fancies a more filling dish, serve ⅄ Blender Borsch, page 140, or Quick Cucumber Soup Cockaigne, page 140.

Very special effects may be achieved in your canned and frozen soup repertory by mixing with them the meat and vegetable stocks which are the by-product of daily cooking (II, 138). Put these regularly by, along with meat glazes, for just this purpose. Occasionally, too, a bouillon cube will add interest. Please read About Soup Stock and Stock Substitutes (II, 138). If you have a plot or some pots of fresh herbs, now is the time to commandeer a clipping all 'round.

➧ One word of caution. Normally, we dilute ready-prepared soups considerably less than their manufacturers recommend, whether we use home-cooked stocks, milk or—less desirably—just plain water. But we find that the more concentrated the soup the more likely it is to taste oversalted. Test your mix and correct this tendency.

For very sturdy potages, casseroles, etc., see suggestions in Brunch, Lunch and Supper Dishes, page 208. There is also the possibility that you are harboring some refrigerator scraps which will respond in a constructive way to ⅄ blender treatment. Before processing, add to them a few mushrooms or a few leaves of spinach, lettuce or cress and a small amount of milk and cream. Be sure, though, if you blend uncooked vegetables, that they are tender and will not spoil the texture of your soup with stringy fibers or bits of hull.

If you have on hand some leftover bones, lean fowl or meat trimmings and have a little extra time, put your ✪ pressure cooker to work, too, at building a soup base. Remember, in this connection, that most fish soups are quick soups, even when you start with raw materials. ➧ Please read About Fish Soups, page 132.

QUICK CANNED CONSOMMÉ VARIATIONS

A clear soup is supposed to be as bracing as a clear conscience.

Add to each serving of consommé, hot or cold:

A slice of lemon or 1 tablespoon sherry or Madeira or diced avocado
A dollop of sour cream

Or add to hot consommé:

Egg Drops, page 145, Marrow Balls, page 150, or Noodles, page 149

QUICK TROPICAL CONSOMMÉ

[About 3 Cups]

Combine and heat the contents of:

1 can condensed consommé
1 can condensed madrilène

Stir in:

The juice of 1 large orange

Serve chilled "on the rocks."

⅄ BLENDER GAZPACHO

[About 1 Cup]

Blend together for 2 or 3 minutes:

¼ cup skinned, seeded cucumbers
¾ cup skinned, seeded tomatoes
¼ cup consommé or water
½ teaspoon red pimiento

Add and blend for a shorter time:

1 teaspoon to 1 tablespoon olive oil

Add, but do not blend, as the flavor would be too strong:

1 teaspoon chopped chives
Correct the seasoning

and serve by pouring the broth over 2 ice cubes. A good garnish is:

Garlic croutons

QUICK VEGETABLE SOUP

[About 2½ Cups]

Utilize the water in which vegetables have been cooked. Melt:

2 tablespoons butter

Add and stir until blended:

1⅓ tablespoons flour

Add and stir until smooth:

1½ cups vegetable water

Bring to a boil and cook for 2 minutes. Lower the heat and add:

½ cup cream or Stock (II, 141)

Add:

½ cup cooked, diced or strained vegetables
2 tablespoons chopped parsley
(A dash of celery salt)
Correct the seasoning

Heat thoroughly ➧ but do not boil if you have chosen to add the cream.

⅄ BLENDER CREAM OF VEGETABLE SOUP

Blend:

1 can condensed cream of vegetable soup
1 can condensed chicken rice soup
1 cup canned or strong asparagus stock
(¼ cup cream)

Heat ➧ but do not boil and serve at once.

QUICK CREAM OF ASPARAGUS SOUP

[4 to 5 Cups]

Combine:

1 can condensed cream of asparagus soup
1 can condensed chicken broth
(1 can condensed cream of mushroom soup)
1 cup milk

Heat, stirring until smooth.

QUICK CHILLED CREAM OF AVOCADO SOUP

[3 Cups]
Stir until smooth and at the boiling point:

2 cups condensed cream of chicken soup

Remove from heat. Chill and add:

½ cup puréed avocado

When ready to serve, stir in:

½ cup chilled cream
⅛ teaspoon white pepper

Serve in cups, sprinkled with:

1 teaspoon chopped chives or chervil

⅄ BLENDER BORSCH

I. [About 4 Cups]
Combine in a blender:

1 can condensed consommé
1 can condensed cream of chicken soup
1 can beets: No. 2½
(1 clove minced garlic)

Half of the liquid from the beets may be drained if a thick soup is desired. Blend until smooth and chill. Serve with a garnish of:

Cultured sour cream and Fines Herbes (II, 220)

II. [About 4 Cups]
Combine in a blender:

2 cups tomato juice
2 cups canned beets
3 dill pickles
3 tablespoons finely grated onion
1 drop hot pepper sauce
(1 clove minced garlic)

Chill the soup and serve garnished with:

4 thinly sliced hard-boiled eggs
Cultured sour cream
Fresh chopped dill or fennel

QUICK PEA SOUP

[About 6 Cups]
Combine and bring to the boiling point:

1 can condensed consommé
1 can clear chicken soup
1 can condensed pea soup

Add:

1⅓ cups water or stock
¼ cup finely diced cooked ham
(4 oz. fine noodles)
(1 tablespoon Worcestershire sauce)
(1 tablespoon chili sauce)

Simmer, covered, until hot or the noodles are done.

QUICK CREAM OF CHICKEN SOUP

Easy to make and very good.
Heat in a double boiler ➧ over, not in, hot water:

Chicken bouillon
Cream—about ¼ the amount of the bouillon

Add, if you wish:

A dash of nutmeg
Chopped parsley

Add, if you want to be really luxurious:

Ground blanched almonds—use about 2 tablespoons to 1 cup soup

QUICK CUCUMBER SOUP COCKAIGNE

[About 5 Cups]
Bring to a boil:

2 cups strong chicken broth

Drop in about:

1½ cups peeled, seeded and diced cucumbers

Simmer until translucent, about 15 minutes. Add:

1 can condensed cream of chicken soup

blended with:

½ cup chicken broth

Again bring to a boil. Now add:

½ cup canned crab meat, shrimp or minced clams
1 teaspoon fresh parsley or chervil

Heat ⧫ but do not boil, and serve at once.

QUICK COLD CUCUMBER SOUP

[About 5 Cups]
Combine in a saucepan:

1 can frozen condensed cream of potato soup
An equal amount of milk
1 chicken bouillon cube
1⅓ cups finely chopped cucumber

Heat slowly, stirring until very hot and until the cucumber is partially cooked, about 10 minutes. ⅄ Blend or put through a food mill and refrigerate, covered, until chilled. Shortly before serving, stir in:

1 cup light cream
½ cup minced cucumber

QUICK CREAM OF CAULIFLOWER SOUP

[About 3½ Cups]
Heat:

2 tablespoons butter

Cook in the butter for 4 minutes:

¼ cup sliced onion
2 minced small ribs celery with leaves

Add:

1½ cups chicken broth
1 cup cooked cauliflower, riced or mashed

Heat to the boiling point. Heat and add:

1 cup rich milk

⧫ Do not let the soup boil after adding the milk.

Correct the seasoning

and serve with:

1 tablespoon chopped parsley
A light grating of nutmeg

QUICK CHEESE SOUP

[About 4 Cups]
Combine and stir over low heat:

1 can condensed celery soup
1 can condensed consommé
1¼ cups water or milk
½ cup grated cheddar or pimiento cheese

Add:

(1 tablespoon chopped onion)
(¼ teaspoon Worcestershire sauce)

Stir over low heat until the cheese is melted. ⧫ Do not let the soup boil. Serve with:

Chopped parsley

QUICK TOMATO CORN CHOWDER

[3 Cups]
Combine and heat, but ⧫ do not boil:

1 can condensed tomato soup
An equal amount of milk
½ cup cream style corn
1 teaspoon sugar
(¼ teaspoon curry powder)
Correct the seasoning

and serve.

QUICK MUSHROOM SOUP

I. [About 4 Cups]
Combine, stir and heat:

1 can condensed mushroom soup
1 cup condensed beef or chicken bouillon or consommé
1¼ cups water or milk

II. [4 Cups]
Soak for 30 minutes:

Dried mushrooms

in:

2 cans condensed consommé

Add:

1 can condensed mushroom soup

Heat and serve.

QUICK ONION SOUP

[About 2 Cups]
Heat:

1 can condensed onion soup

Add:
2 teaspoons lemon juice
A grating of lemon rind
½ clove pressed garlic
⅛ teaspoon nutmeg
(¼ cup sherry)
Correct the seasoning
Top each serving with:
Melba Cheese Rounds

QUICK OXTAIL SOUP WITH WINE

[About 2½ Cups]
Pare thinly in several strips:
The rind of 1 lemon
Add to it:
1 cup water
1 can condensed oxtail soup
1 teaspoon grated onion
➧ Simmer these ingredients for 5 minutes. Remove the lemon rind and
Correct the seasoning
Reduce the heat. Stir in:
½ cup claret or ¼ cup very dry sherry
1 tablespoon minced parsley
Serve at once with:
Toasted crackers

QUICK SPINACH SOUP

[About 2 Cups]
Combine:
½ cup cooked spinach
1 can condensed cream of chicken soup
If the spinach has already been creamed, use instead:
(1 can chicken broth)
You may thin the soup with:
Spinach water, stock or milk
Correct the seasoning
heat and serve.

QUICK TOMATO SOUP

[About 4 Cups]
➧ Simmer, covered, for 15 minutes or steam for 2 minutes in a ⊗ pressure cooker, then strain:
2½ cups canned tomatoes
¼ cup sliced onion
½ cup chopped celery with leaves
Melt:
2 tablespoons butter
Add and stir until blended:
2 tablespoons flour
Add, cook and stir until smooth and boiling:
2 cups Stock (II, 141) or canned bouillon
½ teaspoon sugar
⅛ teaspoon paprika
The strained tomato stock
Correct the seasoning
and add, just before serving:
(1 tablespoon chopped fresh basil or ¾ teaspoon anchovy paste or whipped cream)

QUICK CHILLED FRESH TOMATO CREAM SOUP

⅄ I. [About 3 Cups]
One way to use surplus garden tomatoes. Peel, seed and chop coarsely:
2½ cups fresh, very ripe tomatoes
Blend briefly with:
1 cup cream
1 tablespoon parsley
1 tablespoon basil
Correct the seasoning
Chill and serve with:
Lemon slices

II. [About 3 Cups]
Combine in a cocktail shaker:
2 cups chilled tomato juice
1 cup chilled cream
4 or more ribs raw celery, grated
1 teaspoon grated onion
A few drops hot pepper sauce
A few grains cayenne
Correct the seasoning
and add:
¼ cup chopped ice
Or, you may omit the onion and use:
(¼ teaspoon dry ginger)
(⅛ teaspoon allspice)
Shake well.

QUICK CLAM AND CHICKEN BROTH

Combine equal parts of:

Clam broth
Chicken stock

If the clam broth is very salty, you may have to use more chicken stock or water. You may use both clam and chicken stock canned or one fresh and the other canned. Season lightly with:

White pepper

When the soup reaches a boil, remove from heat and place in hot cups. Add to each cup:

1 tablespoon heavy cream or top it with 1 tablespoon whipped cream

Have the cream at room temperature. Sprinkle the top, for color, with:

Paprika or chopped chives or parsley

Serve at once.

QUICK CRAB OR LOBSTER MONGOLE

[About 4 Cups]

Sprinkle:

3 tablespoons dry white wine or 1 teaspoon Worcestershire sauce

over:

1 cup flaked canned crab or lobster

Combine and heat to the boiling point:

1 can condensed cream of tomato soup
1 can condensed cream of green pea soup

Stir in slowly:

1¼ cups rich hot milk or part cream and part bouillon

Add the crab. Heat the soup ➧ but do not let it boil.

QUICK LOBSTER SUPREME

[About 5 Cups]

Combine:

1 can condensed asparagus soup
1 can condensed mushroom soup

Add:

2 cups light cream

Pick over and add:

6 to 8 oz. canned lobster meat

Heat this soup but do not let it boil. Add:

3 tablespoons dry sherry

QUICK LOBSTER CHOWDER

[About 6 Cups]

An easy-to-get soup meal.

Sauté in a saucepan for about 5 minutes:

¼ cup finely diced onion
½ cup finely diced celery

in:

2 tablespoons butter

Add:

1½ cups water
1 small bay leaf
1 package frozen mixed vegetables, defrosted

➧ Cover and bring to a boil. Cook the vegetables until they are barely tender, about 5 to 10 minutes. Remove the bay leaf. Drain, but reserve the liquor from:

1 can chopped broiled mushrooms: 3 oz.

Stir into the liquor until smooth:

1 tablespoon cornstarch

Add this to the mixture in the saucepan, stirring constantly until it thickens. Add the drained mushrooms and:

1 cup tomato sauce
2 cups milk
1 cup canned rock lobster

Correct the seasoning

and heat slowly ➧ but do not boil. Serve with an assortment of:

Cheese

or, as they do in France, with:

Crusty bread and sweet butter

QUICK SEAFOOD TUREEN

[About 6 Cups]

Melt in a saucepan:

¼ cup butter

Add:

2 cups flounder fillets, cut in pieces
1½ cups dry white wine

➧ Cover and simmer about 10 minutes. Add:

1 cup cooked shrimp
1 cup cooked lobster meat
1 small can sliced mushrooms
1½ cups condensed cream of mushroom soup
2 tablespoons chopped pimientos
1 clove crushed garlic
⅛ teaspoon saffron

Simmer about 5 minutes longer. Add:

(½ cup dry sherry)
Correct the seasoning

and serve in a tureen with:

Buttered toast or French bread

ABOUT GARNISHES FOR SOUP

Changing from marrow balls to a chiffonade of cress in the same clear soup can change the temper of a meal. Scan the parade of breads and garnishes below to determine your pace-setter du jour. If serving an informal buffet, arrange a group of garnishes around a tureen to give your guests a choice between rich, green or lean. Whip up some satisfying dumplings for hungry children or pass a rice ring, flavored with nutmeg. Tempt a finicky appetite with an egg drop. ➧ Be sure none of the garnishes is chilled, unless the soup is an iced one.

FOR CLEAR SOUPS

Drop into the soup:

Thin slices of lemon or orange
Minced parsley, chives, watercress, onion, mint, basil, chervil. For some classic flavor combinations, see Seasonings (II, 216)
Podded peas
Cucumber balls
Croutons, see many varieties, page 151 and 390
Vegetables Brunoise, page 109
Noodles, page 149
Gnocchi, page 156
Won Ton, page 112
Dumplings, page 146
Marrow balls, page 150
Quenelles, page 180
Thin slices of lemon-drenched avocado
Thin slices of cooked root: parsley, chervil or celeriac
Small choux paste puffs (II, 305), farci or plain
Spaetzle, page 179

FOR CREAM SOUPS

Garnish with:

Salted whipped cream or sour cream and a dusting of mixed, finely chopped herbs
Toasted cubed stuffing
Chiffonade
Blanched, shredded, toasted almonds or cashews
Flavored popcorn or puffed cereals

FOR THICK SOUPS

Use:

Thin slices of orange, lemon or lime
Sliced small sausages or thin slices of hard sausages
Sliced hard-cooked eggs
Croutons, page 151
Sour cream
Julienne strips of ham, tongue, chicken or bits of sea food
Grated cheeses or Pesto, (II, 218)

And see Thickenings for Soups, page 108.

BREADS TO SERVE WITH SOUPS

Fancy shapes in toasted white, rye or wholewheat
Melba toast
Toasted rye sticks
Plain or toasted garlic bread or other herbed breads
Crackers, hot and plain or spread with herb butters, cheese spreads or fish pastes
Cheese crackers and straws
Pastry Snails (II, 55)
Hush Puppies (II, 279)
Corn Dodgers (II, 278) or Zephyrs (II, 278)
Croutons, page 151

ABOUT EGG-GARNISHED SOUPS

If your travels have led you to the Mediterranean or China, you probably know the trick of turning a cup of broth into a bracing midmorning pickup or a light nourishing lunch. Our friend Cecily Brownstone gave us these infallible directions.

I. [2]

Heat in a quart pan, until boiling vigorously:

2 cups chicken broth or beef stock

Reduce the heat, so the broth ➧ simmers. This means that the bubbles form slowly and collapse below the surface of the liquid. Break into a cup:

1 egg, which has reached 75°

➧ Beat it with a fork, just long enough to combine yolk and white. When the egg is lifted high, it should run off the tines of the fork in a watery stream. Now, with the broth ➧ simmering, hold the cup with one hand, 5 inches above the rim of the saucepan. Pour a little of the beaten egg slowly in a fine stream into the broth. With a fork in the other hand, describe wide circles on the surface of the broth to catch the egg as it strikes and draw it out into long filmy threads. Rather than pour the egg in one fell swoop, break its fall 3 or 4 times, so as not to disturb the simmering broth. If you have a helper, he can pour the egg through a strainer instead of from a cup. Simmer for about 1 minute.

Add to taste:

Salt
(A squeeze of lemon)

Serve at once in hot cups.

II. [6]

For a quick way to make a Mediterranean egg drop that does not "flower" so profusely, heat to a rolling boil:

3 cups chicken broth
¾ cup cooked rice or fine noodles

Beat in a large bowl, just long enough to combine and be uniform in color:

2 eggs
2 tablespoons lemon juice or wine

From on high ➧ gradually, so as not to curdle the eggs but to allow them to shred, pour the hot soup over them, stirring constantly. Serve at once in hot cups.

III. [8]
A still stauncher mix is made in Germany and is called **Baumwollsuppe.**
➧ Simmer:

4 cups strong brown stock

Mix together:

2 eggs
1 tablespoon flour
¼ cup cream
(1 tablespoon butter)
(Pinch of nutmeg)

Mix and cook as described in **I.** Serve in hot cups.

IV. [4]
In Italy a ragged fluffy drop is made by beating until well combined:

1 egg
1½ teaspoons grated Parmesan cheese
1 tablespoon grated dry bread crumbs
(½ clove pressed garlic)

Stir this mixture rapidly into:

3 cups ➧ simmering consommé

Continue to simmer and stir until egg is set. Serve at once.

SOUP CUSTARD OR ROYALE

Preheat Oven to 325°.
These tender drops are used in clear soups. Bake them as for Cup Custard (II, 437). They may be poured initially to ½-inch thickness into a well-buttered 9-inch pie pan. Because of their fragile consistency, they must always be ➧ well cooled in a mold before handling. Any slight crusting may be trimmed. Beat well:

½ cup milk or stock
⅛ teaspoon each salt; paprika, and nutmeg
1 egg
(1 egg yolk)

Bake about 25 minutes, then ➧ cool, before cutting into dice or fancy shapes. Simmer the soup and drop the royales into it, just long enough to heat them through. Serve at once, allowing 3 or 4 small drops to each cup of broth.

HARD-COOKED EGG DROPS

Crush with a fork:

2 hard-cooked egg yolks

Add to them and blend well:

1 tablespoon soft butter
1 raw egg yolk
A few grains of cayenne
A light grating of nutmeg
⅛ teaspoon salt

Form these ingredients into ½-inch balls. Roll them in:

Flour

Cook the drops in ➧ simmering consommé for about 1 minute.

ABOUT DUMPLINGS

The secret of making light dumplings is to keep them steaming on top of ➧ simmering liquid. And be sure the temperature of the stock, gravy or water in which you are cooking them never goes higher than a simmer. Most dumplings are bound together by egg, and the protein in the egg must not be allowed to toughen. ➧ Use ample liquid in a wide-topped cooking vessel, giving each ball or drop a chance to expand. ➧ Never crowd the pan. The minute the batter is floating in the liquid ➧ cover the pot, so the steam can begin functioning. ➧ Do not lift the lid until the dumpling is done. This is not as hard to do as it sounds if you cover the pan with a tight-fitting heat-resistant glass pie pan or lid, so you can watch the swelling of the batter. When the dumplings look fluffy ➧ test them for doneness, as you would a cake, by inserting a toothpick. If it comes out clean, the dumplings are done. Once you are expert at timing, try simmering dumplings in a ⊗ pressure pan. Proceed to cook as above, but instead of the glass cover use the pressure pan lid. ➧ Keep the vent off the entire time. Some good additions to dumpling dough are parsley or other herbs, cheese or grated onion. We have given ➧ dumpling amounts in cups, for some people like large dumplings, others small. A cup of dough will usually yield about eighteen to twenty 1-inch balls, but marrow, liver and meat balls do not expand as do those high in cereal and egg. ➧ For other dumplings more suitable for luncheon dishes or as an accompaniment to meat dishes, see pages 178–180.

SOUP OR STEW NOCKERLN

[About 1 Cup]

Beat until creamy:

¼ cup soft butter
1 egg

Stir in:

1 cup all-purpose flour
⅛ teaspoon salt

Add gradually, until a firm batter is formed, about:

6 tablespoons milk

Cut out the batter with a teaspoon to form small balls. Drop them into boiling water or directly into the clear soup in which they will be served. Reduce the liquid to a ➧ simmer and continue to simmer, covered, for about 10 minutes. For a stew, cook nockerln in water, drain, and drop them into the meat mixture just before serving.

MATZO OR CRACKER MEAL DUMPLINGS

[About 2 Cups]

These light Passover soup drops are made with the finely crushed crumbs of special unleavened crackers.

Beat until thick and well blended:

2 egg yolks
3 tablespoons soft chicken fat

Pour over them and beat well:

½ cup hot stock

Stir in gently a mixture of:

¾ cup matzo meal or cracker meal
½ teaspoon salt
(⅛ teaspoon ginger)
(⅛ teaspoon nutmeg)
(1 tablespoon finely chopped parsley)
(1 tablespoon finely grated onion)

Beat until ➧ stiff, but not dry:

2 egg whites

Fold the egg whites into the cracker mixture and chill, covered, for ½ to 1 hour. About ½ hour before you are ready to serve, form this dough lightly into small balls. If you wet your hands with cold water, the job will be easier. Drop them into:

6 cups boiling stock

Reduce heat at once to a ➧ simmer and cook, covered, for about 15 minutes.

FARINA BALLS COCKAIGNE

[About 3 Cups]

Serve these stout but light

dumplings with a soup-and-salad meal.
Have ready at about 75°:
2 eggs
Heat to the boiling point:
2 cups milk
Add, stir and cook until thick:
½ cup farina
1 tablespoon butter
½ teaspoon salt
⅛ teaspoon paprika
(⅛ teaspoon nutmeg)
Remove the batter from the heat and beat in the eggs vigorously ➧ one at a time. The heat of the mixture will thicken the eggs. Drop the batter, a generous teaspoon at a time, into ➧ simmering soup stock. Cook, covered, for about 2 minutes and serve.

LIVER DUMPLINGS OR LEBERKLOESSE

[About 3 Cups]
Being the descendants of South Germans, we cannot well compile a cookbook without including a recipe that is typical of that neck of the woods—not exactly a handsome dish, but it has qualities.
Skin and remove the fiber from:
1 lb. calf liver or chicken livers
Grind or chop until very fine. Slightly frozen liver is easy to grind. Soak in water for 3 minutes, then wring the water from:
2 slices white bread: 1 cup
Beat, then stir into liver and bread:
2 egg yolks
¼ cup soft butter
2 teaspoons chopped onion
2 tablespoons chopped parsley
1½ teaspoons salt
½ teaspoon pepper
2 tablespoons flour
Beat until stiff:
2 egg whites
Fold them into the other ingredients. Shape this mixture into 1½-inch balls. Drop them into gently boiling:
Soup Stock (II, 141)
Cook them for 5 or 6 minutes. Serve them with the soup; or drop them into boiling water, drain them and serve with:
Sautéed Onions, page 302

CHOUX PASTE GARNISH

[About 1½ Cups]
You may add:
(4 to 6 tablespoons grated Parmesan cheese)
to the dough, for either of these garnishes.

I. Use a pastry bag with a ¼-inch-diameter tube. Fill with:
Unsweetened or cheese-flavored Choux Paste (II, 306)
Squeeze onto a greased baking tin pea-sized bits of dough. Bake in a preheated 400° oven for about 10 minutes. Add these to the soup the instant before serving.

II. Fill a pastry bag with:
Unsweetened Choux Paste (II, 306)
Make 1-inch rounds. Flatten carefully with a moistened finger any points remaining after the bag is lifted off. Glaze with:
French Egg Wash (II, 433)
Bake in a preheated 400° oven for about 10 minutes. Be sure the puffs are well dried out before removing them from the oven. ➧ Fill them, the last minute before serving, with a farce that combines well with the soup. ➧ Place in soup the instant before serving to avoid sogginess.

FRITTER GARNISH

[About ¾ Cup]
Preheat Deep Fryer to 360°
Beat until light:
1 egg

Add:

- ¼ teaspoon salt
- ⅛ teaspoon paprika
- ½ cup flour
- 2 tablespoons milk

When the fat is ready, page 177, allow the batter to drop into it through a colander. Fry until the garnish is brown. Drain on paper. Place in the soup just before serving.

MEAT PASTRIES FOR SOUPS

Some pastry wrapped meats are used in soup itself, others as accompaniments, but with all of them the aim is the same—to make a covering of dough which is tender, yet strong enough to hold the filling. Chinese Won Ton, page 112, are frequently served in soup. They are very much like ravioli and can also be served with a sauce as an entrée or sautéed in butter and coated with cheese. If made in small sizes, they also make interesting cocktail snacks. Other soup accompaniments of this type are rissoles, turnovers or Piroshki, page 210.

BUTTER DUMPLINGS OR BUTTERKLOESSE

[About ¾ Cup]

Beat until soft:

- 2 tablespoons butter

Beat and add:

- 2 eggs

Stir in:

- 6 tablespoons flour
- ¼ teaspoon salt

Drop the batter from a spoon into ➧ simmering soup and simmer the dumplings, covered, for about 8 minutes. You may also simmer them in the soup for about 4 minutes in a ✪ pressure cooker on which you keep the vent open the entire time.

WHITE OR GREEN NOODLE DOUGH OR FETTUCCINI

[About ½ Lb. Dry or 4 Cups Cooked Noodles]

➧ If you are a beginner, do not try to make noodles in damp weather.

I. On a large pastry board or marble table top make a well (II, 52) of:

- ⅔ cup all-purpose flour

Drop into it:

- 1 egg

barely combined with:

- 1 tablespoon water
- ½ teaspoon salt
- 1 teaspoon oil

Work the mixture with your hands, folding the flour over the egg until the dough can be rolled in a ball and comes clean from the hands. If you want to make green noodles, at this point, add:

- (2 to 4 tablespoons very well pressed and dried, finely chopped cooked spinach)

Knead the dough as for bread (II, 240), about 10 minutes. Then let it stand, covered, for about 1 hour. Now roll the dough, pulling it as you wrap it around the rolling pin, stretching it a little more each time. Continue to sprinkle it

with flour between each rolling and stretching to keep the dough from sticking to the pin or board or developing holes. Repeat this procedure about 10 times or until the dough is paper-thin and translucent. Let it dry for about 30 minutes. You can hang it as the Neapolitans do—like laundry on a line—over a piece of foil or plastic. Before it is brittle, roll it up like a scroll and cut it on the bias into strips of any width you prefer: ⅛ inch for soup or 1 inch for lasagna. Allow about 3 tablespoons uncooked noodles for each quart of soup. Cook the noodles in ➧ rapidly boiling salted water for about 10 minutes. Drain and quickly add them to the soup. If stored for future use, keep them, dry and uncooked, in a closed jar.

II. In making casing for Won Ton, Ravioli, etc., proceed as for above, but ➧ do not allow the dough to dry before cutting. Cut into 3-inch squares, fill and use at once.

SPATZEN FOR SOUP

[About 1½ Cups]

Prepare:

Spatzen or Spaetzle, page 179

making these delicious dumplings in a smaller size. Drop the batter as directed into ➧ simmering soup, instead of water.

MEAT BALLS FOR SOUP

A superb main dish may be had by adding these to vegetable soup. Make up ½ the recipe for:

German Meat Balls, page 518

You may use more bread, if desired. Mix the ingredients lightly with a fork. Shape them without pressure into 1-inch balls and drop into boiling soup or stock. ➧ Simmer them until done for about 10 minutes.

QUENELLES FOR SOUP

Prepare:

Quenelles, page 180

As with all protein-based foods, these delicately poached drops should be added to ➧ simmering soup and cooked only until they are heated through thoroughly.

MARROW BALLS

[About ¾ Cup]

These delicate drops may be prepared several hours in advance and refrigerated.

Combine and beat until creamy:

¼ cup fresh marrow
2 tablespoons butter

Add:

3 egg yolks
¼ teaspoon salt
⅛ teaspoon paprika
2 tablespoons chopped parsley
Cracker crumbs

Use just enough cracker crumbs, at least ½ cup, to make the mixture of the right consistency to shape into balls. Now, fold in:

3 stiffly beaten egg whites

Cook the balls in ➧ simmering soup for about 15 minutes or until they rise to the surface.

LIVER SAUSAGE DUMPLINGS

[About 1 Cup]

Combine and work with a fork:

¼ lb. liver sausage
½ egg or 1 egg white or yolk
½ cup cracker crumbs
1 tablespoon chopped parsley or chives
(1 tablespoon catsup)

Shape the mixture into 1-inch balls. ➧ Simmer gently for about 2 minutes in soup stock.

SAUSAGE BALLS FOR SOUP

[About 1½ Cups]
Good in pea, bean or lentil soup.
Combine:

½ lb. raw sausage meat
1 egg white
2 teaspoons chopped parsley
½ teaspoon fresh basil
¼ teaspoon fresh rosemary
3 tablespoons toasted bread crumbs

Roll this mixture into 1-inch balls. Drop them into boiling stock. Reduce the heat at once and ▶ simmer the soup until the balls are done, for about 30 minutes.

CHEESE BALLS FOR SOUP

[About 1½ Cups]
Combine:

2 beaten egg yolks
2 tablespoons grated cheese: preferably Parmesan
2 tablespoons dry bread crumbs
⅛ teaspoon paprika
½ teaspoon dried herbs, fresh chives or parsley

Beat until stiff ▶ but not dry, then fold in:

2 egg whites
⅛ teaspoon salt

Drop the batter from a spoon into ▶ simmering soup. Simmer for only 1 or 2 minutes.

CHIFFONADE OF HERBS FOR SOUPS

To prepare a chiffonade, always use the freshest and most tender of greens ▶ being sure to remove stems and coarse mid ribs —lettuce, sorrel or parsley, alone or in combination with whatever fresh herbs you have on hand that are compatible with the flavor of your soup. Allow:

1 or 2 tablespoons fresh herbs or greens

to:

1 pint broth

Add the herbs to a small quantity of broth and chop in a ⅄ blender until fine. Combine the blended herbs with the remaining broth. If you have no blender, mince a combination of herbs very, very fine.

ABOUT FANCY BREADS AND CRACKERS FOR SOUP

We suggest in the following recipes a number of quick fancy breads, wafers and crackers, but ask that you consider also Bread Sticks and toasted Cheese Bread (II, 244), and look at things to do with Ready Baked Bread (II, 288).

* PUFFED BREAD BLOCKS

[About Thirty 1½-Inch Blocks]
These may be prepared in advance. Keep at room temperature until soft, then blend well:

½ lb. cheddar cheese
¼ lb. butter: 1 stick

Season palatably with:

Mustard
Curry powder
Caraway or celery seed
Salt and pepper or paprika

Cut bread into 1½ x ¾ x ¾-inch blocks. Cover them with the cheese spread. Keep them chilled until ready for use. Pop them into a 375° oven. They should brown lightly and puff.

SOUP CROUTONS

For other Croutons, see page 390.
To retain the crispness of these ever-popular diced toasts, serve them in individual dishes and let the guests add them to the soup as they are ready for them. Or,

use them diced small, so they are much like buttered toasted crumbs to garnish spinach, noodles or game. They may be flavored by sautéing in:

Butter and olive oil

or dusting them with:

Grated cheese

while still hot.

CHEESE OR BUTTER BREAD CUBES

Preheat Oven to 375°.

I. Beat together:

- **1 egg**
- **1½ tablespoons melted butter**

Cut into cubes or blocks of any size:

Fresh bread

Roll the cubes in the egg mixture, then in:

Finely grated American cheese
Salt and cayenne or paprika

Toast the cubes on a buttered sheet until the cheese is melted. Serve them hot as appetizers. Good with soup or salads.

II. Spread bread cubes with a paste made of:

Butter
Grated Parmesan cheese
Caraway or celery seed
Salt and a few grains cayenne
(Mustard)

Toast and serve, as above.

SEEDED CRACKERS

Brush:

Small crisp salt crackers

with:

Melted butter or partially beaten egg white

Sprinkle lightly with:

Caraway, celery or sesame seeds

Toast and serve.

REFRIGERATOR CHEESE WAFERS OR STRAWS

These keep for weeks in a refrigerator or freezer and are quickly sliced and baked for the unexpected guest. Or just after mixing put the dough in a pastry tube to make straws. Or use the 1½-inch ribbon disk on a cookie press to make ribbons. Cut into 2 inch lengths.

I. [4 Dozen]
Preheat oven to 475°.
Grate or grind:

- **½ lb. aged cheddar cheese**

Combine with:

- **3 tablespoons soft butter**
- **¾ cup all-purpose flour**
- **(1 teaspoon Worcestershire sauce)**
- **½ teaspoon salt**
- **Dash of hot pepper sauce**

Form the dough into 1-inch rolls. Wrap in foil and refrigerate or freeze till cold enough to slice as thin as possible, under a quarter of an inch. Bake for about 10 minutes.

II.
Preheat oven to 475°.
Cream:

- **¼ cup butter**

and mix it well with:

- **¾ cup all-purpose flour**
- **¼ lb. grated aged cheddar cheese**
- **⅛ teaspoon salt**
- **A dash of white pepper**

Shape and bake as above.

MELBA CHEESE ROUNDS

Spread:

Melba rounds

lightly with:

Butter

Sprinkle generously with:

Parmesan cheese

Just before using, run them under a broiler until toasted. Serve at once, floating one or two on:

Onion or other soup

CEREALS AND PASTAS

ABOUT CEREALS

On a train trip from Palermo to Syracuse, a stranger leaned toward us to say in the most casual tone that this was the field where Pluto abducted Persephone and rushed her to his dark abode. This brought to mind the lamentations of her mother Ceres and a speculation as to how much greater those lamentations would have been had she known what today's processing was to do to the grains that bear her name. Until a century ago the entire kernel, including the germ, could be ground between cool millstones without risking rancidity. Today, the heat of steel grinding necessitates removal of the germ.

In spite of the incomplete protein makeup of cereals, they form almost a fourth of the average diet. So let's look at their values more closely. Especially, note that grain mixtures—when served with milk, cheese, egg or even small quantities of meat and fish—have a greatly increased nutritive protein content. If you buy ready-to-eat cereals, the grains have been highly processed. They are either exploded into puffs, under high steam, or malted, sugared and shattered into flakes under rollers; or mixed into pastes and formed. You pay as much for the processing, and the expensive packaging to keep these cereals crisp, as you pay for the cereal itself. You may have to give more time to the proper cooking of whole-grains but there is no question of nutritive and monetary savings. For further details about Whole-Grains, see About Flours (II, 152).

Partially precooked cereals in which the heat has been great enough to destroy the enzymes —which cause rancidity—keep better than raw cereals. They should be finish-cooked according to the directions on the label. ➧ All cereals should be stored covered against insect infestation and moisture absorption. Raw cereals will further profit by storage in a cool place, as even mild heat induces more rapid development of rancidity.

ABOUT COOKING CEREALS

Scientists tell us that cereals are edible as soon as the starch granules swell to their fullest capacity in hot liquid. This state they speak of glibly as gelatinization, although it remains something of a chemical mystery. To cooks, this phenomenon is evident in the thickening of cereals and sauces. While the technical-minded insist that the starch and protein in cereals are adequately cooked in a short period of time, many cooks claim that the results are not so nutty and sweet as when the older, slow-heat methods are used. Whether you back the cook or the scientist, on these points they agree: cereals must be added ➧ slowly to ➧ very rapidly boiling water and ➧ stirred in, so that each individual grain is surrounded and quickly penetrated by the hot liquid.

The boiling point of the water ➧ 212°, must be maintained throughout as the cereal is added.

With cereals that tend to gumminess, this slow addition to the boiling water allows the outer starch layers to stabilize and keeps the grains separated after swelling. Coarsely ground cereals may be added dry. Granular fine cereals may be moistened with part of the measured cold water to form a loose mush and may be poured so slowly into the boiling water that they do not disturb the boiling point. They are then cooked 2 to 3 minutes over direct heat and 5 to 20 minutes more in a double boiler. If you want to cook any of these cereals longer, start out as directed above and, if necessary, add more milk or water during the cooking period. If you cook cereals or starches in an acid liquid like fruit juices with sugar, the thickening power is lowered.

The cereal is done when it looks translucent. The grains should still be separated, retaining their individual shape even though they are soft. Serve at once.

Cereals increase in bulk depending on the amount of water they absorb. You may count 4 to 6 servings for each cup of uncooked cereal. If you cook cereal in advance of serving ➧ cover it at once while it is still hot from the first cooking—so no crust forms on the top. If you plan to use it more than an hour after the first cooking, refrigerate it. ➧ To avoid lumps on reheating, place the cereal over hot water and allow the cereal to become hot all the way through before stirring.

To make a gruel for the baby, cook the cereal with 3 times the called for amount of water or milk and cook twice as long. Strain and serve.

FINELY MILLED CEREALS

[About 4 to 6 Servings]

➧ Please read About Cooking Cereals, page 153. To prepare the fine granular cereals listed below, have water heated in the bottom of a double boiler. In the top of the boiler, over direct heat, bring to a rolling boil, 212°:

4 to 6 cups water or milk
1 teaspoon salt

Very slowly ➧ without disturbing the boiling point, dribble into the water:

1 cup dry corn meal, farina or hominy grits

Continue to cook over direct heat for 2 to 3 minutes, then cook covered over, not in, hot water 5 to 20 minutes. To avoid gumminess ➧ do not stir. If you do not serve at once see About Cooking Cereals, opposite, for reheating or storing. During the last few minutes of cooking, you may fold in lightly:

3 tablespoons dry skim-milk solids
2 teaspoons debittered yeast powder

for each cup dry cereal. These ingredients make no noticeable change in taste and are a great addition in food value. You may at that time also add:

Dates, figs, raisins and cooked dried fruits

Or serve with:

Cold or hot sliced canned or fresh fruits
A cinnamon-sugar mixture
Sugar and cream
Maple sirup
Jams and preserves

COARSELY MILLED CEREALS

[About 4 to 6 Servings]

These coarsely ground or cracked

grains have many different names, but all are cooked the same way. The wheats, whole-grain and cracked, also include bulghur—a parched cracked wheat—and couscous. Groats may be cracked wheat, buckwheat or oats. Coarsely ground buckwheat barley or millet is also called kasha. Cracked corn is called samp. Coarse oats come in a number of forms, steel cut or rolled. Prepare any of these as for the finely milled cereals above. Because they are coarser in grind, you need to use in all:

2 to 4 cups water, milk or fruit juice
1 teaspoon salt

for every:

1 cup dry cereal

Cook about one hour as directed above.

ABOUT WHOLE CEREALS

Whole cereals like rice or barley may be cooked on two principles —the one described above for coarsely ground cereals or by the so-called fried method, in which the cereal is sautéed in oil or clarified butter before the liquid is added. For a detailed description of this method, see Risotto, page 166. For other ways to cook rice, see page 158, and the Index.

ABOUT HOMINY

Hominy is corn with the hull and germ removed. In an attempt to give it calcium values, it is sometimes also soaked in wood ash lye. It has recently gained favor as an antistrontium absorbent. Hominy grits are the broken grains.

HOMINY

I. [Yield 1 Quart]
Shell and wash:

1 quart of dried corn

Put it in an enamel or stainless steel pan. Cover with:

2 quarts water

Add:

2 tablespoons baking soda

Cover the pan and let this mixture set 12 hours. Then bring it to a boil in the liquid in which it has soaked. Simmer about 3 hours or until the hulls loosen. If necessary, add water. Drain. Rub corn until hulls are removed. Bring to a boil in:

2 quarts cold water

Drain. Repeat this boiling process again in fresh water, adding:

1 teaspoon salt

Drain once more and serve. Season with:

Melted butter

II. [6]
Preheat oven to 400°.
Combine and place in a greased baking dish:

2 cups drained, cooked hominy, above
1 cup Cheese Sauce, page 364
½ cup minced green pepper

Cover the top with:

Strips of bacon

Bake the dish for about 20 minutes.

HOMINY CAKES [5]

These cakes are a variation on potatoes.
Drain:

2½ cups cooked or canned hominy

Combine it with:

2 tablespoons flour
1 egg
Salt and pepper

Form these ingredients into flat cakes.
Sauté them until they are brown in:

Butter or drippings

Serve them hot—plain or with:

Honey or sirup

SCALLOPED HOMINY AND HAM [4]

Preheat oven to 375°.
Combine:

- ½ cup water
- 1 can condensed tomato soup or 2 cups Cream Sauce I, page 359

Add:

- 1 cup diced cooked ham
- ½ teaspoon salt
- ½ teaspoon sugar
- ⅛ teaspoon paprika or pepper

Drain and add:

- 2½ cups cooked or canned hominy

Heat these ingredients. Combine:

- 1 cup soft bread crumbs
- 1 cup grated cheese
- ⅛ teaspoon paprika
- ¼ teaspoon salt

Place ½ the hominy mixture in a greased baking dish, cover it with ½ the bread mixture. Dot the top with:

- 1 tablespoon butter

Repeat the process. Bake the dish until the top is brown, about 12 minutes.

CORN MEAL MUSH [4]

Combine and stir:

- 1 cup water-ground corn meal
- 1 cup cold water
- 1 teaspoon salt

Place in the top of a double boiler:

- 4 cups boiling water

Stir corn meal mixture in gradually. Cook and stir the mush over quick heat from 2 to 3 minutes. Steam it, covered, over, not in, hot water about 15 minutes. Stir it frequently. Serve with:

- Maple sirup, honey or molasses

POLENTA

Just as our greatest architectural surprise in Italy was to find St. Francis' first church a log cabin, so were we amazed to discover that the Italians do even more delicious and interesting things with corn meal than you can find in the deep South.
Cheese is sometimes cooked with it, and sometimes it is served sprinkled over it. Tomato sauce, meat or a combination of both is another favorite accompaniment.

I. Prepare:

- Corn Meal Mush, opposite

Add to it for the last 15 minutes of cooking:

- ⅛ teaspoon paprika
- A few grains red pepper
- (½ cup grated cheese)

II. Prepare as above and sauté it in:

- Olive oil or butter

BUCKWHEAT GROATS OR KASHA [4]

I.
Preheat oven to 350°.
Have ready:

- 1 cup kasha

Brown it in hot skillet with:

- 2 tablespoons hot chicken fat or butter

Stir with fork until each grain is coated. Add:

- 3½ cups boiling water

Cover and cook for about 15 minutes, then transfer to greased casserole and bake for about one hour.

II. As a luncheon dish, add:

- Sautéed onions
- Salt and pepper
- Some almonds

and proceed as above.

GNOCCHI WITH FLOUR [4]

Serve as a separate course in place of potatoes or as a soup garnish.

Scald:

1 cup milk

Melt in a skillet:

2 tablespoons butter

Stir and blend in until smooth:

2 tablespoons flour
2 tablespoons cornstarch
½ teaspoon salt

Stir in the scalded milk. Reduce the heat and add:

1 egg yolk
(½ cup grated cheese)

Beat the batter until the egg has thickened and the cheese has melted. Pour it onto a shallow greased platter or pan.

Preheat oven to 375°.

When the batter is cool, cut it into strips 2 inches long. Place the strips in a pan and pour over them:

Melted butter

Sprinkle them with:

(Grated cheese)

Heat them in the oven. We prefer poaching the batter after it has been cut into strips. Poach in gently boiling water or stock for 1 or 2 minutes. Drain the strips and serve them with melted butter.

GNOCCHI WITH FARINA [4]

Scald:

2 cups milk

Stir in, all at once:

¾ cup farina

Stir the mush over low heat until thick. Remove from heat and beat in until smooth:

1 tablespoon butter
1 egg yolk
¼ teaspoon salt

You may spread the mixture evenly in an 8 x 8-inch pan lined with foil to make handling easier. Chill for about 3 hours.

Preheat oven to 425°.

Cut the farina mixture into 1½-inch squares. Place the squares in a well-greased ovenproof dish, letting them overlap slightly. Dot with:

2 tablespoons butter

Pour over them slowly:

1 cup Hunter's Sauce, page 366 or Aurore Sauce, page 362

Sprinkle the top with:

6 tablespoons grated Parmesan cheese

Bake for about 10 minutes.

GNOCCHI WITH POTATOES [6]

➧ The potatoes must be freshly cooked and used at once. Boil, then put through a ricer:

2 medium-sized potatoes

Heat to the boiling point:

½ cup milk
5 tablespoons butter

Stir in, until the dough forms a ball:

1 cup flour

Remove from heat. Beat in:

2 eggs
1 teaspoon salt

¼ teaspoon paprika
(3 tablespoons grated cheese)

and the potatoes. Sprinkle the dough with flour. Roll it into sticks ½ inch thick. Cut it into 1-inch lengths. Drop the gnocchi into simmering salted water. Or force the gnocchi dough through a pastry bag. Cut into desired lengths as shown above before letting the gnocchi fall into the water. Simmer uncovered for 3 to 5 minutes. Drain. Place them on a greased pan in a hot oven for about 3 minutes. The baking is optional. Serve the gnocchi dressed with melted butter and grated cheese.

ABOUT RICE

"May your rice never burn," is the New Year's greeting of the Chinese. "May it never be gummy," is ours. So many people complain to us about the variability of their results in rice cookery. Like flour, it may have more or less moisture in its makeup when you start to use it. In Japan they have a standard ratio, allowing 8 cups of water to 8 cups of rice for the first six weeks after harvest. The amount of water then rises steadily. And when the rice is 11 months old, 8 cups of rice need 10 cups of water.

Not only is there moisture variability in rice, but the type must also be reckoned with. Brown rice, which retains its bran coat and germ, is much slower to tenderize—although more valuable nutritionally—than highly polished white rice.

There are also differences in the grain hybrids. Use short grain types—which cook up tender and moist—in recipes calling for sauces. Long grain types are best for soups, molding or stuffing. Also on the market are preprocessed rices, for which you must follow the directions on the label. Some of these which are parboiled before milling have greater nutritive value than polished white rice. Wild rice is not a true rice. The seed comes from a strictly American plant and needs its own recipes, see page 159.

➧ To keep rice white when cooking in hard water, add 1 teaspoon lemon juice or 1 tablespoon vinegar to the cooking water.

➧ One cup raw rice equals 3½ cups when cooked. If using preprocessed rice, the volume will be less. This is also true for recipes in which rice is browned in a skillet—with or without fat—prior to cooking it with moisture. But this browning helps to keep the granules separate and does contribute to good flavor.

BOILED RICE [6 to 7]

I. Bring to a ➧ rolling boil:

1¾ to 2½ cups water or stock

Add:

¾ teaspoon salt

You may add:

(1 tablespoon melted butter)

to the rice before cooking, to keep it from sticking to the pot. Stir slowly into the water, so as not to disturb the boiling:

1 cup white or brown rice

Cover and cook over slow heat. White rice will take from 20 to 30 minutes, brown from 40 to 50. If the rice becomes too dry, add ¼ cup or more ➧ boiling water. When the grains have swelled to capacity, uncover the pot for about the last 5 minutes of cooking. Continue to cook the rice over ➧ very low heat, shaking the pot from time to time until the grains have separated. Or fluff the cooked rice with a fork.

[3]

II. A moist Oriental-type rice. Wash and drain:

½ cup rice

Place in a deep, heavy kettle with:

1½ cups cold water

Boil for 5 minutes until most of the surface water is gone and air bubbles can be seen on the surface of the rice. ➧ Reduce the heat and continue to cook ➧ uncovered, for about 20 minutes longer. Remove from heat and let the rice stand covered for about 20 minutes more. It is then ready to serve.

BAKED RICE [6 to 7]

Preheat oven to 375°.
Sauté:
½ chopped onion
in:
¼ cup butter
until translucent. Add, and stir until well coated:
1 cup long-grain rice
Add:
2 cups boiling chicken broth or boiling salted water
Cover and bake for about 18 minutes. Gently mix with the rice:
2 tablespoons melted butter
Serve the rice at once.

BAKED GREEN RICE [3]

Outstanding alone or as a stuffing for a veal breast. This amount will fill a 7-inch ring mold.
Preheat oven to 325°.
Beat:
1 egg
Add and mix well:
1 cup milk
½ cup finely chopped parsley
1 finely chopped clove garlic
1 small minced onion
2 cups cooked rice
½ cup sharp grated cheese or 2 tablespoons butter
⅛ teaspoon curry
Salt to taste
Place these ingredients in a baking dish, in which has been poured:
2 tablespoons olive oil
Bake for 30 to 40 minutes.

RICE COOKED IN CHICKEN STOCK [3]

Melt in a saucepan:
2 tablespoons butter
Add and stir until golden brown:
½ chopped onion
Add and shake until the grains are coated:
1 cup rice
Add:
2 cups hot chicken stock
Cover the pot and simmer the rice, or bake it in a 375° oven until the liquid is absorbed.
Add:
2 tablespoons melted butter
Toss the rice with a fork to distribute it.

CURRIED RICE [3]

An unusual and delicious rice dish. Its popularity is undoubtedly due to the restraint with which the spice is used.
Pour:
2 cups hot water
over:
½ cup rice
Place the rice where it will remain hot, but will not cook, for about 45 minutes.
Preheat oven to 350°.
Add to the rice:
½ cup tomatoes
¾ teaspoon salt
¼ cup finely sliced onion
¼ cup sliced green peppers
2 tablespoons melted butter
¾ teaspoon curry powder
Bake these ingredients in a baking dish for 1½ hours or until done. Stir them from time to time. At first, there will be a great preponderance of liquid, but gradually the rice will absorb it. Remove the dish from the oven while the rice is still moist. Good served with beer.

ABOUT WILD RICE

Wild rice is a seed from a grass growing wild in the northern United States and remains a luxury because of the difficulty of harvesting it. For economy, combine cooked wild rice with cooked white or brown rice.
One cup of wild rice equals 3 to 3½ cups of cooked wild rice.
Add 1 teaspoon salt to each cup uncooked rice.

WILD RICE [4]

Wash well in several waters, pouring off the foreign particles from the top:

- 1 cup wild rice

Drain it. Stir it slowly into:

- 4 cups boiling water
- 1 teaspoon salt

Cook it without stirring until tender, for about 40 minutes.

WILD RICE RING [4]

Preheat oven to 350°.
Prepare as above:

- 1 cup wild rice

You may add:

- 1 sliced clove garlic

Cook the rice as above. Add:

- ¼ cup butter
- ½ teaspoon poultry seasoning or freshly grated nutmeg
- (1 cup sautéed onions and mushrooms)
- (¼ cup dry sherry)

Place it in a well-greased 7-inch ring mold. Set the mold in a pan of hot water and bake for about 20 minutes. Loosen the edges with a knife, invert the contents onto a platter and fill the center with:

- Creamed Mushrooms, page 296
- Chicken Livers Lyonnaise, page 534, or Sautéed Onions, page 302

CHINESE FRIED RICE [6]

The rice for this recipe must be ♦ cooked, fluffy and at least one day old. Heat in a heavy skillet:

- ¼ cup cooking oil

Toss in it:

- 3 cups Boiled Rice, page 158

until hot and golden. Add:

- 4 minced scallions
- ¾ teaspoon salt
- (½ cup cooked julienned roast pork or ham or 1 cup cooked diced shrimp)

When these ingredients are well mixed, hollow a center in the rice. Break:

- 3 eggs

into the hollow and scramble until semi-cooked—then stir them into the rice mixture. Sprinkle with:

- 1½ tablespoons soy sauce
- (¼ cup minced Chinese parsley leaves)

and serve with:

- Podded Peas, page 307

CHEESE RICE [6 to 7]

This is a good dish to serve with a cold supper.
Boil, page 158:

- 1 cup rice

When the water is nearly absorbed, add:

- ½ to ¾ cup or more grated cheese
- ¼ teaspoon paprika
- A few grains cayenne

Add:

- 1 can condensed tomato or mushroom soup: 10½ oz.

Stir the rice over low heat until the cheese is melted.

SPANISH RICE [3 to 4]

Sauté until brown:

- 3 slices minced bacon

Remove the bacon. Stir and cook in the drippings until brown:

- ½ cup rice

Add and cook until brown:

- ½ cup thinly sliced onions

Add the bacon and:

- 1¼ cups canned tomatoes
- ½ teaspoon salt
- 1 teaspoon paprika
- 1 seeded and minced green pepper
- (1 clove garlic)

Steam the rice in a double boiler for about 1 hour. Stir it frequently. Add water or stock if the rice becomes too dry. It may be served with:

Cheese Sauce, page 364

RICE LOAF OR CASSEROLE

I. [5]

Boil, page 158:

2/3 cup rice

Line a buttered mold with it. Reserve 1/2 cup for the top. Preheat oven to 375°. Cook:

1 cup Cream Sauce II, page 359

Stir in and thicken over low heat:

1 egg yolk

Add:

1 cup diced canned salmon, cooked fish or meat
1/2 cup bread crumbs
1 tablespoon chopped parsley
1 tablespoon chopped onion
1/2 cup chopped celery
1 teaspoon lemon juice or 1 teaspoon Worcestershire sauce
Salt, paprika, nutmeg

Fill the mold and place the reserved rice over the top. Cover this with a piece of buttered paper. Set the mold in a pan of hot water and bake or steam it until it is set, for about 30 minutes. Invert the loaf onto a platter. Garnish it with:

Sprigs of parsley

Serve it with:

Tomato Sauce, page 376, or Mushroom Sauce, page 367, etc.

II. [6]

Preheat oven to 400°.

The proportions of rice and fish in this dish may be varied. Use about 1/2 as much cream sauce as you do of the other main ingredients combined. Boil, page 158:

2/3 cup rice

There should be about 2 cups cooked rice. Drain:

1 cup tuna fish

Break the tuna into pieces with a fork. Cook:

2 cups Cream Sauce II, page 359

Add:

1/2 teaspoon salt—more if rice is unsalted
1/2 teaspoon paprika
A few grains red pepper

Reduce the heat to low. Stir in until melted:

2 cups grated cheese

Place in a baking dish alternate layers of rice, fish and sauce. Dot the top with:

Au Gratin II, page 389

Bake the dish until the crumbs are brown. If preferred, bake the ingredients in a ring, invert and serve it with the center filled with Sautéed Mushrooms, page 296.

NUT LOAF [4]

Serve with broccoli or any green leafy vegetable.

Preheat oven to 375°.

Melt:

3 tablespoons butter

Sauté in it until soft:

1 minced onion
1 seeded chopped green pepper

Add:

1 cup cooked rice
1/3 cup bread crumbs
1 cup chopped tomatoes
1 cup chopped or ground walnut or other nut meats
1 beaten egg
2 tablespoons chopped parsley
3/4 teaspoon salt
1/4 teaspoon paprika
(1 teaspoon grated lemon peel)

Place these ingredients in a greased baking dish. Bake them for about 30 minutes. Cover the top with:

Mashed potatoes

Dot them generously with:

Butter

Brown them under a broiler.
Serve the loaf with:

Tomato Sauce, page 376

RICE RING OR MOLD

A molded rice ring is a handsome way to enclose your main course. For color, include chopped parsley with the cooked rice, or try some of the following recipes.

I. **[6]**

Preheat oven to 350°.
Boil, page 158:

1 cup rice

Season it with:

½ teaspoon grated nutmeg

Place it in a well-greased 7-inch ring mold. Melt and pour over it:

¼ cup butter

You may add:

(¾ cup blanched, coarsely chopped almonds)

Set the mold in a pan of hot water. Bake the rice for about 20 minutes. Loosen the edges, invert the contents of the mold onto a platter.
Fill the center with:

Creamed Chicken, page 226, Creamed Mushrooms, page 296, or a creamed or buttered vegetable

II. This works fine for any recipe not using egg to bind it. Otherwise use I, above. We have had success packing the hot cooked rice firmly into a well-buttered ring mold. Rest it 3 or 4 minutes and then turn it out onto the serving platter to be filled with the hot entrée.

CHEESE RICE RING [3]

Preheat oven to 350°.
Boil:

½ cup Rice, page 158

Add:

1 beaten egg
2 tablespoons olive oil or melted butter
¼ cup milk
⅓ cup grated cheese
¼ tablespoon grated onion
1 teaspoon Worcestershire sauce
¼ teaspoon salt
3 tablespoons chopped parsley

Grease a 7-inch ring mold. Fill it with the rice mixture. Bake it, set in a pan of hot water, for about 45 minutes.

MUSHROOM RICE RING [6]

No need to bake this mold.
Boil, page 158:

1 cup rice

Grind, chop fine or ⅄ blend:

½ to 1 lb. mushrooms

Sauté them for 2 or 3 minutes in:

2 tablespoons butter

Add:

¼ cup hot stock or water

Combine the mushrooms and rice. Add:

(¾ cup blanched coarsely chopped almonds)
Correct the seasoning

Press the rice firmly in a greased 7-inch ring mold and let stand for 3 or 4 minutes. Invert the rice onto a platter. Fill the center with a buttered vegetable, creamed fish, etc.

RICE AND HAM RING [6]

Preheat oven to 375°.
Combine:

2 cups cooked rice
1 cup diced cooked ham

Combine and beat:

1 egg
⅔ cup condensed mushroom soup
½ cup milk
¼ teaspoon salt
(½ teaspoon dried basil)

Grease a 9-inch ring mold. Place in it layers of rice and ham. Pour the liquid ingredients over them. Sprinkle the top with:

1 cup crushed potato chips or bread crumbs

Bake the ring in 1 inch of hot water, for about ½ hour. Invert it onto a platter. Fill the center with:

A cooked vegetable, carrots and peas, snap beans, etc.

RICE AND ONION CASSEROLE [3 to 4]

Heat in a skillet:

2 tablespoons butter

Sauté in it, until lightly browned:

½ cup uncooked rice
½ cup sliced fresh or canned mushrooms

Stir in:

1 package dried onion soup
1 cup water

Cover and cook over low heat, about 25 minutes, until the rice is tender.

RICE WITH SPINACH AND CHESTNUTS [6 to 8]

Preheat oven to 350°.
Combine:

1 cup cooked rice
1 cup cooked chopped spinach
1 cup cooked chestnuts
½ to 1 cup grated cheese

Cover with:

Au Gratin II, page 389

Bake about 35 minutes or until thoroughly heated. Garnish with:

Sprigs of water cress and ribbons of pimiento

before serving.

BACON AND RICE CUSTARD [4]

Preheat oven to 325°.
Cook until partly done:

8 slices bacon

Use 4 muffin tins. Line each one with 2 slices of bacon. Fill them with the following mixture. Combine:

2 cups cooked rice
1 beaten egg
2 tablespoons cream
1 tablespoon melted butter
1 tablespoon grated onion
1 tablespoon chopped parsley
⅛ teaspoon salt
⅛ teaspoon paprika

Bake the custard until firm, for about ½ hour. Serve with:

Tomato or other sauce

BAKED PINEAPPLE RICE [6]

This good dish may be served with baked ham or fried chicken or as a dessert with cream.
Preheat oven to 350°.
Boil, page 158:

1 cup rice

Drain, then cut into pieces:

3½ cups cubed pineapple

Place in a buttered baking dish ⅓ the rice. Cover with ½ the pineapple. Repeat the layer of rice and pineapple. Place the last ⅓ of the rice on top. Dot each layer with:

1½ tablespoons butter
¼ cup brown sugar

Use in all 5½ tablespoons butter and ¾ cup sugar. Pour over all:

¾ cup pineapple juice

Bake the rice, covered, for about 1 hour.

ROMBAUER RICE DISH [4]

Freely varied each time it is made, but in such demand that we shall try to write a general rule for it.
Prepare:

½ cup Boiled Rice, page 158

Prepare:

Veal stew: 1½ lbs. meat

Pare, slice and add for the last 20 minutes of cooking:

½ parsnip
2 carrots
2 onions
6 sliced ribs celery
3 sprigs parsley

Drain the stew. To make the

gravy, see page 358. There should be about 3 cups of stock. If there is not enough, add chicken bouillon, a bouillon or vegetable cube and water, rice water or sweet or sour cream to make up the difference. If there is not enough fat, add butter. The better the gravy, the better the dish. Combine the rice, meat, vegetable cube and water, rice them. Garnish with:

Parsley

You may add a dash of curry powder and some herbs—thyme, basil, etc. (II, 204). You may use leftover meat, gravy and vegetables. You may serve the stew in a baking dish, au gratin or in individual bakers.

A de luxe dish is this recipe made with rice, chicken, sauce —with cream and chicken gravy —and blanched slivered almonds. An everyday dish is this recipe made with corned beef and some canned soup to substitute for gravy.

VEGETABLE RICE OR JAMBALAYA [4]

Ideal for a picnic supper.

Steam:

2/3 cup rice

Sauté lightly in butter:

3/4 to 1 lb. mushrooms

Chop and add:

2 medium-sized green peppers, seeds and membrane removed
1 medium-sized onion
1 stalk of celery
2 canned pimientos
1 1/4 cups cooked or canned tomatoes

Season these ingredients with:

3/4 teaspoon salt
A few grains cayenne
1/2 teaspoon paprika

Add:

1/4 lb. melted butter

These proportions may be varied.

Preheat oven to 300°.

Combine the rice and other ingredients. Place in a greased baking dish. Bake ◗ covered for about 1 hour. The sautéed mushroom caps and the pimientos may be used to garnish the top of the dish. They are highly decorative with a bunch of parsley in the center.

JAMBALAYA WITH MEAT OR FISH [6 to 8]

Sauté lightly in a saucepan:

2 slices diced bacon

Add and sauté until golden:

1/4 cup chopped onion

Stir in:

1 tablespoon flour

Add:

1 cup tomato pulp
1/3 cup water

Bring these ingredients to the boiling point. Stir in:

3 cups cooked rice
2 cups coarsely diced cooked ham, chicken, sausage, tongue or shrimp, crab, etc., alone or in combination

Season these ingredients with:

1/4 teaspoon thyme
(Worcestershire sauce)
Correct the seasoning

Stir over very low heat for about 10 minutes or heat over boiling water for about 1/2 hour. Serve sprinkled with:

Chopped parsley

CHICKEN JAMBALAYA [4 to 6]

Cut into pieces:

A young chicken

Sauté for about 5 minutes in:

1/4 cup cooking oil or butter

Remove meat from pan. Sauté in the grease, also for about 3 minutes:

1/3 cup minced onion
1/2 cup skinned seeded and chopped tomato

Stir in:

1 diced green pepper, seeds and membrane removed

½ cup diced celery
1 cup rice

When the rice is well coated with grease, stir in the sautéed chicken. Cover these ingredients well with:

Boiling water

Add:

1 bay leaf
¼ teaspoon thyme
¼ cup chopped parsley
1 teaspoon salt
¼ teaspoon pepper

Simmer these ingredients until the chicken is tender and the rice almost done. Add:

½ lb. finely diced cooked ham

Correct the seasoning

Dry out the jambalaya by placing it for about 5 or 10 minutes in a 350° oven.

ITALIAN RICE OR RISOTTO À LA MILANÈSE [8 to 10]

This dish needs fairly constant watching for about 20 minutes and ➧ must be served at once to prevent gumminess. Melt in a heavy pan:

¼ cup Clarified Butter, page 383

Sauté in it, until golden:

1 small minced onion

Add and stir well with a wooden spoon until all the butter is absorbed:

2 cups rice

Have ready:

8 to 10 cups hot beef or chicken stock

After the rice is well coated with the fat, add 1 cup of the stock. Continue to stir, adding about ⅔ of the hot stock over a 10 minute period. Dissolve in a little of the stock:

(A tiny pinch of saffron)

Or add:

(½ teaspoon fennel seed)

Continue to stir and add stock for about 5 to 8 minutes longer, by which time the rice should have absorbed all of the liquid. ➧ Do not let it dry out.

Correct the seasoning

Place the rice in a hot serving dish. Pour over it and mix:

¼ cup melted butter
(Sautéed chicken livers and giblets)

Sprinkle over it:

1 cup grated Parmesan cheese

PAELLA [8]

Preheat oven to 350°.

If you do not own a paellero, the vessel which gives this dish its name, you will need a generous lidded casserole in which to cook and serve it.

Have ready:

2 cups cooked chicken, cut in about 1- to 1½-inch pieces
4 cups hot chicken stock

Heat briefly in the casserole:

¼ cup olive oil
2 cloves garlic

Remove the garlic. Over moderate heat add, stirring until lightly browned:

2 cups rice

Add the hot stock, in which has been dissolved a small quantity of:

Saffron—or up to 2 teaspoons if you are Spanish

Add:

1 cup peas
2 sliced sweet red peppers
(6 artichoke hearts)
8 thin slices chorizo or hard Spanish sausage

Correct the seasoning

Also put in the chicken, arranging it toward the top of the mixture. Cover and bake in a 350° oven for about 15 minutes. Add, arranging them attractively on the top:

8 raw shrimp
16 well-scrubbed clams in their shells

Cover and steam about 10 minutes longer. Serve at once.

PILAF [4]

A rice dish combined with shrimp or chicken livers, etc. It has many variations.

Boil, page 158:

- ⅔ cup long grained rice

Sauté until golden:

- 3 tablespoons chopped onion

in:

- 1 to 2 tablespoons butter

Add to the rice. Simmer until thick:

- 2½ cups tomatoes
- ½ bay leaf
- 3 ribs of celery with leaves
- ⅓ teaspoon salt
- ¼ teaspoon paprika
- ½ teaspoon brown sugar

Strain these ingredients.

Add:

- 1 cup cooked shrimp, lobster meat, crab meat or sautéed or boiled chicken livers

Combine these ingredients with the rice.

Correct the seasoning

Place the rice in a greased baking dish.

Sprinkle with:

- ¼ cup grated cheese and bread crumbs

Run under a heated broiler to brown.

FRUIT, NUT AND RICE CASSEROLE [10]

Cover with water and soak for ½ hour:

- 2 cups dried apricots
- 1 cup white raisins

Boil, page 158:

- 2 cups rice

Preheat oven to 375°.

In a skillet, melt:

- ½ cup butter

Sauté:

- 1 cup minced onion
- ½ cup chopped green pepper
- (½ teaspoon curry powder)

Add:

- (1 cup toasted almonds)

and the drained, chopped apricots and raisins and the cooked rice.

Correct the seasoning

and put into a greased baking dish to bake for about 30 minutes.

RICE TABLE OR RIJSTTAFEL [8]

As this Javanese dish is very filling, it is ideal for suppers. Serve it with ice cold beer, followed by salad. It may be made as elaborate or as simple as you wish. If you object to coconut or if you do not like the flavor of curry, do not discard this dish. Instead, carry out the idea of the rijsttafel by substituting creamed chicken, ragoût fin or a lamb curry you do like, followed by vegetable and condiments served in some attractive way.

Grate:

- A fresh coconut or use about 2 cups canned coconut

Heat but do not scald:

- 4 cups milk or coconut milk

Add the coconut. Permit these ingredients to stand for 2 hours in a cool place. Melt:

- 1 tablespoon butter

Sauté in it, until light brown:

- ½ cup finely chopped onion

Add:

- Chopped gingerroot, a 2-inch length
- 1 chopped clove garlic
- 1½ tablespoons curry powder

Strain and add the coconut. Add to the cooled, strained milk:

- 1 cup milk or Chicken Stock (II, 142)

Mix with 3 tablespoons of the above liquid:

- 1 tablespoon flour
- 1 tablespoon cornstarch

Heat the remaining liquid and

stir the starch paste into it. Cook and stir the sauce until it is hot and thickened.

Correct the seasoning

Place ½ of the sauce in the top of a double boiler. Add the coconut mixture and:

3 cups cooked diced chicken, shrimp, fish, veal, sweetbreads, mushrooms, etc., either alone or in combination

Heat rest of sauce in another double boiler.

Have ready:

2 cups steamed rice, page 158

Have it rather dry and flaky.

The ceremony of serving this dish is part of its charm. In Java one refers to it by the separate dishes, as a "One boy curry" or a "Twenty-two boy curry," each boy representing one dish. Pass the rice first. Spread it generously over your plate, forming a base or "table." Pass the food in the sauce next. Follow this with:

Onion Rings
Sieved hard-cooked eggs
Grated peanuts or toasted almonds
Grated coconut, if there is none in the sauce
Relish
Chutney, raisins, preserved ginger or kumquats
Halved fried bananas
Mixed pickles

Now pass the extra heated sauce.

To simplify matters, the last 4 or 5 dishes may be served from one large condiment dish. Servings from these various dishes are placed upon the rice table. Cut through the layers and proceed to feast.

"LONG RICE" OR HARUSAME

This is not a rice at all, but an oriental pasta made of soy bean powder. It is best described, we feel, as threadlike cellophane noodles, but we infinitely prefer its native name of "Spring Rain." To prepare, pour:

Boiling water

over:

Harusame

Let stand 15 minutes or until it is limp. Cut into desired lengths. Add as a garnish for soup, meat or vegetables. It should then ➧ simmer during the last 15 minutes of the cooking of these foods.

ABOUT SPAGHETTI, MACARONI AND NOODLES

So popular are these hearty fillers that there are over 500 kinds and shapes to choose from. Do we ever graduate from loving the alphabets or sea shells and those large macaronis that can be stuffed? When freshly cooked and tossed in or served with a meat, fish or cheese sauce, pastas need only a salad to make a nutritious, inexpensive and quick meal.

➧ If pastas must be cooked in advance, moisten them with butter, milk, bouillon, tomato juice or a sauce to keep them from drying out. Rarely are any of the pasta types—except Noodles, page 149—made in the home. This is partly because they require unavailable hardwheat flours.

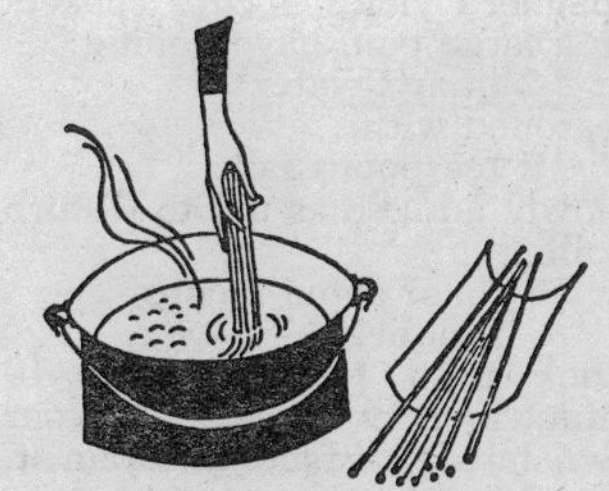

➧ Always use a pot large enough to hold, without boiling over, water 3 times the volume of the pasta to be cooked. For ½ lb. pasta, use not less than 2 qts. water, seasoned with 2 teaspoons salt. Bring water to a ➧ rolling boil. You may put ➧ a tablespoon of fat in the water to help keep the pasta from clumping. It is said this will also deter the water from boiling over, but our experience does not validate this theory. Watch the pot to keep the boil active during the cooking period. The pasta should be ➧ added to the water so gradually that the brisk boiling is not disturbed. To cook long macaroni or spaghetti, hold it as on page 167 and, as it softens, push it into the boiling water.

➧ Do not overcook. Italians usually prefer pasta "al dente," a state in which it still offers some resistance to the teeth. If pastas are freshly made, like homemade noodles, they may require as little as 5 minutes' cooking. If they have been on a shelf a long time, 8 to 10 minutes is long enough for thin types. If thick, they may need all of 15 minutes. Try pastas "al burro," simply tossed in butter with a freshly grated Parmesan cheese topping.

BOILED SPAGHETTI

[4 Cups]

About 2 cups or ½ lb. uncooked spaghetti yields 4 cups cooked. In a large pan, have boiling:

2 quarts water

seasoned with:

2 teaspoons salt

Slowly add, so as not to disturb boiling:

½ lb. or about 2 cups spaghetti

Cook until tender—about 10 minutes more or less—to your own taste satisfaction. Drain it. Keep it hot. Heat a salad or large bowl. Rub it with a cut:

Clove of garlic

Place in it:

¼ teaspoon salt
¼ teaspoon paprika
¼ cup hot oil or melted butter
1 cup grated cheese

Toss the spaghetti in the above dressing like a salad and serve at once.

BAKED SPAGHETTI

Preheat oven to 375°.
Prepare:

Boiled Spaghetti, above

Alternate in a greased baking dish layers of spaghetti and:

1 cup grated cheese

Pour over all:

Tomato Sauce, page 376

Dot with:

Butter

and bake about 15 minutes.

ITALIAN SPAGHETTI WITH SAUCE

[About 6 Servings]

In Italy spaghetti is served in one dish, the sauce in another and grated cheese in a third. The sauce may be poured over the spaghetti, which is tossed until the two are well blended. Prepare:

A Pasta Sauce, page 377

Cook:

1 lb. unbroken spaghetti

When well drained, pour over it:

¼ cup melted butter

Put the spaghetti in a bowl. Pour the sauce over it and toss until well coated.

SPAGHETTI WITH EGG AND CHEESE [4 to 6]

Not the usual cheese sauce, but an Italian version.
Cook in boiling salted water for 8 to 10 minutes:

1 lb. spaghetti

In the meantime, cook in a small skillet:

2 tablespoons olive oil
6 slices finely cut bacon

until the bacon is crisp. Add:

⅓ cup dry white wine

and reduce until the wine has evaporated. Beat together:

3 eggs
⅔ cup mixed Parmesan and Romano grated cheese

Drain the spaghetti and return it to the hot saucepan. Add the egg and cheese mixture and the hot bacon fat and bits, stirring it in quickly. The heat of the spaghetti will cook the egg mixture.

Correct the seasoning

Serve immediately.

QUICK SPAGHETTI WITH TUNA FISH, SALMON OR BEEF [4]

Drain and reserve the oil from:

1 can tuna fish or salmon

Sauté in the oil:

⅓ cup chopped onion

Or use the onion and:

½ lb. ground beef

Sauté in:

¼ cup drippings

Add to the onion the contents of:

1 can condensed tomato soup: 10½ oz.
2½ cups canned spaghetti

Fold in the flaked fish. Season with:

½ teaspoon sugar
A few grains cayenne
Salt and paprika

Cook it until it is thoroughly heated. You may rub a bowl with:

(A cut clove garlic)

Add the spaghetti. Garnish it with:

2 tablespoons chopped parsley

This dish may be served in an ovenproof baking dish, au gratin. Use a hot oven—400°—or a broiler to melt the cheese.

QUICK SPAGHETTI MEAT PIE [4]

Preheat oven to 375°.

Sauté lightly:

2 cups cooked cubed meat
2 teaspoons grated onion

in:

2 tablespoons butter

Add:

¼ cup cream

Season it with:

Salt and pepper
(½ teaspoon basil)

Place in a greased dish the contents of:

1 can spaghetti: 24 oz.

Make a depression in the center. Place the meat in it. Sprinkle the top with:

Au Gratin II, page 389

Bake for about 25 minutes.

QUICK SPAGHETTI WITH SOUP AND BACON [4]

Preheat oven to 375°.

Sauté until nearly crisp:

8 slices bacon or 1 cup chopped tongue, ham or potted meat

Cut them into large pieces. Combine the contents of:

1 can condensed mock turtle or pepper pot soup: 10½ oz.
2½ cups canned spaghetti

If preferred, cook and substitute 1¼ cups spaghetti or use 2½ cups cooked spaghetti. Add:

¼ cup hot water

Place alternate layers of this mixture and the bacon in a greased ovenproof dish. Cover the top with:

Buttered crumbs

Bake the dish for about 20 minutes, until it is thoroughly heated. If you wish, omit the soup and season the spaghetti with:

1 teaspoon prepared mustard
1 teaspoon grated onion

CHICKEN OR TURKEY TETRAZZINI [8 to 10]

A fan writes that she prefers using ¼ lb. macaroni and 1 lb. mushrooms. A bit more extravagant but very good.
Cut the meat from the bones of:
A boiled chicken
There should be 2 to 3 cups of shredded meat. Cook:
½ lb. macaroni or spaghetti
Add to this:
½ to ¾ lb. Sautéed Mushrooms, page 296
(½ cup blanched, slivered almonds)
Make a sauce of:
3 tablespoons butter or chicken fat
2 tablespoons flour
2 cups chicken broth
Seasoning
Remove from heat. Stir in:
1 cup heated whipping cream
3 tablespoons dry white wine
Preheat oven to 375°.
Add ½ the sauce to the chicken and ½ to the macaroni and mushrooms. Place the macaroni in a greased baking dish. Make a hole in the center. Place the chicken in it. Sprinkle the top with:
Grated Parmesan cheese
Bake the dish until it is lightly browned.

SEAFOOD TETRAZZINI [8]

Preheat broiler.
Boil:
½ lb. spaghetti
Sauté until golden:
6 tablespoons chopped onion
in:
2 tablespoons olive oil
Add:
2 cans cream of mushroom soup: 10½ oz.
1⅓ cups water
¼ cup grated Romano cheese
Stir in and heat thoroughly:
2 cups flaked, drained tuna, shrimp, or clams, etc.
⅔ cup sliced pitted ripe olives
Add:
2 tablespoons chopped parsley
2 teaspoons lemon juice
⅛ teaspoon dried thyme and marjoram
In a buttered casserole, mix the sauces and the drained spaghetti. Top with:
¼ cup grated Romano cheese
Heat under the broiler until golden brown.

BOILED MACARONI WITH CHEESE [6]

In a large pan have boiling:
2 quarts water
seasoned with:
2 teaspoons salt
Slowly add so as not to disturb boiling:
½ lb. or about 2 cups macaroni
Cook until tender, about 10 to 12 minutes. Drain. Return to the saucepan. Stir and reheat over slow heat with:
½ cup cream or rich milk
Place it in a dish and sprinkle it with:
½ cup or more grated cheese
Serve it with any of the Pasta Sauces on page 379, or with the Tomato Sauces on page 376.

BAKED MACARONI [4]

I.
Preheat oven to 350°.
Cook:
4 oz. macaroni: 1 cup
Drain it. Place layers of macaroni in a buttered baking dish. Sprinkle the layers with:
1 cup grated cheese
Beat until blended:
1 or 2 eggs

⅔ cup milk
¼ teaspoon salt
⅛ teaspoon paprika
A few grains cayenne

Pour this mixture over the macaroni. Sprinkle the top with:

Au Gratin III, page 389

Bake the macaroni about 40 to 50 minutes.

II. Alternate layers of:

Macaroni, as in I, above

and:

¼ lb. sliced dried beef

III. Follow the above recipe. Substitute for the milk:

½ cup tomato juice
¼ cup cream

Add:

½ teaspoon sugar
(1 tablespoon chopped parsley or 1 teaspoon dried basil or thyme)

IV. One cup well-seasoned Cream Sauce I, page 359, may be substituted for the egg and milk mixture. Bake at 400° about 30 minutes.

MACARONI BAKED WITH SOUR CREAM [4]

Preheat oven to 400°.
Cook:

1½ cups macaroni

Drain it well. Toss it in:

3 tablespoons melted butter

Place it in a greased oven-proof dish. Make a hollow in the center into which pour:

1 cup cultured sour cream

You may sprinkle this with:

½ cup grated cheese

Bake the macaroni until the top is brown.

MACARONI LOAF [5]

Preheat oven to 350°.
This delectable dish is very attractive in appearance. It makes a fine ring dish.
Boil:

5 cups water
1½ teaspoons salt

Add:

¾ cup macaroni or spaghetti

Boil for about 10 minutes. Drain in a colander. Place in a bowl.
Scald:

½ cup milk or cream

Beat into it:

2 or 3 eggs

Melt and add:

3 tablespoons butter

Pour this over the macaroni.
Add:

½ cup soft bread crumbs, without crusts
½ cup grated cheese
1½ sliced pimientos
¼ cup chopped green peppers or 2 tablespoons chopped parsley
1 tablespoon grated onion
¼ teaspoon salt
⅛ teaspoon paprika
A few grains cayenne

Place these ingredients in a buttered baking dish. Bake them for about 1 hour. Serve with:

Mushroom Sauce, page 367, or
Quick Tomato Sauce, page 376

It makes a somewhat lighter dish if you add only the egg yolks to the scalded milk. The whites, beaten until stiff, are then folded into the other ingredients at the last moment.

MACARONI WITH TOMATOES, LIVERS, MUSHROOMS AND CHEESE

[About 2 Quarts]
Preheat oven to 400°.
Cook, page 167:

½ lb. macaroni

Drain. Place in a deep casserole.
Sauté:

½ lb. Mushrooms, page 296

Sauté or boil until tender:

½ cup chicken livers or calf liver

Chop the mushrooms and the liver.

Simmer until fairly thick:
4 cups canned tomatoes
Strain them. Season with:
¾ tablespoon salt
1 teaspoon brown sugar
A few grains cayenne
(1 teaspoon dried basil)
Sauté:
1 minced onion
(½ minced clove garlic)
in:
2 tablespoons butter
Combine these with the other ingredients and pour them over the macaroni. Mix them well with 2 forks. Sprinkle the top with:
Grated cheese
Bake the macaroni until the cheese is golden.

MACARONI WITH SHELLFISH [4]

Preheat oven to 350°.
Cook, page 167:
1½ cups macaroni
Drain it. Sauté:
1 tablespoon minced onion
in:
3 tablespoons butter
Stir in until blended:
1½ tablespoons flour
Stir in until smooth:
1½ cups milk
¾ cup grated cheese
1 teaspoon Worcestershire sauce
½ teaspoon lemon juice
1 teaspoon salt
¼ teaspoon paprika
A few grains cayenne
Have ready:
1½ to 2 cups cleaned shrimp, oysters or clams, etc.
Place layers of macaroni and fish in a baking dish. Pour the sauce over them. Cover the top with:
Au Gratin III, page 389
Bake the dish for about 45 minutes.

MOSTACCIOLI [5]

Melt:
1 tablespoon butter
Stir and brown in it:
¾ to 1 lb. ground round steak
1 large chopped onion
1 clove garlic cut into halves
Cover these ingredients with boiling water. Add:
¾ teaspoon salt
⅛ teaspoon pepper
Simmer covered until almost dry. Fish out the garlic. Add:
2 cups canned tomatoes
Continue to simmer, stirring frequently. Cook until the sauce is thick, from 1 to 1½ hours. Add mushrooms when the sauce is partly done. Wash well in warm water, then drain:
¼ lb. dried reconstituted mushrooms (II, 221)
When the sauce is almost done add:
¼ cup olive oil
Cook until tender, page 167:
½ lb. mostaccioli: about 2 cups
Serve the mostaccioli on a hot platter. First a layer of the pasta, then a layer of sauce, then a layer of the pasta and again a layer of sauce. Sprinkle each meat sauce layer generously with:
Grated Parmesan cheese
Freshly grated black pepper

BOILED NOODLES [5]

Drop:
2 cups Noodles, page 149
into:
3 quarts boiling, salted water—½ teaspoon salt to the quart—or chicken stock, consommé, etc.
Boil for about 8 to 10 minutes, depending on size and your taste preference. Drain in a colander and immediately put back in cooking pot, set over very low heat and moisten them generously with:
Melted butter or cream

(Chicken Stock (II, 142)
Serve with:
Au Gratin II, or III, page 382
Additions may be:
Chopped hard-cooked eggs
Chopped chives
2 tablespoons poppy seeds
(¾ cup cultured sour cream)
or:
½ cup blanched chopped almonds
sautéed in:
1 tablespoon butter
Boiled noodles may be arranged in a ring on a platter and the center filled with a creamed meat, vegetable or a hash.

BUTTERED NOODLES OR FETTUCCINI AL BURRO [4 to 6]

Alfredo II came to Cincinnati to demonstrate the making of those noodles which brought both him and his father fame. He carried along from Italy the hard special flour needed for the dough and the hard Parmesan cheese and sweet butter for tossing. Yet when the noodles were presented, he wished he had brought with him the Roman water in which to cook them.
Cook:
2 cups noodles
In:
3 quarts boiling salted water
for 6 to 8 minutes or until "al dente." Drain. Put on a hot platter:
½ cup butter
Cover with drained noodles. Toss until the noodles are coated with the butter. Have ready:
¾ cup grated Parmesan cheese
to pass at table.

FRIED NOODLES

To be served in the place of a starchy vegetable or as a garnish on vegetables or other dishes, notably Chinese mixtures. Boil in water for about 5 minutes:
Thin noodles
Place them in a colander and rinse them with cold water to rid of surface starch. Drain, separate and dry well.
Preheat deep fryer to 390°.
Fry them, a small amount at a time, until they are a delicate brown. Drain them on absorbent paper. Sprinkle them lightly with:
Salt
Keep them hot or reheat in a 400° oven.

NOODLE BASKETS

Preheat deep fryer to 390°.
For these you need a tea strainer about 3 inches in diameter and a second strainer about ⅜ inch smaller that fits into it but leaves space for the swelling of the noodles. Prepare:
Noodle Dough, page 149
Before the dough is dry fold it over and cut it into ¼-inch strips. Dip the strainers in hot fat to keep the noodles from sticking. Line the larger strainer with 3 layers of noodles, giving them a crisscross effect. Snip off the ragged edges. Place the smaller strainer over the noodle basket. Fry the noodle basket in deep fat, page 75, until lightly browned. Remove it carefully from the strainers and fry the next one. You may fill the fried baskets at once with creamed food, etc., or you may cool them and reheat them later by dipping them briefly in hot fat without the strainers.
Drain them on absorbent paper.

BAKED NOODLE RING [4]

Preheat oven to 350°.
I. Cook:
1½ cups Noodles, page 149

Drain them. Beat:

2 egg yolks
½ cup milk
¾ tablespoon melted butter
¼ teaspoon salt
⅛ teaspoon paprika
(½ cup grated cheese)
(⅛ teaspoon nutmeg)

Combine this mixture with the noodles. Beat until stiff but not dry:

2 egg whites

Fold them lightly into the noodles. Butter a 7-inch ring mold or individual ring molds. Fill them with the noodle mixture and bake them set in a pan of hot water in the oven until done, about 45 minutes for a large mold or 30 minutes for the small ones. Invert the contents of the molds on hot plates and fill the centers with:

Creamed spinach, peas, mushrooms, hash, stewed tomatoes, Chicken à la King, etc.

II. Made with cheese this is our favorite. Follow the above recipe. Use in all:

¾ cup milk

Add to the noodle mixture before folding in the egg whites:

1½ teaspoons Worcestershire sauce
½ tablespoon catsup
¾ cup grated cheese

Also good made with:

Cottage cheese

NOODLE RING WITH WHIPPED CREAM [10]

Preheat oven to 350°.
Use a 9-inch ring. For 5 servings take half the recipe and use a 7-inch ring. Cook:

2 cups fine Noodles, page 149

Drain. Beat and pour over the noodles:

4 egg yolks
¼ teaspoon paprika
¾ cup melted butter

Whip until stiff:

4 egg whites
¼ teaspoon salt

Beat until stiff:

1 cup whipping cream or use 1 cup cultured sour cream

Fold the egg whites and the cream lightly into the noodle mixture. Fill a well-greased ring. Place it in a pan of hot water. Bake it until firm, for about 1 hour or more. Invert the ring and fill it with:

Green peas or creamed food, sweetbreads, fish, etc.

NOODLES, STEWED PRUNES AND CROUTONS

This is a traditional Good Friday dish in a number of European countries. It is a reminder of how good simple food may be in a tempting combination. Prepare:

Boiled Noodles, page 149
Dried Prunes (II, 108)
Croutons, page 390

Serve the noodles hot with the croutons poured over them. Serve the prunes from a separate bowl.

HAM NOODLES [8]

Preheat oven to 350°.
This recipe is capable of a wide interpretation and its proportions may be varied. Cook:

1½ cups Noodles, page 149

Grease a baking dish. Place in it layers of noodles sprinkled with:

¾ cup cooked diced or ground ham
(½ cup grated cheese)
(½ cup shredded green pepper and celery)

Combine:

1½ cups milk
1 or 2 eggs
¼ teaspoon paprika
¼ to ½ teaspoon salt—omit if the ham is very salty

Pour this over the noodles. The top may be covered with:

Bread or cracker crumbs

Bake the dish for about 45 minutes.

LEFTOVER NOODLE DISH

Follow the previous recipe. Substitute for the ham:

Diced cooked roast, chicken, crab, shrimp, chipped beef, mushrooms and other vegetables

Part gravy may be substituted for milk or you may like to try a ham and chicken combination in a Cream Sauce, page 359.

NOODLE RAREBIT

Prepare:

Cheese Rarebit I, page 237

When blended and hot stir in:

1 to 2 cups diced ham or smoked tongue
8 oz. cooked noodles

ROMANIAN NOODLE AND PORK CASSEROLE [8]

Preheat oven to 350°.
Cook until slightly underdone:

1 lb. fine noodles

Combine:

1 lb. ground cooked pork
1 slice bread which has been soaked in milk and wrung out
1 minced leek
½ to 1 teaspoon fennel seeds
¼ cup chopped parsley
1 teaspoon salt
½ teaspoon pepper

In a shallow large baking pan, arrange alternate layers of noodles and pork mixture, ending with noodles. Beat together:

4 eggs
⅔ cup cream
¼ cup grated cheese

Pour this mixture over the noodles and dot with:

¼ cup butter

Bake for about 45 minutes.

QUANTITY NOODLE AND CHEESE LOAF [18]

Preheat oven to 325°.
Cook:

5 cups Noodles, page 149

and drain them. Have ready:

1 lb. grated sharp cheese
1½ cups dry bread crumbs

Mix together half the cheese and one cup of the crumbs with:

¼ cup melted butter

Mix the rest of the crumbs and the cheese and the noodles with:

7 beaten eggs
1¾ cups milk
3 tablespoons grated onion
⅓ cup chopped pimiento
⅓ cup chopped green peppers, seeds and membranes removed
1 teaspoon salt
½ teaspoon white pepper
(1 cup finely chopped celery)
(½ cup sliced stuffed olives)

Divide the mixture in two parts and place in two 9 x 9 inch baking pans. Cover with the cheese, butter and crumb mixture. Bake for about 25 minutes or until the custard sets and the top is golden brown.
To test the custard for doneness, see (II, 436).
Serve with:

Mushroom Sauce, page 367
Tomato Sauce, page 376
Creole Sauce, page 376

TUNA, NOODLE AND MUSHROOM SOUP CASSEROLE

[4 Large Servings]
Preheat oven to 450°.
An excellent emergency dish.
Cook until tender:

2 cups Noodles, page 149

Drain them in a colander. Drain:

1 cup canned tuna fish

Separate it with a fork into large flakes. Do not mince it. Grease an ovenproof dish. Arrange a layer of noodles, then sprinkle it with fish and so on. Have noodles on top. Pour over this mixture:

1 can condensed mushroom soup: 10½ oz.

Season the soup with:

Worcestershire sauce, curry powder, dry sherry, etc.

Cover the top with:

Buttered cornflakes or cracker crumbs

Bake the dish until the top is brown.

LASAGNE [16]

The sauce may be made the day before. Combine in a large saucepan:

2 cans Italian-style peeled tomatoes: No. 2½
4 cans tomato sauce: 8 oz. each
2 teaspoons salt
3 teaspoons dried orégano
(2 teaspoons onion salt)

Start simmering these ingredients uncovered. Sauté until golden:

2 cups minced onions
2 minced cloves garlic

in:

⅓ cup olive oil

Add:

2 lbs. ground chuck roast or round
2 teaspoons salt

and cook until meat loses its red color. Add to the tomato sauce above. Simmer about 2½ hours longer. Prepare:

¾ lb. lasagne noodles

according to package directions—usually in generous quantities of water—and cook for about 25 minutes. Add to the water:

2 tablespoons cooking or olive oil

Stir occasionally. Drain and separate noodles.
Preheat oven to 350°.
Now let's build the lasagne! Put into the bottoms of two 13 x 9 x 2½-inch baking dishes a thin layer of sauce, then a criss-cross layer of the lasagne noodles and a layer of cheese.
In all, use:

¾ lb. Ricotta cheese
⅓ lb. thinly sliced or crumbled Mozzarella cheese
½ lb. grated Parmesan cheese

Repeat twice with sauce, noodles and cheese. The final cheese layer is covered once more with sauce and a dusting of Parmesan.
Bake for about 40 minutes. Remove and let stand for 10 minutes. The lasagne can then be cut for serving.

CANNELONI OR MANICOTTI

[Ten 4 x 6 Inch Rolled Squares]

Wrapped around fillings and served with a sauce, the charm of these "channels" or "little muffs" lies in the freshness of the dough; although the wrappings may be made in advance and held between wax papers in the refrigerator for several hours. Have ready a filling made by mixing together until well blended:

1 cup grated Parmesan cheese
½ cup Mozzarella cheese
1¾ cups Ricotta cheese
⅛ teaspoon nutmeg
1 beaten egg
¼ cup Béchamel Sauce, page 359, or Cream Sauce IV, page 360

You may use instead of the

above filling a good chicken or sausage farce, page 564.

Correct the seasoning

Make a well and mix as described (II, 301).

2 cups flour
¾ teaspoon salt
2 eggs
2 to 4 tablespoons water

Knead for about 10 minutes or until the dough is smooth. Rest the dough ➧ covered under a cloth about 10 minutes. Divide the dough in half and roll each part paper thin. Cut into 4 x 6 inch squares. Have ready in a large pan:

8 quarts boiling water

Cook 5 squares at a time by dropping them into the boiling water ➧ reducing the heat at once and simmering about 5 minutes. Remove with a skimmer, and when drained place between moist towels until all the dough is cooked and ready to fill.

Preheat oven to 400°.

Divide the filling into 10 oval parts. Place on the center of the squares, fold over the two edges and put seam-side down in a greased ovenproof dish, or in individual bakers allowing 2 per person.

Cover generously with:

A tomato sauce or butter and a sprinkling of fresh basil

Bake about 10 minutes.

Serve with:

Grated Parmesan cheese

RAVIOLI

If you are fond of this Italian savory pastry buy a mold for mass-producing it.

Prepare:

Noodle Dough II, page 150

Cover it with a cloth and permit it to stand for 10 minutes. Roll the dough until it is very thin. Cut it into 2 sheets. On one sheet put a teaspoon of one of the ravioli fillings, in little mounds 2 inches apart. Cover them with the second sheet which may be brushed lightly with water. Press the top sheet gently around the ravioli mounds. Press the edges. Cut the dough into squares with a mound in each center. Use a pie jagger. Dry the ravioli for about 2 hours. Drop them into boiling, salted water or into chicken broth. Simmer them for about 10 minutes. Remove them from the liquid with a skimmer onto a hot platter. Sprinkle them with:

Grated Parmesan cheese

Serve with:

A tomato sauce, page 376

RAVIOLI FILLING

This is usually a spinach and meat mixture very finely chopped or put through a purée strainer. Grated cheese and light seasoning may be added. Sometimes the filling is thickened slightly with bread crumbs or egg. There can be much leeway in the composition of the filling and you may use any combination of meat and vegetables you like. For other fillings, see Farces, page 564.

I.

Combine:

¼ cup cooked puréed spinach
¼ cup chopped cooked meat
1 egg
2 tablespoons toasted bread crumbs
2 tablespoons grated cheese
Stock, cream or gravy to form a stiff paste
½ teaspoon dried basil
(½ clove minced garlic)

II.
Combine:
½ cup cooked drained spinach
½ cup cooked minced chicken
2 tablespoons grated cheese
Salt and pepper
½ teaspoon dried basil or ⅛ teaspoon nutmeg
(½ clove minced garlic)

DUMPLINGS [4]

➧ Please read About Dumplings, page 146, where you will find other recipes suitable for use with meats.
Measure, then sift 3 times:
1 cup cake flour
2 teaspoons double-acting baking powder
½ teaspoon salt
Break into a measuring cup:
1 egg
Add until the cup is half full:
Milk
Beat well and stir the liquid slowly into the sifted ingredients. Add more milk if necessary but keep the batter as stiff as possible. Add:
(¼ cup finely chopped parsley or
1 tablespoon fresh chopped herbs) or
(½ teaspoon grated onion and 3 tablespoons minced green peppers)
Thicken:
2 or 3 cups stock
with:
Flour—allow 1½ tablespoons flour to 1 cup stock
Heat the stock in a 9-inch saucepan. To drop dumpling batter from a spoon easily, dip the spoon in water first. Then dip the spoon in the batter, fill it and drop the batter into the stock. Continue doing this until the dumplings are barely touching. Then cover them and simmer for 5 minutes, turn them, cook them 5 minutes longer. They should be served at once. If using a ✪ pressure cooker, drop the batter from a spoon into at least 3 cups hot stock or water. Adjust cover, steam over low heat, vent open, for 5 minutes.

CHEESE DUMPLINGS

To the above recipe for:
Dumplings
Add:
2 tablespoons grated cheese
Cook the dumplings in:
Tomato juice

QUICK CHEESE DUMPLINGS

[Ten 2-Inch Dumplings]
Have ready:
⅔ cup grated cheese
Add 2 tablespoons of this cheese to:
2 cups commercial biscuit mix
and prepare the recipe on the label. Pat out the dough to a ⅛ inch thickness and cut into 3 inch rounds. Place in the center of each round a tablespoon of the cheese. Wet the edges of the rounds with cold water. Gather them up to form a ball. Pinch them well. Have ready in a lidded pot:
6 to 8 cups boiling water
Drop the dumplings in, cover at once and ➧ reduce heat. ➧ Simmer covered about 15 minutes. Meanwhile heat:
Quick Tomato Sauce, page 376
Drain the dumplings and serve at once on hot plates covered with the sauce and:
Finely chopped parsley

CORN MEAL DUMPLINGS

Cooking in the United States is on the up and coming side but it seemed to us that a peak was reached in a small Kentucky town where we were served chicken with dumplings. The latter were like thistledown. "Oh yes!" said the hotel proprietress wearily when we exclaimed over them. "They are always like that when our cook is drunk."

Far be it from us to limit your sources of inspiration, but we are convinced that the following recipe will give you superlative dumplings without dissipation. Have simmering:

5 or 6 cups corned beef stock, consommé or any clear soup or stock

Sift:

1 cup corn meal
¼ cup all-purpose flour
1 teaspoon any baking powder
½ teaspoon salt

Beat:

2 eggs
½ cup milk

Combine the egg mixture and the dry ingredients. Stir in:

1 tablespoon melted butter

Drop the batter from a spoon into the hot stock. Cover the pan closely. Simmer the dumplings for about 15 minutes. Remove them at once from the liquor.

FARINA DUMPLINGS COCKAIGNE [6]

Please read About Dumplings, page 146. Prepare:

Farina Balls Cockaigne, page 147

These remain after many tests the queen of dumplings. Though usually served in soup they may be simmered in stock or boiling water, then served with meat gravy. They may be drained, placed in a greased baking dish and covered with a cup of cream sauce, to which you may add onion juice and parsley, or chopped chives. Sprinkle the top with ¼ cup grated Parmesan cheese, dot it with butter and bake the dish in an oven for about 15 minutes.

SPATZEN, SPAETZLE OR GERMAN EGG DUMPLINGS [4]

Spatzen are good at any time but they are particularly good served with roast veal. Beat:

2 eggs

Combine them with:

1½ cups flour
½ cup water
½ teaspoon salt
¼ teaspoon any baking powder
(A small grating of nutmeg)

Beat these ingredients well. Drop small bits of the batter from a spoon into simmering salted water or stock, or put the batter through a colander, or a sliding cutter as shown below or use a pastry bag as shown on page 157. Spatzen should be very light and delicate. Try out a sample and if it is too heavy, add water to the batter. Simmer them until they are done. Drain them, place them in a dish and cover them with:

Croutons, or ¼ cup bread crumbs sautéed in ½ cup butter

Spatzen may be cooked and served in soup. Pie Dough (II, 293), cut into strips or shapes, simmered in stock, is frequently substituted for a dumpling mixture. Remember the good Vegetable Noodles on page 149.

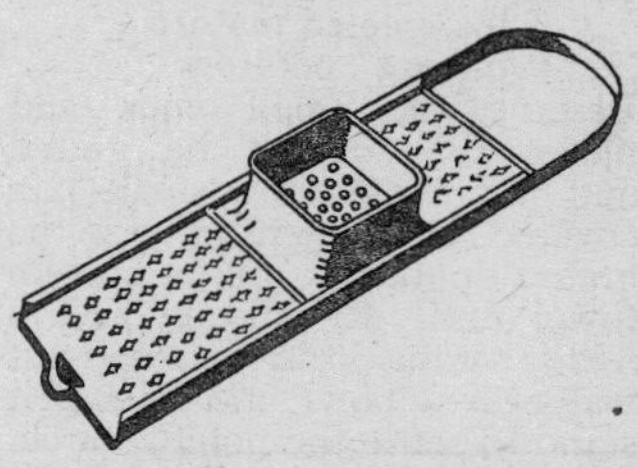

POTATO DUMPLINGS OR KARTOFFELKLOESSE

These are light and tender, especially good with beef à la mode or other roast gravy. It is traditional to serve them with Sauerbraten.

Boil uncovered in their jackets until tender:

6 medium-sized mature baking potatoes

Peel and coarsely grate or rice them. Add:

2 eggs
1½ teaspoons salt
½ cup flour

Beat the batter with a fork until it is fluffy. Roll it lightly into balls 1 inch in diameter. Many cooks prefer to put croutons in the balls. Put 1 crouton into the center of each 1 inch ball. If you wish to make large balls, roll several croutons into each ball. Drop them into gently boiling salted water for about 10 minutes. Drain them well.

Melt:

½ cup butter or drippings

Stir in:

¼ cup dry bread crumbs

Or prepare:

½ cup Croutons, page 390

Pour them over the dumplings.

KARTOFFELKLOESSE WITH RAW POTATOES [6 to 8]

This recipe, contributed by Claire Gregory, is a favorite of her far West German village.

Coarsely grate into a bowl of cold water:

5 lbs. peeled mature baking potatoes

Reserve the small ends and pieces that cannot be grated and put them in a small pan covered with water. Squeeze the grated potatoes in a muslin towel until dry and in a firm ball, saving the pressed-out water in a bowl and letting it stand to settle the potato starch. In the meantime, cook the small pieces of potato in a small amount of water until tender. Drain, mash and add:

3 cups boiling milk

to make a smooth paste.

Correct the seasoning

then add the grated raw potato. Drain off the water from the settled potato starch and add the starch to the potato and paste mixture. Mix together by hand and form patties 3 inches in diameter and about ¼ inch thick. Place in the center of each patty:

Small diced buttered croutons, diced liverwurst or sausage

Then press the potato patty around this to enclose it in the center of the ball. Drop these balls into a large pot of:

Boiling salted water

When the pot begins to boil again ➧ reduce the heat and simmer for 25 to 30 minutes.

Serve with:

Fat meats
Game
Cabbage with hot melted butter

ABOUT QUENELLES

Once eaten, never forgotten is the texture of a well-made quenelle. Success lies not only in the mixing but in the very shaping. The ground mixture, which may be fish, chicken, veal or game, is placed in a large bowl ➧ set in a bowl of ice, see below.

It is then worked into a smooth paste with a wooden spoon.

➧ To shape, you may roll quenelles in flour but this is not the method for best results. We suggest the following classic spoon molding—letting the size of the spoon determine the size of the quenelle. They will expand to about double their original size. Have ready a well-buttered cooking pan and 2 spoons of equal size. Put one spoon in a bowl of hot water. With the other spoon, lightly scoop out enough of the quenelle mixture to just fill it. Invert the other hot, moist spoon over the filled spoon, shaping as shown. ➧ Do not press hard—only smooth the surface. After shaping the point, invert the little egg shapes into the buttered pan. Continue to shape and place the quenelles in neat rows, allowing for expansion space. ➧ To poach the quenelles, pour almost boiling salted water or stock very gently into the pan from the sides so as not to dislodge them. The stock should come half-way up the quenelles. ➧ Simmer gently for 8 to 10 minutes. The water should be barely quivering. As quenelles cook on the bottom, they become light and rise and turn over, but the weight of the uncooked portion will keep them submerged until they are thoroughly done and float.

Although they are not quite as delicate as when served at once, you may hold the quenelles for several hours if you poach them as described above. Place them gently in a bowl of cold water to cool, then drain off onto a cloth and place on a plate. ➧ Butter the surfaces to keep from crusting.

If you want quenelles very small, as a garnish, cut a parchment paper the size of the pan in which you plan to poach them. Use a decorating bag with a small round tip, fill with the quenelle mixture and force out small units on the parchment paper in uniformly spaced rows. Lift the whole paper into the pan and as with larger quenelles, pour the water gently from the side of the pan until the quenelles are only half-covered. As they simmer for 5 to 8 minutes, they will float free and roll over. When floating, skim off and place in a bowl of warm, mildly salted water until ready to use.

If fancy shapes are desired, pack the quenelle mixture into buttered decorative individual molds. To poach, place the molds into a pan of hot water so that they are completely covered. When the quenelle mixture is cooked, it will release itself, rise to the surface and can be removed for serving.

Reheat quenelles by simmering them in the sauce or soup in which they are to be served. Or place the quenelles in a buttered mold in a pan of hot water. Cover with a buttered poaching paper, page 84, and bake for 50 to 60 minutes at 350° until firm.

POACHED OR BAKED QUENELLES [6]

➧ Please read About Quenelles, above.

Run through the finest blade of a food chopper 3 times:

1½ lbs. fresh pike, sole,

shrimp or lobster

Place the ground mixture in a large bowl ➧ set in a bowl of ice. With a wooden spoon, work it to a smooth paste. Gradually ➧ by small additions work in:

2 egg whites

Season with:

Grated fresh nutmeg
Salt
White pepper
Dash of cognac
Dash of cayenne or hot pepper sauce

Mix well. At this point the quenelle mixture should be very firm. Still over ice, add ➧ very, very gradually and mix well with a wooden spoon:

3 cups well-chilled whipping cream

The consistency now should be like a firm whipped cream. To form and poach or bake, follow above directions. Serve with:

Newburg Sauce, page 361
Poulette Sauce, page 362

FISH QUENELLE IN LOBSTER SAUCE [6]

Preheat oven to 350°.

This is a deluxe fish course for a special dinner party.

Prepare the mixture for:

Quenelles, page 180

using:

Dover sole

Put the quenelle mixture into a buttered mold. Place the mold in a pan of hot water. Cover with a buttered poaching paper and bake 50 to 60 minutes until firm. ➧ Test for doneness as for cake (II, 336). Remove the hot mold from the oven, allowing it to rest 5 minutes before unmolding. Then drain off the accumulated liquid and unmold onto a hot deep serving tray and cover with:

Newburg Sauce, page 361

Garnish with:

Parsley

and serve immediately.

YORKSHIRE PUDDING [6]

Preheat oven to 400°.

It was customary to cook this old and delicious dish in the pan with the roast or under the roast, letting the drippings fall upon it. As many of us now cook roast beef in a slow oven and no longer have extravagant drippings, we must revise the preparation of Yorkshire pudding. It is best to cook it separately in the hot oven required to puff it up and brown it quickly. Serve it from the dish in which it was cooked, cut into squares. In Yorkshire it is served before the meat course as a hefty pudding. We always substitute the pudding for the usual starch served with a main course.

➧ The ingredients must be at room temperature when mixed or they will not puff. Sift into a bowl:

⅞ cup flour
½ teaspoon salt

Make a well in the center, into which pour:

½ cup milk

Stir in the milk. Beat until fluffy:

2 eggs

Beat them into the batter. Add:

½ cup water

Beat the batter well until large bubbles rise to the surface. You may permit this to stand covered and refrigerated for 1 hour and then beat it again. Have ready a hot ovenproof dish about 9 x 12, or hot muffin tins containing about ¼ inch hot beef drippings or melted butter. Pour in the batter. It should be about ⅝ inch high. Bake the pudding for about 20 minutes. ➧ Reduce the heat to 350° and bake it 10 to 15 minutes longer. Some cooks recommend a 350° oven for ½ hour or longer. Serve it at once.

EGGS, SOUFFLÉS AND TIMBALES

ABOUT EGG DISHES

Egg dishes are maids of all work in most households. They are nutritious, economical, usually quickly assembled and can be served in any number of appealing combinations—pleasing to the eye and to the palate. Every country in the world seems to have its own special knack of cooking eggs or combining them with something which brings up their flavor. The light, fluffy, golden omelet was born in France. East Indians like their eggs curried. And the Chinese, while partial to Eggs Foo Yoong, are reputed to be connoisseurs of vintage eggs.

To us, no egg dish can be good unless the eggs are "strictly fresh" and cooked with due regard for their delicacy and great sensitivity to heat. Let us not say of an egg, like the curate breakfasting with the bishop, "Oh, no, my Lord, parts of it are excellent!" For more details ➧ please read About Eggs (II, 179). Eggs and egg dishes can be served at any meal in the day: fried, scrambled, boiled, poached, baked or cooked in omelets or soufflés. And almost unlimited variations of meat, vegetables or fish may accompany or be folded into them. They are an excellent means of adding extra protein to a light meal, whether it be hot or cold.

➧ Always keep in mind that eggs must cook on very gentle heat. In combining eggs with soufflés and sauces let them partially cook on the stored heat in the pan. Do not put them back on direct heat—because they never will have as good a texture in sauces and will not function properly in soufflés.

SOFT, HARD-COOKED AND CODDLED EGGS

The difference in soft-cooked, hard-cooked and coddled eggs is more a matter of timing than method.

Place in a sauce pan, preferably glass or enamel:

Unshelled eggs

Cover them with:

Cold water

Put the pan over medium heat and bring the water to boiling point. ➧ Reduce the heat to below boiling point and let the water ➧ simmer. Now watch your time, which will depend on how large and how cold your eggs are. Allow the following times for 70° eggs. If they come right out of the refrigerator, you will have to add at least 2 minutes to the timing given below:

I. Soft-Cooked Eggs

Remove them from the water 2 to 3 minutes after you reduce the heat.

II. Medium-Soft-Cooked Eggs

Allow about 4 minutes after you reduce the heat.

III. Hard-Cooked Eggs

Allow about 15 minutes after you reduce the heat. Plunge the finished hard-cooked eggs in cold water at once to arrest further cooking and to prevent the yolks from discoloring.

IV. Coddled Eggs

Place the eggs in boiling water by lowering them in gently with a tablespoon. Turn off the heat and cover the pan. Allow 6 minutes for delicately coddled eggs; 8 minutes for firmly coddled eggs; and 30 to 35 minutes for hard-cooked eggs. We repeat, plunge hard-cooked eggs, when done, into cold water. If you want the eggs to remain shapely, turn them several times within the first few minutes of coddling so that the white of the egg solidifies evenly in the air space and the yolk is centered.

➧ To shell hard-cooked eggs, crack the shell and roll the egg between the palms of the hands to free the thin tough skin from the egg and make shelling easier. If eggs are very fresh, they are more difficult to shell. If you want to slice the eggs smoothly, dip a knife in water before using.

Soft-cooked eggs may be served shelled, in the various ways suggested for Poached Eggs, opposite.

Recipes and suggestions for serving hard-cooked eggs follow. Others will be found in Hors d'Oeuvre and Salads.

SAUTÉED OR FRIED EGGS [4]

Melt in a skillet over low heat:

1 or 2 tablespoons butter

Break into a saucer one at a time and slip from the saucer into the skillet:

4 eggs

Baste the eggs with the hot butter. Cook them over a very low heat until they are done. To get a firm white ➧ cover the pan with a lid at once. If you like a softer white, you may at once pour over the eggs:

1 tablespoon boiling water

then cover the skillet and cook for about 1 minute. When the eggs are firm, serve them seasoned with:

Salt and pepper

ADDITIONS TO SAUTÉED EGGS

It is the extras that often give punch to eggs, especially in brunch and luncheon dishes. Try eggs on a small mound of:

Boiled rice, noodles, potatoes or rounds of toast

Pour over them:

Well-seasoned leftover gravy
Mushroom, tomato or onion sauce
Canned Soup Sauce, page 375
Cream sauce seasoned with mustard or curry powder, herbs, onion, celery, green peppers, capers, anchovies or cheese, Black Butter, page 383, with a few capers, or Brown Butter, page 383

POACHED EGGS

[Individual Serving]

I. Poached eggs, unless made in individual molds, are apt to produce "streamers" that you may trim off with scissors before serving.

Grease the bottom of a 6 to 8-inch pot. Put in enough slightly salted boiling water to fill to twice the depth of an egg. While the water comes to a boil, put in a small bowl:

1 egg

Swirl the water into a mad vortex with a wooden spoon. Drop the egg into the well formed in the center of the pot. ➧ The swirling water should round the egg. ➧ Reduce the heat. ➧ Simmer 4 to 5 minutes or let stand off the heat for 8 minutes. The white should be firm and the yolk soft by this time. Remove with a skimmer and drain well. If not using the egg immediately, plunge at once into cold water to stop the cooking. Repeat the process for each egg. To reheat the eggs, use hot—not boiling—water.

II. This method will produce a flattened poached egg rather than the rounded "egg-shaped" one described previously.
Put enough water to cover the eggs in a shallow skillet. Add:

½ teaspoon salt
1 teaspoon vinegar

Bring to a boil. Break into a saucer:

1 egg

Take the skillet from the heat and slip the egg into the hot water. Repeat the process for as many eggs as you require. Let the eggs stand in hot water for about 3 to 5 minutes, or until the white is firm. Remove with a skimmer and drain well. Eggs may be poached in a small amount of milk, cream or stock. If these liquids are used, omit the vinegar. For other additions, see below. To store for later use—but not later than 24 hours after the original cooking—put the poached eggs in a bowl of ice-cold water in the refrigerator. This is a good way to prepare eggs in advance for use the following day in Eggs Benedict, page 186, or any other recipe calling for poached eggs. The heat from platter, toast and sauce warms up the egg.

ADDITIONS TO POACHED EGGS

I. Arrange them in a shallow buttered baking dish.
Cover with:

Sauce Mornay, page 361

Sprinkle with:

Grated cheese
Bread crumbs

and brown quickly under a hot broiler.

II. Cover the bottom of a shallow buttered baking dish with:

Creamed Spinach, page 326

Arrange the poached eggs on the spinach and proceed as for Poached Eggs Mornay, above, to produce **Eggs Florentine.**

III. Hollow out a hard roll, insert egg, cover with Seafood Spaghetti Sauce, page 379, and garnish with cooked shrimp, mussels and oysters.

IV. Serve on toast, covered with Hunter's Sauce or Aurore Sauce, pages 366, 362.

V. Poach eggs in:

Creole Sauce, page 380

EGGS POACHED IN SOUP [4]

The following recipe makes a good, attractive, light meal—prepared in a few minutes. Combine in an 8-inch skillet and heat to the boiling point over low heat:

1 can tomato soup: 10½ oz.

diluted with:

½ cup water

Add:

(½ teaspoon dried basil)
(¼ teaspoon sugar)

➧ Reduce the heat and keep the liquid below the boiling point. Add to the soup:

4 eggs

➧ Simmer 4 to 5 minutes or until the eggs firm up. Serve the eggs on:

Rounds of toast

covered with the soup. Sprinkle them with:

Chopped parsley

EGGS POACHED IN WINE [6]

Combine in a skillet:

1 cup dry red wine
1 crushed clove garlic
2 tablespoons minced onion or shallot
¼ teaspoon salt
⅛ teaspoon pepper
A Bouquet Garni (II, 220)

Heat to boiling point ➧ reduce heat and simmer for about 3 minutes, then remove the bouquet garni. Slide into the wine from a saucer, one at a time:

6 eggs

Poach them until the whites are firm. Remove and put them on:

Slices of fried bread (rubbed with garlic)

Strain the wine, put it back into the skillet and thicken with:

Kneaded Butter, page 357

Pour the sauce over the eggs.

EGGS BENEDICT [6]

Toast:

6 rounds of bread or halves of English muffins

Cover each with:

A thin slice of cold or hot ham, minced cooked bacon or deviled ham

Top with:

A Poached Egg, page 184

Serve them hot, covered with:

Hollandaise Sauce, page 369

POACHED EGGS BLACKSTONE [6]

Sauté, then mince:

3 slices bacon

Reserve the drippings. Cut:

6 slices tomato, ½ inch thick

Season them with:

Salt and white pepper

Dip the slices in flour. Sauté them in the bacon fat. Sprinkle them with the minced bacon. Cover each slice with:

A Poached Egg, page 184

Pour over the eggs:

Hollandaise Sauce, page 369

SMOKED SALMON WITH EGGS

A good winter breakfast or luncheon dish. Perpare:

Buttered toast or a slice of pumpernickel bread

Dip into boiling water:

Very thin slices smoked salmon

Dry them. Place them on the toast. Cover them with:

Poached or sautéed eggs

Sprinkle with:

(Dill seed)

HUEVOS RANCHEROS OR COWBOY EGGS [4]

A traditional Spanish and Latin American dish. These eggs can be baked in the following sauce or poached or sautéed with the sauce poured over afterward. Heat in a skillet:

¼ cup olive oil

and sauté in it for 5 minutes:

1 crushed clove garlic

Remove the garlic and add, sautéing until soft:

2 medium-sized finely chopped onions
1 large finely chopped green pepper

Add:

1 cup peeled, seeded and chopped fresh tomatoes
½ teaspoon salt
¼ teaspoon freshly ground black pepper
2 teaspoons chili powder
¼ teaspoon oregano
⅛ teaspoon powdered cumin

Simmer covered until thick and well blended.

Correct the seasoning

The sauce should be very hot and well flavored. At this point, pour it over:

8 poached or sautéed eggs

allowing 2 eggs per serving.

Or, to bake, preheat oven to 450°.

Pour the sauce into a heatproof shallow dish or 4 individual casseroles and nest the uncooked eggs in the same. Garnish with:

Strips of red pimiento

Sprinkle with:

A little grated cheese

Bake until eggs are set. Serve with:

Hot Pepper Sauce, or
Mexican Sauce, page 378

ABOUT OMELETS

The name "omelet" is loosely applied to many kinds of egg dishes. In America, you often get a great puffy, soufflélike, rather dry dish in which the egg whites have been beaten separately and folded into the yolks. In France an entire mystique surrounds a simple process in which the egg is combined as unobtrusively as possible to avoid incorporating air and this marbleized mixture is quickly turned into a three-fold delicacy, filled or unfilled. In an Italian frittata, the food is often mixed at once with the stirred egg and this thin pancakelike mixture is cooked in a little oil, first on one side and then on the other, with a result not unlike a large edition of Eggs Foo Yoong, page 190.

Since omelet making is so rapid, see that you have ready everything you are going to serve the omelet with or on and be sure you have your diners captive. For more details about equipment, see French Omelet, following.

The quality that all of these so-called omelets have in common is that ➧ the pan and the fat in which they are cooked must be hot enough to form an envelope almost at once to hold together the softer egg layers above it, but not too hot to let it toughen before the rest of the egg cooks.

➧ Eggs, therefore, and any food incorporated with them, must be at least 70° before being put in the pan. More omelet failures are due to eggs used direct from the refrigerator than to any other cause. There is always, too, discussion about salting. As salt tends to toughen the egg structure, this flavoring can be allowed to come in the delicate tidbits added to the omelet.

Glazing omelets makes them look prettier but also tends to toughen them. ➧ To glaze an omelet, brush it with butter. Or, if it is a sweet omelet, sprinkle it with sugar and run it under the broiler briefly or use a hot salamander or brander. If you want a real finished job, put the omelet on an ovenproof server. Coat it lightly with a thin Mornay Sauce, page 361, and run it under a broiler for 2 minutes.

➧ To fill and garnish an omelet with mushrooms, seafood, ham, truffles or tongue, put them into the hot butter before the eggs are added. Creamed food, cheese, herbs, garlic or any foods demanding low heat go on top of the eggs the minute the eggs are added to the pan and before stirring begins. Have ready about ½ to ¾ of a cup of the mixture. Place ¼ cup on the upper half of the omelet. Reserve the remaining mixture for the final garnish on top. Or, a simple method is to fold the omelet as sketched on page 188, then cut an incision along the top and insert the hot food. For other fillings, see Additions for Scrambled Eggs, page 191.

ABOUT OMELET PANS

Much fuss is always made about an omelet pan. It is said that it should be kept for that purpose and that alone and should never be washed but simply rubbed with a handful of salt and soft toweling. The argument for a separate pan goes further. For not only should this surface smoothness be maintained, but any pan used for braising is apt to have developed hot spots. But those of us who resent giving kitchen space to a pan for one use only find an all-purpose skillet—cleaned with modern detergents—usable ➧ provided the pan surface is smooth so the eggs can slide freely over it. The pan should be heavy enough to be slowly but thoroughly heated. Otherwise the egg cannot stand what one French authority calls the too great brutality of the quick heat. The next thing to consider is the omelet in relation to the pan size. Since French omelets are made so quickly, we never try more than 2 to 3 eggs at a time—cooked in 1 tablespoon of sweet butter. If more than one omelet is needed, have some extra butter already melted to save preparation time. We use a skillet with a long handle and a 5-inch base flaring gently to a 7-inch top, as shown in the sketches. For larger omelets—and they can be made successfully with up to 8 to 10 eggs—see that the similarly-shaped pan is big enough to keep the egg no deeper than ¼ inch, and add a proportionate amount of butter.

FRENCH OMELET

➧ Please read About Omelets, page 187. Remember that an omelet of this type takes only 30 to 50 seconds to make, depending on your preference for soft or firm results. Mix briefly in a bowl with a dinner fork:

3 eggs

Put in a 7-inch omelet pan:

1 tablespoon clarified sweet butter

To avoid sticking, clarified butter is best. Roll it over the bottom and sides of the pan. When it is hot and ➧ has reached the point of fragrance, but is not brown, pour in the eggs. Meanwhile, agitate the pan forward and backward with the left hand. Keep the egg mass sliding as a whole over the pan bottom. Quickly pick up a dinner fork and swirl the eggs with a circular motion, as shown on the left below. Hold the fork so the tines are parallel to, but not scraping, the base of the pan. At this point, the heat in the pan

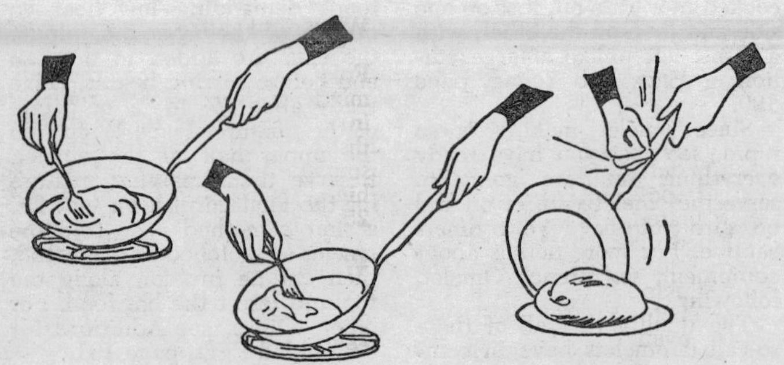

may be sufficient to cook the eggs and you may want to lift the pan from the heat as you gently swirl the eggs, as illustrated, in circular scrolls from the edges to the center. Pay no attention to the ridges formed by the fork. The rhythm of the pan and the stirring is like a child's trick of patting the head while rubbing the stomach. ♦ Have ready a hot serving plate—a heat-resistant one if you plan to glaze the omelet. A heated plate helps to inflate the omelet. To fold it—whether you fill, see page 188, or serve a plain omelet—grasp the handle of the pan so the right palm is up, as shown. Tip the pan down away from the handle and, with the fork, flip about one third of the omelet over, away from the handle, as shown in the center. If the omelet shows any tendency to stick, discard the fork and, by giving the pan handle a sharp rap or two with the fist, as sketched, the omelet will even flip over without the use of a fork and will start to slide. Slant the pan to 90° or more until the omelet makes a second fold in sliding out of the pan and lies with its ends folded under on the plate—ready to serve. Glaze and garnish if you wish and serve at once. For fillings, see About Omelets.

FLUFFY OR SOUFFLÉED OMELET [4]

If you have 1 or 2 extra egg whites, add these and omit the baking powder. You may add some grated Parmesan cheese or chopped parsley, chives and chervil to the egg mixture before cooking it, or sprinkle these on top before putting the omelet in the oven.

Combine and beat with a fork:

¼ cup milk
4 egg yolks
1 teaspoon any baking powder

Beat until stiff, but not dry:

4 egg whites

Melt in a heavy skillet over slow heat:

1 tablespoon butter

Fold the yolk mixture lightly into the egg whites. Pour the batter into the skillet. Cover the skillet with a lid. As the omelet cooks, slash through it several times with a knife to permit the heat to penetrate the lower crust. When the omelet is half done—after about 5 minutes—it may be placed uncovered on the center rack of a 350° oven until the top is set. Jet-propel this to the table as it comes out of the oven, as it will collapse quite quickly. Do not try to fold it as it will crack and become flat and tough. It may be garnished with any of the fillings or sauces suggested for a French omelet, or use poached, drained, chopped oysters. Serve it cut in pie-shaped wedges.

BAKED OMELET [4]

Preheat oven to 325°.
Beat until very light:

4 egg yolks
¼ cup sugar

Add:

½ teaspoon vanilla

Whip until stiff:

4 egg whites

Fold them lightly into the yolk mixture. Place these ingredients in a flat, 8-inch, round baking dish. Slash the top lightly. The soufflé should be about 1-inch high. Bake it until firm, about 25 minutes. Dust it with:

Powdered sugar

Warm and pour over it:

¼ cup rum, Cointreau or kirsch

Ignite the rum at table and let

it burn down. This may be served with:

Crushed sweetened berries

FIRM OMELET [4]

For the beginner, the texture of this omelet is a little more manageable.

Beat with a fork until blended:

4 eggs

Beat in:

¼ cup milk or cream
½ teaspoon salt
⅛ teaspoon paprika

Melt in a skillet:

1½ tablespoons butter

When this is fairly hot, add the egg mixture. Cook it over low heat. Lift the edges with a pancake turner and tilt the skillet to permit the uncooked custard to run to the bottom or stick it with a fork in the soft spots to permit the heat to penetrate the bottom crust. When it is all an even consistency, fold the omelet over and serve it. The Japanese make a good omelet by this rule, substituting stock for milk or cream.

SWEET OMELET

See (II, 448) for other sweet omelets.

I. Follow the preceding recipe for:

Fluffy Omelet

Add to the yolk mixture:

1 tablespoon sugar

Just before serving spread the omelet with:

Jam or jelly

Sprinkle the top with:

Confectioners' sugar

Fruit juice may be substituted for the milk and the omelet may be spread with cooked or raw sweetened fruit instead of jelly.

II. Prepare:

Fluffy Omelet, above

Add to the egg yolks:

1 tablespoon brandy
1 tablespoon curaçao

When finished, sprinkle with:

Castor sugar

and Flambé, page 80.

SHRIMP EGGS FOO YOONG

Foo Yoong is really a rich omelet made with additions of cooked vegetables, fish and meat.

Clean or drain:

2 cups bean sprouts

Heat:

A little cooking oil

in a skillet and stir-fry, page 253, until translucent and crisp:

1 slice minced gingerroot
6 chopped green onions
1 stalk thinly sliced celery
1 cup shredded cooked fish or finely diced cooked meat

Have ready and combine with the above ingredients:

6 well-beaten eggs
1 teaspoon salt
½ teaspoon pepper

Heat an additional:

1 tablespoon cooking oil

in another small skillet. Drop the above mixture into it to form small omelets, golden brown on both sides. Serve with:

Soy sauce

FRITTATA [3]

This Italian omelet usually has the filling mixed into the eggs before they are cooked. You may use any of the suggested fillings for the basic French omelet, except the creamed or sauced ones, allowing about 1 cup of filling to 3 eggs. The frittata is usually turned when the bottom has set firm.

Prepare and keep warm:

2 cups diced cooked vegetables, chicken, seafood, ham, etc., in any combination

Beat with a fork until blended:

6 eggs

Stir in the filling and

Correct the seasoning

How much salt and pepper you add will depend on how highly seasoned your filling is. Have ready a 10-inch greased omelet pan. Into another 10-inch pan which has been heated, put:

1½ tablespoons olive oil

Pour in the egg mixture and proceed as in the basic French Omelet, above, until the bottom of the frittata is set and the top is still like creamy scrambled eggs. Place the greased skillet with the greased side over the frittata like a lid. Reverse the position of the skillets so the ungreased side of the frittata falls into the lid, and this lid then becomes the skillet which is heated to complete the cooking of the dish, a matter of 1 to 2 minutes more. Serve at once on a hot platter.

SCRAMBLED EGGS [2]

Beaten egg whites may be added to whole eggs in the proportion of one additional white to 3 whole eggs.

Melt in a skillet over slow heat or in a well-greased double boiler ➧ over—not in—hot water:

1 tablespoon butter

Beat and pour in:

3 eggs
⅛ teaspoon salt
⅛ teaspoon paprika
(3 tablespoons cream)

When the eggs begin to thicken, break them into shreds with a fork or stir with a wooden spoon. When they have thickened, serve them on:

Hot toast lightly buttered or spread with fish paste, deviled ham or liver sausage; or in a hollowed-out hard roll

An attractive way to serve scrambled eggs is to put them in individual well-buttered ring molds while the eggs are still rather creamy in consistency. Let them finish cooking in their own heat, which will set them. Turn out and fill the center with any of the additions listed below.

ADDITIONS TO SCRAMBLED EGGS

Small amounts of the following may be stirred into the egg mixture before scrambling. They should be at least 70°.

Grated or crumbled cheese
Chopped, peeled, seeded, sautéed tomatoes flavored with basil
Cultured sour cream and chives
Canned chopped sardines
Crab meat, seasoned with curry powder
Capers
Chopped canned anchovies
Chopped sautéed onions
Crisp bacon bits
Small pieces of broiled sausage
Sautéed mushrooms
Poached calf brains

EGGS SCRAMBLED WITH CREAM CHEESE [4]

Melt in a double boiler over simmering water:

1 package cream cheese: 3 oz.
1 tablespoon butter

Scald and stir in:

1 cup cream

Add:

½ teaspoon salt
¼ teaspoon paprika

Break into the sauce:

6 eggs

Before the egg whites are firm, stir the eggs gently with a fork until thick. Add:

1½ tablespoons sherry

SCOTCH WOODCOCK [2]

Toast:

2 slices bread

Cut it into fingers. Butter well and spread with a thin layer of:

Anchovy paste

Beat together:

3 or 4 egg yolks
½ cup cream
⅛ teaspoon pepper
⅛ teaspoon salt

Melt in a double boiler:

2 tablespoons butter

Add the egg mixture and scramble until creamy. Arrange the anchovy toast on a hot dish and cover with the egg mixture. Garnish with:

Chopped parsley

SHIRRED OR BAKED EGGS OR EGGS EN COCOTTE

[Individual Serving]

Baked eggs always have great "eye appeal" served in little ramekins, casseroles or cocotte dishes. Care must be taken that they are not overcooked, as the white can become quite hard and rubbery and the ramekin will retain the heat and continue to cook the egg after it is removed from the oven. If you put a poaching paper, page 83, over the ramekin, this will return enough heat to the topside of the egg to set it. The centers should be soft, the whites just set. Don't try to hurry baked eggs; they must be cooked in gentle oven heat.

Preheat oven to 350°.

Grease small bakers or ramekins.

Break carefully into each one:

1 egg

Add lightly:

Salt

Sprinkle over the top:

1 teaspoon cream or melted butter

Bake for about 8 to 10 minutes.

You may garnish with:

Chopped or sliced truffles

Sautéed pieces of chicken liver

BAKED EGGS ON TOAST

[Individual Serving]

Carefully prepared, this makes a delicious dish.

Preheat oven to 325°.

Grease warmed individual molds with:

Butter

Place in each one:

1 teaspoon chopped celery, chives or parsley

Break into each one:

1 or 2 eggs

Season them with:

Salt and paprika

Cover each mold with a small poaching paper. Place the molds in a pan of hot water, deep enough to reach to within ½ inch of the top of the mold. Bake until the eggs are firm. Turn them out on:

Rounds of hot buttered toast

Serve them with well-seasoned:

Cream Sauce I, page 359, or Tomato Sauce, page 376

Or serve with one of the Additions to Baked Eggs, listed below.

ADDITIONS TO BAKED EGGS

For interesting variations to baked eggs try adding: cooked mushrooms, asparagus tips, tomatoes or other vegetables, such as creamed spinach. Or add chicken hash, small bits of bacon, sausage or anchovy. Or place a round of toast covered with Gruyère cheese in the bottom of the baker before the eggs are added. Instead of butter, you may also cover the eggs with a cheese or tomato sauce before baking. Other tasteful sauce additions are: one cup cream sauce flavored with 1 teaspoon prepared mustard; creamed mushrooms or canned soup—celery, mushroom, asparagus, etc. Dilute the latter with milk or water to the consistency of cream sauce. Eggs are also good baked in 1 cup or more of Creamed Onions, page 301.

EGGS IN A NEST [1 to 2]

A gala-looking dish:
Preheat oven to 350°.
Beat until very stiff.

2 egg whites

Heap them in a greased ovenproof dish. Make 2 cavities an equal distance apart, not too near the edge. Slip into them:

2 unbroken egg yolks

Bake for 10 minutes or until the eggs are set. Season with:

Salt and white pepper

Sprinkle with:

(Chopped chives)

EGGS BAKED IN BACON RINGS

[Individual Servings]
Preheat oven to 325°.
Sauté or broil lightly:

Strips of bacon

Grease the bottom of muffin pans. Line the sides with the bacon. Place in each pan:

(1 tablespoon chili sauce)

Drop into it:

1 egg

Pour over the egg:

1 teaspoon melted butter

Sprinkle with:

Salt and paprika

Bake for about 10 minutes or until the eggs are set. Turn them out onto:

Rounds of toast or slices of drained pineapple

Garnish with:

Parsley

HAM CAKES AND EGGS [4]

Preheat oven to 325°.
Combine:

1 cup cooked ground ham
1 egg
1 tablespoon water
⅛ teaspoon paprika or pepper

Press these ingredients into 4 greased muffin tins. Leave a large hollow in each one. Drop into the hollows:

4 eggs

Bake the cakes until the eggs are firm. Turn out the cakes on:

Rounds of toast

Garnish them with:

Parsley or chopped chervil

HARD-COOKED EGG AND VEGETABLE CASSEROLE [5]

Preheat oven to 350°.
Combine:

1 cup cooked vegetables
1 cup Cream Sauce I, page 359
1 cup Creole Sauce, page 380

You may add:

2 teaspoons chopped fresh parsley, thyme, basil, etc.

Dill or celery seeds are wonderful. Prepare:

5 Hard-Cooked Eggs, page 183

Slice them. Grease a baking dish. Place alternate layers of eggs, etc., and sauce in the dish. Top with:

Au Gratin III, page 389

Bake for about 15 minutes.

CURRIED EGGS [4]

An occasional curry dish is a treat.
Cook:

6 Hard-Cooked Eggs, page 183

Shell and slice them or cut them in half, lengthwise. Prepare:

2 cups Curry Sauce I or II, page 363

You may pound and add:

(¼ cup blanched almonds)

Add the eggs. Heat them well. Serve on:

Hot buttered toast
garnished with:
Parsley

CREAMED EGGS AND ASPARAGUS COCKAIGNE [6]

We use both versions of this, depending on the time at hand. The texture is lovely if the asparagus is well drained and the sauce is not overheated.

I. Drain well and cut in 1-inch pieces:
2 cups cooked or canned asparagus tips
Reserve the liquid. Have ready:
6 hard-cooked, shelled, sliced eggs
Prepare:
2 cups Quick White Sauce, page 360
using milk and the reserved asparagus liquor. When the sauce is hot, gently fold in the asparagus and sliced eggs. Either heat this further in the top of a double boiler ➧ over—not in—hot water or preheat oven to 350° and place in a baker. Cover with:
Au Gratin I, page 389
and bake until the eggs and asparagus are heated through. Serve with:
Slices of ham
Hot French Bread (II, 245)

II. [4]
Preheat oven to 350°.
Have ready:
4 to 6 sliced hard-cooked eggs
1½ cups well-drained canned asparagus, cut in 1-inch lengths
1 can cream of chicken soup
diluted with:
¼ cup asparagus liquor
Place in 4 individual baking dishes. Alternate layers of eggs and asparagus. Cover each dish equally with soup mixture. Cover and bake about 15 minutes or until thoroughly heated.

CREAMED EGGS AU GRATIN [4]

Preheat broiler.
Slice into a baking dish:
4 hard-cooked eggs
Combine:
1½ cups Cream Sauce II, page 359
¼ cup chili sauce
Pour this mixture over the eggs. Top with:
Au Gratin II, page 389
Place the dish under the broiler until the crumbs are golden.

SCOTCH EGGS

[Individual Servings]
Preheat deep fryer to 375°.
➧ Please read About Deep-Fat Frying, pages 75–79.
Some people use pork sausage meat, bound with egg and bread crumbs for the coating. Make a forcemeat with:
Finely chopped or minced cooked ham
2 or 3 mashed anchovies in oil
Fresh bread crumbs
Salt
Pepper
Coat thickly with the forcemeat:
Hard-cooked eggs
Bind with:
Raw egg
Dip in:
Egg and bread crumbs
Deep fry until the coating is brown. Slice in half and serve on:
Croutons

MASKED EGGS

[Allow 1 Egg to a Person]
Chill and shell:
Hard-Cooked Eggs, page 183
Cut them into halves, lengthwise. Place them cut side down on:

Water cress or shredded lettuce

Pour over them:

Mayonnaise thinned with a little lemon juice or cream, Mayonnaise Collé, page 387, or Chaud-Froid Sauce, page 388

Sprinkle them with:

Capers, chopped anchovies, bits of ham or cooked bacon

STUFFED EGGS ON ROSETTES WITH SAVORY SAUCE [8]

This dish is elaborate, but capable of prefabrication. The rosettes, the sauce and eggs may be made the day before they are served.

Prepare:

8 hard-cooked eggs

Cut them crosswise into halves. Remove the yolks. Combine them with an equal part of:

Cooked, finely chopped seasoned spinach or Creamed Spinach, page 326

Fill the egg whites with the mixture. Prepare:

2 cups Cream Sauce I, page 359

Season it with:

2 tablespoons Worcestershire sauce
2 tablespoons dry sherry
¾ cup chili sauce
Salt and pepper

When the sauce is smooth and hot, add:

2 cups cooked or canned shrimp or diced cooked sweetbreads

Prepare:

16 Rosettes, page 209

Place a stuffed egg half on each rosette and cover with sauce. Serve them at once or, if you have made the sauce and the rosettes ahead of time, reheat the sauce in a double boiler. Reheat the rosettes in a 400° oven.

PICKLED EGGS

Prepare:

6 hard-cooked eggs

Shell and stick into each egg:

4 cloves—24 in all

Boil:

2 cups vinegar

Make a smooth paste of:

½ teaspoon ground mustard
½ teaspoon salt
½ teaspoon pepper

with a little cold vinegar and add to the boiling vinegar. Stir for about 1 minute. Put the eggs in a glass fruit jar and pour the boiling vinegar over them. Cover and refrigerate for about 2 weeks. Use with cold cuts and in salads.

DEVILED OR STUFFED EGGS

The blandness of hard-cooked eggs is a challenge to adventurous cooks and a few suggestions to vary this basic ingredient with supplies from your pantry shelves follow:

Prepare:

Hard-Cooked Eggs, page 183

Shell the eggs. Cut them in half lengthwise or slice off both ends, which leaves a barrel-shaped container. Remove yolks carefully so as not to damage the whites. Crush the yolks without packing them and moisten them pleasantly with:

French dressing or mayonnaise, sweet or cultured sour cream, soft butter with vinegar and sugar, lemon juice or sweet pickle juice

Season to taste with:

Salt and paprika

Or one or more of the following:

A little dry mustard
Catsup
A dash of cayenne, curry,

or hot pepper sauce
Worcestershire sauce

Exotic additions to the yolks are:

Anchovy or sardine paste
Liver sausage paste or foie gras
Chopped sautéed chicken livers
Chopped ginger and cream cheese
Chutney
Caviar
Smoked salmon
Deviled ham or tongue
Grated Roquefort
Chopped chives, tarragon, chervil, parsley, burnet or basil

Garnish with:

Olives, capers or truffles

Put the filling back in the whites. You may use a pastry tube for elaborate effects. Remove from the refrigerator ½ hour before serving for improved flavor and texture.

DEVILED EGGS IN SAUCE [4]

Preheat oven to 425°.
Prepare:

4 Deviled Eggs, page 195

Place the halves in a greased dish. Pour over them:

1 cup Tomato Sauce, page 376, Mornay Sauce, page 361, Béchamel Sauce, page 360, or Mushroom Sauce, page 367, or a Shrimp Sauce for Fish, page 377

Coat the sauce with:

Au Gratin II or III, page 389

Bake the dish until the top is brown.

ABOUT SOUFFLÉS AND TIMBALES

The soufflé is considered the prima donna of the culinary world. The timbale is her more even-tempered relative. On closer acquaintance, both become quite tractable and are great glamorizers for leftover foods. ➧ Cooked foods are best to use, as they release less moisture into the mixture than do raw ones.

The soufflé is usually based on a Béchamel or cream sauce, the timbale often on cream and eggs only. The timbale may seem the more fragile of the two, but ➧ steaming—the distinctive process in the timbale—gives this custardlike dish much more stamina. The soufflé, which is baked ➧ must always be kept away from drafts and be served at once in the ovenproof straight-sided dish in which it is cooked.

A timbale is made in a mold and can be reversed onto a hot dish or into a pastry shell that was previously baked and cooled. It looks particularly attractive in a ring mold. It is often coated or served with a sauce. If a delay is even a possibility, turn your ingredients into a timbale, which will even submit to the indignity of reheating.

If your guests are assembled, prepare a soufflé. If not it may be like the beauty Horace Walpole commented on: "She is pretty with the bloom of youth but has no features and her beauty cannot last."

ABOUT SOUFFLÉS

Soufflés have the same kind of life as the "breath" for which they are named, some slightly longer than others, but with a predictable endurance for puffiness. If well made, you can count on about 10 short minutes in a holding oven ➧ but beware of drafts. Since they ➧ depend on egg white and steam for their ascent ➧ no second should be wasted from the beating of the whites until the soufflé is popped quickly into the ➧ preheated oven. With very few exceptions, every action, including ➧ immediate serving after baking, should contribute to hold their "breath" as long as possible. These tours de force, based on cream sauce with egg yolks and whipped whites, are easy to make if the pointers are carefully heeded. The cream sauce should be a rather firm one ➧ heated just to a boil. Remove it from the heat for ½ minute before the 70° eggs and any other ingredients —also at 70°—are added. The egg whites should be ➧ stiff, but not dry (II, 180). ➧ Soufflés can always be made lighter if an extra egg white is added for every 2 whole eggs.

➧ To prepare soufflé dishes for baking, use a straight-sided ovenproof baker. Grease the bottom and sides well with butter and then coat the buttered surfaces with a thorough dusting of flour, sugar or dry grated cheese—depending on the flavor of your soufflé. It will also climb up the sides of an ungreased baker, but it will not rise as high and the lovely brown crust will stick and have to be scraped off the sides rather than form a glossy coating which adds so much to the look of the individual serving.

Next, be sure the oven is heated to the indicated temperature. ➧ A soufflé needs quick bottom heat. ➧ If your electric oven has a top element, be sure to remove it, as the heat in it is often enough to stiffen the top surface of the soufflé too quickly and not allow for its fullest expansion during the baking period. ➧ For oven placement of soufflé bakers, see sketch, page 100. Some recipes suggest making soufflés in the top of a double boiler ➧ over—not in—hot water. This is advisable only if an oven is not available, as the resulting texture is closer to a timbale than a soufflé. ➧ To make a soufflé with a crown—a "high-hat soufflé"—just before putting the soufflé into the oven take a large spoon or a rubber scraper and run a groove about 1½ inches deep all around the top, about 1¼ inches from the edge of the dish. A crown may also be made by extending the height of the baker with a piece of parchment paper tied firmly around the dish. We find this satisfactory only with so-called cold soufflés based on cream gelatins (II, 449).

MADE-IN-ADVANCE CHEESE SOUFFLÉ [6]

Preheat oven to 475°.

You can mix this soufflé as much as 3 hours before baking time, if you like, and set in the refrigerator. Remove it about 20 minutes before putting it in the preheated oven.

Prepare a 10-inch soufflé baker, opposite.

Melt:

½ cup butter

in a double boiler ➧ over—not in—boiling water. Add:

½ cup sifted flour
1½ teaspoons salt
½ teaspoon paprika
Dash cayenne or hot pepper sauce

Mix well. Gradually stir in:

2 cups milk

Cook ➧ stirring constantly until sauce is thick. Dice:

½ lb. sharp cheddar cheese

Stir in cream sauce until cheese melts. Remove from heat. Beat until light:

8 egg yolks

➧ Gradually pour yolks into cheese sauce, stirring constantly. Wash beater. Beat ➧ until stiff, but not dry:

8 egg whites

Fold cheese sauce into egg whites. Pour mixture into baker and refrigerate if you wish. Bake

10 minutes. ➧ Reduce heat to 400° and bake 25 minutes longer. Serve with:

Tossed Green Salad, page 33, or Grapefruit and Orange Salad, page 55

BLENDER CHEESE SOUFFLÉ [4 to 5]

A somewhat firm but acceptable soufflé. ➧ To prepare baker, please read About Soufflés, page 196.

Preheat oven to 325°.

Dice into cubes:

6 oz. sharp cheddar cheese

Heat to just below boiling:

1½ cups milk

Pour the milk into blender container and quickly add:

2 teaspoons butter
6 to 8 pieces crustless bread, torn into large pieces
½ teaspoon salt
⅓ teaspoon pepper or a few grains of cayenne
(⅛ teaspoon mustard)

Blend until thickened. Add the cubed cheese. Beat in a large bowl until lemon colored:

4 egg yolks

Add the blended cheese mixture ➧ very slowly, beating constantly. Beat until stiff, but not dry and fold in gently:

4 egg whites

Place the mixture in a prepared 8-inch soufflé baker and bake about 50 minutes or until set.

ADDITIONS TO CHEESE SOUFFLÉS

For a more complete dish, consider adding one of the following to cheese soufflé:

½ cup ground or finely chopped ham
½ to 1 cup cooked, well-drained and chopped or ground vegetables, such as celery or carrots
3 tablespoons Italian tomato paste

CHEESE SOUFFLÉ COCKAIGNE [4]

Preheat oven to 350°.

➧ Please read About Soufflés, page 196.

Prepare:

1 cup Cream Sauce II, page 359

Bring to a boil. Remove from heat ½ minute. Add, stirring well:

5 tablespoons grated Parmesan cheese
2 tablespoons grated Gruyère cheese
3 beaten egg yolks

Fold into the cheese mixture. Pour into one 7-inch or 4 individual ➧ prepared soufflé bakers. You may decorate the soufflés before baking with:

Paper thin slices of Swiss cheese cut into fancy shapes

Bake for about 25 to 30 minutes or until set.

VEGETABLE SOUFFLÉ [4]

Preheat oven to 350°.

Cooked oyster plant, eggplant, cauliflower, peas, onions, carrots, celery, canned or fresh asparagus, etc., may be used alone or in any good combination. Small quantities of leftover vegetables may be combined with minced raw carrots, celery and onions.

Prepare:

1 cup Cream Sauce II, page 359: ⅓ cup cream and ⅔ cup vegetable stock

When the sauce is boiling, stir in:

1 cup minced drained vegetables

When the vegetables are hot, reduce the heat and add:

3 beaten egg yolks

Cook and stir for 1 minute longer to permit the yolks to

thicken. Season as required with:

Salt and pepper
(Nutmeg)

Cool this mixture slightly. Whip until stiff, but not dry:

3 egg whites

Fold them lightly into the vegetable mixture. Bake the soufflé in a greased 7-inch baking dish for about 40 minutes or until firm. If you wish a dish that is a course in itself, serve the soufflé with:

Mushroom Sauce, page 367

CORN SOUFFLÉ

Follow the preceding recipe. Use in place of the minced vegetables:

¾ cup well-drained corn, canned or cooked, cut from the cob

Add:

(1 chopped pimiento)
(1 chopped green pepper)

ONION SOUFFLÉ [4]

One of our pet accompaniments to an otherwise slim meal.

Preheat oven to 325°.

Prepare:

1 cup Steamed Onions, page 301

Drain and mince them. Melt:

2 tablespoons butter

Stir in until blended:

2 tablespoons flour

Combine and stir in slowly:

½ cup milk
½ cup evaporated milk or cream

When the sauce is smooth and hot, stir in the minced onion. When the onions are hot ➧ remove from the heat and stir in:

3 beaten egg yolks

Cook ➧ but do not boil, and stir for about 1 minute longer to permit the yolks to thicken. Season with:

Salt, paprika and nutmeg
2 tablespoons chopped parsley or ½ teaspoon dried basil

Cook these ingredients slightly. Whip until stiff, but not dry:

3 egg whites

Fold them lightly into the onion mixture. Bake the soufflé in a greased or prepared 7-inch baker until it is firm, about 40 minutes.

SWEET POTATO AND PINEAPPLE OR APPLESAUCE SOUFFLÉ [6]

This is fine with cold or hot ham.

Preheat oven to 350°.

Prepare:

3 cups Boiled Sweet Potatoes, page 322

Add and beat with a fork until the potatoes are fluffy:

3 tablespoons butter
½ teaspoon salt
½ teaspoon grated lemon rind
2 beaten egg yolks

Drain well and fold in:

½ to ¾ cup drained crushed pineapple or tart applesauce

Cool these ingredients slightly. Whip until stiff and fold in:

2 egg whites

Bake the soufflé in a greased 7-inch baker for about 40 minutes.

EGGPLANT SOUFFLÉ

Preheat oven to 325°.

Prepare:

A Stuffed Eggplant, page 292

Combine the cooked mashed pulp with:

¾ cup soft bread crumbs
2 beaten egg yolks
1 tablespoon melted butter
½ cup chopped nut meats or grated cheese
Salt and pepper
Grated nutmeg

If the filling seems stiff, add:

1 tablespoon or more milk

Beat until stiff but not dry:

2 egg whites

Fold them lightly into the other ingredients. Fill the shells. Cover the tops with:

Buttered crumbs or cornflakes

Place them in a pan with a little water and bake for about 30 minutes.

CHICKEN SOUFFLÉ

[16 Individual Soufflés]

This soufflé makes a good luncheon dish, as it has more "body" than most of the other soufflé recipes. Serve in individual bakers.

➧ Please read About Soufflés, page 196.

Preheat oven to 325°.

Mince:

2¼ cups cooked chicken

Prepare:

3 cups Cream Sauce II, page 359

using chicken fat to replace the butter and stock or cream as the liquid. When the sauce is hot, stir in the minced chicken and:

1 cup chopped nut meats

1 cup chopped cooked vegetables or raw celery, carrots and onions

When these ingredients are hot, remove from the heat and add:

9 beaten egg yolks

Season with:

Salt and pepper

Nutmeg

Let cool slightly. Whip ➧ until stiff, but not dry:

9 egg whites

Fold them lightly into the chicken mixture. Pour until ⅔ full into prepared soufflé bakers, page 196. Bake until firm, about 20 to 25 minutes. Serve the soufflé with:

Mushroom Sauce, page 367, or

Poulette Sauce, page 362, etc.

LEFTOVER CHICKEN SOUFFLÉ [5]

A glamorous way to use chicken leftovers.

Preheat oven to 325°.

Prepare:

1 cup Cream Sauce II, page 359

using Chicken Stock and cream for the liquid. When the sauce is hot, add:

1 cup solids: minced chicken, nut meats, minced and drained cooked vegetables

Remove from the heat and add:

3 beaten egg yolks

Season with:

Salt and pepper

Freshly grated nutmeg

Let cook slightly. Whip ➧ until stiff, but not dry:

3 or 4 egg whites

Fold them lightly into the chicken mixture. Bake the soufflé in a prepared 8-inch baker until firm, about 40 minutes.

COOKED FISH OR MEAT SOUFFLÉ [4]

➧ Please read About Soufflés, page 196.

Preheat oven to 325°.

Prepare:

1 cup Cream Sauce II, page 359

When it is smooth and hot, stir in:

¾ to 1 cup flaked cooked fish: tuna, crab, clams, lobster, shrimp, etc., or finely chopped, cooked meat

¼ cup finely chopped raw carrots, celery and parsley

When these ingredients are hot, remove from the heat and stir in:

3 beaten egg yolks

Season with:

Salt and paprika

Nutmeg

Lemon juice, Worcester-

shire sauce or tomato catsup
(⅓ cup sliced olives)

Let cool slightly. Whip ➧ until stiff, but not dry:

3 to 4 egg whites

Fold them lightly into the mixture. Bake in a greased 7-inch soufflé baker until firm, about 40 minutes. Serve the soufflé with:

(Tomato Sauce, page 376)

OYSTER SOUFFLÉ [4]

This soufflé is very delicate.
Preheat oven to 325°.
Drain, but save the liquor from:

½ to 1 pint oysters

Dry on a towel. Prepare:

1 cup Cream Sauce II, page 359, using part cream and part oyster liquor

When it is hot, remove from heat and add the oysters. Add:

3 beaten egg yolks

Season with:

Salt and pepper
Nutmeg
(Lemon juice)

Let cool slightly. Whip ➧ until stiff, but not dry:

3 to 4 egg whites

Fold them lightly into the oyster mixture. Bake in a ➧ prepared 7-inch soufflé baker until firm, about 40 minutes.

SHAD ROE SOUFFLÉ [4]

➧ Please read About Soufflés and Timbales, page 196.
Preheat oven to 375°.
Poach for 3 to 5 minutes:

1 fresh shad roe

Remove outer integument and veins. Crumble the roe and combine it with:

2 beaten eggs
1 cup whipped cream
A grating of nutmeg
Correct the seasoning

Fill individual molds ¾ full of this mixture. Set molds in a pan of hot water. Bake about 25 minutes. Serve with:

Allemande Sauce, page 362, or
Béarnaise Sauce, page 370

ABOUT TIMBALES

➧ Please read About Soufflés and Timbales, page 196.

Butter individual or larger molds lightly. Fill them about two-thirds full with the timbale mixture. ➧ Place them on a rack in a pan of hot, but not boiling, water. The water should be as high as the filling in the molds. If a rack is not available, fold several thicknesses of paper and place the molds on it. ➧ Check the heat occasionally to make sure that the water around the mold never boils—just simmers.

It is wise to protect the top of the timbale with a poaching paper, page 83.

Bake the timbales in a ➧ moderate oven, about 325°, for about 20 to 50 minutes, depending on the size of the mold. The timbales are done when a knife blade inserted in the center of the mold comes out uncoated.

CUSTARD FOR VEGETABLE TIMBALES [4]

In France the salad is served with the meat course and the vegetable is served in solitary state. It is usually worthy of this exalted position. Sometimes it is accompanied by a mound or ring of delicious custard.
Preheat oven to 325°.
Combine and beat with a wire whisk:

1½ cups warm cream or ½ cup cream and 1 cup chicken stock
4 eggs
¾ teaspoon salt
½ teaspoon paprika

(⅛ teaspoon grated nutmeg or celery salt)
(1 tablespoon chopped parsley)
(A few drops onion or lemon juice)

To bake, unmold and serve, see About Soufflés and Timbales, page 196. Serve the timbales with:

Creamed vegetables or Mushroom Sauce, page 367

For a brunch, garnish with:

Crisp bacon
Parsley

LEFTOVER TIMBALES [5 to 6]

Use any good combination of cooked vegetables and meat.
Preheat oven to 325°.
Follow the rule for:

Custard for Vegetable Timbales, above

using milk instead of cream. Omit the seasoning. Cut into small pieces and add:

1 to 1½ cups leftover food
(Chopped parsley)
(Grated onion)

After the food has been added to the timbale mixture, season it to taste. If the food is dry, no additional thickening is needed. If it is slightly moist, add to the leftovers, before combining them with the custard, until they form a moderately thick paste:

Cracker crumbs or bread crumbs

To bake, unmold and serve, see About Soufflés and Timbales, page 196. Serve with:

Tomato Sauce, page 379

BROCCOLI OR CAULIFLOWER TIMBALES [5 to 6]

Preheat oven to 325°.
Prepare:

Custard for Vegetable Timbales, page 201

Add to the custard:

1 to 1½ cups cooked well-drained broccoli or cauliflower, chopped or put through a food mill

Add seasoning if required. To bake, unmold and serve, see About Soufflés and Timbales, page 196. Garnish with:

Hollandaise Sauce, page 369

MUSHROOM TIMBALES [5 to 6]

Preheat oven to 325°.
Prepare:

Custard for Vegetable Timbales, page 201

Add:

2 cups drained, chopped, sautéed mushrooms

To bake, unmold and serve, see About Soufflés and Timbales, page 196.

SPINACH TIMBALES [5 to 6]

Preheat oven to 325°.
Prepare:

Cream Sauce I, page 359

Add to it:

2 cups cooked, drained, finely chopped spinach
3 beaten eggs
½ cup grated cheese
¼ cup Veal Stock or other stock (II, 142)
Salt and pepper
A few grains cayenne

To bake, unmold and serve, see About Soufflés and Timbales, page 196.

CORN, EGG AND CHEESE TIMBALES [4]

Preheat oven to 325°.
Combine:

1⅓ cups canned cream style corn
½ cup grated Swiss cheese
2 to 3 beaten eggs
¼ teaspoon salt
⅛ teaspoon paprika
¼ teaspoon mustard
A few grains cayenne

To bake, unmold and serve, see About Soufflés and Timbales, page 196.

ASPARAGUS TIMBALES [4]

Wonderful balanced by a fruit or vegetable salad.
Preheat oven to 325°.
Grease 4 deep custard cups or a 7-inch ring mold. Place around the sides of each container:

3 to 5 well-drained canned or cooked asparagus tips, heads down

Fill the cups with:

Custard for Vegetable Timbales, page 201

To bake, unmold and serve see About Soufflés and Timbales, page 196. Place between the inverted timbales:

Hollandaise Sauce, page 369

Garnish them with:

Parsley

and surround them with:

Broiled or boiled link sausages

CHEESE TIMBALES OR CRUSTLESS QUICHE

Preheat oven to 325°.
Prepare the filling for:

Cheese Custard Pie, page 214

To bake, unmold and serve, see About Soufflés and Timbales, page 196. Good served with:

Green peas, spinach or broccoli

RICE TIMBALES

A good garnish for a fish platter.
Preheat oven to 350°.
Pack greased molds with leftover:

Vegetable Rice, page 164
Pilaf, page 166
Curried Rice, page 159, or
Spanish Rice, page 160

Bake them in a pan of hot water for 10 minutes. Invert them and garnish with:

Parsley

Serve with:

Onion Sauce, page 363

CHICKEN OR HAM TIMBALES [6]

Preheat oven to 325°.
Grind twice or blend:

2 cups cooked white chicken meat or 1 cup each chicken and cooked ham

Stir into it very slowly to form a paste:

¾ cup cold thick cream
¼ teaspoon salt
⅛ teaspoon paprika

Whip until stiff:

4 egg whites

Fold them lightly into the chicken mixture. Line greased timbale molds with:

(Pieces of truffles, ripe olives or pimiento)

To bake, unmold and serve, see About Soufflés and Timbales, page 196. Serve them with:

Mushroom Sauce, or chicken gravy with chopped parsley

CHICKEN LIVER TIMBALES [4]

Very light and delicate.
Preheat oven to 325°.
Put through a ricer, grinder or ⅄ blender:

¾ cup cooked chicken livers
½ cup Boiled Rice, page 158

Add:

A scant ¼ teaspoon salt
A few grains cayenne and nutmeg
½ teaspoon prepared mustard

Whip until stiff:

2 egg whites

In a separate bowl, whip until stiff:

¼ cup whipping cream

Fold these ingredients lightly

into the chicken-liver mixture. To bake, unmold and serve, see About Soufflés and Timbales, page 196. Serve with:

Mushroom Sauce, page 367, or
Poulette Sauce, page 362

VEAL TIMBALES [4]

Preheat oven to 325°.
Grind twice or blend:

1¼ cups cold cooked veal

Beat slightly and add:

3 egg yolks

Stir the ingredients well. Our French recipe says pound them in a mortar. Continue to stir while adding:

½ cup whipping cream
¼ cup dry white wine or
2 tablespoons lemon juice
⅛ teaspoon paprika
Salt, as needed

Beat until stiff:

3 egg whites
(¼ teaspoon mace)

Fold these into the other ingredients. To bake, unmold and serve, see About Soufflés and Timbales, page 196. Serve with:

Mushroom Sauce, page 367, or
Tomato Sauce, page 376

FISH TIMBALES [5 to 6]

Preheat oven to 325°.
Flake and chop until very fine:

2 cups cooked fish

Season it with:

¼ teaspoon salt
⅛ teaspoon paprika
½ teaspoon grated lemon rind
1½ teaspoons lemon juice

Whip until stiff:

½ cup whipping cream

In a separate bowl, whip until stiff:

3 egg whites

Fold the cream into the fish mixture, then fold in the egg whites. To bake, unmold and serve, see About Soufflés and Timbales, page 196. Serve them with:

Shrimp Sauce, page 377,
Béchamel Sauce, page 359, or Tartare Sauce, page 349

FISH TIMBALES OR MOUSSE [6]

Cooked fish may be substituted, but uncooked fish gives a better result.
➧ Please read About Soufflé and Timbales, page 196.
Preheat oven to 350°.
Grind, put through a ricer or ⅄ blend:

1 lb. uncooked fish: 2 cups

Heat over a low burner:

1½ tablespoons butter

Stir in, until blended:

1 tablespoon flour

Stir in:

¼ cup milk

➧ Remove from heat. Beat and stir in:

2 egg yolks

Season these ingredients with:

½ teaspoon salt
⅛ teaspoon paprika

Stir the yolk mixture for 1 to 2 minutes. Permit it to thicken slightly. Add the ground fish. Cool the mixture. Whip ➧ until stiff, but not dry:

2 egg whites

Whip until stiff:

1 cup whipping cream

Fold these ingredients lightly into the fish mixture. Garnish a greased 9-inch ring mold with:

Strips of pimiento
(Strips of green pepper)

Pour the fish mixture into the mold. Set the mold in a pan of hot water. Bake it for about ½ hour. Serve it with:

Hollandaise Sauce, page 369
Hot Shrimp Sauce, page 377
Horseradish Sauce, page 362
Oyster Sauce, page 361

SPINACH OR BROCCOLI RING MOLD [4]

➧ Please read About Soufflés and Timbales, page 196.
Preheat oven to 325°.
Have ready:

1 cup cooked spinach or broccoli

Drain, chop until fine, put through a purée strainer or ⅄ blend. Melt in a skillet:

3 tablespoons butter

Add and sauté for about 1 minute:

1 tablespoon chopped onion

Stir in until blended:

3 tablespoons flour

Combine and stir in slowly:

½ cup milk or Stock (II, 141)
½ cup cream or evaporated milk

When the sauce is boiling, stir in the spinach. Remove from heat and stir in:

3 beaten egg yolks

Cook and stir for about 1 minute longer to permit the yolks to thicken. Season with:

Salt and pepper
Nutmeg
(½ cup grated cheese)

Cool slightly. You may add just for looks:

A few drops green coloring

Whip until ➧ stiff, but not dry:

3 egg whites

Fold them lightly into the spinach mixture. Place these ingredients in a greased 7-inch ring mold set in a pan of hot water. Bake the mixture until it is firm, about 30 minutes. Invert it on a platter and serve it filled with:

Creamed Mushrooms, page 296
Some other creamed dish

CELERY ROOT RING MOLD [6]

➧ Please read About Soufflés and Timbales, page 196.
Preheat oven to 325°.
Cook, page 283:

4 medium-sized celery roots

Drain them well. Put them through a grinder, using a coarse knife, or through a ricer. Soak:

2 slices white bread

in:

3 tablespoons milk

Stir this into the celery and add:

2 tablespoons melted butter
1 teaspoon grated onion
2 tablespoons cream
4 beaten egg yolks
¾ teaspoon salt
½ teaspoon paprika
A fresh grating nutmeg

Whip until ➧ stiff, but not dry:

4 egg whites

Fold them into the celery mixture. Bake the mixture in a greased ring mold set in a pan of hot water for about 45 minutes. Invert it onto a hot plate. Fill the center with:

Buttered peas, sautéed mushrooms, etc.

CHESTNUT RING MOLD [4]

A delightful way to use chestnuts—the egg white lightens the consistency of the mixture.
➧ Please read About Soufflés and Timbales, page 196.
Preheat oven to 325°.
Combine:

2 tablespoons flour
1 teaspoon salt
¼ teaspoon paprika
1 cup riced Boiled Chestnuts, page 283
½ teaspoon grated onion

Add gradually:

½ cup milk

Stir and cook these ingredients over low heat for about 5 minutes. Cool slightly. Whip until ➧stiff, but not dry, then fold in:

3 egg whites

Bake the mixture in a 7-inch ring mold set in a pan of hot water for about ½ hour. Invert it onto a hot plate. Fill it with:

Buttered green peas
Chopped parsley

It may be served with:

Mushroom Sauce, page 367

to which add:

2 tablespoons dry sherry

MUSHROOM RING MOLD WITH SWEETBREADS OR CHICKEN [8]

➧ Please read About Soufflés and Timbales, page 196.

Preheat oven to 325°.

Parboil, page 537:

1 pair sweetbreads or use
1 cup cooked minced chicken

Remove the skin and membrane and mince the sweetbreads. Prepare:

1 cup Cream Sauce II, page 359

Melt in a pan:

2 tablespoons butter

Add and sauté for about 3 minutes:

2 slices onion

Remove the onion. Add to the pan:

1½ cups finely minced mushrooms

and the sweetbreads or chicken. Heat the cream sauce to the boiling point and combine it with the mushroom mixture. Remove from heat and stir in:

¼ cup dry bread crumbs
1 chopped pimiento
¼ teaspoon salt
2 beaten egg yolks

Cook and stir about 1 minute longer to permit the yolks to thicken. Cool these ingredients slightly. Whip until ➧ stiff, but not dry:

2 egg whites

Fold them lightly into the mushroom mixture. Place the mixture in a greased ring mold set in a pan of hot water and bake covered with a piece of buttered paper for 35 minutes or until firm. Invert the mold onto a platter and serve filled with:

Asparagus spears
Peas, etc.

and pass with:

Suprême Sauce, page 363

STEAMED VEAL MOLD [8]

The following is an excellent pudding.

Combine:

1½ lbs. ground veal
½ lb. ground pork
1½ cups finely rolled cracker crumbs
3 egg yolks
¾ cup milk
¼ teaspoon nutmeg
1 tablespoon melted butter
1 tablespoon onion juice
1¼ teaspoons salt
¼ teaspoon pepper
¼ cup chopped celery
⅛ cup chopped parsley

Beat until ➧ stiff, but not dry:

3 egg whites

Fold them into the other ingredients. Grease a pudding mold, fill it with the mixture, close it tightly and steam for 2½ hours. ➧ Please read about Steamed Puddings (II, 463).

Serve with:

Mushroom Sauce, page 367, or
Poulette Sauce, page 362

or with the always admirable:

Quick Tomato Sauce, page 376

HALIBUT RING MOLD [4]

➧Please read About Soufflés and Timbales, page 196.

Preheat oven to 350°.

Combine and cook to a paste:

1 cup bread crumbs
½ cup cream

When it is hot, add:

½ lb. finely chopped raw halibut

Season with:

teaspoon salt

⅛ teaspoon paprika

Cool these ingredients slightly. Whip until ◆ stiff, but not dry:

2 egg whites

Fold them lightly into the fish mixture. Place the mixture in a 7-inch buttered baking dish; set it in a pan of hot water. Bake it for about 40 minutes. Serve with:

Oyster Sauce, page 361, or
Poulette Sauce, page 362

Garnish with:

Tomatoes
Water cress

BRUNCH, LUNCH AND SUPPER DISHES

This is a chapter, we admit, for which we have a special fondness. In it, we call attention to the many delicious ways you can combine those foods you have already cooked, as well as the staples in your larder—whether they are dried, preserved, canned or frozen. Do not neglect other combinations in the egg, pasta and cereal chapters. From many of these recipes attractive meals may be prepared in less than half an hour's time.

Care in cooking, distinction in seasoning and presentation, can make even a tin of tuna memorable. The large gratinéed casserole, the individual lidded baking dish or one of the following cases for food—as well as garnishes made from simple materials—all lend distinction in making a quick dish a gracious one.

Keep in mind that many fresh fish and shellfish recipes are almost as rapidly cooked as those involving a preprocessed food. For other quick dishes, refer also to the section on Ground Meats, page 514, Variety Meats, page 534, and Vegetables, page 249. For the quickest of sauces, see Soup-Based Sauces, page 375.

ABOUT CASES FOR FOOD

We have left behind the era of trenchers—those coarse loaves that served as dishes and were eaten when empty by trenchermen. But none of us has lost a taste for the sauce-flavored pastry, pancake, tortilla or toast. All manner of creamed foods—meat, vegetable or fish mixtures, cheese concoctions, as well as farces and stews can be placed in one of the following cases and then served with a sauce.

Patty Shells (II, 304)
Popovers (II, 283)
Brioches (II, 258)
Rounds of buttered and toasted bread or French Toast (II, 290)
Rusks lightly buttered and heated
A loaf of bread that has been hollowed, buttered lightly and toasted in a 300° oven
A Rice Loaf, page 161
Pies or Tart Shells (II, 292)
Large or individual Noodle Rings, page 173
Large or individual Rice Rings, page 162
A Pastry Roll, page 311
Biscuits or Shortcakes (II, 283)
A Mashed Potato Ring, page 311
A Bread Dressing Ring, page 225
Stuffed Pancakes (II, 113)
Waffles (II, 118)
Noodle Baskets or Potato Baskets, page 319
Stuffed vegetables
Sandwich Loaf (II, 52)
Barquettes (II, 54)
Turnovers (II, 54)
Leaf Wrappings, page 85

Coconut shells
Sea shells
And the 9 recipes that follow.

ROLL CASES

Preheat oven to 300°.
Hollow out:
Small rolls
Spread the hollows with:
Melted butter
Toast in the oven until crisp.

BREAD CASES

Preheat oven to 300°.
With a biscuit cutter make rounds from:
1¼-inch-thick slices of bread
With a smaller cutter, press out an inner round, but do not let the cutter go beyond 1 inch deep. Hollow out these smaller rounds and brush the hollows with:
Melted butter
Toast in the oven until crisp and golden.

MELBA TOAST BASKETS

Preheat oven to 275°.
Lightly butter on both sides:
Thin crustless bread slices
Press them into muffin tins, letting the corners of the bread protrude slightly. Toast in the oven until crisp and golden.

ROSETTES

[About Thirty-Six 2½-inch Rosettes]
Rosettes are shaped with a small iron made for the purpose. They are very good served as a base for creamed chicken or sweetbreads. For dessert, serve with sweet sauce, stewed fruit or alone with coffee.

➧ This batter makes a thinner, crisper confection if it is allowed to rest refrigerated for 2 hours or more.
Beat until blended:
2 eggs
Add and beat:
¼ teaspoon salt
1 tablespoon sugar
If the rosettes are to be used as patties, omit the sugar. Sift before measuring:
1 cup all-purpose flour
Stir it into the egg mixture, alternately with:
1 cup milk
2 tablespoons melted butter
To deep fry rosettes, prepare the iron by immersing the head of it in deep fat. You can use a rather small deep pan, slightly larger than the head of the iron, with about 2½ inches of fat in it. Heat the fat to 375°. Dip the hot iron in the batter, but do not let it run over the top of the iron, for then it is difficult to get the rosette off when cooked. Return the batter-coated iron to the fat, immersing it completely

from 20 to 35 seconds. Remove the rosette with a fork. Reheat the iron in the deep fat and repeat the process. Drain the rosettes on absorbent paper and, if served as a dessert, dust with:
Confectioners' sugar

TIMBALE CASES FOR FOOD

Select a timbale iron that is fluted, see above. It is easier to handle than a plain one.
Sift:
¾ cup all-purpose flour
½ teaspoon salt
Combine and beat:
1 egg
½ cup milk
Combine the liquid and the

sifted ingredients with a few swift strokes. Add:

1 teaspoon olive oil or melted butter

Let the batter stand for 1 hour to avoid bubbles which disfigure the timbales. For a crisper, thinner case, rest the batter 2 hours or longer covered and refrigerated. To fry timbale cases, prepare the iron by immersing its head in deep fat. Heat the fat to 370°—hot enough to brown a cube of bread in 1 minute. Wipe the iron with a cloth wrapped around a fork. Plunge the iron into the batter, within ¾ inch of the top. Remove it. Allow the batter to dry slightly on the iron. Fry the timbale in the hot fat until it is golden brown, about 1 to 1½ minutes. Remove it from the iron and drain it on a paper towel. Repeat the process.

ABOUT MEAT PASTRIES

How we'd love to judge a competition of housewives, each turning out her native meat pastry! The doughs would range from the resilient to the flaky, with fillings running a full gamut of flavor. They would include: Won Ton, Ravioli, Kreplach, Piroshki, Rissoles, Enchiladas, Pot Pies. It is in such homely functional dishes, varied according to the season and by the individual cook, that the true cuisine of a country dwells. Many of these specialties call for precooked fillings which, already encased, need only a brief cooking of the dough and reheating of the filler, either by simmering in a broth, deep-fat frying, sautéing or baking.

Take your pick of the recipes following and those in hors d'oeuvre and soup garnishes. Size often dictates their placement in the menu.

➧ Cooking method will determine whether or not to vent the pastry. A baked meat pie will need a vent. Some cooks leave a hole in the center by which to add more gravy, if necessary. Others just prick the surface to allow the steam to escape and to prevent a soggy crust. If simmered like Won Ton, page 112, or fried like Rissoles (II, 54) do not vent. If covering a stew with biscuits, allow steam to escape by leaving spaces between the biscuits. This wide spacing also applies to dumpling toppings.

TURNOVERS, PIROSHKI OR ROLLS FILLED WITH MEAT, ETC. [6]

Preheat oven to 450°.

This recipe and the following one make excellent hot canapés. For canapés cut the dough into small, attractive shapes. For hot luncheon sandwiches, make them a more generous size. If prepared in advance, keep them chilled until ready to bake.

Prepare, using about 2 cups of flour:

Biscuit or Pie Dough (II, 283, 292)

Pat or roll it until thin. This is a matter of taste—about ¼ inch for biscuit dough, ⅛ inch for pie dough. Cut it into 3 x 3-inch squares or rounds. Place a filling on each piece of dough—as much as they will hold properly. Moisten the edges, fold over and pinch down with a fork. Place the triangles or crescents in a pan. Brush them lightly with:

(Soft butter)

Bake them until the dough is done, about 20 minutes. This may be served with:

Brown Sauce, page 365

Fillings

I. Lightly moisten:

Ground or minced cooked meat

with:

Gravy or cream, Brown Sauce, page 365, or canned Soup Sauce, page 376

Season it well with:

Salt and pepper
Worcestershire sauce or chili sauce

II. Moisten braunschweiger sausage with chili sauce or tomato soup.

III. Use:

1½ cups cooked ground ham
½ cup Cream Sauce II, page 359
thick cream or evaporated milk
2 tablespoons chopped pickles
1 tablespoon chopped onion
1½ tablespoons catsup
Salt and pepper, if needed

IV. Sauté gently until yellow:

2 cups chopped onions

in:

2 tablespoons olive or anchovy oil

Add:

¼ cup or more chopped ripe olives
6 or 8 chopped anchovies

V. Use any good cooked seafood filling and taste before seasoning.

MEAT PIE ROLL OR PIN WHEELS [4]

Preheat oven to 450°.

This is a palatable, quickly made, everyday dish—an attractive way to serve a small quantity of leftover meat.

Use one of the fillings given in the previous recipe.

Use the recipes on (II, 283, 293), or a biscuit mix to make:

Biscuit Dough or Pie Dough: use 2 cups of flour

If you use biscuit dough, make it a little drier than for ordinary biscuits, otherwise it will be difficult to handle. Roll it until very thin. Cut it into an oblong. Use a pastry brush and brush it lightly with:

1 egg white or soft butter

This will keep the crust from being soggy. Spread the dough with the meat filling, being careful to leave about 1 inch at the sides uncovered. Begin to roll it loosely. Moisten the end with water and plaster it down. Moisten the sides and pinch them together. Bake the roll until it is done, about 20 minutes. Or cut the roll into ¾-inch slices. Place the slices in a lightly greased pan. Dot the tops with:

Butter

This roll may be prepared in advance and placed in the refrigerator until ready for use. Bake the slices until the dough is done. Serve them very hot with:

Brown Sauce, page 365, or Tomato Sauce, page 376

MEAT SHORTCAKES

[10 Cakes]

Preheat oven to 350°.

Prepare, omitting the sugar:

Fluffy Biscuit Dough (II, 286)

If a richer dough is desired, use an additional tablespoon of butter. Combine:

¼ cup cream
¾ cup deviled ham

Ground cooked ham or other meat may be substituted. In that case ¼ teaspoon prepared mustard, 2 teaspoons minced onion or other seasoning may be added. Roll out the dough on a lightly floured board to the thickness of ¼ to ⅓ inch. Spread ½ of it with the ham mixture. Fold over the other ½, so that the ham is between the layers of dough. Cut the dough with a biscuit cutter. Bake the cakes for about 15 minutes until done.

QUICK CHICKEN OR BEEF POT PIE

Preheat oven to 400°.
An easy dish if you have precooked chicken or beef and precooked pie crust shells. We find the precooked shell more convenient and tastier than the crust which has to be exposed to long, slow cooking.
Have ready:

A baked Pie Shell (II, 296)

formed to fit your casserole or individual bakers. Heat:

Creamed chicken, Chicken or Turkey Hash, page 226, or Beef Hash, page 223

Fill the shell with the meat filling and top with:

A prebaked pie topping, Biscuit Dough (II, 284), or slices of bread buttered on both sides

Bake until thoroughly heated and the top is light brown.

CORN BREAD TAMALE PIE [6]

Preheat oven to 425°.
This can be prepared up to the point of adding the corn bread topping; then cooled and refrigerated until 45 minutes before serving time. Place the casserole in the oven and let it warm while you are mixing the corn bread topping.
Sauté in a lightly greased skillet:

1 pound ground beef
1 chopped onion

When the meat is lightly browned and the onion translucent, add:

1 can tomato soup
1 cup water or stock
¼ teaspoon pepper
1 teaspoon salt
1 tablespoon chili powder
1 cup drained whole kernel corn
½ cup chopped green pepper, seeds and fiber removed

Simmer for 15 minutes. Meanwhile, sift and mix together:

¾ cup corn meal
1 tablespoon flour
1 tablespoon sugar
½ teaspoon salt
1½ teaspoons baking powder

Moisten with:

1 beaten egg
⅓ cup milk

Mix lightly and fold in:

1 tablespoon cooking oil

Place meat mixture in a greased 2-quart casserole and cover with the corn bread topping. The topping will disappear into the meat mixture, but will rise during baking and form a good layer of corn bread. Place in oven and bake for about 20 to 25 minutes or until corn bread is brown.

CHINESE EGG ROLLS

[6 Servings or 12 Egg Rolls]

Egg rolls are frequently used for hors d'oeuvre or you may serve them as the main dish at luncheon. The pancake-like skins are available at Chinese grocery stores, although in an emergency you may make a thin Won Ton dough, page 112, or use the following:
Sift into a bowl:

1 cup flour

Beat in:

2 eggs
½ teaspoon salt

Add gradually to make a thin, smooth batter:

2 cups water

Grease a 6-inch-diameter skillet and put over ◆ low heat. Beat the batter again and pour 1 tablespoon into the pan. Let it spread over the surface of the pan to form a very thin, flexible pancake. When it shrinks away from the sides, turn it and let it set on the other side. Do not let it become brown or crisp. Remove each pancake to a dish when done and cover all with a damp cloth until ready to use. You may prepare the filling the day before, as it should be chilled before being enclosed in the pancake envelope. Bring to a boil in ½ cup water, then drain:

½ cup finely chopped celery
¾ cup shredded cabbage

Heat in a skillet:

3 tablespoons salad oil

Stir-fry, see page 253, for 3 minutes:

½ cup diced cooked shrimp
½ cup diced cooked pork

Add and stir-fry for 5 more minutes:

4 finely chopped scallions
½ cup drained and finely chopped water chestnuts
1 minced clove garlic
¼ cup soy sauce

Place 4 tablespoons of filling in rectangular shape on the center of each pancake and fold up envelope-style, sealing the last flap with a paste made of:

1 tablespoon flour
2 tablespoons cold water

Preheat deep fryer to 375°.
Fry rolls until golden brown. Or fill a deep skillet with oil about 1 inch deep up the sides and fry the egg rolls until golden brown.
Serve with:

Chinese Mustard
Soy sauce
Chinese Sweet-Sour Sauce I, page 371

PIZZAS

These Italian pies—pizza is the Italian word for pie—have become very popular luncheon and supper dishes. The pizza began as a use for leftover bread dough. T' Italians some'imes use pastry as the base and, in an emergency, we have successfully used sliced English muffins. A slice of cheese over the whole first—before the sauce—keeps it from getting soggy. To make pizza dough, mix as for Bread (II, 243), using the following ingredients, but do not let it rise a second time:

4 cups sifted flour
1 cake yeast in 1⅓ cups 85° water
2 tablespoons salad or olive oil
1 teaspoon salt

Knead for 10 minutes. Cover with damp cloth and let rise about 2 hours. Have ready two oiled 12-inch pizza pans. Pat and stretch the dough in the pans, pinching up a collar around the edge to hold the filling. Prick dough in about 6 places.
Preheat oven to 400°.
Spread each pizza with your preferred filling and rest it for about 10 minutes. (At this stage the pizzas may be frozen for at least a week before baking.) Bake for about 25 minutes until light brown and serve at once very hot.

I. Spread the pizza with:

(A thin slice of cheese)
Thickened Tomato Sauce, page 376, or Italian Tomato Paste, page 377

Arrange on top:

12 to 14 anchovies or sliced Italian sausage, pepperoni, Prosciutto ham or Salami

Sprinkle with:

Orégano
Olive oil
Chopped parsley
(Parmesan or Romano cheese)

II. Use a highly seasoned:

Meat Sauce for Spaghetti, page 378, or other meat pasta sauce

Cover with a layer of:
Fontina or Mozzarella cheese

III. Use as a base:
Thickened Tomato Sauce, page 376
Add:
1 cup chopped or sliced mushrooms

IV. Cover the base with:
Lightly sautéed onions
Black olives
Anchovies
Brush with:
Olive oil

ENCHILADAS

[About 2 Dozen]
Preheat oven to 350°.
Have ready:
Baked tortillas
In a heavy saucepan, heat:
2 tablespoons olive oil
Sauté until golden:
½ cup chopped onion
1 minced clove garlic
Add:
2 teaspoons to 1 tablespoon chili powder
1 cup tomato purée
½ cup chicken or beef stock
Season with:
Salt and pepper
1 teaspoon cumin
Spread some sauce over the tortillas and fill the centers with equal quantities of:
Chopped raw onion
Chopped Mozzarella cheese
Roll the tortillas and place in an ovenproof dish. Pour more sauce over the tops and sprinkle with:
Chopped Mozzarella cheese
Heat thoroughly about 15 minutes in the oven.

ABOUT QUICHES

Early recipes for Quiche called for bacon and cream, but gradually cheese was added. When sautéed onions were included, the dish was called **Alsacienne.** Cool the onions before adding them.

Quiche makes a hefty brunch or an hors d'oeuvre baked in tiny tarts no larger than the lining of muffin tins. As it is always served lukewarm, time it accordingly. Following are several variations on a Quiche theme.

QUICHE LORRAINE [6]

Preheat oven to 375°.
Prepare a 9-inch pie shell of:
A Pie Crust (II, 293)
Brush it with:
The white of an egg
and prick it well. Slice in 1-inch lengths:
¼ lb. sliced bacon
Cook the bacon in a heavy skillet, stirring constantly, until the fat is almost rendered out but the bacon is not yet crisp. Drain on absorbent toweling. Scald to hasten the cooking time:
2 cups milk or cream
Cool slightly, then beat together with:
3 whole eggs
¼ teaspoon salt
⅛ teaspoon white pepper
A fresh grating of nutmeg
1 teaspoon chopped chives
Sprinkle in the bottom of the pie shell the bacon and:
½ cup diced Swiss cheese
Pour the custard mixture over it. Bake 35 to 40 minutes or until the top is a golden brown. For safety, you may test as for Custard (II, 436).

CHEESE CUSTARD PIE [4]

Preheat oven to 325°.
In Switzerland we had a vile-tempered cook named Marguerite. Her one idea, after being generally disagreeable, was to earn enough to own a small chalet on some high peak where she could cater to moun-

tain climbers. While she was certainly not born with a silver spoon in her mouth—although it was large enough to accommodate several—she did arrive with a cooking spoon in her hand. If she has attained her ideal, many a climber will feel it worth while to scale a perilous peak to reach her kitchen. The following Cheese Custard Pie was always served in solitary state. Its flavor varied with Marguerite's moods and her supply of cheese. It was never twice the same, as she had no written recipe, but we have endeavored to make one like hers, for it would be a pity to relegate so good a dish to inaccessible roosts.

Prepare and bake:

An 8-inch baked Pie Crust (II, 293)

It should be at least 2 inches deep. When cool, brush with:

Egg white

Scald:

1¾ cups milk or cream

Reduce the heat and add:

1 cup grated cheese

Stir until the cheese is melted. Add:

½ teaspoon salt
¼ teaspoon paprika
½ teaspoon grated onion
A few grains cayenne

Remove the mixture from the heat and beat in, one at a time:

3 eggs

Fill the pie crust and bake it until the custard is firm, about 45 minutes.

ONION SHORTCAKE [6]

Preheat oven to 425°.

Peel and slice:

10 medium-sized white onions

Sprinkle them with:

½ teaspoon salt

Melt in a saucepan:

3 tablespoons butter

Add the onions. Cover and simmer until they are tender. Cool them. Prepare ½ the amount on (II, 286):

Fluffy Biscuit Dough

omitting the sugar.

Spread the dough in a deep greased ovenproof dish. Cover it with the cooked onions. Add:

¼ teaspoon paprika
2 teaspoons chopped parsley
(¼ cup diced cooked ham)
A grating nutmeg or white pepper

Prepare:

1 cup Cream Sauce I, page 359

Beat into the sauce:

1 egg

Pour the sauce over the onions. The top may be sprinkled with:

¼ cup grated cheese

Bake the cake for about 20 minutes or until the dough is done.

ONION OR LEEK PIE

Preheat oven to 450°.

Richer and more sophisticated than the preceding Onion Shortcake. Serve Onion Shortcake with a meat course. Have Onion Pie as a main dish with a green salad.

Line a 9-inch pie pan with:

Pie Dough (II, 293)

Prick and chill it. Skin and slice thinly:

2½ lbs. Bermuda onions or leeks

Melt in a heavy saucepan:

3 tablespoons butter

Add the onions. Stir and cook them over low heat until they are clear. Cool them well. Combine and heat slowly until blended:

3 eggs
1 cup cultured sour cream
¼ cup dry sherry
1 teaspoon salt
¼ teaspoon freshly ground pepper
(1 tablespoon minced fresh

herb or 1 teaspoon dill
or celery seed)

Stir this mixture into the onions. Brush the bottom of the cooled pie shell with:

1 slightly beaten egg white

Fill it with the slightly cooled onion mixture. Place over the top:

(4 strips bacon cut into squares)
(Small cooked link sausages)

Bake the pie in a 450° oven for 10 minutes. ◆ Reduce the heat to 300° and bake the pie until the crust is light brown, about ½ hour. Serve it piping hot.

QUICK TOMATO TART [6]

Preheat oven to 350°.
Have ready:

6 baked, unsweetened, 2½-inch tart shells (II, 296)

Slice ½ inch thick:

2 peeled seeded fresh tomatoes

Mix and heat well:

¼ cup sautéed sliced mushrooms
¾ cup canned cream of chicken soup
¼ cup Italian tomato purée
¼ teaspoon sugar
¼ cup softened liver sausage
4 large chopped stuffed olives
2 teaspoons fresh chopped basil
¼ teaspoon salt

First place a layer of this hot sauce in each tart shell, then a tomato slice. Cover with the remaining hot mixture. Dust each tart with:

Grated Parmesan cheese

Heat the filled tarts on a baking sheet in the oven for about 15 minutes or until well heated.

MIXED VEGETABLE GRILL

A good Lenten dish if you omit the bacon and sausages.

Preheat broiler.
Cut into slices:

Tomatoes

Brush them with:

Melted butter

Season them with:

Salt and pepper
Brown sugar

Prepare for cooking:

Mushrooms

Brush them with:

Melted butter or heavy cream

Season them lightly with:

Salt
(Lemon juice)

Grease the broiler. Place on it the tomato slices, mushrooms and:

(Sliced bacon)
(Sausages)

Broil these ingredients until they are done. Meanwhile sauté or poach:

Eggs

Serve the eggs on a hot platter, surrounded by the grilled food. Garnish the platter with:

Parsley, olives, radishes, etc.

ROAST BEEF IN SAUCE [4]

I.
Cut into ½-inch cubes:

2 cups cooked roast beef

Prepare:

Hot Cumberland Sauce, page 372

Add the beef and heat the sauce, but do not boil. Serve at once on:

Hot toast

II. Prepare:

Creole Sauce, page 380, or Curry Sauce II, page 363

Arrange very thin slices of:

Cooked roast beef

on a hot platter. Pour the hot sauce over them. Sprinkle the top with:

Chopped parsley or chopped chives

BOEUF MIROTON

Make a sauce by melting:
2 tablespoons butter
Sauté in it until golden:
1 coarsely sliced onion
Sprinkle over all and mix rapidly with a wooden spoon:
1 tablespoon flour
Add and stir until boiling:
1 cup bouillon
Salt and pepper
Reduce the heat and add:
1 to 2 teaspoons vinegar
Simmer about 15 minutes. Arrange on a heatproof platter:
Thin slices of boiled or roasted beef
Cover the slices with the above hot sauce. Keep on low heat for about 20 minutes and serve.

DEVILED LEFTOVER MEAT

Preheat broiler.
Spread:
Cooked sliced meat
with:
Prepared mustard or catsup
Roll the slices in:
Buttered bread crumbs
Broil them until browned. Serve the meat with:
Leftover gravy, Piquant Sauce, page 367, or Brown Onion Sauce, page 366

CREAMED LEFTOVER VEAL [6]

Melt in a chafing dish or electric skillet:
¼ cup butter
Add and sauté for about 5 minutes:
½ lb. sliced mushrooms
¼ cup diced green pepper, seeds and membranes removed
Add and stir well:
¼ cup flour
Pour over the mixture and stir until thickened:
½ cup cream
1 cup veal or chicken stock
Correct the seasoning and add:
2 cups diced cooked veal
2 tablespoons minced pimiento
¼ teaspoon marjoram
½ cup dry white wine
Simmer about 5 minutes longer and serve over:
Rice, noodles or macaroni
Garnish with:
Chopped parsley

VEAL AND SPINACH DISH

Preheat oven to 425°.
Place in a casserole a 1-inch layer or more of:
Creamed spinach
which has been delicately flavored with a little:
Grated onion
Place over it:
Slices of roast veal or lamb, etc.
If you have gravy, pour a little of it over the meat or use a little thick cream. Cover the top with:
Au Gratin III, page 389
Bake the dish until the top is brown. Garnish it with:
Parsley

COOKED CURRIED VEAL OR LAMB AND RICE [4]

This combination of meat, apple and curry is luscious. Peel and slice:
1 cup onions
(½ cup celery)
Core, peel and slice:
2 medium-sized apples
Melt in a saucepan:
3 tablespoons butter
Add:
½ to 1 teaspoon curry powder
Caution: use only ½ teaspoon curry to begin with if you are unfamiliar with it. Add the onions and apples and sauté until the onions are tender. Re-

move them from the pan. Brown lightly in the pan about:

2 cups sliced or diced cooked veal or lamb

Remove it from the pan. Stir into the pan juices:

2 teaspoons flour

Stir in slowly:

1 cup Stock (II, 141)

When the sauce is smooth and boiling, add the onions, apples and meat. Stir in:

1 tablespoon lemon juice
Correct the seasoning

and serve the meat with:

Steamed or boiled rice

LAMB TERRAPIN [4]

Cut into dice:

2 cups cold cooked lamb

Chop or rice:

2 hard-cooked eggs

Combine the lamb, the eggs and:

2 tablespoons olive oil
1 tablespoon lemon juice

Melt:

2 tablespoons butter

Stir in until blended:

3 tablespoons flour
1 teaspoon dry mustard

Stir in slowly:

2 cups lamb stock or milk

Add:

1 teaspoon Worcestershire sauce
Salt, as needed

Cook and stir the sauce until it is boiling. Add the lamb and egg mixture. Heat the terrapin thoroughly. Serve it on:

Hot toast

CHOP SUEY OR CHOW MEIN [4]

These vaguely Chinese dishes which can be made with cooked pork, chicken or seafood, differ in that Chop Suey is served over steamed rice, and Chow Mein over fried noodles. They resemble some Chinese porcelain patterns originally made strictly for export. To get the feeling of true Chinese food, read Mrs. Buwei Yang Chao's delightful "How to Cook and Eat in Chinese."

Cut into 2-inch julienne strips about ¼ inch in section:

2 cups cooked pork roast

Slice diagonally, see page 484:

½ cup celery with tender leaves
½ cup green onions
1 cup mushrooms

Chop coarsely:

1 green pepper, seeds and membrane removed

Drain:

1 cup bean sprouts

Heat well in a deep heavy skillet:

2 tablespoons cooking oil

Stir-fry, page 253, the onion and celery for about 3 minutes. Then add the mushrooms, pork, peppers and the bean sprouts. Continue to stir-fry for 2 to 3 minutes longer. Then add:

(½ cup fresh, peeled, seeded, and slivered tomatoes)
Jellied juices from the roast or a bit of Meat Glaze (II, 145)
1 cup strong consommé

Season with:

Salt and pepper
1 tablespoon soy sauce
3 tablesoons dry sherry

You may thicken the juices with:

Cornstarch

Serve at once.

LEFTOVERS IN BACON

Preheat oven to 450°.

Measure:

Cooked ground meat, meat loaf, etc.

Add ⅓ this measure of:

Boiled Rice

Moisten it lightly with:

Gravy or cream

Season it well with:

Salt and pepper
Minced onion or onion juice

Roll the mixture into small balls,

flatten them slightly and wrap around them:

Slices of bacon

Secure the bacon with toothpicks. Place the patties in a greased pan or dish and bake them until the bacon is crisp, about 15 minutes. Serve them with:

Tomato Sauce, page 376

HAM LOAF WITH COOKED HAM [6]

Preheat oven to 350°.
Combine:

- 2 cups cooked ground ham
- 1 cup bread or cracker crumbs or crushed cornflakes
- 2 eggs
- 2 tablespoons grated onion
- ⅛ teaspoon pepper
- 1 cup milk
- 2 tablespoons chili sauce
- 2 to 4 tablespoons chopped parsley or celery

Bake these ingredients in a greased loaf pan for about 45 minutes. Serve the loaf with:

Tomato, Horseradish, Mustard, Mushroom or some other sauce, page 367

STUFFED HAM ROLLS [4]

I.

Make these when you have leftover rice. Preheat oven to 400°.
Trim:

8 thin slices baked or boiled ham

Spread them lightly with:

Mustard

Place on each slice part of the following filling. Combine:

- 1½ cups cooked rice
- ⅓ cup chopped raisins
- 1 beaten egg
- ¼ teaspoon paprika
- ½ teaspoon Worcestershire sauce
- (¼ cup chopped celery)
- (½ teaspoon basil)

Roll the slices and secure them with toothpicks. Brush them with:

Milk

Bake the rolls until they are thoroughly heated. Serve them with:

Hot Cumberland Sauce, page 372

II. Prepare, as for above:

Slices of ham

Place on each side:

4 asparagus tips

Roll, brush and heat the ham, as directed. Serve the rolls with:

1½ cups Cheese Sauce, page 364

III. [4]

Preheat oven to 350°.
Prepare, as for above:

8 large slices ham

Combine and mix well:

- ¾ cup cultured sour cream
- 1 cup sieved creamy cottage cheese
- 1 slightly beaten egg
- ¼ cup minced onions
- ½ cup drained chopped cooked spinach
- ½ teaspoon dry mustard
- ¼ teaspoon salt

Place about 2 tablespoons filling on each slice of ham. Roll and tuck in the edges. Put in a shallow baking dish and cover with the following mixture:

- 1 can cream of mushroom soup: 10½ oz.
- ¼ cup cultured sour cream

Bake for 20 to 25 minutes.

GROUND HAM ON PINEAPPLE SLICES [4]

Preheat oven to 400°.
Combine:

- 1 cup cooked ground ham
- 1 teaspoon prepared mustard
- 2 tablespoons mayonnaise

Spread this mixture on:

4 slices drained pineapple

Bake the slices in a greased pan for about 10 minutes.

HAM AND POTATO CAKES [4]

Combine:

1 cup mashed potatoes
1 cup ground cooked ham
1 tablespoon chopped parsley
½ teaspoon grated onion
⅛ teaspoon pepper
Salt, if needed

Shape this mixture into flat cakes. Dip them lightly in:

Flour

Sauté them in:

Bacon drippings or other fat

HAM CAKES WITH PINEAPPLE AND SWEET POTATOES [6]

Boil by the recipe on page 322:

3 large sweet potatoes

Preheat oven to 375°.
Combine:

2 cups cooked chopped or ground ham
½ cup dry bread crumbs
2 eggs
⅛ teaspoon salt
1 teaspoon prepared mustard

Shape these ingredients into 6 flat cakes. Melt in a skillet:

5 tablespoons bacon drippings

Brown lightly in the skillet:

6 slices drained pineapple

Remove them and brown the ham cakes in the skillet. Place the pineapple slices in a baking dish and cover each slice with a ham cake. Peel the sweet potatoes. Cut them lengthwise into halves. Combine and sprinkle over them:

¼ teaspoon cloves
¼ cup brown sugar

Cook them slowly in the skillet until they are well caramelized. Place them in the baking dish. Baste them with:

Pineapple juice

Bake the dish for about 10 minutes.

HAM À LA KING [6]

Prepare:

2 cups Cream Sauce I, page 359

When the sauce is boiling, add:

2 cups cooked diced ham
2 diced hard-cooked eggs
1 cup Sautéed Mushrooms, page 296 or canned mushrooms with sliced stuffed olives
1 tablespoon chopped green pepper
1 tablespoon chopped pimiento

Serve the ham very hot on:

Rounds of toast, on rusks, in bread cases or on corn bread squares

Garnish with:

Chopped parsley

⊟ BARBECUED FRANKFURTERS, WIENERS OR HOT DOGS

Preheat broiler or grill.
Grill or put:

Frankfurters, wieners or hot dogs

on a rack in a roasting pan. During the cooking baste them ➧ constantly with:

Barbecue Sauce, page 374

⊟ FRANKFURTER KEBABS [8]

Preheat grill or broiler.
Cut into about 4 pieces each:

8 frankfurters

Marinate about 30 minutes in:

French Dressing, page 341

Skewer the pieces alternately with bits of:

Bacon
Small canned pickled onions
Green pepper

Grill or broil, turning often.

FRANKFURTERS OR SAUSAGE IN SAUCES

I. [3]

Preheat oven to 400°.
Place in a shallow pan:
6 frankfurter sausages
Prepare:
1 cup Tomato Sauce, page 376, or Barbecue Sauce, page 374
Add:
(Chopped green peppers, seeded and veined)
(Grated onions or chives)
Pour these ingredients over the sausages. Bake them until they swell and the sauce thickens.

II. Prepare, using no salt:
Creole Sauce, page 380, or Quick Tomato Sauce, page 376
Season it well with:
Paprika
Cook:
Vienna Sausages, page 531
Drain them. Heat them in the sauce. Serve with:
Boiled Rice, Noodles, page 192, or Mashed Potatoes, page 311

SAUSAGE BAKED WITH APPLES [4]

Preheat oven to 400°.
Arrange in a baking dish:
8 partially cooked pork sausages
Core:
6 tart apples
Cut them into ¼-inch slices and place them around the sausages. Sprinkle them with:
¾ cup brown sugar
Bake the dish in a hot oven 400° for 10 minutes. ➧ Reduce the heat to 350° and continue baking for about 15 minutes longer. Baste with the drippings.

SAUSAGES AND MUSHROOMS

Fine for brunch.
Prepare:
Mashed Potatoes, page 311, or Boiled Mashed Chestnuts, page 283
Heap them in a mound on a hot platter. Keep them hot. Cook:
Sausages, page 531
Place them around the potatoes. Sauté in the drippings:
Mushrooms, page 296
Garnish the platter with them and:
Sprigs of parsley
Pour the drippings over the potatoes.

SAUSAGE AND ONIONS [4]

Heat in a skillet:
2 tablespoons oil or fat
Add:
1½ cups slivered onions
Cook and stir these over low heat for about 15 minutes until light brown. Cut a lengthwise slit in:
8 wiener sausages or frankfurters
Fill them with the onions. Fasten them with toothpicks. Broil them slowly on both sides. You may place them in:
Lightly toasted buns

LENTIL AND SAUSAGE CASSEROLE [4]

Preheat oven to 400°.
Place in a greased ovenproof dish:
1 cup cooked lentils
Place in boiling water and simmer for 10 minutes:
1 lb. small link or other sausages
Drain them. Place them on top of the lentils. Bake the dish uncovered until the sausages are brown.

PIGS IN POTATOES [3]

Preheat deep-fat fryer to 375°.
Combine and beat well:
1 teaspoon minced onion
1 teaspoon minced parsley

2 cups Mashed Potatoes, page 311
1 egg yolk

Cook:

6 small Vienna sausages

or use:

Precooked pork sausages

Coat them with the potato mixture. Roll in:

Finely crushed bread crumbs

then in:

1 egg diluted with 1 tablespoon water or milk

then again in the crumbs. Fry the piggies until they are a golden brown.

BAKED CORN BEEF

Preheat oven to 350°.
Remove whole from the can:

Corned beef

Stud it with:

Whole cloves

Make a paste by stirring a little water into:

¼ cup brown sugar
1 teaspoon chili powder

Add to it:

2 tablespoons chopped pickles

Spread the beef with the paste. Bake it for about 10 minutes.

CREAMED CHIPPED BEEF

[4 Large Servings]
➧ Do not oversalt.
Pull apart:

8 oz. chipped beef

Melt:

3 tablespoons butter

Sauté in it until light brown:

3 tablespoons minced onion
3 tablespoons minced green pepper

Sprinkle these with:

3 tablespoons flour

Add slowly, stirring constantly:

2 cups milk

Add the beef. Simmer these ingredients until they thicken. Remove from the heat and season with:

1 tablespoon chopped parsley or chives
¼ teaspoon paprika
2 tablespoons dry sherry
(2 tablespoons capers or chopped pickles)

Serve the beef on:

Hot buttered toast

CHIPPED BEEF IN CREOLE SAUCE [3]

➧ Do not oversalt.
Prepare:

Quick Creole Sauce, page 376

Melt:

1 tablespoon butter

Sauté in it for 1 minute:

4 oz. shredded chipped beef

Add the sauce. Heat the dish. Serve it on:

Buttered toast

CHIPPED BEEF IN CHEESE SAUCE [2]

➧ Do not oversalt.
Prepare:

1 cup Cheese Sauce, page 364

Add to it:

4 oz. or more shredded chipped beef

Heat it. Serve it over:

Hot corn bread squares

This may be served in pancakes.

CHIPPED BEEF AND SWEET POTATO CASSEROLE [5]

Preheat oven to 375°.
➧ Do not oversalt.
Cut into cubes:

5 cooked or canned sweet potatoes

Shred:

¼ lb. dried beef

Prepare:

¼ cup grated onion
1½ cups Cream Sauce I, page 359, or canned cream soup

Place these ingredients in layers

in a greased casserole. Cover the top with:

Crushed cornflakes

Dot it with:

Butter or cheese

Bake for ½ hour.

CHIPPED BEEF OR CORNED BEEF IN CANNED SOUP [4 to 5]

➧ Do not oversalt.

Combine and heat:

1 can cream soup—mushroom, celery, asparagus, etc.: 10½ oz.
6 tablespoons milk or Stock (II, 141)
⅛ teaspoon freshly ground nutmeg
A grating of black pepper

Add:

8 oz. shredded chipped beef or 1 cup canned diced corned beef
1 cup leftover vegetables

Heat these ingredients. Serve them on:

Toast or hot biscuits

sprinkled with:

Chopped parsley, chives or grated cheese

Or you may boil until nearly tender:

10 small onions

Drain them and place them in a baking dish, pour the soup and beef mixture over them. Cover the top with:

Crushed potato chips

Bake the dish in a 400° oven for about 15 minutes.

ABOUT HASH

Hash has its ups and downs.

The Irish cook was praised for her hash and she said: "Beef ain't nothing. Onions ain't nothing. Seasoning's nothing. But when I throw myself into my hash, that's hash!" The usual way to make hash is to cut the meat from a chicken or turkey carcass or from a roast beef, combine it with leftover gravy, reheat it briefly and season it acceptably. Never overcook it. There should be about ½ as much gravy as other ingredients. Have sauce or gravy boiling vigorously. Put in the solids ➧ reduce the heat at once and let them warm through thoroughly. If heating hash in the oven, be sure to use a lid or a topping, see Gratins, page 389.

You may add, in addition to the meat, cooked mushrooms, celery or potatoes, chopped olives, green peppers, parsley or some other herb or anything else that seems suitable. The proportions may be varied. This is a matter of taste and expediency. In the absence of gravy, sweet or sour cream or a sauce—cream, tomato, creole, etc.—may be substituted. Or you may add a sauce or cream to the gravy to obtain the desired amount. When using cream, reheat the hash in a double boiler as boiling thins it. Sherry, Madeira or dry wine may be added. Hash may be served in a pastry shell, in a rice or noodle ring, etc.

BEEF AND HAM HASH WITH POTATOES AND MUSHROOMS

Cut into cubes equal parts of:

Cooked roast beef and cooked or smoked ham
Raw pared potatoes

Reserve the beef. Place in a saucepan the ham and potatoes. Cover them with:

Brown Sauce, page 365

Cover these ingredients and simmer for 15 minutes. Add:

½ lb. or more sliced mushrooms

Simmer them covered for 15 minutes longer. Add the beef. Reheat the hash, but do not permit it to boil. Season it with:

Garlic salt

A pinch basil, thyme or savory
Dry sherry
Salt, if needed

Serve it on:

Hot toast

garnished with:

Chopped parsley

This dish may be made without the ham.

SAUTÉED OR BROWNED HASH [4]

Combine and grind:

1½ cups cooked meat
½ cup raw cubed potatoes with or without skins
1 medium-sized onion

Season with:

Salt, pepper, celery seed

Turn these ingredients into a hot well-greased skillet. Cook the hash over medium heat until a crust forms on the bottom, turn it and brown the other side. Stir it from time to time to let the hash brown throughout. Shortly before it is done, pat it down firmly to form an unbroken cake. This requires about ½ hour cooking in all. Serve the hash with:

Catsup or Tomato Sauce, page 376

QUICK HASH [4]

Heat over very low heat:

1 can cream of mushroom soup: 10½ oz.

Stir in gradually:

¼ cup milk

Add:

1 cup cubed cooked ham or meat: frankfurters, hamburgers, etc.
2 sliced hard-cooked eggs

Season the hash with:

A pinch dried basil or thyme
Salt and pepper
(Chopped parsley)

Serve it over:

Hot corn bread or toast

HASH WITH VEGETABLES [6]

This is an excellent combination. If it is not feasible to use all the ingredients given, it will still be good.

Preheat oven to 350°.

Prepare:

½ cup cooked diced potatoes
⅓ cup cooked diced onions
⅓ cup seeded sliced green peppers
⅓ cup cooked chopped celery
3 tablespoons diced pimientos
2 cups cold cooked meat, cut into ⅓-inch cubes

Combine and heat to boiling:

1 cup leftover gravy
⅓ cup tomato purée
1 tablespoon butter
Salt and pepper, as required
1 teaspoon Worcestershire sauce

Add the meat and vegetables. If there is no available gravy, make it with 2 tablespoons butter, 2 tablespoons flour and 1 cup of vegetable stock or water in which 1 beef cube has been dissolved. Pour the hash into 1 large baking dish or into 6 individual baking dishes. Sprinkle the top with:

Au Gratin III, page 389

Or cover it with green pepper rings and seasoned slices of tomatoes dotted with butter. Brown the dish in the oven.

HASH IN CREAMED CABBAGE

Preheat oven to 400°.

Prepare:

Creamed Cabbage III, page 275

Place ½ the cabbage in a greased ovenproof dish. Place on top of it a layer of:

Hash moistened lightly with gravy or cream

Cover it with the remaining cabbage. Sprinkle the top with:
Au Gratin II or III, page 389
Bake the cabbage until the top is light brown.

SHEPHERD'S PIE

I. Preheat oven to 400°.
Prepare:
Hash
Spread it in a baking dish. Cover it with fresh hot:
Mashed Potatoes, page 311
Spread the top with:
Melted butter
Bake the dish until the potatoes are brown.

II. Preheat oven to 400°.
A very good way of using a small quantity of cold mashed potatoes and bits of meat or vegetable scraps.
Line individual molds with a wall ¼ inch thick of:
Leftover mashed potatoes
If the potatoes are very hard, soften them with:
1 or 2 tablespoons hot milk
Brush the inner walls with:
1 egg white
Moisten:
Chopped cooked meat and vegetables
with a small amount of:
Gravy, Tomato Sauce, page 376, Cream Sauce, page 359, or cream
Fill the molds and cover them with a layer of mashed potatoes. Brush the tops with:
Soft butter
Place the molds in a pan of hot water in the oven for 15 minutes or until the potatoes are brown.

BREAD DRESSING IN A RING FILLED WITH HASH, ETC.

Preheat oven to 400°.
Grease a ring mold. Fill it with:
Bread Dressing, page 560, Apple and Onion Dressing, page 563, etc.
Bake it until it is brown. Invert it onto a hot plate. Fill the center with:
Hash, or stewed creamed fresh or leftover vegetables
Good served with:
Leftover gravy or other sauce

CORNED BEEF HASH AND POTATOES [6]

Grind, using coarse blade, or dice:
1½ lbs. cooked or canned corned beef: about 3 cups
Dice:
2 cups boiled potatoes
Melt in a large saucepan:
2 tablespoons butter
Stir in and simmer until tender:
½ cup chopped onion
1 diced green pepper, seeds and fibers removed
2 ribs chopped celery
(1 clove garlic)
(1 cup mushrooms)
Remove the garlic. Add the beef and potatoes and:
1 tablespoon Worcestershire sauce
2 tablespoons minced parsley or chives
Salt and pepper, as needed
Cook and stir lightly over medium heat while adding gradually:
⅓ to ⅔ cup Stock (II, 141), or Cream Sauce III, page 359
Stir and cook till well blended and thoroughly heated. Place on a hot platter and serve topped with:
6 Poached Eggs, page 184
Or sauté the hash in a greased skillet until well browned on the bottom. Remove carefully, folding like an omelet, to serve.

CANNED CORNED BEEF HASH PATTIES [4]

Sauté:

3 tablespoons chopped onion

in:

2 tablespoons butter

Add:

2 tablespoons horseradish
½ teaspoon thyme
2 cups canned corned beef hash

Form patties of this mixture. Sauté them on both sides in:

Hot butter or drippings

Sauté in the same pan:

Slices firm tomato

Season them with:

Brown sugar
Salt and pepper

Arrange the tomatoes and patties on a platter, garnished with:

Parsley

Or serve the patties with:

1½ cups Cream Sauce I, page 359

to which you may add:

2 chopped hard-cooked eggs
2 tablespoons chopped pickles

CHICKEN OR TURKEY HASH [4]

➧ Please read About Hash, page 223.

Combine and heat:

1½ cups diced cooked chicken or turkey
½ cup cooked drained celery or boiled potato cubes
1 cup leftover chicken or turkey gravy or sauce
1 tablespoon chopped parsley or chives
Seasoning, as required

Serve the hash as suggested in About Hash, page 223.

CREAMED CHICKEN OR VEAL [4]

There is no reason why this dish should not be delicious, whether it is made in a luxurious way or with leftover food. Proportions, seasonings, etc., are unimportant, provided that good combinations are chosen.

Prepare:

1 cup Cream Sauce I, page 359

Use cream and chicken stock or vegetable water, with part gravy and part milk, etc. Add:

2 tablespoons chopped parsley
2 cups minced cooked chicken or veal
(½ cup Sautéed Mushrooms, page 296)

Part of this may be cooked or canned vegetables. Season these ingredients with:

1 teaspoon lemon juice or ½ teaspoon Worcestershire sauce or 2 teaspoons dry sherry
(3 tablespoons chopped pickles or olives)

Add:

Salt and pepper
(Celery salt)

Grease a baking dish and put the creamed mixture in it. Sprinkle the top with:

Au Gratin II or III, page 389
(½ cup blanched shredded almonds)

Place the dish under the broiler until the crumbs are brown. The creamed ingredients may be served unbreaded on:

Hot Waffles or in a Noodle or Rice Ring, pages 173, 162

CHICKEN À LA KING [4]

Cut into dice:

1 cup cooked chicken
½ cup Sautéed Mushrooms, page 296
¼ cup canned pimiento

Melt:

3 tablespoons chicken fat or butter

Stir in and blend:

3 tablespoons flour

Add slowly:

1½ cups Chicken Stock (II, 142), or cream

When the sauce is smooth and boiling, add the chicken, mushrooms and pimiento. Reduce the heat. Pour some sauce over:

1 egg yolk

Return mixture to pan. Stir and permit it to thicken slightly. Add:

Seasoning, if required
(¼ cup blanched slivered almonds)
(1 tablespoon dry sherry)

Serve the chicken at once. To reheat, place in a saucepan over boiling water.

TURKEY OR CHICKEN CASSEROLE WITH VEGETABLES [4]

Prepare by cutting into cubes:

2 cups cooked turkey or chicken

Melt:

3 tablespoons butter

Stir in and sauté gently until lightly browned:

½ cup diced celery
⅓ cup thinly sliced onions
⅓ cup thinly sliced green pepper, seeds and fibrous portions removed

Sprinkle over the top, stir in and cook slowly for 5 minutes:

3 tablespoons flour

Stir in gradually:

1½ cups turkey or chicken stock

Remove the pot from the heat. Stir in:

2 lightly beaten egg yolks
Seasoning, as required

and the turkey meat. Stir over low heat just long enough to let the sauce thicken slightly. You may add:

3 tablespoons dry white wine
Correct the seasoning

Place the mixture in one large or in individual casseroles. Sprinkle the top with:

Minced chives or parsley, nut meats or grated cheese

Serve at once. Good with rice or spoon bread or on toast.

QUICK CHICKEN CREOLE [8]

Melt:

3 tablespoons chicken fat

Sauté in it:

2 tablespoons chopped onion
2 tablespoons chopped green pepper
(1 minced clove garlic)

Stir in:

3 tablespoons flour
¼ teaspoon salt
¼ teaspoon paprika

Add:

½ cup tomato purée or strained tomatoes
1 cup chicken broth

Stir and cook these ingredients until they boil. Add:

1 teaspoon lemon juice
½ teaspoon horseradish
2 cups cooked diced chicken meat
½ cup sliced Sautéed Mushrooms, page 296
½ cup chopped pimiento
Salt, as needed

Serve the chicken in a:

Rice Ring, page 162, or
Noodle Ring, page 173

Just before serving, top with:

(1 cup cultured sour cream)

COOKED TURKEY, CHICKEN OR VEAL LOAF [4 to 6]

Preheat oven to 350°.

Cook and stir for 1 minute:

1½ tablespoons grated onion

in:

1 tablespoon butter

Add it to:

2 cups diced cooked turkey, chicken or veal
¾ teaspoon salt
1 cup cracker crumbs

¾ cup gravy or thickened Chicken Stock (II, 142)
¾ cup milk
2 beaten eggs
(½ cup finely chopped celery)
(¾ teaspoon chili powder)

Place these ingredients in a well-greased loaf pan set in a pan of hot water. Bake the loaf for about 50 minutes. Serve it with:

Leftover gravy with chopped olives
Mushroom Sauce, page 367, or cream sauce with lots of chopped parsley or chives

QUANTITY CHICKEN LOAF [16 to 24]

This is a wonderfully stretchable recipe to serve at group meetings. It is rather firm and serves well sliced, covered with a sauce. Preheat oven to 350°. Remove meat carefully from:

A 4 to 5 lb. stewed chicken

Shred it. Combine lightly with a fork:

2 to 4 cups dry bread crumbs
1 to 3 cups cooked rice
1½ to 2 cups chicken broth, depending on how much rice and crumbs are added
3 to 4 lightly beaten eggs
Correct the seasoning
(½ cup chopped ripe olives)
(½ cup slivered pistachio nuts)

Bake ➧ uncovered for about 25 to 30 minutes. Serve with:

Chicken pan gravy, page 359, seasoned with a little lemon rind, parsley and 1/16 teaspoon saffron

or with:

Quick à la King Sauce, page 375, or Mushroom Sauce, page 367, or Poulette Sauce, page 362

SWEETBREAD AND CHICKEN IN PATTY SHELLS OR BOUCHÉES À LA REINE [4]

A good party dish.
Prepare and keep warm:

Timbale Cases, Bread Cases, page 209, or Patty Shells, page 596

Prepare:

1 cup Cream Sauce I, page 359

seasoned with a small amount of:

Chablis or dry sherry

Add:

½ cup blanched button mushroom caps
¾ cup coarsely chopped cooked white chicken meat
1 pair coarsely diced cooked sweetbreads

Heat thoroughly, but do not boil and, just before serving, fill the above cases to overflowing with the creamed mixture. Garnish with:

Chopped parsley

CHICKEN OR TURKEY DIVAN [4]

Preheat oven to 400°.
Butter a 12 x 9-inch shallow heatproof dish or use individual oval steak platters. Place on the dish:

(4 slices hot buttered toast or make a layer of buttered crackers)

Next place a layer of:

Slices of cooked chicken or turkey

The white meat is best. Allow 2 or 3 slices per serving. Partially cook and lay on top of the meat:

1 package frozen broccoli or asparagus spears, cooked and well drained

Or use leftover cooked broccoli or asparagus. Cover the whole with:

2 cups Mornay Sauce, page 361

Sprinkle with:

Grated Parmesan cheese

and heat in the oven until the sauce is browned and bubbling. Serve at once.

DUCK PILAF [4]

A leftover duck and rice dish. Remove the meat from:

Roast duck

There should be about 2 cups. Break the carcasses apart. Add to them:

4 cups water
1 chopped onion
Some celery leaves

Simmer this stock covered for 1 hour. Strain. Bring to boiling point. Stir in slowly, not disturbing the boiling:

⅔ cup rice

Cook the rice until it is tender, for about ½ hour. Strain it. Reserve the liquor. Melt:

2 tablespoons butter

Add and sauté covered for 5 minutes:

¾ cup finely chopped celery
1 teaspoon grated onion

Add the duck scraps, the rice and:

1 cup leftover gravy, duck liquor or cream combined

Mix these ingredients well with a fork. Season them, if needed, with:

Salt and paprika

Serve the pilaf hot with:

Stewed plums or apricots

SEAFOOD À LA KING [4]

Combine:

1 cup canned lobster, crab meat, etc.
3 peeled, diced, hard-cooked eggs
1 chopped pimiento

Sauté, page 296, and add:

½ cup chopped mushrooms

Cook until tender in boiling water, drain and add:

¼ cup chopped sweet red peppers

Prepare:

Cream Sauce I, page 359

When the sauce is smooth and boiling, add the other ingredients.

Correct the seasoning

and add:

1 teaspoon Worcestershire sauce, 1 tablespoon lemon juice or 2 tablespoons dry white wine

Serve the seafood over:

French Toast (II, 290) rusks, or in a patty shell or au gratin in ramekins

Or toast bread triangles and spread with:

Mashed avocado and lemon juice

CREAMED SEAFOOD AU GRATIN [6]

Preheat oven to 350°.
Combine 3 or 4 kinds of raw fish or shellfish.
For example:

½ lb. chopped lobster meat
1 cup drained oysters
1 cup minced fillet of haddock

Prepare:

1½ cups Sautéed Mushrooms, page 296
4 cups Cream Sauce I, page 359

using cream as the liquid. When the sauce is smooth and hot, fold in the fish. Add the mushrooms.

Correct the seasoning

Fill ramekins or shells with the mixture. Cover the tops with:

Au Gratin II, page 389

Bake the fish for about 25 minutes.

QUICK TUNA OR SEAFOOD CASSEROLE [4]

Prepare:

1½ cups Cream Sauce I,

page 359, or Poulette Sauce, page 362

Add:

1 cup canned tuna, shrimp, clams, etc.

Just before serving, heat through and add:

½ to 1 cup coarsely chopped watercress
1 diced avocado

Serve over:

Toast or rusks

CREAMED SEAFOOD AND VEGETABLES [4]

Preheat broiler.
Cook:

1 cup chopped celery, eggplant or cucumber

Drain it well. Prepare:

¾ cup Cream Sauce I, page 359

When the sauce is boiling, add the celery and:

¾ lb. cooked shrimp, crab meat, etc.

Season with:

Salt, if needed
⅛ teaspoon paprika
(½ teaspoon Worcestershire sauce)

Place these ingredients in greased ramekins. Cover with:

Au Gratin I, page 389

Brown them under the broiler.

SHRIMP WITH CHEESE AND ONION SAUCE [4]

Preheat broiler.
Shell and clean:

1 lb. poached Shrimp, page 442

Melt:

¼ cup butter

Add:

½ cup minced onion

Sauté the onion for about 3 minutes. Stir in:

½ cup grated cheese
½ teaspoon dry mustard
½ teaspoon salt
(½ minced clove garlic)

Cook and stir these ingredients over very low heat until the cheese has melted. Add the shrimp and:

6 tablespoons dry sherry

Butter individual baking dishes. Place the shrimp in them. Brown lightly under a broiler. Shortly before they are done sprinkle the tops with:

Grated coconut

Serve very hot when the coconut is light brown.

KEDGEREE OF LOBSTER OR OTHER FISH [6]

Combine:

2 cups cooked rice
1 lb. cooked flaked lobster or cod fillets
4 minced hard-cooked eggs
¼ cup butter
¼ cup cream
2 tablespoons minced parsley
Salt and cayenne

Heat these ingredients in a double boiler.

SEAFOOD CASSEROLE IN CREOLE SAUCE [4]

Prepare:

¾ lb. cooked shrimp or other seafood

Melt in a skillet:

2 tablespoons butter

Add the shrimp. Stir and cook over high heat for about 2 minutes. Add:

2 cups Creole Sauce, page 380
¼ cup dry white wine

Simmer the shrimp covered for about 5 minutes. You may add:

(Salt and pepper)
(A few grains cayenne)
(3 diced hard-cooked eggs)

Serve the shrimp with:

Boiled Rice

LOBSTER OR SEAFOOD CURRY [4]

Heat in a double boiler:

2 cups Curry Sauce I, page 363

Add, stir and cook for about 3 minutes:

2 cups boiled diced lobster meat or 2 cups cooked seafood

You may add:

(3 chopped sautéed ribs celery)

(½ chopped sautéed green pepper, seeds and fibrous portions removed)

(1 teaspoon grated sautéed onion)

Correct the seasoning

➧ Simmer until well heated. May be served at once with:

Boiled Rice, Chutney (II, 592), or slivered almonds

Or place in individual baking dishes or a casserole and cover with:

Au Gratin II, page 389

Heat in a 425° oven until the crumbs are lightly browned.

LOBSTER OR SEAFOOD NEWBURG [4]

I.

Melt in a double boiler:

4 tablespoons butter

Add, stir and cook for 3 minutes:

2 cups boiled diced lobster meat

Add:

¼ cup dry sherry or Madeira

Cook gently about 2 minutes more. Add:

½ teaspoon paprika

(⅓ teaspoon nutmeg)

Beat and add:

3 egg yolks

1 cup cream

Cook and stir these ingredients until they thicken. Do not permit them to boil.

Correct the seasoning

Serve the lobster at once on:

Hot buttered toast

II. Heat in a double boiler:

2 cups Newburg Sauce, page 361

Add, stir and cook for about 3 minutes:

2 cups boiled diced lobster meat or 2 cups cooked seafood

You may add:

(1 lb. sliced sautéed mushrooms)

Correct the seasoning

Serve at once on:

Hot buttered toast or Boiled Rice

QUICK SEAFOOD DIVAN [4]

Preheat oven to 325°.

Prepare and heat:

1½ cups Cream Sauce I, page 359, condensed cream of celery or mushroom soup sauce, or Quick Creole Sauce, page 380

Have ready:

1 cup cooked shrimp, crab meat, etc.

Correct the seasoning

Put in a hot baking dish:

2 cups cooked asparagus, broccoli, cauliflower, etc.

½ cup Sautéed Mushrooms

2 teaspoons diced pimientos

Cover the vegetables with a close layer of the seafood. Pour the hot sauce over the seafood. Sprinkle lightly all over:

Grated cheese

Bake for about 25 minutes.

QUICK CRAB MEAT OR LOBSTER MONGOLE [4]

For a perfect luncheon or supper, serve with rice and a salad. Combine and heat in a double boiler:

¾ cup canned tomato soup

¾ cup canned pea soup

¾ cup cream

Heat in a double boiler:

1 cup canned crab or lobster meat

Pour a little of the sauce over

it. Serve it garnished with:

Parsley

Boiled Rice, page 158

and the remaining sauce. All the sauce may be added to the crab. In that case, the dish becomes a thick soup.

CRAB MEAT CUSTARD [8]

Preheat oven to 325°.
In the bottom of a large buttered casserole place:

- 4 slices crustless bread

Place on top of the bread:

- 1 large can flaked crab meat: 2 cups
- ½ cup grated American cheese
- Salt and pepper

Beat together:

- 4 eggs
- 3 cups milk
- ½ teaspoon salt
- Dash of cayenne

Pour this mixture over the fish and top with:

- ½ cup grated American cheese

Bake as for a Custard (II, 437), until done. Serve with:

- A mixed green salad

DEVILED CRAB [4]

Flake and pick over:

- 1½ cups canned or cooked crab meat

Melt in a saucepan:

- 1 tablespoon butter

Add:

- 1½ tablespoons cracker crumbs
- ¾ cup milk or cream

Cook these ingredients until they are thick. Remove from the heat. Beat and add:

- 2 small eggs
- ¼ teaspoon salt
- 1½ teaspoons prepared mustard
- A few grains cayenne

Add the crab meat. Pack these ingredients into crab shells or ramekins. Brush the tops with:

- Melted butter

Brown them in a 400° oven or under a broiler.

INDIVIDUAL TUNA FISH PIES [6]

Any other fish or seafood may be substituted. Bake 6 individual Pie Shells (II, 296).
Combine:

- 1 cup flaked tuna fish
- 1 or 1½ cups thick Cream Sauce II, page 359, or condensed cream soup slightly diluted with milk

Heat this mixture. Season it with a choice of:

- 2 tablespoons fresh chopped parsley or chervil
- ¼ teaspoon curry powder
- ½ teaspoon Worcestershire sauce

Place the hot tuna mixture in the hot pie shells. Serve them garnished with:

- Parsley sprigs

sprinkle with:

- Parmesan cheese or chives

TUNA AND POTATO CHIP LOAF [4]

Preheat oven to 350°.
Pat lightly until broken:

- 3 oz. potato chips

Flake and add:

- 1 cup canned tuna fish

Combine these ingredients lightly with:

- 1 can mushroom soup: 10½ oz.

Add, if desired:

- Chopped pimiento, stuffed olives or chopped parsley

Bake the loaf in a greased pan for about ½ hour.

⅄ LOBSTER PARFAIT [6]

This is an exceedingly elegant way of serving cold lobster—fit

for a pavilion! Serve with iced champagne.
Purée in the ⅄ blender:

The meat of 1 freshly killed and cooked 2½ lb. lobster or 2 cups cooked meat from frozen lobster tails

with:

3 tablespoons tomato purée
2 tablespoons lemon juice
1 tablespoon dry sherry
2 teaspoons cognac
½ cup water

Mix in:

1 minced clove garlic
1 finely chopped shallot

Cook the mixture over a low heat until reduced by ⅓. Cool, then add:

2 cups mayonnaise
1½ tablespoons heavy cream
½ teaspoon paprika
1 teaspoon salt
½ teaspoon monosodium glutamate

Chill for 1½ hours. Arrange additional:

4 oz. lobster meat per serving

in 6 parfait glasses. Cover the meat with the above sauce, letting it trickle down in parfait style. Garnish with:

Chilled whipped cream
Water cress

Serve at once.

HOT LOBSTER RING [5]

Preheat oven to 325°.
Melt:

2 tablespoons butter

Stir in, until blended:

3 tablespoons flour

Stir in gradually:

2 cups chicken bouillon or 1 cup bouillon and 1 cup cream

Add:

1 tablespoon minced parsley
½ cup grated bread crumbs —not toasted
4 beaten egg yolks
2 cups boiled diced lobster meat
Salt and white pepper

Whip until stiff, but not dry:

4 egg whites

Fold lightly into the other ingredients. Bake the lobster mixture in a well-oiled 9-inch ring mold until firm, about 20 minutes. Unmold and serve with:

Mushroom Sauce, page 367

QUICK FISH LOAF [4]

Preheat oven to 400°.
Drain, then flake:

1 lb. cooked or canned fish: 2 cups

Combine and beat:

1 egg
¼ cup undiluted evaporated milk or rich cream
¾ cup soft bread crumbs
½ teaspoon salt
¼ teaspoon paprika
2 teaspoons lemon juice or 1 teaspoon Worcestershire sauce
1 tablespoon melted butter
3 tablespoons minced parsley
2 tablespoons chopped celery, onion, green pepper or olives

Add the fish. Place these ingredients in a greased baking dish. Bake them for about 30 minutes. This loaf may be served hot with:

Cream, Tomato or Cheese Sauce, or Caper Sauce

or cold with:

Mayonnaise

TUNA FISH BALLS

[About 4 Servings]
Also use as a hot hors d'oeuvre.
Combine and mix well:

1 cup grated or flaked tuna fish
1 cup mashed potatoes
4 or 6 chopped olives

6 or 8 capers
½ minced clove garlic or 1 teaspoon grated onion
1 tablespoon minced parsley
Salt and paprika
1 teaspoon brandy or dry sherry
(1 teaspoon dried basil)

Shape the mixture into 1-inch balls. Sauté them for 2 or 3 minutes in:

½ cup hot olive oil or butter

Drain the balls, roll them in:

¾ cup ground nut meats

EMERGENCY FISH CAKES

Excellent cakes may be made quickly by combining cooked seafood with condensed cream soup. Keep your mixture rather stiff. Treat it as you would any other fish ball or cake.

CRAB, CLAM OR OYSTER CAKES

[Six 3-Inch Cakes]

You may combine the fish or use them separately.

Melt:

2 tablespoons butter

Add, stir and simmer for 3 minutes:

2 tablespoons minced onion
½ cup soft bread crumbs

Combine and add:

2 beaten eggs
½ cup cream
2 cups minced oysters, canned clams or flaked crab meat
½ cup minced celery
½ teaspoon dry mustard or 1 tablespoon lemon juice
2 tablespoons chopped parsley
½ teaspoon salt
½ teaspoon paprika

Chill this mixture for 2 hours. Shape into cakes. Dust them lightly with:

Flour or bread crumbs

Melt in a skillet:

1 tablespoon butter

Quickly brown the cakes on both sides. ◆ Lower the heat and cook the cakes slowly for about 6 minutes longer. You may dip the cakes in crumbs, then in 1 egg diluted with 1 tablespoon water and again in crumbs. If you do, permit them to dry for 15 minutes, then fry until golden in deep fat heated to 375°.

SALMON CAKES [6]

Flake the contents of:

2 cups canned salmon

Stir in:

½ cup cracker crumbs
2 beaten eggs
½ teaspoon salt
⅛ teaspoon paprika

Form these ingredients into cakes. Sauté them until brown in:

Butter

Serve the cakes with:

Mushroom Sauce, page 367
Celery Soup Sauce III, page 375, etc.

SALMON POTATO CAKES [6]

Prepare:

Leftover Potato Cakes, page 320

Use the egg and 2 cups mashed potatoes. Add in small flakes:

1 cup or more cooked salmon

Season with:

Chopped parsley, onion juice or celery seed

Shape the mixture into cakes. Dip them in:

Crushed cornflakes or bread crumbs

Sauté them slowly in:

Butter, oil or drippings

SALMON PUFFS [6]

Preheat oven to 350°.

Remove skin and bones, drain, then flake:

2 cups canned salmon
Add and stir lightly to blend:
½ cup fresh bread crumbs
2 tablespoons grated onion
1 tablespoon lemon juice
1 tablespoon melted butter
¼ teaspoon salt
¼ teaspoon pepper
Beat:
1 egg
Add and beat in:
½ cup milk
Combine with the salmon mixture. Place in 6 well-greased baking cups set in hot water. Bake for about 45 minutes. Unmold onto a hot platter. Serve with:
Velouté Sauce, page 362

SALMON CASSEROLE [4]

Preheat oven to 425°.
Skin, bone and flake:
2 cups cooked or canned salmon or other fish
Add:
Salt—lightly
Freshly ground pepper
Freshly ground nutmeg
Place the fish in a greased baking dish. Pour over it:
Béchamel Sauce, page 359, Cream Sauce, page 359, or Canned Soup Sauce, page 375, etc.
Cover the top with:
Au Gratin II, page 389
You may add a border of:
Mashed potatoes
Bake the dish until the top is lightly browned.

SALMON LOAF WITH CHEESE SAUCE [6]

Preheat oven to 350°.
Prepare:
1 cup Cream Sauce I, page 359
Stir in over low heat until melted:
¼ lb. grated cheese
Season the sauce with:
¼ teaspoon salt
⅛ teaspoon paprika
A few grains cayenne
Prepare:
1½ cups Mashed Potatoes, page 311
Grease a baking dish and spread the mashed potatoes in it. Cover them with ½ the sauce. Drain, skin, then flake the contents of:
2 cups canned salmon
Place it over the sauce. Cover it with the remaining sauce. Bake the dish for about 30 minutes. Serve it with:
Tomato Sauce, page 376
The cheese may be omitted in the cream sauce and a well-seasoned Cream Sauce I, page 359, may be used. Add herbs.

SALMON POT PIE [8]

Preheat oven to 425°.
A meal in one dish. The salmon mixture may be prepared in advance, so may the dough, and combined shortly before baking. A fine thing for the hurry-up housekeeper. Canned vegetables —peas, asparagus, etc.—and, of course, other fish—crab, shrimp, tuna, etc.—may be substituted.
Drain, reserving the oil:
2 cups canned salmon
Prepare:
Biscuit Dough (II, 284)
Prepare:
1 cup cooked celery
1 cup cooked peas
Drain the vegetables, reserving the liquid. Melt:
¼ cup butter
Sauté in it for about 2 minutes:
1½ tablespoons minced onion
Stir in until smooth:
6 tablespoons flour
Stir in until boiling:
¾ cup vegetable water
1½ cups milk
Add:
1 teaspoon salt
⅛ teaspoon paprika
1 tablespoon lemon juice or 1 teaspoon Worcestershire sauce

1 teaspoon or more chopped parsley or chives

Break the salmon into large pieces. Fold the vegetables and the salmon into the cream sauce. Add, if needed, more salt and flavoring. Place the mixture in a large casserole. Roll the biscuit dough to the thickness of about ¼ inch. Cut it into rounds. Top the salmon mixture with biscuits. Bake until it is done, for about 12 minutes.

SALMON AND TOMATO SCALLOP

[4 Large Servings]
Preheat oven to 375°.
Drain:

2 cups canned salmon

Combine them with:

3 cups soft bread crumbs
2 tablespoons butter
¼ cup chopped onion
½ teaspoon salt
1 teaspoon sugar
¼ teaspoon paprika or pepper
2½ cups tomatoes
(1 chopped seeded green pepper)
(1 beaten egg)
(1 teaspoon Worcestershire sauce or lemon juice)
(¼ cup white wine)

Place these ingredients in a greased baking dish. The top may be sprinkled with:

Grated cheese

Bake the dish until the top is brown and the interior heated.

SALMON IN PARSLEY SAUCE WITH RICE OR NOODLE RING [6]

Drain:

2 cups canned salmon

Remove skin and bones. Break the fish into large flakes. Combine:

1½ teaspoons dry mustard
1½ teaspoons salt
⅛ teaspoon pepper
½ teaspoon paprika
3 tablespoons flour

Combine and beat into the dry ingredients:

1 cup milk
¾ cup salmon liquid and water

Place in double boiler ♦ over—not in—boiling water and beat with a wire whisk:

1 egg
2 tablespoons lemon juice

Add the milk mixture and stir and cook until the sauce has thickened. Add the salmon and:

2 tablespoons butter
½ cup finely minced parsley
1 teaspoon Worcestershire sauce

Heat well and serve in:

Rice Ring, page 162, or
Noodle Ring, page 173

CREAMED CANNED SHAD ROE [2]

Sauté:

1 cup canned shad roe

in:

Butter

with:

½ teaspoon curry powder

Add:

Salt and paprika
¾ cup cream

Reheat but do not boil the roe. Serve it on:

Toast

See other roe recipes on page 416.

BROILED CANNED SHAD ROE [2]

Preheat broiler.
Separate into pieces:

1 cup canned shad roe or other canned fish roe

Dry them with a paper towel. Brush them with:

Melted butter

Sprinkle them with:

Lemon juice
Paprika

Place them in a shallow greased pan or on a greased broiler. Broil the roe gently for about

10 minutes. Turn it once. Baste it frequently with:

Melted butter

Serve it on toast, garnished with:

Slices of lemon
Chopped parsley

CANNED FISH ROE IN RAMEKINS [3]

Preheat oven to 325°.
Combine:

1 cup drained canned fish roe
1½ teaspoons bread crumbs
1½ teaspoons butter
1 beaten egg
Salt, if needed
¼ teaspoon paprika
2 teaspoons chopped parsley
½ cup milk

Fill four greased ramekins. Bake them in a pan of hot water until firm—about 20 minutes. Serve the roe with:

Slices of lemon

ABOUT CHEESE DISHES

If you want to know the secrets of cheese cookery, please read About Cheese (II, 175).

WELSH RAREBITS

Our correspondence is closed on the subject of rarebit vs. rabbit. We stick to rarebit because rabbit already means something else. But we can only answer the controversy with a story. A stranger mollifying a small crying boy: "I wouldn't cry like that if I were you!" Small boy, "You cry your way and I'll cry mine." Good Welsh rarebit can now be bought canned, ready to be heated and served.

I. With Beer [6 to 8]

Grate or grind:

1 lb. aged yellow cheese

Melt in a double boiler:

1 tablespoon butter

Stir in:

1 cup beer

When the beer is warm, stir in the cheese. Stir constantly with a fork until the cheese is melted. Beat slightly and add:

1 whole egg

Season the rarebit with:

1 teaspoon Worcestershire sauce
1 teaspoon salt
(½ teaspoon paprika)
A few grains red pepper
(¼ teaspoon curry powder)
¼ teaspoon mustard

Serve the rarebit at once on:

Crackers, hot toast or Grilled Tomatoes

II. With Milk [4]

Melt in a pan over hot water:

1 tablespoon butter

Stir in and melt:

1½ cups diced aged cheese

Add:

⅓ teaspoon salt
¼ teaspoon dry mustard
A few grains cayenne
1 teaspoon Worcestershire sauce

Stir in slowly:

½ to ¾ cup cream or top milk

When the mixture is hot, remove the pan from the heat. Beat in:

1 egg yolk

Serve the rarebit at once over:

Hot toasted crackers or bread

TOMATO RAREBIT OR WOODCHUCK [4]

I.

Combine and bring to the boiling point:

1 can tomato soup: 10½ oz.
½ cup water

Add and cook slowly until tender:

(¾ cup thinly sliced onions)

Add and stir until melted:

¾ lb. or more thinly sliced aged cheese

Remove the pan from the heat. Combine, beat and add:

2 egg yolks
1 teaspoon Worcestershire sauce
1 teaspoon dry mustard
1 teaspoon salt
¼ teaspoon paprika
⅛ teaspoon white pepper

Stir these ingredients over low heat for 1 or 2 minutes to permit the yolks to thicken slightly. Whip until ♦ stiff, but not dry:

2 egg whites

Fold them into the hot cheese mixture. Serve the rarebit on:

Hot toast or crackers

II. [4]

Stir and melt over low heat:

½ lb. grated aged cheese: 2 cups

Add, stir and heat:

1 can condensed tomato soup: 10½ oz.
3 tablespoons water
½ teaspoon salt
A few grains cayenne

Serve the rarebit on:

Toast or toasted crackers

CHEESE CASSEROLE

This inexpensive luncheon or supper dish is good balanced by a green vegetable, a salad or orange and grapefruit cups. A fine addition to this dish is ½ pound cooked or canned shrimp.

I. [4]

Preheat oven to 350°.
Cut ½ inch thick:

7 slices bread

Spread the slices lightly with:

Butter

Cut 2 of the slices twice across on the bias, making 8 triangular pieces. Cut the remaining bread into cubes. There should be about 4 cups of diced buttered bread. Place layers of diced bread in a buttered baking dish. Sprinkle the layers with:

1 cup grated cheese

Combine and beat:

2 eggs
1 cup milk
1 teaspoon salt
¼ teaspoon paprika
A few grains cayenne
½ teaspoon dry mustard

Pour these ingredients over the cheese. Place the triangle of bread upright around the edge to form a crown. Bake the dish for about 25 minutes. Serve at once.

II. [4]

Preheat oven to 350°.
Trim the crust from:

8 slices bread

Cut them in half on the bias. Place ½ of them in the bottom of a greased 8-inch ovenproof dish, spiral fashion, not letting them overlap. They should resemble a pinwheel. Cut into slices ¼-inch thick:

6 oz. cheese: cheddar, American, Swiss, etc.

Cover the bread layer with the cheese slices, not letting them overlap. Cover the cheese with the rest of the bread, again in spiral fashion. Beat lightly:

3 eggs

Add and beat well:

¼ teaspoon salt
⅛ teaspoon paprika
A few grains cayenne
2 cups rich milk
(1 teaspoon grated onion, 1 tablespoon parsley or chives or ¼ teaspoon mustard)

Pour this mixture over the bread. Permit the dish to stand for 1 hour. Bake it for about 1 hour or until well browned. Serve it hot.

CHEESE NUT AND BREAD LOAF [6]

Preheat oven to 350°.
Combine well:

2 cups fresh bread crumbs

1 cup minced walnut or pecan meats
1 cup grated American cheese
1 cup milk
¾ teaspoon salt
½ teaspoon paprika
1 tablespoon finely chopped onion
1 tablespoon minced parsley
1 beaten egg

Shape these ingredients in a loaf by placing them in a bread pan. Bake the loaf for about 25 minutes. Serve it with:

Quick Tomato Sauce, page 376,
Mushroom Sauce, page 367, or
Onion Sauce, page 363

ABOUT FONDUE

For so simple an affair, the controversy involved in the making of this dish is vast indeed. Its confecting is a ritual that varies with each Swiss household. Experiment has led to the following conclusions, no matter how simple or how complex a version you choose to make. The cheese or combination of cheeses used must be ➧ natural cheese, not pasteurized types. Whatever kind of wine, it must be ➧ a dry white wine. Although kirsch is de rigueur, you may substitute a nonsweet liqueur like slivovitz, a cognac or an applejack. ➧ Measure all ingredients and have them ready to add with one hand. For your other hand will be busy stirring the mixture with a wooden spoon—from the time the wine is hot enough for the cheese until the fondue is ready to be eaten. Altogether, this is a matter of about 10 minutes of cooking.

Have ready a bread basket or bowl filled with crusty French or Italian bread cut into 1 x 1 x ¾-inch pieces, making sure that each piece has one side of crust. At this point the guests, each equipped with a heatproof-handled fork—preferably two or three-tined—spear the bread from the soft side and dip the impaled bit into the well-warmed cheese. The fondue will at first be on the thin side, but will thicken as the process progresses. There is seldom much left by the time another 10 minutes has elapsed. Serve with fresh fruit and tea.

FONDUE [4]

Grate:

1 lb. Emmenthaler or ½ lb. Emmenthaler and ½ lb. Gruyère cheese

Rub a heavy saucepan with:

A clove of garlic

Put into the pan:

2 cups dry white wine

While this is heating ➧ uncovered, over moderately high heat, pour into a cup:

3 tablespoons kirsch

This is the classic flavoring, although one of the other dry liqueurs mentioned above may be used. Stir into the kirsch until well dissolved:

1 teaspoon cornstarch

By this time the wine will begin to show small foamy bubbles over its surface. When it is almost covered with this fine foam

▸ but is not yet boiling, add the coarsely shredded cheese gradually ▸ stirring constantly. Keep the heat high, but do not let the fondue boil. Continue to add the cheese until you can feel a very slight resistance to the spoon as you stir. Then, still stirring vigorously, add the kirsch and cornstarch mixture. Continue to cook until the fondue begins to thicken. Add to taste:

Nutmeg, white pepper or paprika

Quickly transfer it to a heat-proof heavy pan which can be placed over an alcohol lamp or chafing dish or transfer it to an electric skillet adjusted to ▸ low heat. After this transferral the cooking continues on low heat and the guests take over as described previously.

ABOUT SANDWICHES

Innumerable hostesses—not to mention quick-lunch stands—keep green the memory of Lord Sandwich, whose mania for gambling gave the world the well-known concoction that bears his name.

Sandwiches range in size and complexity until they rival a Dagwood. But don't neglect the Canapé chapter, where many delectable smaller versions are found. To keep sandwiches fresh, wrap in wax paper, foil or a dampened cloth.

TOASTED SANDWICHES

These are offered as luncheon suggestions. Many of the sandwich fillings given in the chapter on Canapés (II, 59), may be spread between slices of toast. The sandwiches may be served with a hot sauce or a cold dressing.

Put between:

2 slices toast

any of the following combinations:

Sliced chicken
2 strips sautéed bacon
Grated cheese
Mushroom Sauce, page 367

Creamed chicken
Parmesan cheese
Grilled tomatoes and bacon

Baked ham
Creamed chicken and mushrooms

Ham, chicken and lettuce, with mayonnaise

Braunschweiger
Sliced tomatoes
Lettuce
Tart mayonnaise

Sliced tongue
Sliced tomatoes
Mayonnaise
Sautéed bacon

Creamed mushrooms
Sliced tomatoes
Grated cheese on top, broiled until it is melted

Sliced ham
Creamed mushrooms

Lettuce, French dressing
Sliced tomato and avocado
2 slices crisp sautéed bacon

Asparagus tips
2 slices crisp bacon
Welsh Rareibt, page 237

Lettuce, sliced tomato
Sliced chicken
Crumbled Roquefort cheese
2 slices crisp bacon

SAUTÉED OR GRILLED SANDWICHES

Melt in a small skillet large

enough to accommodate one sandwich:

1½ teaspoons butter

Sauté a sandwich slowly on one side until browned. Add to the skillet:

1½ teaspoons butter

Brown the second side. Especially good with a thin slice of cheese, mustard, salt and paprika between the bread slices or with deviled ham, meat mixtures, jam or jelly.

WAFFLE OR TOASTED SANDWICHES

Cut into thin slices:

White or dark bread

Spread it lightly with:

Soft butter

Cut off the crusts and spread between the slices:

Cheese Spread or other sandwich fillings, pages (II, 59) and 240

Cut the sandwiches to fit the sections of a waffle iron. Wrap them in a moist cloth until ready to toast. Heat a waffle iron, arrange the sandwiches upon the iron, lower the top and toast them until they are crisp.

FINGER ROLL FILLINGS

Very good picnic sandwiches.
Cut into lengthwise halves:

Soft finger rolls

Hollow them slightly. Fill the hollows with any palatable sandwich spread. These are easy to handle. They are delicious filled with:

Chicken Salad, page 51
Tuna Fish Salad, page 51
Braunschweiger sausage
Canapé Filling (II, 63)
Chopped celery and mayonnaise
Chopped olives and cream cheese, etc.

Also see the many spreads in Canapés (II, 59 to 62).

HOT BISCUITS BAKED WITH FILLINGS

[About Eighteen 2½-Inch Biscuits]

Combine:

1 cup cooked, shredded meat: chicken, fish, ham, veal, roast, etc.
½ cup thick gravy, cream sauce or condensed soup
1 tablespoon grated onion
1 chopped hard-cooked egg
2 tablespoons chopped pickles or olives
Seasoning

Prepare:

Baking Powder Biscuit Dough (II, 284)

Roll it to the thickness of ¼ inch. Cut it into rounds. Place on one round 1 tablespoon of the above meat mixture.
Moisten the edges and cover it with another round. Seal the edges with a fork. Prick the tops. Place the biscuits on a baking sheet and bake them until brown in a very hot oven —450°. You may serve these with:

Mushroom Sauce, page 367

MEAL-IN-ONE SANDWICH

[4 Servings—But Better Call It 2]

On your toes when you make this. It's easy if you have all your ingredients ready before you poach the eggs.
Prepare:

4 large slices of toast
8 sautéed bacon slices
4 skinned and sliced large tomatoes
½ cup French dressing
1 cup Cream Sauce I, page 359
1 cup grated cheese

Place the toast on a baking sheet, cover it with the bacon, tomatoes and dressing.
Poach:

4 eggs

Place an egg on each piece of garnished toast, cover it with ¼ of the cream sauce and ¼ of the grated cheese. Place the toast under the broiler until the cheese melts. Serve the sandwiches piping hot.

HOT ROAST BEEF SANDWICH [4]

Slice:

Cold roast beef

Prepare:

1 cup Brown Sauce, page 365

Add to it:

1 tablespoon finely minced sour pickle or ½ cup chopped olives

Cut:

6 thin slices of light or dark bread

Beat until soft:

2 tablespoons butter
¼ teaspoon prepared mustard or 1 teaspoon horseradish

Spread the bread with this mixture. Dip the beef slices in the hot sauce. Place them between the slices of bread. Serve the sandwiches on a hot platter, covered with remaining sauce.

CORNED BEEF OR DRIED BEEF AND CHEESE SANDWICHES [6]

Cut into tiny slivers:

¼ cup sharp American cheese

Cream the cheese well with:

2 tablespoons mayonnaise

Shred finely and add:

4 oz. canned corned beef or dried beef

Chop until fine and add:

¼ cup sweet-sour pickles
1 tablespoon grated onion
(2 tablespoons minced celery or parsley)

Season the spread, as needed, with:

Salt and pepper
Curry powder, mustard or Worcestershire sauce

Spread it between:

Slices of bread

The sandwiches may be toasted or served with sliced tomatoes and lettuce between the layers.

CORNED BEEF AND TOMATO SANDWICHES

Preheat broiler.
Prepare:

Slices of buttered toast

Cover them with:

Sliced corned beef

seasoned with:

Mustard or horseradish
Tomatoes seasoned with French dressing

Sprinkle the tops with:

Grated cheese

Broil the sandwiches until the cheese is melted.

SANDWICH SAVOYARDE [1]

Preheat broiler.
Place on a shallow baker:

½ English muffin

Then add:

A large thin slice of ham

Make a:

2 egg French Omelet, page 188

large enough to cover the ham. Do not fold the omelet, but slip it flat onto the above. Sprinkle with:

Grated Swiss cheese

Run under broiler until cheese melts. Serve at once.

HAM OR TONGUE SALAD SANDWICHES

I. Combine:

Ground cooked ham or tongue
Chopped onion or chives
Chopped celery

Moisten them with:

Cream or salad dressing

If cream is used, season with:

Paprika and salt, if needed

Spread the filling between:

Thin slices of bread

II. Combine and mix:

2 tablespoons chopped onion
2 tablespoons catsup
2 tablespoons chopped green pepper
2 tablespoons chopped pickles
½ lb. chopped sharp cheese
3 oz. deviled ham or ½ cup finely cut cooked ham
¼ cup cream, melted butter or oil

Serve in hollowed hard rolls.

HAWAIIAN TOAST WITH BACON SANDWICH [4]

Cut:

4 to 6 slices stale bread, ½ inch thick

Beat until light:

2 eggs

Beat in:

1 cup pineapple juice
½ teaspoon salt

Dip the bread in the egg mixture. Soak it well. Sauté in a skillet:

8 slices bacon

Remove them to a hot platter. Keep them hot. Fry the bread in the bacon drippings, brown one side and then the other. Remove the bread to the hot platter. Sauté in the bacon drippings:

4 slices drained pineapple, cut into halves

Garnish the platter with the bacon and the pineapple. Serve the toast at once.

HAM, TOMATO AND EGG SANDWICH

Slice and butter:

Rye bread

Place on it:

Slices boiled ham
Lettuce leaves
Sliced tomatoes

Garnish the sandwiches with:

Slices hard-cooked egg
Sprigs parsley

Serve them with:

Horseradish Dressing, page 343, or Russian Dressing, page 349

TOAST ROLLS WITH HAM AND ASPARAGUS [4]

A fine luncheon or supper dish with a molded grapefruit salad and coffee.

Preheat oven to 400°.

Drain:

2 cups asparagus tips

Remove the crusts from:

8 thin slices bread

Brush them lightly on both sides with:

Melted butter

Place on each slice:

A slice boiled ham
Several asparagus tips

Roll the bread around the tips or bring 2 corners together. Fasten the bread with toothpicks. Bake these rolls on a baking sheet until they are lightly browned. Use the asparagus water and cream to make:

Cream Sauce, page 359

Serve the rolls piping hot with the sauce.

HAM AND PINEAPPLE FRENCH TOAST SANDWICH

Combine equal parts:

Ground ham
Crushed pineapple

Season these ingredients with:

French mustard

Spread this filling between slices of:

Buttered bread

See French Toast (II, 290). Spread the outside of the sandwiches with the egg mixture and sauté them as directed.

TOASTED DEVILED HAM AND CHEESE SANDWICHES

Cover:

Thin slices of toast

with a paste made of:

Deviled ham, French mustard or horseradish

Or use:

(Thin slices boiled ham)

Cover the ham with thin slices of:

American cheese

Dot with:

Capers

Press the sandwiches and refrigerate 6 hours. Then sauté until toasted in:

Butter

Serve hot.

POOR BOY, SUBMARINE OR HERO SANDWICH [4]

Cut in half lengthwise a long loaf of:

French Bread (II, 245)

Spread both cuts with:

Butter

On the bottom half, arrange layers of:

Sliced salami sausage
Sliced sharp cheese
Thinly sliced boiled ham
(Thin slices tomato)

Put the top half of bread on to make a sandwich and cut into 4 pieces. Mix together:

¼ cup dry mustard
1 tablespoon dry white wine

Serve this with the sandwich.

TOASTED BRAUNSCHWEIGER SANDWICH

Braunschweiger is a refined version of the rather heavy smoked liver sausage.

Combine and stir to a smooth paste:

Braunschweiger sausage
Canned tomato soup or tomato paste
(A few drops of cream or Worcestershire sauce)

Cut the crusts from:

Thin slices of bread

Spread them with the sausage mixture. Roll the bread or make double-deck sandwiches. Toast and serve them very hot.

BACON AND CHEESE SANDWICH [4]

Preheat broiler.

Toast on either one or both sides, or use untoasted:

4 slices bread

Place on each slice:

(A thick slice tomato)
(Chopped onion and green peppers)
(Sliced olives or pickles)
A slice of American cheese

Spread the cheese with:

Mustard or chili sauce

Cover each sandwich with:

2 slices bacon

Crisp the slices of bacon under the broiler and serve immediately. Also good with:

(Hot Cheese Sauce)

EGG AND CHEESE SANDWICH WITH TOMATO SAUCE [4]

Rub:

4 slices French bread

with:

(Garlic)

Dip them quickly in:

Milk seasoned with a pinch of salt

Brown them in:

Olive oil

Place them on a hot ovenproof plate. Cover them with:

4 chopped hard-cooked eggs
1 cup or more grated cheese
6 or more chopped olives
Dots of butter

Place the slices under a broiler until the cheese is melted. Serve them with:

Tomato Sauce, page 376

FRENCH TOAST AND CHEESE [4]

Preheat oven to 350°.
Prepare, omitting the sugar:
French Toast (II, 290)
Toast the bread in the oven on a buttered ovenproof plate for about 5 minutes. Stir over very low heat until smooth:
½ lb. grated or minced cheese
½ teaspoon salt
A few grains cayenne
¼ cup milk
3 tablespoons butter
Spread the toast with the cheese mixture. Return it to the oven to brown lightly.

FRENCH TOMATO TOAST

Beat until light:
2 eggs
½ teaspoon salt
¼ teaspoon paprika
½ cup condensed tomato soup
Dip in this:
6 slices of bread
Sauté the slices in hot:
Butter or drippings
When a good brown, serve them with:
Cheese Sauce, page 364
Minced parsley or chives

CHEESE SANDWICH WITH MUSHROOM SAUCE

Trim the crusts from:
Slices light or dark bread
Spread them with:
Butter
Place on each piece:
Slices of cheese
Lettuce leaves
Slices tomato or cucumber
Slices hard-cooked egg
Sliced olives or pickles
Serve the sandwiches with:
Mushroom Sauce, page 367

PUFFED CHEESE WITH MUSHROOMS ON TOAST [4]

Preheat oven to 375°.
Melt in a saucepan:
1 tablespoon butter
Add and sauté until tender:
½ cup finely sliced mushrooms
1 teaspoon grated onion
Combine:
2 unbeaten egg yolks
½ lb. grated Swiss cheese: 2 cups
¾ teaspoon salt
¼ teaspoon pepper
A few grains cayenne
Stir in the mushroom and onion mixture. Beat until stiff, but not dry:
2 egg whites
Fold them into the mixture. Toast on one side:
6 slices bread
Place them toasted side down on a cookie sheet. Spread the untoasted sides lightly with:
Butter
Heap the cheese mixture on the bread. Bake the slices until they are firm to the touch and well puffed.

PEANUT BUTTER AND TOMATO SANDWICH

Preheat broiler.
Toast on one side:
A slice of bread
Spread the untoasted side with:
Peanut butter
mixed with:
Chopped cooked bacon
Bacon drippings
You may top this with:
A thick slice of tomato
Season the tomato with:
¼ teaspoon brown sugar
Salt and paprika
Put the sandwich under a broiler for a minute or two.

PEANUT BUTTER AND BACON SANDWICH [4]

Preheat broiler.
Virtue, however admirable, is

frequently dull. Peanut butter needs enlivening. Try this mixture on the unconverted.
Combine:

¾ cup peanut butter
¼ cup mayonnaise
¼ teaspoon salt
2 tablespoons pickle relish or chili sauce
¼ cup cooked minced bacon

Toast on one side:

4 slices bread

Spread the untoasted side with the mixture. Broil the sandwiches until the tops are brown. Slice them diagonally.

CLUB SANDWICH

[Individual Serving]
Prepare:

3 large square slices of toast

Cover slice 1 with:

A lettuce leaf
3 crisp slices hot bacon
Slices of tomato
1 tablespoon mayonnaise
(Drained slices pineapple)

Place slice 2 over slice 1 mixture and cover it with:

Slices of cold cooked chicken
1 tablespoon mayonnaise

Place slice 3 over slice 2 mixture and cut the sandwich on the bias.

FRUIT STICKS

I. Cut into strips 3 by 1½ inches wide and ½ inch thick:

White bread

Toast them on 3 sides. Place them on a baking sheet with the untoasted side up. Drain:

Pineapple or apricot slices

Place them on the untoasted sides. Sprinkle them well with a mixture of:

Brown sugar and cinnamon

Dot them with:

Butter

Brown them under a broiler.

II. Preheat oven to 450°.
Prepare:

Pie Dough (II, 293)

Roll it until very thin. Cut it into oblongs. Sprinkle:

Pineapple or apricot slices

with:

Cinnamon and brown sugar

Wrap the slices in the oblongs. Moisten the edges with water. Bake the slices for about 20 minutes.

LAMB OR CHICKEN SANDWICH

Trim the crusts from:

Large slices rye bread

Spread them with:

Butter

Place on each piece:

Slices cold lamb or chicken
Lettuce leaves
Slices tomato
Slices hard-cooked egg

Serve the sandwich with:

Russian Dressing, page 349

CHICKEN AND CREAM CHEESE SANDWICHES

Spread:

Slices of whole-wheat bread

with:

Cream cheese softened with cream

Add:

Slices of cooked chicken
Chopped green olives
Salt

HOT CHICKEN SANDWICHES

I. Cut into slices:

Cold cooked chicken

Dip the slices in:

Mayonnaise

Prepare:

Biscuits (II, 284)

While hot, open and spread them with:

Butter

Place the chicken slices in the biscuits. Serve them hot with:

Chicken gravy, Cheese Sauce, page 364, or Mushroom Sauce, page 367

II. Using biscuits, as in the previous recipe, fill with:

Chicken Salad, page 51

or combine:

½ cup cooked minced chicken
1 chopped hard-cooked egg
6 chopped stuffed olives
¼ cup mayonnaise
(2 tablespoons chopped parsley)

Serve hot with one of the sauces mentioned previously.

III.

Preheat oven to 375°.

Prepare:

Buttered toast

Cover the toast with:

Sliced chicken

Sprinkle it with:

Crumbled Roquefort cheese

Cover it with:

Strips of notched bacon

Bake for about 10 minutes, until the bacon is crisp. Sliced tomatoes may be placed on the toast.

OPEN-FACED SEAFOOD SALAD AND TOMATO SANDWICHES

I. Prepare:

Slices of buttered bread

Cover them with:

Slices of tomato

Top the tomatoes with mounds of:

Tuna Salad, page 51, or other seafood

Garnish with:

Chopped parsley, olives or chives
Chopped sautéed bacon

II. Cut crosswise into 2 sections:

A large round loaf of bread

Spread cut sides with:

Butter

Place around the outer edges of each piece:

Thinly sliced tomatoes

Sprinkle with:

Salt and pepper
Chopped fresh basil or chives

Arrange like spokes of a wagon wheel, in the center of each piece:

Canned sardines

Decorate with:

Sliced black olives

Sprinkle some of the sardine oil over all, cut the pieces into 6 wedges each and serve.

TOASTED ROLLS WITH CRAB MEAT AND CHEESE [4]

Fine with beer or cider.

Preheat broiler.

Cut into halves:

4 rolls

Cover the 4 lower halves with:

Lettuce leaves

Combine:

¾ cup canned crab meat
¼ cup mayonnaise

Spread this on the lettuce. Spread the remaining halves with:

Butter
Slices of cheese
(Mustard)

Toast the cheese under a broiler until it is soft. Combine the halves.

LOBSTER SANDWICHES

Flake:

6 oz. canned lobster or other seafood

Sprinkle over it:

1 teaspoon lemon juice

Add:

½ cup minced celery

1 tablespoon minced onion or chives
½ cup mayonnaise

Mayonnaise, if too thick, is fine thinned with sour cream. Season with:

(Worcestershire sauce, curry powder or freshly grated nutmeg)

Add:

(Capers, chopped olives, pickles or parsley, etc.)

Spread these ingredients on:

Buttered rye bread

You may add:

Crisp lettuce leaves

SHRIMP SANDWICHES WITH CHEESE SAUCE [3]

Clean:

1½ cups cooked shrimp

Melt:

2 tablespoons butter

Add:

1 tablespoon grated onion
(1 sliced pimiento)

and the shrimp. Stir over low heat for 1 minute. Prepare:

6 slices toast

Heap the shrimp on the toast. Serve with:

Cheese Sauce, page 364

VEGETABLES

It is probably true that more outrages are perpetrated against vegetables than against any other basic foods. These outrages often begin when the seeds are sown —in impoverished ground; they may continue during the plant's development, because of inadequate moisture; and then reach some sort of climax in the almost uniformly careless handling that produce is subjected to on its way to the point of sale.

To preserve their true, delicate flavor, as well as their natural sugars and nutrients and to enjoy green vegetables at their wholesome best, they should be ➧ washed just before cooking ➧ cooked just after picking ➧ just to the point of doneness, not a moment more, and ➧ eaten just off the heat.

➧ The longer vegetables take to reach maturity, the coarser their cellulose. The greater the period between picking and cooking, the longer the time needed to make them palatable. Naturally, longer cooking periods impair nutritive values, color and especially flavor—that quality a family considers first.

Here are ways to get the best out of the less than perfect vegetables we are often forced to buy. Market on days when supplies reach your store—buying so that you hold them the least possible time before use. ➧ Apply to each kind of vegetable the tests for ripeness we describe later.

If stocks are limited, always prefer a fresh, fluffy, country or garden lettuce over a bruised Bibb and a crisp bunch of carrots over darkened, leathery artichokes. Care in cooking, piquancy of seasoning and ingenuity in combining familiar varieties can compensate for the more commonplace choice.

If the vegetable is old, dress it up with seasoned butters, herbs, spices and sauces. If young, drain it, toss it in butter, allowing 1 tablespoon to every cup of vegetable and season it very lightly, so that its own tender flavor prevails. You will find that young vegetables have an abundance of natural sugars but that ➧ older ones often profit by an added pinch of sugar in cooking. You will notice varied seasonings suggested in our individual recipes. Add them with a light hand; the exception being dried legumes and canned vegetables, which are greatly improved by a bold and imaginative approach. ➧ Salting just after the onset of cooking will slightly firm vegetable structure and help retain color and flavor. ➧ Allow about ¼ teaspoon of salt to each cup of water. But see the steaming method we prefer, page 252.

ABOUT STORING VEGETABLES

Certain vegetables and fruits should not be stored together. Apples give off an ethylene gas that makes carrots bitter, for example, and onions hasten the spoilage of potatoes. Watch for other such relationships. Do not wash vegetables until you are ready to use them and then do not soak them, except as indicated, because moisture tends to leach away the water-soluble vitamins.

A good general rule ➧ for leaf vegetables, peas and green beans is to store them unwashed at about 45° in plastic bags. There is enough moisture within the vegetables to keep them fresh this way. The exception is water cress, page 31. Cut the leaves from root vegetables before storing, for the flow of sap continues to the leaf at the expense of the root. Store thick-skinned vegetables like potatoes, rutabagas and turnips unwashed in a dry, dark, cool place. The ideal temperature is 55° to 65°.

ABOUT PREPARING VEGETABLES FOR COOKING

Some vegetables may simply be scrubbed and steamed or baked unpeeled. These methods keep vitamin losses to a minimum, provided cooking is not overly prolonged. Sometimes vegetables are scrubbed, scraped or thinly pared before cooking. Remember that most of the vitamins lie near the skin and that deep paring will mean losing them. Prepare peeled vegetables and cook them immediately to minimize their exposure to air. ➧ Never soak after slicing, if the greatest amount of nutrient values is to be retained. Whether you cook vegetables whole or sliced ➧ see that pieces are uniform in size, so they will all be done and tender simultaneously.

Many chopping and slicing devices are advertised, but nothing can replace a skilled relaxed wrist and a sharp French knife. Acquire this indispensable trick and you will be forever grateful. Practice with a mushroom, which is yielding and not slippery when placed cap down, and work up to an onion, which is resistant and evasive. In either case ➧ to slice, first cut the onion or apple or whatever you are slicing, so that it rests on a flat, not a rolling base, then hold this object as shown in the sketch below. For a good view, showing how the knife handle is held relaxed between the thumb and forefinger, see Soufflé Potatoes, page 317. ➧ The point of the knife is never lifted from the cutting board but forms a pivot. The cutting edge is never lifted above the first joint of the left forefinger.

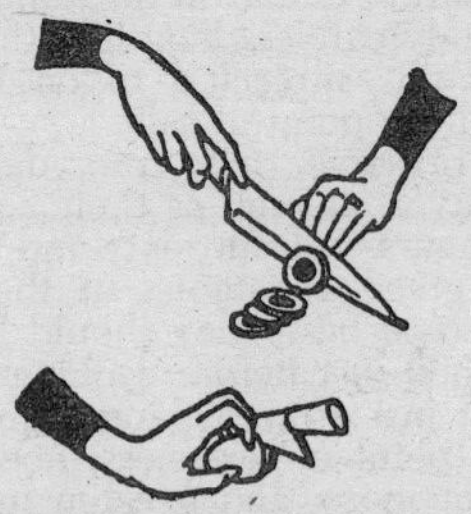

The handle end of the knife is raised high enough to be eased gently up and down, its wide blade guided by the perpendicular left forefinger and midfinger. As the slicing progresses, inch a slow retreat with the left hand without releasing a firm grasp on the object.

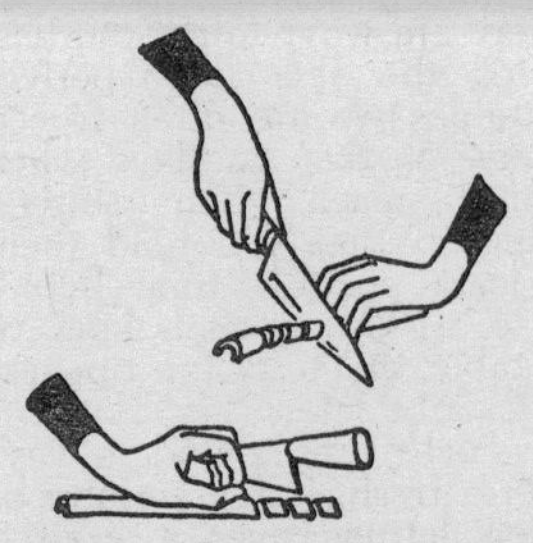

If celery or Chinese cabbage, for instance, are to be sliced on the diagonal, the two guide fingers are set at an angle, as shown next. But the knife in the right hand continues its relaxed accurate slicing, while the left makes way without losing control of the stalks. To peel very hard, round vegetables, see a trick sketched on page 338.

If you are really determined to lure your family into eating vegetables, you will find they will respond more readily if the vegetables are attractive in shape and perhaps rather sparse in number. Think of the irresistible charm of vegetables floating like flowers in a Japanese lacquered bowl. The French are also very adept at presentation, if more lavish, and they disguise the same old carrots, beans and potatoes under a mass of impressive aliases. As **printanière**, they are spring-grown, young, tender and thinly sliced. As **brunoise, salpicon, mirepoix** and **macédoine**, they are ageless, and sliced respectively from ⅛ to ¼ to ⅜ inch, which latter size we call just plain "diced." As **jardinière, julienne** or **allumette**, they are taller and thinner, about 2 to 3 inches long and ⅛ inch through. When they are round in shape and small, you may call them **pearls**; if they are elliptical, call them **olivette** at ⅜ inch, **noisette** at ½ inch and **Parisienne**, if about 1 inch at their narrowest diameter. Utilize whatever scraps are left over in ⅄ blender soups or, unless they are starchy ones, in the stockpot.

ABOUT MAINTAINING FLAVOR AND COLOR DURING VEGETABLE COOKING

There are bound to be some nutritional losses, especially of vitamin C, in any cooking process. It does not follow that eating vegetables raw is the whole answer. Cooked carrots and spinach, in spite of losses during cooking, will have more nutrients available for absorption by the body than raw. ➧ The greatest losses probably come in mashing and puréeing. If done when the vegetables are hot, exposure to air during these processes will involve losses of ¼ to ½ of the vitamin C content. If you prepare mashed or puréed vegetables, compensate by serving a salad or citrus fruit at the same meal. All in all, you will do best nutritionally with fresh vegetables; next, with frozen ones that have been held below 0° for less than 2 months; last, with canned vegetables, provided the liquid in the can is utilized. Dehydrated vegetables, frozen and nonfrozen, suffer great loss of nutrients, the latter, especially, if improperly packaged. For cooking frozen vegetables, see page 254.

No one method of vegetable cooking can claim superiority over all other methods, but ➧ those processes which retain the best color and flavor are most apt to retain the most nutrients.

➧ Color should never be maintained by the addition of baking soda, for this method not only destroys nutrient values but makes the vegetable mushy in texture. Color may, however, be lost without accompanying nutrient loss if you cook in hard water, see (II, 147). ➧ The addition of vinegar or lemon juice to the cooking water will stabilize color. Greens, cauliflower, cabbage, onions, turnips and beets will need about 1 teaspoon for each 2 cups of water. Another method of preserving color without losing nutrients is to cook vegetables in milk. This tenderizes them more rapidly too, although sometimes, due to acid in the vegetable, the milk may curdle harmlessly.

It is advisable to cook most vegetables ➧ covered and with a small amount of water. ➧ Exceptions are the cabbage and onion tribes, turnips, parsnips, beets and wild greens which, when boiled, require water to cover. All are cooked uncovered. They react adversely under too great heat and too long a period of cooking. The greens become slimy and the strong, volatile oils of all these vegetables give off unpleasant odors—and they discolor. It is often wise to parblanch, page 88, this whole group of vegetables, briefly. ➧ Both when putting them into hot water which has reached a rolling boil for the blanching and again for the cooking, add them gradually so as not to disturb the boiling. These vegetables also tend to discolor badly, especially if covered. Blanching, page 88, helps to retain their color, as does cooking Cauliflower à blanc (II, 147). Do not cover any vegetable completely after the cooking is over, but allow the steam to escape and the dish will have much better color.

No matter which method of cooking you use, be sure ➧ to keep the vegetable waters unless they taste too strong. Use them for their invaluable nutritional qualities and flavoring powers (II, 138).

ABOUT STEAMING VEGETABLES

Steaming vegetables, we find, gives the most consistently good results. See the sketches of steamers on page 253. Our favorite method ➧ when time is short, is a French steamer used with a pressure cooker. If you ⊗ pressure-steam, add a minute or two to the time we indicate for pressure cooked vegetables. Expel all air from the pan before closing the vent, Time carefully, for vegetables may be quickly overcooked by this method. Or use regular heat under a double boiler with a specially built steamer inset—sketched on page 253. Steaming is such a superior method, we feel, that, if you have no adequate equipment, it is worthwhile to improvise a steamer by placing a colander in any pot with a tight-fitting lid.

In any steaming, not matter what accessory you use, be sure that ➧ the water is boiling before you set the perforated container over it. ➧ Cover at once and cook 3 to 5 minutes longer than when vegetables are processed in boiling water.

ABOUT PANNING VEGETABLES

Panning, also known as braising or covered-skillet cooking, as well as stir-frying—discussed later—are very good and quick methods for tender vegetables and those very finely and evenly sliced. ➧ They are prepared the same way for both methods: sliced fine and usually cut on the diagonal for any that tend to be stringy. If leaves are coarse, remove mid-ribs and stem ends. For 4 servings, allow about 1 lb. kale, cabbage, okra, celery or celery cabbage, about 1½ lbs. of spinach or chard, ¾ lb. beans.

Skillet and panning cookery requires about 1 tablespoon of oil or butter per pound of vegetables. If the vegetables are dry, sprinkle them lightly with water before adding them to the hot fat. To pan, braise or skillet-cook any tender vegetable, have ready a pan with a tight-fitting lid. Heat the pan, put in the fat and heat to the point of fragrance. Quickly add the ▶ uniformly sliced vegetables and clap the lid on at once to retain as much steam as possible. When the steam comes up vigorously ▶ reduce the heat at once and cook over low heat until the vegetable is just tender. Shake the pan repeatedly to be sure the contents do not stick.

The braising or panning method is also an effective, if somewhat slower, way to do small quantities of podded vegetables. Let them remain in the pod and shell them just before serving. Allow about 1½ to 2 lbs. of these vegetables—depending on how full the pods are—for 4 servings. Depending also on the thickness of the pod, add from ⅓ to ¾ cup boiling water for each pound of vegetables and cook 15 to 20 minutes or until tender. No fat is necessary if the vegetables are podded. Butter them after shelling.

ABOUT STIR-FRYING

This is the method so typical of Chinese cooking, which allows the vegetables to remain tender, crisp and of very good color. They are traditionally stirred in a big open conical pan held erect by a ring stand ▶ over really fierce heat. Stir-frying is an ideal way to cook mixed tender vegetables quickly—the whole process lasting only 3 or 4 minutes. Preparation is the slow part, as the vegetables must all be cut uniformly as for panning, page 252. Those which need longer cooking are put in first and the tenderer ones later, so they are all done at the same time.

Use any cooking oil, other than olive. Allow 2 teaspoons of oil to 1 pound of vegetables. ▶ Have the pan very hot and heat the oil to the point of fragrance. A slice or two of fresh ginger root or garlic may be put in at this time and discarded before the vegetables are added. Stir the vegetables rapidly to make sure they are well coated with the oil. Continue to cook ▶ uncovered, over high heat, stirring constantly until the vegetables are just tender.

Watery vegetables like cucumber, tomato and zucchini, and thin-leafed types like spinach, Chinese cabbage, bean sprouts and salad greens may need no water. Beans and root vegetables will require about ¾ cup of stock or water for each pound. Cook these a little longer —about 5 to 8 minutes in all.

When the vegetables are just tender, you may add Chinese Sauce for Vegetables, page 372. Stir it into the vegetables—and cooked meat, if you are using any. ▶ Cover the pan briefly until the sauce reaches the boiling point and serve at once.

▶ To ensure crispness, bring your guests to the table the moment you have finished cooking. Be sure also ▶ to preheat lidded

dishes from which to serve the food.

The preceding description applies primarily to meat-and-vegetable dishes, but it may be ➧ adapted to meat combinations, too—although ➧ we do not recommend it for raw pork. First, cook thin slices or slivers of lean meat briefly in the pan. Remove the meat and set it aside—keeping it warm. Cook the vegetables in the same fat with the meat juices. When they are ready, add the meat to them just before serving. It is advisable to cook no more than one pound of meat at a time by this method.

⊙ ABOUT PRESSURE COOKED VEGETABLES

Please see About Pressure Cooking, page 81. Rather than cook directly in a small amount of water, we prefer to pressure steam, as described previously in About Steamed Vegetables. For pressure timing, see individual recipes. Be sure to save the cooking juices for the stock pot.

⅄ ABOUT BLENDED PURÉED VEGETABLES

The blender is a real find for mothers of young children who want to cook fresh vegetables all at once for the whole family and then purée the very young children's portion. As an alternative, well-washed and scrubbed, tender, raw vegetables may be blended and then cooked to the boiling point. Tough ones should be briefly parboiled, cooled and then blended. You may reheat briefly in butter or cream before serving.

⊟ ABOUT CAMPFIRE VEGETABLES

Here are 2 simple, potless ways to cook vegetables for an outdoor barbecue. For the first, use frozen or sliced and washed vegetables. Place them on heavy-weight aluminum foil and season them. Use the drugstore wrap (II, 550). Place the foil-wrapped vegetables on a grill or under or on hot coals for 10 to 15 minutes.

For the second method, place—directly on a greased grill above the coals—thick slices of tomato, mushroom, pepper, parboiled onion. Cover with an inverted colander. Cook until tender.

❄ ABOUT COOKING FROZEN VEGETABLES

➧ Please read about Thawing and Cooking of Frozen Foods (II, 552). To cook these convenience foods so they are all heated through at the same time, use a frozen-food steamer.

⊙ To pressure cook frozen foods, allow about ½ as long as for the regular pressure cooking times given in individual recipes, but use the same amounts of water.

If using an electric skillet, place the hard-frozen vegetables, except for spinach and corn on the cob, which must be partially thawed, in the skillet and cover. Set at 350° until steam escapes. Then turn to 300° until the vegetable is tender.

▲ ABOUT COOKING VEGETABLES AT HIGH ALTITUDES

In baking vegetables at high altitudes, use approximately the same temperatures and timing given for sea-level cooking. In cooking vegetables at high altitude by any process involving moisture, both more liquid and a longer cooking time are needed, as the vegetables boil at lower temperatures. Frequently, the longer time can be reduced if the vegetables are thinly sliced or cut into small units. To avoid tough stems and overcooked leaves on leafy vegetables, remove the mid rib and use it in the stock pot.

Make these adjustments as an approximate time guide: for each 1000 feet of elevation, add to the cooking time given in the recipes about 10% for whole beets, carrots and onions, and about 7% for green beans, squash, green cabbage, turnips and parsnips. ▲ ✻ In cooking frozen vegetables at high altitudes, whole carrots and beans may require as much as 5 to 12 minutes of additional cooking, while other frozen vegetables may need only 1 to 2 more minutes.

The extension division of most land grant colleges will test the gauge of your pressure cooker and probably provide a pressure chart for youı area free of charge.

In pressuring vegetables at high altitude, you will have to increase the liquid in your cooker ¼ to ½ cup for every 2 cups of vegetables, depending on their respective length of cooking time. As with other vegetable-cooking at high altitudes, sliced or shredded vegetables, as well as peas, corn and spinach may cook almost as rapidly as at sea level, at 15 lbs. pressure. But you may find that, with some of the leafy greens, 10 lbs. of pressure and a slightly longer cooking period gives a better result. This has been found true for asparagus, celery, turnips and cauliflower. Don't be surprised if whole potatoes, beets, yams and beans need considerably more time than at sea level.

ABOUT REHEATED VEGETABLES

Reheating vegetables is frowned on—both from a culinary and health standpoint. If you do reheat them, put them with a few teaspoons of water or stock in the top of a covered double boiler or reheat or bake them in a hot sauce. Allow about ¼ to ½ as much sauce as vegetables. Reheating in a sauce is one of the best ways to serve vegetables which must be held. The sautéing and browning of cooked vegetables diminish vitamins. Try serving leftover vegetables vinaigretted in a salad, remembering—contrary to at least one precept we learned at mother's knee—that cold food is as nutritious as hot.

Canned or frozen vegetables have, of course, already suffered some loss of flavor and vitamins. Reheating before serving increases this loss. ➧ Be sure to retain the canning or cooking water for use in soup or sauce or as the medium in which to reheat.

➧ Always clean off tops before opening cans, as they may be dusty or have been sprayed with poisonous insecticides while in the store. Also ➧ avoid metal slivers in opening a can, by starting to open it beyond the side seam and stopping before you cut through it. Food may be stored safely in opened cans, covered and refrigerated, but a metallic taste results, especially if the food is acid.

ABOUT CREAMED, BUTTERED AND SAUCED VEGETABLES

Practically any vegetables may be served in or with a sauce. They may be steamed or even deep fried before saucing. ➧ Drain them well before combining with sauces or butter.

The amount to allow for garnishing will depend so largely on the richness of the sauce, from ½ to 1 tablespoon of butter per cup of cooked vegetables —on up to 4 tablespoons of a cream sauce garnish. If the vegetable is heated in the sauce, allow about 2 to 3 tablespoons for each cup of vegetables, using less if it is a rich sour cream dressing—more, perhaps, if based on cream soup. Consider, too, if the vegetable is to be presented in individual deep dishes or from a big serving bowl onto a flat plate.

If you are casseroling the vegetable in a sauce, allow enough sauce to just cover the vegetables. Such casseroles are often finished off Au Gratin, page 389.

Add to vegetable butters and sauces, if not already indicated in the recipe, citrus juices and pinches of zests (II, 219), fresh or dried herbs, curry powder, mustard, chili powder, horseradish or grated cheese; and don't forget the onion (II, 209).

ABOUT VEGETABLES FONDUES

Although the term fondue is usually associated with cheese, page 239, or Boeuf Fondu Bourguignonne, page 475, it applies also to vegetables reduced to a pulp by very, very slow cooking in butter, as for Tomato Pudding II. Some other vegetables that lend themselves well to such dishes are carrots, celery, eggplant, sweet pepper, onion, leek and lettuce.

To prepare them for this method of cooking, first rid them of excess moisture in one of the following ways. Except for tomatoes, they may be parblanched, page 88, from 3 to 5 minutes. Eggplant and cucumber may be sliced, salted generously and allowed to drain on a rack. Salting clears them of a rather unpleasant astringent quality they sometimes acquire. They may also be thinly sliced, salted, placed in a bowl and weighted to force out excess moisture.

Mushrooms and green onions may be wrapped in a dish towel and wrung out. If you are strong enough, you may be able to extract enough juices for the stock pot.

Tomatoes for fondues may be cut at the stem end and squeezed toward the cut end to get rid of both moisture and seeds.

Cook fondue vegetables covered, until they reach a naturally puréed state.

ABOUT STUFFED VEGETABLES

Tomatoes, peppers, squashes, cucumbers, onions, mushrooms, all make decorative and delicious vegetable cases. For a "new dimension," fill them with other vegetables, contrasting in color or flavor; or point up the bland ones with a farce of cooked food, with buttered, crumbed, cooked vegetables or with creamed mixtures. Raw foods needing long cooking should not be used in vegetable stuffings.

As vegetable cases need different timing for blanching, see recipes under individual vegetables for this information. Other factors remain the same. After draining, place the filled cases on a rack, in a pan containing about ¼ inch of water.

Heat the cases through in a 400° oven, unless otherwise indicated, before serving. Or, if you want to serve them Au Gratin I or II, page 389, you may find they have better color if you run them first under a broiler and then bake as above to heat them. With Au Gratin III, the cheese will probably brown the tops sufficiently in the baking alone without using a broiler at all.

ABOUT VEGETABLES À LA GRECQUE

These mixed vegetables, left whole if small or cut into attractive shapes, see page 250, become aromatic as the result of being boiled in a court bouillon of highly seasoned oil and water. They are served at between 70° and 90° or, at most, slightly chilled, so that the oil will not be evident. They make convenient hors d'oeuvre, meat tray or salad garnishes, as they keep well if covered and refrigerated. They are excellent for an antipasto tray. Prepare one of the following court bouillons in which to cook:

1 lb. mixed vegetables

Suitable vegetables include artichoke hearts, julienned carrots, cauliflower florets, celery, fennel, green beans, leeks, mushrooms, pearl onions, peppers and pickled whole olives. Cucumber and eggplant slices or strips are delicious but these should have excess moisture removed, see page 288.

Squeeze over the cut vegetables, to keep them white:

Juice of 2 lemons

I. Place in a 3-quart stainless or enamel pan:

4 cups water
1/3 to 1/2 cup olive oil
1 teaspoon salt
2 peeled cloves garlic
(3 peeled shallots)

and the following herbs and spices, tied in a cheesecloth bag:

6 sprigs parsley
2 teaspoons fresh thyme
12 peppercorns
(3 coriander seeds or 1/4 teaspoon orégano)
(1/8 teaspoon fennel or celery seeds)

Add for flavor 2 of the squeezed lemon halves. Bring the mixture to a boil, then remove from the heat to season for about 15 minutes. Remove the spice bag and garlic. Bring the court bouillon again slowly to a ♦ simmer. Add in turn the most delicately flavored of the prepared vegetables. Once more bring the oil just to a boil, reduce the heat and let the vegetables heat through and then cool in the marinade. Drain them and place them in a jar, using a slotted wooden spoon. Now, use the marinade to cook the next most delicately flavored vegetable. Continue till each one has been cooked and cooled in the marinade. When they are all in the jar, mixed or separate, cover them with the marinade to store. After the vegetables have been eaten, use the marinade for sauces.

II. Combine in a stainless or enamel pan:

1 cup wine
2 cups olive oil
1/2 cup vinegar
1/2 to 3/4 cup water
2 cloves garlic
3 sprigs parsley
6 peppercorns
2 sliced lemons
1/4 teaspoon salt

Cook the vegetables in the heated mixture, as in I.

III. This rather off-beat version is a pleasant change.

Combine in a stainless or enamel pan:

3/4 cup olive oil
1/2 cup wine vinegar
3/4 cup catsup
1/2 cup chili sauce
1 clove garlic
1 teaspoon Worcestershire sauce

Cook the vegetables in the heated mixture, as in I.

ABOUT VEGETABLES BAKED UNPEELED

We have always liked the snug phrase "baked in their jackets" to describe this process. But we are told that at least one young cook, after encountering it, called a home economist of the local utility company and complained that her grocer was unable to supply her with potato-jackets!

Only to a degree true is the concept that unpeeled baking is the very best way of cooking to preserve vitamins in vegetables. Since most vitamins lie just under the skin ➧ those most sensitive to heat will be destroyed if baking is too protracted and the skin becomes too crusty. Proper baking, however, destroys few and we can cheefully put up with the loss in gaining the distinctive baked flavor.

ABOUT VEGETABLES FOR A ROAST

To cook vegetables for a roast, it is better on several scores to process them separately. For one thing, if they are placed in the roasting pan, the steam they exude tends to give a moister oven heat than is desirable for meat roasting. For another, typical root vegtables such as potatoes, carrots, onions and turnips themselves profit by separate cooking. Steam them, page 252, first, then drain and dry. Cook them in butter in a ➧ heavy, covered pan until almost tender and finish browning them uncovered.

GLAZED ROOT VEGETABLES

Choose:

2 cups young vegetables—onions, carrots, turnips or potatoes

Simmer, covered, in a very heavy pan with:

1 cup veal or chicken stock
½ teaspoon salt
2 teaspoons sugar
2 tablespoons butter

When the vegetables are tender and the liquid has been almost absorbed ➧ uncover and continue to cook, shaking the pan constantly over brisk heat until they are coated with a golden glaze.

ABOUT DEEP FAT FRIED VEGETABLES

The French have made the fried potato famous in floured strips, page 318, the English in **chips,** page 401. The Italians, by using either a beaten egg coating or a batter, produce their famous vegetable and other mixtures as **fritto misto**—and the Japanese, who learned this trick from Portuguese sailors way back in the 16th century, prepare them today under the term **tempura.**

Since success depends so largely on the ➧ quality of the fat and avoiding its excess absorption, please read About Deep Fat Frying, page 75.

➧ Be sure to have the vegetables dry before applying the coating. It is also best to let the coating dry for about 10 minutes before immersing the food in fat brought to between 350° and 375°. Cook until the vegetables are golden.

Vegetables suitable for this type of cooking are long green beans; ⅓ inch thick eggplant slices—barely nicked with tiny knife marks at ½ inch intervals, all around the bands of skin; mushrooms and tiny green peppers—whole or cut in half vertically; cucumber, squash, zucchini or sweet potato rounds, cut lotus roots or bamboo shoots, small bundles of julienned onions, asparagus tips, finely shredded cabbage, cauliflower or broccoli florets, artichoke hearts or stems.

After preparing the vegetables, be sure to sprinkle any which may discolor with lemon juice.

ARTICHOKES

Artichokes of the globe type, sketched, differ in shape, taste and method of cooking from Jerusalem artichokes, page 260. If the leaves are spreading or discolored, the artichokes are not tender. They are served whole or cored and eaten with the fingers after cooking. Serve one to each diner. The leaves are dipped, one at a time, in a sauce and the lower end is simply pulled through the teeth to extract the tender edible portion. The leaf is then discarded. Continue to eat them until a light-colored cone of young leaves appears. Pull this up with one movement. Then lift the fuzzy center out and discard it. Eat the remaining heart with a fork, dipping each piece in sauce first.

To prepare, hold by the stem end and dash up and down, quickly, in a deep bowl of water:

Artichokes

Cut off the stems. Pull off the tough bottom row of leaves and cut off ¼ of the tops. For this, you may use scissors. To avoid discoloration, dip the cut parts in:

Lemon juice

➧ Steam, page 252, or place the artichokes upright on a trivet, with 1 to 2 inches of boiling water beneath. Add:

1 sliced onion or 1 mashed clove garlic
2 celery ribs with leaves
1½ tablespoons lemon juice, wine or vinegar
(2 tablespoons salad oil)
(A bay leaf)

Cook them covered for 45 minutes or until tender. Drain and serve them hot with:

Melted butter, Mayonnaise, page 345, Hollandaise Sauce, page 368, Béchamel Sauce, page 359, or Vinaigrette Sauce, page 341

Cooked artichokes may be served chilled. ⊗ Pressure cook large artichokes at 15 lbs. about 15 minutes, small ones 8 minutes at 15 lbs.

CORED ARTICHOKES

Clean and trim, as described previously

Artichokes

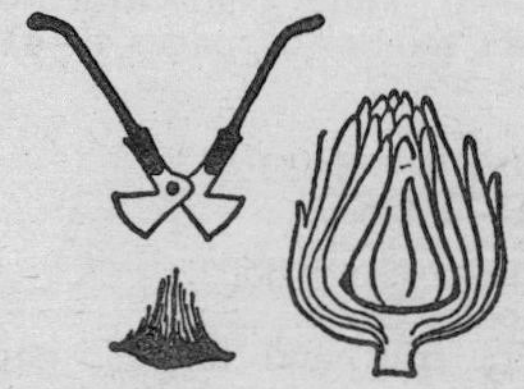

Turn them upside down. Press hard to force the leaves apart. Reverse and insert a grapefruit corer. Press the handles down to cut out the choke. Remove it. Tie artichokes into shape with string. ➧ Steam them, page 252, or cook as in previous recipe. Drain them well, untie and serve either warm or cold, the centers filled with:

Hollandaise Sauce, page 368

If they are too hot when filled, the Hollandaise may separate. Or serve cold with:

Marinated shrimp and mayonnaise

ARTICHOKE HEARTS

Remove all leaves and chokes from:

Artichokes

Steam them, page 252, or drop the hearts into 1 inch of:

Boiling water

to which you may add:

Lemon juice

Simmer them, covered, for 20 minutes or until tender. Serve them with:

Brown Butter, page 383, or Hollandaise Sauce, page 368

Cooked or canned artichoke hearts, well drained, may be sautéed until hot in:

Butter or drippings

to which you may add:

Garlic, shallots or onions

Season them with:

Salt and paprika
Lemon juice

Serve hot or cold. For a good way to stuff cold artichoke hearts, see Salads, pages 40–41.

STUFFED BAKED ARTICHOKES

Preheat oven to 350°.

I. Roman Style

Clean, trim and blanch, page 88:

Artichokes

Drain them well. Make a dressing of:

Bread crumbs
Minced garlic or onion
Chopped celery
Chopped anchovies or anchovy paste
Grated Parmesan cheese
Chopped parsley
Salt and paprika

Push the dressing down between the leaves. The choke may be removed, as described previously, if desired, and the center filled with the dressing. Pour over the artichokes a little:

Olive oil

Place them in a baking dish and cover the bottom of the dish with ½ inch of:

Boiling water or stock

Bake them, covered, until they are done, about 1 hour.

II. Or fill the artichokes with either:

Ham or sausage stuffing, or Stuffed Mushrooms, page 297, or Creamed Spinach, page 326, and grated cheese

JERUSALEM ARTICHOKES

This tall, yellow blooming composite of our roadsides has been miraculously hybridized and should be better known. Its nubbly roots proliferate to furnish us that extra vegetable we always wish we could find. They do need watching while being cooked.

Wash:

1½ lbs. Jerusalem artichokes

➧ Steam them, page 252, or drop them into:

Boiling water

To prevent discoloration, add:

1 teaspoon mild vinegar or white wine

Cook them ➧ covered, until they are tender only. If permitted to cook beyond this point, they will again become tough. Test them with a toothpick after 15 minutes. Drain them. Remove the peel. Melt:

2 to 3 tablespoons butter

Add:

2 drops hot pepper sauce
2 tablespoons chopped parsley

Pour these ingredients over the artichokes or cream them, page 255. Or, cut into halves and ⊗ pressure cook at 15 lbs. for 10 minutes.

ASPARAGUS

The Romans used to say if they wanted to do something in a

hurry, "Do it in less time than it takes to cook asparagus."

I. 4 to 6 Servings

Wash:

2 lbs. asparagus

Cut off or snap off the lower part of the stalks. Keep the trimmings for soup. It is seldom necessary to skin green asparagus. If it is white, skin from below the head, increasing the depth of cut into the stalk as you approach the base to remove any bitter flavor in the skin. Tie the asparagus in serving bunches with white string. Place them upright in a deep stewpan or in the bottom part of a double boiler, the lower ends in:

½ cup boiling water

Cook the asparagus ▸ closely covered 12 minutes or until tender.

An inverted double boiler top may be used. The steam will cook the tips. Drain the asparagus well. Reserve the liquor. Add:

½ teaspoon salt

Melt:

⅓ cup butter

Sauté in it, for 1 minute:

1 cup bread crumbs

Pour this mixture over the tips of the asparagus or serve them with:

1 cup Cream Sauce I, page 359, made with half cream and half asparagus liquor, Egg Sauce, page 360, or Hollandaise Sauce, page 368

II. Sometimes, if asparagus must be held, both the color and texture are improved if this recipe is used—although we do not guarantee nutritive value.

Arrange in a flat pan:

2 lbs. cleaned asparagus

Place them not more than 3 or 4 deep. Add:

½ teaspoon salt

Cover with cold water. Prepare and cover with a poaching paper, page 83. Bring them to a boil, reduce the heat at once and ▸ simmer about 15 minutes. Keep lukewarm until ready to serve.

Drain when ready to serve.

BAMBOO SHOOTS

These slightly acid shoots, which complement mushrooms and meat, must be young and tender and from an edible bamboo plant.

If fresh, boil:

Bamboo shoots

in:

Water

about 10 to 15 minutes. Discard the water and then the shoots are ready to use. If using canned shoots, scrape off the calcium deposits. If you want to use only part of a can, store the remainder by first draining. Re-cover with cold water and refrigerate ▸ covered, for about 1 week.

ABOUT FRESH BEANS

Green or snap beans, formerly called string because their strings had to be removed, have in many instances been hybridized so that now they snap clean and need only have the ends snipped off. Kentucky wonders and wax beans, however, still need both snipping and stringing. To prepare broad beans, see Lima Beans, page 268. To prepare immature fava beans or marrow-fat beans, see Podded Peas, page 307. For mature green favas, see Lima Beans. For dried favas, see Dried Legumes, page 264. Haricots verts, with their okra-like flavored overtones, are otherwise much like green beans. ➧ To avoid toughening any beans, salt when cooking is half finished.

GREEN OR SNAP BEANS [4]

This vegetable is available fresh the year around and lends itself to endless variations.
Wash:

1 lb. green beans

Snip off the ends. You may then sliver them, French them on the diagonal or leave them whole. If the latter, tie them in individual bunches before cooking. When cooked and drained, arrange them on a platter and cover with one of the garnishes or sauces suggested below. To cook green beans ➧ steam, page 252, or drop them into:

Boiling water or part water and part stock

Reduce the heat at once. Place on top of the beans:

(1 whole peeled onion)

Cook partially covered, page 251, if you wish to preserve the color; or covered, if you wish to preserve more nutrients. Simmer until barely tender, no longer—about 20 minutes. Before draining, you may remove the onion.

Correct the seasoning

Cover with:

1 tablespoon melted butter

ADDITIONS TO GREEN BEANS

To further flavor beans during the cooking, add:

(1 small cut-up onion)
(1- to 2-inch cube of salt pork)

To garnish or sauce, use for 1 lb. of beans:

1 tablespoon butter or browned butter, or ¼ cup buttered crumbs, or 2 tablespoons brown onion butter, or 2 tablespoons crumbled bacon and drippings

Add to the above fats:

(1 teaspoon celery or dill seed) or (1 teaspoon fresh summer savory or basil)

Or garnish with:

Anchovy Butter or Oil, page 384, or Almond Garnish, page 390

Or add:

½ cup sautéed mushrooms
⅓ to ½ cup cultured sour cream
2 tablespoons chopped parsley

Or add:

2 tablespoons wine vinegar
¼ teaspoon mustard
1 tablespoon Worcestershire sauce
A drop of hot pepper sauce

Or add:

2 tablespoons butter
¼ cup toasted slivered almonds
¼ cup sliced water chestnuts
¼ cup sliced cooked mushrooms

If the beans are left long, cover with:

A Cream Sauce Variation, page 359, or 1 can Cream of Chicken or Mushroom Soup and herbs, or Quick Tomato Sauce, page 376 or Egg Sauce I, page 360

CASSEROLE GREEN BEANS [6]

I.

Preheat oven to 350°.
What becomes of the onions and peppers? They frequently disappear, leaving marvelously seasoned beans. An easy dish for

the hostess who cooks her own dinner.

Trim:

1 lb. green beans

Skin and chop:

4 medium-size white onions

Remove the seeds and membrane from:

2 medium-size green peppers

Chop the peppers. Butter a baking dish. Place in it alternate layers of the vegetables, beginning and ending with a layer of beans. Sprinkle each layer with:

Salt and paprika

Dot each layer with:

Butter

Bake the vegetables ➧ covered, for about 1¼ hours or until the beans are tender. Before serving, garnish with:

Au Gratin II, page 389

II. Preheat oven to 350°.

Prepare for cooking:

1 lb. green beans

Place them in a greased casserole. Cover with:

1 can cream of tomato soup
3 tablespoons prepared horseradish
2 teaspoons Worcestershire sauce
¼ teaspoon salt
¼ teaspoon paprika

Bake ➧ covered, for about 1 hour or until tender. Remove the lid and garnish with:

Au Gratin III, page 389

Serve when the cheese is melted.

GREEN BEANS, POTATOES AND SMOKED MEAT [4]

Cook until nearly tender in water to cover:

A piece of smoked meat: ham, picnic, Canadian bacon, etc.

If using already cooked or left-over ham or bone, just bring to a boil before adding:

1 lb. green beans
4 halved, pared, medium potatoes
(1 onion)

Simmer, covered, about 20 to 25 minutes.

Correct the seasoning.

Serve from a large platter, garnished with:

Lemon wedges

SWEET-SOUR BEANS [4]

Trim and shred lengthwise:

1 lb. green beans

➧Steam them, page 252, or drop them into:

Boiling water

to barely cover. Cook them, covered, about 20 minutes. Now, render the fat slowly from:

3 pieces lean bacon

Cook with it:

2 tablespoons chopped onions

When the bacon is crisp, remove it and swirl in the pan:

1 tablespoon white wine vinegar
1 tablespoon sugar
½ teaspoon salt

Drain the liquid from the beans and add it to the skillet mixture. Then combine with the beans and cut-up bacon and serve. A good variation to this dish is the addition of:

Bean sprouts

PURÉED GREEN BEANS, PEAS OR LIMAS

In winter, these are a fresh note if used as a base for soup, as a lining in serving sautéed mushrooms or as a puréed vegetable, garnished with parsley.

Purée:

2 cups cooked beans or peas

Use a ⅄ blender or a food mill.

Add:

2 tablespoons butter
Correct the seasoning

and serve as soon as possible after puréeing. If the purée must be held over, cover it while hot with whipping cream and, in reheating in a double boiler ➧ over hot water, beat in the cream before serving.

COOKED BEAN SPROUTS [4]

As with other vegetables, cooked sprouted beans have less vitamin C than if eaten raw just after sprouting.

Bring to a boil:

¾ cup water

Add:

4 cups sprouted beans, Mung or edible soybeans or lentils

➧ Simmer, covered, until almost soft, just long enough to remove the raw bean flavor. Season with:

Salt
(Soy sauce)

ABOUT DRIED LEGUMES

Dried peas and beans, being rather on the dull side, much like dull people respond readily to the right contacts. Do not scorn them, for they have valuable, if incomplete, proteins, see page 2. Combine them with tomatoes, onions, chili and cheese. They are also much more temperamental than one would think. Their cooking time depends on the locality in which they were grown and on their age—usually two unknowns for the cook; plus the type of water used in cooking them, see About Water (II, 147). Wash, unless the package states otherwise. Do not use soda, see About Soda (II, 164). Soak in 3 to 4 times as much water as beans. Remove any beans that float. If the beans are not preprocessed, usually they are soaked overnight. Bring the beans to a slow boil in the water in which they were soaked, unless it is bitter, as happens sometimes with soybeans. Reduce the heat and ➧ simmer them. All beans should be cooked until tender. One test, provided you discard the beans you have tested, is to blow on a few of them in a spoon. If the skins burst, they are sufficiently cooked.

If you have forgotten to soak, a quick method to tenderize them for cooking is to cover with cold water. Bring up to a boil and simmer for 2 minutes. Remove from heat and let stand, tightly covered, for 1 hour. Or, blanching the beans for 2 minutes is almost equivalent to 8 hours of soaking.

You may use pre-processed beans which require no soaking. But remember that some nutrients have been lost in the preparation. Lentils and split peas are better for soaking, but do not require it.

Remember that 1 cup of beans, peas or lentils will expand to 2 to 2½ cups after cooking.

There are over 25 types of beans and peas available in our stores. They include red, kidney, black-eyed peas or beans, edible soys, pinto, strawberry, cow peas or Mexican frijoles, chick peas or Garbanzos or flageolets—which is the French haricot, dried and shelled.

White beans, which the white man learned of from the Indians and then took sailing, became our navy beans. They are usually the toughest beans and take up to 3 hours simmering. Dried Limas, after soaking for 8 hours, may cook almost as rapidly as the fresh ones—in about ½ hour. Lentils take about 1½ hours to cook.

Other people know a trick or two with navy beans. In Europe, where chestnuts are highly prized, bean purée often replaces chestnut purée in strongly seasoned chestnut dishes. ✪ Dried legumes can be pressure cooked, but can be dangerous, see page 81; therefore, long, slow cooking is preferable. Never fill the pressure cooker more than ¾ full of liquid. Pressure cook at 15 lbs.: black-eyed peas for 10 minutes; Great Northern beans for 20 minutes; kidney beans for 30 minutes; lentils for 20 minutes; Lima beans, small, for 25 minutes—large for 30 minutes; navy beans for 30 minutes; pea beans for 20 minutes and soy beans for 35 minutes. Cool pan normally for all dried vegetables for about 5 minutes, then place under cold water faucet.

PURÉE OF DRIED LEGUMES

Cook until tender:

Dried Lentils, Beans or Peas, page 264

You may add:

A clove of garlic

After draining the lentils, put them through a fine sieve, a purée strainer or ⅄ blender. Allow to every cup of purée:

1 tablespoon butter
A scant ½ teaspoon salt
¼ teaspoon pepper or paprika or a dash of clove

You may brown in the butter:

1 tablespoon flour

Whip the purée over a high heat. Serve in a mound, garnished with:

Sautéed onions
Chopped parsley

⊗ For pressure cooking time, see About Dried Legumes, above.

DRIED BEAN PATTIES [4]

Grind and mash:

2 cups cooked dried beans: soy, Lima, navy

Add to them:

1 chopped onion
¼ cup chopped parsley

Beat and add:

2 egg yolks
2 tablespoons cream or evaporated milk
¼ teaspoon pepper
1 teaspoon salt

Shape these ingredients into balls. Flatten them. Dip them in:

Flour

Chill the patties for 1 hour or more. Sauté them slowly, until brown, in:

Butter, drippings or other fat

Serve them with any:

Barbecue Sauce, page 374

GREEN SOY BEANS

Use the young vegetable type, not field varieties of beans. The fuzzy pods should still be green. Immerse them in boiling water. ▸ Cover the pot. After 5 minutes, drain and cool them. Squeeze the pods to press out the beans. Cook the beans in boiling water until tender, approximately 10 to 15 minutes. Use them as directed in About Lima Beans, etc., page 268.

The cooked beans may also be spread in a greased pan, dotted with butter and roasted in a 350° oven until brown or they may be browned in deep fat, pages 75–76.

Soy milk, see page 487, and cheese can also be made from them.

BEAN DINNER IN ONE DISH [4]

Preheat oven to 350°.

Combine:

1 cup cooked corn
1 cup cooked navy beans
1 cup lightly drained canned tomatoes
¾ teaspoon salt
¼ teaspoon paprika
½ teaspoon brown sugar
1 teaspoon grated onion

Place in a greased baking dish.
Sprinkle the top with:
Browned bread crumbs or grated peanuts
Bake ➧ covered, for about 45 minutes.

BAKED BEANS [4]

Did you know that baked beans are as traditional in Sweden as they are in Boston?
➧ Please read About Dried Legumes, pages 264–265.
If quick-cooking or precooked beans are used, follow the directions on the package. Otherwise, soak:
1½ cups dried beans
Cover them with water. Bring them to a boil, then simmer them slowly for ½ hour or more, until tender.
Preheat oven to 250°.
Drain the beans, reserving the cooking water and add:
¼ cup chopped onion
2 tablespoons or more dark molasses
2 or 3 tablespoons catsup
1 tablespoon dry mustard
1 teaspoon salt
½ cup boiling bean water or beer
(½ teaspoon vinegar)
(1 teaspoon curry powder)
(1 tablespoon Worcestershire sauce)
Place them in a greased baker, decorate them with:
¼ lb. sliced salt pork
and bake them, covered, for 6 to 9 hours. If they become dry, add a little:
Well-seasoned stock or reserved bean water
Uncover the beans for the last hour of cooking.

CANNED BAKED BEANS WITH FRUIT [6]

This is a good brunch dish.
Preheat oven to 250°.
Arrange:
2 cans beans without sauce
in layers in a casserole with:
2 sliced apples
2 sliced oranges or 4 canned apricot halves or pineapple slices
(2 large onions, sliced)
Top with:
½ lb. salt pork
Cover with:
1 cup molasses
Bake about 1 to 3 hours.

BOILED BEANS [5]

Soak, page 264, then drain:
1 lb. dried beans: kidney, navy, marrow-fat or Limas
Place them in a heavy saucepan. Cover them with water. Add:
6 tablespoons butter
⅓ cup chopped onion
3 whole cloves
2 teaspoons salt
¼ teaspoon freshly ground pepper
¼ teaspoon dried thyme
Simmer the beans, covered, from 1 to 1½ hours. Stir them from time to time. Add and cook for about 20 minutes longer:
1 cup dry red wine or stock
When the beans are tender, serve them hot, garnished with:
Chopped chives or parsley
✪ We do not recommend the pressure cooking of dried beans, because of the danger of frothing.

⊟ CAMPFIRE BEANS

Have ready at least 2 to 3 quarts of hot coals. Dig a hole deep enough and wide enough to hold a covered iron kettle, allowing about 4 extra inches to the depth of the hole. Get ready for cooking:
Baked Beans
Put half the coals in the bottom of the hole. Sink the covered kettle. Cover the lid with a large piece of foil to keep out dirt. Put the rest of the coals on the ket-

tle lid. Now, fill in the rest of the hole with dirt and put at least 3 inches of dirt on top of the kettle. Don't dig in to peek for at least 4 hours.

CANNED BAKED BEANS AND BACON OR FRANKFURTERS [6]

Preheat oven to 350°.
To jazz up pepless canned beans, add to:

2½ cups canned beans

approximately:

¼ cup catsup
2 tablespoons molasses
2 tablespoons brown sugar
2 tablespoons bacon drippings
Minced onion, celery and green pepper
Salt if needed
(3 drops hot pepper sauce, a few grains of red pepper or 1 tablespoon mustard)

to make them moist and palatable. Place the beans in a greased, shallow, ovenproof dish. Cover the top with:

Bacon, very thin strips of salt pork or skinned sliced frankfurters

Bake beans ➧ covered, about 30 minutes. ➧ Uncover. Bake 30 minutes more.

CANNED KIDNEY BEANS AND TOMATOES

[4 Large Servings]
Preheat oven to 350°.
Grease a baking dish. Have ready:

2½ cups canned red kidney beans
1 cup canned tomatoes or diluted tomato soup
¼ cup chopped onion
¼ lb. chopped bacon

Cover the bottom of the dish with a layer of beans. Sprinkle it with some of the bacon and onions. Repeat the process. Pour the tomatoes over the whole. Cover the top with:

Bread crumbs or cornflakes

Dot it with:

Butter

or sprinkle it with:

Grated cheese

Bake the dish until the top is browned, for about 30 minutes.

PINTO BEANS AND RICE [4]

A combination often found in South American countries.
Soak:

½ cup pinto beans

in:

3 cups ham broth

Gently boil the beans in the broth until they are almost done. Add:

½ cup chopped cooked ham
½ cup rice

Cover and cook for about 20 to 30 minutes, until the rice is tender.

LENTILS [6]

➧ Please read About Dried Legumes, page 264.

I. Add to:

2 cups lentils
3 sprigs parsley or a celery rib with leaves
¼ cup sliced onions
½ bay leaf
(A piece of fat corned beef, ham skin or bacon rind, tried-out pork fat or smoked sausage)
(2 cloves without heads)
(A slice of garlic)

Cover with:

4 cups water

Cook, covered, about 1½ hours. Add boiling water, if necessary, during the cooking. Drain the lentils and serve with:

Tomato Sauce, page 376

Or serve as a Purée, page 254. If you omit the bacon or pork flavorings above, serve the lentils with:

Roast Pork, page 485

II. Wash but do not soak:

1 cup lentils

Sauté, until golden brown:

1 minced onion

in:

¼ cup olive oil

Add the lentils and let them absorb the oil. Pour over them:

3½ cups boiling water

Cover the pan and simmer about 1½ hours.

Correct the seasoning

and serve hot or cold. If used for a salad, serve with French dressing and hard-cooked egg slices.

LENTILS AND PRUNES [4]

Please read About Dried Legumes, pages 264–265. Wash and cook:

1 cup lentils

Cook:

1 cup Stewed Dried Prunes (II, 108)

Pit the prunes and mash them. Add them to the lentils with:

¼ cup dry sherry
1 teaspoon salt
(Lemon juice and spices)

Cook over low heat until thoroughly heated.

ABOUT LIMA, BUTTER OR BROAD BEANS

The following cooked beans, whether canned, frozen, fresh or dry, may be substituted for one another in most recipes: Fordhooks or baby Limas, Sieva types or fava beans and the European broad beans—which really taste more like peas.

If you are hulling fresh Limas, cut a thin strip along inner edge of the pod to which the beans are attached. The beans will pop out easily. One pound in the pods will yield 2 servings.

For that famous combination called Succotash, see page 286.

LIMA BEANS [6]

➧ Steam, page 252, or cover:

1 quart fresh shelled Lima beans

with:

1 inch boiling water

Add:

1 tablespoon butter

Simmer the beans for 15 minutes. Add:

1 teaspoon salt

Simmer the beans, covered, until tender, for about 20 minutes more. Add:

1 tablespoon butter or olive oil
1½ tablespoons lemon juice
1 tablespoon chopped parsley, chives or dill

Or dress them with:

Warm cultured sour cream and freshly ground white pepper

Or serve them with:

Sautéed onions, creamed mushrooms or a spirnkling of crisp bacon

⊗ Pressure cook Lima beans at 15 lbs. for about 2 minutes.

LIMA BEANS WITH PIQUANT SAUCE [4]

In order to provide a canned Lima bean with glamor, you must do a fan dance with it!

Drain:

1½ cups canned or cooked Lima beans

Reserve the liquor. If necessary,

add to it, to make 1½ cups of liquid:

Cream

Melt:

3 tablespoons butter or drippings

Sauté in it until golden brown:

¼ cup chopped onion
(¼ cup chopped celery)

Stir in, until it bubbles:

2½ tablespoons flour

Stir in the liquid slowly. Reduce the heat and stir in until melted:

¼ cup or more minced cheese

Season the sauce with:

½ teaspoon salt
⅛ teaspoon paprika
A few grains red pepper
¼ teaspoon mustard
2 teaspoons Worcestershire sauce
A pinch of 3 herbs—marjoram, thyme, savory, etc.

Add the beans and heat them. Serve them garnished with:

Chopped parsley

FRENCH LIMA BEANS [4]

Place in a heavy saucepan:

1 quart fresh Lima beans
1 small clove garlic
2 tablespoons peeled, seeded, finely diced tomatoes

Barely cover with:

1 inch water or half water and half olive oil

Cover and simmer about 15 minutes. Remove garlic. Add:

2 tablespoons butter
¼ teaspoon salt
1 tablespoon chopped parsley

Continue cooking, covered, until beans are tender.

LIMA BEAN CASSEROLE [4]

This is a fine main dish.
Preheat oven to 375°.
To:

1 cup cooked or canned Lima beans

add:

6 sliced frankfurters or sausages
1 chopped and seeded green pepper
2 chopped tomatoes

You may wish to purée the beans, page 254. Place these ingredients in a baking dish and cover the top with:

Au Gratin II, page 389

Bake the beans for about 15 minutes. This dish, puréed, makes a fine stuffing for peppers or onions.

LIMA BEANS WITH CHEESE [4]

Preheat oven to 350°.
Prepare:

2½ cups cooked Lima beans

Stir into them:

½ cup chicken stock

Or melt:

2 tablespoons butter

Add and sauté for 3 minutes:

¼ cup minced onion

Stir into the stock or butter, over low heat, until melted:

½ lb. grated cheese

Add the beans and:

½ teaspoon salt
¼ teaspoon pepper
1 teaspoon dried basil or thyme
A few grains cayenne
(1 cup chopped nut meats)

Bake the beans for about ½ hour. Serve them with:

Tomato Sauce, page 376

CHILI LIMA BEANS [6]

Preheat oven to 350°.
Drain:

2 cups cooked Lima beans

Add:

¼ lb. salt pork, cut in strips
1 large minced onion
1 tablespoon molasses
2 cups cooked tomatoes
1 tablespoon brown sugar

¼ teaspoon chili powder or pepper
1 teaspoon salt

Bake these ingredients in a greased casserole for about 1 hour.

LIMA BEANS AND MUSHROOMS [6]

Serve this with crisp bacon and grapefruit salad.
Have ready:

2 cups fresh, cooked or canned Lima beans

Drain them. Sauté:

½ lb. mushrooms

Drain them, saving the liquor if there is any. Add to the liquor and melt:

1 tablespoon butter

Stir in:

2 tablespoons flour

Cook and stir these ingredients until they are well blended. Stir in slowly:

½ cup Chicken Stock (II, 142), or stock and bean liquor
½ cup top milk
Correct the seasoning.

Add the beans and mushrooms. Heat them. Add before serving:

(1 tablespoon sherry)

The dish may be served with:

Au Gratin II, page 389

Place it under a broiler until the crumbs are brown.

BEETS [8]

Cut the tops from:

2 lbs. beets

leaving 1 inch of stem. Wash the beeets. ➧ Steam them, page 252, or half cover them with:

Boiling water

Cover pot and cook until tender. Allow ½ to 1 hour for young beets, 1 to 2 hours for old beets. Add boiling water as needed. When the beets are done, cool them slightly and slip off the skins. Cut them into quarters, chop or put them through a ricer.

Correct the seasoning

Then either pour over them:

Melted butter
Chopped parsley

or serve the beets in:

Cream Sauce II, page 359

seasoned with:

Mustard, curry powder, horseradish or ¼ cup sautéed onions

or prepare:

Cream Sauce II, page 359

using in place of the milk, half orange juice and half water. Add:

3 tablespoons brown sugar
2 teaspoons grated orange rind

⊗ Pressure cook small beets 12 minutes, large beets 18 minutes at 15 lbs.

CASSEROLED BEETS [8]

Preheat oven to 400°.
Pare, then slice or chop fine:

16 medium-sized beets

Grease a 7-inch baking dish. Place the beets in it in layers. Season them with:

¼ cup sugar
¾ teaspoon salt
¼ teaspoon paprika

Dot them with:

3 tablespoons butter

Add:

1 tablespoon lemon juice or a sliver of fresh ginger
⅓ cup water
(Grated or sliced onions)

Cover the dish closely and bake the beets for 30 minutes or until they are tender. Stir them twice.

SWEET-SOUR OR HARVARD BEETS [6]

For a cold version of sweet-sour, see Pickled Beet Salad, page 42.
Slice or dice:

3 cups freshly cooked or canned beets

Stir in a double boiler until smooth:

½ cup sugar
1 tablespoon cornstarch
½ teaspoon salt
2 whole cloves
½ cup mild cider vinegar or dry white wine

Cook and stir these ingredients until they are clear. Add the beets and place them over hot water for about 30 minutes. Just before serving, heat, but do not boil, the beets and add:

2 tablespoons butter
(1 tablespoon orange marmalade)

BOILED BEETS IN SOUR CREAM [4]

Combine in a double boiler:

3 cups cooked or canned sliced beets
½ cup cultured sour cream
1 tablespoon prepared horseradish
1 tablespoon chopped chives
Salt, as needed
(1 teaspoon grated onion)

Heat these ingredients ➧ over hot water.

SWEET-SOUR APPLE BEETS [4]

Preheat oven to 325°.
Grease a casserole. Mix together and put into it:

2 cups chopped cooked beets
2 cups chopped tart apples
¼ to ½ cup thinly sliced onions
1½ teaspoons salt
A generous grating of nutmeg

If the apples are very tart, add:

(1 tablespoon sugar)

If they are bland:

(2 tablespoons lemon juice)

Dot with:

2 to 3 tablespoons butter

Cover and bake for about 1 hour.

BAKED BEETS

I. Beets may be baked like potatoes—in their jackets.
Preheat oven to 325°.
Wash:

Beets

Trim the tops, leaving 1 inch of stem. Place them on a pan and bake them until they are tender. Allow at least ½ hour for young beets and 1 hour for old beets. Pull off the skins. Season the beets with:

Salt and paprika

Serve them with:

Melted butter

II. Have ready a preheated 325° oven or ⊟ hot coals in the grill.
Pare and slice:

Beets
Correct the seasoning

and add:

Butter

to each serving, before wrapping in aluminum foil. Bake until tender.

YOUNG BEETS AND LEAVES [4]

Scrub well and dice, unpared, into ¼-inch cubes:

6 or 8 beet roots

Drop them into:

¾ cup hot milk

Stir until you are sure that all surfaces have been coated with the milk. Cook, covered, over slow heat, 8 to 12 minutes, depending on age of beets. Cut into ½-inch shreds:

Beet leaves

Add them to the diced beets. Re-cover the pan and continue to simmer 6 to 8 minutes longer. Season with:

Salt and paprika
Freshly ground nutmeg or cloves

BEET GREENS [4]

Beet greens may be prepared like Spinach, page 325. Put the

beets in a ring, serve the greens in the center, dressed with melted butter, and garnish with horseradish sauce. Or, heat in a frying pan:

2 tablespoons butter or cooking oil

Add and simmer:

2 cups cooked, chopped beet greens
1 teaspoon grated onion
¼ teaspoon salt
½ tablespoon prepared mustard
1 tablespoon horseradish

Remove from the heat and add:

½ cup cultured sour cream

⊗ Pressure cook at 15 lbs. for about 3 minutes.

BREADFRUIT

If ever your fate is that of Robinson Crusoe, remember that you can eat raw any breadfruit that has seeds. The seeds are treated like Chestnuts, page 283. All seedless varieties must be cooked.

The breadfruit is one of the most beautiful of tropical trees, with a highly romantic history. The fruit is 6 to 8 inches in diameter and greenish brown or yellow when ripe. The slightly fibrous meat is light yellow and sweet. You may remove the center core with its seed, if it has one, before or after cooking. Season and serve it as you would sweet potato.

I. To boil, choose mature, firm fruit, with rind still green in color. Core and dice:

4 cups peeled breadfruit

Drop into:

3 cups boiling water

and simmer, covered, about 1 hour, until tender. Drain, season and serve.

II. Preheat oven to 375°.
To bake, place in a baking pan:

1 unpeeled breadfruit

Have enough water in the pan to keep it from burning. Bake until tender, about 1 hour, then the stem and core will pull out easily. Cut in half. Season with:

Salt and pepper or sugar and butter

III. To steam, remove skin, stem and core:

1 breadfruit

Cut into halves or quarters and place the pieces in a pan to steam, covered, page 252, for 2 hours. Season with:

Butter
Salt and pepper

You may steam ¾-inch-thick breadfruit slices, roll in flour and fry in deep fat until a golden brown color.

BREADFRUIT SEEDS

These are so close to chestnuts in flavor and texture that they may be substituted in any chestnut recipe.
Wash well:

1 lb. breadfruit seeds

Drop them into:

1 quart boiling water
3 tablespoons salt

Cook covered for about 45 minutes. Drain and serve hot.

BROCCOLI [4]

Choose heads that are all green. If yellow appears, the bloom is coming up and the broccoli is apt to be tough. Soak for 10 minutes in cold water:

2 lbs. broccoli

Drain it well. Remove the large leaves and the tough part of the stalks. Cut deep gashes in the bottom of the stalks. If the broccoli is mature, cook it like cabbage, page 274. If it is young ▸ steam it, page 252, or place it upright so only the stems are in water and the heads steam, see Asparagus, page 260. Or, to retain excellent color, use a poaching paper, page 83. Add:

1 inch boiling water

Cook it ◆ closely covered, until it is barely tender, 10 to 12 minutes. Drain and sprinkle with:

½ teaspoon salt

Serve it with:

Buttered crumbs, melted butter or lemon juice

to which add:

(¼ cup chopped salted almonds)

or try serving it:

Au Gratin II, page 389

or with one of the following sauces:

Hot Vinaigrette Sauce, page 341
Hollandaise Sauce, page 368
Cheese Sauce, page 364
Onion Sauce, page 363
Sour Cream Dressing, page 351
Allemande Sauce, page 362

⊗ Pressure cook broccoli at 15 lbs. for about 2 minutes.

QUICK CREAMED BROCCOLI [4]

Preheat broiler to 550°.
Prepare:

2 cups hot, cooked broccoli

Drain. Either cover it with:

Hot canned cream soup sauce

or dice the broccoli and fold it gently into the sauce. Place it in a buttered casserole and sprinkle with:

Crushed cornflakes
(Grated Romano cheese)

Run it under the broiler until golden.

DEEP FRIED BROCCOLI

Preheat deep fryer to 375°.
Prepare:

Cooked broccoli

Drain it before it is tender. Cut it into quarters. Dip in:

Batter for Vegetables (II, 126)

Fry the broccoli in deep fat, page 75, until golden brown.

BRAISED BROCCOLI [6]

Preheat oven to 350°.
Cut off the tough stems and slice:

2 lbs. broccoli

Wash and drain it. Prepare and place in a baking dish:

¼ cup chopped celery or carrots
¼ cup chopped onions

Add the broccoli, cover it with:

Well-seasoned Chicken Stock (II, 142)

Bake the vegetables, covered, until they are tender—about 1 hour. Serve:

Au Gratin I or III, page 389

⊗ Pressure cook broccoli at 15 lbs. for about 2 minutes.

BRUSSELS SPROUTS [6]

If wilted, pull the outer leaves from:

1 lb. Brussels sprouts

Cut off the stems. Soak the sprouts for 10 minutes in cold water to which a little salt has been added. Drain them. Cut crosswise gashes into the stem ends. ◆ Steam, page 252, or drop them into a quantity of rapidly boiling:

Water

◆ Reduce heat and simmer, uncovered, until they are barely tender, about 10 minutes. Do not overcook. Drain and serve with:

1 tablespoon melted butter
(Grated Parmesan cheese and chopped parsley or 1 tablespoon lemon juice or a grating of nutmeg)

or sauté in the butter:

1 tablespoon grated onion, or 2 tablespoons bread crumbs and ¼ teaspoon mustard

or serve with:

Canned Cream Soup

Sauce, page 375
into which you may put at the last moment:
(½ cup finely chopped fresh celery)
or, best of all, with lots of:
Hollandaise Sauce, page 369
⊗ Pressure cook Brussels sprouts at 15 lbs. for about 3 minutes.

BAKED BRUSSELS SPROUTS AND CHESTNUTS [6]

Preheat oven to 350°.
Have ready:
2 cups cooked Brussels sprouts
½ lb. cooked chestnuts
Butter a baking dish. Fill it with alternate layers of sprouts and chestnuts. Dot the layers with:
Butter
Correct the seasoning
Moisten them lightly with:
Stock
Cover with:
Au Gratin II, page 389
Bake them, uncovered, for about 20 to 30 minutes.

ABOUT CABBAGE

Cabbage types are as different as the uses of the word. In France, "mon petit chou" is a term of endearment—but call anyone a cabbage in English and see what happens!

Savoys, which are a loose-leaved cabbage, endear themselves to us for their elegance of texture. They are usually available only in the fall. As a rule, whether cabbage is green or red, choose a head that is firm. Cabbage lends itself to stuffing as do the leaves, see Dolmas, page 522.

All cabbage types, if fresh, are a high and inexpensive source for vitamin C. To preserve the vitamins, keep cabbage wrapped before cooking. And use the cooked cabbage water in sauces and soups. The old way of cooking cabbage is to cut it in sections and boil it for hours. The new way is to shred it finely or quarter it and barely cook it—allowing only 7 minutes if shredded, 15 if quartered. ▸ To shred cabbage, cut the head in half and place flat side down on a board. Hold the cabbage with the left hand and slice into long shreds with a sharp knife. The longer growing periods required for winter and Savoy cabbages demand in turn more time to break down their coarser cellulose. Use a longer cooking period, about 20 minutes. ⊗ Pressure cook 2- to 3-inch wedges of cabbage at 15 lbs. pressure for 3 to 5 minutes.

I. Remove the outer leaves from:
½ head cabbage
Drop it into a quantity of rapidly boiling:
Water
▸ Reduce the heat to a simmer. Cook it ▸ uncovered, until it is tender but still crisp. Drain it. Add:
½ teaspoon salt
Place it in a serving dish and pour over it:
Melted butter—1 tablespoon to 1 cup cabbage
Add to the butter:
(Bread crumbs or caraway, chilis, or poppy seeds or a few drops lemon juice and a tablespoon chopped parsley)
or place the cooked cabbage in a baking dish and cover with:
A Creole Sauce, page 380, or Au Gratin III, page 389
Heat through in a 350° oven.

II. All rules have exceptions, so try out this cabbage dish which calls for little water. Cut into wedges:

A head of cabbage

Trim off part of the core. Drop the wedges into:

½ inch boiling water

Cover and cook the cabbage for about 10 minutes. Drain it well. Dress it with:

1 cup Cream Sauce I, page 359

to which has been added:

½ teaspoon freshly grated nutmeg or 2 teaspoons prepared mustard or ½ cup grated cheese

or use:

1 cup Horseradish Cream Sauce, page 362, or 1 cup creamed canned condensed soup, or Allemande Sauce, page 362

No matter which sauce you use, combine it with the cabbage and serve at once.

III. [6]

This method makes young cabbage very delicate and is a great help in disguising the age of a mature cabbage, but you may be losing some nutrients. Cut into very fine shreds:

3 cups cabbage

Drop it gradually into:

¾ cup boiling milk

Boil it for 2 minutes. Drain and discard the milk. Drop the cabbage into hot:

Cream Sauce I, page 359

Simmer for 3 minutes longer and serve at once with:

Broiled sausages

CABBAGE, POTATOES AND HAM [4]

Cook until nearly tender, in water to cover:

A piece of smoked ham: Cali, picnic, butt, shank or cottage ham or roll

If using already cooked or left-over ham or bone, just bring to a boil before adding:

1 large quartered cabbage
4 halved and pared medium size potatoes

Simmer, covered, about 20 to 25 minutes.

Correct the seasoning

Serve from a large platter, garnished with:

Lemon wedges

BAKED CABBAGE [4]

Preheat oven to 325°.
Put in a buttered baking dish:

3 cups shredded cabbage

Pour over it a mixture of:

¾ cup cream
1 tablespoon sugar
½ teaspoon salt
½ teaspoon paprika
(½ cup chopped nuts)

Sprinkle the top with:

½ cup bread crumbs

Bake for about 45 minutes. Just before serving, sprinkle the top with:

⅓ cup grated cheese

and run under the broiler until melted.

SAUTÉED CABBAGE [4]

Preheat oven to 375°.
Shred:

A small head cabbage

Sauté it lightly in:

Butter or bacon drippings

Add to the hot fat:

½ teaspoon salt
¼ teaspoon paprika
Minced garlic or onion

Place the cabbage in a greased baking dish. Pour over it:

1 cup cultured sour or sweet cream

Bake it for about 20 minutes.

FRENCH FRIED CABBAGE

Preheat deep fryer to 375°.
Crisp in cold water:

Finely shredded cabbage

Drain and dry it. Dip it in:

Milk

then in:

Flour

Fry a small amount at a time in deep fat, see page 258. Drain it on absorbent paper.

Correct the seasoning

CABBAGE OR LETTUCE AND RICE DISH [6]

This is a good dish to make in the trail of a salad luncheon. You may use the outer leaves of lettuce. Melt:

2 tablespoons bacon drippings
2 tablespoons butter or 3 tablespoons other fat

Stir in, cover and cook gently for about 10 minutes:

3 cups finely shredded cabbage or lettuce
½ cup finely chopped onion
1 seeded, chopped green pepper

Stir these ingredients frequently. Stir in and cook until well heated:

1 cup cooked rice
2 cups tomato pulp or thick stewed tomatoes
Salt and pepper

This is good served with:

Crisp bacon or cold ham

CABBAGE OR SAVORY STRUDEL [12 to 14]

Prepare:

Strudel Dough (II, 307)

Steam blanch, page 89, for 5 minutes:

4 lbs. shredded cabbage

Press out any excess moisture and place on the dough with:

1½ cups heavy cultured sour cream
(teaspoon caraway seed)
(4 chopped hard-cooked eggs)

To roll and bake the strudel, see (II, 307).

SCALLOPED CABBAGE [8]

Rather luxurious treatment for this good bourgeois vegetable. Preheat oven to 375°.

Chop, then cook:

1 medium-sized head cabbage

Drain it well. Prepare:

1½ cups Cream Sauce I (II, 359)

Prepare:

2 tablespoons chopped seeded green peppers
2 tablespoons chopped pimientos

Sauté and mince:

(6 slices bacon)

Melt:

2 tablespoons bacon fat or butter

Toss lightly in this:

½ cup bread crumbs

Place layers of drained cabbage in a greased baking dish. Sprinkle them with the minced bacon and peppers and:

1 cup or less grated cheese

Cover them with the cream sauce. Top the dish with the sautéed bread crumbs. Bake the cabbage for about 10 minutes.

CABBAGE WITH TOMATO SAUCE [6]

A practical, all-purpose vegetable dish. Good made with Brussels sprouts as well. Prepare by any recipe for Cooked Cabbage, page 274:

A small, firm head cabbage

While the cabbage boils, prepare this sauce. Dice and sauté until crisp:

4 slices bacon

Remove and reserve the bacon. Sauté in the bacon fat, until tender:

1 small minced onion

Add:

1 cup tomato purée
Salt and pepper
(2 teaspoons brown sugar)

When the sauce is boiling, add the well-drained cabbage and the bits of bacon. Serve very hot, garnished with:

2 tablespoons minced parsley

CABBAGE, TOMATO AND CHEESE DISH [6]

Preheat oven to 325°.
Cook for 5 minutes, page 274:

3 cups finely shredded cabbage

Drain it well. Cook:

1½ cups Stewed Tomatoes, page 332
¾ teaspoon salt
¼ teaspoon paprika
(2 teaspoons brown sugar)

Butter a baking dish. Place in it alternate layers of tomatoes and cabbage, beginning with tomatoes. Sprinkle the layers with:

Au Gratin III, page 389

Bake the dish for about ½ hour or until the crumbs are brown.

CABBAGE ROLLS STUFFED WITH RICE AND CHEESE [6]

To prepare, see:

Dolmas, page 522

Omit the vegetables if desired. Substitute for the meat:

¾ cup grated American cheese

Season well with:

Cayenne, paprika and salt

CABBAGE STUFFED WITH CORNED BEEF HASH [4]

Trim the outer leaves and the stem from:

A medium-sized head of cabbage

Cook it, uncovered, until it is barely tender in:

2 quarts boiling water

Do not overcook cabbage. It is best when still slightly crisp. Drain it well. Scoop out the inside, leaving a 1½-inch shell. Place the shell in a greased ovenproof dish. Keep it hot. Chop the removed part. Add it to the contents of:

1 can minced corned beef hash: 16 oz.
¼ cup or more sautéed onions
A pinch of thyme

Moisten it with:

(Cream, evaporated milk or bacon drippings)

Heat these ingredients. Fill the shell. Cover the top with:

Buttered cornflakes

The cabbage may be heated in a 425° oven for about 10 minutes. It may be served with:

Dried Onion Soup Sauce, page 375

CABBAGE STUFFED WITH HAM AND CHEESE [6]

Trim the loose outer leaves from:

A firm head cabbage

Cut out enough from the stem end to make a deep well. Prepare a filling by combining:

2 cups cooked ground or chopped ham
1 cup bread crumbs
¾ cup grated American cheese
½ teaspoon dry mustard
Salt
½ teaspoon paprika
A few grains cayenne

Fill the center of the cabbage with this filling. Steam in an improvised steamer made of a colander or frying basket, if necessary, until it is tender—from 1 to 2 hours. Place it over boiling water. Cover it with a bowl or lid or wrap the cabbage in heavy foil and bake it from 1 to 2 hours. Serve it with:

Cheese Sauce, page 364, or Tomato Cheese Sauce, page 376

RED CABBAGE

An old favorite to serve with game—cooked either for a long time as in this recipe or for a shorter time as in the next. Pull the outer leaves from:

A head of red cabbage: about 2 lbs.

Cut it into sections. Remove the hard core, shred the cabbage and soak in cold water. Cook over low heat until some fat is rendered out:

4 slices chopped bacon or use 3 tablespoons melted butter

Sauté with the bacon or butter, until golden:

3 or 4 tablespoons finely chopped onions

Lift the cabbage from the water with the hands, leaving it moist. Place it in a heatproof glass or enameled iron casserole, cover it and let it simmer for 10 minutes. Core and cut into very thin slices:

2 apples
(1/8 teaspoon caraway seeds)

Add them to the cabbage with:

1/4 teaspoon salt, if bacon is used, or 1 teaspoon salt, if unsalted butter is used
1/4 cup vinegar or 1/2 cup red wine or a mixture of 2 tablespoons honey and 2 tablespoons vinegar

Add the sautéed onion and stir these ingredients. Cover the pan and simmer the cabbage very slowly for 1 hour and 20 minutes. Add boiling water during cooking, if necessary. If the water has not been absorbed when the cabbage is done, uncover the pot and cook it gently until it is absorbed.

RED CABBAGE AND CHESTNUTS [6]

In "The House of Exile," the Chinese serve red cabbage in green peppers, see Stuffed Peppers, page 307. This dish is attractive. Have ready:

1 cup blanched chopped chestnuts

Shred until very fine:

1 small head red cabbage

Place it in a bowl. Cover it with:

Boiling water

Add:

1/4 cup dry white wine or vinegar

Permit it to soak for 15 minutes. Drain it well. Heat in a saucepan:

2 1/2 tablespoons bacon drippings or butter

Add the cabbage. Sprinkle it lightly with:

Salt and pepper

Sauté the cabbage until it is limp. Cover and simmer for ten minutes. Sprinkle over the cabbage:

1 tablespoon flour

Meanwhile, in a separate saucepan, combine the chestnuts with:

1 cup water
1 1/2 tablespoons sugar
1/4 cup dry white wine or vinegar
1/3 cup seedless raisins
1 peeled, thinly sliced apple

Simmer these ingredients, covered, until the chestnuts are tender. Add to the cabbage mixture. Cook these ingredients until they are well blended.

Correct the seasoning

and serve them hot.

SAUERKRAUT [6]

The healthful quality of sauerkraut was recognized in 200 B.C. when, history records, it was served to the laborers working on the Great Wall of China. To retain its full flavor, serve it raw or barely heated through. Cooking makes kraut milder. Melt in a skillet:

2 tablespoons butter or bacon drippings

Add and sauté until clear:

1/2 cup sliced onion or shallots

Add and sauté for about 5 minutes:

1 quart fresh or canned sauerkraut

Peel, grate and add:

1 medium-sized potato or tart apple

Cover the kraut with:

Boiling Stock (II, 141), or water

(¼ cup dry wine)

Cook the kraut, uncovered, for 30 minutes, cover it and cook or bake it in a 325° oven for about 30 minutes longer. It may be seasoned with:

1 or 2 tablespoons brown sugar

1 teaspoon caraway or celery seed

Serve with:

Frankfurters, roast pork or spareribs

SAUERKRAUT AND TOMATO CASSEROLE [8]

Lovers of sauerkraut will welcome this old friend in a new guise.

Preheat oven to 350°.

Drain well:

4 cups canned sauerkraut

Put through a strainer:

3½ cups canned tomatoes

Melt:

2 tablespoons bacon or other fat

Add, cook and stir about until golden:

1 small chopped onion

Add the strained tomatoes and:

¼ cup brown sugar

Freshly ground pepper

Add the drained sauerkraut. Place the mixture in a covered casserole and bake for about 1 hour. ➧ Uncover the last 20 minutes of cooking. Garnish the top with:

Crumbled crisp bacon

CARDOONS

A vegetable of the thistle family, like artichoke—but the tender stalks and root are eaten, rather than the flower. Generally used for soups. Wash well. Discard outside stalks, trim the strings as for celery. Leave the heart whole. Cut into 3-inch pieces:

Tender stalks of cardoon

Parblanch, page 88, in:

Court Bouillon Blanc (II, 146)

for 5 to 7 minutes, to keep it from discoloring. Drain and rinse at once in cold water to remove bitterness. Simmer, covered, for about 1½ to 2 hours or until tender in:

Boiling Acidulated Water (II, 148) to cover

Correct the seasoning

and serve with:

Cream, butter or Cream Sauce I, page 359

Slice the heart and arrange it as a garnish.

CARROTS

Carrots are frequently boring—but that may be the cook's fault. For good results, combine them with onions, celery, green peppers, olives, mushrooms, etc. Peel or scrape them; or use unpeeled, cut into slices, or diced. If small, they may be served whole. If large, they may be more attractive if cut Parisienne, page 250. Wash and scrape:

Carrots

➧ Steam, page 252, or place them in a small quantity of:

Boiling water or stock

Cook them, covered, until they are tender, from 20 to 30 minutes. Allow a shorter cooking period for cut-up carrots. Permit them to absorb the water in which they are cooked. If necessary, add a small quantity of boiling water. Celery, onions, etc., may be cooked with peeled carrots or they may be cooked separately and added later. Serve the carrots with:

(Seasoned chopped parsley)

Bercy Butter, page 384, or

Cream Sauce, page 359

or add to 2 cups cooked carrots:

1 or 2 tablespoons butter
1 or 2 tablespoons sugar, honey or orange marmalade
(½ teaspoon ginger, ginger root or cinnamon)

Simmer the carrots in this mixture until well glazed. Or try the glaze in:

Candied Sweet Potatoes, page 323

⊗ Pressure cook carrots whole for 4 minutes—sliced, 2 minutes—at 15 lbs.

CARROTS IN BUNCHES

Steam or cook as in preceding recipe:

Small, shapely carrots in their jackets

Cool them. Skin them. Reheat them by placing them over steam or by sautéing them for about 12 minutes in a little butter. Serve them in 2 bunches—one at each end of a meat platter. Place at the blunt ends, to represent carrot greens:

Sprigs of parsley

Pour over them:

Melted seasoned butter

Season with:

A dash of cloves

MASHED CARROTS OR CARROT RING [4]

Cook as above:

2 bunches young carrots in their jackets

Skin the carrots and use a ⅄ blender or put them through a ricer or mash them with a potato masher. Beat in:

1 tablespoon butter
Salt and pepper
1 tablespoon chopped parsley or chives
(A dash of cloves)

Heap the carrots in a mound or in individual mounds. Garnish them with:

Sprigs of parsley

To make a ring, beat in:

1 to 2 egg yolks

Place in a greased mold and heat over hot water in a 350° oven until set, for about 20 to 30 minutes. Invert the mold. Fill the center of the ring with:

Green Peas, page 305

CARROTS VICHY [4]

Place in a saucepan:

2 cups scraped, sliced carrots
½ cup boiling water
2 tablespoons butter
1 tablespoon sugar
¼ teaspoon salt
(1 teaspoon lemon juice)

Cover the pan closely. Cook the carrots over quick heat until the water evaporates. Permit them to brown in the butter. Serve them sprinkled with:

Chopped chives or parsley

BAKED CARROTS [4]

Preheat oven to 350°.

Melt:

3 tablespoons butter

Sauté in it for about 3 minutes:

¼ cup chopped onion

Add:

2 cups peeled, shredded carrots

Place these ingredients in a baking dish. Sprinkle them with:

¾ teaspoon salt
1 teaspoon sugar

Pour over them:

½ cup water or stock

Cover the dish. Bake the carrots until they are tender.

WATERLESS CARROTS [5]

Peel or scrape:

2 bunches carrots

Slice them in long, thin strips. Place them in a heavy saucepan with:

2 tablespoons butter
½ teaspoon sugar
½ teaspoon salt

1 tablespoon chopped parsley

You may sauté in the butter:

3 tablespoons chopped onion

Cover the pan closely. Simmer the carrots on top of the stove for about 20 minutes or place them in a 350° oven until they are done. Add:

1 tablespoon cream

Cook them about 2 minutes longer.

CARAMELIZED CARROTS

A good way to treat mature carrots.

Steam in their jackets, page 252:

Carrots

Skin them. Cut them into halves or quarters. Dip them in:

Melted butter

Sprinkle them with:

Salt, paprika and brown sugar

Place them in a heavy skillet over low heat until they are well glazed. Baste them from time to time with a little melted butter.

CAULIFLOWER [4]

Cut off the tough end of the stem, remove the leaves and soak in cold salted water, head down for 10 minutes:

1 medium-sized head cauliflower

Drain it. You may break it into florets. Cut deep gashes into the stalks. ➧ Steam, page 252, or place it uncovered, head up, in about 1 inch of:

Boiling water or milk

The milk will help keep it white, as will:

(Juice of ½ lemon)

Reduce the heat to a simmer and cook ➧ partially covered, until the stalk is barely tender. Test for tenderness after 12 minutes. Drain the cauliflower well and place it in a serving dish. Serve it with:

Brown Buttered Bread Crumbs (II, 159)

and you have prepared **Cauliflower Polonaise.**

Or cream it, page 255. Or use:

Hollandaise Sauce, page 368

Egg Sauce I, page 360 (with crumbled bacon)

Creole Sauce, page 380

Lemon Butter, page 384

⊗ Pressure cook whole cauliflower at 15 lbs. for about 7 minutes.

SAUTÉED CAULIFLOWER [5]

Cook as above:

Boiled or steamed cauliflower

Break it into florets. Heat:

2 tablespoons butter

2 tablespoons salad oil

Add and cook for 2 minutes:

½ clove garlic or

2 teaspoons grated onion

Remove the garlic. Sauté the florets in the fat until they are well coated. Cover and cook for several minutes. Season with:

Salt and paprika

A fresh grating of nutmeg

or serve the cauliflower with:

Chopped parsley or chives

DEEP FRIED CAULIFLOWER

Drain:

Cooked cauliflower

Separate the florets.

Preheat deep fryer to 380°.

Dip each section of cauliflower in:

Fritter Batter for Vegetables (II, 125)

Drain, and deep fry, page 75, until golden. Serve with:

Hollandaise Sauce, page 368, or Sour Cream Dressing, page 351

or cream them, page 255

CAULIFLOWER AND MUSHROOMS IN CHEESE SAUCE [6]

Cook:

1 large cauliflower

Drain it well and put it in a greased baking dish. Place it where it will keep hot. Melt in a skillet:

2 tablespoons butter

Sauté in it for 2 minutes:

½ lb. mushrooms

Cook:

1½ cups Cream Sauce I, page 359

Stir into the hot sauce ➧ off the heat:

¾ cup grated cheese

When the cheese is melted, add the sautéed sauce and pour the sauce over the cauliflower. Serve it at once.

CELERY [4]

Wash:

2 cups chopped celery

➧ Steam, page 252, or drop it gradually into:

½ inch boiling water

Cook it, covered, until it is tender, for about 8 minutes, allowing it to absorb the water. Should there be any liquid, drain the celery and reserve the liquid for the sauce. Brown the celery in:

Seasoned butter

Or, drop the celery into:

1 cup Cream Sauce I, page 359, made with cream and celery liquor

Season the sauce with:

Curry powder
Celery, dill or sunflower seeds
Freshly grated nutmeg
Herbs (II, 200)

Serve:

Au Gratin III, page 389

⊗ Pressure cook celery at 15 lbs. pressure for 1½ minutes.

BRAISED OR GLAZED CELERY [4]

Not only celery, but Belgian endive and Boston lettuce are choice prepared in this way. Do blanch the endive and lettuce briefly first.

Wash and trim:

1½ lbs. celery

Cut into 3- to 4-inch lengths. Arrange them attractively in the bottom of a buttered heatproof ➧ glass, enamel or stainless steel casserole. Squeeze over them:

3 tablespoons lemon juice

Add:

½ cup chicken or veal stock
½ teaspoon salt
1 tablespoon sugar
2 tablespoons butter

Bring the liquid to a boil, then cover with a poaching paper, page 83. Now, cover the casserole with a lid and simmer for about 25 minutes or until tender. Place the celery on a heated serving dish and keep warm. Reduce the pan liquid to about ½ a cup. Add:

1 tablespoon butter or Beurre Manié, page 357

Pour this glaze over the celery.

CELERY CABBAGE OR CHINESE CABBAGE

Use raw as a salad or prepare this vegetable by any of the recipes for cabbage; or stir-fry it as the Chinese do, page 372. If young, it may require only a few minutes' cooking.

➧ Steam, page 252, or place a stalk of:

Whole or shredded celery cabbage

in:

½ cup boiling water

Cook until it is barely tender. Drain thoroughly. Add:

½ teaspoon salt

Serve it with:

Melted butter or Mock Hollandaise Sauce, page 370

or season with:

½ **teaspoon turmeric**

and garnish with:

¼ **cup freshly grated coconut**

CELERY ROOT OR CELERIAC [4]

This knobby tough root, also called **celerirave,** is often woody if too old, but can be one of the most subtly flavored vegetables. It is difficult to peel, so cut into slices first. See page 338. To make the flavor more delicate for use in salads and hors d'oeuvre, blanch 1 to 2 minutes after peeling to keep it white—by using lemon juice or ascorbic acid in the water. Scrub well:

1½ **lbs. celery root**

Steam, page 252, or cover it with:

Boiling water

Cook uncovered, until it is tender—about 25 minutes. Drain the celery root. Cover with:

1½ **cups Cream Sauce II, page 359**

or serve with:

Au Gratin III, page 389

Pressure cook at 15 lbs. about 5 minutes.

SWISS CHARD

Prepare:

Chard leaves

as you would spinach, but remove the coarse middle rib before cooking. If cooking the ribs, cook as for asparagus.

CHAYOTES [4]

This pear-shaped vegetable belongs to the gourd family and is also called **Christophenes.** Treat it much as you would zucchini or other squash. It may be served chilled with mayonnaise, combines well with meats, seafoods and is even good in some desserts.

Pare and cut crosswise in ¾-inch slices:

1 **lb. chayotes**

Drop into:

Boiling water to cover

Reduce the heat at once and simmer 45 minutes, if young, or as long as 1 hour, if mature—or until tender. Drain it. You mya also pressure cook whole chayotes at 15 lbs. for 6 to 8 minutes and, if diced, for 2 minutes. Dress with:

Salt
Butter
Black Butter, page 383, etc., or cream sauce and grated cheese

They are delicious if steamed whole and stuffed with:

Mushrooms and cheese

BOILED CHESTNUTS [4]

I. To use as a vegetable, shell and skin (II, 188):

1 **lb. chestnuts**

or use ½ lb. dried chestnuts that have been soaked overnight. Use this water. Drop the chestnuts into:

Boiling water or milk

To which add:

3 **chopped ribs celery**
1 **small, peeled, chopped onion**
(1 **tablespoon vinegar)**
(⅛ **teaspoon anise)**

Cook them until they are tender. Drain them well. Mash them with:

1 **tablespoon butter**
Correct the seasoning

Add:

2 **or more tablespoons warm cream**

Beat the chestnuts until they are fluffy. Keep them hot over hot water. Immediately before serving them, stir in:

(1 **cup or more finely diced raw celery)**

II. To use as a compote, shell, skin, boil, as above:

1 **lb. chestnuts**

in:

Boiling water or milk

Drain. Save the liquid and add sufficient to make about 2 cups. Make a sirup by adding:

2 cups sugar
Juice and grated rind of 2 lemons
Juice and grated rind of 1 orange
4 whole cloves
1 stick cinnamon
¼ teaspoon ground ginger
(½ cup raisins)
(½ cup chopped nuts)

Simmer the sirup gently until slightly reduced, then fold into the mashed chestnuts and serve.

BAKED CHESTNUTS [4]

Preheat oven to 325°.
Prepare and cook:

3 cups chestnuts, above

Season them with:

(2 tablespoons or more brown sugar)

Grease a baking dish. Place the chestnuts in it. Pour over them:

1¾ cups chicken stock

Cover them and bake for about 3 hours. Pour off the stock and reserve. Melt:

2 tablespoons butter

Stir in until blended:

1 tablespoon flour

Stir the stock in slowly. When the sauce is smooth and boiling, pour it over the chestnuts and serve them.

CHICORY

Witloof chicory and French or Belgian endive may be treated just as for any recipe calling for cooked lettuce or celery. Differentiate the above from the sunburst-centered, highly ruffled or frisée endive, common in our store and usually used raw only.

ABOUT CORN

Some years ago a Frenchman wrote to the Paris Herald to ask: "Why do Americans put their elbows on the table?" The answer, published the following day, was conclusive: "It comes from eating green corn."

When cooked corn is called for in the following recipes, it can be canned, fresh cooked or frozen cooked. Cooked just after picking, young corn is naturally sweet. A few hours off the stalk brings about changes which lessen this flavor. Try cutting fresh corn for puddings and fritters by scraping with either of the tools sketched here—and notice the superior results this

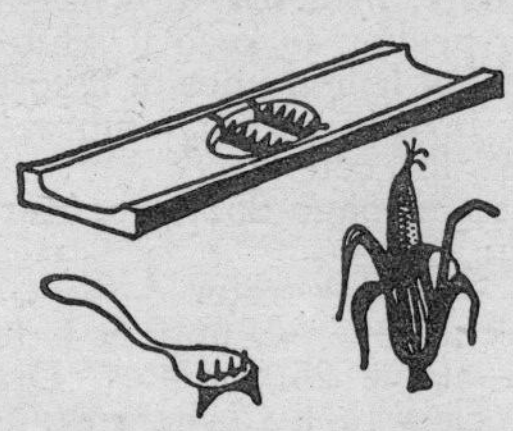

preparation gives. If you must use a knife to cut off the kernels, do not cut deeply. Then press along the rows with the dull side of a knife to retrieve the richly flavored juice and heart of the kernel. ▶ To avoid toughness in cooking corn, add salt when the cooking period is half over.

If ⊗ pressure cooking ❄ frozen corn on the cob ▶ be sure to thaw partially before cooking at 15 lbs. for about 4 minutes.

CORN ON THE COB

I. Remove the husks and silk from:

Ears of fresh corn

▶ Steam, page 252, or drop them, ear by ear, so as not to disturb the boiling, into:

1 inch boiling water or half milk and half water

Add:

(1 tablespoon or more sugar)

Cover the kettle and boil the corn rapidly until it is tender, from 4 to 10 minutes, depending on maturity. Drain and serve it with:

Butter
Salt
Freshly ground pepper

II. Remove the husks and silk from:

Very young, freshly picked corn

In a large kettle which you can cover tightly, bring to a rolling boil:

Enough water to cover corn generously

Slip the ears into the water one by one. Cover the kettle and remove it from the heat at once. Allow the corn to remain in the hot water for about 5 minutes or until tender. Drain and serve at once.

FRESH CORN CUT FROM THE COB

Cut or grate from the cob:

Fresh corn

Simmer it, covered, for several minutes, until it is tender, in its own juice and a little:

Butter

Season it with:

Salt and white pepper

Moisten it with:

Milk or cream

You may devil it by adding:

1 tablespoon Worcestershire sauce
Minced garlic

⊟ GRILLED OR ROASTED CORN

Preheat oven to 400° or have ready a good bed of coals.

I. Pull down husk to remove silk and any damaged portions of the ear on:

Young roasting corn

Replace the husk. Run into the husk as much:

Water

as it will hold. Drain and close the husk by twisting it. Put the ears on a rack over the hot coals or in the preheated oven and bake 20 to 25 minutes. Husk before serving.

II. Strip the husk and silk from:

Roasting ears

Remove any damaged portions. Rub with:

Butter
Salt and pepper

Wrap in foil and roast 20 to 30 minutes, depending on the size of the ears.

FRESH CORN PUDDING COCKAIGNE [8]

This is a luscious dish, but it is a little difficult to give an exact recipe for it because the corn differs with the season. If the corn is watery when scraped, it is sometimes necessary to add a tablespoon of flour. This is apt to be the case early in the season. Later on, it may be necessary to use more cream—up to 1 cup. When the corn mixture is right, it looks like thick, curdled cream when scraped.

Preheat oven to 325°.

Scrape, but ➧ do not cut:

2 cups fresh corn

Add:

1 teaspoon sugar
½ to ¾ cup cream
Salt and white pepper

Place these ingredients in a generously buttered flat baking dish. Dot the top with:

Butter

Bake the pudding for about 1 hour. ✻ This dish may be frozen.

CORN PUDDING [5]

A good hefty corn dish.

Preheat oven to 350°.

Drain:

1 No. 2 can kernel corn: 2½ cups

Reserve the liquid. Melt:

2 tablespoons butter

Stir in until blended:

2 tablespoons flour

Combine and stir in slowly:

The corn liquid and enough cream to make 1 cup

When the sauce is smooth and hot, stir in the drained corn and:

¼ cup chopped seeded green pepper
1 chopped pimiento

When this mixture reaches a boil ➧ reduce heat. Beat well:

2 egg yolks

Pour part of the corn mixture over them off the heat. Beat it and return to corn mixture. Stir and cook for several minutes to permit the yolks to thicken slightly.

Add:

¾ teaspoon salt
¼ teaspoon paprika
(¼ cup crisply cooked, crumbled bacon)

or you may cover the bottom of the dish with:

(Minced ham)

Place on a platter and whip ➧ until stiff, but not dry:

2 egg whites

Fold them lightly into the corn mixture. Bake the pudding in a baking dish ➧ prepared as for a soufflé baker, page 196, for about 30 minutes.

SCALLOPED CORN [4]

Preheat oven to 325°.

Combine:

2 cups uncooked corn, scraped or cut from the ear
2 beaten eggs
½ teaspoon salt
(¼ cup minced seeded green peppers with membrane removed, or chopped olives)
¾ cup cream

Place in a baking dish, prepared as for a soufflé baker, page 196.

Sprinkle with:

Au Gratin II, page 389

Bake the corn for about ½ hour.

CORN SUCCOTASH [4]

This is also good made with canned or frozen vegetables. Combine, then heat in a double boiler ➧ over—not in—hot water.

1 cup cooked fresh corn
1 cup cooked fresh Lima or finely shredded green beans
2 tablespoons butter
½ teaspoon salt
⅛ teaspoon paprika
Chopped parsley

CORN CREOLE [6]

Seed, remove membranes and chop:

¼ cup green pepper

Skin and chop:

1 small onion

Melt:

2 tablespoons butter

Sauté the vegetables in the butter until they are translucent. Heat in the top of a double boiler:

1 cup drained canned or fresh cooked tomatoes

Add the sautéed vegetables and:

½ teaspoon salt
⅛ teaspoon pepper
A few grains cayenne

Cook and stir these ingredients ➧ over—not in—boiling water about 5 minutes. Add:

⅔ cup cooked corn

Heat 2 minutes longer. Stir in, until melted:

1⅓ cups grated cheese

COhN FRITTERS WITH FRESH CORN

For a short period one of our local newspapers devoted a column to masculine taste in culinary matters. The author of the following graciously permitted us to use it when we told him how much it pleased us.

"When I was a child, one of eight, my father frequently promised us a marvelous treat. He, being an amateur horticulturist and arboriculturist, would tell us of a fritter tree he was going to plant on the banks of a small lake filled with molasses, maple sirup or honey, to be located in our back yard. When one of us children felt the urge for the most delectable repast, all we had to do was to shake the tree, the fritters would drop into the lake and we could fish them out and eat fritters to our hearts' content.

"Mother was a good cook and a good helpmate, so she developed the fritter that was to grow on and fall from the tree into the lake of molasses or maple sirup or honey, as the case might be. Her recipe, as preserved in our family, is:

"Grate 12 ears of corn, preferably sugar corn, then beat the yolks of 3 eggs with a very small amount of flour—about a teaspoonful—and a scant teaspoon of salt; beat the whites thoroughly. Mix the grated corn and yolks, then fold in the beaten whites.

"Fry in butter like pancakes and serve hot. You will want more; so will your guests."

Who could resist the delightful idea of a fritter tree in full fruit?

For 4 Servings

Grate:

2½ cups fresh corn

Add:

1 well-beaten egg yolk
(2 teaspoons flour)
¼ teaspoon salt

Whip until ◆ stiff, but not dry:

1 egg white

Fold the egg white into the corn mixture. Into a hot buttered skillet, drop the mixture as for pancakes and sauté until light brown and fluffy. Do not overcook.

CORN FRITTERS OR CORN OYSTERS WITH FRESH OR CANNED CORN

[About 16 Fritters]

For best results, make the batter immediately before using it. Drain, then mash with a potato masher:

1 cup freshly scraped corn or canned, cream-style corn

Beat until light and add:

2 eggs

Add:

6 tablespoons flour
½ teaspoon double-acting baking powder
¼ teaspoon salt
⅛ teaspoon nutmeg

Melt in a small skillet:

3 tablespoons butter

When it has reached the point of fragrance, add the batter with a tablespoon. Permit the bottom of the cakes to brown, reverse them and brown the other side. Serve at once with:

Mushroom Sauce, page 367, or maple sirup

TAMALES

[20 Tamales]

A curious call used to rend the air on hot summer nights, one that brought a sense of adventure to our limited childhood world. It was the Mexican tamale man, whose forbidden, hence desirable, wares long remained a mystery. These varied, leaf-wrapped confections, like individual puddings, may be spicy as mole, filled with cheese and peppers, or sweet with almond, citron and coconut.

Tamales steam slowly to allow the wrapping, either corn husks or banana leaves, to both protect and flavor the contents. Soften the leaves by soaking for 5 minutes in hot water and then draining before using. Most tamales have two ingredients not easily available. First a pastate or tortilla base—that moistened mixture of unslaked lime and dried corn which is ground into flour in a matate; and second, a combination of tequesquite and transparent green tomato parings which make the puddings puff up. The following tamale filling, for which we can get authentic ingredients, is made from fresh corn.

Remove the husks from 20 ears of:

Tender corn

and reserve the largest leaves. Soak for 5 minutes in hot water and drain. You will need 3 to 4 large leaves for each tamale. Scrape the kernels from the cobs, using the scraper illustrated on page 284. Mix these tender bits with:

¾ cup cultured sour cream
1 to 1¼ cups milk

Use the larger quantity if the corn is absolutely not fresh picked. Add:

¼ cup sugar
½ teaspoon salt
½ cup raisins

Overlap 3 or 4 leaves, see page 86. Place about 3 tablespoons of the corn mixture lengthwise down the center of the overlapped leaves. Roll the filling so the husks completely encase it, tucking up the short ends and tying with a white string. Put several layers of the remaining husks in the bottom element of the steamer and cover with about 1 to 1½ inches of boiling water. Place the carefully wrapped rolls ▸ upright in some form of vegetable steamer, see types illustrated on page 252. Close the steamer tightly and steam the tamales over low heat for about 1 hour. Remove the strings, allow the puddings to cool slightly and serve still wrapped in the inedible husks. The fillings should be firm enough to leave the husks easily. You may pass as a garnish:

Cultured sour cream
Cinnamon

ABOUT CUCUMBERS

How often the Japanese draw these decorative plants! That their formal values were missed when the cold weather came was poignantly noted by Isaiah when he said, "as desolate as a cottage in a cucumber garden abandoned in winter."

A cucumber ready to use is rigid and all green. It should have a lustrous skin—but do not be misled by the heavy, waxy, man-applied finish on some of those now in the markets. Never use a skin so waxed. If not waxed, it is perfectly edible. Some people who are allergic to this delicious vegetable find they can enjoy it if it is cooked. ▸ Use any recipe for summer squash or one of the following:

MULLED CUCUMBERS

I. [4]

Pare, seed and cut into strips:

2 cups cucumbers

Drop them into:

1½ cups boiling water

▸ Simmer them until they are nearly tender—but no longer, as they will not retain their color. Drain them well. Place in a double boiler:

¾ cup Cream Sauce I, page 359

Season the sauce with:

Salt and white pepper
Freshly grated nutmeg or
1 teaspoon chopped fresh herbs or dill or celery seeds
1 teaspoon or more lemon juice

When the sauce reaches a boil, add the drained cucumbers. Place the pan over hot water and steam them, uncovered, for a few minutes before serving.

II. Prepare:

Mulled Cucumbers I, above

substituting for the Cream Sauce:

Lemon Butter, page 384, with capers or Tomato Sauce, page 376, with basil or Soubise or Onion Sauce, page 363

CUCUMBER OR MOCK-OYSTER CASSEROLE [4]

Preheat oven to 400°.
Prepare:

2 cups Mulled Cucumbers, as above

Drain the vegetable well. Prepare:

1 cup Cream Sauce, page 359

seasoned with:

1 tablespoon anchovy paste

Place the vegetable in a baking dish. Pour the hot sauce over it. Cover the top with:

Au Gratin III, page 389

Bake the dish until the top is brown.

CUCUMBER CREOLE CASSEROLE [4]

Preheat oven to 375°.
Pare and seed:

3 large cucumbers

Cut them into ¼-inch slices. Combine with half the recipe for:

Creole Sauce, page 380

Place in the bottom of a greased ovenproof dish:

½ cup dry bread crumbs

Add the cucumbers. Pour the sauce over them. Cover it with:

Au Gratin I, page 389

Bake the dish for about 35 minutes.

ABOUT DASHEEN OR TARO

This versatile vegetable, a form of the elephant ears we all know as a decorative plant, has a potato-like root that becomes grayish or violet when cooked. It is used as a vegetable or as a base for puddings and confections. Fermented, it is the famous poi of tropical countries, see following recipe. The spinach-flavored leaves are boiled as for greens but must be cooked from 45 minutes to 1 hour.

To bake, parboil the unpared root for 15 minutes and then time as for potato baking, but make certain the oven is not over 375°.

POI

[About 5 Cups]

Poi may be held at room temperature if unmixed with water. If refrigerated, mix with water. Dice into 1-inch cubes:

2½ lbs. cooked taro roots, above

Mash in a wooden bowl with a wooden potato masher until starchy paste forms. Work in gradually with the hands:

2½ cups water

To remove lumps and fiber, force through several thicknesses of cheesecloth. Store in a cool place and serve at once or let it stand 2 to 3 days until it ferments and has a sour taste.

ABOUT EGGPLANT OR AUBERGINE

These vegetables, lovely when stuffed, also make beautiful individual servings with their green caps against the polished purple of the cases. We have tried alternating them with green and red stuffed peppers for an effective buffet platter.

There are several important things to keep in mind in cooking eggplant. ➧ It may become very watery. Get rid of excess moisture by salting and draining on a rack before using in unthickened recipes; or stack the slices, cover with a plate, place a heavy weight on top and let stand until moisture is squeezed out. ◆ Eggplant discolors quickly when cut and should be sprinkled or rubbed with lemon juice. Also, because of discoloration ◆ cook in pottery, enamel, glass or stainless steel. One lb. of eggplant equals 3 cups diced.

Eggplant has a blotter-like capacity for oil or butter, well pointed up by this Near East tale. The imam or priest was so fetched by the eggplant dish his fiancée prepared that he asked that her dowry be the oil in which to cook it. Great Ali Baba jars of oil were stored in their new home. The first night the eggplant was delicious, also the second; but on the third night, his favorite dish was not waiting for him. "Alas," said the wife, "the first two nights have exhausted the supply of oil." And then the priest fainted! Imam Baaldi, the current and classic dish which carries the priest's name, calls for halved egg-plant, stuffed and completely covered in oil and casseroled covered, page 84, for 1½ hours.

EGGPLANT SLICES

These slices, after frying, sautéeing or broiling, are used in many ways.

I. Top with:

Creamed Spinach, page 326

Sprinkle with:

Gruyère cheese

and run under broiler.

II. Put in a casserole and cover with:

Creole Sauce, page 380

Sprinkle with:

Au Gratin I, page 389

Run under a broiler.

III. Place on each slice:

A slice of Tomato Provençale, page 333

IV. Place on eggplant slice:

A grilled tomato slice

Cover with:

A poached egg

Serve with:

Cheese Sauce, page 364

V. Place on an eggplant slice:

Creamed ham or hash

BAKED EGGPLANT SLICES [4]

Preheat oven to 400°.
Pare:

An eggplant

Cut it crosswise into slices ½ inch thick. Spread the slices on both sides with a mixture of:

Soft butter or salad oil

Seasoned with:

Salt and pepper
Grated onion, lemon juice or basil

Place them on a baking sheet and bake until tender, about 12 minutes, turning them once. Garnish with:

Chopped parsley or chervil

BAKED EGGPLANT HALVES [4]

Preheat oven to 400°.
Wash, dry, then cut into halves lengthwise:

An eggplant

Crisscross the top with gashes about 1 inch deep. Sauté the halves cut side down for about 10 minutes in:

3 tablespoons hot olive oil

Set them upright in a shallow ovenproof dish. Make a paste by mashing together until well blended:

8 flat, minced anchovy fillets
2 skinned, chopped cloves garlic
¼ cup bread crumbs
2 tablespoons strong beef stock
⅛ teaspoon freshly ground pepper

Spread this over the tops of the eggplant. Sprinkle them with:

Dry bread crumbs
Finely minced parsley
A little oil or dabs of butter

Bake the dish for about ½ hour.

SCALLOPED EGGPLANT [4]

Preheat oven to 375°.
Pare and cut into dice:

A medium-sized eggplant

Simmer it until tender in:

½ cup boiling water

Drain it well. Sprinkle it with:

(2 tablespoons chopped parsley)

Chop until very fine:

1 small onion

Melt:

1 tablespoon butter

Sauté the onion in this until it is golden. Add it to the eggplant with:

½ cup milk
(2 well-beaten eggs)

Melt:

3 tablespoons butter

Stir into it, until the butter is absorbed:

¾ cup cracker crumbs or
½ cup bread crumbs

Place layers of eggplant and layers of crumbs in a baking dish. Season them, if the crackers are unsalted, with:

¼ teaspoon salt
⅛ teaspoon paprika

Halve the top layer of crumbs. Place on the top:

(Thin slices of cheese or grated cheese)

Bake the eggplant for about ½ hour. Garnish it with:

Crisp crumbled bacon, page 491, or thin strips of pepperoni

DEEP FRIED EGGPLANT SLICES [4]

The classic method is to dip eggplant in batter and fry it in deep fat.

➧ Please read About Deep Fat Fried Vegetables, page 258.
Preheat deep fryer to 370°.
Pare, cut into ½-inch slices or sticks:

An eggplant

Dip it in:

Fritter Batter for Vegetables (II, 125)

Fry it in deep fat until golden. Drain on absorbent paper and serve after adding:

Salt

SAUTÉED EGGPLANT SLICES [4]

Peel and cut into ½-inch slices, cubes or sticks:

An eggplant

Dip the pieces in:

Milk

Dredge them in:

Seasoned flour, crumbs or cornmeal

For easier handling, place slices on a rack to dry for 15 minutes before cooking: Melt in a skillet:

Butter or oil

Sauté the pieces until tender. Serve while very hot with:

Chopped parsley or tarragon
A sliced lemon or Tomato Sauce, page 376

EGGPLANT CASSEROLE OR RATATOUILLE PROVENÇALE [8]

This ends up looking in color like a Braque still life.
Put in a deep skillet or heavy casserole:

⅓ cup olive oil

Sauté until golden:

¾ cup thinly sliced onions
2 cloves garlic

Remove the onions and garlic from the casserole and combine in layers with:

4 julienned green peppers
2½ cups peeled, diced eggplant
3 cups zucchini in ½-inch slices

2 cups peeled, seeded, quartered tomatoes

Add to each layer:

Salt and pepper

Sprinkle the top with:

Olive oil

Simmer, covered, over very low heat 35 to 45 minutes. ➧ Uncover and continue to heat 10 minutes longer to reduce the amount of liquid. Serve hot or cold.

STUFFED EGGPLANT OR EGGPLANT FARCIE [4]

Eggplant makes a wonderful "background" food, due to its color and shape. Cut eggplant, just under and following the lines of the leafy green cap. This then forms an attractive lid. Or slice it into two oval halves. The cases may be filled with any desired combination of food, to which the cooked eggplant pulp is added.

Preheat oven to 400°.

Cut as described:

A medium-sized eggplant

Scoop out the pulp, leaving a thick shell. Then, drop the pulp into a small quantity of boiling water or stock and cook it until it is tender. Drain it well and mash it. Combine with:

Farce, page 564, or chopped or ground cooked meat: lamb or ham or rice and shrimp

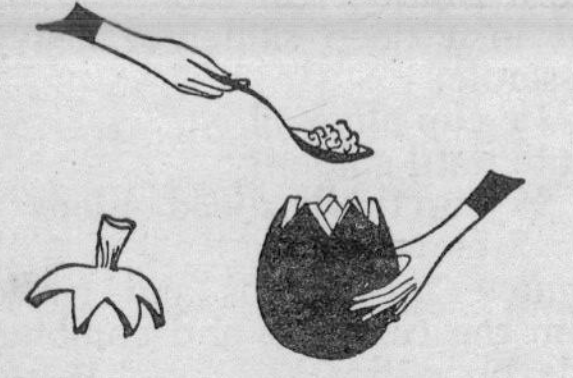

Fill the shell. Cover the top with the cap or

Au Gratin II or III, page 389

Bake the eggplant until filling is heated.

STUFFED EGGPLANT CREOLE [4]

Cut into halves:

A small eggplant

Scoop out the pulp and chop it. Leave a shell ¼ inch thick. Mince and heat in a skillet:

2 strips bacon

Add to it and sauté until the bacon is cooked:

¼ cup minced onion
¼ cup minced seeded green pepper with membrane removed

Add the eggplant pulp and:

2 cups drained canned tomatoes
¼ cup diced celery

Simmer these ingredients until the eggplant is tender. Beat them with a fork until they are well blended. Thicken them with:

⅓ cup bread crumbs

Season them with:

Salt and freshly ground pepper

Add to them:

½ cup Sautéed Mushrooms, page 296

Preheat oven to 350°.

Fill the eggplant shells with the mixture. Cover the tops with:

Au Gratin III, page 389

Place the eggplant in a pan with a very little water and bake until it is thoroughly heated, about 15 minutes.

BRAISED OR GLAZED ENDIVE

Prepare as for:

Braised Celery, page 282

ABOUT FENNEL OR ANISE

Florence fennel, which is found in season at Italian markets, can be eaten raw and is a choice hors d'oeuvre or a substitute for celery with rice in stuffings. If you enjoy the anise flavor, use the bulbous root and stalk as for celery and try seasoning with olive oil. The leaves can also be used discreetly for seasoning, but the usual plant for this purpose is Foeniculium vulgare (II, 206).

ABOUT FERN SHOOTS OR FRESH BRACKEN

In the Spring, cut ferns while the shoots are still curled in crosiers. Wash and tie in bundles of 6 to 8 fronds. Stand upright and steam about 20 minutes or until just tender.
Serve with:

Hollandaise Sauce, page 368

ABOUT GREENS

Greens, such as turnips, mustard, kale, collards, corn salad, comfrey, borage, etc.—are seldom creamed. However, there is no reason why they should not be. The old-fashioned custom is to cook them to death, for an hour or more, with bacon, salt pork or ham hocks and to serve them with vinegar. To retain color and nutrients, try cooking by the following methods.

I. Prepare greens by washing carefully to remove grit and cut out any blemished areas or tough stems. Simmer for 2 hours in water to cover:

A 2 lb. piece side meat: bacon or cottage ham

Add:

2 to 3 lbs. greens

And simmer about 35 to 40 minutes, until just tender.

II. If the greens are very young, cook them as for:

Panned Spinach, page 326

allowing about 15 minutes cooking time.

ABOUT WILD GREENS

If you are in earnest about pursuing the hobby of greens collecting, try to consult a local enthusiast. If he is not available, make a slow approach, trying the greens you are absolutely sure of, like dandelion. Then experiment with poke, dock, lambs quarters, marsh marigold leaves, emerging ferns, yellow rocket cress, young milkweed shoots, pigweed, mustard, purslane.

Many plants are poisonous in part or in whole and most wild greens are bitter unless blanched, page 88, sometimes more than once before cooking. Young milkweeds, marsh marigold, plantains, purslane and nettles are relatively mild, while dock and dandelion, even when young, are better blanched.

Poke, for instance, has a poisonous root and leaf, although the shoot is both edible and delicious. In any case, use these wild greens in small quantities until you know your own reaction to them.

KOHLRABI [4]

Wash:

8 large kohlrabi

Cut off the tops and pare the roots. Slice the roots and drop them into a quantity of rapidly:

Boiling water

Cook them, uncovered, until they are barely tender. Drain them well. Boil the tops separately in the same manner. Drain them well, chop them until they are very fine or purée them and combine them with the roots.
Prepare:

Cream Sauce I, page 359

Add:

(A grating of nutmeg)

When the sauce is smooth and hot, add the kohlrabi.

ABOUT LEEKS OR POIREAUX

How we wish that leeks were as common here as in France, where they are known as the "asparagus of the poor." Leeks, like other onion types (II, 209), make a wonderful seasoning. When cooked as a vegetable, they must be carefully washed to free the interlacing leaves from grit; and only the white portion is used. Cook as for Asparagus, page 260, or braise as for Celery, page 282.

PURÉE OF LEEKS

Good as a meat garnish or stuffing in tomatoes.
Prepare and cook:

Leeks, as above

Drain them well. Chop them coarsely. For each cup add:

2 tablespoons butter
½ cup fresh bread crumbs
Salt and pepper

Stir and simmer them gently until blended. If they become too thick, add:

A little cream

Serve the purée very hot with:

Finely chopped parsley

COOKED LETTUCE

Home gardeners in their enthusiasm find themselves with sudden surpluses of lettuce and wish they had rabbits instead of children—failing to realize that nibbling is not the only approach to this vegetable. Try these delectable alternatives: cook lettuce as a Cream Soup, page 131; cream it like Spinach, page 326; cook with peas; stuff it like Cabbage, page 277; cook and smother it with stewed tomatoes or braise as for Celery, page 282, allowing the lettuce to simmer only a few minutes before reducing the sauce.

ABOUT MUSHROOMS

Who would expect a lot of sunshine vitamin D in plants that flourish in cellars and caves? Yet this is only one of the many valuable nutrients in mushrooms. They delight us too with their almost total lack of calories and then promptly fool us by a blotter-like capacity for butter, oil and cream.

They can fool the experts in other ways. Some of the poisonous types resemble edible forms during various stages of development. ➧ There is no simple way to identify mushrooms and other edible fungi. Experts prefer to have about 10 specimens for identification before committing themselves.

The amanitas, for instance, include types so deadly they may well have been the rumored secret poison of the Borgias. These rather common growths are white gilled and they have a ruptured basal cup and a torn veil or ring left by that veil on the stem. So, collectors should stick to a safer family, like the **puffballs,** which have neither stems nor gills. They are edible if they grow above ground and the flesh inside is white. Lycoperdon giganteum, shown first on the left, varies from marble to canteloupe size and Lycoperdon craniforme resembles a skull slightly shrivelled, even when in prime eating condition.

Rural families return, season after season, to the same mushroom clumps and fairy rings which appear like magic when moisture conditions are just right. The hidden roots of mushrooms are often as stable as an oak. To preserve these seasonal mushrooms, see (II, 221).

➧ Never use any mushroom that shows signs of decay. It harbors ptomaines and toxins just like any other decaying vegetation. ➧ Never cook light-colored mushrooms in aluminum as it darkens them. And don't worry about mushrooms packaged by reputable firms. These firms guard their beds intensively against harmful invading spores. Don't bother to buy spawn blocks to grow your own mushrooms if your cellar is warmer than about 55°.

Agaricus campestris, shown in the center, is the type most often found fresh at the market. The young, pale buttons are succulent, the older, drier ones are best for sauces, as the flavor lies in the dark gills. The completely dried **Gyromitra esculenta** usually imported from Europe is also very strong in flavor when reconstituted, see below. Strangely enough, it can never be eaten raw as it has a poisonous alkaloid which, with this mushroom, disappears entirely in drying or parboiling. But cooking will not destroy the poison ➧ with the most poisonous types.

Shown second from the left, page 294 are a **morel,** a spring growth, and second from the right, **chanterelle,** a summer one. On the far right is **Boletus edulis,** a great European favorite known to gourmets as cèpe or Steinpilz. For truffles, those diamonds of the kitchen, see page 299.

➧ To prepare fresh mushrooms, brush or wipe with a cloth. If they must be washed, dry thoroughly. As the most intense flavor lies in the skin, do not remove it. Some people use only the caps, as the stems tend to be tougher. Should you be so extravagant, turn the mushroom on its side and cut the stem so enough is left within the cap to prevent subsequent shrinkage at the center during the cooking. Be sure to use the stems in Stock Making (II, 139) in Farces, page 564, or in Duxelles, page 540. Another way to keep the mushroom plump and to use most of the stem is to turn it, as sketched, and slice lengthwise.

One of the choicest garnishes for looks is the channelled mushroom. To channel these curving lines on the rather firm but spongy textured mushroom evenly with a sharp knife requires considerable skill, but we find the point of a curved grapefruit knife is quick and easy for the amateur. We have even been tempted to use a V-shaped linoleum carving tool.

➧ To keep mushrooms light in color, sprinkle with lemon juice or white wine or cook À Blanc (II, 146). ➧ To reconstitute dried mushrooms, soak from ½ to 4 hours in tepid water to cover. Drain and use as for fresh mushrooms. Use the water for sauces or soups. Store dried mushrooms, uncovered, in a glass container in a light place. ➧ 3 oz. dried mushrooms reconstituted equal 1 lb.

To keep mushrooms or truffles impaled on food as a garnish, use tiny lemon thyme branches as picks.

STEAMED MUSHROOMS

This is a fine way to prepare very large mushrooms for stuffing.
➧ Please read About Mushrooms, page 294.
Prepare:

1 lb. mushrooms

Place them in the top of a double boiler ➧ over—not in—hot water. Dot them with:

2 tablespoons butter

Add:

¼ teaspoon salt
⅛ teaspoon paprika
(½ cup milk)

Cover closely. Steam for about 20 minutes or until tender. The broth that results is superlative. Serve with salt or use this broth in sauces.

SAUTÉED MUSHROOMS [4]

Prepare for cooking, using caps or pieces sliced to uniform thickness:

1 lb. mushrooms

Melt in a skillet over moderately high heat until they reach the point of fragrance:

2 tablespoons butter
1 tablespoon cooking oil

or use:

(3 tablespoons clarified butter)

Add the mushrooms and ➧ shake the pan, so the mushrooms are coated without scorching. Drop in:

(1 clove garlic)

Continue to cook over moderately high heat ➧ uncovered, shaking the pan frequently. At first the mushrooms will seem dry and will almost invisibly absorb the fat. Continue to shake the pan for 3 to 5 minutes, depending on the size of the pieces. Remove the garlic. If you are holding the mushrooms to add to other food, do not cover, as this will draw out their juices. If using as a garnish or vegetable, serve at once on:

Toast rounds
Grilled tomatoes or eggplant

or on a bed of:

Puréed Peas, page 306

CREAMED MUSHROOMS [4]

Sauté, as for Sautéed Mushrooms, above:

1 lb. sliced mushrooms
1 tablespoon finely chopped onion

Combine the above with:

1 cup hot Cream Sauce II, page 359, or Velouté Sauce, page 362

Season with:

Salt and paprika
2 tablespoons dry white wine
A pinch of herbs

Marjoram is the traditional touch. Chives and parsley are recommended too. Serve over a baked potato or serve in a casserole, covered with:

Au Gratin II, page 389

MUSHROOMS À LA SCHOENER [4]

A Viennese specialty.
Wipe off with a clean cloth:

1 lb. button mushrooms

Choose mushrooms with about a 1- to 1½-inch cap and cut off the stems ¼ to ½ inch below the caps. Sprinkle with:

Lemon juice
Salt

Dip them in:

Fritter Batter with Beer (II, 126)

and deep-fat fry them at 375°, until a golden brown. You may hold them for a very short time in a 200° oven, covered with a paper towel. Just before serving, dust them with:

Chopped parsley or chervil

Serve with:

Cold Tartare Sauce, page 349

BROILED MUSHROOMS

Preheat broiler.

Wipe with a dry cloth and remove the stems from:

Mushrooms

Brush them lightly with:

Butter or oil

Place them cap side down on a hot greased broiler and broil them for about 2½ minutes to a side, turning them once. Put in each cap a small lump of:

Butter or a square of bacon

Season the mushrooms with:

Salt, as needed and paprika
Chopped parsley and lemon juice

They are usually done when the butter has been absorbed. Serve them at once on:

Hot toast

After adding the butter, keep the cap side up to preserve the juices.

BROILED STUFFED MUSHROOMS COCKAIGNE

[4 Small Servings]

Preheat broiler.

There are wonderful farces of sweetbreads, sausages or just seasoned puréed peas with a sprig of lemon thyme. The mushroom stems may be incorporated with them to form the stuffings. Our particular favorite is given below.

Remove stems. Wipe with a damp cloth:

12 large mushroom caps

Chop the stems. Simmer them for 2 minutes in:

1 tablespoon butter

or, if the stems are very large, cook them, first in the top of a double boiler in:

Milk

Add:

1½ cups dry bread crumbs
¼ cup chopped blanched almonds, pecans or other nut meats
(1 pressed clove garlic)
1½ tablespoons chopped chives, basil or tarragon

Bind these ingredients with:

2 tablespoons cream, stock or part stock and part sherry

Season with:

Salt and paprika

Brush the caps with:

Butter or olive oil

Fill them with the above dressing and sprinkle with:

Grated Parmesan cheese

Place them cap side up on a well-greased pan. Broil for about 5 minutes and serve them sizzling hot on:

Toast

MUSHROOMS STUFFED WITH CLAMS OR OYSTERS

Preheat broiler.

Remove the stems and wipe with a dry cloth:

Large mushrooms

Dip the caps in:

Melted butter

Place on each one:

A clam or oyster

Cover each clam with:

1 teaspoon horseradish
1 teaspoon or more mayonnaise
A drop or 2 hot pepper sauce or Worcestershire sauce

Place the mushrooms in a pan.

Broil them about 6 inches from the source of heat, until the tops begin to color. Serve them hot.

MUSHROOMS FLORENTINE [4]

Preheat broiler.
Prepare as for Broiled Stuffed Mushrooms Cockaigne, page 297:

12 large mushrooms

Add to the stems and the juice in the pan:

2 teaspoons grated onion
2 tablespoons chopped parsley
(1 teaspoon anchovy paste)

Cook these ingredients gently for about 3 minutes. Add:

⅓ cup or more creamed spinach

Brush the caps with:

Butter or olive oil

Fill them with the above mixture and broil them cap side up on a greased pan for about 5 minutes. Serve as a garnish for individual steaks or scrambled eggs.

MUSHROOMS STUFFED WITH SEAFOOD OR SNAILS [4]

Preheat broiler.
Remove the stems from:

8 large mushrooms

Wipe caps and stems with a dry cloth. Chop the stems. Shell, then chop:

½ lb. cooked shrimp, snails or crab meat

Prepare the sauce. Melt:

3 tablespoons olive oil or butter

Stir in:

¼ cup flour

Add:

2 cups shrimp, chicken or clam stock

Add the mushroom stems. ➧ Lower the heat. Stir and simmer the sauce for 2 minutes. Add the seafood and:

2 teaspoons chopped chives, parsley or other herb

Stir gently until well blended.

Correct the seasoning

and add:

⅛ teaspoon curry powder or 1 tablespoon sherry

Brush the caps with:

Butter or olive oil

Fill them with the above dressing, place cap side up on a well-greased pan and broil for about 5 minutes. While the caps are cooking, prepare:

8 rounds of buttered toast, about same size as mushrooms

Place the cooked caps on the toast. Put the remaining filling in the center of a platter and surround it with the caps on toast. Garnish with:

Parsley

If you want to make this a main dish, add curls of:

Broiled bacon

MUSHROOMS AND ONIONS IN WINE [4]

Fine for a chafing dish.
Prepare for cooking:

1 lb. mushrooms

Melt:

½ cup butter

Skin, add, stir and sauté for 5 minutes:

16 tiny white onions

Add the mushrooms. When they are coated with butter add:

2 tablespoons flour
¼ cup chopped parsley
½ bay leaf
¼ teaspoon freshly grated nutmeg
½ cup bouillon or stock

Cook and stir these ingredients until the onions are tender. Add:

¼ cup Madeira or dry sherry

Serve garnished with:

Croutons, page 390
Sprigs of parsley

MUSHROOM RING OR MOUSSE [6]

Preheat oven to 325°.
Put through a food chopper:

1 lb. mushrooms

Melt:

2 tablespoons butter

Stir in:

2 tablespoons flour

Brown the flour slightly. Sauté the mushrooms in this mixture for 2 minutes. Cool them. Beat in:

4 beaten egg yolks
½ teaspoon salt
¼ teaspoon paprika

Whip until stiff:

1 cup heavy cream

In another bowl ◆ whip until stiff, but not dry:

2 egg whites

Fold the cream lightly into the mushroom mixture. Fold in the egg whites. Butter a 9-inch ring mold. Pour in the mousse. Cover it with a piece of buttered paper. Place the ring mold in a pan of hot water. Bake it for about 1 hour. Invert the mousse onto a platter. Fill center with:

Buttered peas and parsley

MUSHROOMS UNDER GLASS [4]

In former years the following dish was always a mark of extreme luxury. Today it is within the reach of anyone with an ovenproof glass bowl that fits closely over a baking dish.
Preheat oven to 375°.
Trim the stems from and channel, page 295:

1 lb. mushrooms

Beat until creamy:

¼ cup butter

Stir in very slowly:

2 teaspoons lemon juice

Add:

1 tablespoon chopped celery
⅓ teaspoon salt
¼ teaspoon paprika

Cut with a biscuit cutter and toast:

4 rounds bread, ½ inch thick

When cold, spread them on both sides with ½ the butter mixture. Spread the rest on the tops of the mushroom caps. Place the toast in the bottom of a small baking dish and heap the mushrooms upon them. Pour over them:

½ cup cream

Cover them closely with a glass bowl. Bake them for about 25 minutes. Add more cream if they become dry. Just before serving, add:

2 tablespoons dry sherry

Serve the mushrooms garnished with:

Parsley

ABOUT TRUFFLES

When we found them at a gas stop in the Indiana hills one winter day, in their imported cans, both as rubbings and whole, we knew they had become common currency. So common that when a friend asked the proprietor of a small fruit market if he had any truffles, he, being a little hard of hearing, shrugged his shoulders eloquently and replied, "And who hasn't?"

Like other "storied" foods, truffles are best appreciated where they are grown: in Périgord, they lock them up in hotel safes. For even where they are most plentiful they are expensive and treasured, as they defy cultivation. French are the black truffles, rooted from their underground depths by trick pigs. Dogs are used in Italy for digging the whites. They are called white only in contrast to the best French ones, for they are really pale brown and beige and are in season from October to March.

Too bad there isn't a truffle Geiger counter, but since these fungi have a symbiotic relationship to oak trees, that's the place to start digging.

The terms **Périgordine, Piémontaise** or **Lucullus** are often applied to truffled dishes. Famous dishes seasoned with truffles are:

Pâté de foie in pastry
Scrambled eggs
Garnishes for hors d'oeuvres
Farce for artichokes

➧ To prepare truffles, wash fresh ones in several waters. As the skin is rough, scrub them. They should be sliced very thin, for their aroma is overpowering. To take advantage of it, place thin slices on food and store overnight in a closed container in the refrigerator. Save all parings and mince finely for sauce or soup. Add truffles to dishes at the end of the cooking period, as they should be cooked with the food to flavor it—but not overcooked. If using canned truffles, merely heat with the food or use as a garnish. If you open a can and use only a portion, cover the remainder with oil or sherry. It will keep refrigerated a month.

✲ Truffles may be frozen in their own juice; or add some Madeira wine if juice is lacking.

⅄ TRUFFLE GARNISHES

I. To get truffles in economical quantity for decorating, put in a blender:

7 tablespoons truffle bits, peelings and juice
1 tablespoon gelatin

Dissolved in:

¾ cup water

If this blended mixture is not dark enough to suit you, heat it over hot water until it colors to your satisfaction. Spread the mixture thin on a cookie tin and cool it in the refrigerator. Cut into any desired form and use on cold food, see Chaud-froid, page 388. This same process may be used for pimientos.

II. White truffles can be used raw over risotto or fondue, puréed for canapés, processed in foie gras or cooked 2 to 3 minutes in butter with Parmesan cheese.

ABOUT OKRA

This vegetable is often combined in stews, where its gluey sap helps thicken the sauce and gives to such dishes the name of **Gumbo.** See also page 118.

STEWED OKRA [3]

Wash:

2 cups young okra

If the pods are small, leave them whole, in which case less sap is released. If they are large, cut off the stems and slice into 1-inch pieces. Drop the okra into a small amount of:

Boiling water

enough to cover the bottom of the pan by ⅛ inch. Simmer it, covered, until tender. If whole, it will take about 8 minutes—if cut, about 5. Or the okra may be cooked until half tender, drained and then cooked, covered, in the butter over low heat until it is tender. Drain it.

Correct the seasoning

Serve it hot with:

Melted butter—1 tablespoon to 1 cup okra

or serve with:

Hollandaise Sauce, page 368

or serve it:

Vinaigrette, page 341

⊗ Pressure cook okra cut into 1-inch slices at 15 lbs. for 4 minutes.

SAUTÉED OKRA [6]

Wash:

1 quart okra: 1 lb.

Dry it well, cut off the stem ends and slice the okra crosswise in thin slices. Melt:

2 tablespoons butter

Add the okra, cover it and simmer gently for about 10 minutes. Stir it frequently. Remove the cover and continue cooking the okra until it is tender and a golden brown.

ABOUT ONIONS

Onions are supposed to be the secret of health. But how can they keep that secret? For various suggestions to disguise their lesser virtues and exploit their potential ➧ please read About Onions as Seasoning (II, 209), where you will also find a full discussion of this marvelous family with the qualities each member contributes.

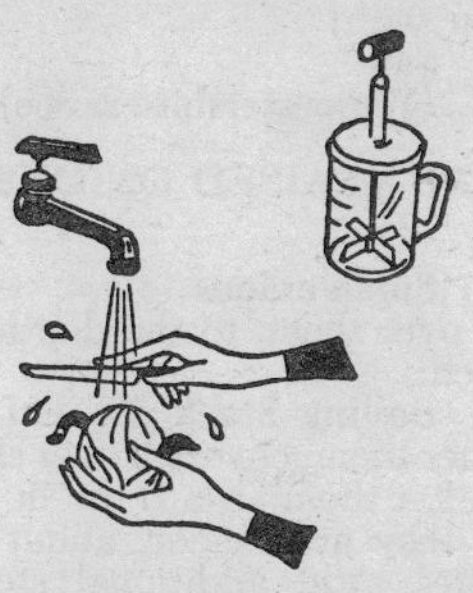

A pleasant way to skin onions is to drop them into rapidly boiling water and leave for about 8 seconds. Drain, chill; and the skin should slip off.

To avoid weeping, you may also pare them under running water, as sketched. Onions all rebel under high heat or too long a cooking period by both discoloring and releasing an unpleasant clinging odor from their sulphur compounds. In sautéing them, be sure they are evenly sliced so they all cook golden at the same time and none remains raw and unpleasant in taste. Give them care in cooking and you will be amply rewarded by the flavor that results.

STEAMED ONIONS [4]

This method is recommended in place of stewing because onion, like cabbage, releases sulphur compounds under too great heat, causing odors and discoloration. Place on a rack ➧ over—not in—hot water:

10 medium, dry, unpeeled onions

Cover the pan and cook them until tender, for 30 minutes or more. Peel and serve with:

(1 cup browned buttered bread crumbs (II, 159)

or dress them with:

¼ cup melted butter
½ teaspoon salt
½ teaspoon cinnamon or cloves
(1 teaspoon sugar)

CREAMED ONIONS [4]

Prepare:

Steamed Onions, above

Cover with:

1 cup Cream Sauce I, page 359, and Au Gratin III, page 389, 1 cup Allemande Sauce, page 362, or 1 cup Tomato Sauce, page 376

You may use ¼ onion water and ¾ cream. Cook the onions and the sauce together for 1 minute. Add:

¼ cup chopped parsley
A dash of cloves
¼ teaspoon paprika
(2 tablespoons sherry)

A wonderful addition is:

(½ cup Sautéed Mushrooms, page 296)

or:

(Minced celery, cooked or raw)

If using one of the above sauces, you may serve the onions on:

(Toast)

YOUNG GREEN ONIONS OR SCALLIONS

Place:

Young green onions

in a very small quantity of:

Boiling water

Cook them, uncovered, until they are nearly tender, about 25 minutes. Drain them well. Place them in rows, on very thin:

Slices of toast

Season them with:

Salt and freshly grated white pepper or nutmeg

Pour over them:

Melted butter or Hollandaise Sauce, page 369

Or cut the onions into small pieces, cook them and combine them with other cooked vegetables—peas, beans, or new potatoes.

WHOLE BAKED ONIONS

I. Preheat oven to 375°.

Wash:

Medium-sized onions

Bake them in a buttered baking dish until they are tender, for about 1½ hours. Cut a slice from the root end. Squeeze the onions to force out the centers. Discard the outer shells. Pour over the onions:

Melted butter

Season them with:

Salt and paprika

Cover them with:

(Grated cheese or chopped parsley)

II. ⊟ Cook, as you would potatoes, in a bed of coals for about 45 minutes:

Whole onions

The outer skin forms a protection. When they are tender, puncture the skin to let the steam escape. Scoop out the centers and serve with:

Salt and pepper

SAUTÉED ONIONS [2]

These can be useful also as a garnish for a greater number than two.

Skin:

4 medium-sized onions

Cut them into very thin slices or chop them. Melt in a skillet:

2 tablespoons butter or bacon drippings

Add the onions and sauté them until they are golden brown. Stir them frequently to keep them from burning. Before serving, season with:

Salt

(Worcestershire sauce)

SMALL BRAISED ONIONS

Skin:

Small onions

Pour over them, to the depth of ½ inch:

Boiling Stock (II, 141)

Simmer them, covered, over slow heat. Let them absorb the liquid until they are tender, about 35 minutes. Add additional stock, if necessary. When they are tender

Correct the seasoning

and add:

(Seeded raisins)

GLAZED ONIONS [4]

These onions are good with pork roast.

Skin:

12 small onions

Prick them through the center and place them on a rack above:

1 inch boiling water

Cook them, covered, until they are nearly tender, for about 25 minutes. Dry them on a cloth.

Melt:

¼ cup butter

Add:

½ teaspoon salt
2 tablespoons brown sugar

Cook this sirup for 1 minute. Add the onions and move them about until they are well coated. Cook them over low heat for about 15 minutes, using an asbestos mat under the pot, if needed, toward the end.

SCALLOPED ONIONS WITH CHEESE [4]

Preheat oven to 350°.

I. Peel, slice crosswise and poach in:

Milk

until tender:

6 large white onions

Drain them well. Place in a buttered baking dish:

4 slices buttered toast

Arrange the onions on the toast. Sprinkle them with:

½ cup grated American cheese

Beat well:

1 egg
1 cup milk
½ teaspoon salt
⅓ teaspoon paprika

Pour this mixture over the onions. Dot the top with:

1 tablespoon butter

Bake the dish for 40 minutes. Serve with:

Crisp bacon
Parsley

II. Or, as a substitute for scalloping which gives much the same result, cook the onions, as described above, until tender. Then make a generous spread of grated cheese, Worcestershire sauce and seasonings. Place the parboiled onions on the toast, spread them with the paste, broil them until the cheese is melted.

FRENCH FRIED ONION RINGS OR SHOESTRING ONIONS [4]

➧ Please read About Deep-Fat Frying, pages 75–79.

Skin and cut crosswise into ¼-inch slices or shred paper-thin.

2 large onions

Combine:

1 cup milk
1 cup water

Soak the onions in this for ½ hour. Drain them, spread them on absorbent paper and dredge them with:

Fritter Batter for Vegetables (II, 125)

Fry in a deep fryer, preheated to 350°–370°, until light brown. Drain on absorbent paper.

STUFFED ONIONS

Onions make attractive garnishes or individual servings when filled.

➧ Please read About Stuffed Vegetables, page 256.

Skin and parboil, page 88, for about 10 minutes:

Medium-sized onions

Drain well. Cut a slice from the top and remove all but ¾ inch of shell. Chop the removed pulp with:

Bread crumbs or cooked rice, chopped cooked fish, meat or sausage, baked beans, mushrooms and bacon, deviled ham or nutmeats

Moisten these ingredients with:

Cream Sauce I, page 359, melted butter, stock, cream or gravy
Correct the seasoning

and add:

Chopped fresh herbs

Fill the onion cases. Cover the tops with:

Au Gratin III, page 389

Place the filled onions in a pan with enough water to keep them from scorching and bake them in a preheated 375° oven until they are tender, about 30 to 40 minutes, depending on size and type. If they are too soft to hold their shape well, bake them in well-greased muffin tins.

ONIONS STUFFED WITH SAUERKRAUT [4]

Preheat oven to 400°.
Prepare:
6 onion cases, above
Combine the chopped pulp and:
1 cup drained sauerkraut
½ cup soft bread crumbs
¼ teaspoon salt
(¼ teaspoon caraway or celery seed)
Heap the mixture into the onion cases. Sprinkle the tops generously with:
Buttered crumbs
Bake the onions in a pan with a very little water until they are well heated and tender, about 35 minutes.

ONION AND APPLE CASSEROLE [4]

This is a complete meal served with green salad, a beverage and bread.
Preheat oven to 375°.
Peel and cut crosswise into ⅛-inch slices:
6 medium-sized onions
Peel, core and cut in the same way.
4 medium-sized apples
Sauté, remove from the pan and mince:
8 slices bacon
Take out 2 tablespoons of the bacon fat. In the remainder, toss:
½ cup soft bread crumbs
Grease a baking dish. Arrange the onions, apples and bacon in alternate layers. Combine and pour over them:
¾ cup hot Stock (II, 141), or water
½ teaspoon salt
Cover the top with the bread crumbs. Cover the dish and bake it for 30 minutes. Uncover and cook it about 15 minutes longer.

ABOUT OYSTER PLANT OR SALSIFY

Salsify, as usually found in the market, is white-skinned. If you plan growing a salsify, pick scorzonera—the black-skinned type which is better flavored. The best flavor results if the vegetable is stored for several weeks at temperatures just above 32°.

This root discolors on exposure to air. To avoid this, cook it unpeeled or, if peeled, cook it à blanc, as below.

OYSTER PLANT À BLANC

Have ready:
3 cups boiling water
in which you have dissolved:
1 tablespoon flour
2 teaspoons lemon juice
½ teaspoon salt
Drop in:
2 cups peeled oyster plant
and cook for 7 to 10 minutes.
Serve in:
Cream Sauce I, page 359
or with:
2 tablespoons melted butter
(Chopped chives or parsley)
or season it with:
1 tablespoon brown sugar
A grating of nutmeg
½ cup whipping cream

SAUTÉED OYSTER PLANT

Wash and peel:
Oyster plant
Dip at once in:
Milk
Drain and season it with:
Salt and pepper
Roll it in:
Flour, bread crumbs or crushed cornflakes
Sauté it slowly until golden in:
Butter

ABOUT HEARTS OF PALM

This ivory-layered vegetable, also known as swamp cabbage, usually weighs between 2 to 3 lbs. when trimmed. Unless available where grown, it is found canned—for it loses flavor and discolors quickly after removal from its sheath.

➧ To boil, remove the outer covering of the heart, leaving a cylindrical portion, the base of which should be tested for bitterness. Remove fibrous upper portion. Slice thin and soak for 1 hour. Use the same water to blanch à blanc (II, 146), the palm for 5 minutes—if there is any trace of bitterness. Now drain and plunge into boiling water again. Cook, covered, about 45 minutes. Drain and serve with:

Hollandaise Sauce, page 368

or in:

Cream Sauce I, page 359

➧ To roast, leave the heart in its sheath. Roast in a 400° oven until tender. Lay back the sheath. Slice the heart crosswise and serve with:

Lemon juice and salt

DEEP FRIED PARSLEY

➧ Please read About Deep-Fat Frying, pages 75–79.

Fried parsley was used merely as a decoration by Ranhofer, the great chef at Delmonicos, who wrote "The Epicurean." Today, try to keep guests from eating it! This is so delicious if properly fried, but becomes limp if the fat is not hot enough and olive green if the fat is too hot. It should be both crisp and a bright dark green. To obtain this crispness and color have at least 2 to 3 inches of fat per cup of parsley and bring the fat you are using just to the smoking point. The parsley must be carefully stemmed, washed and placed between towels until absolutely dry. Put in a frying basket:

1 cup clean, fresh, well-dried, stemmed parsley

Immerse the basket in:

Hot cooking oil

which has just reached the smoking point and leave it 1 to 2 minutes or until no hissing noise is heard. Remove and drain on paper. Serve immediately!

PARSNIPS [4]

To bring out the best flavor of this vegetable, store for several weeks at temperatures just above 32°. Parsnips discolor easily. To avoid this see Oyster Plant, page 304.

Preheat oven to 375°.

Pare, then cut into halves:

4 medium-sized parsnips: 1 lb.

Place them in a buttered ovenproof dish. Brush them with:

2½ tablespoons butter

Sprinkle them with:

½ teaspoon salt

Add to the dish:

¾ cup stock or water

Cover the dish and bake until the parsnips are tender, for about 45 minutes. Serve with:

Parsley butter

⊗ Pressure cook parsnips at 15 lbs. for 7 minutes.

FRENCH PARSNIPS

Prepare as for:

Carrots Vichy, page 280

GREEN PEAS [2 to 3]

Young peas have always elicited paeans of praise, but what to do with old ones? The skins toughen easily. Try salting when cooking is about half over or try Puréed Peas I, below. ➧ One pound of fairly well-filled pods will yield about 1 cup hulled peas. Wash, then hull:

1 lb. green peas

Steam them, page 252, or cook them, covered, in:

⅛ inch boiling water or light stock

to keep them from scorching. Add:

½ teaspoon lemon juice

to help preserve color. There is a tradition that one must add to peas:

(A pinch of sugar)

Two or three pea pods may be cooked with the peas for flavor. Simmer 10 to 15 minutes. When the peas are tender, drain them if there is any water left. Season them with:

Melted butter or hot cream

to which you may add:

Chopped parsley or mint

⊗ Pressure cook peas at 15 lbs. for 2 minutes.

GREEN PEAS AND LETTUCE

I. [2 to 3]

Wash, and remove the heart from:

A head of lettuce

Wash, then hull:

1 cup green peas

Season them with:

Salt and pepper
Pinch of sugar

Fill the head of lettuce with the peas, tie up the leaves and place the head in a small quantity of:

Boiling water

Steam the peas, covered, until tender, about 30 minutes. Serve them with:

Melted butter or cream

The lettuce leaves may be chopped and served with the peas.

II. [2 to 3]

Wash, then hull:

1 cup green peas

Place them in the top of a double boiler. Cover them with large moist:

Lettuce leaves or purslane

Cook them, covered, until tender, over boiling water. This is sometimes a slow process, dependent upon the size of the peas, about ¾ of an hour. Remove the lettuce or purslane.

Correct the seasoning

and add:

Butter or cream

Serve the peas sprinkled with:

Chopped parsley

PURÉE OF PEAS

These make a lovely base on which to place stuffed mushrooms.

I. Prepare:

2 cups cooked frozen peas

⅄ Blend them, when tender, with:

3 tablespoons cream
Correct the seasoning

and serve at once.

II. Prepare:

¼ cup minced onions, scallions or chives

Sauté them until tender in:

3 tablespoons butter

Heat in a double boiler the contents of:

2 cans condensed cream of pea soup: 21 oz.

Stir in the onions. Serve:

Au Gratin, page 389

PEAS AND CARROTS

Prepare:

Hot, drained Carrots, page 279

Combine them in any proportion with:

Hot canned or cooked green peas

Drain the vegetables well.

Correct the seasoning

Pour over them:

Melted butter:
1 tablespoon to 1 cup vegetables
Chopped parsley

Serve at once.

PEAS AND MUSHROOMS

Prepare as for:

Peas and Carrots, above

substituting for the carrots:

Sautéed Mushrooms, page 279

PODDED PEAS

These sought-after varieties, known also as sugar peas, snow peas and mange-tout, are often available in Chinese shops. If they are not young, slice them diagonally, page 250.
Wash, cut off the ends, string and cook as for:

Green or Snap Beans, page 262

or you may stir-fry, page 253, about 5 minutes. Serve while still crisp.

ABOUT SWEET PEPPERS OR PIMIENTOS

Many people in the Midwest call sweet bell peppers mangoes. Do not confuse them with the tropical fruit of the same name (II, 103). Peppers and their hot cousins (II, 213) are chock-full of vitamin C and are also reported as having antibacterial values as well. The seeds cause excruciating pain when in contact with eyes or lips, so ➧ always remove, before use, the stem and fibrous portions that hold the seeds. ➧ To peel peppers, put under the broiler and turn often until they blister.

These are one of the few vegetables that can be ✻ frozen without blanching. So buy when they are plentiful. Peppers are delicious stuffed, but ➧ never overcook them as they become bitter.

GREEN PEPPERS IN SAUCE

Stewed green peppers combine well with other vegetables—for example, green peppers with celery or onions. Remove stem, seeds and fibrous portions from:

Green peppers

Cut the peppers into oblongs or strips. Drop them into:

½ inch boiling water

Boil them until they are tender, for about 10 minutes. Drain them well. Serve them in:

Cheese sauce or a canned soup sauce

Season either one with:

Salt
Worcestershire sauce

Allow about ½ as much sauce as peppers.

ONIONS AND GREEN PEPPERS [4]

This is a good accompaniment to cold meat.
Skin, then cut into thin slices:

6 medium-sized onions

Cut coarsely, after removing seeds and membranes:

3 green peppers

Melt in a large skillet:

3 tablespoon butter, ham fat or olive oil

Sauté the onions and peppers in this for about 10 minutes. Add:

2 tablespoons stock or water
Correct the seasoning

Cover the skillet. Simmer the vegetables until the onions are tender, for about 10 minutes. Serve with:

Tomato Sauce, page 376

STUFFED PEPPERS

Should you want to fill peppers with heated, precooked food, blanch them, page 88, for about 5 minutes. Fill and serve. Or, cover the filling with Au Gratin I, II, or III, page 389, and run briefly under broiler until the crumbs are golden. You may fill pepper cases with any of the fillings suggested for Stuffed Tomato, page 336, or one of the following: parslied, buttered Lima beans; creamed spinach, peas or celery; creamed asparagus with shredded almonds; Stuffings of precooked food; Macaroni and Cheese au Gratin, page 170, or Corn Creole, page 286.

PEPPERS STUFFED WITH ANCHOVY DRESSING [4]

➧ Please read About Stuffed Vegetables, page 256.
Preheat oven to 350°.
Prepare:

4 pepper cases

Fill the pepper cases with a mixture of:

1⅔ cups dried bread crumbs
2 tablespoons melted butter
3 crushed anchovy fillets
2 tablespoons capers
½ cup sliced green olives
½ teaspoon salt
1¼ cups undrained canned tomatoes

Bake, as directed, about 10 to 15 minutes.

PEPPERS STUFFED WITH RICE [4]

➧ Please read About Stuffed Vegetables, page 256.
Preheat broiler.
Prepare:

4 pepper cases

Have ready:

1 cup hot cooked rice

Add:

½ cup stock, cream or tomato pulp
Salt and pepper
A few grains cayenne
½ teaspoon curry powder or a bare pinch of oregano
½ cup or more grated cheese

Fill the pepper cases. Cover tops with:

Au Gratin I or II, page 389

Brown briefly under a broiler.

PEPPERS STUFFED WITH FISH OR MEAT

Fine for creamed turkey or shrimp.
➧ Please read About Stuffed Vegetables, page 256.
Line individual molds with:

Pimientos, whole or in strips

Prepare in Cream Sauce II, page 359.

Chopped cooked fish or meat

Use ½ as much cream sauce as fish or meat. Season these ingredients with:

Worcestershire sauce, lemon juice or sherry

Fill the molds and place them in a pan of hot water on top of the stove. Steam them gently until they are well heated, about 10 minutes. Serve them hot with:

Thickened Tomato Sauce, page 376

to which add:

2 tablespoons chopped parsley

Or chill them, unmold and serve cold with:

Mayonnaise

PEPPERS STUFFED WITH MEAT AND RICE [4]

➧ Please read About Stuffed Vegetables, page 256.
Preheat oven to 350°.
Cook until nearly tender:

4 pepper cases

Melt:

2 tablespoons drippings or butter

Add, stir and sauté until light colored:

½ lb. ground beef
3 tablespoons minced onions

Add:

1 cup hot cooked rice
2 well-beaten eggs
½ teaspoon salt
⅛ teaspoon paprika
¼ teaspoon celery seed, curry powder, dried

herb or Worcestershire sauce

Fill the pepper cases. Bake, as directed, about 10 or 15 minutes.

PEPPERS STUFFED WITH CORN À LA KING [6]

➧ Please read About Stuffed Vegetables, page 256.

Prepare:

6 pepper cases

Place in a double boiler and cook for 20 minutes:

2½ cups corn niblets: 1 No. 2 can
1 shredded green pepper
1 chopped pimiento

You may add:

(4 slices sautéed minced bacon)
2 tablespoons minced onion that has been sautéed in the bacon fat and drained

Combine and beat:

1 egg
½ cup milk
1 tablespoon soft butter
¾ teaspoon salt
⅛ teaspoon paprika

Add these ingredients to the vegetables. Cook and stir over low heat until they are slightly thickened. Fill the peppers with this hot mixture and serve.

PEPPERS STUFFED WITH CREAMED OYSTERS [4]

➧ Please read About Stuffed Vegetables, page 256.

Preheat broiler.

Prepare:

4 pepper cases
½ pint Creamed Oysters, page 424, using ½ the amount

Add:

2 tablespoons chopped parsley

Fill the pepper cases with the hot oysters. Cover the tops with:

Au Gratin II or III, page 389

Brown the tops briefly under a broiler.

ABOUT PLANTAIN

These 9- to 12-inch bananas must be cooked to avoid a starchy, raw flavor. They are not sweet, even when ripe. They get bitter when overcooked, due to a tannin component, but can be put into omelets, soups or stews if finely diced and added the last minutes before serving.

Remove the fibrous strings before cooking, as they darken. Peel green plantains under running water to keep from staining the hands. ➧ Simmer 30 minutes in rapidly boiling water. Season and serve with butter. If plantains are ripe, slice fine and deep-fat fry as for Potato Chips, page 319, or cook as for Candied Sweet Potatoes, page 323. The purple bud end of the banana can be roasted in its husk. Only the heart is eaten. Serve with crumbled bacon or cracklings.

ABOUT POTATOES

Anyone who has visited Hirschhorn, in the sweetly romantic Neckar Valley, and who has climbed the hill to the partly ruined castle that dominates the little village, will remember being confronted by a "Potato Monument" dedicated piously "To God and Francis Drake, who brought to Europe for the everlasting benefit of the poor—the Potato."

But, in recent years, potatoes have been maligned as too caloric—although they are only equal to the same-sized apple or a baking powder biscuit. They are full of B, C, and G vitamins, plus many minerals and even some high-class protein. Do include them regularly in the diet, but don't use potatoes whose skins are greenish, as they are apt to be bitter, or sprouted potatoes or frost-bitten ones, which are watery and have a black ring under the skin when cut in cross sections.

If you wonder why there are no recommendations for ✻ freezing potatoes in this chapter, let us say that this operation is not possible with success in home freezers. Potatoes purchased frozen have all been treated to a quick-vacuum partial dehydration and instant freezing, to which home freezing equipment does not lend itself.

In the following recipes we have tried to give these delicious vegetables a renewed status. ➧ Be sure, if a potato type is specified, to use that type only—and remember that ➧ once a potato is cold, mealiness can never be returned to it.

Potatoes are often combined and mashed with other cooked vegetables, as: ⅔ celeriac, ⅓ potato, or in equal parts with turnips or ¼ fresh avocado, ¾ potato.

BOILED MATURE POTATOES [4]

Wash well, remove sprouts and blemishes, then pare:

6 medium-sized potatoes

When in haste, cut them into quarters. Cook them, covered, from 20 to 40 minutes in:

4 cups boiling water
½ teaspoon salt

When they are tender, drain them well. Reserve the stock for a thick soup base.

To make the potatoes mealy, place a folded towel over the pot for 5 minutes. Shake the pot well. Remove the towel, which will have absorbed excess steam. Roll the potatoes in:

2 to 3 tablespoons melted butter
3 to 4 tablespoons chopped parsley or chives

⊗ Pressure cook large potatoes at 15 lbs. for about 15 minutes.

BOILED NEW POTATOES [4]

There are many lovely things to do with small new potatoes, one of which is serving them in their skins, so all of their delicate goodness is held until the very moment they are eaten.

Wash well:

12 new potatoes

Drop them in:

Boiling water to cover

Cook them, covered, until they are tender, from 20 to 30 minutes. Remove the skins and serve the potatoes with:

Chopped parsley, mint or chives

Or melt in a skillet:

3 to 6 tablespoons butter

Add the potatoes and shake them gently over low heat until they are well coated. Serve them sprinkled with:

Salt
Chopped parsley or chopped fresh dill or fennel

Or add to the butter in the pan:

3 to 4 tablespoons freshly grated horseradish

and shake the potatoes until coated. This last is particularly good with cold cuts.

⊗ Pressure cook small new potatoes at 15 lbs. for about 2½ minutes.

RICED POTATOES [6]

A fine foil for meat with a rich gravy.

Prepare:

Boiled Mature Potatoes, this page

When the potatoes are tender and dried, put them through a food mill, ricer or strainer. Heap them on a dish and pour over them:

(2 tablespoons melted butter)

MASHED POTATOES [6]

Mashed potatoes should be served at once but, in a pinch, can be kept warm by placing the pan in a larger pan of hot water. Or put them in a greased casserole, run a slight film of cream over the top and keep in a warm oven. The cream should brown to an attractive color.
Prepare:

Boiled Mature Potatoes, page 310

You may add to the water a small onion or a cut clove of garlic, a piece of bay leaf and a rib of celery with leaves. Remove these extraneous ingredients. Mash the potatoes with a fork or a potato masher or put them through a food mill, ⅄ blender or electric mixer. Add to them:

3 tablespoons butter
1 teaspoon salt
⅓ cup hot milk or cream

Beat them with a fork or heavy whisk until they are creamy. Grated or sautéed onions with the drippings, minced crisp bacon, chopped parsley, chives or water cress are good additions to mashed potatoes. To help fluff the potatoes, cover the pan after they are mashed and place over very slow heat for about 5 minutes.

MASHED POTATO CHEESE PUFFS

[6 Puffs]
This is a tempting potato dish and a good-looking one.
Preheat oven to 350°.
Beat:

2 egg yolks

Add and beat until fluffy:

1⅓ cups hot or cold Mashed Potatoes, above
3 tablespoons hot milk
⅓ cup grated cheese

Season these ingredients with:

¼ teaspoon salt
¼ teaspoon paprika
¼ teaspoon celery salt
½ teaspoon finely grated onion
1 teaspoon chopped green pepper or parsley

Beat until stiff, then fold in:

2 egg whites

Place the batter in mounds in a greased pan. Brush the tops with:

1½ tablespoons soft butter

Bake the potatoes for about 20 minutes.

CHANTILLY POTATOES [6]

The use of whipping cream is what makes a dish Chantilly.
Preheat oven to 375°.
Prepare:

3 cups Mashed Potatoes, this page

Whip until stiff:

½ cup whipping cream

Season it with:

Salt and white pepper
A few grains cayenne

Combine it with:

½ cup grated cheese

Shape the potatoes into a mound on an ovenproof plate. Cover the mound with the whipped cream mixture. Bake the plate until the cheese is melted and the potatoes are lightly browned.

BAKED MASHED POTATO BALLS [4]

Preheat oven to 350°.
Have ready:

2 cups well-seasoned, hot Mashed Potatoes, this page: 4 medium-sized potatoes

Beat in:

2 egg yolks
1 tablespoon chopped parsley

Cool these ingredients slightly.
Beat until stiff:

2 egg whites

Fold them lightly into the potato mixture. Shape the mixture into balls. Bake the potatoes in lightly greased muffin tins or drop them on a greased sheet. Bake them until crisp. Turn them to brown evenly.

CREAMED POTATOES

Prepare:

Boiled New Potatoes, page 310

Drain and dry off potatoes over very low heat. Peel and cut into ½-inch dice. Serve at once in:

Cream Sauce II, page 359

flavored with:

Dill seed

CREAMED POTATO CASSEROLE

Prepare as for:

Boiled New Potatoes, page 310

using mature baking potatoes. When nearly done, in about 35 to 40 minutes, drain and dry off the potatoes by shaking the pan over low heat. Peel and cut into ½-inch dice.

Preheat oven to 400°.

Prepare, for every 2 cups diced potatoes:

1 cup Cream Sauce II, page 359

Line a buttered casserole with the potatoes. Add the cream sauce and sprinkle the top with:

Au Gratin III, page 389

Bake the potatoes for 20 minutes, longer if the casserole has been refrigerated.

SCALLOPED POTATOES [4]

Preheat oven to 350°.

I. Grease a 10-inch baking dish. Place in it, in 3 layers:

3 cups pared, very thinly sliced potatoes

Dredge the layers with flour and dot them with butter. Use in all:

2 tablespoons flour
3 to 6 tablespoons butter

There are many tidbits you can put between the layers. Try:

(¼ cup finely chopped chives or onions)
(12 anchovies or 3 slices minced crisp bacon—but then reduce the salt in the recipe)
(¼ cup finely sliced sweet peppers)

Heat:

1¼ cups milk or cream

Season with:

1¼ teaspoons salt
¼ teaspoon paprika
(¼ teaspoon mustard)

Pour the milk over the potatoes. Bake them for about 1½ hours. They may be covered for the first ½ hour.

II. Prepare:

Scalloped Potatoes I, above

Omit the flour, using, instead of the hot milk mixture:

1¼ cups hot condensed mushroom or celery soup or hot Cheese Sauce, page 364

Bake, as directed above.

POTATOES SCALLOPED IN BUTTER [6]

Preheat oven to 425°.

Wash and pare:

4 cups mature baking potatoes

Cut them in slices ⅛ inch thick. Place them in cold water to cover for 15 minutes. Drain them. Dry them between towels. Butter a shallow 9-inch baking dish generously. Sprinkle it with:

Fine dry bread crumbs

Cover the bottom carefully with the potato slices. Dot them generously with:

Butter

Use in all about ⅓ cup. Sprinkle them lightly with:

Salt and white pepper
(Grated Swiss cheese)

Repeat this process until the dish is filled. Cover the dish. Bake the potatoes for about ¾ hour or until tender. Turn them out onto a platter. Garnish them with:

Parsley

BAKED POTATOES

The best baked potatoes are flaky when served—so start with mature baking types like Idahos. Although new potatoes can be used, they will never have the desired quality and will need only half as much baking time. The present rage for wrapping potatoes in foil will not allow them to become flaky as too much moisture is retained. In fact, to draw moisture out of bakers, they are often placed on a bed of rock salt. One of the treats of baked potatoes is eating the skin, under which the greatest proportion of its minerals, vitamins and protein lie.

Preheat oven to 425°.

Wash and scrub even-sized, shapely:

Baking potatoes

Dry them and grease them lightly with:

Butter

Bake the potatoes for 40 minutes to 1 hour, depending on their size. When potatoes are ½ done, pull out rack, quickly puncture skin once with fork, permitting steam to escape. Return to oven and finish baking. When done, serve them at once with:

Butter or thick sweet or cultured sour cream
Chopped chives or parsley
1 tablespoon deviled ham

or serve with:

Cheese Sauce, page 364

STUFFED POTATOES [6]

Prepare:

6 Baked Potatoes, above

Cut them in halves crosswise, lengthwise like boats, or leave them whole, cutting a small ellipse on the flat top. Scoop out the pulp. Add to the pulp:

3 to 4 tablespoons butter
3 tablespoons hot milk or cream
1 teaspoon salt

Sauté:

(2 tablespoons grated onion)

in the butter or, if you plan to serve these with fish, add, for piquancy:

(1 tablespoon horseradish)

along with the butter and cream. Beat these ingredients until they are smooth. Whip until stiff:

(2 egg whites)

Fold them into the potato mixture. Fill the potato shells. Sprinkle the exposed potato with:

½ cup grated cheese
Paprika

Broil them under low heat until the cheese is melted.

BAKED POTATOES STUFFED WITH VEGETABLES [8]

Preheat oven to 400°.

Prepare:

4 Baked Potatoes, this page

Have ready:

1 cup Cream Sauce I, page 359

Mix into the sauce:

¼ teaspoon salt
½ cup grated cheese
½ cup cooked peas
½ cup cooked chopped carrots
¼ cup diced green peppers
2 tablespoons diced pimientos

Cut the potatoes lengthwise into halves. Remove the pulp without breaking the skin. Mash the pulp and fold in the sauce and vegetables. Fill the potato shells with the mixture. Cover them with:

Au Gratin II, page 389

Place the potato shells in the oven until the tops are brown. Serve with:

Hot or cold meat

BAKED POTATOES STUFFED WITH HASH [6]

Creamed leftover vegetables and/or meat or fish may be substituted.

Preheat oven to 400°.

Bake:

6 medium-sized baking potatoes

Cut a thin slice off the flat side. With a spoon, remove as much as you can of the potato without breaking the skin. Do not mash the potato. Add to it and work lightly with a fork until blended:

1 tablespoon butter
1 tablespoon cream
½ teaspoon salt
¼ teaspoon paprika
1 teaspoon onion juice
1 tablespoon minced parsley
1 cup chopped cooked meat
(¼ minced celery)

Moisten these ingredients with:

Gravy or stock

Season them with:

2 teaspoons Worcestershire sauce

Combine them with the potato mixture. Fill the skins, heap the tops. Place on each potato:

½ teaspoon butter

or sprinkle it with:

Grated cheese

Brown the potatoes in the oven.

STUFFED POTATO CUPS

⧫ Please read About Deep-Fat Frying, pages 75–79.

Preheat deep fryer to 385°.

Pare oval:

Potatoes

Hollow out the centers to make cups or boat shapes. Parboil for 10 minutes in:

Boiling water

Drain and dry them. Fry the potato cups in the hot deep fat until they are well browned. Drain well and sprinkle them with:

Salt

Fill them with hot:

Creamed meat, fish or vegetables

TINY NEW POTATOES, SAUTÉED [4]

Scrub and scrape well:

24 very small whole new potatoes

Heat in a heavy saucepan:

2 to 3 tablespoons olive oil or clarified butter

Turn the potatoes in the oil, cover them closely and cook them slowly until tender. Shake the pan from time to time. Sprinkle the potatoes with:

Salt and paprika
(Chopped chives or parsley)

LYONNAISE POTATOES

Prepare:

6 medium, waxy, Boiled New Potatoes, page 310

While hot, peel and slice thinly. Sauté them to an even brown in a heavy skillet in:

2 tablespoons butter
2 tablespoons cooking oil

While they are cooking, sauté until golden in another pan:

½ cup finely sliced onions

in:

2 tablespoons butter

Mix onions and potatoes together gently.

Correct the seasoning

Sprinkle with:

Parsley

and serve at once.

FRANCONIA OR BROWNED POTATOES

We love browned potatoes, but

have an aversion to the hard-crusted, grease-soaked variety so often served. To insure a tender crust, we suggest preparing:

6 boiled mature potatoes, about 2-inch diameter

Cook them until they are ◆ not quite done, so that there is still resistance to the testing fork. Preheat oven to 350°.
Melt in a small, heavy iron skillet or casserole a mixture of:

Butter and cooking oil

to the depth of about ¼ inch. When the fat is hot, but not quite to the point of fragrance, put in the potatoes. Let them cook ◆ covered, in the oven for about 20 minutes, turning them for even coloring. On the last turn, put in:

2 tablespoons finely chopped parsley

Bake them ◆ uncovered, about 10 minutes longer.

POTATOES ANNA [6]

One of the most beautiful of all culinary wares is the lidded copper Potatoes Anna dish, about 8 inches in diameter and 3½ inches high. The lid, which has side handles, fits down over it to a 1½ inch depth during the oven period, but is reversed to hold the potatoes for serving. You may substitute a heavy skillet.
To get even rounds, cut cylinders from big potatoes with a corer the size of a small biscuit cutter. Cut the cylinders into 3/16-inch even slices to make:

4 cups potatoes

Soak them in ice water for 10 minutes. Drain. Dry carefully in a towel. Heat in an 8-inch skillet with sloping sides:

2 to 3 tablespoons butter
2 tablespoons cooking oil

Do not brown the fats, but let them just reach the point of fragrance. Put the potatoes in the butter in slightly overlapping spirals until the base of the pan is filled. Shake vigorously while filling, so the potatoes will not stick. Add a sprinkling of:

Salt
Grated onion
Parmesan cheese

The butter will bubble up. But make sure, before adding another layer of slightly overlapping potato slices, that the first layer is coated with additional:

Butter

Continue this process for the first 2 layers, letting the potatoes color slightly. Be sure the layers are welded together. Add a sprinkling of salt, onion and butter each time. It is not necessary to continue adding butter if you have used about ½ cup. The moisture from the cooking potatoes will make it bubble up. In building the next layer or two, omit the butter. Shake the pan constantly to make sure the contents are not sticking. Cover the pan and bake in a 375° oven for 45 minutes to 1 hour. Just before the potatoes are done, turn the entire mass over—to brown the upper side.

HASHED BROWN POTATOES [4]

Combine with a fork:

3 cups finely diced raw potatoes
1 teaspoon grated onion
1 tablespoon chopped parsley
½ teaspoon salt
¼ teaspoon black pepper
(1 teaspoon lemon juice)

Heat in a 9-inch skillet:

3 tablespoons bacon drippings, oil or other fat

Spread the potato mixture over this. Press it with a broad knife into a cake. Sauté the potatoes slowly, shaking them from time to time to keep them from sticking. When the bottom is brown, cut the potato layer in half and turn each half with 2 spatulas. Pour over them slowly:

¼ cup cream

Brown the second side and serve the potatoes piping hot.

POTATO PANCAKES

[About Twelve 3-Inch Cakes]

➧ This recipe demands mature potatoes.

Pare and grate coarsely until you have:

2 cups grated mature potatoes

Place the gratings on a muslin towel and wring the towel to extract as much moisture from the potatoes as possible. Place them in a bowl. Beat well, then stir in:

3 eggs

Combine and sift:

1½ tablespoons all-purpose flour
1¼ teaspoons salt

Add the flour to the potato mixture with:

(1 to 3 teaspoons grated onion)

Shape it into ¼-inch thick 3-inch diameter patties. Sauté in ¼ inch or more hot fat. Turn and brown the second side until crisp. These are usually served hot with:

Applesauce (II, 95)

They are best, like all pancakes, served hot out of the pan. If you must hold them until all the batter is cooked, place them on a rack above a baking sheet in a 200° oven. Then serve all of them at once after draining on absorbent paper to remove any excess grease.

GRATED POTATOES, PAN-BROILED [4]

Very good, quick—something like a potato pancake. Wash, grate on a medium grater, skin and all:

3 medium-sized mature baking potatoes
(2 tablespoons grated onion)

Melt in a skillet to the point of fragrance:

2 tablespoons butter
2 tablespoons cooking oil

Spread the potatoes in the skillet to a depth of about ¼ inch. Cook, covered, over medium slow heat until the bottom is brown. Reverse and brown the other side. Season with:

Salt

Serve piping hot.

SOUFFLÉ OR PUFFED POTATOES [6]

➧ Please read About Deep-Fat Frying, pages 75–79.

Legendary or not, we like this version of the origin of these delicacies. Louis XIV, diverted for the moment by his favorite pastime of fighting the Dutch, was inspecting his army at the front. He was to dine at a given point, at a given time, and a fitting repast had been prepared for him.

His sumptuous traveling coach, that little palace on wheels which was the scene of so many intrigues—or so many tender affairs—was swinging along on its great springs when it was delayed by torrential rains that made the rough roads almost impassable.

Whenever the King made his entrance he would undoubtedly demand food at once to appease his phenomenal appetite. The cook was frantic. His delicious dinner was kept hot over steam, but the potatoes, unfortunately fried ones, appeared limp and cold. A tremendous bustle heralded the arrival of the King and, in despair, the unfortunate cook immersed the potatoes in the hot fat for the second time, agitated them madly, and, behold—the dish that was to make him rich and famous!

There were several more coincidences that the cook may not have been aware of. His potatoes must have been old, so that the starch content was just right to make them puff. He must have had a very systematic apprentice who cut the potatoes all with the grain and to a very uniform thickness, as sketched. In his relief at having something to serve, he evidently didn't mind a 10% failure, for even experts who make these daily count on that great a percentage of duds. All this is just to encourage you if, like us, you expect a 100% return on your efforts. The duds, by the way, are edible as good French fries, if not as glamorous as the puffs. Choose:

8 large mature potatoes

Restaurants famous for this dish age their own to the point where you can no longer pierce or scrape the skin off with your fingernail, but must use a knife to pierce it. There should be about 80% starch in the potato. Idahos and Burbanks are especially recommended, although Pierre Adrian, who is very expert at this, says there is nothing like a Holland potato, grown on Spanish soil. Cut from the unpared potato the largest possible

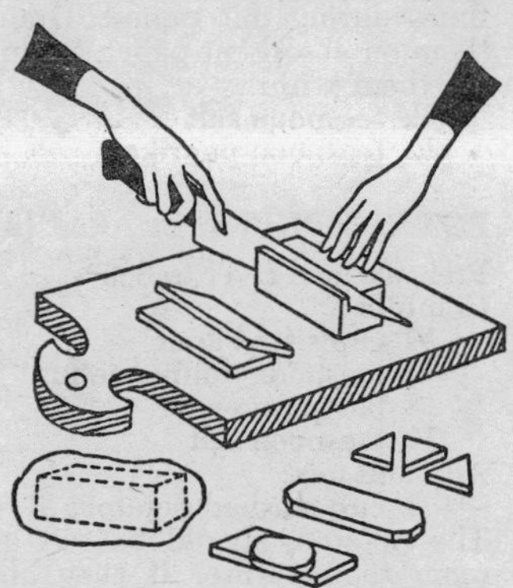

oblong ➧ with the grain—that is, the long way, as sketched—into ➧ ⅛-inch slices that are of uniform thickness from one end to the other. In restaurants, this accuracy is produced by a slicing machine. Once you have these long, even slices, you can cut them into the classic shape with polygonal ends, as sketched, or into triangles, circles or fancy ovals with crimped edges. ➧ But whatever the final shape, always start with the long piece—cut with the grain—and have it ⅛ inch thick for its entire length. Soak the slices for at least 25 minutes in:

Ice water

Dry them thoroughly. Have ready a deep-fat frying kettle ⅓ filled with:

Rendered kidney suet or cooking oil

heated to 250°. Drop the slices in separately. ➧ Do not crowd the pan. The slices will sink. This next admonition is not without danger for the unskilled. ➧ When, after a few seconds, they rise, use a continuous shaking motion with the pan, which will set up a wave-like action to keep the floating strips bathed in the fat. Continue to cook them at 250° until they begin to clarify toward the centers and show a marked difference in texture at the cut edges, to a depth of about 1⁄16 of an inch. Drain them on absorbent paper. If you do not want to use them at once, they may be refrigerated before the second cooking, but ➧ bring them to room temperature before immersing in the hot fat the second time. If you want to proceed at once, let them cool off and drain for about 5 minutes before the second cooking.

Just before you are ready to serve them, drop them again one by one into a kettle filled ⅓ full with frying oil which has reached 375°. Again agitate the pan, as described. The once-fried slices should puff at once, although they always retain a seam wherever you have made an original perimeter cut. Cook to a golden brown. Drain. Dry them on absorbent paper. Salt and serve the puffed ones at once. If they are not crisp enough, return them to the fat for a few seconds. Drain again. Sometimes it is worth trying the duds once more, after they have cooled.

NEVER-FAIL FRENCH FRIES

The following recipe, like Soufflé Potatoes, calls for a two-stage frying operation. After the first stage, you may drain and cool the potatoes on absorbent paper. Cook the second stage just before serving.

➧ Please read About Deep-Fat Frying, pages 75–79.

Preheat deep fryer to 300° to 330°.

As with all successful potato frying, much depends on the maturity of the potato, so choose:

Mature baking potatoes

Pare and slice them into strips about 2¼ inches long and about ⅜ inches through. If you are using cold storage potatoes and want a good, light-colored result, soak the potatoes for 15 minutes in 90° water. Wipe well with a towel to remove surface moisture and excess starch. Slowly heat to 300° to 330°:

Cooking oil or rendered beef kidney fat

When the fat is ready, drop in the potatoes—about 1 cup at a time—and cook about 2 minutes, until all sputtering ceases. Skim out the rather limp potatoes, drain on absorbent paper and cool at least 5 minutes before starting the second stage. ➧ Heat the oil to 375°. Place the potatoes in a frying basket. This will assure quick and easy removal for them, in just the right condition. Finish frying them for about 3 minutes. They should be golden brown and will be crisp when drained on absorbent paper. ➧ Never cover them, as they will get flabby. Serve at once, in a napkin-lined basket.

SHOESTRING POTATOES

Cut into very thin strips, not more than 3/16 inch thick:

Mature baking potatoes

Cook as for:

Never-Fail French Fries, above

BAKED "FRENCH FRIED" POTATOES [4]

Preheat oven to 450°.

Pare:

4 medium-sized potatoes: 2 cups

Cut them lengthwise into strips about ½ inch thick. You may soak them in cold water for 10 minutes. Dry them well between towels. Spread them in a single layer in a flat ovenproof dish. Pour over them:

¼ cup melted butter, bacon drippings or cooking oil

Stir them about until coated. Bake them for about 30 to 40 minutes. Turn them several times during this period. Drain them on absorbent paper. Sprinkle them with:

½ teaspoon salt
¼ teaspoon paprika

POTATO PUFFS [4]

Preheat deep fryer to 385°.

Combine:

½ cup sifted flour
1 teaspoon double-acting baking powder
¼ teaspoon salt

Add and mix:

1 cup mashed potatoes

The potatoes should be soft at room temperature. If they are not, add a little hot milk or water and beat. Add:

1 slightly beaten egg
1 teaspoon minced parsley

Drop by spoonfuls into hot fat. Fry to a golden brown. Drain on absorbent paper.

BAKED POTATO WAFERS

Potatoes prepared in this way have a distinctive flavor.
Preheat oven to 375°.
Select large, well-shaped:

Potatoes

Scrub them well. Rub them with:

Butter

Cut them, without peeling, in rounds ¼ inch thick. Place them in a generously buttered skillet or baking pan, flat side down. Sprinkle them with:

Salt and white pepper

Cover and bake for 20 minutes or until they are tender. Turn the slices as they brown. Serve them, garnished with:

Minced parsley

POTATO OR SARATOGA CHIPS

➧ Please read About Deep-Fat Frying, pages 75–79.
As with Soufflé Potatoes, page 316, and French Fries, page 318, it is very important to have properly aged potatoes. Or try unpeeled sweet potatoes. Use either of these chips as a vegetable, a garnish or a cocktail snack.
Using a vegetable slicer, slice as thin as possible:

Peeled Idaho potatoes

Soak the slices for 2 hours in cold water, changing the water twice. Drain and dry well. ➧ Very slowly, heat to 380°:

Peanut or corn oil

If you want a good luster on your cooled chips, bring the cooking oil to 75° before heating it. Drop the separated slices into the hot fat in a frying basket. Shake the basket or stir the potatoes several times to prevent the chips from sticking together. Cook until they are golden. Drain and place on absorbent paper to get rid of excess fat.

POTATO BASKETS

➧ Please read About Noodle Baskets, page 173.
Preheat deep fryer to 390°.
Use a shredder to cut into long ¼-inch strips:

Peeled potatoes

Soak them for 30 minutes in ice water. Drain them well and dry them between towels. Line the larger strainer, as directed for noodle baskets. Fit the smaller strainer over it. Fry the potato basket 3 to 4 minutes. Remove from the fat and drain. Bring the fryer up to 390° again and immerse basket for 1 minute more. Drain on absorbent paper and serve at once.

DUCHESS POTATOES [4]

I. Prepare:

Riced Potatoes, page 310

Add:

¼ cup butter
2 beaten egg yolks
(A dash of mustard)
Correct the seasoning

and allow this mixture to cool briefly.
Preheat oven to 400°.
Now shape the potato mixture into flat cakes on a floured board. Place the cakes on a buttered baking sheet. Brush with:

A slightly beaten egg

Bake until golden and serve at once.

II. This version is for decorating the edges of planks or baking dishes.
Prepare:

Duchess Potatoes I, above

using:

1 egg yolk
3 to 4 tablespoons milk

Be sure there are no lumps to block the nozzle of the pastry tube or to destroy the smooth surface. Use a fluted tube to shape ruffles or wavy scallops. Brown in oven.

DAUPHINE POTATOES

If you add about 2 tablespoons of grated Gruyère cheese to each cup of potatoes called for in this recipe, you will have Potatoes **Lorette.**

➧ Please read About Deep-Fat Frying, pages 75–79.

For every cup:

Freshly Mashed Potatoes, page 311

add:

⅓ to ½ cup Pâte à Choux (II, 305)

made without sugar and seasoned with:

A grating of nutmeg

Shape the potato mixture into 1 to 1½ inch balls or fill into a pastry bag with a large plain tube. If you use the tube, shape as for Spaetzle, page 179.

Roll in:

(White dry bread crumbs)

Deep-fat fry for 3 or 4 minutes and allow the heat of the fat to increase to 370° until the potato balls are golden. Drain on absorbent paper. Add:

Salt

and serve at once.

FRIED POTATO BALLS [6]

A simpler version, not unlike Dauphine Potatoes.

➧ Please read About Deep-Fat Frying, pages 75–79.

Preheat deep fryer to 385°.

Prepare:

2 cups hot Riced Potatoes, page 310: 4 medium-sized potatoes

Add to them:

2 tablespoons butter
½ cup grated cheese
½ teaspoon salt
A few grains cayenne
2 tablespoons cream
2 beaten egg yolks
½ teaspoon any baking powder

Whip these ingredients until they are light. Shape them into balls. Roll the balls in:

Flour

then in:

1 egg, diluted and beaten with 2 tablespoons water

and in:

Sifted bread crumbs

Fry the balls in deep fat. Drain them on absorbent paper. Serve at once.

ABOUT LEFTOVER POTATOES

Not for nothing do we use the phrase "cold potato" as a disagreeable appellation. Once cold after cooking, potatoes lose their mealiness and the good, earthy flavor of a freshly cooked potato is forever gone. They are probably most frugally used ⅄ blended into or used with a soup base. If you do use them, see that the base liquid is hot before combining with the cold potato. We give the following recipes as rather sorry bargains.

LEFTOVER MASHED POTATOES

To reheat, try placing in the top of a double boiler:

Leftover mashed potatoes

Add, if necessary:

A little hot milk

Beat the mixture well with a fork. Cover and cook ➧ over—not in—hot water until thoroughly heated.

LEFTOVER BAKED POTATOES

Have ready:

2 baked potatoes, 24 hours old

Grate them on the coarsest side of a hand grater. Melt in a 10-inch skillet:

2 tablespoons cooking oil

When the oil is hot, sprinkle the potato evenly and thinly over the bottom of the pan. Cook until the entire mass can be turned as one. Before turning, dribble over the uncooked surface of the potatoes:

2 tablespoons melted butter

Now cook the second side until glazed and brown. Serve at once, garnished with:

2 tablespoons yogurt and chives

LEFTOVER GERMAN FRIED POTATOES [4]

Melt in a skillet:

2 or more tablespoons fat

Add:

2 cups cold, sliced, boiled potatoes
Salt and paprika
(1 or more teaspoons minced onion)

Sauté the potatoes slowly until they are light brown. Turn them frequently.

LEFTOVER POTATOES O'BRIEN [6]

Preheat oven to 350°.
Dice:

6 medium-sized leftover boiled potatoes

Add:

1 chopped seeded green pepper
1 chopped onion
1 tablespoon flour
Salt and pepper
A few grains cayenne
(¾ cup grated cheese)

Place these ingredients in a greased baking dish. Pour over them:

1 cup hot milk

Cover them with:

Au Gratin II, page 389

Bake them for about 30 minutes.

LEFTOVER POTATO CAKES

I. Shape into little cakes:

Leftover mashed potatoes

Add:

(A beaten egg)
(Chopped parsley)
(Chopped celery)
(Celery seed)
(Grated onion or ¼ cup chopped sautéed onions)
(A grating of nutmeg)

Dip the cakes in:

Flour, bread crumbs or crushed cornflakes

Melt in a skillet:

Butter or other fat

Brown the cakes in this on one side, reverse them and brown the other side.

II. Preheat oven to 375°.
Have ready:

2 cups leftover mashed potatoes

Roll the potatoes into balls and flatten them. Dip in:

Melted butter

Roll in:

Crushed cornflakes

Place them in a greased pan. Bake the balls until they are well heated.

LEFTOVER AU GRATIN POTATOES

Cut into dice:

Leftover boiled potatoes

Prepare:

Cream Sauce—½ as much sauce as there are potatoes, page 359

Combine the potatoes and the sauce. Add:

(Chopped parsley, minced onion or chives)

Heat these ingredients in a double boiler for 30 minutes or put them in a greased baking dish. Cover them with:

Au Gratin II, page 389

Bake them in a 400° oven until the crumbs are brown. To prepare the potatoes with cheese, omit the parsley, etc., and substitute grated cheese or place alternate layers of potatoes and cream sauce in a baking dish and sprinkle the layers with:

Grated cheese

Season with:

Paprika or a dash of cayenne

Cover top with:

Au Gratin III, page 389

Bake the potatoes, as directed.

ABOUT SWEET POTATOES OR YAMS

It was George Washington Carver who really brought attention to the many ways in which this highly nutritious tuber could increase the health of our South. Sweet potatoes, whether the light yellow, dryish Jersey types or the orangey, moist varieties affectionately called yams, are both extremely high in vitamin A. Buy only enough for immediate use as they spoil rather easily.

They lend themselves to most of the cooking methods used for potatoes, and are especially good when combined with fruits and fruit flavoring.

Six medium-sized sweet potatoes will yield about 2 cups of riced sweet potatoes. Cooked sweet potatoes lend themselves to reheating better than leftover "Irish" potatoes, page 255.

BOILED SWEET POTATOES

To cook sweet potatoes in their jackets, drop them into boiling water to cover and cook ➧ covered, until tender, about 25 minutes. They may also be pared, dropped in ¼ cup boiling water and cook ➧ uncovered, until tender, about 15 minutes. Salt before serving.

MASHED SWEET POTATOES [4]

Prepare:

6 Boiled Sweet Potatoes, above

Put them through a ricer or mash them with a potato masher. Add:

2 tablespoons butter
½ teaspoon salt
A little hot milk, cream, lemon juice or dry sherry
(2 teaspoons brown sugar)

Beat them with a fork or whisk until they are very light. Sprinkle them with:

Grated orange or lemon rind, cloves or cinnamon

Chopped dates and nut meats may be added. Good served with ham.

BAKED SWEET POTATOES

Follow the recipe for:

Baked Potatoes, page 313

➧ Be sure to cut a small slice off one end or to puncture a sweet potato when half cooked, as a safety valve to prevent its bursting.

STUFFED SWEET POTATOES [4 to 6]

Preheat oven to 375°.

I. Prepare and bake as for Baked Potatoes, page 313:

6 shapely sweet potatoes

Cut them lengthwise into halves and scrape out the pulp. Add:

2 tablespoons butter
¼ cup hot cream or ¾ cup crushed pineapple
½ teaspoon salt
(1 tablespoon dry sherry)

Southern people say "use lots of butter, some brown sugar, nutmeg and black walnut meats; and replace the sherry with 2 tablespoons bourbon whisky." Beat these ingredients with a fork until they are fluffy. Fill the shells and cover the tops with:

Au Gratin III, page 389

Marshmallows may be substituted for the bread crumbs and butter. These are a matter of taste, or lack of taste. Bake the potatoes until they are brown.

II. These make a good cold weather lunch. Bake:

Sweet potatoes

Just before serving, insert in each potato:

1 tablespoon deviled ham

CANDIED SWEET POTATOES [4]

Cook, covered, in boiling water to cover until nearly tender:

6 sweet potatoes

Preheat oven to 375°.
Pare and cut them lengthwise in ½-inch slices. Place them in a shallow greased baking dish. Season with:

Salt and paprika

Sprinkle with:

¾ cup brown sugar or ⅓ cup maple sirup
½ teaspoon grated lemon rind
1½ tablespoons lemon juice or ⅛ teaspoon ginger

Dot them with:

2 tablespoons butter

Bake them, uncovered, for about 20 minutes.

CARAMELIZED SWEET POTATOES

Slice:

4 medium-sized boiled sweet potatoes

Melt:

3 tablespoons orange marmalade or Sauce Cockaigne (II, 474)

Cook the sweet potatoes gently in the sauce until they are glazed and brown.

SAUTÉED SWEET POTATOES

Dice into a skillet:

4 medium-sized boiled or baked hot sweet potatoes

Add to them:

3 tablespoons melted butter
Grated rind and juice of 1 small orange
½ cup brown sugar
2 tablespoons chopped parsley or chives

Shake the sweet potatoes over quick heat until they are hot.

DEEP-FRIED SWEET POTATOES

➧ Please read About Deep-Fat Frying, pages 75–79.
Preheat deep fryer to 380°.
I. Wash, then parboil for 10 minutes:

Large sweet potatoes

Pare and cut them into strips. Fry the sweet potato strips in the deep fat until they are a golden brown. Drain them on absorbent paper. Sprinkle with:

Salt

➧ To flambé, just before serving, put the drained potatoes in a pan. Sprinkle over them:

2 tablespoons warm brandy, applejack or rum

Light and tilt the pan back and forth until the flame burns low.

II. Pare, then cut into ¼-inch slices:

Sweet potatoes

Deep fry them in hot fat until done. Drain them on absorbent paper. Sprinkle with:

Brown sugar
Salt
Freshly grated nutmeg

SWEET POTATO PUFFS

Preheat oven to 500°.
Have ready:

2 cups riced, cooked sweet potatoes

Peel, mash and add:

1 large ripe banana

Combine these ingredients and beat them into:

1½ tablespoons melted butter

1 egg yolk
1½ teaspoons salt
⅕ to ¼ cup hot milk or cream
(⅛ teaspoon nutmeg or ginger)

Beat until stiff:

1 egg white

Fold it lightly into the potato mixture. Drop the batter with a tablespoon in mounds—well apart—on a greased tin, or place the mixture in buttered ramekins. Bake the puffs for about 12 minutes.

SWEET POTATOES AND APPLES [4]

This tart dish is exceptionally good with roast pork, baked ham or game. Cook, covered, until nearly done in boiling water to cover:

6 medium-sized sweet potatoes

Peel and cut them into ½-inch slices. Cook, covered, until nearly done in a very little boiling water:

1½ to 2 cups thinly sliced apples

If the apples are not tart, sprinkle them with:

Lemon juice

Preheat oven to 350°.
Grease a baking dish and place in it alternate layers of sweet potatoes and apples. Sprinkle the layers with:

½ cup or more brown sugar
A dash cinnamon or grated lemon rind

Dot them with:

¼ cup butter

Pour over them:

½ cup apple water or water

Bake them for about 1 hour.

SWEET POTATOES WITH OTHER FRUITS

Follow the recipe for:

Sweet Potatoes and Apples, above

Omit the sugar and substitute for the apples:

½ cup puréed, sweetened, dried apricots (II, 96), ½ cup Sauce Cockaigne (II, 474), or ½ cup crushed pineapple

SWEET POTATOES AND ORANGE JUICE

Preheat oven to 375°.
Cook and mash:

Sweet potatoes

Allow to every cup of potatoes:

1¼ tablespoons butter
1 tablespoon brown sugar
½ teaspoon grated orange or lemon rind
3 tablespoons orange juice
½ teaspoon salt

Combine these ingredients and place them in a baking dish or in hollow orange rinds made into cups, placed in a baking pan. Sprinkle the top with:

Brown sugar
Paprika

Cover the dish or the cups closely. Bake the potatoes for 30 minutes in the dish, 15 minutes in the cups. Remove the cover and bake them until they are brown.

PURSLANE [3]

Wash well:

2 lbs. purslane

Use only the tender tips and leaves. Blanch, page 88, briefly in

Salted boiling water

Drain well. Reheat in:

2 tablespoons butter
Correct the seasoning

and serve at once.

ABOUT RADISHES

We all enjoy red and white radish garnishes and, if we've read Pepys, we know he ate them buttered at William Penn's—worth trying, too, especially with black radishes. Radishes are also good prepared as for

Celeriac Remoulade, page 43. The large Japanese radish, Daikon, and the red and white ones, if you have a plethora in your garden, are good cooked by any recipe for Turnips, pages 338–339.

To store radishes before using, cut off the leaves.

COOKED RADISHES

Peel and slice:
Radishes
Drop them into:
Boiling salted water to cover
Simmer, uncovered, about 6 to 8 minutes or until tender. Drain.
Correct the seasoning
Serve in:
Cream or Cream Sauce I, page 359

RUTABAGAS OR SWEDES [4]

These may be French fried as for Shoestring Potatoes, page 318, or baked like Potatoes, page 313.
To boil, pare and dice:
4 medium rutabagas
➧ Do not use the leaves. Drop the pieces into:
Boiling water
Cook them, uncovered, until tender, about ½ hour. Drain them well. Add:
½ teaspoon salt
Serve them with:
Melted butter
to which you have added generously:
Lemon juice
Chopped parsley
or mash the turnips and add them in any proportion to mashed potatoes with lots of:
Chopped parsley or cultured sour cream and nutmeg

ABOUT SKIRRET

Cook as for any recipe using carrots, but never peel before boiling as the flavor is lost. Be sure to remove the inner hard core before serving.

ABOUT SORREL

Rather heavy in oxalic acid, this vegetable is seldom served by itself, but is combined with spinach, chard or other greens. It lends itself to flavoring with meat glaze, eggs and cream.

Prepare as for Panned Spinach, page 326, and season with butter; or purée it and season with mustard and tarragon as a bed for fish.

ABOUT SPINACH

Forced down the throats of a generation as a source of iron, spinach is today in bad repute for its calcium-robbing activity. Perhaps we had better forget both these factors and just eat it in moderation for its true goodness. It is a special treat as a garnish with other foods, where its presence is usually heralded by the title **Florentine.**

We suggest 3 servings to the pound as the cooked amount is so variable—depending on age.

Spinach requires little salt. Its astringent taste comes from alum and iron. Never serve it in silver.

* If using frozen spinach, thaw partially before cooking.

⊙ Pressure cook spinach at 15 lbs. for 1 minute.

BOILED SPINACH [3 to 4]

Pick over and cut the roots and tough stems from:
¼ peck spinach: 1 lb.
Wash it quickly in several waters until it is free from sand and soil. If it is young and tender, cook it as for Panned Spinach, page 326. If old, place the spinach in:
2 cups rapidly boiling water
➧ Reduce heat and simmer, cov-

ered, until tender, for about 20 minutes. Discard the water if it is strong in flavor. If not, keep it for use in soups and sauces. Drain the spinach well. ⅄ Blend briefly or cut up the spinach with 2 sharp knives or a triple chopper until it is as fine as you like it. Sauté:

2 tablespoons diced sweet red pepper, 2 tablespoons minced onion or a clove of garlic

in:

Butter or drippings

Add:

Lemon juice
Correct the seasoning

➧ being careful not to over salt. Serve the seasonings over the spinach. Other garnishes for spinach include:

Hard-boiled egg
Crumbled bacon
Fine buttered croutons
Hollandaise Sauce, page 369
Au Gratin III, page 349

CREAMED SPINACH [3]

Prepare:

2 cups Boiled Spinach, above

⅄ Blend, rice or chop it until it is a fine purée. Melt in a skillet which may be rubbed lightly with a clove of garlic:

1½ to 2 tablespoons butter

Add and cook for 1 minute or, if preferred, until golden:

(1 tablespoon or more very finely chopped onion)

Stir in, until blended:

1 tablespoon flour or 2 tablespoons browned flour

Stir in slowly:

½ cup hot cream, top milk or stock
1 teaspoon sugar

When the sauce is smooth and hot, add the spinach. Stir and cook it for 3 minutes. Season it well with:

Salt and pepper
(Freshly grated nutmeg or grated rind of ½ lemon)

Serve it garnished with slices of:

1 hard-cooked egg

PANNED OR SICILIAN SPINACH [3]

The seasonings in this dish are also good used with canned spinach.

Wash well and remove the coarse stems from:

1 lb. spinach

Shake off as much water as possible. Heat in a large, heavy skillet:

1 tablespoon butter
2 tablespoons olive oil

Add:

(1 clove minced garlic)

Add the spinach. Cover at once and cook over high heat until steam appears. ➧ Reduce the heat and simmer until tender, 5 to 6 minutes in all.

Correct the seasoning

To turn this into Sicilian Spinach, add:

(2 or more chopped anchovies)

SPINACH WITH TOMATOES [4]

Cook:

1 lb. spinach

Drain and ⅄ blend or chop fine. Add:

6 or 8 oz. Italian tomato paste or tomato purée

Sauté:

1 pressed clove garlic or 3 tablespoons minced onion

in:

3 or 4 tablespoons olive oil

Add the spinach mixture and

Correct the seasoning

SPINACH, TOMATO AND CHEESE LOAF [8]

Preheat oven to 350°.

Place in a bowl:

2 cups cooked, drained spinach
2¼ cups canned tomatoes
¼ cup chili sauce
½ lb. grated cheese
1 cup cracker crumbs
Juice of ½ onion
¼ teaspoon salt
¼ teaspoon freshly ground pepper

Toss these ingredients until they are blended. Place them in a greased loaf pan. Bake the dish for about 1 hour. Serve it garnished with:

Crisp Bacon, page 491

SPINACH IN PANCAKES

Prepare:

Creamed Spinach, page 326

Prepare:

French Pancakes (II, 113)
Chopped Sautéed Mushrooms, page 296

Place the spinach and mushrooms on the pancakes. Roll them like a jelly roll. The tops may be sprinkled with:

Grated cheese

Place the rolls under a broiler until the cheese is melted. Serve at once.

⅄ BLENDER SPINACH [3]

Cook and drain:

Boiled Spinach, page 325

Put it very briefly through a blender. Stir into it:

¼ cup cultured sour cream or condensed cream of chicken soup
A grinding of nutmeg or ⅛ teaspoon prepared mustard
(1 teaspoon horseradish)
Correct the seasoning

Heat briefly and serve.

GROUND SPINACH [3]

Cooked in this way, spinach seems to retain all its flavor.

Wash:

1 lb. spinach

Drain it well. Shortly before you are ready to serve the spinach, run it through a food chopper with:

1 small onion

Reserve the juices. Place it in a saucepan with the juices and:

½ teaspoon sugar

Cover and cook it slowly for 3 minutes. Add before serving:

1½ to 2 tablespoons butter
(2 teaspoons lemon juice)
Correct the seasoning

ABOUT SQUASHES

Perhaps no other vegetable has so wide a tolerance of growing conditions. You will quickly know after cooking if the variety you have is cultivated, for the wild ones are very bitter. Cross-pollination from wild species grown in subtropical climates may explain the occasional bitterness you find in squash from the market.

These plants divide into summer and winter types. We often call for special varieties of each type in the recipes which follow; but others may be substituted, as long as they belong to the respective type.

SUMMER SQUASHES OR CYMLINGS

Whether green, yellow, white, long, round or scalloped, these are all thin-skinned and easily punctured with a fingernail—the classic marketer's gesture and the grocer's despair. They should be firm and heavy. Avoid them if the rind is tough or the stem dry or black. If they are young, there is no need to pare nor to discard the seeds. If only hard-rinded ones are available, do both. Summer squash do not store well.

You may have your favorites. Ours are undoubtedly zucchini or the closely related cocozelle.

Remember these squash may also be prepared by recipes for cucumber and eggplant. As shown above, from left to right, they are **straight neck, crooked neck, cymling, cocozelle** and **zucchini.**

WINTER SQUASHES

These are of many colors and shapes and remain on the market from fall to early spring. Except for butternut, they have hard-shelled skins. Choose the others for their hard rinds. Avoid winter squash with watery spots which indicate decay. The winter types sketched from left to right below, are **Golden Delicious, acorn, buttercup** or **turban, butternut** and **Hubbard.** For ways to cook pumpkin, the most famous winter squash, see (II, 319). Unless you bake them whole, remove the seeds and stringy portions. Peel and cut into small pieces. They need from 10 to 45 minutes of cooking.

Because squash is so bland in flavor, it can stand a good deal of "doctoring" and is ideal for stuffing. Cut small squash into boats and fill. ➧ To stuff a whole squash cut off the ends, core the center and, after stuffing, secure the ends with toothpick closures. For fillings, see Farces, page 564.

If it is a tender summer type, you may combine the removed portion with the farce, which may include vegetables, bread crumbs, nuts, mushrooms or cooked meat.

STEAMED SUMMER SQUASH [4]

➧ Please read About Squashes, page 327.

I. Wash and cut into small pieces:

2 cups any summer squash: zucchini, yellow crooked neck, etc.

If very tender, the squash may even be left whole. Steam it, covered, in a strainer over boiling water until it is tender. Drain it very well. Sprinkle it generously with:

Grated Parmesan cheese and melted butter

II. Prepare the squash as above, then mash it with a fork. Beat it until it is fluffy. Beat in:

1 tablespoon cream

1 tablespoon butter or olive oil
1/8 teaspoon pepper
(1 teaspoon grated onion or chopped fresh herb or a touch of saffron)

Reheat the squash briefly and serve.

STUFFED SQUASH BLOSSOMS

Do you wonder why so many of your squash blossoms fall off without maturing? These are male blooms and after they close and drop make decorative, as well as edible, cases for Forcemeat, see page 564. Open each flower and put in only enough of the forcemeat to allow the petals to close again. Place stuffed blossoms side by side in a greased baking dish, in a moderate oven, until thoroughly heated. Serve them alone or as a platter garnish.

BAKED SUMMER SQUASH [4]

➧ Please read About Squashes, page 327.

Preheat oven to 350°.

If summer squash is young, it need not be pared. Cut into strips:

3 cups any summer squash

Place in a greased baking dish. Dot with:

2 tablespoons butter

Sprinkle with:

1 teaspoon salt
1/4 teaspoon paprika
(A grating of nutmeg or 1 teaspoon fresh lemon thyme)

Pour over it:

1/4 cup milk
(1 teaspoon grated onion)

Cover the dish. Bake the squash for about 1/2 hour or until it is tender. Garnish with:

Crisp crumbled bacon

SAUTÉED SUMMER SQUASH [4]

➧ Please read About Squashes, page 327.

Wash and cut into dice:

2 cups any summer squash

Melt in a saucepan:

3 tablespoons butter or olive oil

Add and sauté until golden:

1 cup minced onion

Add the squash and:

1/2 teaspoon salt
1/4 teaspoon freshly ground white pepper

Cover the pan and cook the squash until tender, for about 10 minutes, shaking the pan occasionally to keep from sticking. Serve it sprinkled with:

Chopped parsley or basil
Grated Parmesan cheese
or Tomato Sauce, page 376

STUFFED COOKED SUMMER SQUASH

I. [4]

➧ Please read About Squashes, page 327.

Wash thoroughly, then cut the stem ends from:

4 small summer squashes

Steam them as for Steamed Summer Squash, but leave them whole. When almost tender, drain the squashes, cool them. Scoop out the centers, leaving a shell about 1/2 inch thick. Chop the removed pulp. Add to it:

1/4 teaspoon paprika
1/2 teaspoon Worcestershire sauce
Minced garlic or onion
1/4 teaspoon salt
1 tablespoon butter
3 tablespoons dry bread crumbs
1/4 cup grated cheese
A few grains cayenne
1/8 teaspoon curry powder or dry mustard

Preheat oven to 400°.

Refill the shells. Place them in a pan, in a very little water or on a rack above the water. Bake until hot, about 10 minutes.

II. Or fill these cooked squash cases while hot with:

Heated creamed chicken, ham, fish or spinach

Garnish with:

Parsley or tiny sprigs of lemon thyme

STUFFED RAW SUMMER SQUASH [4]

▶ Please read About Squashes, page 327.
Preheat oven to 350°.
Wash:

4 small squashes

Cut them down the middle, either crosswise or horizontally. Scoop out the pulp, leaving a ½-inch shell. Combine the squash pulp and:

2 tablespoons chopped sautéed onions
½ cup grated cheese
½ teaspoon salt
¼ teaspoon paprika
A dash of nutmeg or cloves

Stir and cook these ingredients until hot. Remove from the heat. Add:

1 beaten egg
½ cup dry bread crumbs

You may rub the squash shells with:

Butter or drippings

Fill them with the stuffing. Place them in an ovenproof dish. Cover the bottom with ⅛ inch water or stock. Sprinkle the tops with:

Au Gratin II, page 389

Bake the squashes until tender, about 20 to 25 minutes, depending on their size.

SUMMER SQUASH CREOLE

▶ Please read About Squashes, page 327.
Have ready:

2½ cups well-drained, cooked zucchini, yellow crooked neck, etc. summer squash

Place it in a greased baking dish and proceed as for:

Stuffed Eggplant Creole, page 292

substituting the squash for the eggplant.

DEEP FRIED ZUCCHINI

▶ Please read About Deep-Fat Frying, pages 75–79, and About Squashes, page 327.
Preheat deep fryer to 365°.
Wash, dry and slice into ¼- to ½-inch slices:

Zucchini

Dry it well. Dip it in:

Fritter Batter for Vegetables (II, 125)

Fry it in deep fat until golden. Serve at once.

SUMMER SQUASH CASSEROLE COCKAIGNE [4]

We are particularly fond of zucchini in this dish.
▶ Please read About Squashes, page 327.
Cut into small pieces:

3 cups summer squash

Simmer the squash, covered, until tender, for about 6 to 8 minutes, in a small amount of boiling water. Shake the pan to keep from sticking. Drain well. Combine:

¼ cup cultured sour cream
1 tablespoon butter
1 tablespoon grated cheese
½ teaspoon salt
⅛ teaspoon paprika

Stir this mixture over low heat until the cheese is melted. Remove it from the heat. Stir in:

1 beaten egg yolk
1 tablespoon chopped chives

Add the squash. Place the mixture in a baking dish. Cover the top with:

Au Gratin III, page 389

Brown it in a heated 375° oven.

BAKED WINTER SQUASH

➧ Please read About Squashes, page 327.

Preheat oven to 375°.

If the squash is small, like:

Acorn or butternut squash

it may be washed, dried, greased and treated just like Baked Potatoes, page 313. Bake at least 1 to 1½ hours. The smaller baked winter squashes make attractive cases for:

Creamed spinach, ham, etc., or buttered vegetables

Serve garnished with:

(Pimiento strips or Au Gratin, page 389)

MASHED WINTER SQUASH

➧ Please read About Squashes, page 327.

I.

Preheat oven to 375°.

Scrub:

A 3 to 4 lb. Hubbard or other winter squash

Place it on a rack and bake it until it can be pierced easily with a toothpick. Cut it in halves, remove the seeds. Peel the squash and mash the pulp. To:

1 cup squash

add:

1 tablespoon butter
1 teaspoon brown sugar
¼ teaspoon salt
⅛ teaspoon ginger

Beat this well, with enough:

Warm cream or orange juice

to make it a good consistency. Place it in a serving dish. Sprinkle it with:

Raisins or nut meats
¼ cup crushed pineapple

II. ✲ If using frozen or canned squash, season with:

Sautéed onions
Cultured sour cream
A pinch allspice
Chopped parsley

Heat it in a double boiler.

STUFFED WINTER SQUASH

Small acorn or butternut squash are ideal for individual service. You may fill the raw shell as in I or make it first, as in Baked Winter Squash, and then fill it with the hot, creamed foods suggested below.

➧ Please read About Stuffed Vegetables, page 256, and About Squashes, page 327.

I. Preheat oven to 375°.

Prepare uncooked:

Acorn squash cases

by washing, cutting the squash in half lengthwise and scooping out the seeds. Fill them with:

Sausage meat or Ham à la King, page 220

Bake them for about 1 hour.

II. Prepare cooked:

Acorn squash cases, see above

Fill them with:

Creamed oysters, chicken, chipped beef, crab, fish, mushrooms, hash, hash and vegetables, hot applesauce or crushed pineapple

Garnish the tops with:

Parsley

Reheat for 10 to 15 minutes in a 350° oven.

ABOUT PUMPKIN

We think of this squash first as pie (II, 319), and next as soup, but it is also good as a vegetable. Cook by any recipe calling for a winter squash. About ½ lb. will serve 1 person.

ABOUT TOMATOES

Really a fruit, beautifully colored and unsurpassed for flavoring, tomatoes, like lemons, are one of the most satisfactory things to have on hand fresh or canned—also in the form of juice, purée, paste, catsup or chili sauce. Since they are an acid fruit and often home grown, they can be easily home processed (II, 537). Try growing the more meaty pear-shaped Italian varieties, which are both sweeter and sharper than American types.

To use fresh tomatoes in cooking where their juiciness is sometimes not an asset, slit the stem end and remove it. Holding your hand palm down above a bowl, press the tomato tightly in the palm to eject excess juice and seeds. To skin tomatoes, see pages 48 and (II, 537).

When the recipes call for strained, canned tomatoes, watch for 2 things: Be sure to force the pulp through the sieve well, so you make the most of its thickening and seasoning powers; also watch your brands: the cheaper ones are often watery.

We cannot leave this eulogy without comment on the high vitamin C and A values of tomatoes. To retain them and the best color ➧ store in good light, not sunlight, unwrapped, between 65° and 75°. If you have any choice in the matter, do not pick until they have reached their full size. Ripened 5 to 6 days off the vine, unless overripe, they retain good vitamin values. Once ripe, store refrigerated. ➧ Immature green tomatoes will not ripen off the vine, so use at once for pickles. To retain food value, prepare tomatoes just before using.

Prepare them stuffed, not only for Salads, page 48, but as cases for other Vegetables, page 256.

STEWED TOMATOES [4]

Wash and skin (II, 537):

6 large quartered tomatoes
or 2½ cups canned tomatoes

Place them in a heavy pan over slow heat, about 20 minutes for the fresh tomatoes—10 for the canned. You may add:

(1 teaspoon minced onion)
(½ cup chopped celery)
(2 or 3 cloves)

Stir them occasionally to keep them from scorching. Season them with:

¾ teaspoon salt
¼ teaspoon paprika
2 teaspoons white or brown sugar
⅛ teaspoon curry powder or 1 teaspoon chopped parsley or basil
1 tablespoon butter

Tomatoes may be thickened with:

(½ cup bread crumbs)

STEWED GREEN TOMATOES [4]

Sauté until light brown:

2 tablespoons minced onion

in:

2 tablespoons butter

Add:

2 cups sliced green tomatoes

Stir and cook the tomatoes slowly until they are tender. Season with:

¾ teaspoon salt
¼ teaspoon paprika
½ teaspoon curry powder

Garnish the tomatoes with:

1 tablespoon chopped parsley

SEASONED SAUTÉED TOMATOES [4]

This recipe is much like the preceding one, but it may be useful when broiling or baking is out of the question. Wash:

6 firm, medium-sized, red or green tomatoes

Slice them in ¼-inch slices. Bread them with:

Seasoned Flour (II, 160)

Rub a skillet with garlic. Melt in it:

3 tablespoons butter or bacon drippings

Add the tomato slices. Sauté them gently on both sides. Place the tomatoes on:

Rounds of toast or squares of corn bread

Blend the butter and crumbs left in the skillet with:

¾ cup cream
1 teaspoon chopped fresh basil or chopped parsley

When the sauce is smooth and hot ➧ but not boiling, pour it over the tomatoes.

CREAMED CANNED TOMATOES [4]

Simmer gently for about 10 minutes:

2 cups canned tomatoes
2 tablespoons minced onion
¾ teaspoon salt
¼ teaspoon paprika
2 teaspoons brown sugar
(½ cup chopped celery)

Combine until smooth and bring just to a boil:

1 tablespoon flour
½ cup cream or milk

If you use the milk, add 2 tablespoons of butter to the tomato mixture. Add the tomato mixture slowly to the cream or milk. ➧ To avoid curdling, be careful not to reverse the process, and stir constantly over very low heat until the raw-flour taste is gone, about 3 to 5 minutes.

BAKED TOMATOES [4]

Preheat oven to 400°.
Cut deep, narrow holes in:

6 firm tomatoes

Season them—pushing the seasoning into the hollows—with:

3 tablespoons brown sugar
1½ teaspoons salt
2 tablespoons butter

Fill the remaining space with:

(¼ cup Au Gratin II, page 389)

Place the tomatoes in a well-buttered shallow baking dish on a rack or in greased muffin tins. Bake them for about 15 minutes. You may top each tomato with:

Crisp crumbled bacon

TOMATO PROVENCALE

This garnish looks very professional if you have a broiler and an oven you can use in quick succession. Choose:

Firm ripe tomatoes

Slice off a deep enough section horizontally on the stem end to get an even surface. Do the same on the base. Divide the remaining tomato horizontally. Place these thick slices on a rack to drain. Sprinkle on top of each:

Salt and black pepper
Sweet basil
A slight pinch of orégano

Melt enough:

Butter

to coat the tomato slices. Place in the butter

A split clove of garlic

Or, as an alternative to the butter, squeeze a little garlic on a thin square of:

(Parmesan cheese)

that will almost cover the tomato slice. Allow the seasoned tomatoes to remain at 70° for 1 hour.
Preheat broiler and preheat oven to 350°
Put the slices on a greased baking sheet. Run them under a broiler first to brown slightly and then bake them for 15 minutes. Serve at once.

GRILLED TOMATOES [4]

Preheat broiler.
Wash:

4 large, firm tomatoes

Cut them crosswise into even ½-inch slices. Season them well with:

1 teaspoon salt
¼ teaspoon pepper
White or brown sugar
(Celery salt)

Place in a greased pan and cover them closely with:

About 1 cup Au Gratin III, page 389
(2 tablespoons or more grated onion)

Broil them for about 10 minutes ➧ about 5 inches from the heat source.

BROILED BREADED TOMATOES

Preheat oven to 375°.
Wash and cut a piece off the stem end horizontally, so the surface is even, and cut another off the base of:

Tomatoes

Cut them in half, crosswise and sprinkle the halves with:

Salt and pepper
(Brown sugar)

Dip them in:

Bound Breading III (II, 160)

Bake them on a greased sheet until they are nearly soft, then broil them under moderate heat, turning them once, until they are brown.

CANDIED TOMATOES [4]

Melt:

2 tablespoons butter

Sauté in the butter until brown:

¼ cup chopped onion

Add:

1 quart canned tomatoes
6 tablespoons brown sugar

Cook these ingredients very slowly, using an asbestos mat, until the juice has been absorbed. Place the tomatoes in a baking dish. Sprinkle them with:

¾ teaspoon salt
2 tablespoons brown sugar
1½ cups buttered bread crumbs

Bake them in a 375° oven until the crumbs are brown.

TOMATOES CREOLE [4]

In contrast to the above, a very good quickie!
Melt in a saucepan:

2 tablespoons butter

Add:

4 large, skinned, sliced, tomatoes or 1½ cups canned tomatoes
1 large minced onion
2 tablespoons minced celery
(1 shredded green pepper)

Cook the vegetables until they are tender, about 12 minutes.
Add:

¾ teaspoon salt
¼ teaspoon paprika
2½ teaspoons brown sugar
(¾ teaspoon curry powder)

Strain the juice from the vegetables and add to it enough:

Cream

to make 1½ cups of liquid. Stir in:

1½ teaspoons flour

Simmer and stir the sauce until it is thick and smooth. Combine it with the vegetables and serve them hot on:

Toast

with:

Sautéed bacon

Or use to fill pepper or squash cases.

TOMATO OLIVE CASSEROLE [3]

If you have any prejudice against tapioca, please dismiss it long enough to try out this fine dish. Serve it with ham, scrambled eggs, omelet, etc.
Preheat oven to 350°.
Heat and ➧ strain well, discarding the seeds:

1½ cups canned tomatoes

Melt in the top of a double boiler:

1 tablespoon butter

Add and sauté until golden:

¼ cup minced onion or 1 pressed clove garlic

Add the strained tomato and:

3 tablespoons quick-cooking tapioca
½ teaspoon salt
½ teaspoon sugar
⅛ teaspoon paprika

Cook and stir these ingredients in a double boiler ➧ over—not in—hot water for about 7 minutes. Chop coarsely:

18 stuffed or ripe olives

Grease a baking dish. Fill it with alternate layers of tomato mixture and olives. Sprinkle the layers with:

(½ cup grated cheese)

Cover the top with:

Au Gratin I, page 389

Bake the dish for about 30 minutes.

TOMATO CUSTARD [6]

Preheat oven to 325°.
Skin and squeeze well, page 331, to rid them of excess liquid and seeds and put through a coarse sieve:

Enough tomatoes to make 2 cups

Beat together with:

3 eggs
1 cup milk
¼ to ½ cup sugar
½ teaspoon salt
⅛ teaspoon nutmeg

Bake in custard cups for about 30 minutes or until set. Serve hot or cold.

TOMATO PUDDING COCKAIGNE

Either of these recipes should serve 6, but we find the demand for this favorite makes 4 servings a safer count.

I. Preheat oven to 375°.
In winter, place in a saucepan:

1¼ cups tomato purée
¼ cup boiling water

Heat to the boiling point and add:

¼ teaspoon salt
6 tablespoons brown sugar
½ teaspoon dried basil

Place in a 9-inch baking dish:

1 cup fresh white bread crumbs (II, 159)

Pour over them:

¼ cup melted butter

Add the tomato mixture and:

(2 tablespoons chopped stuffed olives)

➧ Cover the dish closely. Bake the pudding about 30 minutes. Do not lift the lid until ready to serve.

II. Preheat oven to 325°.
In summer, substitute for the dried basil:

1½ to 2 teaspoons fresh chopped basil
1 teaspoon chopped chives
1 teaspoon chopped parsley

and for the tomato purée and water, substitute:

14 skinned, seeded, sliced tomatoes

Bake the dish for 2½ to 3 hours until it has cooked down to a pastelike consistency.

TOMATO TART [6]

Have ready:

6 baked 2-inch Tart Shells (II, 296)

Prepare a filling of:

¾ cup tomato purée
¾ cup Cream Sauce III, page 359
3 tablespoons sautéed chopped onions
½ cup sautéed chopped chicken livers
2 tablespoons chopped stuffed olives

Just before serving, preheat the oven to 400°. Fill the tarts and bake until thoroughly heated. Serve at once.

ABOUT HOT STUFFED TOMATOES

➧ Please read About Stuffed Vegetables, page 256.
To prepare cases for hot food, cut large hollows in very firm unpeeled tomatoes. Salt them

and invert them on a rack to drain for about 15 minutes. Fill the tomato cases with any of the following cooked foods and cover the tops with:

Au Gratin I, II, or III, page 389

Place the tomato cases in a pan with enough water to keep them from scorching and bake them in a preheated 350° oven for 10 or 15 minutes. If they are too soft to hold their shape, bake them in well-greased muffin tins. For fillings, try:

Creamed ham or sausage and mushrooms
Bread crumbs and deviled ham
Chestnuts and rice or wild rice, seasoned with salt and brown sugar
Creamed green peas, parsley or mushrooms
Mashed potatoes and nuts
Creamed Spinach, or Florentine

Or see Farces, page 564, Fillings for Vegetable Cases, page 48; or use one of the following recipes.

TOMATOES STUFFED WITH PINEAPPLE [4]

➧ Please read About Stuffed Tomatoes, above.
Preheat oven to 350°.
Prepare:

4 medium-sized tomato cases

Sprinkle each hollow with:

1 teaspoon brown sugar

Place in each hollow some of the following mixture:

1 tablespoon chili sauce
1 cup drained crushed pineapple
2 tablespoons dry bread crumbs

Sprinkle the tops with:

Au Gratin II, page 389

Bake, as directed above and serve on:

Toast rounds

TOMATOES STUFFED WITH CORN [4]

➧ Please read About Stuffed Tomatoes, page 335.
Preheat oven to 350°.
Prepare:

4 tomato cases

Sauté, then mince:

4 slices bacon

Combine:

1 cup cooked, drained corn
1 chopped pimiento
½ chopped green pepper
2 tablespoons chopped celery
½ cup bread crumbs
2 tablespoons corn liquor or cream
½ teaspoon salt
¼ teaspoon paprika
½ teaspoon sugar, if the corn is green

Add the minced bacon. Fill the tomato cases. Sprinkle the tops with:

Au Gratin I or III, page 389

Bake as directed above.

TOMATOES FILLED WITH ONIONS [6]

➧ Please read About Stuffed Tomatoes, page 335.
Preheat oven to 350°.
Prepare:

6 tomato cases

Melt:

2 tablespoons bacon drippings or butter

Add and sauté until golden:

½ cup finely chopped onion

Chop the pulp taken from the tomatoes and combine it with the onions. Add:

1½ teaspoons brown sugar
½ teaspoon salt
1 tablespoon celery seed

Simmer these ingredients for about 10 minutes. If the filling is too moist, it may be thickened with:

(Bread crumbs)

If it is too dry, it may be moistened with:

Cream or milk

Fill the tomato cases. Cover the tops with:

Au Gratin II or III, page 389

Bake them, as directed above.

TOMATOES STUFFED WITH BREAD CRUMBS AND ANCHOVIES [6]

➧ Please read About Stuffed Tomatoes, page 335.
Preheat oven to 350°.
Prepare:

6 medium-sized tomato cases

Season the cases with:

3 tablespoons brown sugar

Chop the pulp taken from the tomatoes. Combine it with an equal amount of:

Soft bread crumbs

add:

2 tablespoons sautéed chopped onion
2 tablespoons sautéed chopped pepper
4 chopped anchovies

Taste before

Correcting the seasoning

as anchovies are salty. Fill the tomato cases. Bake, as directed above.

TOMATOES STUFFED WITH CREAMED SWEETBREADS [6]

➧ Please read About Stuffed Tomatoes, page 335.
Prepare:

6 tomato cases

Sauté:

¼ lb. Mushrooms, page 296

Cook:

¼ lb. Sweetbreads, page 537

The mushrooms and sweetbread proportions may be varied. Cook by the recipe on page 389:

Cream Sauce I—as much as there are mushrooms and sweetbreads combined

Add the other ingredients to the boiling cream sauce. Thicken them with:

(¼ cup bread crumbs)

Preheat oven to 350°.
Fill the tomato cases. Cover the tops with:

Au Gratin II or III, page 389

Bake them, as directed above.

TOMATOES STUFFED WITH CRAB MEAT [6]

➧ Please read About Stuffed Tomatoes, page 335.
Preheat oven to 350°.
Prepare:

6 tomato cases

Melt over low heat:

1½ tablespoons butter

Add and cook for 3 minutes:

3 tablespoons minced green pepper
3 tablespoons minced onion

Stir in, until blended:

1½ tablespoons flour

Stir in slowly:

1½ cups milk

When sauce is thick and hot, add:

1½ cups crab meat
⅓ teaspoon salt
A few grains red pepper
2 teaspoons Worcestershire sauce
1 cup grated American cheese

Simmer and stir these ingredients until the cheese is melted. Fill the tomato cases with this mixture. Bake, as directed above.

TOMATOES STUFFED WITH SHRIMP [6]

➧ Please read About Stuffed Tomatoes, page 335.
Preheat oven to 350°.
Prepare:

6 tomato cases

Chop the tomato pulp removed from the centers. Melt:

1 tablespoon butter

Sauté in it for 2 minutes:

2 tablespoons finely chopped onion

Add the tomato pulp and:

1 cup chopped, cooked or canned shrimp

Stir in:

1 tablespoon chopped parsley
3 tablespoons crushed cracker crumbs
Paprika and salt, if needed

Fill the tomatoes with this mixture. Dust the tops with:

Au Gratin I or II, page 389

Bake them, as directed in the 2 previous recipes.

ABOUT TURNIPS

A turnip is not necessarily a depressant, as so many people seem to feel. Children often enjoy them well-washed and raw, like apples; and the knowing choose them as an accompaniment to game They make a good change, if browned, to serve instead of potatoes around a roast, page 258. A favorite peasanty dish, **Himmel und Erde**, is made of mashed turnips, potatoes and seasoned apples, combined in any proportion.

Discard woody turnips and parblanch old ones for 3 to 5 minutes before cooking. ➧ One pound turnips will yield about 3½ cups sliced and 2½ cups cooked.

Cut off the tops at once and store in a dark cool place. The tops, if tender, may be used as greens, page 293

✪ Pressure cook turnips at 15 lbs. for 5 minutes.

COOKED TURNIPS [4]

I. If young, wash, pare and place in a steamer:

1 lb. sliced young turnips

Steam, page 252, for 20 to 30 minutes. Drain.

Correct the seasoning

and dress with:

Butter
Lemon juice and vinegar

or mash or cream as for Potatoes, page 311.

II. If old, you may parblanch, page 88, 3 to 5 minutes:

Sliced or whole turnips

Drop them into rapidly boiling water to cover. Add:

½ teaspoon salt
½ teaspoon sugar

Cook, uncovered, 15 to 20 minutes if sliced, 20 to 25 minutes if whole or until tender. Proceed as for I.

SCALLOPED TURNIPS

Prepare:

Scalloped Potatoes, page 312

substituting just turnips or turnips and sliced onions for the potatoes.

GLAZED TURNIPS

Cook as directed previously:

Young turnips

Drain and dry them well. Brown them in:

Hot melted butter

Season them with:

Paprika and sugar

The sugar helps with the browning. Use Meat Glaze (II, 145), or dissolve in a little boiling water:

A beef cube

Pour it over the turnips.

Correct the seasoning

Serve them at once, rolled in:

Chopped parsley

STUFFED TURNIP CUPS [8]

◆ Please read About Stuffed Vegetables, page 256.
Preheat oven to 350°.
I. Pare, then blanch, page 88, for 3 to 5 minutes:

8 medium-sized turnips

Hollow into cups, reserving and chopping the pulp. Melt:

1 tablespoon butter

Sauté in it for about 3 minutes:

1 tablespoon grated onion
2 tablespoons cooked, seasoned peas

You may use the peas alone, omitting the onion. Combine the pulp with the onion and peas. Season with:

Salt and pepper

Thicken it slightly with:

Cracker crumbs or bread crumbs

Fill the turnip cups with this mixture. Place them in a greased baking dish. Combine and pour around them:

½ cup milk
⅛ teaspoon salt

Bake until tender, about 15 minutes.

II. Proceed as above, using a filling of leftover sauced foods, a cooked Farce, page 564, or creamed peas.

ABOUT WATER CRESS

Usually thought of only as salad and sandwich material, water cress not only adds greatly in flavoring soups and vegetables but is good cooked with other greens or by itself. Prepare as for Creamed Spinach, page 326. Serve with grills or chops.

WATER CHESTNUTS

Please read About Water Chestnuts (II, 188).
These crisp vegetables are added usually as a garnish to other vegetables.
◆ Add for the last 2 or 3 minutes of cooking only.

SALAD DRESSINGS, SAUCES, GRAVIES, MARINADES, GLAZES AND SEASONED BUTTERS

ABOUT COLD SAUCES AND DRESSINGS

Some dressings seem designed to turn a salad into a costume piece. To demonstrate how welcome a switch to simplicity can be—after more elaborate recipes—follow our instructions for Tossed Salad, page 33. This dressing consists of nothing whatever but oil and vinegar, both of first quality, plus a sprinkling of salt. Good salad dressings should complement—never repeat—the salad ingredients they grace.

A word to dieters: while a salad is an unimpeachable slenderizer, a salad dressing most definitely is not. The fat content in commercial French dressings may be 35% and generally goes up to 40%; commercial mayonnaise must, by law, consist of 65% fat; and these amounts are almost always exceeded in their homemade counterparts. If you diet, then, be a spendthrift with the greenstuff, a miser with dressing. To help along, we have included in this section some low calorie formulas. The recipes given later may inspire you to make spiced or herb vinegars in quantity; also to add to individual bottles of salad dressing that certain something which gives them a personalized appeal. ➧ Store refrigerated, in closed containers, all egg-based dressings like mayonnaise. Please read About Salads, page 30, About Oil (II, 173) and Vinegar (II, 150). For heavier dressings, see Dips (II, 83).

ABOUT SAUCE TOOLS

Handy-size simple tools hanging above the cooking area encourage the addition of interesting ingredients to sauces. ➧ The 3 hand-beaters, sketched on the left, make lumps vanish. The third from the left is particularly useful for beating an egg in a cup. For that little grating of cheese, onion or bread crumbs, try the rotary grater shown next. Kitchen shears with a self-releasing hinge are easy to keep clean and unrusted. Use them to snip herbs quickly, right into the sauce.

A garlic press, center, will squeeze enough juice to give an ineffable flavor to your sauces, and the hand grater is good for a shaving of lemon rind or nutmeg. Also have ready a bar-type strainer for the quick clearing of very small quantities of sauce. For larger ones, use a Chinese hat or conical strainer, shown on page 145, and for very careful straining, line this with muslin.

By all means have some very hard wooden spoons for delicate sauces which may be broken

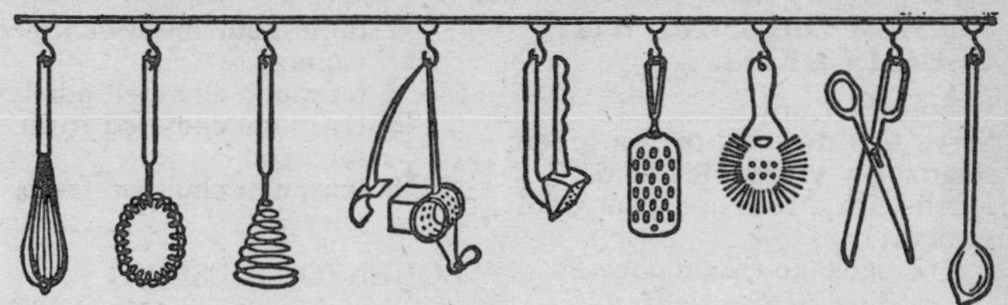

down by the more vigorous metal tools. A sauce spoon with one pointed end will scrape the pan edges clean easily and help avoid lumping. If you should use a metal spoon, make sure it is stainless steel, so as not to discolor a delicate sauce.

➧ If the recipe calls for beating over ice, please see illustration, page 180.

Electric beaters and ⅄ blenders are great labor-savers in the kitchen and will beat out lumps very quickly. They do, however, change the texture and flavor of the sauce as they whip in a great deal of air and will make a thickened sauce foamy and less tasty and a brown sauce much lighter in color.

OIL DRESSING

Pour the following over salad greens:

½ cup olive oil
1 clove garlic
½ teaspoon salt

Before serving, grate over greens:

Fresh lemon peel

FRENCH DRESSING OR SAUCE VINAIGRETTE

[About ½ Cup]

The dressing is best made just before use and can become part of the salad-making if you like. See Tossed Salad, page 33. The classic proportions are 3 to 4 parts of oil to one part lemon juice, lime juice or vinegar, and salt and pepper to taste. Many other condiments may be added, including Worcestershire sauce, chili sauce, chutney, Roquefort cheese, spices, sweet and sour cream and, of course, herbs and garlic. The garlic clove should be removed after 24 hours if the dressing is to be stored refrigerated. ➧ Fresh herbs should be added only when the sauce is to be used at once, because they become strong and unpleasant if left in the oil for any length of time.

Combine in a small bowl:

¼ teaspoon salt
¼ teaspoon pepper
1 tablespoon olive oil
1 tablespoon vinegar or lemon juice
(¼ teaspoon dry mustard)

Beat these ingredients well with a wire whisk or a fork until they are smooth. Add:

2 tablespoons olive oil

Beat well again. Add:

1 tablespoon vinegar or lemon juice
3 tablespoons olive oil

Peel and add:

(1 clove garlic)

Place the dressing in a jar, cover it well. Put it in a cold place ready for use. Shake well before using.

FRENCH FRUIT-SALAD DRESSING

[About ⅔ Cup]

Prepare:

½ cup French dressing

Substitute for the vinegar:

3 tablespoons grapefruit or lemon juice

FRENCH DRESSING WITH CREAM CHEESE

[About ⅞ Cup]
Serve this dressing over a green salad or a vegetable salad.
Mash with a fork and beat until smooth:

1 package cream cheese: 3 oz.

Beat in:

1 teaspoon finely minced onion
½ teaspoon dry mustard
1 teaspoon salt
Freshly ground black pepper
2 tablespoons chopped parsley

Beat in gradually:

¼ cup salad oil
1½ tablespoons vinegar

AVOCADO DRESSING

I. [About ¾ Cup]
Good on sliced tomatoes.
Peel and mash:

½ avocado

Add gradually:

½ cup French dressing

and beat until smooth. Use immediately.

II. Use this as a heavy dressing or as a filling for tomatoes, cucumbers, celery or endive. See Salads, page 33, and Hors d'Oeuvre (II, 66).
Mash:

A ripe avocado

with:

Lemon juice or vinegar to taste

and

Correct the seasoning.

RAVIGOTE SAUCE

[About 1⅓ Cups]
Good with cold meat or fish.
Prepare:

1 cup French dressing

Add:

½ cup finely chopped onion
1 tablespoon finely chopped capers
1 teaspoon chopped parsley
½ teaspoon chopped fresh tarragon
½ teaspoon chopped fresh chervil

LORENZO DRESSING

[About ½ Cup]
Combine:

½ cup French dressing
2 tablespoons chili sauce
2 tablespoons chopped water cress

ANCHOVY DRESSING

[About ½ Cup]
Prepare:

½ cup French dressing

Beat into it:

1 tablespoon or more anchovy or other fish paste

ANCHOVY AND BEET DRESSING

[About 1 Cup]
Place in a jar with a screw top:

½ cup French dressing
3 or 4 chopped anchovies
2 small chopped cooked beets
1 chopped hard-cooked egg

Season the dressing highly. Shake the jar well. Pour the dressing over a large bowlful of:

Endive or lettuce

SALSA VERDE

[About ¾ Cup]
To be used with salads and fish.
Combine:

½ cup chopped parsley
1½ tablespoons capers
2 garlic cloves
3 anchovy fillets or ½ teaspoon anchovy paste

Add:

1 crustless slice white bread

soaked in:

¼ cup vinegar
3 tablespoons olive oil

2 tablespoons sugar
Correct the seasoning

Any of the following may be added:

(Horseradish, pickles, green olives, green peppers)

ROQUEFORT OR BLEU CHEESE FRENCH DRESSING

[About ⅔ Cup]

Prepare:

½ cup French dressing

Beat into it:

2 tablespoons or more crumbled Roquefort or bleu cheese

⅄ BLENDER ANCHOVY AND ROQUEFORT DRESSING

[About 1½ Cups]

Place in container of electric blender and blend until smooth:

⅔ cup olive oil
1 can anchovies with oil
3 tablespoons vinegar
3 tablespoons lemon juice
¼ teaspoon paprika
(1 clove garlic)
½ teaspoon mustard
½ teaspoon sugar
½ teaspoon celery salt
A dash of Worcestershire sauce and hot pepper sauce
A 3-inch wedge Roquefort cheese

HORSERADISH DRESSING

[About ½ Cup]

Prepare:

½ cup French dressing

Beat into it:

1 tablespoon or more fresh or prepared horseradish

FROZEN HORSERADISH SAUCE

[About 1½ Cups]

This comes out rather like a sherbet and is delicious with boiled beef.

Combine:

¼ cup grated horseradish
¼ cup fresh orange juice
1 teaspoon sugar

and fold into:

1 cup stiffly whipped cream

Freeze about 3 to 4 hours in a tray and spoon out into a bowl to serve. Do not hold frozen for long periods.

CUMBERLAND SAUCE

[About ¾ Cup]

Good with cold ham and game.

Combine and blend well:

Grated rind of 1 lemon
Juice of 1 lemon
Grated rind of 1 orange
1 tablespoon confectioners' sugar
1 teaspoon prepared mustard
½ cup melted red currant jelly
1 tablespoon port wine

If the jelly is very stiff, it may have to be diluted over heat with:

(1 or 2 tablespoons hot water)

WATER CRESS DRESSING

[About 2 Cups]

Excellent over salad greens or Cucumber Gelatin Salad, page 64, and Shrimp, page 441.

Combine:

2 tablespoons lemon juice
1 tablespoon tarragon vinegar
½ cup olive oil
1 teaspoon salt
⅛ teaspoon pepper

Stir in:

2 finely chopped bunches water cress

⅄ BLENDER CRESS DRESSING

Blend to a paste in an electric blender:

2 hard-cooked eggs
2 tablespoons olive oil
¾ cup cut water cress, packed lightly

Dilute this paste with:

French dressing

to the consistency you like.

⅄ BLENDER VEGETABLE SAUCE

[About 1 Cup]

Serve this sauce over bland foods, sweetbreads, cold veal, hot or cold fish.

Combine:

¾ cup tomato purée or 2 large, raw, skinned tomatoes—the juice pressed from them
1 medium-sized onion
1 green pepper, seeds and membrane removed
¼ cup celery or 1 teaspoon celery and/or dill seeds
2 tablespoons parsley or chives
½ teaspoon salt
¼ teaspoon freshly ground pepper
(2 tablespoons French dressing)

Chill the sauce for about ½ hour.

CHIFFONADE DRESSING

[About 1½ Cups]

Prepare:

½ cup French dressing

Add to it:

2 chopped hard-cooked eggs
2 tablespoons julienned cooked beet root
2 tablespoons chopped parsley
2 teaspoons chopped chives
1 teaspoon chopped onion

COCKTAIL SAUCE

[About 1 Cup]

Good for dunking or garnishing shellfish, small sausages or other hors d'oeuvre.

Combine:

¾ cup catsup
⅛ to ¼ cup prepared horseradish
Juice of 1 lemon
1 dash hot pepper sauce

CHUTNEY DRESSING

[About 1 Cup]

Combine in a bottle and chill:

1 tablespoon chopped hard-cooked egg
1 tablespoon chopped chutney
¼ teaspoon curry powder
1 tablespoon lemon juice
½ cup olive oil
3 tablespoons vinegar
¼ teaspoon salt
1 teaspoon sugar
A few grains black pepper

Shortly before serving the dressing, beat it well with a fork.

COLD MUSTARD SAUCE

I.

For boiled or cold meats or fish. This is in the nature of a relish.

Combine:

2 teaspoons grated onion
1 tablespoon prepared mustard
1½ teaspoons sugar
1 to 2 tablespoons oil
2 tablespoons vinegar
(2 hard-cooked egg yolks)
(1 tablespoon cream)

II. [About 1 Cup]

Try this over raw or cooked vegetables or seafood.

Combine:

¾ cup Italian tomato paste
1 teaspoon dry mustard
1 tablespoon sugar
½ teaspoon salt
1 tablespoon vinegar
1 tablespoon drained horseradish
(1 tablespoon chopped onion, chives or fresh herbs)

III.

A highly seasoned sauce for cold meats or broiled sausages. Blend gradually:

2 tablespoons or more dry mustard

with a little:

Water

until it is the consistency of thick cream. Fold this paste into:

½ cup heavy cream or evaporated milk, whipped (II, 133)

Season the sauce, if desired, with:

Salt and paprika

DRESSING WITHOUT OIL

[About ¾ Cup]

No, it isn't particularly good, but it may be eaten by the bulging with a clear conscience.

Soak:

1 teaspoon gelatin

in:

1 tablespoon cold water

Dissolve it in:

¼ cup boiling water

Add:

1 tablespoon sugar
½ teaspoon salt

Cool this mixture. Add:

1 teaspoon grated lemon rind
½ cup lemon juice
⅛ teaspoon dry mustard
¼ teaspoon paprika
A few grains cayenne
⅛ teaspoon pepper
¼ teaspoon onion juice
(⅛ teaspoon curry powder)

Shake the dressing. Chill it. Before serving it, beat it well with a wire beater. Add, if you wish:

2 tablespoons minced parsley
1 tablespoon minced chives

SWEET-SOUR LOW CALORIE DRESSING

[1 Cup]

Serve on a green salad.

Combine:

⅓ cup lemon juice
⅔ cup water
1 teaspoon sugar
¼ teaspoon salt

CHINESE LOW CALORIE DRESSING

[About ½ Cup]

Good on sliced cucumber and tomato.

Combine:

3 tablespoons lemon juice
3 tablespoons soy sauce
1 tablespoon sugar
(1 teaspoon finely chopped candied ginger)

LOW CALORIE THOUSAND ISLAND DRESSING

[About 2 Cups]

Combine in a large screw-top jar:

¾ cup tarragon vinegar
1 can condensed tomato soup: 10½ oz.
1 minced garlic clove
A few grains cayenne
2 tablespoons chopped dill pickle
2 tablespoons finely chopped celery
2 tablespoons finely chopped parsley
1 tablespoon Worcestershire sauce
1 teaspoon paprika
1 teaspoon prepared mustard

MAYONNAISE

The making of a perfect mayonnaise is the Sunday job for Papa in France and rivalry for quality between households is intense. Mayonnaise or Mahonnaise—as it was first called, after a French victory over the British at Port Mahon on the Island of Minorca —is a great favorite, not only as a dressing, but for combining with other foods. It has been made by hand for some 300 years. But, with care, we can now make it with an electric mixer or in the ⅄ blender. Blender mayonnaise is made more quickly, has greater volume and fluffier texture, but cannot duplicate the smooth, rich-looking glisten of hand-beaten mayonnaise. We believe it is slightly less adaptable to some mayonnaise variations, such as mayonnaise collée. Care must be used in ➧ storing all mayonnaise combinations under refrigeration, as they are subject to bacterial activity which may be very toxic without showing any evidence of spoilage. Cooked foods to be mixed with mayonnaise keep much better and help deter bacteria if they have been marinated in vinegar or lemon juice or are mixed with pickle. But, even if they have this added acid content, they must be kept thoroughly refrigerated. Freezing mayonnaise combinations is also chancy, as the spoilage is only arrested and not destroyed and then accelerates when the food is defrosted. ➧ Don't try to make mayonnaise if a thunderstorm threatens or is in progress, as it simply will not bind.

If you have to resort to bottled mayonnaise, beating in 1 to 2 tablespoons good olive oil until all trace of it has disappeared will give it a good flavor and make it stiffer and heavier. Sour cream, according to taste, can also do wonders for commercial mayonnaise—if well beaten in. Please note that commercial "Salad Dressing" is not mayonnaise and the above suggestions will not work if it is used.

➧ Eggs, oil, bowl and mixer must all be at room temperature, 70°. Warm the oil slightly if it has been refrigerated, rinse your bowl in hot water and dry it.

I. [About 1¼ Cups]

Place in a medium-sized bowl and beat with a wire whisk or wooden spoon until lemon color:

2 egg yolks

Beat in:

¼ to ½ teaspoon dry mustard
½ teaspoon salt
A few grains cayenne
½ teaspoon vinegar or lemon juice
½ teaspoon confectioners' sugar

Beat in, very slowly, ½ teaspoon at a time:

½ cup olive oil

The mixture will begin to thicken and emulsify. Now you can relax! Combine in a cup or small pitcher:

1½ tablespoons vinegar
2 tablespoons lemon juice

Have ready:

½ cup olive oil

Alternate the oil ➧ drop by drop, with a few drops of the lemon and vinegar mixture. If the oil is added slowly during constant beating, this will make a good thick sauce. Sometimes the sauce will break, because you have either added your oil too fast toward the end or added too much of it—figure no more than ½ to ¾ cup oil to each large yolk. It may also break if your oil has been cold and your egg yolks warm. Do not despair: a curdled mayonnaise can be reconstituted by placing 1 egg yolk in a bowl. Stir it constantly and add the curdled dressing to it very, very slowly at first and continue slowly as the mixture thickens. If the dressing is too heavy, thin it with cream.

II. ⅄ [About 1¾ Cups]

You may make the above recipe following exactly the same procedure, in the same order, using an electric mixer on medium speed or the speed indicated for whipping cream.

III. ⅄ [About 1¾ Cups]

Blender mayonnaise differs from the first recipe in that it uses a whole egg. If your beating arm is rather weak, we suggest you try this method as the emulsifying is taken care of by the action of the blender.

Put in blender container:

- 1 egg
- 1 teaspoon ground mustard
- 1 teaspoon salt
- A dash of cayenne
- 1 teaspoon sugar
- ¼ cup salad oil

Cover and blend until thoroughly combined. With blender still running, take off the cover and slowly add:

- ½ cup salad oil

and then:

- 3 tablespoons lemon juice

until thoroughly blended. Then add slowly:

- ½ cup salad oil

and blend until thick. You may have to stop and start the blender to stir down the mayonnaise.

AIOLI OR GARLIC SAUCE

[1 Cup]

This is a garlic sauce very popular in France where it is sometimes known as "Beurre de Provence." Some recipes omit the eggs. Serve over fish, cold boiled potatoes, beet rounds and boiled beef.

Skin, then chop very finely the:

- 4 garlic clove sections

that give the sauce its name. Beat in:

- 2 egg yolks
- ⅛ teaspoon salt
- (1 slice dry French bread without crust, soaked in milk and wrung out)

Add, as for mayonnaise, very slowly and beating constantly:

- 1 cup olive oil

As the sauce thickens, beat in:

- ½ teaspoon cold water
- 1 teaspoon lemon juice

In the case the sauce fails to thicken, treat as a defeated Mayonnaise, above.

SKORDALIA

[1 Cup]

Prepare:

Aioli Sauce, as above

adding, after the sauce has thickened:

- ¼ cup ground almonds
- ¼ cup fresh bread crumbs
- 3 teaspoons lemon juice
- 2 tablespoons chopped parsley

ROUILLE SAUCE

A strongly flavored sauce, served with Mediterranean fish soups or bouillabaisse. Pound together in a bowl or mortar to make a smooth paste:

- 1 blanched, seeded, skinned red pimiento or 1 canned pimiento
- 1 small red chili, boiled until tender or a dash of hot pepper sauce
- ¼ cup white bread crumbs soaked in water and squeezed dry
- 2 mashed cloves garlic

Beat in, very slowly, as in Mayonnaise:

- ¼ cup olive oil

Thin the sauce just before serving with:

- 2 to 3 tablespoons of the soup you are serving

Pass with the soup.

SAUCE FOR SMOKED FOOD

Combine:

- 2 tablespoons mayonnaise
- 1 teaspoon horseradish
- 1 tablespoon cultured sour cream

ANDALOUSE SAUCE

[2 Cups]

For vegetable salads, cold fish or egg dishes.

Combine:

- 2 cups mayonnaise
- 1 chopped tomato, with

seeds and juice removed or ½ cup tomato purée
¼ julienned red pimiento

FRUIT-SALAD MAYONNAISE

[1½ Cups]
Combine:
1 cup mayonnaise
½ cup pineapple juice
1 teaspoon grated orange rind
1 tablespoon orange curaçao

CREAM OR CHANTILLY MAYONNAISE

[2 Cups]
Serve with fruit salad.
Prepare:
1 cup mayonnaise
Add to it, shortly before serving:
1 cup whipped cream

CURRY MAYONNAISE

[About 1 Cup]
For fruit or fish.
Combine:
1 cup mayonnaise
¼ teaspoon ginger
½ to 1 teaspoon curry powder
1 mashed clove garlic
1 teaspoon honey
1 tablespoon lime juice
It is very good for molded chicken salad or shrimp with these additions:
(1 tablespoon chopped chutney)
(1 tablespoon chopped kumquats)
(1 tablespoon blanched slivered almonds)

MAYONNAISE GRENACHE

[About 2½ Cups]
Serve with smoked turkey or smoked tongue.
Combine:
1 cup mayonnaise
½ cup red currant jelly
3 tablespoons grated horseradish
¼ teaspoon salt
⅛ teaspoon freshly ground pepper
2 tablespoons dessert sherry or Madeira
Fold in:
½ cup whipped cream

GREEN GODDESS DRESSING

[About 2 Cups]
Use on fish or shellfish.
Combine:
1 cup mayonnaise
1 minced clove garlic
3 minced anchovy fillets
¼ cup finely minced chives or green onions
¼ cup minced parsley
1 tablespoon lemon juice
1 tablespoon tarragon vinegar
½ teaspoon salt
Ground black pepper
½ cup cultured sour cream

GREEN MAYONNAISE OR SAUCE VERTE

[1 Cup]
For cold shellfish or vegetables.
Chop, blanch, page 88, for 2 minutes and drain:
2 tablespoons parsley
2 tablespoons tarragon, fennel or dill
2 tablespoons chives
2 tablespoons spinach or finely chopped cucumber
2 tablespoons water cress
Rub through a sieve and combine to make a paste with:
2 hard-cooked egg yolks
Add to:
1 cup stiff mayonnaise

HARD-COOKED EGG MAYONNAISE OR SAUCE GRIBICHE

[About 3 Cups]
For fish and cold meat.

Mash in a bowl until smooth:
3 hard-cooked egg yolks
Add:
½ teaspoon salt
A dash of pepper
1 teaspoon prepared Dijon-type mustard
Add very gradually and beat constantly:
1½ cups olive oil
½ cup vinegar
The mixture will thicken. Then stir in:
3 finely julienned egg whites
½ cup mixed, finely chopped sour pickles and capers, with the moisture squeezed out
2 tablespoons finely chopped mixed parsley, chervil, tarragon and chives

REMOULADE SAUCE

[About 1⅓ Cups]
For cold meat and poultry—also shellfish, with which it is especially good.
Combine:
1 cup mayonnaise
1 tablespoon drained, finely chopped cucumber pickle
1 tablespoon drained, chopped capers
2 teaspoons French mustard
1 teaspoon finely chopped parsley
½ teaspoon chopped fresh tarragon
½ teaspoon chervil
(½ teaspoon anchovy paste)

RUSSIAN DRESSING

[About 1¾ Cups]
Use on arranged salads, eggs, shellfish or in chicken sandwiches, instead of butter or mayonnaise.
Combine:
1 cup mayonnaise
1 tablespoon grated horseradish
(3 tablespoons imported caviar)
(1 teaspoon Worcestershire sauce)
¼ cup chili sauce or catsup
1 teaspoon grated onion

TARTARE SAUCE

[About 1⅓ Cups]
A good old stand-by for fried fish.
Combine:
1 cup firm mayonnaise
1 teaspoon French mustard
1 tablespoon finely chopped parsley
1 teaspoon minced shallots
1 tablespoon chopped, drained sweet pickle
(1 tablespoon chopped, drained green olives)
1 finely chopped hard-boiled egg
1 tablespoon chopped, drained capers
Correct the seasoning
You may thin the sauce with:
A little wine vinegar or lemon juice

THOUSAND ISLAND DRESSING

[About 1½ Cups]
Serve over iceberg lettuce wedges, eggs, etc.
Combine:
1 cup mayonnaise
¼ cup chili sauce or catsup
2 tablespoons minced stuffed olives
1 tablespoon chopped green pepper
1 tablespoon minced onion or chives
1 chopped hard-cooked egg
2 teaspoons chopped parsley

WATER CRESS SAUCE OR SAUCE AU CRESSON

[About 1 Cup]
This is excellent with cold fish dishes.

Combine:

- 1/4 cup finely chopped water cress
- 3/4 cup mayonnaise
- 1 tablespoon lemon juice
- Correct the seasoning

SAUCE LOUIS

[About 2 Cups]

This is good with stuffed artichokes, shrimp or crab. It is the sauce used for Crab Louis, page 50.

Combine:

- 1 cup mayonnaise
- 1/4 cup heavy cream
- 1/4 cup chili sauce
- 1 teaspoon Worcestershire sauce
- 1/4 cup chopped green pepper
- 1/4 cup chopped green onion
- 2 tablespoons lemon juice
- Correct the seasoning

HALF AND HALF DRESSING

[About 2 1/2 Cups]

Serve on tossed salad, combination salads or hearts of lettuce.

Combine:

- 1 cup mayonnaise
- 1 cup French dressing
- 1 minced garlic clove
- 1 teaspoon mashed anchovies
- 1/2 cup Parmesan cheese

BOILED SALAD DRESSINGS

Three recipes for boiled salad dressings are given. No. I, made with 1 egg or 2 yolks, is a very economical, acceptable boiled dressing. It may be thinned with cream, but is good as it is over vegetable and potato salad. No. II is made with milk and whole eggs. Use this dressing over slaw, tomatoes, aspics, etc. No. III is a fruit salad dressing. Keep these dressings well refrigerated.

I. [About 1 1/4 Cups]

Dissolve:

- 1/2 to 1 teaspoon dry mustard
- 1 to 2 tablespoons sugar
- 1/2 teaspoon salt
- 2 tablespoons flour
- 1/4 teaspoon paprika

in:

- 1/2 cup cold water

Beat in the top of double boiler:

- 1 whole egg or 2 yolks
- 1/4 cup vinegar

Add the dissolved ingredients. Cook and stir the dressing ♦ over—not in—boiling water, until it is thick and smooth. Add:

- 2 tablespoons butter

Chill the dressing. It may be thinned with:

- Sweet or cultured sour cream

II. [About 1 1/2 Cups]

Beat in the top of a double boiler:

- 2 egg yolks
- 2 teaspoons sugar
- 1 tablespoon melted butter
- 2/3 cup milk
- 1/4 cup vinegar
- 2 teaspoons salt
- A few grains cayenne
- 1 teaspoon dry mustard

Dissolve:

- 2 teaspoons cornstarch

in:

- 1/3 cup milk

Add it to the ingredients in the double boiler. Cook and stir the dressing ♦ over—not in—boiling water, until it is thick. Cool it. You may add chopped parsley, chives or other herbs, celery or dill seeds, etc. Fold it into:

- 2 stiffly beaten egg whites

III. [About 1 1/4 Cups]

Beat in the top of a double boiler:

- 1 teaspoon salt
- 1/3 teaspoon paprika
- 1/4 to 1/2 cup sugar
- 2 tablespoons melted butter

6 tablespoons cream
3 eggs
(½ teaspoon mustard)

Stir and cook the dressing ◆ over—not in—boiling water, until it is thick. Add slowly:

6 tablespoons lemon juice

The dressing may be thinned with:

Fruit juice or cream

SOUR CREAM HORSERADISH DRESSING OR DRESDEN SAUCE

[1 Cup]

A fine change from the well-liked but often monotonous butter or cream sauce. Usually served with smoked or boiled fish. Combine and stir:

1 cup cultured sour cream
½ teaspoon prepared mustard
½ teaspoon horseradish
¼ teaspoon salt

CREAM HORSERADISH DRESSING

[About 1¼ Cups]

This dressing is good with cold meat.

Beat until stiff:

½ cup heavy cream

Add slowly, beating constantly:

3 tablespoons lemon juice or vinegar
¼ teaspoon salt
⅛ teaspoon paprika
A few grains cayenne
2 tablespoons grated horseradish
(3 tablespoons mayonnaise)

SOUR CREAM DRESSING FOR VEGETABLE SALAD

[About 1 Cup]

Beat until smooth:

1 cup thick cultured sour cream

Add to it:

1 teaspoon grated onion or fresh onion juice
1 teaspoon celery or dill seed
½ teaspoon salt
A fresh grating of white pepper
(2 tablespoons chopped green or sweet red pepper)

CUCUMBER SAUCE

[About 1½ Cups]

For fish or meat, preferably cold food, such as salmon.

Beat until stiff:

¾ cup heavy sweet or cultured sour cream

If the cream is sweet, add slowly:

2 tablespoons vinegar or lemon juice

Season the sauce with:

¼ teaspoon salt
⅛ teaspoon paprika

Pare, seed, cut finely and drain well:

1 large cucumber

Add it to the sauce with:

(2 teaspoons finely chopped chives or dill)

YOGURT DRESSING

Yogurt (II, 135), simple and unadorned, is excellent on honeydew and cantaloupe melon balls in a lettuce cup. Try it on other fresh fruits or on crisp salad greens on hot summer days. Good for dieters, too.

SOUR CREAM SAUCE FOR BAKED POTATOES

[1 Cup]

Combine:

1 cup cultured sour cream
1 teaspoon Worcestershire sauce
A dash of hot pepper sauce
½ teaspoon monosodium glutamate
½ teaspoon salt
Freshly ground black pepper

Garnish with:

Chopped chives

CAVIAR SAUCE

[About 1⅓ Cups]

Try on baked potatoes or as a dip for cold vegetables in hors d'oeuvre or salad.

Combine:

1 cup cultured sour cream
1 teaspoon onion or shallot juice
2 teaspoons capers
¼ cup red caviar

HONEY DRESSING

[1 Cup]

For fruit salads:

Combine:

½ cup honey
½ cup lime juice
(A pinch of ground ginger)

CELERY SEED DRESSING

[About 2 Cups]

Add to fruit salad just before serving. This may be made with an electric ⅄ blender or mixer. Constant beating to blend the ingredients is the secret of success here.

Combine:

½ cup sugar
1 teaspoon dry mustard
1 teaspoon salt
1 to 2 teaspoons celery seed

Add:

3 tablespoons grated onion

Gradually add, beating constantly:

1 cup salad oil
⅓ cup vinegar

Garnish with:

(A few finely cut sprigs lemon thyme)

CREAM CHEESE DRESSING FOR FRUIT SALAD

[About 1¼ Cups]

Mash with a fork and beat until smooth:

1 package cream cheese: 3 oz.

Beat in slowly:

1 tablespoon lemon juice
2 tablespoons currant jelly
½ cup cream

Chill the dressing for 1 hour or more before serving it.

LEMON AND SHERRY DRESSING FOR FRUIT SALAD

[About ½ Cup]

Delightful over tart fruit, apples, grapefruit, etc.

Combine:

¼ cup lemon juice
⅛ teaspoon salt

Stir in slowly:

¼ cup sugar

Add:

2 tablespoons dry sherry

CURRY DRESSING FOR FRUIT SALAD

[About 1 Cup]

Combine:

2 tablespoons mild vinegar
1 tablespoon lemon juice
¼ to ½ teaspoon curry
1 teaspoon sugar

Stir in:

1 cup cultured sour cream

See also Curry Mayonnaise, page 348.

ABOUT HOT SAUCE TYPES

There are certain old dowagers who try to dominate "sauciety." Call them the mother sauces, as the French do, if you like. Each has her strong peculiarities of individual makeup; each traditionally queens it over a whole coterie of dishes. The ubiquitous member of the clan—the one who is always close by—is pan gravy: she knows what's cooking, because she carries its essence.

Her roux-based cousins have more solid and dependable backgrounds and take more abuse in heating, reheating and storing—for their flour and butter base combines into as stable an ingredient as any in the kitchen. There are the delicate pale members of the roux family, descended from Béchamel, who accept the company of eggs, cream and even shallots. There are the robust characters originating in browned flours, who have picked up acquaintanceships with strange foreign spices, who love tomatoes and who, on occasion, set their caps for garlic. Both rely for authenticity on two principles. Their roux base must be cooked to rid it and them of any trace of plebeian floury origin and must always be hot when added to cold liquids or cold when added to hot.

There are the plush sauce aristocracy who scorn flour altogether and derive their stamina from eggs. Like a lot of other sauces for cold food, the mayonnaise branch performs this elegant trick without requiring heat. While its cousins, the Hollandaise-Béarnaise group, must have heat, they need it only in small doses and for short periods.

Most showy and demonstrative of all are the wine sauces, the vinaigrettes, the playful tenderizing sweet-sours or agrodulces, the marinades, the barbecues and, of course, the truly sweet dessert sauces (II, 473), which are the simpering sentimentalists of the whole colony.

Although these rather simple divisions mark the major sauce families, don't feel overconfident about your acquaintanceship until you can spot a rare nonidentical twin—with arrowroot as thickener—or an occasional reveler in fancy dress, tricked out with beurre manié or butter swirls. These wayward collaterals are among the most treasured, if fleeting, personalities of all.

When you once feel at home in sauce circles, you will learn rapidly how to make them welcome members of your culinary life. You will learn how to skillfully blend the hot ingredients, so that they may receive food without thinning. You will discover that adding the wine before—not after—the eggs and cream will avoid curdling and that a mixture can be stabilized with that extra bit of cream when separation threatens.

Of course, there is always the ⅄ blender to fall back on in a crisis of this kind, but the texture of the sauce can never be as smooth or thick as if it had been properly made in the first place. In sauces based on cornstarch, overbeating itself can disturb consistency—and this factor alone may cause thinning. The use of a light whisk or a wooden spoon is a help in avoiding this condition. Another reason for thinning in sauces may be the addition of acid in the form of fruit juice or wine. Sauces will also lose body if covered and held heated, for the excess steam created thins them and tends to cause separation. ➧ To lessen separation in frozen sauces, see Waxy Rice Flour (II, 157).

ABOUT COLOR IN SAUCES

A well-prepared sauce really has its color built in and should need no artificial coloring. ➧ To maintain and develop color for sauces, see page 353.

Rich beef stock combined with some tomato, browned meat—in the case of a stew—browned onions and carrots and a brown roux will result in a rich brown sauce needing no addition of caramel to bring up the color. If you feel obliged to add caramel to gravies, add it sparingly. Some cooks use yellow coloring for chicken gravies and sauces to try to hide the omission of chicken fat and egg yolks. Should you use saffron, do beware of its overpowering flavor. A tomato sauce will keep a good color if you do not cook it too quickly or too long.

ABOUT SAUCES IN QUANTITY

➧ If you are making gravies or sauces in quantity, it will take considerably longer to get rid of the raw flour taste after the liquid has been added to the roux than when you are making only 1 or 2 cups for immediate family use. We advise heating these larger amounts ➧ uncovered, in a slow oven for ½ to ¾ of an hour and straining the sauce before serving, to remove any crusting or lumps. But if you stir the sauce from time to time, it may not be necessary to strain it.

When doubling the ingredients in sauce recipes, taste before adding the full amount of seasoning. It is easy to overdo it.

ABOUT KEEPING SAUCES

You may keep Velouté, Tomato and Brown Sauces in the refrigerator for at least a week. To store, strain the sauce, pour it into a container and cover with a thin layer of fat or sherry. If you have not used all the sauce at the end of a week, you may reheat it, put it in a clean jar, cover again with a little melted fat and return it to the refrigerator, where it will keep at least another week.

You can also ✻ freeze the sauces mentioned above, as well as Béchamel, in ice-cube trays and keep the cubes in your freezer in a plastic bag, taking out as many as you need for immediate use. They may be melted in a double boiler—4 large cubes melt down to about ½ cup of sauce. You may also freeze Hollandaise Sauce, page 369, but be very careful when reheating. Do not try to freeze mayonnaise; it will break. And, in general, do not try to keep sauces made with eggs, cream or milk for more than 2 or 3 days in the refrigerator.

ABOUT SAUCE INGREDIENTS

Sauces in general are spoken of as savory or sweet. Many of those in the first category are made with some sort of pan gravy. Pan residues, unless from fish or from strong variety meats, like kidneys, are a most desirable flavoring ingredient. ➧ To make pan gravies, see page 358.

Pan residues for sauces also include those which are left over from browning and sautéing meats. Browning lends attractive color and the addition of some rendered fat serves to intensify the characteristic meat flavor. It is always best, if you sauté with butter—and the butter should be sweet, not salted —to clarify it, page 383, or to combine it with a little cooking oil to raise its smoking point, so as to prevent scorching and bitter overtones. If economy is a factor and margarine has been substituted for butter, you may wish to improve the flavor of the final product by finishing the sauce off with a Butter Swirl, page 357.

Good strong, fat-free Stocks (II, 138) are invaluable sauce ingredients, too, especially when reduced to a Glaze (II, 145). Where possible, the stock should reflect the food it is to flavor: chicken stock for chicken, lamb stock for lamb, etc. Although meat stocks, including those of poultry and game, are often combined in sauce-making—favorites being those of chicken—and veal—fish and shellfish Fumets (II, 143) should be reserved only for fish and shellfish dishes.

Such broths always make better sauce ingredients if left to stand refrigerated for 24 hours and then de-fatted.

When pan residues or stocks are scanty, turn to wine. ➧ Please read About Cooking With Wine (II, 149). Use, as a rule of thumb, dry white wines in sauces for fish or white meats; dry red wines for red meats. Strong game sauces sometimes support stronger liquors like rum, brandy or Madeira, but whisky is never added to them. ➧ In any wine sauce, add egg, milk, cream or butter swirls after the wine has been incorporated.

ABOUT THICKENERS FOR SAUCES

Sauces not made by deglazing with liquids, as described above, are generally ➧ thickened just enough to coat food lightly and yet not run off.

ROUX

The most common thickeners for savory sauces are the ➧ roux —white, blonde or brown. All of these are made of the same ingredients to begin with, but change in character as heat is applied. These mixtures of flour and fats are blended gently ➧ over very low heat from 5 minutes to a much longer period, depending on your available time and your patience. White roux should not color; blonde, barely; and brown should reach the color of hazelnut and smell deliciously baked. ➧ Unless a roux is cooked long enough to dispel the raw taste of flour, this unpleasant flavor will dominate the strongest stocks and seasonings. And unless the flour and butter are stirred to distribute the heat and to allow the starch granules to swell evenly, they will later fail to absorb the liquid. Therefore the sauce will be thin. ➧ This heated blending period is important. Using too high heat to try hurrying it will burn the flour, giving it a bitter taste and it will shrink the starch, making it incapable of continuing to swell.

For white roux-based sauces, see Béchamel, page 359; for blonde, see Blanquette de Veau, page 504; for brown, see Sauce Espagnole, page 365. Since most cooks use some form of roux every day, you may find it a time-saver to make one in advance and store it in tablespoon-sized units under refrigeration. It will keep in the ❄ freezer, too, for several months if you do the following: when the roux has been cooked to the desired color and is still soft, measure it by tablespoons on a baking sheet and freeze. Transfer the frozen wafers to a plastic bag or wide-topped container and store in the freezer. To thicken sauce, drop several wafers of the original roux in the sauce to reach the thickness desired. Or you may soften the wafers in a double boiler over hot water and proceed as usual with the making of the sauce.

BROWNED FLOUR

This variant is used in gravies to enhance color and flavor. The slow but inexpensive procedure by which it is made is worth trying. Place:

1 cup all-purpose flour

in a heavy dry skillet. ➧ Stir constantly over very low direct heat until golden brown; or place the skillet in a 350° oven until the flour is golden brown, about 30 minutes. Stir frequently, scraping the flour from the sides and bottom of the pan. In a very slow oven, the flour, when ready, should smell nutty and baked. Do not let it get too dark or, as with brown roux, it will become bitter and lose its thickening power altogether. ➧ Even properly browned flour has only about ½ the thickening power of all-purpose flour. It may be stored in a tightly covered jar in a cool place.

FLOUR PASTE

This is sometimes pressed into service to thicken emergency gravies and sauces, but the results are never as palatable as when even a quick roux is used. Make a paste of flour and cold water or stock. Use about 2 parts water and one part flour. Stir as much of the paste as needed into the boiling stock or drippings. Permit the sauce to heat until it thickens and ➧ simmer for at least 3 minutes more to reduce the raw taste of the flour. Stir frequently with a wire whisk.

CORNSTARCH

Cornstarch is often used where translucency is desirable, as in some Chinese or dessert sauces. It should be mixed with a little cold water before being added to the hot liquid. One tablespoon cornstarch will thicken 1½ to 2 cups of liquid. Most Chinese sauces are finished over direct heat. But dessert sauces are better cooked in the top of a double boiler ➧ over—not in—hot water until the raw taste of the cornstarch disappears. ➧ Do not overbeat cornstarch-based sauces for this thins them.

ARROWROOT

Of all the thickeners, this makes the most delicately textured sauces. ➧ But use it only when the sauce is to be served within 10 minutes of thickening. It will not hold, nor will it reheat. Since the flavor of arrowroot is neutral and it does not have to be cooked to remove rawness, as do flour and cornstarch, and since it thickens at a lower temperature than either of them, it is ideal for use in egg and other sauces which should not boil. Allow 2½ teaspoons to 1 cup liquid. See also (II, 158).

POTATO STARCH OR FECULA

This is preferred by some cooks, rather than flour, as a thickener in certain delicate sauces. When it is used, less simmering is required and the sauce gains some transparency. ➧ Heated beyond 176° the sauce will thin out. Serve soon after it has thickened, as it has no holding power. One tablespoon of potato starch will moderately thicken 1 cup of liquid.

EGG YOLKS

Egg yolks not only thicken but also enrich a sauce. ➧ Never add egg yolks directly to hot liquid. Stir them into a little cream, then incorporate with them some of the hot sauce you want to thicken. Stir this mixture into the remainder of the hot liquid and continue to stir over low heat until the sauce thickens. ➧ Do not allow the sauce to boil, or it will curdle. If this happens, plunge pot into cold water and stir; or beat in a small amount of chilled cream. It is generally safer to add egg yolks to a mixture in a double boiler ➧ over—not in—hot water, unless you can control the heat source very exactly. Two or three egg yolks with a little cream will thicken 1 cup of liquid. Egg yolks added very slowly to melted butter or oil with constant stirring will produce an emulsion which is quite thick. Suitably seasoned, this becomes the base for Hollandaise or mayonnaise. Hard-cooked egg yolks and oil will also emulsify, see Sauce Gribiche, page 349.

BLOOD

Blood from the animal or bird the sauce is to accompany is a desirable thickener. To save the blood from a freshly killed hare, rabbit or chicken, see (II, 540). You may store it refrigerated for a day or two, mixed with 1 or 2 tablespoons vinegar to prevent clotting. Strain it and add it to the sauce at the last minute just before serving, swirling it in as you would butter, below. Simmer gently, but ➧ never allow the sauce to boil after the blood is added. For other thickening suggestions, see Thickeners for Soups, page 108, and Ingredients.

REDUCTION

This is another classic way to thicken sauces. Béchamel and Espagnole may be thickened during very slow simmering by the evaporation of liquid to achieve a more perfect consistency. If you intend to thicken a sauce by reducing it, season ➧ after you have brought it down to the right viscosity, otherwise you may find it highly overseasoned or unpleasantly salty. There are a good many recipes for tomato sauces which demand long cooking and reducing. Unless you can keep these sauces—or, in fact, any thickened sauces—on very low heat, they will cook too fast and flavor will be impaired. In the case of roux-thickened sauces which call for reducing, do use an oven. It is a great labor-saver and the heat can be controlled much more exactly. ➧ Almost all reduced sauces, to be perfect in texture, should be strained before serving.

BUTTER SWIRLS

These finish off many fine, rich sauces, both white and brown, after straining and final heating. This can only be done if the sauce is to be served at once. ➧ It must not be reheated after the butter has been added. In addition to improving the flavor, the butter swirl also, very slightly, thickens the sauce. To make a sauce "finie au beurre" after straining and heating, add ➧ unsalted, unmelted butter bit by bit to the sauce, moving the pan in a circular motion, so that the butter makes an actual swirl in the hot sauce as it melts. Remove the pan from the heat before the butter is fully melted and continue to swirl. ➧ Do not use a spoon to stir it and do not try to reheat it. About 1 tablespoon butter is generally used to "finish" 1 cup of sauce.

KNEADED BUTTER OR BEURRE MANIÉ

This a magic panacea for rectifying sauces or thickening thin ones at the end of the cooking process. Do not use it for those which require long simmering. After adding kneaded butter ➧ do not boil the sauce. Simmer only long enough to dispel the floury taste. Manipulate with your fingers, as though you were rubbing for fine pastry, 2 tablespoons butter and 2 tablespoons flour. Form into small balls and drop into the hot liquid, stirring constantly until the ingredients are well blended and the sauce thickens. This amount will be sufficient for 1 cup of thin liquid.

ABOUT ATTRACTIVE WAYS TO SERVE SAUCES

Apart from the usual gravy boat or deep bowl and ladle, there are a number of attractive ways to serve sauces. Cold sauces and dips with a mayonnaise or sour cream base may be served in a crisp hollowed-out cabbage (II, 67), or individually in tomato or pepper cases, page 39. Suggest the marine flavor of cold shrimp or poached salmon with a delicate pink mayonnaise or Remoulade Sauce in a large sea shell.

Hot sauces can be served in ramekins, tin-lined copper pans or other small heatproof containers. The doll house instinct rises in all of us at the sight of these miniature individual pitchers and pots that are so appropriate when serving hot lobster, artichokes or asparagus. Sauces on the buffet table may be kept hot in small French three-legged saucepans, placed over a candle or—in the case of egg-based sauces—in wide-mouthed vacuum bottles or in chafing dishes. Like the food it accompanies, sauce, if it is meant to be hot, must be kept hot. However, ➧ any sauce that is worth its salt won't keep indefinitely on a steam table or in a casserole. There is a point of maximum goodness at which it should be served.

Cold sauces and seasoned butters can be kept chilled on a mound of crushed ice. Molds and pats of seasoned butter may be placed directly on the ice. Don't use ice cubes—the butter slips down between them.

ABOUT SAUCES MADE BY DEGLAZING

These are such a welcome change after the monotonous flour-thickened type. Pan juices and scrapings are precious and are frequently used as the base for many delicious sauces accompanying sautéed as well as roasted fowl and meat dishes. In initially roasting meat, be sure to grease the pans lightly to keep from burning any juices which may drip, before the fats from the meat have covered the bottom of the roasting pan. The addition of a cup of Mirepoix (II, 221) to the pan after the browning period will make both roast and pan gravy more flavorful. When the meat is done, remove it from the pan and pour off the fat. Add ¼ cup or more hot water or stock to the pan and cook on top of the stove—stirring and scraping the solidified juices from the bottom and sides. The addition of wine or dry sherry will hasten the deglazing process and heighten the flavorful aroma. Use the stock appropriate to your meat or fowl and the kind of wine you would normally drink with it. This, with a Butter Swirl, page 357, or Beurre Manié, page 357, or a little cream or more wine, can make the finest of all sauces.

ABOUT PAN GRAVY

If you use drippings for sauces, you may want to strain them first and remove excess fat. Reheat some of the fat because it will absorb the flour better. Add flour until it has the consistency of heavy cream.

PAN GRAVY

[1 Cup]

Remove the meat from the pan. Place it where it will remain hot. Pour off all but:

2 tablespoons drippings

Blend into them:

1 or 2 tablespoons flour

Stir with a wire whisk until the

flour has thickened and until well combined and smooth. Continue to cook slowly and stir constantly, while adding:

The degreased pan juices and enough milk, water, stock, cream or beer to make 1 cup

The beer may be "still." Season the gravy with:

Salt
Pepper
Fresh or dried minced herbs
Grated lemon rind, etc.

Color, if necessary, with:

A few drops Caramel (II, 169)

You may strain the gravy, reheat and serve it. If you are using a thickener other than flour, please read About Thickeners, page 355, for the correct amount of cornstarch or arrowroot to be added for the above amount of liquid.

CHICKEN PAN GRAVY

[About 2 Cups]

Strain the juices from the roast chicken. Pour off the fat. Heat:

¼ cup fat

Add and stir until blended:

¼ cup flour

Stir in slowly:

2 cups pan juices and Chicken Stock (II, 142)

Cook and stir the gravy until smooth and ➧ simmer for 5 minutes. Add:

The cooked chopped chicken giblets
(¼ cup or more cream)

➧ If the gravy is very rich, it may separate. Add the cream slowly. Stir it constantly. This will usually forestall any difficulty.

Correct the seasoning

and serve.

CREAM SAUCE I OR BÉCHAMEL

[1 Cup]

This sauce, actually made with milk, is used for creaming foods like vegetables and fish and as a base for other sauces. Melt over low heat:

2 tablespoons butter

For a delicate flavor, even commercial establishments have found no substitute for butter. Add and blend over low heat for 3 to 5 minutes:

1½ to 2 tablespoons flour

Stir in slowly:

1 cup milk

For better consistency, you may scald the milk beforehand; but be sure—to avoid lumping—that the roux is cool when you add it. Add:

1 small onion studded with 2 or 3 whole cloves
½ small bay leaf

Cook and stir the sauce with a wire whisk or wooden spoon until thickened and smooth. Place in a 350° oven for 20 minutes to cook slowly. The oven interval also saves your time and hands for other kitchen jobs. Strain the sauce,

Correct the seasoning

and serve. For creamed dishes, use about ½ as much sauce as solids.

CREAM SAUCE II OR HEAVY BÉCHAMEL

[1 Cup]

This sauce is used in soufflés. Prepare:

Cream Sauce I

Use in all:

3 tablespoons butter
3 tablespoons flour
1 cup liquid

CREAM SAUCE III OR BINDING BÉCHAMEL

[1 Cup]

This sauce is used in croquettes. Prepare:

Cream Sauce I, above

Use in all:

3 tablespoons butter

⅓ cup flour
1 cup liquid

CREAM SAUCE IV OR ENRICHED BÉCHAMEL

Reduce:
1 cup Cream Sauce I
to ¾ of its volume. Stir in:
¼ cup heavy cream
and bring to boiling point. If the sauce is for fish, add:
(½ to 1 teaspoon lemon juice)

QUICK WHITE SAUCE

If you are in a hurry, this base can be flavored and modified in many ways. Melt over low heat:
2 tablespoons butter
Add ➧ still over low heat and stirring about 3 to 4 minutes or until well blended and the taste of raw flour has vanished:
1½ to 2 tablespoons flour
Stir in slowly:
1 cup milk, milk and light stock, light stock or light stock and cream
Correct the seasoning
and vary the flavor with one or more of the following:
Celery salt
A grating of nutmeg
1 teaspoon lemon juice
½ teaspoon Worcestershire sauce
1 teaspoon sherry
1 teaspoon onion juice
2 tablespoons chopped parsley
2 tablespoons chopped chives
➧ Simmer and stir the sauce with a wire whisk until it has thickened and is smooth and hot. Combine it with other ingredients just as it boils, so that it will not become watery. For creamed dishes, use about ½ as much sauce as there are solids.

CREAM SAUCE MIX

[4 Cups Dry Mix]
This can be stored in a covered container, refrigerated several months. It will thicken, in all, about 2½ to 3 quarts of sauce.
Rub:
1 cup butter
into:
1 cup flour
Stir in and blend thoroughly:
2 cups nonfat milk solids
To make sauce, stir to a paste in a saucepan ⅓ cup of the above mixture with:
⅓ cup water or stock
then add:
⅔ cup water or stock
gradually over low heat and stir constantly until the sauce thickens.
Correct the seasoning

EGG CREAM SAUCE

[1¼ Cups]
This is good made with chicken stock and cream.
Prepare:
Cream Sauce I, page 359
Add to it:
2 chopped hard-cooked eggs
1 tablespoon capers or chopped pickles

FLORENTINE SAUCE

[About 2 Cups]
Combine:
1 cup Cream Sauce I, page 359
A dash of hot pepper sauce
2 drops Worcestershire sauce
(A dash of monosodium glutamate)
1 cup finely chopped spinach
A fresh grating of nutmeg
1 tablespoon finely chopped parsley
If using cold for fish, do not thin. If you use it hot, you may thin it with:
Cream or dry white wine

MORNAY SAUCE

[About 1¼ Cups]
Excellent for masking fish, egg and vegetable dishes. If you are using it in a dish to be browned in the oven or under the broiler, sprinkle a little grated cheese over the top first. Prepare:

1 cup Cream Sauce I, flavored with onion or shallot, page 359

Beat together until blended:

1 egg yolk
2 tablespoons cream

➧ Add a little of the sauce to the egg yolk and cream, stirring constantly, then return the mixture to the rest of the sauce and cook until well heated. Then add:

2 tablespoons grated Parmesan cheese
2 tablespoons grated Gruyère cheese

Keep stirring with a small whisk to help melt the cheese and keep the sauce smooth while it thickens.

Correct the seasoning

with:

Salt and a few grains of cayenne

NANTUA SAUCE

[About 1½ Cups]
For fish.
Prepare:

1 cup Cream Sauce I, page 359

Add:

½ cup whipping cream

Rub through a fine sieve:

2 tablespoons Shrimp Buttter, page 385

Instead of the shrimp butter, you may add 1 tablespoon finely ground shrimp made into a smooth paste with 1 tablespoon butter. Heat to boiling point.

Correct the seasoning

Garnish with:

Finely chopped shrimp

NEWBURG SAUCE

I. [About 1 Cup]
Melt in a double boiler:

½ cup Lobster Butter, page 385

Add and cook gently until translucent:

1 teaspoon finely chopped shallots

Add and continue to cook about 3 minutes:

¼ cup sherry or Madeira

Into:

1 cup cream

beat:

3 egg yolks

Add the two mixtures, stirring constantly until the sauce thickens. Use at once.

II. If you want a pink sauce for shrimp or lobster, add to the above:

1 tablespoon tomato paste
(1 tablespoon cognac or brandy)

OYSTER SAUCE FOR FISH

[About 2 Cups]
Prepare:

1 cup Cream Sauce II, page 359

Season it well with:

Salt
(1 teaspoon Worcestershire sauce)

Shortly before serving, bring the sauce to the boiling point and add:

3 tablespoons chopped parsley
1 cup finely chopped poached oysters and juice

ANCHOVY SAUCE FOR FISH

[1 Cup]
Prepare:

Cream Sauce I, page 359

Add to it:

3 fillets of anchovy, washed and pounded to a paste

Blend it well with the sauce.

HORSERADISH SAUCE OR SAUCE ALBERT

[1 Cup]
Usually used with boiled beef or corned beef.
Prepare:

Cream Sauce I, page 359

Remove it from the heat. Add:

- **3 tablespoons prepared horseradish**
- **2 tablespoons whipping cream**
- **1 teaspoon sugar**
- **1 teaspoon dry mustard**
- **1 tablespoon vinegar**

Reheat but do not boil. Serve immediately.

VELOUTÉ SAUCE OR SAUCE BLANCHE

[1½ Cups]
This is a white cream sauce made from a roux and stock base. The stock may be chicken, veal or fish, depending on the dish the sauce is to accompany. A quick Velouté may be made like Cream Sauce I, using stock in place of milk, but for a classic sauce of fine texture, proceed as directed below. ➧ The sauce should never be cooked in aluminum pans because they discolor it badly. Melt in the top of a double boiler:

- **2 tablespoons butter**

Stir in:

- **2 tablespoons flour**

When blended, add gradually:

- **2 cups chicken, veal or fish stock**

and stir over low heat until well combined and thickened. Add:

- **¼ cup mushroom peelings**

Place in the double boiler and simmer ➧ over—not in—hot water for about 1 hour, stirring occasionally. Strain through a fine sieve, then add:

A pinch of nutmeg
Correct the seasoning

and stir occasionally during the cooling process to prevent a crust from forming.

AURORE SAUCE

[About 2 Cups]
Fine with fish.
Prepare:

Velouté Sauce

Add:

- **2 tablespoons tomato purée**

to the sauce and mix. Let boil a little before pouring through a sieve and adding:

A Butter Swirl

ALLEMANDE SAUCE OR THICKENED VELOUTÉ

[1½ Cups]
This is an enriched Velouté Sauce, to be used with poached chicken or vegetables. ➧ Do not let this sauce boil or it will curdle.
Prepare:

- **1½ cups Velouté Sauce, above**

Stir in:

- **¾ cup strong chicken stock**

Blend well and reduce on medium heat to ⅔ of its original volume. Remove from the heat and add:

- **1 egg yolk mixed with 2 tablespoons cream**

Stir the sauce until it is slightly thickened. Just before serving, stir in:

- **1 tablespoon lemon juice**
- **1 tablespoon butter**

POULETTE SAUCE

[1½ Cups]
Prepare:

- **1½ cups Allemande Sauce, above**

Just before serving, add:

- **1 tablespoon finely chopped parsley**

PAPRIKA OR HUNGARIAN SAUCE

[About 1½ Cups]
Use for fish, poultry or veal.
Sauté until golden:

- **1 finely chopped onion**

in:

1 tablespoon butter

Add:

2 tablespoons mild Hungarian paprika

and stir for 1 minute. Add gradually, stirring constantly:

1 cup cream
⅓ cup Velouté Sauce, above
Correct the seasoning

CAPER SAUCE

[1½ Cups]

For poached or broiled fish, or mutton.

Prepare:

1½ cups Velouté or Allemande Sauce, above

Just before serving, add:

2 tablespoons drained chopped capers

CURRY SAUCE

I. [1½ Cups]

Pour over whole poached fish or fish fillets.

Prepare:

1½ cups Allemande Sauce, page 362

A few minutes before serving, stir in:

1 teaspoon good curry powder

II. [About 2 Cups]

Sauté slowly until tender:

¼ cup chopped onion
¼ cup chopped tart apple

in:

¼ cup butter

Stir in and cook, without browning, for 4 or 5 minutes:

2½ tablespoons flour
½ to 2 teaspoons curry powder

Add slowly, stirring constantly and simmer until well blended:

1 cup chicken broth
1 cup cream
½ teaspoon grated lemon peel

If you wish to have a perfectly smooth sauce, add the chicken broth and grated lemon peel only, cook for 10 minutes, strain through a sieve, add the cream and bring back to a boil. You may liven up this sauce, if you like a hot curry, with dashes of:

Hot pepper sauce
Cayenne
Ginger
Chopped chutney
Dry sherry

MUSTARD SAUCE

[1½ Cups]

Serve with poached or broiled fish.

Prepare:

1½ cups Allemande Sauce, page 362

Add, just before serving:

½ teaspoon dry mustard or 1 teaspoon prepared mustard
¼ teaspoon salt
½ teaspoon freshly ground black pepper

SOUBISE OR WHITE ONION SAUCE

[About 1½ Cups]

This is a delicate onion-flavored sauce for fish, poultry or vegetables.

Prepare:

1½ cups Velouté Sauce, page 362

Sauté until transparent:

2 medium chopped onions

in:

2 tablespoons butter

Add the onions to the Velouté Sauce and simmer over low heat for 30 minutes, stirring occasionally. Rub the whole sauce through a fine sieve. Finish off the sauce with:

2 tablespoons whipping cream
Correct the seasoning

SUPREME SAUCE

[About 2 Cups]

For fish, poultry and eggs. The special characteristics of Supreme Sauce are its perfect

whiteness and delicacy.
Prepare:

1½ cups Velouté Sauce, page 362, made with chicken stock

Add:

1 cup strong white chicken stock
¼ cup mushroom peelings

Bring to a boil, reduce the heat and simmer, stirring occasionally, until the sauce is reduced to 1½ cups. Strain through a fine sieve and add, stirring constantly:

½ cup whipping cream

Stir in:

1 tablespoon butter
Correct the seasoning

HOT RAVIGOTE SAUCE

This sauce is served lukewarm over variety meats, boiled fish, light meats and poultry. Chop until very fine:

2 shallots

Add:

1 tablespoon wine vinegar

Cook these ingredients rapidly, stirring constantly for about 3 minutes. Add:

1 cup Velouté Sauce, page 362

to the shallots and simmer the sauce for about 10 minutes. Stir it from time to time. Add:

Salt and freshly ground pepper

Cool the sauce to lukewarm. Add:

1 tablespoon chopped parsley
(1 teaspoon prepared mustard)
1 tablespoon chopped chervil
1 tablespoon chopped capers
½ teaspoon chopped chives
½ teaspoon chopped tarragon
(A grating of fresh nutmeg)

SMITANE SAUCE

[About 2 Cups]
Use for roast poultry or game—especially pheasant.
Melt in a saucepan:

1 tablespoon butter

Add:

¼ cup finely chopped onions

and cook until transparent, then add:

½ cup dry white wine

and cook until the mixture is reduced to ½. Add:

1 cup Velouté, page 362 or Brown Sauce, page 365

Blend and simmer 5 minutes then add:

1 cup cultured sour cream
Correct the seasoning

If a sourer effect is wanted, add:

(A little lemon juice)

Do not allow the sauce to boil after adding the sour cream or it will curdle.

BREAD SAUCE

[About 3 Cups]
Usually served with small roasted wild birds or roast meat.
Skin:

A small onion

Stud it with:

3 whole cloves

Place the onion in a saucepan with:

2 cups milk
2 tablespoons butter

Bring the milk to a boil. Add:

1 cup fresh white bread crumbs

Simmer for 15 minutes. Remove the onion. Beat the sauce smooth and stir in, until blended:

3 tablespoons cream

CHEESE SAUCE

[About 2 Cups]
Melt in a saucepan:

3 tablespoons butter

Stir in, until blended:

3 tablespoons flour

Stir in slowly:

1½ **cups milk**

When the sauce is smooth and hot, reduce the heat and stir in:

1 **cup or less mild grated cheese or diced processed cheese**

Season the sauce with:

½ **teaspoon salt**
⅛ **teaspoon paprika**
A few grains cayenne
(½ **teaspoon dry mustard)**

Stir the sauce until the cheese is melted.

BROWN SAUCE OR SAUCE ESPAGNOLE

[About 6 Cups]

This is one of the "sauces mères" of the French cuisine, the basis for many other sauces and dishes. Diat has said that the making of a good Espagnole is the mark of an accomplished saucier.

➧ Always stir, never whip, a Brown Sauce and use good, strong, clear beef stock. The flavor comes from the gradual "reduction" of the sauce by very slow simmering, which, if you are a perfectionist, can be 8 to 12 hours. Here is a rather more time-saving method.

Melt in a heavy saucepan:

½ **cup beef or veal drippings**

Add:

1 **cup Mirepoix (II, 221)**

When this begins to brown, add:

½ **cup flour**

and stir until the flour is a good brown. Then add:

10 **black peppercorns**
2 **cups drained, peeled tomatoes or 2 cups tomato purée**
½ **cup coarsely chopped parsley**

Stir and mix well, then add:

8 **cups good beef stock**

Simmer on the stove for about 2 to 2½ hours or until reduced by ½. Stir occasionally and skim off the fat as it rises to the top. Strain the sauce and stir occasionally as it cools to prevent a skin forming. The sauce should be the consistency of whipping cream, no thicker. If you are using this sauce "as is,"

Correct the seasoning

DEMI-GLAZE SAUCE

[About 4½ Cups]

This is the Espagnole, above, reduced to the nth degree. Serve with filet mignon or any meat with which Madeira Sauce is generally used.

Combine in a heavy saucepan:

4 **cups Brown Sauce, above**
4 **cups good beef stock, flavored with mushroom trimmings**

Simmer slowly, until reduced by half. Strain into a double boiler and keep warm, over hot water, while adding:

½ **cup dry sherry**

ORANGE SAUCE FOR DUCK OR GOOSE

[About 2 Cups]

For a true Bigarade, see page 588.

Pour off the fat from the pan in which you have roasted the bird. Deglaze the pan with:

1 **cup Game Stock (II, 143)**

Thicken with:

1 **teaspoon arrowroot or cornstarch**

mixed first with a little of the stock. In another pan, cook together until light brown:

2 **tablespoons vinegar**
2 **tablespoons sugar**

Add the sauce from the roasting pan and cook 4 or 5 minutes, then add:

1 **tablespoon julienned and blanched orange rind**
½ **cup hot orange juice**
1 **teaspoon lemon juice**

2 tablespoons curaçao
Correct the seasoning

Serve immediately over goose or wild or domestic duck and garnish with:

Orange sections

BORDELAISE SAUCE

For sweetbreads, chops, steaks, grilled meats.
Cook together in a saucepan:

½ cup dry red wine
4 or 5 crushed black peppercorns

until reduced to ¾, then add:

1 cup Brown Sauce, above

Simmer for 15 minutes. Add, just before serving:

¼ cup diced beef marrow, poached for a few minutes and drained
(½ teaspoon lemon juice)
½ teaspoon chopped parsley

QUICK BROWN SAUCE OR GRAVY

[About 1 Cup]
You may rub your pan with:

½ clove garlic

Melt:

2 tablespoons butter

Stir in, until blended:

2 tablespoons flour

Stir in:

1 cup canned bouillon or 1 or 2 bouillon cubes dissolved in 1 cup boiling water

Permit the gravy to reach the boiling point. Stir it constantly. Season it as required with:

Salt and pepper or paprika
Dry sherry or Worcestershire sauce
Lemon juice, catsup or chili sauce
Dried herbs

HUNTER'S SAUCE OR SAUCE CHASSEUR

[About 2 Cups]
Sauté gently until very tender:

2 tablespoons minced onion or shallots

in:

2 tablespoons butter

Stir in and sauté gently for about 2 minutes:

1 cup sliced mushrooms

Add:

½ cup dry white wine
(2 tablespoons brandy)

Simmer until reduced by ½. Add:

½ cup tomato sauce or purée
1 cup Brown Sauce, page 365

Cook for 5 minutes, then:

Correct the seasoning

and add:

1 teaspoon chopped parsley

MADEIRA SAUCE

[About 1 Cup]
This sauce may also be made with dry sherry. It is good with game or fillet of beef.
Reduce:

1 cup Brown Sauce, page 365

to ¾ its volume, then add:

¼ cup Madeira
(1 teaspoon Meat Glaze (II, 145))

Finish with a:

Butter Swirl, page 357

and another:

2 tablespoons Madeira

Keep hot, but do not allow to boil after adding the butter. You may also make this in the pan in which you have sautéed the meat. Remove the meat and pour off the fat. Deglaze the pan with the above quantity of Madeira until the wine is reduced by half, then add the Brown Sauce and cook for 10 minutes before finishing, as described above.

LYONNAISE SAUCE OR BROWN ONION SAUCE

[1¼ Cups]

A good sauce to use for leftover meat.

Melt in a saucepan:

2 tablespoons butter

Add:

2 finely chopped onions

and cook until golden brown. Add:

⅓ cup dry white wine or 2 tablespoons vinegar

If you use the wine, simmer until reduced by ½. Then add:

1 cup Brown Sauce, page 365

and simmer for 15 minutes. Just before serving, add:

1 tablespoon finely chopped parsley

MARCHAND DE VIN SAUCE

[About 2 Cups]

Serve with broiled steak.

Sauté:

1 cup finely sliced mushrooms

in:

2 tablespoons butter

Add:

½ cup hot beef stock

➧ Simmer for 10 minutes. Add:

1 cup Brown Sauce, page 365

½ cup dry red wine

➧ Simmer for 20 minutes, then:

Correct the seasoning

You may add:

(Juice of ½ lemon)

MUSHROOM SAUCE

[About 2 Cups]

For roast meat, chicken and casseroles.

Sauté:

¼ lb. sliced mushrooms

in:

2 tablespoons butter

Remove the mushrooms from the skillet. Add to the drippings:

1 cup Brown Sauce, page 365, or Quick Brown Sauce, page 366

When the sauce is heated, add the sautéed mushrooms.

SAUCE PÉRIGUEUX

[1 Cup]

Use for croquettes, shirred eggs and chicken.

Prepare:

Madeira Sauce, page 366

Just before adding the butter swirl, stir in:

1 tablespoon chopped truffles

Very similar is **Sauce Périgourdine**, but the truffles are finely diced instead of chopped and a dice of foie gras is added.

PIQUANT SAUCE

[About 1¼ Cups]

This sauce is excellent for giving extra zip to bland meats and for reheating leftover meat. A good sauce for pork and pigs' feet.

Lightly brown:

2 tablespoons minced onion

in:

1 tablespoon butter

Add:

2 tablespoons dry white wine or 2 tablespoons vinegar or lemon juice

and cook until the liquid is almost evaporated. Add:

1 cup Brown Sauce, page 365

and simmer for 10 minutes. Just before serving, add:

1 tablespoon chopped parsley or chopped mixed parsley, tarragon and chervil

1 tablespoon chopped sour pickles

1 tablespoon chopped capers

Correct the seasoning

SAUCE ROBERT

[1¼ Cups]

Prepare:

Piquant Sauce, above

doubling the amount of onion and omitting the parsley, chervil and tarragon. Just before serving, stir in:

1 teaspoon prepared Dijon-type mustard
A pinch of powdered sugar

POIVRADE OR PEPPER SAUCE

[3 Cups]
This is the traditional sauce to serve with venison and constitutes the basis of several other game sauces. As the name suggests, it is quite peppery.
Heat:
¼ cup cooking oil
Sauté in it, until brown:
1 chopped carrot
1 chopped onion
(Game bones, trimmings and giblets, if available)
Add:
3 sprigs parsley
1 bay leaf
A pinch of thyme
¼ cup vinegar or ¼ cup marinade liquid, if the game has been marinated before cooking
Simmer until reduced to ⅓ original quantity. Add:
3 cups Brown Sauce, page 365
Bring to a boil ➧ reduce heat and simmer for 1 hour. Add:
10 peppercorns
and simmer 5 more minutes. Strain the sauce into another saucepan and add again:
¼ cup marinade liquid
Cook slowly for 30 minutes more, then add:
½ cup dry red wine
Correct the seasoning
Add enough:
Freshly ground black pepper
to make a hot sauce.

ROSEMARY WINE SAUCE

[1 Cup]
Serve with Calf's Head, or turtle meat.
Heat to boiling point:
½ cup good Madeira or dry sherry
Add:
1 teaspoon mixed dried marjoram, rosemary, sage, bay leaf, thyme and basil
This strongly flavored combination of herbs is known as herbs "à tortue" in France. Remove from heat and let stand 5 to 10 minutes. Strain off the herb-flavored wine and add it to:
1 cup hot Brown Sauce, page 365

ABOUT HOLLANDAISE AND OTHER EGG-THICKENED SAUCES

These delicious sauces, loaded with calories, make a superb dish out of the plainest and simplest cooked vegetables or broiled or roasted meat. But nothing can make a cook more frenzied than a Hollandaise which suddenly breaks or fails to thicken just as dinner is to be served. To avoid such disasters, here are a few tricks. Don't try to make Hollandaise or Béarnaise, on a very humid day, unless you use Clarified Butter, page 383. You will remove the cords from the egg yolks as they make the sauce lumpy. Cook these sauces ➧ over—not in—hot, but not boiling, water. If you use a heatproof glass double boiler you can see when the water begins to boil and add 1 or 2 tablespoons of cold water. ➧ Keep stirring the sauce all the time and ➧ add the melted butter very, very slowly at first. Scrape the mixture away from the sides and bottom of the pan as you stir, to keep the sauce smooth. As with Mayonnaise, page 345, a wooden spoon or a whisk is the best tool for making Hollandaise. A professional chef will make Hollandaise over low direct heat, but don't try this unless you have a drummer's quick wrist—as it needs both fast and practiced stirring. ➧ To hold egg sauces for several hours, prepare and stir in wide-mouthed vacuum bottles, as sketched. Some of our friends freeze Hollandaise just as one can roux-based sauces.

Reheat it in a double boiler ➧ over—not in—hot water, stirring constantly so that it does not break. Should any of these egg sauces break, beat into them at once 1 to 2 tablespoons cream. Or a slightly curdled sauce can be rescued in a blender, although the texture will not be as good as an originally well-made sauce. Or it can be reconstituted, using a fresh egg yolk as for Mayonnaise, page 345.

NEVER-FAIL HOLLANDAISE SAUCE

➧ Please read About Hollandaise Sauce, page 369

[1 Cup]

Our cook calls this "holiday sauce"—isn't that a grand name for it?

Melt slowly and keep warm:

½ cup butter

Barely heat:

1½ tablespoons lemon juice, dry sherry or tarragon vinegar

Have ready a small saucepan of boiling water and a tablespoon with which to measure it when ready. Place in the top of a double boiler ➧ over—not in—hot water:

3 egg yolks

Beat the yolks with a wire whisk until they begin to thicken. Add:

1 tablespoon boiling water

Beat again until the eggs begin to thicken. Repeat this process until you have added:

3 more tablespoons water

Then beat in the warm lemon juice. Remove the double boiler from the heat. Beat the sauce well with a wire whisk. Beat constantly while adding the melted butter slowly and:

¼ teaspoon salt
A few grains cayenne

Beat until the sauce is thick. Serve at once.

⅄ BLENDER HOLLANDAISE

[About 1 Cup]

This is easy, but not as flavorful as handmade Hollandaise. It is also paler in color. ➧ Do not make in a smaller quantity than given here, as there is, then, not enough heat to cook the eggs properly.

Have ready in your blender:

3 egg yolks
2 tablespoons lemon juice
A pinch of cayenne
¼ teaspoon salt

Heat to bubbling stage, but do not brown:

½ cup butter

Cover container and turn motor on "High." After 3 seconds, remove the lid and pour the butter over the eggs in a steady stream. By the time the butter is poured in—about 30 seconds—the sauce should be finished. If not, blend on "High" about 5 seconds longer. Serve at once or keep warm by immersing blender container in warm water. This sauce may be frozen and reconstituted over hot water.

MOCK HOLLANDAISE

For less rich versions, try one of the following or if you are in a hurry, prepare Hot Mayonnaise.

I. [About 1¼ Cups]
Mix in the top of a double boiler:

1 cup cultured sour cream
Juice of 1 lemon
2 egg yolks
½ teaspoon salt
¼ teaspoon paprika

Stir ➧ over—not in—hot water until thick.

II. [4]
Good over vegetables such as Cauliflower, see page 281.
Place in a double boiler ➧ over—not in—boiling water:

2 beaten eggs
¼ cup cream
⅛ teaspoon salt
⅛ teaspoon freshly ground nutmeg
1 tablespoon lemon juice

Cook and stir these ingredients until they are thick, then add a little at a time:

2 tablespoons butter

Serve at once.

HOT MAYONNAISE SAUCE

[About 1 Cup]
Good over steak and fish.
Heat in a double boiler and stir:

1 cup mayonnaise

Add:

Lemon juice and capers

MOUSSELINE SAUCE

[1¼ Cups]
Use for any vegetable or fish on which Hollandaise is served.
Just before serving, add:

½ cup whipped cream

to:

1 cup Hollandaise Sauce, above

Serve hot or cold.

FIGARO SAUCE

Prepare:

1 cup Hollandaise Sauce, above

Beat in very slowly:

¼ cup warm tomato purée

Add:

1 to 2 tablespoons chopped parsley
Correct the seasoning

and serve.

MALTAISE SAUCE

[About 1 Cup]
Interesting on asparagus.
Add:

2 to 3 tablespoons orange juice
1 teaspoon grated orange rind

to:

1 cup Hollandaise Sauce, above

SAUCE BÉARNAISE

[About 1½ Cups]
Heavenly on most broiled red meat, especially beef tenderloin. It is also quite at home on fish and eggs.
Combine in the top of a double boiler:

½ cup white wine or red wine
2 tablespoons tarragon vinegar
1 tablespoon finely chopped shallots or onion
2 crushed peppercorns
2 sprigs chopped tarragon
1 sprig finely chopped chervil
(1 sprig parsley)

Cook over direct heat until reduced by half. ➧ If you have used dried tarragon or coarsely chopped onion, now strain the mixture. Allow it to cool. Then, beating briskly ➧ over—not in—hot water, add alternately a little at a time and beat steadily so that they are well combined before you add in all:

3 egg yolks
¾ cup melted butter
Correct the seasoning

When you have added all the butter, the sauce should have the consistency of Hollandaise.

SOUFFLÉD MAYONNAISE SAUCE FOR FISH [6]

This is also good as a masking for broiled tomatoes.

Broil until nearly done, see page 399:

3 lbs. fish

Transfer them to a hot ovenproof dish. Combine and beat well:

½ cup mayonnaise
¼ cup pickle relish
2 tablespoons chopped parsley
1 tablespoon lemon juice
¼ teaspoon salt
A few grains cayenne

Beat until stiff, but not dry:

2 egg whites

Fold them into the mayonnaise mixture. Spread the sauce evenly on the fish. Broil it until the sauce is puffed and golden.

MINT SAUCE

[About 1 Cup]

The usual accompaniment to roast lamb.

Heat:

3 tablespoons water

Dissolve in it:

1½ tablespoons confectioners' sugar

Cool the sirup and add:

⅓ cup finely chopped mint leaves
½ cup strong vinegar

This is best made ½ hour before serving.

SWEET-SOUR MUSTARD SAUCE

[About 2½ Cups]

Use for ham or tongue.

Combine in a double boiler ◆ over—not in—hot water:

½ cup sugar
1 tablespoon flour
4 teaspoons dry mustard

Add gradually:

2 cups cream

mixed with:

2 egg yolks

Cook until thick. Stir in, gradually:

½ cup vinegar

SWEET-SOUR CREAM DRESSING

[About 1 Cup]

For snap beans, cabbage, etc.

Combine and stir over very low heat until the sauce thickens slightly:

1 beaten egg
½ cup cultured sour cream
2 tablespoons sugar
¼ cup vinegar
½ teaspoon salt
¼ teaspoon paprika

Serve it hot over hot vegetables or cold over chilled vegetables.

SWEET-SOUR BACON SAUCE

[About 1 Cup]

Fine for green beans.

Slowly render, until crisp:

4 thin slices of cut-up bacon

At the same time, you may cook until transparent:

(1 teaspoon minced onion)

Remove the bacon and onion and pour off all but:

2 tablespoons bacon grease

Add to the grease:

¾ cup of the bean or vegetable stock
2 tablespoons vinegar
1 to 2 tablespoons sugar

CHINESE SWEET-SOUR SAUCE

I. [1 Cup]

Heat:

½ cup pineapple juice

3 tablespoons oil
2 tablespoons brown sugar
1 teaspoon soy sauce or salt
½ teaspoon pepper
¼ cup mild vinegar

II. [2½ to 3 Cups]
Serve with Chinese Meat Balls, page 519, or Sweet-Sour Pork, page 488.
Have ready a paste of:
2 tablespoons cornstarch
½ cup chicken broth
2 tablespoons soy sauce
Melt in a heavy pan:
2 tablespoons butter
Add:
1 cup chicken broth
¾ to 1 cup diced green peppers
6 slices diced canned pineapple
Cover and simmer for 5 minutes. Add the cornstarch paste and the following ingredients to the peppers and pineapple:
½ cup vinegar
¾ cup pineapple juice
½ cup sugar
½ teaspoon salt
¼ teaspoon ginger
Simmer, stirring constantly, until the mixture thickens.

CHINESE SAUCE FOR VEGETABLES

[For About 1 lb. Vegetables]
Blend until smooth:
1 tablespoon cornstarch
3 tablespoons cold water
Add:
½ teaspoon salt
1 tablespoon soy sauce
½ teaspoon finely grated gingerroot
Pour over vegetables that are cooking. Stir well until the whole mixture comes to a boil.

CURRANT JELLY SAUCES

I. [About 1¼ Cups]
For game or cold meat.
Heat in a double boiler just before serving:
¾ cup currant jelly
Stir in:
½ cup Indian chutney
1 teaspoon lemon juice
1 tablespoon brandy
Salt

II. [About ½ Cup]
Make a simplified version by mixing:
½ cup jelly
2 tablespoons horseradish
½ teaspoon dry mustard

HOT CUMBERLAND SAUCE

[About 2 Cups]
This calls for many ingredients, but you may omit some or substitute others.
Combine:
1 teaspoon dry mustard
1 tablespoon brown sugar
¼ teaspoon powdered ginger
A few grains cayenne
¼ teaspoon salt
¼ teaspoon ground cloves
1½ cups red wine, preferably port
(½ cup seedless raisins)
(½ cup blanched slivered almonds)
Simmer the sauce, covered, for 8 minutes.
Dissolve:
2 tablespoons cornstarch
in:
2 tablespoons cold water
Stir this into the sauce. Let it simmer for about 2 minutes.
Stir in:
¼ cup red currant jelly
1 tablespoon grated orange and lemon rind
¼ cup orange juice
2 tablespoons lemon juice

BURGUNDY SAUCE OR SAUCE BOURGUIGNONNE

[1 Cup]
For snails and egg dishes.
Reduce by ½ a mixture of:

2 cups dry red wine, preferably red Burgundy
2 minced shallots
A few sprigs parsley
A pinch of thyme
¼ bay leaf
(Mushroom peelings)

Strain the mixture. When ready to serve, heat and add:

1 to 1½ tablespoons Kneaded Butter, page 357
(A dash of cayenne)

RAISIN CIDER OR BEER SAUCE

[About 1½ Cups]
Good with hot or cold ham or smoked tongue.
Combine in a saucepan:

¼ cup firmly packed brown sugar
1½ tablespoons cornstarch
⅛ teaspoon salt

Stir in:

1 cup fresh cider or beer
¼ cup raisins, cut in halves

Put in a cheese cloth bag and hang it in the cooking sauce from the edge of the pan:

8 whole cloves
1 two-inch stick cinnamon

Cook and stir for about 10 minutes. Add:

1 tablespoon butter

Remove the spices. Serve the sauce very hot.

SAUCE FOR LIGHT MEAT GAME

After roasting the game bird, which is barded with salt pork or bacon and basted with equal quantities of butter and white wine, flame it in:

⅛ cup cognac: 1 oz.

Remove the game and keep warm. Degrease the pan juices and reduce them over low heat for 1 minute. Then add, for each small bird:

1 egg yolk

Beat in:

½ cup whipping cream

Stir until thickened ◆ but do not allow the sauce to boil. Season well.

BERCY SAUCE

[¼ Cup]
White wine is best for this sauce, which is served on fish.
Cook until transparent:

1 teaspoon finely chopped shallots

in:

1 tablespoon butter

Add:

¼ cup dry white or red wine
¼ cup Fish Fumet (II, 143)

and simmer until reduced by ½.
Thicken the mixture with:

Kneaded butter, made by creaming together 1 teaspoon flour and 2 tablespoons butter

stirring it in briskly until well blended.
Add:

1 teaspoon chopped parsley
Correct the seasoning

WHITE WINE SAUCE FOR FISH

[About 1¼ Cups]
Reduce by ½ over medium heat a mixture of:

¼ cup white wine
1 bay leaf
2 cloves
2 black peppercorns
(1½-inch piece gingerroot)
¼ cup fish stock
1 teaspoon chopped shallot

Strain and add to:

1 cup strained Cream Sauce I, page 359

To make a sauce that coats well and browns beautifully, add:

2 tablespoons whipped cream

WHITE WINE SAUCE FOR LIGHT MEATS

[About 1 Cup]
Serve over Sautéed Brains, page

540, or other light meats.
Add to the pan drippings and sauté until light yellow:

1 **tablespoon chopped onion**

Stir in until smooth:

1½ **tablespoons flour**

Stir in gradually, until the sauce is smooth and very hot:

½ **cup chicken or veal stock**
½ **cup dry white wine**

Add:

1 **tablespoon chopped parsley or chives**
Salt, as needed

SOYER'S UNIVERSAL DEVIL SAUCE

We have chosen this sauce from Alexis Soyer's "Culinary Campaign," a fabulous account of the Crimean War, through which he cooked his way with abandon. No one brought more conviction to his work, whether changing the diet of the British armed forces, cooking at the Reform Club or remolding the cooking habits of the English lower classes—which he attempted through his Shilling Cook Book. The original recipe called for a tablespoon of cayenne pepper. We have changed it to a small pinch, for in Soyer's day cayenne was baked into a sort of bread and then ground, making it about the same strength as a mild paprika.
Rub any deviled food with the following mixture:

1 **good tablespoon Durham mustard**
¼ **cup chili vinegar**
1 **tablespoon grated horseradish**
2 **bruised shallots**
1 **teaspoon salt**
A few grains cayenne
½ **teaspoon black pepper**
1 **teaspooon sugar**
(2 teaspoons chopped chilies)
(2 raw egg yolks)

Soyer's instructions are to "broil slowly at first and end as near as possible the Pandemonium Fire."

BARBECUE SAUCES

Please read About Skewer Cooking, pages 74–75. It is important to ♦ baste with barbecue sauces only during the last 15 minutes of cooking. Too long cooking of the sauce will make the spices bitter.

I. [About 2 Cups]
Sauté until brown:

¼ **cup chopped onions**

in:

1 **tablespoon drippings or other fat**

Add and simmer for 20 minutes:

½ **cup water**
2 **tablespoons vinegar**
1 **tablespoon Worchestershire sauce**
¼ **cup lemon juice**
2 **tablespoons brown sugar**
1 **cup chili sauce**
½ **teaspoon salt**
¼ **teaspoon paprika**
1 **teaspoon pepper**
1 **teaspoon mustard**

II. [About 1½ Cups]
Simmer for 15 minutes, stirring frequently:

12 **to 14 oz. tomato catsup**
½ **cup white distilled vinegar**
1 **teaspoon sugar**
A liberal seasoning of red and black pepper
⅛ **teaspoon salt**

FEROCIOUS BARBECUE SAUCE

Combine and heat:

1½ **cups Barbecue Sauce II, above**
¼ **of a seeded lemon, diced fine**
½ **teaspoon ground cumin**
1 **teaspoon ground coriander**
⅛ **teaspoon Spanish paprika**

⅛ teaspoon saffron
¼ teaspoon ground ginger

BARBECUE SAUCE FOR FOWL

[For 1 Fowl]
I. Combine and heat:
4 teaspoons lemon juice
1 teaspoon Worcestershire sauce
1 teaspoon tomato catsup
1 tablespoon butter

II. Cook slowly until golden:
1 medium chopped onion
1 minced clove garlic
in:
3 tablespoons fat
Add and simmer for 30 minutes:
3 tablespoons soy or Worcestershire sauce
1 cup water
1 red pepper
2 tablespoons vinegar
2 to 4 tablespoons brown sugar
1 cup catsup
1 teaspoon prepared mustard
½ cup celery
½ teaspoon salt
Then add:
¼ cup lemon juice

QUICK CANNED SOUP SAUCES

Not only can the thin canned consommés and broths be used for flavoring sauces, but some of the condensed cream soups can be quickly made into acceptable sauces. ➧ Taste before salting them.
I. [1¼ Cups]
For chicken, veal and fish.
Heat:
1 cup condensed cream of chicken soup
2 tablespoons butter
2 to 4 tablespoons rich chicken or vegetable stock
A grating of lemon rind

II. [1¼ Cups]
For beef hash.
Heat:
1 cup cream of mushroom soup
2 to 4 tablespoons strong beef stock
½ teaspoon meat glaze
Few drops garlic juice
1 tablespoon butter

III. [1¼ Cups]
For creaming vegetables.
Heat:
1 cup cream of celery soup
2 tablespoons butter
2 to 4 tablespoons chicken stock
1 tablespoon chopped chives

DRIED SOUP SAUCES [4]

These are not as quick as the canned ones but can provide a well-flavored base when reconstituted with half the amount of liquid called for normally. Use in making sauces for casseroles. The dried vegetables swell as the casserole cooks.
Try heating:
1 package dried cream of leek, cream of mushroom or smoky pea soup
1½ cups light cream or top milk
Use with leftover chicken or veal, with rice or noodles in a casserole. Or combine and heat:
1 package dried onion soup
1½ to 2 cups water
and add to meat and vegetables in a casserole. Again, do not salt—and go easy on other seasonings in these sauces—until they have cooked for about 20 minutes and you have tasted them.

QUICK À LA KING SAUCE

[About 1½ Cups]
To the rescue, whenever this type of sauce is required.
Sauté until tender:

1 minced green pepper

in:

1 tablespoon butter

Add the contents of:

1 can condensed mushroom soup: 10½ oz.
¼ cup milk

Heat the sauce and add:

1 pimiento, cut into strips
(2 tablespoons dry sherry)

QUICK CREOLE SAUCE

[2½ Cups]

To:

2 cups Quick Tomato Sauce, page 377

Add:

½ cup finely chopped green peppers, onion, celery, olives and pimiento

QUICK TOMATO CHEESE SAUCE

[About 1½ Cups]

Good over eggs.

Heat in a double boiler:

1 can condensed tomato soup: 10½ oz.

Add:

¼ teaspoon salt
¼ teaspoon pepper or paprika

Stir and cook these ingredients until they are hot. Beat in:

1 cup or more grated cheese

Use a wire whisk. Beat the sauce until the cheese is melted.

UNTHICKENED TOMATO SAUCE

[About 4 Cups]

Place over low heat:

3 tablespoons olive oil

Add and stir for about 3 minutes:

1 large chopped Bermuda onion
2 chopped celery ribs with leaves
1 carrot, cut in small pieces
(½ chopped green pepper, seeds and fibrous portions removed)
(1 chopped clove garlic)

Add:

4 cups canned tomatoes or
6 large fresh tomatoes

If these are very juicy, peel and squeeze slightly to get rid of excess liquid and seeds. Add:

1 sprig thyme, basil or tarragon
1 teaspoon salt
⅛ teaspoon pepper
1 teaspoon sugar

Cook the sauce gently, uncovered, until thick, for about 45 minutes. ➧ Watch it, so that it does not burn. Put it through a fine strainer. Add seasoning, if needed. This sauce will keep for several days.

THICKENED TOMATO SAUCE

[About 1½ Cups]

Bring to a boil and then ➧ simmer for 30 minutes before sieving:

2 cups canned tomatoes
1 onion, stuck with 3 cloves
2 chopped celery ribs with leaves
1 diced carrot
1 Bouquet Garni (II, 220)
1 bay leaf
(½ chopped green pepper)

➧ Be sure to get all the pulpy residue when sieving, so that only cloves, leaves and seeds remain in the sieve. This well-flavored pulp helps thicken the sauce. Melt in a saucepan:

3 tablespoons butter

Stir in, until blended:

2 tablespoons flour

Add the strained thickish stock slowly with:

¼ teaspoon sugar

➧ Simmer and stir the stock for about 5 to 10 minutes.

Correct the seasoning

Flavor with:

(1 tablespoon fresh basil)

QUICK TOMATO SAUCE

[About 3 Cups]

Strain:
1 large can Italian tomatoes
Add:
½ can tomato paste: 6 oz.
½ teaspoon salt
1 tablespoon onion juice or 2 tablespoons finely grated onion
½ teaspoon sugar
Bring to a boil and simmer gently for 15 to 20 minutes.

SHRIMP SAUCE FOR FISH

[3½ Cups]
This is an elaborate sauce. Do not hesitate to deduct from, add to or alter it.
Prepare:
2 cups Thickened Tomato Sauce, page 376, or 2 cups Cream Sauce I, page 359
Season the sauce well. Add and heat to the boiling point:
1 teaspoon Worcestershire or 2 teaspoons chili sauce
2 tablespoons chopped parsley
¼ cup chopped olives
½ cup boiled or canned shrimp
½ cup sautéed or canned mushrooms
¼ cup finely chopped celery
Serve the sauce with baked or boiled fish or place the fish on a platter and pour the sauce over it. Heat it under a broiler.

ITALIAN TOMATO PASTE

This flavorful paste is diluted in a little boiling water or stock and added to sauces and soups. Fine in spaghetti and noodle dishes and as a dressing for cooked vegetables or salads.
Wash and cut into slices:
1½ pecks ripe Italian tomatoes: 6 quarts
Add:
3 teaspoons salt
You may add:
1 large celery stalk, cut up with some leaves
¾ cup chopped onion
3 tablespoons fresh herbs or 1 tablespoon dried herbs
¾ teaspoon peppercorns
12 cloves
1 two-inch stick cinnamon
(1 minced clove garlic)
Simmer these ingredients until the tomatoes are soft. Stir frequently. Put the vegetables through a fine sieve. Simmer the pulp over hot water or simmer it over direct heat with some means of protecting it from the bottom by using an asbestos pad. Stir it frequently, as it burns easily. After several hours, when the pulp is thick and reduced by about ½, spread the paste to the depth of ½ inch on moist plates. Cut into the paste to permit the air to penetrate. Place the paste in the sun to dry or dry it in a 250° oven. When the paste is dry enough, roll it into balls. They may be dipped in salad oil. Store them in airtight jars or store the paste in a tin box with waxed paper between the layers.

TOMATO PASTE OR VELVET

[About ¾ Cup]
Wash, then mash:
6 large ripe tomatoes
Melt:
2 tablespoons butter
Add the tomatoes and:
1 teaspoon brown sugar
¼ teaspoon paprika
¾ teaspoon salt
Cook the tomatoes over low heat, stirring constantly or in a double boiler, until they are the consistency of thick paste. Put the paste through a strainer. This makes a relish or fine addition to sauces.

MEXICAN SAUCE

[About 1 Cup]

Just what you might expect. You will feel hot inside, down to your toes. Use with Cowboy Eggs, page 186.

Place in a small saucepan and simmer until fairly thick:

- ¾ cup canned tomatoes or about 3 large, skinned and quartered, peeled and seeded fresh tomatoes
- 6 tablespoons chili sauce
- 2 teaspoons dry mustard
- 3 tablespoons grated or prepared horseradish
- ½ teaspoon sugar
- ¾ teaspoon salt
- ¼ teaspoon pepper
- A few grains cayenne
- ¾ teaspoon curry powder
- 6 tablespoons vinegar
- 1 teaspoon onion juice
- 1 sliced clove garlic

Strain the sauce. Add:

- 1 teaspoon dried or 1 tablespoon fresh herbs

This may be served—in discreet quantities—by itself but it combines excellently with hot cream sauce or hot or cold mayonnaise. Use as much of the Mexican sauce as you find palatable.

SPAGHETTI MEAT SAUCE

[About 2½ Quarts]

Mince and cook over very slow heat:

- 3 slices bacon

Stir in and sauté:

- ¼ cup chopped onion
- ½ lb. ground round steak

When the meat is nearly done, add:

- 2½ cups pressed drained tomatoes
- ½ cup chopped green peppers
- 1 cup chopped mushrooms or ½ lb. to 1 lb. fresh sliced Sautéed Mushrooms, page 296
- Salt, cayenne or paprika
- ½ lb. grated cheese: 2 cups

Simmer ◆ uncovered 20 or 30 minutes. If more liquid is needed after adding the spaghetti, add:

- ½ cup hot stock or canned bouillon

ITALIAN MEAT SAUCE FOR SPAGHETTI

[About 1 Quart]

Heat:

- ½ cup olive oil

Add:

- 1 pressed clove garlic
- 1 lb. ground round steak
- ¼ lb. ground lean pork
- 2 cups Italian tomatoes
- ½ cup Italian tomato paste
- ½ cup beef or veal stock
- 1½ teaspoons salt
- ¼ teaspoon pepper
- 1 bay leaf

Simmer the sauce uncovered for about 1 hour. Add the last 15 minutes:

- (½ cup sliced mushrooms)

Season it with:

- 1 to 2 tablespoons fresh basil

Serve over:

- Cooked spaghetti or noodles

with:

- Grated Parmesan cheese

SPAGHETTI SAUCE WITH LIVER [4]

Melt:

- 2 tablespoons butter or drippings

Sauté in it until light brown:

- ½ cup chopped onions

Add and sauté very lightly:

- 1 cup cubed liver or chicken livers

Add and simmer for about 15 minutes:

- ½ cup tomato sauce

Season with:

- 1 teaspoon salt
- ⅛ teaspoon pepper
- (¼ teaspoon basil)

Serve the sauce over noodles,

spaghetti, etc., garnished with:
Parsley

BOLOGNESE SAUCE

[About 2 Cups]
This is an interesting variation on the usual meat sauce for pasta.
Melt in a large saucepan:
⅓ cup butter
Add:
¼ cup minced lean ham or Canadian bacon
¼ cup finely chopped carrot
¼ cup finely chopped onion
Stir and cook for 1 or 2 minutes. Add:
1 cup chopped lean beef
and brown it over medium heat, stirring occasionally, then add:
2 tablespoons tomato paste
1 strip lemon peel
A pinch of nutmeg
1 cup beef stock
(½ cup dry white wine)
Partially cover and simmer slowly for 1 hour. Remove from heat, take out the lemon peel and stir in:
¼ cup whipping cream
just before serving with:
Green Noodles, page 149, or Lasagne, page 176

MARINARA SAUCE

[About 1½ Cups]
Keep this sauce on hand. Use a little on green beans or serve over meatless spaghetti.
Sauté lightly:
1 minced clove garlic
in:
2 tablespoons olive oil and the oil from the anchovies
Add slowly:
2½ cups canned pressed and drained whole or Italian tomatoes
then stir in:
6 finely chopped anchovies
½ teaspoon orégano
1 tablespoon chopped parsley
Bring to a boil then ➧ reduce heat and simmer uncovered 15 to 20 minutes, stirring occasionally. If served with spaghetti, pass with:
Grated Parmesan cheese
Try omitting the orégano and adding:
(5 chopped canned artichoke hearts)
Simmer 3 or 4 minutes more.

SEA FOOD SPAGHETTI SAUCE

[About 1 Quart]
Heat:
1½ cups condensed tomato soup
Melt in a saucepan over slow heat:
¼ cup olive oil or butter
Stir in and cook until transparent:
¼ cup or more chopped onion
¾ cup chopped green pepper
Stir in slowly:
½ cup Stock (II, 141)
When the sauce is hot, add very slowly, stirring constantly:
½ lb. cooked or canned diced lobster, crab, shrimp or tuna
Remove from heat and add:
½ lb. diced cheese: Mozzarella or Scamorza
Correct the seasoning
and stir in cheese until melted. Pour over cooked spaghetti.

QUICK SHRIMP AND CLAM SAUCE FOR PASTA

[Enough for 1 lb. Pasta]
Heat in a skillet:
6 tablespoons olive oil
Add:
3 minced cloves garlic
and cook gently for 5 minutes. Add:
¾ cup finely chopped parsley
1 cup minced clams or mussels with liquid

½ lb. shelled raw shrimp, cut in bite size pieces
(⅛ teaspoon orégano)

Heat until bubbling and the shrimp is pink. Serve at once over hot cooked sea shell pasta—conchiglie—to complete the marine flavor. This goes down well with seafood addicts who don't care for the usual tomato sauces. Pass with:

Grated Parmesan or Romano cheese

OCTOPUS PASTA SAUCE

[For 1 lb. Linguini Pasta]

Heat in a large saucepan:

1 to 1¼ cups olive oil

Add:

1¼ cups seeded, peeled fresh tomatoes
⅔ to 1 cup finely chopped parsley
1 teaspoon salt
2 cloves garlic

To remove the garlic before serving, see (II, 210). Simmer the mixture for 15 to 20 minutes. Add:

1½ cups cooked octopus, cut into bite size pieces

Simmer for another 15 to 20 minutes. Toss with the cooked, drained pasta and serve at once.

CREOLE SAUCE

[About 2 Cups]

Melt over low heat:

2 tablespoons butter

Add and cook, covered, for about 2 minutes:

¼ cup chopped onion
1 minced clove garlic
6 shredded green olives

Add and cook until the sauce is thick, about 50 minutes:

1½ cups canned tomatoes or ½ cup tomatoes and 1 cup Brown Sauce, page 365
½ chopped green pepper, with seeds and membranes removed
½ bay leaf
A pinch of thyme
1 teaspoon chopped parsley
1 teaspoon white or brown sugar
⅓ teaspoon salt
A few grains cayenne
(1 tablespoon dry sherry)
(¼ cup chili sauce)
(2 tablespoons diced ham)
(½ cup sliced mushrooms)

ABOUT MARINADES

Never underestimate the power of a marinade. ➧ Choose your type carefully if an originally delicate food flavor is to be preserved. These aromatic tenderizing liquids are easily abused. There is usually an acid in their make-up, so any dish in which they are soaked should be glass, glazed or impervious metal—like stainless steel or stainless enamel. Use wooden spoons in stirring or turning.

The simplest marinades are, first, a means of spreading flavor or preserving a better color; and immersion may last only a few minutes. Spicier, stronger marinades may be devised to make bland food more interesting or to mask off-flavor. But perhaps the most important function of a marinade is to tenderize tougher foods. Sometimes these replace and sometimes are combined with papaya extract, which tenderizes.

Marinades may be either raw or cooked. ➧ The cooked ones make their flavor more available to the food and should be prepared in advance and ➧ thoroughly chilled before use. They are best to use if the marinade exceeds 12 hours. Marinating is hastened by higher temperatures, but so is the danger of bacterial activity.

➧ Refrigerate any foods in their marinade if the marination period indicated is 1 hour or more or if the weather is hot or stormy.

A marinade is also used in finishing a sauce. So do not discard it before deciding whether you need it for your meat when it has been cooked. Sauce Poivrade for venison is an example. And some dishes, such as Hasenpfeffer and Sauerbraten, are cooked in the marinade, which is then converted into a sauce proper—just before serving.

When using the same marinade for cubed meat or one whole piece, soak the cubes for only 2 to 3 hours and the whole 4- or 5-lb. piece overnight. Longer marination may be too pungent and kill the flavor of the meat. In an emergency, try mixing oil and vinegar with packaged dried salad seasonings for a quickly prepared marinade.

MARINADES FOR VEGETABLES

Marinated vegetables are usually served cold as hors d'oeuvre or salads. French dressing seasoned with herbs, Vinaigrette and Ravigote Sauces are all suitable for the short-term marinating of vegetables. See also Vegetables à la Grecque, page 257.

FISH OR LAMB MARINADE

[Enough for 1 lb. Lamb Kebabs]

I. Combine:

- 2 tablespoons lemon juice
- ¼ cup olive oil
- 1 teaspoon salt
- ⅛ teaspoon pepper

Marinate refrigerated and covered for at least 3 hours. Turn frequently.

II. Combine:

- ½ teaspoon turmeric
- ½ teaspoon powdered ginger
- 1 small pressed clove garlic
- 1 tablespoon lemon juice
- ½ teaspoon grated lemon rind

Toss the meat in this mixture and leave to marinate covered and refrigerated for 24 hours.

II. Combine:

- ¼ cup pineapple juice
- 2 teaspoons soy sauce
- 2 teaspoons lemon juice
- 1 minced clove garlic

Marinate covered and refrigerated for 2 hours, turning the meat frequently.

LAMB OR GAME MARINADE

[About 1 Cup]

For marinated leg of lamb.

Combine:

- ½ cup dry red wine
- ¼ cup vinegar
- ¼ cup olive oil
- 3 to 4 juniper berries
- A sprig of parsley
- A sprig of thyme
- 2 bay leaves
- 1 crushed clove garlic
- 2 slices onion
- A pinch of nutmeg
- 1 tablespoon sugar
- 1 teaspoon salt
- A dash of hot pepper sauce

Marinate the meat, covered and refrigerated, for 24 hours.

MARINADE FOR VENISON

[For 5 lbs. Meat]

Cover venison with:

- 1 cup each of water and dry red wine

Add:

- 6 or 8 black peppercorns
- 1 bay leaf
- 8 to 10 whole cloves
- 1 sliced onion
- (1 small sprig rosemary)

Permit the meat to remain in the marinade, covered and refrigerated, from 1 to 3 days. Turn it from time to time.

SASSATIES SAUCE OR MARINADE

[For a 3-lb. Lamb]
Soak overnight:

½ cup dried apricots

Cook them until soft and press through a sieve or purée in the ⅄ blender. Sauté until golden:

3 large sliced onions
1 minced clove garlic

in:

2 tablespoons butter

Add and cook for a minute longer:

1 tablespoon curry powder

Then add the apricot purée with:

1 tablespoon sugar
½ teaspoon salt
3 tablespoons vinegar
A few grains cayenne
6 lemon or orange leaves

Bring to a boil, then remove from heat, cool and pour over raw meat, which marinates overnight in the sauce. Fry or grill the meat, which should be cut into small, thin, round pieces. Heat the sauce to boiling and pour over the grilled pieces of meat. Serve with rice.

COOKED MARINADE FOR GAME

[About 8 Cups]
This is a cooked marinade, which can be stored in the refrigerator and used as needed for venison, mutton or hare.
Sauté a combination of:

1 cup chopped celery
1 cup chopped carrot
1 cup chopped onion

in:

¼ cup cooking oil

until they begin to color. Then add:

8 cups vinegar
4 cups water
½ cup coarsely chopped parsley
3 bay leaves
1 tablespoon thyme
1 tablespoon basil
1 tablespoon cloves
1 tablespoon allspice berries
A pinch of mace
1 tablespoon crushed peppercorns
6 crushed cloves garlic

Simmer for 1 hour. Strain and cool.

BEER MARINADE

I. [2 Cups]
Use for beef.
Combine:

1½ cups beer
½ cup salad oil

stirring the oil in slowly. Then add:

1 clove garlic
2 tablespoons lemon juice
1 tablespoon sugar
1 teaspoon salt
3 cloves

II. [2 Cups]
A more pungent mix for beef or pork.
Combine:

1½ cups beer
½ teaspoon salt
1 tablespoon dry mustard
1 teaspoon ground ginger
3 tablespoons soy sauce
⅛ teaspoon hot pepper sauce
2 tablespoons sugar
4 tablespoons marmalade
2 cloves minced garlic

PORK MARINADE

[Enough for 1 lb. of Pork Chops]
Combine:

3 tablespoons chili sauce
1½ tablespoons lemon juice
1 tablespoon grated onion
¼ teaspoon dry mustard
2 teaspoons Worcestershire sauce
½ teaspoon salt
¼ teaspoon paprika

MARINADE FOR CHICKEN

[¾ Cup]

Use for chicken to be broiled or grilled.
Combine:

- **¼ cup cooking oil**
- **½ cup dry white wine**
- **1 minced clove garlic**
- **1 finely chopped medium-sized onion**
- **½ teaspoon celery salt**
- **½ teaspoon salt**
- **½ teaspoon coarsely ground black pepper**
- **¼ teaspoon dried thyme, tarragon or rosemary**

Mix well. Chill several hours in covered jar or dish. Shake well, then pour over chicken pieces. Chill about 3 hours, turning pieces at least once.

ABOUT SEASONED BUTTERS AND BUTTER SAUCES

Butter sauces are quick, tasty and simple. The main thing is to use fresh, good butter, preferably unsalted. For other seasoned butters used as Spreads, see (II, 56). For Snail Butters, see page 384.

Allow about 1 tablespoon butter per serving for butter sauces. A few butter sauces are melted, but most seasoned butters are creamed and served in solid form, being allowed to melt on the hot fish, meat or vegetables. You may form the butter into fancy shapes and molds, see page 56. Most of the solid seasoned butters may be prepared more quickly and taste almost as good, when made, as melted butter sauces. But if you use melted butter, dress the food in the kitchen. Make sure you spoon out the seasonings with the butter. They will sink to the bottom if you serve the melted butter at table in a sauce boat. There are some butters, such as shrimp and lobster, which are used to flavor and finish sauces, but rarely are served by themselves as sauces.

Seasoned butters may be ✻ frozen for several weeks. But they ◆ should not be refrigerated longer than 24 hours, as the herbs deteriorate quickly.

DRAWN OR CLARIFIED BUTTER

There is no mystery about drawn or clarified butter. It is merely melted butter with the sediment removed. But, as it is used in so many different ways—as a sauce for cooked lobster, to make brown and black butter and as a baking ingredient—here is the recipe.
Melt over low heat:

Butter

When completely melted, remove from heat, let stand for a few minutes, allowing the milk solids to settle to the bottom. Skim the butter fat from the top and place in a container. This is the clarified drawn butter ready for use.

BROWN BUTTER OR BEURRE NOISETTE [4]

Brown and black butters can only be made successfully with clarified butter. The sediment in unclarified butter will tend to brown and make sauce speckled and bitter. Use for asparagus, broccoli and brains.
Melt in a saucepan and cook slowly until light brown:

¼ cup clarified butter

BLACK BUTTER OR BEURRE NOIR [4]

Use for fish, eggs, vegetables and brains. Melt very slowly, until very dark brown:

¼ cup clarified butter

Stir in at once:

1 teaspoon vinegar or lemon juice

If served with brains or fish, you may add:

1 tablespoon chopped capers

Serve immediately.

MEUNIÈRE OR LEMON BUTTER [4]

Prepare:

Brown Butter, page 383

Add:

1 tablespoon chopped parsley
1 teaspoon lemon juice
Correct the seasoning

ALMOND BUTTER

[⅓ Cup]

This is often used in cream sauces, for sautéed chicken and other "amandine" dishes. Another version for such dishes is Amandine Garnish, page 390.

Cream:

¼ cup butter

Blanch:

¼ cup Almonds (II, 189)

Remove the skins and pound the almonds to a paste with:

1 teaspoon water

Add gradually to the butter, blending well. Rub through a fine sieve.

ANCHOVY BUTTER [4]

Fine spread on hot broiled fish, steak or canapés.

Cream until soft:

¼ cup butter

Beat in:

1 teaspoon anchovy paste
⅛ teaspoon onion juice
¼ teaspoon lemon juice
A few grains cayenne

BERCY BUTTER [4]

Simmer in a saucepan:

2 teaspoons finely chopped shallots
¾ cup dry white wine

until reduced to ¼ original quantity. Cool. Cream together and blend into the wine and shallot mixture:

¼ cup butter
2 teaspoons finely chopped parsley
Correct the seasoning

and serve on broiled meats.

CAVIAR BUTTER [6 to 8]

A lovely fish garnish.

Cream:

½ cup butter

Add:

1 tablespoon lemon juice
¼ cup black caviar
Salt, if necessary

Chill slightly, mold or cut into shapes and serve.

MAÎTRE D'HÔTEL BUTTER [4]

Good over broiled steak.

Cream until it is soft:

¼ cup butter

Add:

½ teaspoon salt
⅛ teaspoon white pepper
1 teaspoon chopped parsley

Add very slowly, stirring the sauce constantly:

¾ to 1½ tablespoons lemon juice

COLBERT BUTTER [4]

Use on fish and roasted meats.

Cream together:

¼ cup Maître d'Hôtel Butter, above
½ teaspoon melted beef extract or meat glaze
¼ teaspoon finely chopped fresh tarragon

SNAIL BUTTER

[About 1 Cup]

Should any of this be left from stuffing the snails ❋ freeze for a short period for use on steaks, fish or vegetables.

Cream until soft:

¾ cup butter

Work into it:

1 to 2 tablespoons minced shallots
1 to 2 well-crushed cloves garlic
(1 tablespoon minced celery)
1 tablespoon minced parsley
½ teaspoon salt
Freshly ground pepper

DEVILED BUTTER FOR SEAFOOD [4]

Work until soft:
¼ cup butter
Combine it with:
½ teaspoon dry mustard
2 teaspoons wine vinegar
2 teaspoons Worcestershire sauce
¼ teaspoon salt
1/16 teaspoon cayenne
2 egg yolks
Beat well.

GARLIC BUTTER [4]

This is good on steak, if you are a garlic fancier, or it can be used for garlic bread. Boil in a little water for 5 or 6 minutes:
1 to 3 cloves garlic
Drain, crush and pound well in a mortar with:
¼ cup butter

GREEN OR RAVIGOTE BUTTER

Use for broiled fish, to give sauces a green color or in the making of Ravigote Sauce, page 364.
Chop until fine:
2 shallots
1 teaspoon fresh tarragon
1 teaspoon fresh chervil
1 teaspoon fresh parsley
6 to 8 spinach leaves
Blanch these ingredients for 5 minutes, then plunge in cold water, drain and dry in a towel. Pound them in a mortar or bowl. Work in gradually:
¼ cup butter
Salt, if needed

SHRIMP OR LOBSTER BUTTER

[½ Cup]
This should appeal to frugal cooks. It uses every last bit of your shellfish, and a deliciously flavored pinkish butter is the result. Use for finishing cream sauces served with fish or with the shellfish you have used for the butter.
Dry the shells from:
1 lb. shrimp or 1 large lobster
in a low oven for a short time. Pound them in a mortar or put them through the food grinder, so that they are broken up as finely as possible. Melt:
½ cup butter
in a double boiler ➧ over—not in—hot water. Add the shells and:
2 tablespoons water
Simmer for 10 minutes. ➧ Do not let the butter boil. Line a sieve with cheesecloth or fine muslin and strain the hot butter into a bowl of ice water. Refrigerate and skim off the butter when it hardens.

WHITE BUTTER [4]

Use for poached fish, making the fumet required from the same type of fish. Simmer together, until reduced to ¼ original volume:
1 teaspoon finely chopped shallots
¼ cup wine vinegar
¼ cup Fish Fumet (II, 143)
Cool and add, a little at a time:
¼ cup softened butter
beating constantly with a sauce whisk until the sauce is creamy and whitened, rather like whipped cream.
Correct the seasoning
Add:
(1 teaspoon chopped parsley)
2 tablespoons mixture of

chopped fresh fennel, parsley, chives, basil, chervil or tarragon or 1 tablespoon of the dried herbs

POLONAISE OR BROWNED CRUMB SAUCE [4]

A garnish for vegetables.
Brown:

⅓ **cup fine dry bread crumbs**

in:

Meunière Butter, page 384

Garnish the vegetable with:

Hard-cooked, finely chopped egg

and pour the sauce over it. If you wish, you may sauté:

(**1 tablespoon minced onion**)

in the butter, until transparent, before adding the bread crumbs.

BUTTER SAUCE FOR CANNED OR BOILED VEGETABLES

Drain the vegetables. Permit the stock or juice to boil until it is reduced by ½. Add to it:

Melted butter
Seasonings

ABOUT GLAZES AND GLAÇAGE

These terms are among the very trickiest in the cooking vocabulary and we might try to straighten them out right here. They apply to both glazes for candies, nuts and desserts and to the desserts themselves. They also apply to a number of important processes and coatings for savory items.

Let's get rid of the sweet ones first, by referring to the following: Glacé or Ice (II, 493); Crème Glacé or Ice Cream (II, 483); Glacé, as in Meringue (II, 522); Fruit Glaze for Tarts (II, 434); and Caramel Glaze as in Crème Brulée (II, 438); transparent glaze as in Nuts Glacé (II, 515) and Fruits Glacé (II, 523).

And then turn to the non-sweet processes and coatings, which do so much to add color and flavor to food. ➧ To glaze meats is an expression that can be interpreted in a number of ways. If food has been Braised, page 538, or prepared à l'étouffée, page 85, it acquires, in the cooking, reduced juices which may be further reduced. Place it ➧ uncovered in an oven if the food was braised. Or hold it ➧ covered in the skillet or poêle if the food is covered with a poaching paper, before lidding. Meats may also be glazed by the use of Glacé de Viande, or Meat Glaze (II, 145)—a specially prepared, potent and wonderful substance to use with discretion.

➧ To glaze a sauce can mean to run it under a hot broiler until it becomes golden brown.

➧ To glaze an hors d'oeuvre or sandwich may mean to apply to it an aspic jelly coating.

➧ You can, in cooking vegetables, let the butter in which they are cooked combine with their reduced juices to form a glaze. This is usually done over carefully controlled heat. Often a little sugar or honey is added, see page 387.

➧ You can coat eggs or fish with a rich white sauce—which process can be referred to as glazing them.

And last but not least, let's read about ➧ deglazing, a most vital process—usually neglected—but one that can mean so much, see page 358.

TO GLAZE A SAUCE ON A CASSEROLE

Preheat broiler.
Try this only if you have preheated your broiler well. Then

run your dish quickly under the heat, until it browns delicately. Should the broiler not be hot enough and your sauce boil before it colors, it will separate into an oily, watery mass. ➧ Be sure the sauce does not touch the edge of the pot. Allow an empty area all around for expansion. It is also a wise precaution to protect the casserole by putting it in a pan of hot water. Do not leave it longer than 3 minutes. A perfect all-over brown glaze on the sauce coating fish dishes or Chicken Divan can be achieved by the following method: Reserve some of the Béchamel or Mornay Sauce and fold in whipped cream, at least 4 tablespoons to 1 cup of sauce. The more whipped cream, the smoother the browning. Put under the hot broiler and watch closely.

SPIRIT GLAZE FOR HAM

Combine:

½ to 1 cup dry red wine
½ to 1 cup bourbon whisky
1 cup brown sugar
6 cloves
2 tablespoons grated orange peel

Spread on the ham after it is skinned and continue to baste during the last ½ hour of cooking.

CRANBERRY GLAZE FOR FOWL

Combine:

1 cup canned cranberries
½ cup brown sugar
2 tablespoons lemon juice

HONEY GLAZE FOR MEAT OR ONIONS

Combine:

¼ cup honey
¼ cup soy sauce
1 teaspoon mustard

ASPIC GLAZE

Use this for cold meats, fish, salads and canapés.

Soak:

1 tablespoon gelatin

in:

½ cup meat or vegetable stock

Dissolve it over hot water. Add it to:

1½ cups clarified stock

Season it mildly. Chill it until it thickens somewhat. Spoon it over cold roast, cold fish, canapés, etc.

MAYONNAISE COLLÉE OR GELATIN MAYONNAISE

This coating, also known as Mayonnaise Chaud-Froid, is ordinarily used to coat or mask aspics, cold fish, meat or fowl dishes. But if you make it fairly stiff, it can be piped through a pastry tube and you can achieve the same rococo flights of fancy as when icing a wedding cake. You may also use delicately tinted mayonnaise collée, made from Green Mayonnaise, see page 348, but please avoid highly colored mayonnaise which looks unappetizingly artificial. Note that this stiffened mayonnaise serves much the same purpose as the Béchamel-based Chaud-Froid Sauce on page 388, but it does not hold as well or as long for the heavy oil content may cause oozing. ➧ Have the dish you wish to coat well chilled and dry.

I. Soak:

1½ to 2 teaspoons gelatin

in:

1½ to tablespoons water

Beat into:

1 cup heavy mayonnaise

II. Or beat:

1 cup mayonnaise

into:

¼ cup Aspic Glaze, above

The Aspic Glaze should be at

about 70°—tepid and still liquid. Once it has begun to jell, it will not beat into the mayonnaise properly. Spread it as you would frosting, with firm strokes of a spatula. Work quickly, for this mayonnaise will set at room temperature. Chill the dish until the mayonnaise is set, then decorate as described later. After the decorations have set, place the whole dish on a rack with a platter under it and glaze it with aspic glaze, which should be about the consistency of thick sirup. Your food should be very cold, so that the aspic almost sets at the moment of contact. Use a ladle which holds about 1 cup glaze and pour it on with the motion illustrated for Petits Fours (II, 360). You should give the whole dish two or three coats, which should be perfectly smooth. There should be no streaks or lumps if you have used aspic of the consistency described. You may re-use the aspic which has fallen through the rack onto the platter, after straining, for the second and third coats.

SAUCE CHAUD-FROID

Chaud-Froid is so-called because it begins as a heated sauce and is served as a cold one. It has an advantage over Mayonnaise Collée, because it emphasizes the flavor of the dish it coats—for you make the sauce with the stock resulting from the dish itself. It is often used to coat whole cooked chickens, ham or veal roasts, fish or other cold buffet items.

Prepare:

2 cups Béchamel Sauce, page 359, slightly overseasoned

using chicken or veal stock or Fish Fumet (II, 143)—according to the dish you intend to mask. Chaud-Froid may also be made with a Brown Sauce for meats or chicken. The brown color is more appetizing to many people. Add:

2 tablespoons gelatin

softened in:

3 or 4 tablespoons stock

again using the appropriate flavor for the dish. Stir constantly over medium heat until thoroughly combined. Remove from heat and cool, stirring from time to time to prevent a skin forming. ➧ When cool enough to coat a spoon, but not set, ladle it over the cold chicken or fish in the way described above. Chill to set. The dish may need more than one coat of the sauce. Decorate and glaze.

ABOUT DECORATIONS FOR CHAUD-FROID

Decorations on dishes masked with Sauce Chaud-Froid or Mayonnaise Collée, can be as fanciful as you wish. And professional chefs achieve masterful effects. With a little practice, you can produce the same elegantly curving sprays of flowers, leaves and stems from leeks, chives, eggplant skin or green peppers. To make them pliable, they must be blanched for about 3 minutes in salted water, then cooled immediately on crushed ice to retain their color. Chives form the stems, and leeks, etc. can be cut into leaf shapes—free-hand or with fancy cutters sketched in the illustration on page 39.

Lemon rind, carrot and red pepper, blanched as above, can be used for flower petals. Or use paper-thin slices of ham. Other materials suitable for decoration are: truffles; black olives—you can use the skins of ripe olives as a truffle substitute; pickles, hard-cooked eggs and grapes; parsley and other herbs

—blanched for 1 minute; peas, capers and wilted cucumber slices.

The decorations are first dipped in clear Aspic Glaze, page 387, then applied to the dish to be ornamented, as described on page 387. If they slip after the first application of clear glaze, replace carefully with tweezers. If the decorating proves slow, be sure to chill periodically so that the chaud-froid does not darken.

Chaud-froids are often garnished with aspic jelly, chopped or cut in fancy shapes; and you may use on a suitable meat dish, foie gras balls rolled in chopped Truffles, see page 299. Lemon wedges, sprinkled with finely chopped parsley and other fancy lemon shapes are shown (II, 101). To garnish with hard-cooked eggs, see (II, 74).

ABOUT AU GRATIN

"Au gratin" is a term that, in America, is usually associated with cheese. But the term may merely refer to a light but thorough coating of fine fresh or dry bread crumbs or even crushed corn flakes, cracker crumbs or finely ground nuts placed on top of scalloped or sauced dishes. These are then browned in the oven or under the broiler to form a crisp golden crust. Such dishes are usually combinations of cooked shellfish, fish, meats, vegetables or eggs, bound by a white or brown sauce and served in the dish in which they are cooked. If the sauce is heavy in fat, it is wise to place the scalloped dish in a pan of hot water before running it under a broiler. Or you may set the casserole or baking dish on a piece of foil, with the shiny side down to deflect the heat. Or just put the casserole in a baking tin.

Raw food may also be covered with one of the above toppings before cooking. See Scalloped Potatoes, page 312. ♦ To make au gratin mixtures quickly, put them in a blender ⅄ in the proportion and amount you need.

AU GRATIN

I. Place:

Dry bread crumbs

in a thorough, but light, covering over the sauced food. Bake in a 350° to 375° oven—or run it under a preheated broiler, 3 inches below the source of heat until a golden brown crisp crust forms.

II. Place:

Dry bread crumbs and dots of butter

to make a thorough but light covering over the food, before baking it in a 350° oven—or running it under a preheated broiler, 5 inches from the source of heat, to produce a crisp golden crust.

III. Completely cover the food to be au gratined with:

Dry bread crumbs, dots of butter and grated cheese

Run it under a preheated broiler, 5 inches below the source of heat, to form a glazed golden crust. The finished result should be neither powdery nor rubbery but "fondant." It will be more "fondant" if you use natural-aged American or cheddar cheese, and dried if you use Parmesan or Romano.

BUTTERED CRUMBS

Sauté

1 cup bread crumbs

in:

⅓ cup hot butter or bacon drippings

You may add a choice of:

Chopped minced bacon
Minced onions
Chopped parsley
Chopped nut meats
Curry powder
Paprika
Grated cheese

CROUTONS

These dry or fried seasoned fresh breads come in all sizes. As coarse crumbs, they are an attractive garnish for noodles, dumplings or Spaetzle. In small dice, they add glamour to pea and other soups. Use in tiny dice and mound them around game, or, as larger toasts, under game or a chop. They can be spread with a pâté or be used as a spongy surface for the natural juices. In large size, they can also be placed under a dripping rack during the roasting of meats to catch and hold the juices.

I. Dice bread, fresh or dry, and sauté it in butter until it is an even brown. Or butter slices of bread, cut them into dice and brown them in a 375° oven.

II. When croutons have been sautéed or browned in the oven, drop them while still hot into a bag containing:

1 teaspoon salt
1 teaspoon paprika
Ground Parmesan cheese or very finely minced fresh herbs

Close the bag. Shake it until the croutons are evenly coated. Add them to hot soup.

III. Use for soup, noodles or Caesar Salad. Cut into ½-inch cubes:

Bread

Sauté the cubes in:

Hot butter or olive oil

You may rub the skillet with garlic or add grated onion to the butter. Stir them gently or shake the skillet until they are coated. Sprinkle with:

Grated cheese or herbs

ELABORATE TOPPING OR GRATIN

[About 1½ Cups]

Combine:

¼ cup melted butter
2 tablespoons crumbled potato chips
½ cup cracker or bread crumbs
½ teaspoon paprika
2 tablespoons grated Parmesan
½ cup dry sherry

ALMOND OR AMANDINE GARNISH

[A Scant ½ Cup]

This garnish is a classic. It glorifies the most commonplace dish.

Melt:

¼ cup butter

Stir and sauté in it over low heat, to avoid scorching, until lightly browned:

¼ cup blanched shredded almonds
Salt, as needed

As a variation on almonds as a vegetable garnish, try:

(Roasted pumpkin, squash or sesame seeds)

EGG AND CHEESE GRATIN

[About 1 Cup]

This is a good topping for spaghetti or noodle casserole dishes which have to wait for tardy guests, as it prevents the spaghetti from drying out.

Beat until light yellow and foamy:

3 eggs

Stir in, to form a thick paste:

⅔ cup grated Parmesan cheese

Spread over the top of the dish and bake in a 400° oven until the eggs and cheese are set and browned.

CHICKEN LIVER TOPPING FOR PASTA DISHES

Sauté until just done:

1 cup chicken livers

in:

¼ cup cooking or olive oil

Remove the livers from the pan and cut up coarsely. In the same pan, sauté for 5 minutes:

1 cup sliced mushrooms

then add:

½ cup halved, ripe, pitted olives

and the chicken liver pieces. Stir and deglaze the pan with:

½ cup dry sherry

Spread the topping over the spaghetti in an even layer and sprinkle as evenly as possible with:

½ cup chopped hard New York cheese

Run under the broiler until the cheese is toasted, about 2 minutes.

FISH

ABOUT FISH

As demographers concern themselves about our exploding population they begin more and more to consider—as a source of abundant high-grade protein—the creatures of the lakes, the rivers, and the seven seas. There are schemes for reaping the fantastically numerous, infinitely tiny plankton. There are projects for fertilizing the spawning ground of the world's more conventionally edible water-life and so harvesting familiar species more intensively than ever before.

The amateur angler, too, has been doing his bit. With America gone fishing-crazy, no housewife knows when she will answer a knock at the kitchen door and be suddenly faced with a neighbor's surplus catch in all its chill, scaly impersonality. This need not be a moment of consternation. If it happens to you, judge the gift—after, of course, enthusiastically thanking the donor—as critically as you would judge a fish offered at market. To test its freshness ➧ make sure that its eyes are bulging and its gills are reddish, that the scales are adhering firmly to the skin, and that the flesh, when you press it, is firm to the touch. The scales should have a high sheen. Also be certain that the fish has no offensive odor—especially around the gills or the belly. If it is very fresh, and you cannot use it at once ➧ see directions for freezing fish and for cooking frozen fish, page 397, and (II, 562). Should you be buying fish, remember that in some stores ➧ thawed frozen fish is sold with no sign or comment to indicate the important fact that it should be used at once and never refrozen. If you are in doubt about the freshness of a fish, place it in cold water. A fresh fish will float.

➧ To choose a method of cooking appropriate to a particular type of fish and to the kind of meat at hand—whether whole, filleted or cut for steaks—see the generalized recipes which come first in this chapter.

Many fish are seasonal delicacies. Available all year round are rock bass, carp, cod, eel, flounder, grouper, haddock, hake, halibut, herring, mullet, red snapper, sole and tuna.

If you are adventuring with eel, herring, some types of sole—or an officious stranger like octopus—consult the Index to see if we have some extra special suggestions for preparing, cooking or seasoning them.

SEAFISH

These include: bass, bluefish, butterfish, cod, croaker, cusk, flounder, grouper, haddock, hake, halibut, Atlantic herring, Pacific herring, lingcod, mackerel, mullet, pilchard, pollock, pompano, porgy, red snapper, rosefish, sea bass, sea trout, shad, the soles, swordfish, tuna, turbot and whiting.

FRESH-WATER FISH

These include: buffalo fish, carp, catfish, crappie, lake herring, mullet, muskellunge, yellow perch, yellow pike, pickerel, sheepshead, sucker, sunfish, brook trout, lake trout, and whitefish.

Either sea or fresh fish—depending on age and season—are eel, elver and salmon.

For those of you concerned with lean and fat fish, the following are considered in the fattest category: bloaters, bluefish, herring, kipper, pilchard, salmon, sardine, shad, smelt, and sprat, beginning at 15% fat and achieving about 30% with eel.

Now, a few more general comments. Many fish respond to Deep Fat Frying, pages 75–79, Sautéing, page 79, Pan-Frying, page 80, Broiling, page 399 and Baking, page 402. And there are fish that steam or poach well. In the latter category—a more descriptive term with which we like to replace the word "boiled"—are: cod, buffalo fish, hake, haddock, sheepshead, red snapper, grouper, pollock, halibut and salmon. Some very oily fish respond to smoking (II, 545). Some others are available fresh or salted, page 407. Some fish, strong in flavor or dry in texture, respond to Marinating, pages 409, 411.

Whatever kind of fish you choose ➧ don't overcook it.

ABOUT CLEANING AND PREPARING FISH

➧ To prepare a fish for baking and stuffing, begin by spreading on a firm work surface several layers of newsprint covered with 3 thicknesses of brown paper. If the fish needs scaling, cut off the fins with scissors so they will not nick you while you are working. Wash the fish briefly in cold water—scales are more easily removed from a wet fish. Grasp the fish firmly near the base of the tail. If it is very slippery you may want to hold it in a cloth. Begin at the tail, pressing a rigid knife blade at a slight angle from the vertical position to raise the scales as you strip them off. Work against the "nap"—up toward the head. A serrated scaler or a grater will be of great help in scaling. Be sure to remove the scales around the base of the head and the fins. After scaling, discard the first layer of brown paper with the scales on it. Next draw the fish. Cut the entire length of the belly from the vent to the head and remove the entrails. As they are all contained in a pouch-like integument which is easily freed from the flesh, evisceration need not be a messy job. Now, cut around the pelvic and ventral fins on the lower side and remove them. If you are removing the head, cut above the collarbone and break

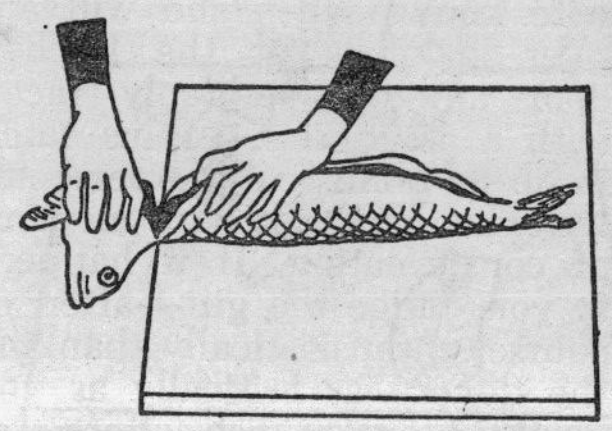

the backbone by snapping it off on the edge of the work surface as shown above. The head and pectoral fins, if they were not previously cut off, should come with it. Then remove the tail by slicing right through the body just above it. Wrap and discard the entrails, keeping the choicer trimmings for making Fumet (II, 143).

If the fish does not need scaling and you are preparing it for stuffing, you can remove the dorsal fin in such a way as to release unwanted bones. Cut first down to either side of it for its full length. Then give a quick pull forward toward the head end to release it, and with it the bones that are attached to it, as sketched below.

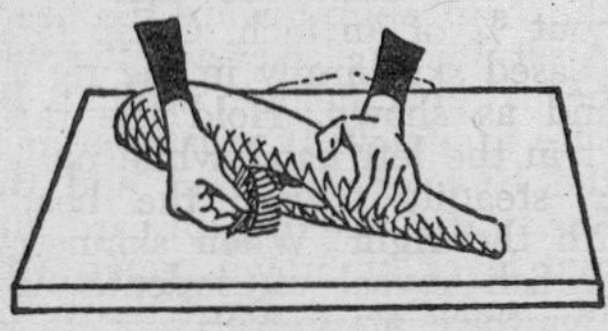

Wash the fish in cold running water, removing any blood, bits of viscera or membrane. ➧ Be sure the blood line under the backbone has been removed. Dry the fish well. It is then ready to use steamed, baked, stuffed or unstuffed, or as steaks.

➧ To cut a fish into steaks or darnes, begin at the head end and cut evenly, as shown, into cross sections of desired thickness.

➧ To clean small fish like smelts, spread open the outer gills, take hold of the inner gills with the forefinger and pull gently. The parts unfit for food are all attached to these inner gills and come out together, leaving the fish ready to cook after rinsing.

If you cannot use a fish at once, store it at 39° temperature, preferably lidded, so that its penetrating odor does not permeate other foods in the refrigerator. Fish may be kept directly on ice if drainage is provided to prevent it from soaking up water. Length of fish storage depends largely on the condition in which it reaches you. The sooner it can be used the better, for its fragile gelatinous substances break down and dry out quickly as the fish ages, destroying flavor as they dry.

ABOUT FILLETING FISH

To prepare skinned fillets, you need not scale the fish, remove its fins, or draw it.

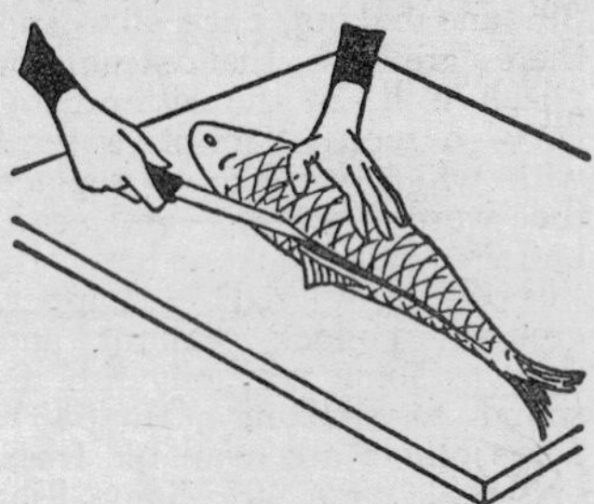

➧ To fillet—place on the work surface several thicknesses of newsprint covered by brown paper. Cut the fish, as shown, along the back ridge from the tail to a point just behind the head. Then slice down at a slight angle behind the collar bone beyond the gill—until you feel the backbone against the knife. Turn the knife flat with the cutting edge toward the tail and the point toward the cut edge of the backbone. Keep the blade flat and in the same plane with the backbone. Now, cut with a sliding motion along the backbone until you have freed the fillet all the way to the tail, see below. It should come off in one piece.

➧ To skin, place the fillet skin side down. Hold the tail firmly with your free hand as shown. Cut through the flesh of the fillet about ½ inch above the tail. Flatten the knife against the skin with the blade pointing toward the top of the fillet. Work the knife forward, keeping in the same plane and close against the skin while your left hand continues to hold the skin taut.

An exception to the above procedure must be made with a certain group of very flat fish, some of which, rather disconcertingly, have both eyes on their upper surface. All of them are skinned and filleted in a special way; and they may all be cooked by recipes for sole or flounder, including turbot, which is less flat than most.

The true English or Dover sole, whose eyes are normally situated, has the most delicate flavor and texture of them all. But fillets of flounder, plaice, dab, lemon or gray sole are often palmed off on the unsuspecting purchaser as the genuine article.

➧ To fillet these flat varieties, first skin the fish by cutting a gash through the skin above the tail. Peel back the skin for about ¾ of an inch. Grasp the released skin firmly in the right hand as shown. Hold the tail flat in the left hand while pulling steadily toward the head with the right. When skinned, flat fish reveal an indentation down the center which separates a double set of fillets—2 on the dark side and 2 on the light side. Cut through the flesh on either side of the spine. Slip the knife under the fillet—close to the bone—and cut the fillet loose from the backbone toward the outside edge of the fish. Having freed the fillets, refrigerate them, and wrap for discard in the papers on which you were working all the unusable entrails. You may keep the bone structure, skin, heads and tails for Fumet (II, 143), unless the fish is a strong-flavored or oily one.

ABOUT COOKING FISH

➧ While in cooking and timing, the size and shape of the fish, and whether it is whole or divided, must be taken into consideration, the methods themselves are much the same. A good cook knows through experience how long to cook her fish, but even she will watch the proceedings with a vigilant eye to guard against overdoneness. For details of each method of cooking see the following pages. ▶ Cooking times in individual recipes apply to fish which has been removed from the refrigerator long enough to reach 70°; but no warmer.

You will sometimes see ▶ suggestions for gashing fish before cooking. This procedure is adopted chiefly for firm-fleshed fish when cooked unskinned, to prevent them from curling. Slashes may be made, too, before baking, if the fish is a very tough-skinned one, to allow the heat to penetrate, or when the area of skin is large, as in turbot, to keep the skin from bursting.

▶ To test a fish for doneness you may insert a thermometer at an angle in the thickest portion of the flesh behind the gills. Fish is edible when the internal heat reaches 140°. At 150° its tissues begin to break down, allowing both juices and flavor to escape. Remove the fish from the heat, surely by 145°. Remember that because fish needs so little heat to cook, it will continue to do so on a hot platter.

If you have no thermometer, stick a toothpick into the thickest part of the fish near the backbone and separate the meat from the bone. The fish is done when the flesh is no longer translucent and flakes readily. One of the best ways ▶ to test a soft-fleshed fish is to touch it as you would a cake to see if the flesh responds by returning to its original shape after imprinting a finger.

Many fish are bland in flavor and profit by a sauce. If, on the contrary, the fish is strong in flavor, many expert cooks ▶ discard the butter or cooking oil in which it has been cooked. Otherwise, deglaze the pan, page 358.

▶ Most of our fish recipes call for cooking in ovenproof dishes. Service is simplified if such dishes are attractive enough to appear at table. This way, fish—being fragile—undergoes less handling, and you have fewer "fishy" dishes to clean up later. Single-dish service also, of course, keeps the fish warmer; but do watch for overcooking from the added heat of the dish.

▶ To keep a whole fish warm, put it on a heated serving platter in a very low oven. Leave the door ajar. For fillets, treat as above, but cover them with a damp warm paper towel or cloth. ▶ Be sure that any sauce served on the fish is very hot.

▶ To keep a sauced fish warm, use a double boiler ▶ uncovered, or place the baker in which you plan to serve the fish in a pan of boiling water and hold ▶ uncovered.

▶ If cooked fish is to be served cold keep refrigerated until the very last minute. If served buffet, place it over cracked ice.

▶ Allow per serving 1 lb. whole small fish, ¾ lb. if entrails, head, tail and fins are removed; ½ lb. fish steaks; or ⅓ lb. fish fillets.

▶ To minimize fish tastes and odors, use lemon, wine, vinegar, ginger, spring onions, or garlic in the marinating or cooking.

To remove the odor of fish from utensils and dishcloths use a solution of 1 teaspoon baking soda to 1 quart water. Pans may be washed in hot suds, rinsed and dried, and then scalded with a little vinegar. To remove the odor of fish from the hands, rub them with lemon juice, vinegar or salt before washing them.

FROZEN FISH

Frozen fish should preferably be thawed before cooking but may be cooked while still frozen.

Use thawed fish immediately, and do not re-freeze. You may also thaw at room temperature if you are in a hurry, and speed up the process even more by covering the fish and placing it in front of an electric fan, see (II, 562). ➧ Frozen fish, when thawed, may be cooked in the same way as its fresh counterpart. ➧ If cooked frozen, it is best baked, broiled, or cooked "en papillote" or in aluminum foil. Double the cooking time given for fresh fish, and in foil cooking add another 15 minutes to allow the heat to penetrate the foil. Freezing processes for fish have improved greatly in the last few years, and have brought us varieties hitherto not available, such as rainbow trout. But we still think that frozen fish cannot compare with fresh fish for flavor and texture. It is apt to be dry, as the gelatins lose their delicate quality, and thus needs a well-flavored sauce or a good deal of moisture or fat in the cooking process. ➧ If you are buying frozen fish from frozen food cabinets, buy only solidly frozen packages. They should not be torn or misshapen or show evidence of refreezing. ➧ Skin frozen fish before cooking it.

CURED FISH

Smoked, dried, salted or pickled—some of these cured fish can be eaten as they come, others must be cooked first. Haddock and several kinds of herring are usually ➧ Cold-Smoked (II, 545). They have been salted and smoked over a smoldering fire to the dry stage, but have not been cooked. Whitefish, chub and salmon are usually ➧ Hot-Smoked (II, 545), so that they cook in the heat of the smoking fire, and so can be used without further cooking. Haddock, when smoked, becomes finnan haddie. A smoked herring is known as a kipper—actually, the general term for any smoked fish. An unsalted, smoked herring is known as a bloater. It will not keep as long as a kipper. ➧ Store all smoked fish refrigerated in airtight containers to lengthen their keeping period.

Cod, mackerel and herring are often ➧ salted and air-dried, and before cooking should be soaked in water for several hours—skin side down. If soaking in fresh running water is not practical, change the water frequently during the soaking period. For ways to cook, see Salt Cod, page 408. Fish was often ➧ pickled in the days before refrigeration, and in eighteenth century English and American cookbooks you will find recipes for "caveaching" fish in spices, oil and vinegar. We imagine there is a close relationship between the French "Escabèche," and its Spanish variant, page 406, in both word derivation and method. Nowadays, herring and mackerel are usually reserved for pickling, although Escabèche can be used for small fish, like fresh anchovies, sardines, young mullet and whiting.

➧ To prepare fish dishes based on cooked fish and shellfish, see Luncheon Dishes, pages 229–237, and Hors d'Oeuvre (II, 79) and Canapés (II, 63). ➧ To prepare Fish Stews and Soups, see pages 132–138.

There are any number of attractive ways to serve and garnish fish. Handsome bases for cold dishes are salmon, lake trout, chicken halibut, turbot, filleted Dover sole, wall-eyed pike and carp. For directions for Cold Salmon, see page 415.

A gala way to serve a hot fish in summer is to place it on a grill above a bed of dry fennel stalks and flame it for several seconds before serving. This may also be done directly on a heatproof platter. Another decorative and delicious addition to fish is Fried Parsley, page 305.

ABOUT STEAMING, POACHING OR BRAISING FISH

Steaming is one of the better ways to treat a delicate lean fish as far as retaining flavor is concerned; although—unlike meat—fish will lose more weight processed in this way than in poaching. Poaching—sometimes also called braising in fish cookery—runs steaming a close second.

A steamer has a perforated tray support designed to hold the fish above the water level. In a poacher, which is otherwise very similar, the tray is not elevated and allows the fish to be immersed in the liquid. ➧ A poaching tray is always greased before the fish is placed on it. Fish may be poached in Fumets (II, 143), Court Bouillons (II, 146), in Light Stocks (II, 142), or à Blanc (II, 146)—depending on the flavor you wish to impart or the degree of whiteness you desire. If you are chiefly concerned with preserving the true flavor of the fish, salted water may be all you care to use. Allow 1 tablespoon of salt for every quart of water. For details, see individual recipes.

➧ If fumet or light stock is used for the steaming or poaching liquid, you may want to use some of it either as it is, or reduced, in the fish sauce. ➧ Court bouillons are not used in this way, nor are à blanc liquids, because they are both apt to contain too much vinegar and salt.

➧ Please read the general principles of Poaching, page 83, which apply here. Small fish or cut pieces are started in a boiling liquid which is at once reduced to a simmer. ➧ Large pieces are started in cold liquid. This is especially important because immersing a fish of any considerable size in boiling water causes the skin to shrink and burst. Fragile fillets profit by the use of a poaching paper. Large fish will tolerate more liquid. In either case, allow about 5 to 8 minutes to the pound, depending on the size of the fish, from the moment the cooking liquid reaches the boiling point, and then ➧ reduce to a simmer for the remainder of the cooking period. If you do not have a poacher there is the problem, with large fish, of keeping them constantly bathed in liquid; and after cooking, of lifting them out of the pan without breaking them. Both can be solved either by cooking them tied in a muslin cloth or by using a cloth as described below.

A roasting or baking pan is

best. If a large pan is not available, cut the fish in two and place it in a smaller pan with the halves dovetailed. The fish can be reassembled on a platter later. If served hot or cold, it can be masked with a sauce without anyone being the wiser for your subterfuge. Put in the pan with the fish several onion and lemon slices, a chopped carrot and a few celery stalks. Fill the pan with Court Bouillon (II, 146) to within an inch of the top. Cover the fish completely with a piece of turkish toweling or a heavy muslin which is large enough to hang down into the liquid. Baste the cloth with the court bouillon in which the fish is cooking as it ➧ simmers on the stove or in the oven. ➧ See that the cloth is always completely soaked. The top of the fish will then cook as quickly as the bottom. If you have already wrapped the fish in muslin as described previously, it will serve exactly the same purpose as a piece of cloth over the top; so will a close-fitting domed lid or a poaching paper if the pot is sufficiently deep.

After the cooking period the fish is sometimes allowed to cool in the water. We do not recommend this practice, as it leads to overcooking and waterlogging. ➧ If the fish is to be served cold it is easier to remove the skin and trim the fish while it is still warm.

ABOUT COOKING FISH "AU BLEU"

It is the skin of the fish only, of course, which turns blue during this cooking process. The important point about cooking "au bleu" is to have available a very fresh fish—alive, if possible. The fish should not be washed or scaled, and should be handled as little as possible, merely being eviscerated. Small fish are sometimes cleaned through the gills, see page 393. Larger ones, such as carp and pike, are slit along the belly to clean them. And, if this involves less handling, slit the small fish, too. Both may then be poached in a vinegar Court Bouillon (II, 146). The natural slime of the fish, coupled if you wish with a preliminary sprinkling of boiling hot vinegar all over, "blues" the skin. See Blue Trout, page 419. They may be served hot or cold.

ABOUT BROILING FISH

"Ruling a large kingdom," observed Lao-Tzu, "is like cooking a small fish." What he meant was that both should be gently handled, and the treatment never overdone. We have usually respected the old philosopher's advice. But in broiling fish we have discovered that they taste even better when they can be subjected to quite high and intense, rather than gentle, heat. The following cooking procedure, for instance, is most effective.

For a 2½-lb. fish, unskinned, broil in the bottom of a preheated broiler at 400° for 5 minutes, then move to a top broiler for 5 minutes more at a preheated 800°. The 800° is not

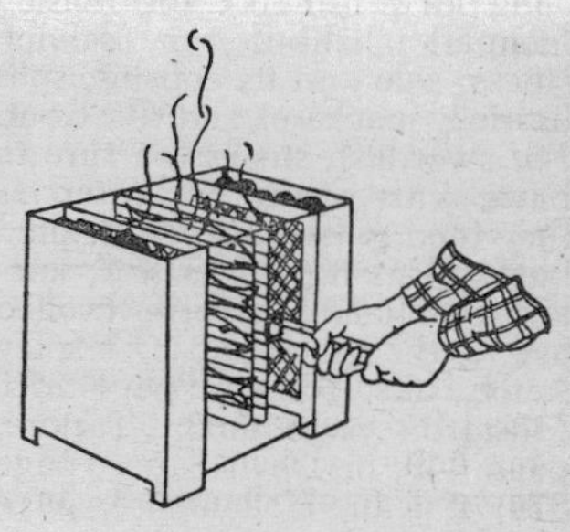

a misprint. But it requires coil or burner capacity that most household ranges are simply not equipped to supply, see page 74. The closest practical home approach is to use a vertical pair of charcoal grills—set as sketched—which produce what is known in France as a "roti" rather than a grill. But most of us must be content with our range broilers preheated to 550°. ➧ It helps to warm up the broiling rack in advance—thus transferring some heat at once to the fish; but be sure to ➧ grease the rack after heating so the fish will not stick. If the fish is to be turned, the hinged rack which fits into the vertical grill, as sketched, may also be conveniently used in the oven broiler pan. Grease it with cooking oil, and the fish with clarified butter. A lean fish may be floured before dotting with butter.

Fillets, flat and split fish are usually placed about two inches from the source of heat. If unskinned, place them skin side down. It is not necessary to turn them, but advisable to baste several times during the cooking period.

If thick fish steaks or large fish are being broiled, place the rack about 6 inches from the source of heat. They may take as long to cook as 5 or 6 minutes to a side.

Types of fish good for broiling include: halibut or salmon steaks, sole and its cousins, split herring, mackerel and sea trout. For swordfish steaks, be sure to baste with plenty of butter, as they tend to become dry. Melted butter, lemon wedges and parsley adequately garnish broiled fish. If the fish is fat, try a spicy sauce, like Tomato, page 376, Mustard, page 363, Tartare, page 349, or Devil Sauce, page 374; if lean, Hollandaise, page 368, Béarnaise, page 370, or one of the seasoned butters.

⊟ FISH KEBABS

[Serves 6]

Prepare:

2 lbs. firm-fleshed fish: swordfish, halibut, cod or haddock

Cut into 1-inch cubes. Place in a glass, enameled or stainless steel pan and marinate for 30 minutes in:

¾ cup cooking oil
½ cup lemon juice
¼ teaspoon powdered bay leaf
4 drops soy sauce

Stir once or twice to thoroughly coat fish. Preheat broiler. Thread on skewers alternating with thick slices of:

2 cucumbers, and
Stuffed olives

Broil or grill for 10 minutes, turning frequently and basting with the marinade.

FRIED FISH

Scale, if necessary, and clean, page 393:

A large fish or several small pan fish: crappie, brook trout, sun fish, or perch

Cut the large fish into Steaks or Darnes, page 394, before rolling them in:

Seasoned flour or corn meal or Bound Breading (II, 160)

Melt in a skillet to the depth of ⅛ inch:

Clarified butter and cooking oil

➧ It is inadvisable to use butter, when sautéing large fish, without the addition of cooking oil, as it burns more readily than other shortening or drippings. When the fat is hot place the fish in it. To keep the fat from spattering your hands you may cover the pan with an inverted colander. Reduce the heat slightly and cook the fish until done, from 3 to 5 minutes. Our former cook, Virginia Turner, taught us to complete cooking one side of the fish entirely before turning and cooking the other side until done. Larger fish may be sautéed on both sides until seared, then placed in a 375° oven about 10 minutes.

DEEP FAT FRIED FISH

[Allow About ⅓ Pound Per Serving]

Preheat deep fryer to 370°

➧ Please read About Deep Fat Frying, pages 75–79. Have fish at 70°. Clean and prepare for cooking:

Small fish or pieces of fish not thicker than 1 inch

Dip them in:

Fritter Batter for Fish (II, 125), or Bound Breading (II, 160)

Fry in deep fat for 5 to 8 minutes, or until a golden brown. The fish will rise to the surface when done. Drain on absorbent paper. Serve very hot with:

Lemon wedges or Tartare Sauce, page 349

MARINATED DEEP FAT FRIED FISH [3]

Preheat deep fryer to 370°.

➧ Please read About Deep Fat Frying, pages 75–79. Skin and cut into pieces:

1½ lbs. fish steaks

Marinate for 30 minutes in:

6 tablespoons dry white wine or

2 tablespoons lemon juice

Drain dry and dip each piece separately in:

6 tablespoons cream

then in:

Flour

Fry the fish in deep fat for about 7 minutes. Serve with:

Tartare Sauce, page 349

FISH AND CHIPS [4]

Preheat deep fryer to 375°.

➧ Please read About Deep Fat Frying, pages 75–79.

Cut into uniform serving pieces:

1½ lbs. fillet of flounder

Coat with:

Fritter Battter for Fish (II, 125)

Cut into thick uniform strips, slightly larger than for French fries:

1½ lbs. mature baking potatoes

Soak in cold water for ½ hour. Drain and dry thoroughly. Fry in the hot fat until golden brown. Remove, drain and keep warm. Deep fry the breaded fish until golden brown. Arrange the potatoes and fish on a platter and serve as a dip:

Hot cider vinegar

OVEN-FRIED SMALL FISH FILLETS OR STICKS

[Allow About ⅓ Pound Per Serving]

Preheat for cooking:

Small fish, pieces of fish or fish fillets

Dip the fish in:

¼ cup rich milk or cream

then in:

Seasoned bread crumbs or crushed cornflakes

Let the fish dry on a rack for ½ hour. Preheat oven to 350°. Bake in an ovenproof dish until firm and golden. Baste twice during the cooking period with:

Melted butter

FILLETS OF FISH SAUTÉED AMANDINE

[Allow ⅓ Pound Per Serving]

Dip:

Fillets of Sole

in:

Milk

Dust with:

Flour

Melt in a skillet enough to cover the bottom well:

Butter

Sauté the fillets in the pan. Turn once. Place on a hot platter. Melt additional:

Butter

Brown in it lightly:

Blanched shredded almonds

Pour them over the fillets. Garnish the dish with:

Lemon and parsley

FRESH FILLETS SAUTÉED PALM BEACH [2]

Bread if you like:

2 small skinned fish fillets

Sauté until golden brown in:

2 tablespoons clarified butter

Serve with 3 or 4 alternate sections of:

Grapefruit and orange

on each fillet. Pour the pan gravy over the garnished fillets and serve at once.

BAKED UNSTUFFED FISH

[Allow ½ Pound Per Person]

Preheat oven to 325°.

Scale, remove the entrails and clean:

A 3-lb. fish

A larger fish may be used, but will require longer, but not proportionately longer, baking, see page 395. If the fish has a tough skin slash it in several places. Place it on a well-greased ovenproof platter. Rub generously with:

Clarified Butter, page 383

If the fish is ➧ lean, you may bard it, page 453. If it is not barded, baste it frequently with:

Clarified Butter

Bake about 30 minutes or until done. Serve on a hot platter garnished with:

Slices of lemon
Sprigs of parsley
Stuffed Tomatoes, page 335

Suitable sauces are:

Almond Sauce, page 390, Shrimp Sauce, page 377, or Mustard Sauce, page 363

➧ To carve an unstuffed fish, remove the skin and cut a line down the middle of the exposed side from head to tail. To either side of this line, cut pieces 2½ to 3 inches wide. Lift off above the bone structure and serve. Pry up the backbone, beginning at the tail. Slide it up and out the dorsal ridge. Break the spine at the neck. Lift it out and lay it aside. The exposed lower fillet will then be ready to carve just as the upper one was.

POACHED FISH STEAKS [3]

Cut into pieces suitable for individual servings:

1½ lbs. halibut or other fish steak

Place it in a skillet. Cover with:

Boiling water

Season with:

4 whole peppercorns
½ bay leaf
2 teaspoons lemon juice

Simmer about 10 minutes, or until tender. Remove to a hot platter. Strain the stock and use it to make the sauce. Try:

Curry Sauce I, page 363, or Poulette Sauce, page 362, or Mustard Sauce, page 363, or Anchovy Sauce for Fish, page 361

FISH FILLETS À LA BONNE FEMME [4]

Cut, wipe with a damp cloth and dry:

4 Flatfish Fillets, page 395

Place in a buttered shallow casserole. Cover with:

¾ cup finely sliced mushrooms
1 minced shallot

1 teaspoon chopped parsley

Pour gently into the dish:

⅔ cup dry white wine

Cover with a Poaching Paper, page 86, and ⧫ simmer 10 to 15 minutes. Remove the fish onto a hot shallow ovenproof serving dish. Reduce the wine by half. Stir into it gradually until well blended:

⅔ cup Velouté Sauce, page 362

using fish stock. You may swirl in:

2 tablespoons butter

Pour the sauce over the fillets and run them under a broiler until the sauce is lightly browned. Serve with:

Boiled New Potatoes, page 310

FISH STEAKS OR FILLETS MARGUÉRY BAKED IN SEA FOOD SAUCE [6]

Preheat oven to 350°.

Place in boiling water or milk and simmer until nearly tender:

6 fillets or 3 steaks

This will be a quick process if the fillets are thin. Drain the fillets. Place in a greased baking dish or platter. Keep them where they will remain hot. Melt:

¼ cup butter

Stir and sauté in it until done:

½ lb. mushrooms

Stir in:

¼ cup flour

Stir in gradually:

1¾ cups milk

Simmer in their liquor until plump:

½ pint oysters: 1 cup

Strain and reserve the liquor. Dry in a towel and add the oysters to the hot cream sauce. Stir in:

¼ lb. cooked shelled shrimp, split lengthwise

Remove the sauce from the heat. Add the oyster liquor and:

½ cup dry white wine

Correct the seasoning

Pour the sauce over the fillets. Bake about 10 minutes or until firm when pressed.

FILLETS OF FISH ON SPINACH WITH SHRIMP AND MUSHROOMS [3]

Cook, page 359, drain and chop:

1 lb. spinach or broccoli

Poach, page 398:

1 lb. fish fillets

Cook, then shell, page 441:

½ lb. shrimp cut lengthwise

Sauté:

½ lb. mushrooms

Prepare:

1 cup Cream Sauce, page 359

using part of the stock in which the fish was poached, and part cream. Combine:

1 egg yolk

¼ cup dry white wine

Add these ingredients to the cream sauce. Thicken the sauce by stirring over low heat, but do not let it boil. Place the spinach on a buttered ovenproof dish, place the fillets on it. Pour the sauce over them. Surround them with the mushrooms and shrimp. Place the dish in a preheated 400° oven until well heated.

QUICK BAKED FILLETS OF FISH [3]

Preheat oven to 350°.

Place in an ovenproof dish:

1 lb. small skinned fish fillets

Stir and heat until smooth:

⅔ cup condensed soup: tomato, celery, mushroom or asparagus

2 tablespoons milk, stock, or dry white wine

Add:

A few grains cayenne

Pour the sauce over the fish.

Bake ▸ uncovered 10 minutes. Serve with:

Steamed Rice

BAKED STUFFED FISH [6]

▸ If you bone a fish before stuffing be sure to leave the skin intact. Stuffed fish, like stuffed meats, need a longer baking period to the pound. See About Cooking Fish, page 395.

Dressing for fish should not be so bold in seasoning as to destroy the naturally delicate fish flavor. Scandinavians would object to this counsel, and make lavish use of fennel in preparing many of their traditional seafood dishes.

Scale, eviscerate and clean:

A 3-lb. fish

Preheat oven to 325°.

Stuff fish with:

1½ cups Oyster Bread Dressing, page 561, or Bread Dressing for Fish, page 561, or Green Dressing, page 562

or with a combination of:

Pressed cucumbers, bread crumbs and almonds

Bake about 40 minutes or until done.

Serve with a sauce of equal parts of:

Butter and sauterne

and:

Lime wedges

BAKED FILLETS OF FISH IN WINE [4]

Preheat oven to 350°.

Place in a greased ovenproof dish:

1½ lbs. fillets of sole or other fish

If the fillets are large they may be cut in half. Pour over them:

1 cup dry white wine
(2 tablespoons dry sherry)

Bake until just done, see page 396. Serve covered with the liquid from the dish, which you may reduce slightly. Garnish with:

Lemon wedges
Sautéed mushroom caps

BAKED FISH WITH SOUR CREAM [8]

Preheat oven to 350°.

Split and remove the bones from:

A 4-lb. whitefish

Flatten it out. Rub inside and out with:

Paprika and butter

Place on an ovenproof dish. Cover with:

2 cups cultured sour cream

Lid the dish. Bake the fish for about ¾ hour, or until done, see page 396. Before serving sprinkle with:

Chopped parsley

FISH BAKED IN A COVERED DISH [4]

Preheat oven to 350°.

This is a simple way to bring out the flavor of a delicate fish.

Combine:

2 tablespoons Clarified Butter, page 383
¼ teaspoon pepper or paprika
A fresh grating of nutmeg

Rub well over:

2 lbs. fish, preferably in 1 chunky piece

Place the fish in an ovenproof dish. Cover with a closely fitting lid. Bake 20 to 25 minutes, or until done. The time depends largely on the shape of the fish.

Add while cooking:

(2 tablespoons dry white wine)

Place the fish on a hot platter.

Melt:

3 tablespoons butter

Add:

2 tablespoons capers
1 teaspoon chopped parsley
1 teaspoon chopped chives

2 teaspoons lemon juice
Correct the seasoning

Pour this or some other suitable sauce over the fish.

FISH BAKED IN FOIL

[Individual Serving]

Preheat oven to 350°.

Clean a small fish. Rub with:

Seasoned Butter, page 383

Place on a piece of buttered aluminum foil large enough to make a generous fold at the edges. Do not include more than 1 lb. in each packet. Bake 35 to 40 minutes to the pound.

MOLDED FILLED FILLETS OF FISH OR PAUPIETTES [4]

Preheat oven to 375°.

Have ready:

8 fillets of Dover sole or blue fish, or any other very thin fillet

Butter 4 individual molds. Line each mold by placing 2 fillets crisscrossed at right angles, filling the center with the farce below, or with a Fish Quenelle Mixture, page 180, and overlapping the ends of the fillets to make a casing. Combine and stir with a fork a farce made of:

¼ cup melted butter
1½ cups soft bread crumbs
¼ cup chopped celery
1 teaspoon grated onion
1 tablespoon chopped parsley
(⅛ teaspoon dried burnet or basil)
¼ teaspoon salt

Fill the molds with this filling. Place the molds in a pan of hot water. Bake for about ½ hour. Unmold on a hot platter. Garnish with:

Lemon wedges
Parsley or watercress

Serve with:

Lemon Butter, page 384, or a seafood sauce, page 377, or Oyster Sauce for Fish, page 361

PLANKED FISH [6]

Please read About Planking, page 80.

Preheat oven to 350°.

Scale, clean, wash in running water and dry:

A 3 to 4 lb. fish

Brush with:

Clarified butter or cooking oil

Place the fish on a well-greased ovenproof or metal platter, about 18 x 13 inches. A Seasoned Plank, page 80, may be used but if used, should in the future be reserved solely for fish. Bake the fish 40 to 60 minutes; if stuffed, about 10 minutes longer.

Preheat broiler.

Garnish the platter with a decorative edging of:

Duchess Potatoes, page 319

Broil 6 to 8 minutes, 8 inches from the source of heat or until the potato garnish is delicately browned. Further garnish the plank with:

A stuffed vegetable
Parsley, fennel or watercress

and serve.

FISH IN ASPIC COCKAIGNE [5]

Prepare for cooking, page 393, then cut into 4 or 5 pieces:

A fish weighing about 2½ lbs.

Bring to the boiling point:

5 cups water
3 or 4 ribs celery with leaves
1 small sliced onion
4 or 5 sprigs parsley
3 tablespoons lemon juice
1 inch lemon rind
3 peppercorns
½ teaspoon dried herbs: tarragon, basil, etc.

½ teaspoon paprika
1 teaspoon salt

Drop the fish into the boiling stock. ➧ Simmer until tender. Do not let it boil at any time. This is a quick process, requiring only 12 to 15 minutes or so. To test for doneness, see page 396. Remove it at once from the stock. Strain the stock. There should be about 3½ cups. If there is not, add water or chicken stock to make up the difference. Soak:

2 tablespoons gelatin

in:

¼ cup cold fish stock

Dissolve it in the hot stock. Add:

2 tablespoons or more capers
2 to 3 tablespoons lemon juice or dry white wine
Correct the seasoning

Chill until it begins to thicken. Remove the skin and bone from the fish. Leave it in large flakes or pieces. Place a layer of aspic in a wet mold, cover it with flaked fish and repeat this process, winding up with aspic on top. Chill. Serve the aspic very cold with:

Mayonnaise, page 345, or cultured sour cream

to either of which you may add:

1 to 2 tablespoons chopped herbs: chives, tarragon, parsley, etc.
Diced cucumbers

Decorate the platter with watercress or shredded lettuce, and surround it with deviled eggs, radishes and olives. Serve with:

Brioche Loaf Cockaigne (II, 245), or Garlic Bread (II, 289)

PICKLED FISH OR ESCABÈCHE

[Allow ½ Pound Per Serving]

Preheat deep fryer to 375°.

➧ Please read About Deep Fat Frying, pages 75–79.

Use smelts, fresh anchovies, sardines, whitings or mullets not over ½ inch thick. For an alternate method, see (II, 79). Clean, wash, dry and flour:

1 lb. small whole fish

Plunge them into:

Hot cooking oil

for 5 to 10 seconds, according to size. Remove them, drain, and arrange in a shallow ovenproof glass or earthenware dish. Using 3 tablespoons of the oil, sauté until the onion is translucent:

2 tablespoons finely minced carrot
1 small finely minced onion
4 whole cloves garlic

Add:

⅔ cup wine vinegar
¼ cup water
A small bay leaf
A sprig of thyme
Salt
2 small red hot peppers

Simmer for 10 minutes, then pour sauce over the fish. When cooled, refrigerate for 24 hours. Serve the fish in the same dish in which it was marinated.

GEFÜLLTE FISH OR POACHED FISH BALLS

[Allow ½ Pound Per Person]

Using two varieties of fish, lean and fat, remove the skin and bone from:

3 lbs. of fish: jack salmon and white

Put the fish through a fine food chopper with:

3 large onions

Place this ground mixture in a large bowl. Slowly add, mixing well until fluffy:

1 well-beaten egg
¾ cup cold water
1 teaspoon salt
¼ cup soft white bread crumbs or matzo meal
½ teaspoon pepper

Place heads, skins and bones of fish in a large pan and add:

Water to cover
1 large sliced onion
2 thinly sliced carrots
Salt and pepper

Bring to a boil. Wet hands to facilitate handling. Form the ground fish mixture into small balls. Drop the balls into the boiling stock. Reduce the heat, cover the kettle and ➧ simmer for 2 hours. Remove the fish balls. The fish liquid may be strained and thickened with egg yolks, page 356, to make the sauce.

SOUTHERN FRIED CATFISH

Preheat deep fryer to 370°.
Clean and skin:

A catfish

Dredge with:

Seasoned white corn meal

Fry in hot fat until golden brown. Serve with:

Hush Puppies (II, 279)
Sliced Tomatoes, page 47

ABOUT CARP

These great, languid, soft-finned fish, whose portraits we admire on Chinese scrolls, can be admirable eating too. But be sure to hold them alive for several days in clear, running water—to rid them of the muddiness they acquire in their native haunts. To enjoy carp at their best, they should be killed just before cooking. If you cannot appoint a Lord High Executioner and must perform the act yourself, we recommend a preliminary perusal of the chapter called "Murder in the Kitchen," in Alice B. Toklas' weird and wonderful "Cookbook."

Carp lend themselves to cooking Au Bleu, page 399; are delicious baked, stuffed or braised; in red wine (II, 149); and eaten hot or cold. Serve with new potatoes and Celeriac, page 283.

ABOUT COD

Through the ages cod has been one of the mainstays of the Lenten diet. It has endless variations. Salt cod, often very tough, is pounded before desalting. To freshen salt cod, leave it under running water for 6 hours; or soak it up to 48 hours in several changes of water in a glass, enamel or stainless steel pan.

Salt cod is most often used flaked. To prepare for flaking, put the desalted fish in cold unsalted Court Bouillon (II, 146) to cover, then bring it to a boil and ➧ simmer for 20 to 30 minutes. Skin, bone and flake it. One lb. dried salt cod will yield about 2 cups cooked flaked fish.

SCALLOPED COD [4]

Preheat oven to 375°.
➧ Please read About Cod, above.
Cook and flake:

1 lb. dried salt cod

Combine:

1 tablespoon flour
2 cups milk
1 well-beaten egg

Cook and stir these ingredients until they are thick in the top of a double boiler ➧ over, not in, hot water.

Correct the seasoning

Prepare:

1½ cups bread crumbs
1½ cups finely chopped celery

Grease a baking dish. Place in it ½ the fish and a layer of ⅓ the crumbs and celery. Cover with ½ the sauce and repeat the process. Sprinkle the remaining crumbs on the top. Dot with:

Butter or grated cheese

Bake for about 20 minutes, or until the crumbs are golden brown.

CODFISH BALLS OR CAKES [4]

◆ Please read About Cod, page 407.
Soak in water for 12 hours, drain, place in boiling water, and simmer for 15 minutes:

1 cup salt cod

Drain and flake it. Rice or mash:

6 medium-sized boiled potatoes

Combine the fish and potatoes. Beat in one at a time:

2 eggs

Beat in until fluffy:

2 tablespoons cream
(1 teaspoon grated onion)
Correct the seasoning

Shape the mixture into balls or patties, and use one of the following cooking methods.

I. Form the mixture into 2-inch cakes, dip in flour and sauté in butter until brown. Serve at once.

II. Preheat deep fryer to 375°. Form into 1-inch balls, dip in milk, roll in flour. Fry until golden brown.

III. Preheat oven to 375°. Form into patties and bake in a greased pan about ½ hour. Dot with butter and serve.

FRESH COD À LA PORTUGAISE [4]

Season:

4 thick cod fillets

with:

Pepper

Place the fish in a heavy saucepan. Add:

1 finely chopped onion
1 crushed clove garlic
¼ cup coarsely chopped parsley
A sprig of thyme
3 peeled, seeded and coarsely chopped tomatoes
½ cup dry white wine

Bring to boiling point, ◆ reduce the heat and simmer gently ◆ covered for about 10 minutes. Remove the fish carefully. Arrange it on a hot serving dish and keep warm. Reduce the cooking liquid by ⅓,

Correct the seasoning

and finish with a Butter Swirl, page 357. Pour the sauce over the fish and serve at once.

SALT COD OR MORUE À LA PROVENÇALE [4]

◆ Please read About Cod, page 407.
Cook, drain, cut into 2-inch cubes and reserve:

1 lb. salt cod

In a large saucepan fry gently until golden:

3 tablespoons olive oil
1 minced clove garlic
3 large chopped onions
1 large sliced leek, white part only

Add and simmer gently for about 15 minutes:

1 quart hot water
¼ cup tomato paste
¼ teaspoon each dried sage, thyme, and rosemary
1 bay leaf
1 small hot Spanish pepper
1 chopped green pepper, seeds and membrane removed

Add to the sauce and simmer until tender:

2 cups peeled potatoes cut Parisienne, page 250

Add the cod to the hot sauce and set the pan over very low heat until the cod is heated through. Garnish with:

Triangles of fried French bread
Chopped parsley

COD SOUNDS AND TONGUES

[Allow About ¼ Pound Per Serving]

Sounds—or cheeks—and tongues

may come fresh or salted. If salted, they must be soaked overnight, drained, simmered for 5 minutes in water started cold, then drained again. To poach, cover with boiling water, ➧ reduce the heat and simmer about 5 minutes. Drain. Serve this way with Mornay Sauce, page 361, or Poulette Sauce, page 362. Or you may sauté them until golden brown. Serve with Maître d'Hôtel Butter, page 384.

FRESH COD BOULANGÈRE [4]

Preheat oven to 350°.
Parboil in separate pans:

16 small peeled potatoes
12 small white onions

Place in a shallow buttered heatproof dish:

A center cut of cod or a whole small cleaned cod

Arrange the onions and potatoes around it and sprinkle with:

A pinch of thyme
Correct the seasoning

Brush with:

Melted butter

Baste frequently with melted butter during the baking process. Bake about ½ hour. Serve in the same dish garnished with:

Chopped parsley
Slices of lemon

BROILED FRESH SCROD

[Allow ½ Pound Per Serving]
Split, then remove the bones from:

A young codfish: scrod

Leave it whole, flatten it out, or cut it in pieces. Broil as described on page 399.

ABOUT EEL

The eel is a fish which believes in long journeys. It is spawned in the Sargasso Sea in the western Atlantic, and from there will travel back to its fresh water haunts in this country or in Europe to feed and grow up in the rivers and streams frequented by its parents. The young eel or elver is still only 2 or 3 inches longer after its immense journey, and is transparent and yellowish. Little eels can be cooked and larger ones smoked or pickled to make a delicious addition to Hors d'Oeuvre or Antipasto (II, 69). As with cats, there is more than one way to skin a fresh eel. We prefer the following. Slip a noose around the eel's head and hang the other end of the cord on a hook, high on the wall. Cut the eel skin about 3 inches below the head all around, so as not to penetrate the gall bladder which lies close to the head. Peel the skin back, pulling down hard—if necessary with a pair of pliers—until the whole skin comes off like a glove. Clean the fish by slitting the white belly and removing the gut which lies close to the thin belly skin.
Eel may be sautéed as for:

Trout à la Meunière, page 419

poached for 9 to 10 minutes and then served with a:

Velouté Sauce, page 362

or one of its variations, made from the eel stock. Skinned, cleaned, boned and cut into 3-inch pieces and dried, eel may be dipped in:

Batter (II, 125)
Bound Breading (II, 160)

and deep fried until golden brown. Serve this way with:

Fried Parsley, page 305
and lemon wedges,
Tartare Sauce or Tomato Sauce, page 376

Eel may also be broiled as for any fat fish, page 399.

MARINATED FLOUNDER FILLETS [6]

Marinate for 10 minutes:

2 lbs. flounder fillets

in:

1 cup tarragon vinegar

Drain, and coat with a mixture of:

½ cup yellow corn meal
½ cup flour
¼ teaspoon salt
⅛ teaspoon freshly ground pepper

Sauté the fillets in:

¼ cup butter

until golden brown, about 4 minutes on each side. Serve with:

Hot Ravigote Sauce, page 364, or Cucumber Sauce, page 251

ABOUT HADDOCK

Fresh haddock may be prepared as in any recipe for cod, flounder or other lean white fish. It may be baked plain or stuffed, its fillets fried, sautéed, or poached. Smoked haddock—or finnan haddie—may be broiled, well basted in butter, or baked, as in the following recipe.

CREAMED FINNAN HADDIE

Barely cover:

Finnan haddie: smoked haddock

with:

Milk

Soak for 1 hour. Bring slowly to the boiling point. Simmer for 20 minutes. Drain. Flake and remove the skin and bones. Place the fish in very hot:

Cream Sauce I, page 359

Use about ⅔ as much sauce as you have fish. Add for each cup of flaked fish:

1 chopped hard-cooked egg
1 teaspoon chopped green pepper, seeds and membrane removed
1 teaspoon chopped pimiento

Serve fish on:

Rounds of toast

sprinkled with:

Lemon juice
Chopped chives or parsley

BAKED STUFFED FRESH HADDOCK [6]

Preheat oven to 375°.

Sauté in a large saucepan for about 5 minutes:

½ cup chopped onion
¼ cup chopped celery
½ cup chopped fresh mushrooms

in:

3 tablespoons butter

Stir into the sautéed vegetables:

2 cups soft bread crumbs
1 teaspoon salt
⅛ teaspoon pepper
A pinch of dried tarragon
(A pinch of dried rosemary)

Arrange in a layer on a greased large shallow baking dish:

2 lbs. haddock fillets

Sprinkle the fish with:

Lemon juice

and spread the stuffing over it. Cover with:

3 or 4 peeled sliced tomatoes

Bake uncovered for 35 to 40 minutes.

Serve with:

Boiled Potatoes, page 310

BAKED FINNAN HADDIE [6]

Preheat oven to 350°.

Prepare for cooking:

2 lbs. finnan haddie: smoked haddock

Soak it in warm water for ½ hour, skin side down. Pour off the water. Put the fish on a greased ovenproof pan and cover it with:

1 cup cream

Dot generously with:

Butter

Sprinkle with:

¼ cup chopped onions
Paprika

Bake for about 40 minutes. If cream evaporates, use additional cream. The dish may be served with:

Cream Sauce I, page 359

BAKED FRESH FILLETS OF HADDOCK IN CREAM SAUCE [4]

Preheat oven to 350°

Place on an ovenproof dish:

4 haddock or other lean fish fillets

Prepare:

2 cups Cream Sauce I, page 359, or Cheese Sauce, page 364

Season the sauce well, adding:

1 teaspoon Worcestershire sauce or ½ teaspoon dry mustard or 1 teaspoon fennel, dill or celery seed
(2 tablespoons dry sherry)

Pour it over the fillets. Bake the fish until done, see page 396. You may sprinkle over it:

1 cup or more freshly cooked or canned shrimp or crab meat

Place the dish under a broiler until the top is heated. Sprinkle with:

Chopped parsley

ABOUT HERRING

Herring is one of the cheapest, most nutritious and plentiful fish one can buy. It is very fat, with a calcium content twice that of milk. Split, salted and smoked, it is known as a **kipper;** smoke-cured without salt, as a **bloater.** Bloaters are very perishable and should be eaten right after curing. Perhaps the reason herring is not more popular is because it has innumerable tiny, fine bones. If you split a herring down the center of the back with a sharp knife, lever up the backbone and carefully pull it out, most of these small bones will come with it. After cleaning, page 393, you may then cook the herring in one piece or split it in two.

Marinated herring comes in various disguises. **Rollmops** are fresh herring fillets seasoned and rolled—like Paupiettes, page 405—around a pickle or cucumber. **Bismarck herring** is the flat fillet in a sour marinade; **matjes** or virgin herring can be sour or salted. Herring also comes with the roe or milt sieved and thinned with sour cream as a dressing over the fish, pages 351 and 416.

BAKED HERRING AND POTATOES [4]

Preheat oven to 375°.

I. To prepare salt herring, soak overnight in water or milk to cover:

2 large salt herring

Drain and split them. Remove and discard skin and bones. They can now be used as a garnish for hors d'oeuvre, on lasagne; or as follows. Cut fillets into 1-inch-wide pieces. Pare and slice very thinly:

6 raw potatoes
2 medium-sized onions

Butter a baking dish. Place in it alternate layers of potatoes, onions and herring, beginning and ending with potatoes. Cover the top with:

Au Gratin II, page 389

Bake for 45 minutes or more.

II. A Yorkshire version substitutes:

Sour apples

for the onions, and uses:

Fresh herring

In this case, prepare as above, but season with:

Salt and pepper

after each layer of herring.

MARINATED HERRING [12]

Soak for 3 hours in water to cover:

24 milter herring

Change the water twice. Cut off the heads and tails. Split the herring. Remove the milt, page 416. Reserve it. Remove the bones as described, page 411. Discard them. Cut the fillets into pieces about 3 inches long. Place in a crock in alternate layers with the herring:

½ the milt
2 very thinly sliced lemons
2 skinned and thinly sliced onions
⅓ cup mixed pickle spices
1 tablespoon sugar

Cover these ingredients with:

Malt vinegar or other vinegar

Crush with a fork and add:

The remaining milt

Dilute the vinegar with a little water if it is very strong. ➧ Cover the crock and put it in a cool place. The herring will be ready to serve after 2 weeks.

MARINATED HERRING WITH SOUR CREAM

Prepare, as above:

6 milter herring

using only 1 lemon, 1 onion, 2½ tablespoons mixed spices and ¼ cup vinegar.

Add:

1 cup cultured sour cream

Keep in a cool place. Serve after 48 hours.

SCOTCH FRIED HERRING

[Allow 1 Herring Per Serving]

This must be made with:

Fresh caught herring

You may fry them whole but they are better split down the backbone and boned, as described, page 411. Cut off head, tail and fins. Roll in:

Medium-ground seasoned Scotch oatmeal

pressing a little to make it stick. Fry the herring on both sides in:

Bacon fat or olive oil

Serve with:

Lemon wedges
A pat of butter

or with:

Mustard Sauce, page 363

Garnish with:

Parsley

GRILLED OR BAKED KIPPERS OR BLOATERS

[Allow ½ Pound Per Serving]

Preheat broiler.

An excellent breakfast dish with scrambled eggs. Do not try to grill canned kippers; they are too wet. Place:

Kippers or bloaters

skin side down on a hot oiled grill. Dot with:

Butter

Grill 5 to 7 minutes. Serve very hot. You may also bake them in a 350° oven for 10 minutes, or En Papillote, page 87, for 15 minutes at the same temperature. Season with:

A little lemon juice
Pepper

ABOUT OCTOPUS AND SQUID

These fish are similar in shape, treatment and taste. They both have long edible arms, a body that can be formed into a natural sack for stuffing if desired, and an ink-expelling mechanism. The transparent cartilage must be removed from squid and octopus before they are ready for the kitchen; and some of it, after heating and drying, becomes the cuttlebone one sees in birdcages.

Of much greater importance to us is the ink. Not only does it furnish the pigment known as sepia, but it may be used in recipes just as blood is used, page 357, to color, flavor and give body to a sauce. When the ink is not available, it is sometimes "faked" by the use of chocolate, as in Mole Sauce, page 586.

To prepare octopus and squid, remove the beaklike mouth, anal portion and the eyes—being careful not to pierce the ink sack which lies close by. If inkfish are small, this may be done with scissors; if large and tough, you will need a knife to penetrate far enough to slip them inside out and remove and discard the yellowish pouch and the attached membranes. On octopus the very ends of the tentacles are also discarded. Wash well in running water to remove gelatinous portions. Octopus, which has 8 arms, comes in enormous sizes, but is apt to be very tough if over 2 to 2½ lbs. in weight. Both these and the 8 to 12 inch squid, which have 6 arms and 2 tentacles, need tenderizing. This can be done in 2 ways: by merciless beating—native fishermen pound them on the rocks—or by adding tenderizer to a marinade.

The arms and tentacles are cut crosswise in 1 to 1¼ inch rounds and the white portions of the body meat are often cut in diamond shapes of about the same size to equalize the cooking time. ➧ To skin these sections, Parblanch, page 88, briefly 1 to 2 minutes, and arrest further cooking by plunging them into cold water. If you do not deep fat fry as for other fish, page 401—a matter of 3 to 4 minutes at 375°—long slow cooking is necessary. Even after marinating, the simmering time may run close to 3 hours, unless the specimens are very young and well pounded, when 45 minutes should suffice.

Squid is available ready to use in cans and is sometimes found frozen or dried. ➧ To use dried squid, marinate in a combination of water, gin and ginger for 45 minutes and then use in recipes as for the fresh meat. ➧ Allow about ½ lb. of fresh squid or octopus per serving.

CASSEROLED OCTOPUS

[Allow ½ lb. Per Person]

Clean, pound, and cut up as described previously and place in a casserole:

- **6 small octopus**
- **½ cup olive oil**
- **⅓ cup vinegar or ½ cup dry wine**
- **2 cups julienned mushrooms**
- **1 cup chopped onions**
- **1 pressed clove garlic**
- **1 tablespoon each fresh chopped parsley, chervil and basil**
- **⅓ bay leaf**

Cover and bring just to a boil. ➧ Reduce the heat at once and ➧ simmer, very tightly covered, 2½ to 3 hours. You may add the ink to the pan drippings just before serving. ➧ Do not boil. Serve with:

Creamed Spinach, page 326

BOILED SALT MACKEREL

[Allow ⅓ to ½ Pound Per Serving]

Soak overnight, skin side up, well covered with cold water:

Salt mackerel

Drain, place in a shallow pan, cover with water and simmer until tender, for about 12 minutes. Drain well. Place on a hot platter. Pour over the fish:

Melted butter

to which add:

Chopped chives or parsley, lemon juice or Worcestershire sauce

BROILED FRESH MACKEREL

Preheat broiler.

Split and bone:

A Mackerel, page 392

Place it skin down in a greased pan. Sprinkle with:

Paprika

Brush with:

Melted butter or olive oil

Broil slowly on one side only until firm, about 20 minutes. Baste with the drippings while cooking. Remove to a hot platter. Spread with:

Anchovy Butter, page 384

Garnish with:

Parsley and lemon slices

BROILED SALT MACKEREL

[Allow ⅓ to ½ Pound Per Serving]

Soak by the preceding recipe:

Salt mackerel

Drain, then wipe dry.
Preheat broiler.
Brush with:

Melted butter

Broil, skin side down. Baste twice with melted butter while cooking. Remove to a hot platter. Pour over the fish:

½ cup Cream Sauce I, page 359

Garnish with:

Chopped parsley

ABOUT PIKE, PICKEREL AND MUSKELLUNGE

These fish, which are naturally dry, may be marinated or not, as desired, before cooking. Many cooks prefer to bake or braise them, page 398.

POMPANO EN PAPILLOTE

[Individual Serving]

Preheat oven to 450°.
Place on heart-shaped parchment paper, page 86.

2 medium-sized skinned pompano fillets

Cover with:

2 tablespoons Velouté Sauce, page 362
2 chopped cooked shrimp
2 tablespoons chopped cooked crab meat

Close the parchment paper, fold the edge and bake for about 15 minutes until the paper is browned and puffed. Serve immediately. For a party, make individual packets ahead of time, allow them to reach about 60°. Preheat oven and bake as above.

ABOUT SALMON

Atlantic salmon, pink and prized, comes to our markets mainly in fresh form. Pacific salmon reaches us in many forms. These include the choice King or Chinook from Alaska and the Columbia River areas. They may be pink or white-fleshed, and are about 17% fat. Included also are the red-fleshed sockeye, the pinkish silver Coho and the yellowish-fleshed, almost fat-free, dog salmon. ▸ All smoked salmon is highly perishable and should be kept refrigerated even when canned. Regular canned salmon, if in tall cans, is tail meat; if in squat cans it comes from the center cuts.

BROILED SALMON STEAKS OR DARNES

[Allow ½ Pound Per Serving]

Preheat broiler.
To cut steaks or darnes, see page 394.
Brush preheated broiler rack and:

¾-inch-thick salmon steaks

well with:

Clarified Butter, page 383

Place rack 6 inches from the source of heat. Broil 5 minutes. Baste, turn, baste again and continue to broil 5 to 8 minutes. To test for doneness, see if you can lift out the central bone without bringing any of the flesh with it. Serve with:

Freshly grated horseradish

The steak shape lends itself to attractive service as the hollow may be filled with:

A stuffed tomato, or
A mound of vegetables, or
Potatoes garnished with parsley

COLD GLAZED SALMON

[Allow ½ Pound Per Serving]

This method of preparation applies to any fish you wish to glaze and serve cold.

Poach, page 398, leaving head and tail on:

1 large cleaned salmon

Remove from the poaching water as soon as it is done. Leaving the head and tail as it is, and working with the grain, skin and trim the rest of the fish, removing the fins and the gray, fatty portions until just the pink flesh is left. Place on a large serving platter and refrigerate. If you have an emergency, the fish may be eaten just this way with mayonnaise. But to glaze—read on. ➧ Work quickly to prevent the glaze from darkening, and keep chilling between processes. Coat the visible pink portion of the fish evenly and smoothly with:

Mayonnaise Collée, page 387, or
Sauce Chaud-Froid, page 388

Rechill until this sauce has set. Decorate as described in the Sauce Chaud-Froid recipe. Chill again. Coat the whole surface, head and tail too, with:

Aspic Glaze, page 387

Chill and continue coating and chilling until you have built up an even clear ¼ inch of aspic. Clean the platter by removing aspic dribbles. Save any leftover aspic and chill it in sheet form. Chop it fine and surround the fish with an edging of little sparkling tidbits. Serve the fish with:

Cold Mousseline Sauce, page 370, or
Green Mayonnaise, page 348

The classic garnish is:

Tiny tomatoes stuffed with Russian Salad, page 40

We suggest also:

Cold Leeks Vinaigrette

ABOUT SARDINES

Sardines were to us something that came out of a can on laundry day until one summer we had a Breton guest. Her family had for centuries lived an amicably divided life in seaside castles on opposite sides of a river inlet. Her uncle's fleets dredged seaweed from which chemicals were produced. Her father's fleet sailed from Maine to Spain—following those Atlantic sardines which were fit even for the Czar of Russia, himself, to whom they were purveyed. But fish, like people, may change habits suddenly. For three years the fleet failed to find the sardine runs. Sonar might have changed Odette's fate, but Brittany's loss was our vivacious and warmhearted gain.

Pacific sardines are almost twice as large as the Atlantic kind, and both are bigger than the type of pilchards originally caught off Sardinia. **Anchovies** are even smaller sardines. When smoked, sardines are referred to as **sprats.** Treat fresh sardines as for Smelts, page 417.

If you want to present canned sardines in an interesting way, skin and bone:

12 canned sardines

Mash 6 of them with:

1 teaspoon minced onion
2 teaspoons butter
½ teaspoon prepared mustard
1 teaspoon lemon juice

Spread:

6 narrow toasts

with this mixture. Place a whole sardine on each toast and run under the broiler. Before serving garnish with:

Finely chopped fennel
A grating of black pepper

ABOUT SEA SQUAB OR BLOWFISH

These puffers are related to the sought after Japanese fugu. As the ovaries and liver are very poisonous be sure to discard all but the back flesh before cooking. Prepare as for any delicate fish.

ABOUT ROE AND MILT

The eggs of the female fish are known as roe or hard roe; the male fish's sperm is known as milt or soft roe, as its texture is creamy rather than grainy. Both types are used in cooking and the roe of certain fish is more valued than the fish itself, see Caviar (II, 79).

Shad roe is considered choice. You may serve the roe or milt of other fish such as herring, mackerel, flounder, salmon, or cod as in the following recipes for shad roe. The milt of salmon must have the vein removed.

Hard roe, to be cooked and served alone, should be pricked with a needle to prevent the membrane from bursting and splattering the little eggs. Cook roe gently with very slow heat. Overcooked, it is hard, dry, and tasteless. It may be served as a luncheon dish; as a savory; as stuffing or garnish for the fish from which it comes. Or it may be used raw, as in Marinated Herring, page 411, or as an hors d'oeuvre. Also see Canned Roe Dishes, page 236.

➧ Allow 6 oz. Per Serving.

PARBOILED SHAD ROE

➧ Please read About Roe, above. Prick with a needle in several places and cover with boiling water:

Shad roe

Add to it:

2 tablespoons lemon juice or 3 tablespoons dry white wine

Simmer from 3 to 12 minutes, according to size. Drain and cool. Remove the membrane. Add salt if needed. The roe is now ready to be sautéed, sauced, or used in a garnish or hors d'oeuvre.

BAKED SHAD ROE

Preheat oven to 375°.

Parboil:

Shad roe

Place in a buttered pan. Cover with:

Creole Sauce, page 376, or
Mushroom Sauce, page 367

Bake for 15 or 20 minutes, basting every 5 minutes.

SAUTÉED SHAD ROE

Heat until light brown:

2 tablespoons Clarified Butter, page 383

Sauté in this until delicately browned on both sides:

Parboiled Shad Roe, see above
Correct the seasoning

Remove to a hot platter. Add to the drippings and heat:

2 teaspoons lemon juice
½ teaspoon chopped chives
½ teaspoon chopped parsley
1 minced shallot
½ teaspoon dried tarragon, chervil or basil

Pour the sauce over the roe. Sautéed roe is frequently served with Tartare Sauce, page 349. Or sprinkle with:

Chopped parsley, lemon juice and Brown Butter, page 383

Surround with:

Orange sections

BROILED SHAD ROE

Preheat broiler.
Parboil, page 88, wipe dry and place on a greased rack:

Shad roe

Sprinkle with:

Lemon juice

Bard with:

Bacon

Broil from 5 to 7 minutes. If the roe is large, you may have to turn it, baste with drippings and cook until firm. Serve on toast garnished with:

Maître d'Hôtel Butter, page 384
Parsley

BAKED SHAD WITH CREAMED ROE [6 to 8]

Preheat oven to 350°.
Parboil, page 88:

Shad roe

➧ Simmer for 15 minutes. Drain. Remove the outside membrane. Mash the roe. Melt in a saucepan:

2 tablespoons butter

You may add and sauté for about 3 minutes:

1 tablespoon grated onion

Add the roe and stir in:

2 tablespoons flour
½ cup cream

When these ingredients begin to boil, remove from heat. Stir in:

2 egg yolks

Season the roe mixture well with:

Dry white wine or lemon juice

Keep hot. Bone, page 395:

A 3 or 4 lb. shad

Place it skin side down on a well-greased broiler rack or a flat pan. Brush it with:

Melted butter

Bake, allowing about 8 minutes per pound. Remove from the oven and spread the thin part of the fish with the creamed roe. Cover the fish with:

Au Gratin Sauce II, page 389

Return to the broiler and brown evenly. Serve at once garnished with:

Lemon slices
Parsley or water cress
Pickled beets or cucumbers

ABOUT CARVING SHAD

Carving shad is a very direct process. Before cooking, every effort must be made to remove as many bones as possible. Even tweezers may be resorted to. When carving time comes, the fish is sliced completely through its entire thickness in about 4-inch parallel widths. Any exposed bones may again be removed with tweezers before the cut pieces are put on the individual plates.

ABOUT SHARK

If you care to adventure, you will find that shark meat—close to and along the backbone—responds to recipes for Fish Fillets, pages 401–405, or to Poaching, page 490. The belly sections need long simmering.

SMELTS [2]

Clean, see page 393, rinse thoroughly and wipe dry:

12 smelts

Leave whole. Season with:

Lemon juice

Let them stand covered for 15 minutes. Roll the smelts in:

Cream

Dip in:

Flour or corn meal

I. Melt:

¼ cup butter

Sauté the smelts gently until they are done.

II. Bake smelts in a buttered pan in a 450° oven for about 5 minutes. Place them on a hot platter. Add to the butter in the pan:

Juice of 1 lemon
2 tablespoons chopped parsley or chives

Pour the sauce over the smelts.

III. ➧ Please read About Deep Fat Frying, pages 75–79. Smelts may be dipped in crumbs or egg and crumbs and fried in deep fat at 370° about 3 minutes. Serve with:

Tartare Sauce, page 349

BAKED RED SNAPPER WITH SAVORY TOMATO SAUCE [4 to 6]

Preheat oven to 350°.
Prepare for cooking:

A 3-lb. red snapper or other large fish

Dredge it inside and out with:

Seasoned flour

Place in a baking pan. Melt:

6 tablespoons butter

Add and simmer for 15 minutes:

½ cup chopped onion
2 cups chopped celery
¼ cup chopped green pepper, seeds and membrane removed

Add and simmer until the celery is tender:

3 cups canned tomatoes
1 tablespoon Worcestershire sauce
1 tablespoon catsup
1 teaspoon chili powder
½ finely sliced lemon
2 bay leaves
1 minced clove garlic
1 teaspoon salt
A few grains red pepper

Press these ingredients through a potato ricer or food mill. Pour the sauce around the fish. Bake the fish for about ¾ hour, basting frequently with the sauce.

SOLE AMBASSADOR

[Allow ½ lb. Per Person]

Prepare for poaching:

10 fillets of sole, lemon or English, trout or halibut

Place them in a buttered heatproof dish or skillet and sprinkle with:

1 tablespoon finely chopped shallot or onion
Salt and pepper

Add:

½ cup dry white wine
Juice of 1 lemon

Cover with a buttered poaching paper, page 84, and simmer until the fillets are done, see page 395. While they are cooking, melt in a heavy casserole:

1 tablespoon butter

Sauté:

1 cup finely chopped mushrooms
Juice of ½ lemon
Salt and pepper

Cook over high heat for about 3 minutes, until the juices disappear. Reduce heat.
Add:

½ cup whipping cream

➧ Simmer until reduced by ⅓. Remove from the heat and beat in:

1 egg yolk

Drain and save the stock from the fish. On a heatproof serving platter, spread the mushroom mixture, and arrange the fillets over it. Heat the fish stock and add:

Kneaded Butter, page 357

Beat in well until thickened.
Add:

½ cup whipping cream

Heat to the boiling point. ➧ Remove from the heat and add:

3 egg yolks

Strain the sauce and pour it over the fish fillets. Glaze under the broiler until brown. Serve at once.

FILLET OF SOLE FLORENTINE [6]

Poach, page 398:

6 fillets of sole or other fish

In the bottom of an ovenproof platter, put a layer of:

1½ cups Creamed Spinach, page 398

Arrange the poached, drained fillets on top. Cover with:

1 cup seasoned Cream Sauce II, page 359

Sprinkle over it:

Au Gratin III, page 389

Run under the broiler to heat through until the sauce is glazed.

SWORDFISH STEAKS

Prepare as for:

Salmon Steaks, page 414

As this fish dries out even when in prime condition, be sure to use plenty of butter in the cooking.

BROOK TROUT MEUNIÈRE [4]

Clean and wash:

4 brook trout: 8 inches each

Cut off the fins. Leave the head and tail on. Dip in:

Seasoned flour

Melt:

¼ cup Clarified Butter, page 383

Sauté the trout until they are firm and nicely browned. Remove to a hot platter. Add to the drippings in the pan:

3 tablespoons clarified butter

Let it brown. Cover the fish with:

Chopped parsley

Pour the browned butter over the fish. Garnish with:

Lemon wedges

BROILED LAKE TROUT OR WHITEFISH

[Allow About ½ Pound Per Serving]

Preheat broiler.

Bone, page 393:

A large fish, lake trout, whitefish, etc.

Flatten it out or cut it into pieces. Rub a saucer with

Garlic

Place in it and mix:

1 or 2 tablespoons olive oil
¼ teaspoon white pepper

Rub the fish on both sides with these ingredients. Place it in a greased shallow pan. Broil until brown, turning it once. Spread with:

Maître d'Hôtel Butter, page 384, or Lemon Butter, page 384

Garnish with:

Parsley
Cucumbers in Sour Cream, page 44

BLUE TROUT OR TRUITE AU BLEU

[Allow One 4 to 6½ Ounce Trout Per Person]

Please read About Cooking Fish "Au Bleu," page 399. The amazingly brilliant blue color of this dish can be achieved only if your fish is alive when ready for the pot. We ate these first in the Black Forest at an inn bordering a stream, but we think of them always in connection with Joseph Wechsberg's zestful book, "Blue Trout and Black Truffles."

Have ready and boiling:

Seasoned Acidulated Water with lemon juice or vinegar (II, 148)

allowing 2 tablespoons acid per fish. Kill the fish with one sharp blow on the head. Split and clean it with one stroke if possible. Be careful not to disturb the slime on the body of the fish. Plunge it at once into the boiling water. Let this come to a boil again, then remove the pan from the heat and cover it. Let stand for about 5 minutes. Slightly larger fish may need another 2 or 3 minutes. The white eyeballs pop out when the fish is done. Remove the fish and drain well. The classic service is on a napkin on your best silver salver, accompanied by a garnish of:

Parsley

with:

Boiled or steamed potatoes and sweet butter balls, or melted butter

You may also serve other fancy butters or:

Hollandaise Sauce, page 368

But why add earrings to an elephant? If you serve the fish cold, pass:

Gribiche Sauce, page 348 or
Ravigote Sauce, page 342

FRESH TUNA OR BONITO

[Allow ½ Pound Per Serving]

Clean:

A fresh tuna or bonito

Braise or roast as for veal, or brush the delicate stomach sections with:

Cooking oil

and broil. For recipes for canned tuna, see Index.

POACHED TURBOT

[Allow ½ Pound Per Serving]

This firm-fleshed, very white flat fish may be skinned and filleted, page 395, and poached in Court Bouillon (II, 146), part wine or part milk to reinforce its whiteness, and cooked as for any recipe for Sole, page 418. As both the skin and the gelatinous areas near the fins are considered delicacies, turbot is often prepared and served unskinned. To keep it from curling or bursting cut a long gash down the center of the under or brown side before poaching.

To cook in the skin, place the fish in a greased pan; float it in a cool:

Court Bouillon

Cover with a poaching paper, page 84. Bring the liquid to a boil. ➧ Reduce the heat at once. Barely simmer for about 30 minutes, basting several times during the cooking. Be sure to replace the paper after each basting.

WHALE

[Allow ½ Pound Per Serving]

Last—but vast.

If whale meat is frozen, thaw before cooking. Whether fresh or frozen, soak for 1 hour in a solution of:

1 tablespoon baking soda to
1 quart water

Rinse well and marinate 1 to 2 hours ➧ covered with a liquid made up of:

3 cups water
1 cup vinegar

Cut across the grain into thin steaks not over ½-inch thick. Sprinkle with:

Lemon juice

and pound, page 452, to tenderize further. Stew, braise or sauté as for beef, which it resembles more than it does fish.

SHELLFISH

ABOUT MOLLUSKS AND CRUSTACEANS

Connoisseurs dispute as to which stretches of the world's seacoast provide the best breeding grounds for shellfish and are ready to do battle over the relative merits of oysters and mussels versus lobsters and crabs. We hope to sidestep most of these controversies in the pages which follow. We hope also to clarify the distinction, along the way, between lobster, page 436, langouste, page 436, and langoustine, page 441, and between crevettes, scampi, page 437, and écrevisses, page 444; sneaking in a few succulent freshwater anomalies like crawfish and frogs, as well as the land-based snail. And we will put our chief emphasis on how to cook so as to retain a just-caught flavor. Details for handling and keeping are given in each shellfish category.

In cooking, we beg you to ➧ use low heat, unless otherwise indicated, to ➧ use the shortest possible cooking period and to serve at once. If these delicacies are eaten raw, be sure they are served properly chilled. Shrimps, prawns, lobsters and crabs are regarded as rather indigestible. Consider an accompanying citrus or vinegar sauce, which will both stimulate the gastric juices and help break down food fibers. Keep in mind that ➧ commercial shellfish collection is permitted only in areas where the waters are unpolluted and that if you collect on your own, be sure the water in the area is safe. ➧ Recipes for mussels, oysters and clams are fairly interchangeable; and some exciting dishes may be created by combining mollusks and crustaceans.

Seafood is often seasoned with wines. For every 6 servings, allow 2 tablespoons dry sherry, 4 tablespoons white wine or 1 tablespoon cognac.

SHELLFISH COCKTAILS

Serve these well chilled, preferably in glasses imbedded in ice. If serving individually, allow about ⅓ cup of seafood per person with about ¼ cup sauce. You may pour the sauce over the seafood, serve it separately for dipping or toss the seafood in the sauce and serve it on lettuce, endive or cress. For appropriate sauces, see:

Russian, page 349, or
Seafood Dips and Sauces, pages (II, 84) and 343

Serve with these cocktails:

Oyster crackers
Cheese crackers
Pretzel sticks
Potato chips
Olives

ADDED COLOR AND FLAVOR IN SEAFOOD DISHES

To 3 well crushed lobster shells and 2 lbs. shrimp shells, add ½ bottle of white wine. Reduce to ½ to ⅓. A bright red sauce results which, when tepid, can be added with puréed shrimp or lobster to Hollandaise Sauce. Purée of pimiento can also be used.

ABOUT OYSTERS

These shellfish, edible at any time, are best in flavor when they are not spawning. As Southern oysters spawn all during the year, they do not have the fine flavor of Northern types and are, therefore, often served highly condimented. These bivalves have one shallow and one deep shell and it is in the deeper shell that they are served raw or baked. Some canny diners have been known to ask for them in restaurants on the shallow shell, in the hope of getting them absolutely freshly opened. Oysters in the shell should be alive. If they gape and do not close quickly in handling, discard them. Also discard any with broken shells.

➧ To open oyster shells, provide yourself first with a strainer and a bowl in which to catch the juices. Hold a well-scrubbed oyster, deep shell down, in a folded napkin in the palm of one hand—work over the strainer and bowl. Insert the edge of an oyster knife into the hinge of the shell. Turn the knife to pry and lift the upper shell enough to insert the knife to cut the hinge muscle. Then run the knife along between the shells to open. The oysters are then ready to be served on the half shell. This procedure is not easy until you have the knack. Should you grow desperate in this shucking process, you may be willing to sacrifice some flavor for convenience. If so, place the oysters in a 400° oven from 5 to 7 minutes, depending on size, drop them briefly into ice water and drain. They should open easily. ➧ To shuck, no matter how you open them, release the oysters from the shell with a knife. Examine each oyster with your fingers to be sure no bit of shell is adhering to it. Drop the oyster into a strainer. If the oysters are sandy, you may rinse them in a separate bowl, allowing ½ cup cold water to each quart of shucked oysters. Pour it over the oysters and reserve the water. In using the oyster liquor and the water mixture, be sure to strain it through a fine muslin to free it from grit. ➧ Before using oysters in any fried or creamed dish, dry them carefully in an absorbent towel.

If oysters have been bought already opened, in bulk, be sure to free them of bits of shell. They should be plump and creamy in color. The liquor should be clear, not cloudy, and should have no sour or unpleasant odor. If plump oysters burst during the cooking, they have been previously soaked in fresh water to plump them and their flavor as well as their texture has been ruined. Oystermen claim they can easily tell the sex of oysters and insist that females should be fried and males should be stewed. ➧ Allow 1 quart undrained, shucked oysters for 6 servings. It is hard to estimate amounts for oysters on the shell, as they vary in size—6 moderate-sized Eastern oysters would equal about 20 Olympia West Coast oysters.

➧ To store oysters in the shell, refrigerate at 39°, not directly on ice. Keep dry. Store shucked oysters at the same temperature, covered by their liquor, in a closed container. The container may be put in crushed ice, up to about ¾ its height. If you received them fresh, oysters may be stored in this way up to 5 days.

For other oyster suggestions, see Hors d'Oeuvre and Canapés (II, 64, 81 and 82). For cooked oyster suggestions and oyster cakes, see Luncheon Dishes, page 229. Champagne is a fine accompaniment.

OYSTERS ON THE HALF SHELL

[Allow 5 to 6 Oysters per Serving]

➧ Please read About Oysters, page 422.

Scrub well and ➧ open just before serving:

Oysters

Chill them well. Arrange them in cracked ice on the serving plates. You may place, in the center, a small glass of:

Cocktail Sauce, page 344, or Lorenzo Dressing, page 342

or you may serve them with:

Lemon wedges and horseradish sauce

BROILED OYSTERS

[Allow 6 Oysters per Serving]

➧ Please read About Oysters, page 422.

Preheat broiler.

Shuck, drain and dry in a towel:

Oysters

Place them on a well-buttered baking sheet. Broil them for about 3 minutes, turning once during this time. They should be lightly browned. Serve them with:

Lemon wedges, Parsley or Lemon Butter

▤ GRILLED OYSTERS

[Allow 6 Oysters per Serving]

You may grill Western oysters—except Olympias—right on the coals without toughening them, but if you have Eastern oysters put them on a piece of foil in which you have punched holes, before placing them on your grill over a bed of coals.

I. Put on the foil:

Scrubbed, unopened oysters in their shells

Grill until the shells pop. Season and serve with:

Lemon wedges
Melted butter

II. Open:

Scrubbed oysters

Sprinkle them with a:

Gremolata (II, 222)

Heat for a few minutes on the grill over moderate coals.

DEEP-FAT FRIED OYSTERS [2]

➧ Please read About Deep-Fat Frying, pages 75–79.

Preheat deep fryer to 375°.

Drain:

12 large shucked oysters

Dry them well between towels.

Beat together:

1 egg
2 tablespoons water

Inserting a fork in the tough muscle of the oysters, dip them in the egg, then in:

Seasoned bread crumbs

in the egg again and again in the crumbs. Permit the oysters to dry on a rack for ½ hour. Fry them in deep fat for about 4 minutes.

SAUTÉED OYSTERS [2]

Bread, as above, for Deep-Fat Fried Oysters:

12 large shucked oysters

When they are dry, sauté them until they are golden in a combination of:

3 tablespoons cooking oil
2 tablespoons butter

Serve at once.

BAKED OYSTERS

[6 Oysters per Serving]

Preheat oven to 475°.

Have ready:

Oysters on the half shell

Cover them with:

1 tablespoon Creamed Seafood, page 425

Sprinkle them with:

Bread crumbs

Bake for about 10 minutes or until golden.

CREAMED OYSTERS [4]

➧ Please read About Oysters, page 422.

Drain and dry:

1 pint oysters

Reserve the liquor. Melt in a saucepan:

2 tablespoons butter

Add and stir until blended:

2 tablespoons flour

Stir in slowly:

1 cup oyster liquor or oyster liquor and cream, milk or chicken stock

Add:

½ teaspoon salt
⅛ teaspoon paprika or cayenne
(½ to 1 teaspoon curry powder)

When the sauce is smooth and hot, add the drained oysters. Heat them to the boiling point, but do not allow the sauce to boil. When the oysters are thoroughly heated, season them with:

1 teaspoon lemon juice, ½ teaspoon Worcestershire sauce or 2 tablespoons dry sherry

Serve them at once in:

Bread Cases, page 209, patty shells or on hot buttered toast

Sprinkle them generously with:

Chopped parsley

SCALLOPED OYSTERS [6]

Preheat oven to 350°.

Have ready:

1 quart shucked oysters in their liquor

and a deep buttered casserole. Place in the bottom a:

½-inch layer of coarsely crushed soda crackers

Put in a layer of the oysters. Season with:

Salt and pepper
Bits of butter
2 cups cream

Sprinkle with another layer of:

Crushed crackers

Bake 45 to 50 minutes.

OYSTERS SCALLOPED IN CANNED SOUP [6]

➧ Please read About Oysters, page 422.

Preheat broiler.

Drain and dry, reserving the liquor:

1 pint small oysters: 2 cups

Combine:

1 cup dry bread or cracker crumbs
3 tablespoons melted butter
¼ teaspoon salt
1 teaspoon minced parsley

Heat to the boiling point:

1 can cream of celery, mushroom or chicken soup: 10½ oz.
The oyster liquor or 4 tablespoons water

or replace 1 tablespoon of the liquor with:

(Catsup)

Add the oysters. Cook them until the edges begin to curl. Place ½ the buttered crumbs in a hot casserole, add the oysters and soup. Top with the remaining crumbs. Place the dish under a broiler until the top is brown.

OYSTER CELERY [4]

Preheat oven to 350°.
Prepare:
Creamed Oysters, page 424
Before adding the oysters thicken with:
2 egg yolks
Season with:
Dry sherry
Place in a baking dish:
¾ cup white, peeled, diced celery
Cover with the creamed oysters and dust with:
Parmesan cheese
Bake until golden, about 15 minutes.

BAKED CREAMED OYSTERS AND SEAFOOD [6]

Do not take this dish too literally. Change the proportions and substitute crab, tuna, etc., to suit yourself. It's a grand basic dish with which to work.
Preheat oven to 375°.
Prepare:
Creamed Oysters, page 424
Add:
1 cup cooked chopped shrimp, lobster, crab meat, tuna, scallops or leftover cooked fish
Cover with:
Au Gratin II or III, page 389
Bake about 10 minutes.

OYSTERS IN MUSHROOMS AU GRATIN [4]

Preheat oven to 375°.
Sauté, page 296:
20 large mushroom caps
in:
3 tablespoons butter
Place the mushrooms, cavity side up, in a greased baking dish. Fill them with:
20 large drained oysters
and cover them with:
1 cup hot Cream Sauce I, page 359
seasoned with:
Dry sherry
Sprinkle the top with:
Grated Parmesan cheese
Place the dish in the oven until the top is brown or omit the cream sauce and dot each oyster with:
¼ teaspoon butter
A few drops lemon juice
Bake about 10 minutes, until the oysters are plump. Serve on:
Creamed Spinach, page 326

OYSTER RAREBIT [4]

Cook in their liquor until plump:
2 cups oysters: 1 pint
Drain. Keep them hot and reserve the liquor. Cook in a double boiler and stir until smooth:
2 tablespoons butter
¼ lb. diced Swiss or Gruyère cheese
½ teaspoon salt
A few grains cayenne
Add and stir until thick:
The oyster liquor
If there is not enough oyster liquor to make a good sauce, add rich milk until it is the right consistency. Add:
2 beaten eggs
Add the oysters and:
Salt
1 teaspoon Worcestershire sauce or 2 tablespoons dry sherry
Serve it on:
Toast or rusks
Garnish it with a sprinkling of:
Paprika

OYSTERS ROCKEFELLER

[Allow 6 Oysters per Serving]
Preheat oven to 475°.
I. This dish is best with oysters in the shell but, if they are not available, this recipe is a good way to dress up bulk oysters in separately bought shells.
Season and cover the oysters in turn with:

Butter, creamed with onion juice and chopped parsley—reserve some of this
Salt
A few grains cayenne
Cooked, minced bacon
Puréed spinach
Bread crumbs and some of the remaining butter
A dash of Spice Parisienne

It is a New Orleans idea to sprinkle the oysters with absinthe. The shells are then imbedded in pans of rock salt. Bake for about 10 minutes or until plump. Run them under a broiler to brown and serve at once.

II. A simpler version.
Half fill a shell with:
Creamed Spinach, page 326
Place on spinach:
1 large oyster
Cover with:
1 teaspoon chopped parsley
A few drops lemon juice and Worcestershire sauce
A square inch of bacon
Cook as in I.

III. Fill half the shell, as above, with:
Creamed Spinach, page 326
Place the oyster on the spinach and cover with:
1 teaspoon well-seasoned Cream Sauce I, page 359
1 teaspoon grated Parmesan Cheese
Bake as above.

OYSTERS CASINO [4]

➧ Please read About Oysters, page 422.
Preheat oven to 450°.
Prepare:
24 oysters on the half shell
Imbed them in pans of rock salt.
Cream together:
½ cup sweet butter
⅓ cup finely chopped shallots
¼ cup finely chopped parsley
¼ cup finely chopped green pepper
¼ cup finely chopped white celery
Juice of 1 lemon
Put a piece of the butter mixture on each oyster, plus:
½ teaspoon of chopped pimiento
Small square of partially cooked bacon
Bake until the bacon is browned, from 5 to 8 minutes.

ABOUT MUSSELS

Mussels are sometimes called "the oysters of the poor," which only goes to show that there are various definitions of poverty. These delicious mollusks do, however, deteriorate rapidly and, if uncooked, may be the cause of infections.

➧ To test mussels for freshness, try to slide the two halves of the shell across each other. If they budge, the shell is probably filled with mud, not mussel. Mussels are distinguished by a beard. They may be served either with or without it.

Wash mussels in a colander in running water. Keep agitating the colander, so as to keep them from opening their shells and dying. Scrub them with a stiff brush. You may clip the beards with scissors. Mussels may be steamed, removed from the shell, bearded and served much like oysters or clams or served with a sauce, shell and all. It is permissible—probably because it is necessary—to use the hands in separating the shells. Gourmets suggest that a half shell be used to spoon up the liquor to the last drop. ➧ For 4 servings allow about 1 quart undrained shucked or 3 quarts unshucked mussels. Cockles may also be cooked as for mussels.

STEAMED MUSSELS OR MOULES MARINIÈRE [3 to 4]

➧ Please read About Mussels, page 426.
In:

- ¼ cup butter

sauté until golden:

- 6 chopped shallots
- 1 clove garlic

Cook in a deep, heavy skillet for about 2 minutes:

- ¼ cup dry white wine
- ⅓ bay leaf

Add the sautéed shallots and:

- 3 quarts scrubbed, bearded mussels

Cook ➧ closely covered, over lively heat about 6 to 8 minutes. Agitate the pan sufficiently during this time to cook the mussels evenly but ➧ remove from heat the moment the shells are open. Pour the mussels, shells and all, and the sauce into heated bowls and serve garnished with:

- ¼ cup chopped parsley

If you prefer, you may drain the sauce off and quickly thicken it with:

- 2 tablespoons fresh bread crumbs

before pouring it over the mussels.

BAKED BUTTERED MUSSELS

Preheat oven to 450°.
Place well-cleaned mussels in a large pan, in:

- 2 tablespoons olive oil

in the oven until the shells open. Do not overcook them. Remove the upper shell and beard or fringe. Reserve the liquor. If any has escaped to the pan, strain and add it to the reserved liquor from the shell. Serve the mussels on the lower shell with:

- Melted butter or melted garlic butter

and the liquor in small cups or glasses. See Steamed Clams, page 430.

ABOUT CLAMS

All clams arc sandy, especially surf clams. Unshucked, they should be scrubbed and washed in several waters, then soaked in a cold brine of ⅓ cup salt to 1 gallon of water; and it may even be necessary later to put the cooked clams under cold running water to rid them completely of sand. Clams are sold in the shell or shucked. If in the shell ➧ test to see that the clams are tightly closed or, if slightly open, that they close tightly at once upon being touched. ➧ Discard any that float, or have broken shells.

➧ Eight quarts of clams in the shell will yield about 1 quart of clams shucked. ➧ Allow about 1 quart of unshucked clams per person for steamed clams, 6 to 8 clams if served in some other way.

SOFT OR LONGNECK CLAMS

Found mostly north of Cape Cod, these are the preferred East Coast type for eating raw or steamed whole. They are easily opened by running a sharp knife along the edge of the top shell. Work over a bowl, so as to trap the juices. Cut the meat from the bottom shell. Slit the skin of

the neck or siphon, as sketched, and pull off the neck skin.

This skin is too tough to eat as it is, but may be chopped or ground and used in chowders or creamed dishes with other clam meat.

HARD-SHELL CLAMS

These include **butter clams** and **quahogs** which in turn are called **cherrystones** in junior sizes; in medium sizes, they are called **littlenecks.** The large, strongly flavored hard-shells are preferred for chowders. The smaller sizes are suitable for eating on the half shell. If in the shell, you may wash them in several waters. Then cover them with a cold brine of ⅓ cup salt for each gallon of water and sprinkle on the top ¼ cup corn meal to every quart of clams. Leave them in this bath 3 to, preferably, 12 hours. This whitens them, rids them of sand and causes them to eject the black material in their stomachs. After soaking, wash them again in clear water.

Quahogs are difficult to open but, if covered for 5 minutes with water and then gently picked up, you may be able to insert a knife quickly in the opening. Or, if you are using them in a cooked dish and do

not mind a small loss in flavor, you may place them in a pan in a moderate oven until they open. After opening, cut through the muscle holding the shells together. If they have not had a corn meal bath, open the stomachs with sharp shears and scrape out and discard the contents. Large hard-shelled clams have a tough portion, which may be separated from the tender portion, chopped or ground and used in various dishes, creamed, scalloped, in fritters, chowders, etc., using any of the recipes for oysters, or any of the following clam recipes.

RAZOR CLAMS

Especially the Pacific Coast variety, these are unsurpassed for flavor.

SURF CLAMS

These may be used in chowders, broth or cocktails, but their sweetness should be counteracted with salt. They are the sandiest of all clams.

➧ For other recipes, see Soups and Chowders, page 135, or Luncheon Dishes, page 229.

ABOUT CLAMBAKES

Whatever the size of your bake, dig your clams the day before. Scrub them well to remove sand. Put them in a bucket, well covered with sea water. Add corn meal, allowing ½ cup to 2 quarts water. The cereal helps rid the clams of sand and internal waste. Leave the clams in a ➧ cool place. Rinse and drain them just before using. A big bake is described in I; a smaller one, often more practical, in II, with amounts proportionately cut.

⊟ CLAMBAKE

I. **[20]**

Allow:

200 soft-shell clams
(50 hard-shell clams)

Start preparations at least 4 hours before you plan to serve. Dig a sand pit about 1 foot deep and 3½ feet across. Line it with smooth round rocks. ▶ Be sure the rocks have not been baked before. Have a wet tarpaulin—generous enough to overlap the pit area by 1 foot all around—and a few rocks handy to weight the edges. Build a fire over the rock surface, using hardwood, and keep feeding it for the next 2½ to 3 hours while the rocks are heating. Gather and wash about 4 bushels of wet rock seaweed. In fact, it is wise to soak the seaweed for at least 45 minutes before use. Have a pail of sea water at hand. Partially husk about:

4 dozen ears of corn

Do not pull them quite clean but leave on the last layer or two. Rip these back far enough to remove the silk. Then replace them, so the kernels are fully protected. Reserve the pulled husks. Quarter:

5 broiling chickens

Have ready:

10 sweet potatoes
(20 frankfurters)

You may wrap the chicken pieces in cheesecloth or divide the food into 20 individual cheesecloth-wrapped servings, so that each person's food can later be removed as one unit. Scrub:

20 1½-lb. lobsters or 5 pecks soft-shell crabs

Now you are ready to arrange for the "bake." Rake the embers free of the hot stones, remove them from the pit and line it with the wet seaweed covering the stones. The lining should be about six inches deep. Put over it, if you wish, a piece of chicken wire. If you haven't wrapped the individual servings in cheesecloth, now pack the pit in layers. For added flavor, put down first a layer of hard-shell clams, then the frankfurters if you use them, then the lobsters or crabs, the chicken, the corn and the soft-shell clams. You may also put seaweed between the layers. Cover the layered food with the reserved corn husks and sprinkle the whole with the bucket of sea water. Quickly cover with the wet tarp. ▶ Weight the tarp down well with rocks. The whole should steam ▶ covered, about 1 hour. During the steaming, it will puff up, which is a sign of a satisfactory "bake." To test, lift the tarp carefully at one corner ▶ so as not to get sand into the pit and see if the clams have opened. If so, the whole feast should be cooked just to the right point. Have handy plenty of towels and:

Melted butter

Serve with the "bake":

Beer

and afterwards:

Watermelon
Coffee

II. [8]

A well-timed bake in a wash boiler on a stove or outdoor grill. Soak for 45 minutes and remove sand from seaweed in several rinsings. Line the bottom of the boiler with a 4-inch layer of it. Add about:

1 quart water

When water boils, add:

8 foil-wrapped potatoes

▶ Cover boiler and cook gently 15 minutes. Wrap in cheesecloth:

2 cut-up broiler chickens

and place on top of the potatoes. Cook 15 minutes more, before adding:

8 well-scrubbed 1½ lb. lobsters

Cover and cook 8 minutes more, then place on top of the lobsters:

8 shucked foil-wrapped ears of corn

Cook 10 minutes, still covered and add:

48 well-scrubbed soft-shell clams

Cover and steam until the clams open, from 5 to 10 minutes longer. In serving, use:

Melted butter

The drained kettle liquid is to be drunk, but it is wise to drain this through a cloth-lined sieve before serving.

III. [4]

For amounts, cut those in II in half. Use a clean 8-inch stove pipe, about 20 inches deep. Dig and line a circular 18-inch-diameter pit with stones, as described in I—about 12 inches deep—and build the same type fire. When ready to cook, center the stove pipe over the embers. Put in an 8-inch layer of well-soaked seaweed, followed by 4 units of food wrapped in cheesecloth, as described in I, placing seaweed between them. Top with 8 inches of seaweed and heap sand against the stove pipe in volcano shape. Put a wet tarp over the top and weight with rocks. Cook about 1 hour.

STEAMED SOFT-SHELL CLAMS WITH BROTH

[Allow 2 Dozen Unshucked Clams per Serving]

Scrub thoroughly with a brush and wash in several waters:

Soft-shell clams

Place them close together in the top of a steamer, as sketched on the right, page 398, or on a rack in a stock pot with a spigot, as shown on (II, 139). Place in the bottom of the steamer or stock pot:

½ inch water

Cover the kettle closely. Steam the clams over moderate heat until they open, but no longer—from 5 to 10 minutes. Overcooking makes clams tough. Lift them out. Place in individual soup bowls. Serve with individual dishes of:

Melted butter
Lemon wedges

The broth is served in cups along with the clams or it is used for clam juice cocktail later. ➧ To eat clams, pick them up from the shell by the neck with the fingers, dip in broth to remove any possible sand, then in butter. All of the clam is edible, except the neck sheath. The broth is delicious to drink, but don't entirely drain the cup, so as to avoid the sand at the bottom.

BAKED SOFT-SHELL CLAMS [4]

Preheat oven to 425°.

Scrub with a brush and wash in several waters:

36 soft-shell clams

Place them flat in a pan in depressions in crumpled foil or rock salt to keep shells steady. Bake them about 15 minutes until the shells open. Remove the top shell carefully to avoid spilling the juices. Serve the clams in individual plates with:

Butter and celery salt
Pepper and lemon wedges

CLAMS BROILED ON THE HALF SHELL

[Allow 6 to 8 Clams per Person]

Preheat broiler.

Place on an ovenproof dish, in which foil has been crumpled to keep shells steady:

Cherrystone clams on the half shell

Cover each clam with:

A dash of Worcestershire sauce
A square of bacon

Broil the clams until the bacon is done.

FRIED CLAMS

[Allow 6 to 8 Clams per Person]

➧ Please read About Clams, page 427.

Shuck, wash well in a colander under running water:

Soft-shell clams

Dry them between towels. Cut

away the black skin of the neck or siphon. Prepare as for Fried Oysters, page 423. Serve with

Tartare Sauce, page 349, or catsup

CLAM BROTH FROM STEAMED HARD-SHELL CLAMS

The meat of these clams is used for chowder, fritters or sauced dishes, the broth for soup or as sauce stock. Prepare as for:

Steamed Soft-Shell Clams, opposite

Strain the broth through 2 thicknesses of cheesecloth. You will have about 1 quart of strong broth. It may be diluted with scalded cream or milk but do not boil it after these additions. Or it may be combined with:

Water, chicken broth, consommé or tomato juice

Each cup of broth may be topped with a spoonful of:

(Unsweetened whipped cream)

Sprinkled with:

(Chopped chives)

To prepare the clam meat for use ➧ please read About Hard-Shell Clams, page 428, and add to broth, if desired.

ABOUT SCALLOPS

These beautiful mollusks known on menus as Coquilles St. Jacques are emblematic of the pilgrims who visited the shrine of St. James of Compostella. They ate the mollusks as penance—surely not a rigorous one—and afterwards fastened the cockle shells to their hats. Scallops are also responsible for the cooking term "scalloped," which originally meant seafood creamed, heated and served in a shell. If you get scallops in the shell, wash and scrub them thoroughly. Place in a 300° oven, deep shell down, until they open. Remove the hinge muscle. In Europe, the handsome beanlike coral and beard are both used. The former is treated as for any roe and the latter cut up, sautéed briefly and then simmered ➧ covered, in white wine for ½ hour. When you buy scallops, try for the small, tender, creamy pink or tan **bay scallops** rather than the large, firmer, whiter **sea scallops.** Both types are illustrated on (II, 80). If only the large ones are available, slice them—after cooking—in 3 parts, against the grain, for use in salads and creamed dishes or sauces.

➧ To test scallops for freshness, see that they have a sweetish odor. If in bulk, they should be free of liquid. Allow about ⅓ lb. of sea scallops or ¼ lb. of bay scallops per serving for sautéing or broiling. Cooked scallops may be used in any recipe for fish salads or creamed fish or may be skewered and grilled, see below. See the seafood suggestions in Luncheon Dishes, page 229.

SCALLOPS MEUNIÈRE [4]

In:

A Bound Breading (II, 160)

dip:

1 lb. bay or sea scallops

You may let them dry on a rack about 15 minutes. Heat in a heavy skillet large enough so the scallops will be only 1 layer deep:

2 tablespoons butter
2 tablespoons cooking oil

Sauté ➧ agitating frequently, about 5 minutes for bay scallops, 8 minutes for sea scallops. Just before the cooking time is over, sprinkle with:

Lemon juice
Finely chopped parsley

Serve with:

Tomatoes Florentine, page 336

BAY SCALLOPS FONDU BOURGUIGNONNE [4]

➧ Please read about Boeuf Fondu Bourguignonne, page 473, using instead of beef:

1 lb. bay scallops

Serve as sauces:

Seasoned Butters for Fish, page 383, or Hollandaise Sauce, page 368
Tartare Sauce, page 349, Béarnaise Sauce, page 370, or Tomato Sauce, page 376

⊟ SCALLOP KEBABS

[Allow ¼ lb. Bay or ⅓ lb. Sea Scallops per Person]

Preheat broiler or grill.

If scallops are large or old, drop into boiling water and allow them to stay immersed, but removed from heat, for 1 minute. Drain and dry. If tender, simply brush:

Scallops

with:

Cooking oil

Dip in:

Fine bread crumbs

Skewer alternately with:

1-inch squares of bacon

Grill over moderate heat for 10 minutes or until golden brown or broil 4 inches from the source of heat, turning several times during the cooking period. Serve with:

Lemon wedges
Fried Parsley, page 305

DEEP-FAT FRIED SCALLOPS [6 to 8]

Preheat deep fryer to 385°.

Wash and pick over:

1 quart scallops: about 2 lbs.

Drain. Dry between towels. Season with:

White pepper
Celery salt

Dip them in a:

Bound Breading (II, 160)

Fry for 2 minutes in deep fat. Drain on absorbent paper. Serve with:

Tartare Sauce, page 349, Béarnaise Sauce, page 370, or Tomato Sauce, page 376

SCALLOPS IN WINE [6 to 8]

Wash well:

2 lbs. scallops

➧ Simmer in:

2 cups dry white wine

Drain and reserve the liquid. Melt:

¼ cup butter

Sauté:

4 finely chopped shallots
24 finely sliced mushroom caps
2 tablespoons minced parsley

Stir in, until blended:

2 tablespoons flour

Add the reserved liquid and:

2 to 4 tablespoons whipping cream

Add the scallops to the hot sauce. Place in a shallow casserole. Cover with:

Au Gratin II, page 389

and run under a broiler until golden brown.

CREAMED SCALLOPS OR OYSTERS AND MUSHROOMS [4]

Simmer until tender, for about 5 minutes:

2 cups scallops

in:

Water or light stock to cover

Drain well. Sauté for 5 minutes:

½ lb. mushrooms

in:

2 tablespoons butter

Prepare:

1 cup Cream Sauce I, page 359

using half cream and half chicken broth or milk. When the sauce is smooth and hot, stir in the scallops and the mushrooms. Simmer gently for about

3 minutes if bay scallops, 5 minutes if sea scallops.

Correct the seasoning

An unusual variation is to add:

2 cups of minced cooked ham

to the above mixture. When oysters are substituted, cook them in their own juice until the edges begin to curl. Drain. Substitute the juice for part of the milk.

SCALLOPED SCALLOPS OR SCALLOPS MORNAY [6]

Preheat broiler.
Poach:

3 cups scallops

in:

1½ cups dry white wine and Light Stock (II, 142), or Fumet (II, 143)

Drain and slice the scallops. Coat each of the deep halves of 12 scallop shells with:

1 tablespoon hot Mornay Sauce, page 361

You may edge the shell, using a forcing bag, with a decorative rim of:

(Duchess Potato, page 319)

Almost fill the shell with the sliced scallops. Coat each shell, staying within the rim of the potatoes, with:

Hot Mornay Sauce, page 361

Dust the sauce coating with:

Grated Parmesan or Gruyère cheese

Run under a broiler until the sauce is lightly browned. Serve at once.

ABOUT ABALONE

The foot of this delicious shellfish—contraband if shipped from California—comes to our markets canned or frozen from Mexico and Japan, shelled, pounded and ready to cook. If you get it in the shell, remove the edible portion by running a knife between the shell and the meat. Trim off the dark portion. Abalone, like inkfish, needs prodigious pounding to tenderize it, if it has died in a state of tension. Leave it whole or cut it in ¼-inch strips for pounding with an even, not too hard, motion. The meat is ready to cook when it looks like Dali's limp watches. ➧ For steaks, slice against the grain. Bread it if you like and sauté or boil as for any fish, page 399. Beat and chop it for Chowder, or for Fritters (II, 125). ➧Allow 1 lb. for 2 to 3 servings.

SAUTÉED ABALONE [2 to 3]

Cut into ⅜-inch-thick steaks across the grain and pound:

1 lb. abalone

Dip in a:

Bound Breading (II, 160)

Melt in a heavy skillet:

2 tablespoons cooking oil or clarified butter

When the fat reaches the point of fragrance, sauté the abalone steaks, allowing 1½ to 2 minutes to each side.

ABOUT CRABS

Recipes for cooking crab meat apply to almost all species of edible crab, but both the type of crab and the part of the crab from which the meat is taken may make a difference in color, taste and texture.

BLUE CRABS

These comprise three-fourths of the fresh crabs in the market. Lump or back-fin meat, taken from the body, is choice for looks and white in color. Flake meat, while less shapely, is also white. Claw meat is brownish, but very choice as to taste.

DUNGENESS AND ROCK CRABS

These are both packaged in one grade, combining body and claw meat. The rock crab flesh is brownish. Dungeness is best in 2½ to 3 lb. size.

KING CRABS

These are pinkish in tone, and consist mainly of leg meat.

OYSTER CRABS AND HERMIT CRABS

There are two edible types of miniature crabs. Oyster crabs are crispy ½-inch pinkish "boarders," found living right in the shell with live oysters and may be eaten raw. They may also be sautéed or deep-fat fried, as is. When deep fried, several dozen may be served with several dozen fried whitebait as one portion. Tiny hermit crabs are found in vacated univalve shells and respond to deep-fat frying and sautéing, but not to being eaten raw.

Preheat deep fryer to 390°.

To deep fry either of these crabs or whitebait, keep them on ice until the last minute. Wash and dry carefully and put in a bag to dust with flour (II, 160), then in a sieve to bounce off as much flour as possible. Place a few at a time in a frying basket and cook only 2 to 3 seconds until crisp.

HARD-SHELL CRABS

These do not ship well. ➧ From a 5 oz. hard crab, you can expect about 1½ oz. of crab meat. ➧ Crabs must be alive and lively when cooked.

SOFT-SHELL OR EASTERN BLUE CRABS

These are crabs that have just molted and not yet hardened.

Their hardening up is a matter of only a few days. They ship very satisfactorily.

➧ Freshly cooked crab meat in partially aerated cans must be under constant refrigeration until used. It should have no ammonialike odor. The completely sealed canned crab meats, Japanese and Korean, are all nonperishable until the cans are opened.

➧ To prepare crab shells for restuffing, select large, perfect shells and scrub them well with a brush until clean. Place them in a large kettle, covered with hot water. Add one teaspoon baking soda. Cover the kettle closely. Bring to a boil and simmer for 20 minutes. Drain, wash and dry. They are then ready for refilling.

➧ For crab dishes made with cooked or canned crab, see page 231. In using canned meat, be sure to pick it over for small bits of shell and bone.

➧ To prepare soft-shell crabs, wash them in several waters. Place live crab face down on a board. Make an incision just back of the eyes and cut out the face. Lift the tapering points on each side of the back shell to remove sandbag and spongy gills, as shown in sketch. Turn crab on its back and with a pointed knife remove the small pointed apron at the lower part of the shell. These crabs, since the shell is edible, are usually broiled or breaded and sautéed, or are deep-fat fried as follows.

DEEP-FAT FRIED SOFT-SHELL CRABS

Preheat Deep Fryer to 375°.
➧ Please read About Deep-Fat Frying, pages 75–79. Dip:

Cleaned soft-shell crabs

in:

A Bound Breading (II, 160)

Fry from 3 to 5 minutes or until golden brown, in deep fat. Turn them once while they are frying. Drain on absorbent paper. Sprinkle well with:

Salt and pepper

Serve at once with:

Tartare Sauce, page 349
Remoulade Sauce, page 349, with parsley

BROILED SOFT-SHELL CRABS

Preheat broiler.
Prepare for cooking:

Soft-shell crabs

Combine:

¼ cup butter
2 tablespoons lemon juice
A few grains cayenne
A few grains pepper

Roll the crabs in the butter mixture, then lightly in:

Flour

Place them on the broiling rack, 2 inches from the heat. Broil for about 10 minutes. Turn once.

SAUTÉED SOFT-SHELL CRABS

Follow the above recipe for:

Broiled Soft-Shell Crabs

Sauté them in butter or other fat over moderate heat. Place on a platter. Serve with:

Fried Parsley, page 305

STEAMED HARD-SHELL CRABS

We are very grateful to a Maryland fan who put us wise to handling this type of crab. She says, "When I moved into this crab country, I began to boil hard crabs and threw the natives into fainting fits. They were right."

This is the way she describes the Maryland method: "Dump the crabs into a large vessel or deep sink and cover them with water a little hotter than the hand can bear. The crabs sometimes drop their claws at the contact with hot water—but it is no matter—just pile the claws on top when steaming.

"This hot water bath anesthetizes them quickly with 2 good results: first, you can handle them safely, like soft-shells; and second, they do not appear to suffer when they are placed over the steam. Otherwise they struggle woefully in the pot while the steam is rising. I scrub the muck from each crab with a vegetable brush. This is my own discovery—the natives do not bother. But somehow I like to suck a clean crab better. If you have a suitable rack, place it in a large pot with a close lid and put a little water in the bottom, but not nearly enough to touch the rack. If a rack is lacking, moisten the bottom of the vessel with 2 or 3 tablespoons of water. In any case, lay in the crabs and set upon the heat. Sprinkle well with:

About 1 teaspoon red pepper
2 tablespoons salt
½ cup vinegar or lemon juice
(2 tablespoons Crab Boil)
1 tablespoon monosodium glutamate
½ cup beer or what-have-you

Have no fear that the pot will get dry while steaming. It never does, for the crabs put out a lot of moisture. The problem, on the contrary, is to keep them from getting sodden. Cover and steam until the aprons begin to rise, about 30 minutes or a little more. Eat hot or cold, preferably over newspapers, and dip each bit in melted butter. Some people use simple French dressing, but not me. If you pull off the apron and open the crab from that point with the fingers, it is easy.

"For the uninitiated we might interpolate: eat only the meat and discard the intestines and spongy gills. Otherwise, a knife is useful to pry off the shell. A mallet or hammer is better than crackers for opening the claws. And don't forget to pry in the points of the top shell for a bite of fat. Some crabs are lean, but some are not. Many crabs—followed by a general hand washing—and then green salad, French bread and dessert make a fine dinner for the fanciest guests."

ABOUT LOBSTERS

The **Northern lobster** or French "homard," with its great delicious claw meat, is sketched on page 438. It is caught from New England to the Carolinas and in North European waters.

The **spiny rock lobster**, or **langouste**, as it is called, is shipped from Florida, California, Australia, South Africa and the Mediterranean. It has extra-long antennae and most of the meat is in the heavy tail. These are also sometimes called crawfish, in contradistinction to the freshwater écrevisses or crayfish of both continents. The Northerns are reputed most delicious when served hot. The spinys, when frozen, especially if over 10 oz., may be tough. If fresh, they are often preferred in cold dishes. The Northerns, when caught, are a dark mottled blue green. The spinys vary from tan to reddish orange and maroon with more or less light spotting and more or fewer spines. Both kinds require about the same cooking time and may be cut and cleaned as shown on page 438. But as lobster ritual is more complicated in the Northern type, we will discuss it in further detail below.

The female is considered finer in flavor. Look for the soft, leathery, finlike appendages on the underside, just where the body and tail meet. In the male, these appendages are bony. In opening the female lobster, you may find a delicious roe or coral that reddens in cooking. Use it as a garnish or to color a sauce. The flesh of the male stays firmer when boiled. The greenish substance in both of them is the liver or tomalley.

➧ Allow ½ large lobster or 1 small lobster per serving. Buy active live lobsters weighing from 1¼ to 2½ pounds. Lobsters weighing 3 pounds and over are apt to be coarse and tough. A 2½-pound lobster will yield about 2 cups of cooked meat.

➧ To store live lobsters until ready to use, place them in the refrigerator, but not directly on ice. The claws should be plugged with a small piece of wood and held together with rubber bands. Before cooking, test to make sure lobsters are lively and that, when picked up, if the tail is stretched out flat, it snaps back.

POACHED OR "BOILED" LOBSTER

I. To boil or poach lobster for hot family-type table service, put a folded towel on the bottom of a large, heavy pan. Place on it:

> **A 1½ to 2½ lb. live lobster**

Cover with:

Cold sea or salted water

Bring the water to a boil and cook for 5 minutes. ➧ Reduce the heat and simmer for 15 minutes, slightly less if the lobsters have recently shed and are soft. Drain. Serve at once, leaving the head, body and tail intact, and surrounding this portion with the claws. Garnish with a small bowl of:

Drawn Butter, page 383
Lemon wedges

And provide each person with a finger bowl, a bib and abundant napkins. The uninitiated are sometimes balked by the ferocious appearance of a lobster at table. They may take comfort from the little cannibal who, threading his way through the jungle one day at his mother's side, saw a strange object roar overhead. "Ma, what's that?" he quavered. "Don't worry, sonny," said Ma. "It's an airplane. Airplanes are pretty much like lobsters. There's an awful lot you have to throw away, but the insides are delicious."

All the lobster components lie on your plate—the body, head and tail intact, arched shell up, surrounded by the large claws which, on removal before serving, have been cracked to allow excess moisture to drain off. Pick the lobster up in your fingers, turn it soft side up and arch it until the tail cracks off the body. Then break off and discard the tail flippers by bending them back. Pick up the tail piece, again upside down, and push the meat at the small flipper end of the tail with the oyster fork. The tail meat should emerge in one piece out of the large end. Unhinge the back from the back shell and crack open the back by pulling it open. Be sure to eat the greenish tomalley or liver and all the meat. At this point, we call your attention to the finger bowl.

II. To boil lobster for salad, hors d'oeuvre or sauced dishes, prepare as for I, using:

A 2½ to 3 lb. lobster

Larger ones are apt to be tough. After the cooking period, drain and plunge into cold water to arrest further cooking. When cool ➧ to remove the meat from the shell, place the lobster on its back. With sharp scissors cut a lengthwise gash in the soft underside as sketched on page 439. Draw out the tail meat in one piece. Remove and discard the lady, or sandbag, and the intestinal vein, as well as the spongy lungs which, while harmless, are tough. Add the red coral, if any, and the green liver, or tomalley, to the lobster meat or reserve it for use in sauces.

If you buy pre-boiled lobster in the shell, see that the color is bright red and that it has a fresh seashore aroma. ➧ Most important of all, the tail should be curled and, when pulled, should roll back into place under the body. This means the lobster was alive, as it should have been, when cooked.

To remove lobster meat from the large claws, crack them with a nutcracker or a mallet. If you want them in a single piece for garnish, break the claw off at the first joint. Place it on a flat surface, the lighter underside up. Using a mallet, hit the shell at the inner hump. This will crack it, so that the meat in the entire larger pincer claw is released. Crack off the small pincer shell and its meat will slide out. For attractive service, you may want to keep the lobster shell to refill with the seasoned sauced meat or you may want to use it to make Lobster Butter, page 385.

⊟ BROILED LOBSTER [1]

Preheat broiler.
Prepare for broiling:

A 1¼ lb. live lobster

Sever the vein at the base of the neck. Place the lobster on his back. Hold him with your left hand firmly over the head. Be sure to protect your hand with a towel. Draw the knife from the head down through the base of the abdomen, as shown below, so the lobster will lie flat with the meat evenly exposed to the heat. All the lobster meat is edible, except for the stomach, or lady—a hard

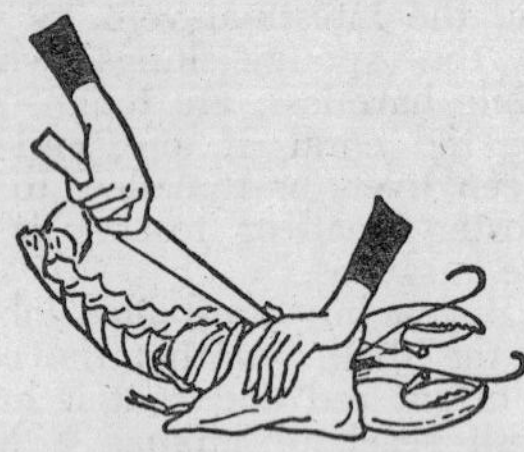

sac near the head—and the intestinal vein that runs through the middle of the underside of the tail meat. Remove and discard these inedible parts. The spongy substance to either side of the body—the lungs—is harmless. It may or may not be removed when the lobster is cooked in the half shell. Beyond a doubt edible are the delicious red coral and the greenish liver or tomalley. You may prepare a stuffing by removing and mixing together:

The coral
The tomalley
1 tablespoon toasted bread crumbs
1 teaspoon of lemon juice
or
dry sherry

Replace in the cavity and brush with:

Melted butter

Also brush with:

Melted butter

the exposed lobster meat. ➧ If broiling stuffed, place shell side down on the oven grill and broil about 16 minutes. If broiling unstuffed or grilling over charcoal, place shell side toward heat for 7 to 8 minutes, turn and broil, flesh side to heat, for about 8 minutes more. In either case serve with:

Lemon wedges and
Drawn Butter,
page 383

➧ To eat broiled lobster served to you on the half-shell, begin with the tail meat first, using the small, sharp-pronged lobster or oyster fork,—see sketches below. You may twist off bite-size pieces with the fork. This needs some skill, and we often wish when dining out, for a good European fish knife. Dip the pieces in the sauce. You may also squeeze lemon juice from the garnish wedges over the lobster meat. Twist off a large claw with the fingers and, if necessary, also use the cracker which should always be provided.

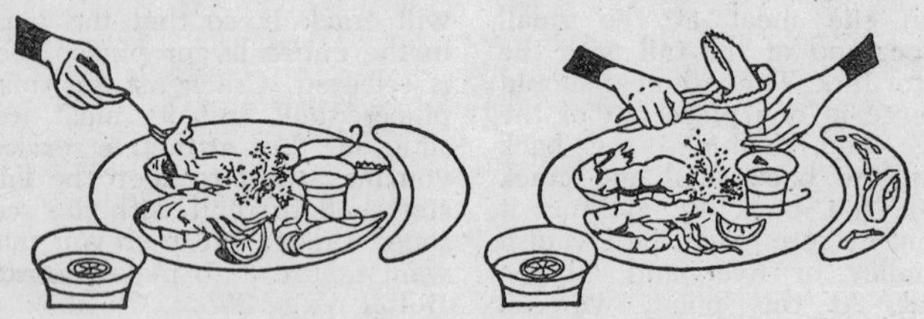

Crack the claw, as shown, to release the delicate rich meat. You may then pull off the small side claws, one by one, with the fingers, and suck out the meat. As you empty the shells, place them on the bone tray or extra plate and make use of the finger bowl when needed. Continue to eat the contents of the shell: it is good to the last shred. Some people even suck the knuckle after releasing it from the grey gristle.

LOBSTER AMÉRICAINE OR ARMORICAINE [2]

Who really cares how it's spelled? This method of cooking lobster is good enough to credit regional inventiveness on both sides of the Atlantic.
Have ready:

½ cup Fish Fumet (II, 143)

Place on a flat pan, so as to be able to reserve any juice that results from cutting:

2 live 1½ lb. hen lobsters

With a sharp knife, sever the vein at the base of the neck. Cut off the claws. Divide the body at the tail and cut the tail in 3 or 4 pieces at the segmentations. Divide the shell in half, lengthwise. Remove and discard the sac. Reserve the coral, if any, and the tomalley, for the sauce.
Have ready 2 heavy skillets. In one, sauté:

3 tablespoons butter
1 cup Mirepoix (II, 221)
½ cup chopped shallots

Heat in the other, to the point of fragrance:

½ cup olive oil
1 clove garlic

Sauté in the oil for about 4 minutes ➧ still in the shell, the cut-up lobster. Keep the pan moving. When the lobster shell is red and the flesh firm, add it to the mirepoix in the first skillet. Flambé, page 80, the lobster mixture in:

1 oz. brandy

Place in the second skillet and simmer about 5 minutes:

½ cup tomato purée
1 cup white wine
3 peeled, seeded, chopped tomatoes

In winter use the small Italian-type canned tomatoes.
Add the sautéed lobster pieces still in the shell, the fumet and:

1 teaspoon chopped fresh tarragon
The juice or "blood" of lobster
The coral and tomalley

to the tomato mixture. Heat the sauce.

Correct the seasoning

Thicken the sauce slightly with:

(Beurre Manié, page 357)

Serve the lobster with the hot sauce poured over it and garnish with:

Chopped parsley

⊟ GRILLED LOBSTER TAILS [4]

Preheat broiler or grill.
Marinate for several hours:

4 spiny lobster tails

in a mixture of:

¼ cup lemon or lime juice
¼ cup salad oil
1 teaspoon each salt and paprika
¼ cup minced shallots

Remove with scissors the soft under-cover of the lobster tails, as sketched above.

Slightly crack the hard upper shell with a cleaver so the tails will lie flat, and grease the meat lightly. Broil for about 5 minutes to a side, basting the exposed side well with the marinade. Hold about 4 inches above coals or under broiler. These make an attractive plate when served with:

Asparagus spears

placed to either side and garnished with:

Polonaise Sauce, page 386

▤ CHARCOAL-GRILLED BAHAMIAN LOBSTER TAILS WITH LIME BUTTER SAUCE

You can use fresh or frozen lobster tails for this recipe and grill them outdoors or in a broiler. Split:

Lobster tails

Do not remove meat from the shells. Several hours before cooking, marinate lobster tails in:

Melted butter or olive oil

or a mixture of the two, allowing 2 to 3 tablespoons of fat for each lobster, plus:

Freshly ground black pepper
1 teaspoon lime or lemon juice

Broil until top is crisp and golden brown, 10 to 15 minutes. Keep basting with the marinade. Serve hot, with the drippings or extra butter and cut limes or lemons, if desired.

BAKED STUFFED LOBSTER [2]

Split in half, as for Broiled Lobster, page 438:

A freshly Boiled Lobster, page 437: about 2 lbs.

Remove the meat. Chop it. Melt:

¾ tablespoon butter

Stir in until blended:

¾ tablespoon flour

Stir in slowly:

½ cup Chicken Stock (II, 142), or Fumet (II, 143)

Season the sauce with:

1¼ teaspoons dry mustard
1 teaspoon chopped onion
Salt
Paprika

Melt in a separate saucepan:

2 tablespoons butter

Sauté the lobster meat in the butter until it is heated. Add the boiling sauce. Simmer these ingredients for about 2 minutes. Remove them from the heat. Preheat broiler.

Beat, then stir in:

1 tablespoon cream
2 egg yolks

Add:

(½ cup chopped Sautéed Mushrooms, page 296)

Fill the lobster shells with the mixture. Cover them with:

Buttered Crumbs (II, 159), or Au Gratin I or II, page 389

Broil the lobster until the crumbs are brown. Season it, as it is removed from the oven, by pouring over it:

(2 tablespoons sherry)

LOBSTER THERMIDOR [2]

This calls for cream, as well as stock. Split in halves:

2 freshly Boiled Lobsters, page 436: 1 to 1½ lbs. each

Remove the meat, as directed. Dice the meat. Melt:

2 teaspoons butter

Stir in, until blended:

2 teaspoons flour

Add the lobster meat. Stir in slowly:

¼ cup rich cream
1 cup Stock (II, 141)

Simmer these ingredients for about 10 minutes. Stir them frequently. Season them lightly, if required, with:

Salt, paprika and celery salt
A few grains cayenne

Preheat broiler.

Remove the lobster from the pan. Add:

1 tablespoon dry sherry

Melt:

3 tablespoons butter

Add:

1½ cups shredded white bread

Cook and stir these ingredients until all the butter is absorbed. Wash the lobster shells thoroughly. Fill them with the mixture. Spread the tops with the bread crumbs. Brown them under a broiler. Serve the lobster with:

Wilted Cucumbers, page 43

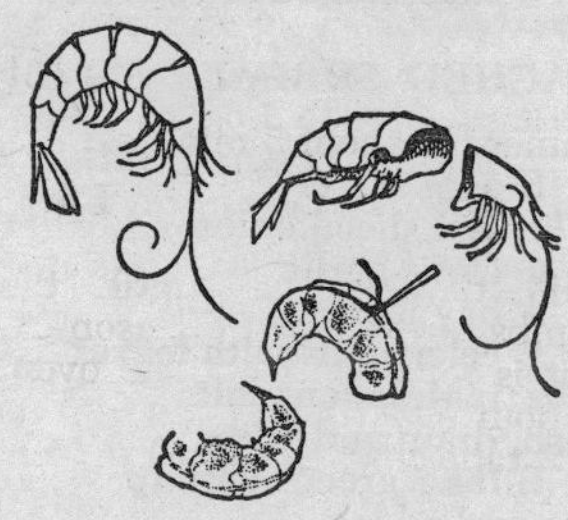

ABOUT SHRIMP

Formerly our Southern shrimp or **crevette** was the only one available in most of our markets. Today we can buy many members of this family. So let us remind you of the tiny forms from our West coast and from Scandinavia—now widely used as hors d'oeuvre; **scampi, Dublin prawns** or **langoustines**—all large—from Europe; and the giants from India—shrimp so large that 2 or 3 suffice for a serving. In spite of slight differences in flavor and texture, all can be substituted for one another if size is taken into consideration for serving amounts and cooking time. If poaching, cooking varies from 3 to 8 minutes.

➧ To test shrimp for freshness, see that they are dry and firm. Allow about 1 pound of shrimp in the shell—these are called "green" shrimp—½ pound of cooked shrimp without shells for 3 servings. In buying, remember, 2 to 2½ lbs. of shrimp in the shell gives only about 1 lb. cooked, shelled shrimp, or 2 cups. While shrimp may be cooked in the shell or unshelled, the shells add considerable flavor. Shelling is easy—either before or after cooking. A slight tug releases the body shell from the tail.

Devein before or after cooking, using a small pointed knife or the end of a toothpick, as sketched. This is essential.

➧ If using canned shrimp, you may rinse briefly in cold water to remove excess salt. Large shrimp may be made more decorative by slicing lengthwise, as shown below. ➧ To

butterfly shrimp, peel the shrimp down to the tail, leaving it on. Devein. Hold so the underside is up. Slice down its length, almost to the vein, to form the hinge. Spread and flatten to form the butterfly shape.

➧ Never overcook shrimp. If they are fresh, drop them into boiling stock or water ➧ reduce the heat at once and simmer 3 to 4 minutes. But be sure to remove them from the heat before they begin to curl up. ➧ Drain at once, to prevent curling and also overcooking. To cook frozen shrimp, peeled and deveined, and also the "green" types, start from the frozen state, drop into boiling stock or water and count the time when the stock comes to a boil again.

For other shrimp recipes, see Hors d'Oeuvre chapter (II, 82).

BUTTERFLY SHRIMP

➧ Please read About Deep-Fat Frying, pages 75–79. To cut for butterfly shape, see About Shrimp, page 441.
Preheat deep fryer to 370°.
Don't flour or crumb the tails, but do coat the body of the shrimp with:

Bread crumbs or grated coconut or flour or egg or both; or in a batter

Fry 8 to 10 minutes or until golden. Drain on absorbent paper. Serve at once with:

Soy Sauce, Tartare Sauce, page 349, or Chinese Sweet-Sour Sauce, page 371

POTTED SHRIMP OR LOBSTER

This terrine can be used as a luncheon or hors d'oeuvre spread. Cook:

Raw shrimp or lobster

Drain and remove meat from shells. Chop coarsely. Reserve shells. Allow for every cup of seafood:

2 to 3 tablespoons butter

To ½ the butter, add the reserved shells to make:

Shrimp or Lobster Butter, page 385

Season with:

⅛ teaspoon mustard or mace
⅛ teaspoon salt
A few grains cayenne

Stir the seafood into the heated shrimp or lobster butter until well coated. Place it in a small terrine. Clarify the remaining butter. ➧ Do not let it color. Pour it while hot over the seafood, making sure the food is well covered. Refrigerate covered.

⊟ SHRIMP TERIYAKI [3]

Marinate:

1 lb. shelled, deveined "green" shrimp

for about 15 minutes, in:

½ cup pineapple juice
2 to 4 tablespoons soy sauce
½ cup bland cooking oil

Drain and broil or grill 3 or 4 minutes on each side, 4 inches from heat. Serve with:

Rice, page 158

POACHED SHRIMP [6]

Simmer for about 5 minutes:

8 cups water
¼ cup sliced onion
1 clove garlic
1 bay leaf
2 celery ribs with leaves
1½ tablespoons salt

Wash, drain and add:

2 lbs. "green" shrimp

Slice and add:

½ lemon

Simmer the shrimp for about 5 minutes or till pink. Drain immediately and chill. Serve very cold in their shells—to be shelled at table—with a bowl of:

Russian Dressing, page 349, or Remoulade Sauce, page 349

or shell them, remove the intestinal vein and use them as desired.

SHRIMP CASSEROLE WITH SNAIL BUTTER [4]

Preheat oven to 400°.
Prepare:

1½ lbs. Poached Shrimp, see above

Have ready in refrigerator:

Colbert or Snail Butter, page 384

Put a ¼-inch layer of the butter in the bottom of a shallow casserole. Lay shrimp in rows and press into the butter. Cover the shrimp with the remaining butter and bake about 10 minutes. Broil for a few minutes to let top brown. Serve at once.

DEEP-FAT FRIED SHRIMP [3]

Shell:

1 lb. raw shrimp

Remove the intestinal vein. Combine:

⅔ cup milk
⅛ teaspoon paprika
¼ teaspoon salt

Soak the shrimp in the milk for 30 minutes.
Preheat deep fryer to 375°.
Drain the shrimp well. Sprinkle with:

Lemon juice
Salt

Roll in:

Corn meal

Fry in deep fat until golden brown. Drain on absorbent paper. Serve hot with:

Lemon juice or mayonnaise seasoned with puréed chutney

DEEP-FAT FRIED STUFFED SHRIMP

[2 Dozen Shrimp]
Shell and devein:

10 jumbo-size shrimp

Chop them into a pulp and add:

6 water chestnuts

which have been smashed with a cleaver and finely chopped. Shell, leaving the tails intact, and devein:

14 jumbo-size shrimp

Split lengthwise along the deveined edge ➧ but not far enough to separate. Spread them flat and lay along each crevice:

A thin julienne of Prosciutto or Westphalian ham

Spread the shrimp and chestnut mixture in the crevices above the ham and mold it into the form of a wide beveled edge when you partially reclose the shrimp for breading. Dip into:

Beaten egg

then into:

Flour

Allow to dry on a rack 15 to 20 minutes.
➧ Please read About Deep-Fat Frying, pages 75–79.
Preheat deep fryer to 370°.
Lift the shrimp by the tails and slide them gently into the heated fat. Fry for about 5 minutes or until golden. Drain on absorbent paper. Serve at once with:

Chinese Sweet-Sour Sauce, page 371

adding some:

Plum jam

SHRIMP FRIED IN BATTER [3]

Preheat deep fryer to 370°.
Shell and clean, page 441:

1 lb. "green" shrimp

You may leave the tails on. Prepare:

Fritter Batter for Fish (II, 125)

Dip a few shrimp at a time in the batter, holding them by the tail. ➧ Do not cover the tail with batter. Fry in deep fat until golden brown. Drain on absorbent paper. Serve with:

Lemon wedges or mayonnaise seasoned with catsup and mustard

SHRIMP TEMPURA

➧ Please read About Deep-Fat Frying, pages 75–79.

Preheat deep fat fryer to 350°.
Prepare:

Butterfly Shrimp, page 442

Dip them in:

Fritter Batter for Fish (II, 125)

Fry until golden.
Serve with:

Hot Mustard Sauce, page 363, soy sauce, Chinese Sweet-Sour Sauce, page 371

NEW ORLEANS SHRIMP [4 to 6]

Poach:

2 lbs. fresh shrimp, page 442

Shell and clean them. Serve well chilled on:

Lettuce

Prepare the following sauce. Rub a bowl with:

Garlic

Add:

½ cup finely chopped celery
1 stalk finely chopped green onion
1 tablespoon chopped chives
6 tablespoons olive oil
3 tablespoons lemon juice
¼ teaspoon hot pepper sauce
5 tablespoons horseradish
2 tablespoons prepared mustard
¼ teaspoon paprika
¾ teaspoon salt
½ teaspoon white pepper

You may marinate the shrimp in this sauce for 12 hours, or the time may be much shorter. A clove of garlic may be added to the mixture for 2 hours.

SHRIMP NEWBURG [3 to 4]

Prepare, page 442:

1 lb. Poached Shrimp

Serve with:

Newburg Sauce, page 361

using 1 to 1½ cups of sauce. Serve in a:

Rice Ring, page 162

or over:

Baked Green Rice, page 159

ABOUT CRAYFISH, CRAWFISH, OR ÉCREVISSES

[➧ Allow about one dozen per serving]

One of the thrills of our grandparents was to find in Missouri streams the crayfish they had so relished in Europe. These crustaceans, looking like miniature lobsters, were brought to the table in great steaming crimson mounds, garnished with dill or swimming in their own juices, that is, "à la nage."

To cook, wash well in several waters:

Crayfish

If they have been kept in fresh running water for several days, they need not be eviscerated. If they have not, they are cleaned while still alive. Grasp the middle tail fin, as sketched, give a long firm twist and pull to remove the stomach and intestinal vein. Have ready a large pot of:

Boiling water

seasoned with:

A leek—white part only
Parsley
1 chopped carrot

Drop the crayfish one by one into the boiling water at a rate which will not disturb the boiling. Cook not longer than 5 to 7 minutes. Serve in the shell. Have on the side plenty of:

Melted butter

seasoned with:

Fresh dill

They are eaten with the fingers. Separate tail from body. Crack open tail by holding between thumb and finger of both hands and force it back against the curve of the shell. Be sure to serve with finger bowls. If you are preparing them for hors d'oeuvre, cook only until the water is boiling well after they are all immersed. Then remove

from heat. Let them cool in the liquid. Shelled, they lend themselves to all kinds of combinations and sauces, but the connoisseur usually wants them for themselves alone.

ABOUT SNAILS

The Romans, who were addicted to snails, grew them on ranches where they were fed special foods like bay, wine and spicy soups to preseason them. Only snail types that are sealed in their opercula before hibernating are edible. If your snails are less privileged than the Roman ones, be sure to ➧ let them fast for about 10 days to get rid of any possible poisons they may have imbibed from foliage inimical to humans. After the fast, they may be fattened for the feast before cooking. ➧ Allow about 1 dozen snails per serving.

Before cooking, scrub and remove the membrane which closes them. Place in water to cover and add ½ cup salt or ¼ cup vinegar for every 50 snails. Change the water several times during this 3 to 4 hour soaking. Then rinse in several waters until the slime is removed. Blanch à blanc (II, 147), 8 minutes. After draining from the cold water, place the snails in a court bouillon to cover, made with:

½ water or stock and ½ white wine

seasoned with:

A Bouquet Garni (II, 220)
An onion stuck with cloves
2 cloves garlic

➧ Simmer gently for 3 to 4 hours, depending on the size of the snails. After cooling in the court bouillon, drain.

I. Remove snails from shells. Cut off and discard the black end. Dry the snails and shells in a cloth. Place a dab of Snail Butter, page 384, in each shell. Replace the snails. Pack them firmly in the shell, so generously covered that only the lovely green herbed butter is visible at the opening. You may chill the snails for later use or bake them at once on a pan lightly sprinkled with water in a 425° oven just long enough to get them piping hot—a matter of a few minutes only. Have ready heated, grooved, snail dishes. The shell holder has a spring in the handle which allows you to regulate its viselike end to the size of the snail. The long, closely tined fork is used with a slight twist to remove the snail. See sketch above.

II. For those of us who have to rely on canned snails, the following is a snail rejuvenation. Prepare enough to fill 48 snails:

Snail Butter, page 384

Reduce to 1 cup over high heat:

1 cup consommé
1 cup dry white wine

cooked with:

½ bay leaf
1 clove garlic

Put in a colander:

48 canned snails

Pour over them:

1 quart warm water

Drain well. Simmer the snails briefly in the hot reduced consommé and wine. Wash the snail shells well and drain. Pack, as above, with:

Snail Butter, page 384

Heat and serve as for I.

III. Or, replace the shells with:

Sautéed Mushroom Caps, page 296

Fill the mushrooms with one or more snails, depending on size. Coat the snails with:

Snail Butter, page 384

and run under a broiler briefly until heated.

ABOUT FROG LEGS

Frog legs resemble chicken in texture and flavor. They are usually bought skinned and ready to use. Allow 2 large or 6 small frog legs per person. If the frogs are not prepared, cut off the hind legs—the only part of the frog used—close to the body. Separate and wash them in cold water. Begin at the top and strip off the skin like a glove. Through an experiment with a twitching frog leg, Galvani discovered the electric current that bears his name. Should you prefer keeping your kitchen and your scientific activities separate and distinct, chill the frog legs before skinning.

BRAISED FROG LEGS [4]

Clean:

8 large frog legs

Roll them in:

Seasoned flour

Melt in a skillet:

6 tablespoons clarified butter

Add to it:

½ cup chopped onions

Brown the frog legs in the butter. Reduce the heat and add:

¾ cup boiling Stock (II, 141)

Cover the skillet closely and cook the frog legs until they are tender, for about 10 minutes. Melt:

6 tablespoons butter

Sauté in the butter:

1¼ cups seasoned bread crumbs
¾ cup finely chopped hazelnuts

Add:

1 teaspoon lemon juice

Roll the frog legs in the bread crumbs and serve them garnished with:

Fennel

or, if you have used the hazelnuts, with:

Parsley

DEEP-FAT FRIED FROG LEGS

➧ Please read About Deep-Fat Frying, pages 75–79.

Preheat deep fryer to 375°.

Clean:

Frog legs

Dip them in:

A Bound Breading (II, 160)

Let dry for 1 hour. Fry the frog legs until golden. Drain. Serve with:

Tartare Sauce, page 349

FROG LEGS IN MUSHROOM SAUCE [3]

Clean:

6 large frog legs

Cut the meat into 3 or 4 pieces. Place in a saucepan. Cover with:

Boiling water or Light Stock (II, 142)

Add:

2 thin slices lemon
⅛ teaspoon white pepper
(Celery, parsley, onion or

vegetables suitable for soup)

Simmer the frog meat, covered, until it is tender. Drain well. Melt in a saucepan:

3 tablespoons butter

Add to it and sauté until light brown:

1 cup sliced mushrooms

Stir in:

1½ tablespoons flour

Stir in slowly:

1½ cups chicken stock or stock in which the frog legs were cooked

Correct the seasoning

When the sauce is hot, add the frog meat. Reduce the heat to low. Beat well:

3 egg yolks

3 tablespoons rich cream

Stir these ingredients into the sauce. Let them thicken off the heat. Add:

1½ teaspoons lemon juice or 2 teaspoons dry sherry

Serve the meat at once, covered with the sauce.

FROG LEGS FORESTIÈRE

[Allow 5 Per Serving]

Sprinkle small frog legs with:

Brandy

Let stand about 2 hours and wipe dry. Sauté them in:

Clarified Butter, page 383

During the last few minutes of cooking when the frog legs become firm to the touch, sauté with the meat for each portion:

2 thinly sliced mushrooms

(1 tablespoon very finely sliced fresh sweet red pepper)

1 tablespoon chopped parsley

1 teaspoon lemon juice

Correct the seasoning

ABOUT TURTLES AND TERRAPIN

Sea turtles attain huge size and their habits are nowhere more fascinatingly described than in "The Windward Road" by Archie Carr.

Handling and cooking these monsters, some of which weigh over 100 pounds, is not a usual household procedure. Therefore most of us are content to enjoy their highly prized, highly priced, gelatinous meat ready-diced and in cans. The greenish meat from the top shell is considered the best—that taken from the bottom is whitish.

The **terrapin** is a freshwater snapping turtle: our children bring them home from the creeks in our neighborhood, as yours may, too. If you cannot use them at once or wish to keep them at least long enough to make certain that they are rid of waste or pollution, you may put them in a deep open box—and don't forget a wire screening on top—give them a dish of water and feed them for a week or so on 3 or 4 small handouts of ground meat.

➧ To cook, place in a pan of cold water:

A 7-inch terrapin

Bring water slowly to a boil and parblanch for at least 10 minutes. Drain. Plunge into cold water and leave until cool enough to handle. Scrub the terrapin well. Place it in rapidly boiling water, and add:

(A Bouquet Garni (II, 220))

(An onion stuck with cloves)

(3 stalks celery)

➧ Reduce the heat at once and simmer 35 to 45 minutes or until the claws can be removed by pulling. Drain, reserving the stock. Allow the terrapin to cool on its back in order to trap the juices as it cools. When cool, pry the flat plastron free from the curved carapace—easier said than done. Near the head you will find the liver. ➧ Free it carefully from the gall. Discard the gall. Slice the liver thin and reserve it, as well as the eggs, if any. You may or may not want to reserve the small intestines, which may be chopped and added to the meat or sauce. Remove the meat both from the carapace and the skinned legs. When ready to serve, you may toss the meat, including the ground liver and intestines, in:

6 tablespoons melted butter

until heated. Garnish with parsley and serve with:

Sherry, as a drink

or you may heat the meat briefly over very low heat or in the top of a double boiler ➧ over—not in—hot water in a sauce made by combining:

1 cup Brown Sauce, page 365
The chopped, cooked eggs, if any
1 teaspoon mixed herbs: including basil, sweet marjoram, thyme, with a touch of rosemary, bay and sage
3 tablespoons Madeira or dry sherry

MEAT

ABOUT MEATS

When a novice approaches the meat counter, she may also approach a state of panic. The friendly informative butcher of a generation ago has often been succeeded by an automaton, mysteriously cutting, grinding, and packaging behind a glass partition. The meats he so impersonally presents in transparent film look bafflingly similar and equally attractive. As a result, they often react in the pan or on the palate in a totally unexpected way. We hope, if you are a rank amateur, that the charts in this chapter will give you the skill of an expert in choosing the right cut for the right dish. For each animal, the charts show you first the general layout of the bone structure; next, the relation of bone to common commercial cuts.

Tender cuts, you will note, lie in those sections where the least body movement and stress occurs and respond to dry heat cooking: roasting, broiling, panbroiling and sautéing.

Meats with more connective tissue will need very slow cooking with moisture: braising, stewing, fricasseeing, pot roasting or poaching. ➧ In these processes, the liquid should never go above the simmering point, 185°. For this reason, we do not recommend the pressure cooking of meats, although expediency sometimes overcomes our better judgment. If you pressure cook meat, follow the directions given by the manufacturer of your appliance.

The third chart shows how these commercial cuts are further subdivided into the meat shapes we are familiar with at table. Listed nearby are the recipes appropriate for each cut. Meat cuts and their names vary not only from country to country but even from region to region in the United States. This makes us wish that there were, as in plants, a sound Linnaean classification. We hope that the charts will not only identify the names most commonly used, but correlate for you the meat and bone relationships involved and—along with the government grading—give you some relative ideas of fat and lean content.

But there is much about meat that must be learned the hard way. How the animal was fed—on grass or corn—and how it was aged, are important factors. Also important are the temperatures at which meat has been held; whether it is watered, or whether treated with preservatives, page 515; how long it has been packaged; and whether it is fairly priced. These are all factors in which you must rely partly on experience and mostly on ➧ the integrity of the butcher.

ABOUT THE GRADING OF MEAT

Before you plunge into purchasing, a word about ➧ grades and prices. The U.S. Government gives you grade protection by stamping all meat sold in interstate commerce. And some states and cities have their own inspection laws. Federal standards of sanitation are rigid, but do be critical of any uninspected locally butchered meats. U.S. grading falls into six classes.

PRIME

This is not commonly available in neighborhood markets. Lean portions, unless the meat is aged, are bright red and well-marbled with fat. Because it comes from young, specially fed cattle, "prime" is well-flavored, fine-textured, tender and encased in white fat. It is very expensive because you pay for the excess fat, much of which is rendered out in cooking.

CHOICE

This grade has less fat than "prime" in its marbling of the lean portions. And, in its coloring, it has a slightly darker tone in both of these portions, but retains high, tender, juicy eating quality.

GOOD

This is still a relatively tender grade, but has a higher ratio of lean to fat meat than either of the above. The lean meat is darker, with little fat marbling, the encasing fat is yellowish and thin.

STANDARD

This grade is cut from young low-quality animals with a very thin fat covering and virtually no marbling in the lean portions. The youth of the animals gives this meat a bland flavor. Tenderness cannot be counted on.

COMMERCIAL AND UTILITY

These are very lean grades and come from old animals. While they are by reason of maturity better in flavor than those in "standard," such meats are coarse in flesh texture and tough, even when carefully cooked, because of their great proportion of connective tissue and their lack of fat.

Although we are always being assured that ▶ the food value of the meat from older animals is comparable to that from younger, more tender ones, we know that they rarely match them in eating quality. One definite exception applies to stocks and soups (II, 138). Both are enhanced by extractives from more mature animals. Whatever grade or cut of meat you buy, there is a great deal that you as a cook can do to make less tender cuts pleasanter to eat.

But before we discuss the cook's role, let's consider ▶ how much to purchase per serving. ▶ While price may go down for bonier cuts, the amount you need per serving goes up. So that ▶ for highly processed and canned meats you need less poundage per person. Another thing to watch is the weight of meat, trimmed and untrimmed. In buying trimmed meats, allow: ▶ for boneless cuts, ¼ to ⅓ lb. per serving. This category includes ground beef, lamb and veal, boneless stew, boned roasts and steaks, flank tenderloin and most variety meats. ▶ For meat with some bone, allow ⅓ to ½ lb. per serving. These cuts include rib roasts, unboned steaks, chops and ham. ▶ For bony cuts, allow ¾ to 1 lb. per serving. In this bracket are short ribs, spareribs, lamb shanks, shoulder, breast and plate cuts, brisket and hock.

ABOUT STORING MEAT BEFORE COOKING

We assume that the meat you buy is properly aged (II, 561). ➧ Raw meat should be stored at once at 42° loosely wrapped; or, if encased in fat, uncovered. You will see a typical butcher wrap illustrated on (II, 551). If you simply pull out the ends of the paper and loosen them, adequate protection and proper ventilation are usually ensured. As a general rule, the larger the piece of meat the longer it will store.

Ground meat, fresh sausage and variety meats are among the most perishable kinds—both as to flavor-retention and safety. Use them within 24 hours of purchase; and, if the ground meat is in amounts over a pound, make sure it is stored, loosely covered, in a container not more than 2½ inches thick in depth, so that the chill of the refrigerator penetrates it quickly. Uncooked diced and cubed meats should be used within 48 hours or so. Roasts will hold 3 to 5 days, steaks 2 to 4.

Pork, lamb and veal are slightly less stable than beef. Prepackaged cured or smoked meat and sausages may be stored refrigerated in the original wrapper. Tenderized hams can be kept much longer in the refrigerator—about 2 weeks—provided the seal of the original wrapper is not broken; only one week otherwise. Once opened, the cut surfaces should be protected. The only exception to an invariable rule is so-called "dry sausage," which need not be refrigerated.

ABOUT SEASONING MEAT

Early salting brings the juices of meat to the surface and into the pan. These juices, which are themselves quite salty, are retained if the meat is seared before seasoning. If meat is breaded or dredged (II, 160), or if it is browned before stewing and the pan drippings or liquors used in gravy, salt may be added when cooking begins. In cooking ground meat, allow ¾ teaspoon salt to 1 pound, but do not apply it to patties until the first side is seared and turned. Allow 1 teaspoon to 2 pounds of solid meat with bone.

There are other ways to accent flavor. About half an hour before cooking, either rub meat with garlic, onion, herbs or spices or insert slivers of garlic or onion near the bone of a roast or else distribute them over a cut surface of steak or roast. Remove any exposed garlic before cooking, as its scorched flavor is not attractive.

Delicacy of flavor may be preserved in meat heavy with fat by pouring off any excess grease after the first half hour of cooking.

ABOUT COOKING TOUGH MEATS

Tenderness in raw meats depends not only on the comparative youth of the animal, but on the strain of cattle to which it belongs and the way it was fed. ➧ Toughness is due to the presence of connective tissues and lack of fat in the muscle. Larding and Barding, page 453, can help to make up somewhat for the lack of fat. The best way to convert stringy to tenderer tissue is by very long and ➧ very slow covered cooking in the presence of moisture. See Braising, Pot-Roasting and Stewing, page 493. Grinding and mincing make chewing easier. But the texture of the meat, if basically tough, remains so and it should never be used in luxury dishes like galantines or, for that matter, even in those as humdrum as hamburger.

Any meat can be made more palatable by seasonings and by added fats or dressings. Pounding and scoring are a help in cuts that are normally treated by dry heat methods, like sautéing and pan-frying. Another favorite technique is marinating, although it involves nutritive losses, some of which can be recaptured if the marinade itself is subsequently used in making up the dish.

Chemical tenderizing is a modern development. One controversial innovation of this type is beyond the control of the consumer. The live animal is given an injection of vegetable enzyme, the tenderizing effects of which are carried throughout the body before butchering. Special aging and storing techniques must accompany this method. The enzyme is reactivated at 130° and reduces the cooking time. A 22-lb. piece of beef will cook at 400° in about 1 hour.

Unfortunately all meat tissues—those which need it and those which do not—are affected by enzyme injection. As a result, the prime portions are usually flabby and somewhat tasteless and the meat generally has a jellied consistency which we find unpleasant. Nor can we say much for the older methods of injecting or dusting the meat with papain, a derivative of papaya, which also tenderizes. We feel that both the flavor and the texture of the meat itself are adversely affected. Meat may be tenderized with a papain derivative of the household type. Usually it is sprinkled on both sides, allowing 1 teaspoon of tenderizer per lb. Prick the meat all over with a fork after applying the tenderizer. Recent studies indicate that papain enzymes seem to tenderize meat as it warms up to between 140° and 176°, so apply the tenderizer as the meat is put in the oven.

ABOUT MINCING, GRINDING AND POUNDING MEAT

The effect of the first two processes is quite different. Particles of minced meat remain separate in further preparation; but ground meat, especially if ground 2 or 3 times, tends to pack. ➧ Always handle ground meat lightly to avoid a dense finished texture.

Pounding, which breaks down the tough fibers of the meat, may be done with a wooden mallet or the flat side of a cleaver. Shown below is a Chinese cleaver which can also be used for chopping, just like a French knife, page 250. ➧ If you are inexperienced, hold the cleaver in both hands and be sure the handle projects beyond the board or table surface—so that you don't pound your fingers.

If you strike with a glancing motion or if you slightly moisten the cleaver, the meat is not so apt to stick. If you are pounding something delicate, like capon breasts, and don't want the fillets to separate, put them in a fold of oiled parchment paper. This allows a sliding and slipping comparable to the glancing action the professional achieves and keeps the meat intact, even when it is pounded paper thin. A chef friend has suggested that if you find the appearance of a very thin piece of meat disappointing, it can be pounded and then folded over for the cooking —to make it more presentable when served.

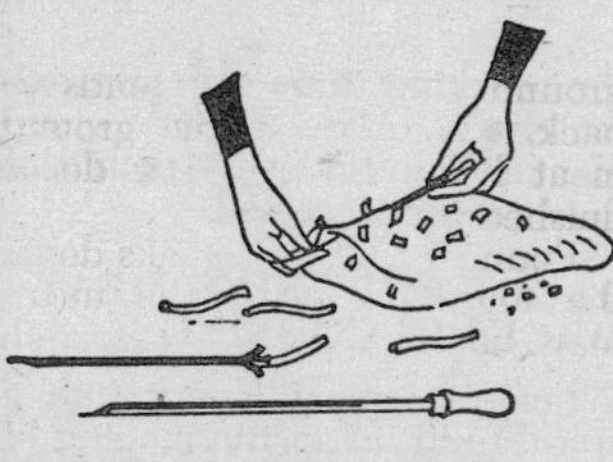

ABOUT LARDING AND BARDING MEAT

Lean meat is frequently "larded" to give it additional juiciness and flavor. ➧ Lardoons are thin strips of salted pork or bacon. They may be first blanched briefly, page 88, and dried before use. French cooks rub them with garlic and other herbs or dust them with cloves and cinnamon. They are cut into 2- or 3-inch strips ¼ inch thick for heavy meat cuts, ⅛ inch thick for small fowl. A larding needle may be used to draw lardoons through the surface of the meat or, as a stopgap measure, a thin knife or ice pick can be pressed into service. Insert lardoons about 1 inch apart. When larding a fowl, place the lardoons at right angles to the breast bone. Larger strips of salt pork may be forced through such meat cuts as chuck and round from surface to surface. After pulling the lardoons through, the ends may be cut off. Allow about 3 oz. of fat per pound of meat.

Lardoons are sometimes placed so their ends form rosettes or decorations. Larding needles are of 2 types. The one in use opposite is also shown, center left, before the lardoon is firmly tightened in it by pinching the pliable fringed ends together. The lower needle has a more than semicircular profile and can be used to form the lardoon itself by plunging it into the salt pork. Then turn the needle to cut the lardoon free. It is shown loaded and ready to run through the meat. To keep the lardoon in the meat, after forcing the needle in, place your thumb or forefinger at the base of the needle groove and slip the needle out with an even, steady pressure. If salt pork is used to lard a meat, as in Galantine, page 529, the lardoons are placed with the grain of the meat, as sketched above. Then, in carving, the pork shows attractively in cross section.

LARDOONS

[Enough for 2½ Lbs. of Meat]

I. Rub:

¼ lb. salt pork or bacon

with a cut:

Clove of garlic

Cut into small strips. Dip into:

Freshly ground pepper
Ground cloves
Minced parsley or chives

II. Marinate:

¼ lb. salt pork lardoons

in:

A few tablespoons of brandy

Just before using, sprinkle with:

Nutmeg
Chopped parsley

III. Lardoons or Cracklings

These are also called grattons. Dice:

Salt pork

Try it out (II, 174) in a skillet until brown and crisp or place the dice in a very slow oven until golden brown. Use for garnishing.

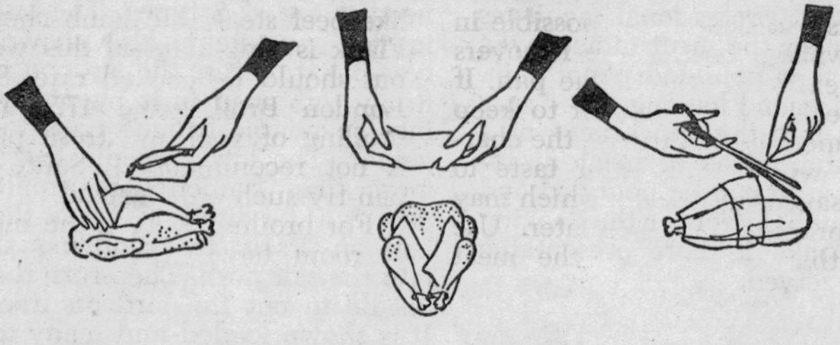

Any lean meat or that of fowl, like guinea or partridge, which is low in fat content, or any fowl from which the skin has been removed can profit by barding before roasting. Meat cuts are simply covered with slices of salt pork, about ¼ inch thick, or fat bacon, as shown on the left in the sketch. For fowl, truss the bird. For each small bird, use 4 pieces of ¼-inch-thick salt pork or fat bacon about 3 x 3½ inches square. Slip one on either side between the leg and breast, see sketch above, left and center. Cover the bird—legs and all—with 2 other pieces and tie, as shown on the right, ▶ making sure that the high exposed surfaces of the bird are blanketed. After cooking, the salt pork or bacon which has served its protective purpose is discarded.

ABOUT MARINATING MEAT

Although you may gain tenderness through marination, you also stand to lose substantial nutritive value, since, by this method, a good many proteins and vitamins are leached away. Marinades are made of both raw and cooked materials and ▶ just to remind you of the importance of using them in making up the finished dish, you will find them in Sauces, page 380. ▶ Marinating for 12 hours or more cuts the cooking time by approximately ⅓. Allow about ½ cup of marinade for every pound of food to be processed.

ABOUT RETAINING MEAT JUICES IN COOKING

When raw meat is put into a cold liquid, as in the making of stocks (II, 138), the meat juices are released into the liquid. But when we cook meat for the table, we want these juices to stay in the meat itself. ▶ Do not cook chilled meats or ✱ frozen meat unthawed. Temperature and cooking times in all of our recipes are given for meat at 70°. Of course, this method does not apply if the meat is salt, like ham and tongue, when it may first be blanched, page 88, or unless the broth is being used for stock. In a stew, one approved method of preparation is to drop the meat into boiling water—disturbing the boiling as little as possible— ▶ and as soon as the meat turns in color, to reduce the heat to a simmer. This method is effective with veal or poultry and is called cooking "à blanc."

But the proper browning, see below, of most meats not only does a sealing job but adds immeasurably to flavor.

ABOUT SEARING OR BROWNING MEAT

Before browning meat, be sure that it is wiped ▶ dry. It is best to use as little fat as possible in browning, but be sure it covers the entire bottom of the pan. If there is not enough fat to keep the meat from burning, the charring will give a bitter taste to the sauces or gravies which may be prepared from it later. Use fat that comes from the meat you are browning or one that complements it in flavor. The ➧ heavy pan should be thoroughly and slowly heated before the fat is added and the meat ➧ slowly browned. Turn it frequently. ➧ Be sure not to crowd the pan, because this lowers the heat and the meat becomes greyish rather than the desired brown. If necessary, until you learn to brown without burning, use a little more fat and pour it off after the searing. In fact, it is always wise to pour off most of the excess grease which may accumulate in the pan before adding a liquid for stewing. When browning a meat, it is often desirable to cook a few chopped onions or other vegetables with it. Since vegetables are apt to cook more rapidly, the meat may be partially browned before they are added. Keep the vegetables moving so they, too, cook without scorching. You may, if you prefer, brown them separately in order to control the heat more easily and then add them to the meat pan. If you are cooking the onions separately, sprinkle them with a very small amount of sugar. It caramelizes them attractively and gives good color to a stew. For vegetables used as meat flavoring, see Mirepoix (II, 221).

To braise, stew or pot-roast, see page 493.

ABOUT BROILING MEAT

➧ Please read About Broiling, page 74, then choose tender cuts, see Chart, pages 464–471, like beef steak and lamb chops. Flank is also handled this way, but should be cooked rare. See London Broil, page 475. The broiling of veal and fresh pork is not recommended. Sauté or pan-fry such cuts instead.

For broiling ➧ have the meat at room temperature. Score it about every 2 inches around the edge to keep it from curling. Cut off excess fat, if any.

Place the meat ➧ on a cold rack to keep it from sticking or, should your rack be hot, grease the meat or rack. Set the meat on the middle of the broiler rack, 3 inches from the heating unit.

Broil the meat until the top side is well browned. Turn, season and broil until the second side is browned. ➧ Only one turning is necessary for a 1-inch steak or chop. Turn frequently for thicker ones and lower the rack about 1 inch for each successive inch of meat thickness—although 2 inches is considered the limit for broiling. Season and serve the meat on a hot platter. Broiling time depends largely upon the thickness of the meat, the length of time it has been hung, its fat content and the degree of doneness desired. If you use a thermometer, rare steaks are broiled to an internal temperature of 130°; medium to 160°. Lamb chops are broiled to 155° for rare and to 170° if well done. Ham is cooked well done. The time for broiling bacon is influenced by personal preference as to crispness, but ➧ to keep it from curling, the heat should be low. Should your broiler be an infrared one, follow manufacturer's directions.

ABOUT PANBROILING MEAT

➧ Preheat a heavy skillet. Rub the pan with a small quantity of fat if the meat is not prime. Sear the meat on one side until the blood rises to the surface. Then turn at once and sear it on the other side. ➧ Reduce the heat and continue to process the meat uncovered. If cooked too long, it toughens badly and dries out. In the case of a steak about 1½ inches thick, cooking time may be 10 minutes or more if you want it medium to well done. During the cooking, pour excess fat from the pan for, if allowed to accumulate, the meat is "fried" rather than "broiled" in quality.

If meat is solid and well-marbled or if fat has been incorporated with it—as is often the case with ground meats, like hamburger—it can go directly into a preheated ungreased pan. Sometimes a salt base is suggested, allowing 1 teaspoon salt for each pound of meat. This rather surprising technique works but is, in our judgment, best avoided, since the salt extracts meat juices which, of course, are promptly discarded when broiling is over. If you are obliged to follow fat-free procedures, try oven broiling, a soapstone griddle or a pan whose surface has been specially treated for fat-free frying. With such treated pans, follow the manufacturer's directions.

ABOUT ROASTING MEAT

After trying out different methods of roasting meat over a long period of years, we are convinced that the quality of the meat is the decisive factor. We suggest you choose a method best suited to the meat at hand. ➧ To cook vegetables with a roast, see page 258.

I. If the meat is Prime or Choice, we get the best flav.. by placing not less than 2 ribs at about 70° temperature ➧ on a rack in a pan greased with suet or oil, in a preheated 500° oven, fat side up. The rack allows proper circulation of air. As soon as the oven door is closed ➧ reduce the heat to 350° and time the cooking from that point, depending on the size of the roast and the degree of doneness wanted. Timings are given in the individual recipes.

No basting is necessary in this procedure, there being sufficient fat in the meat. You will get minimal, but very precious, juice in the pan. To make gravy from pan drippings, see page 358.

II. ➧ If meat is Good or Standard grade and its weight not under 4 lbs., place it when it has reached 70° ➧ uncovered in a preheated 325° oven—except for pork, for which we prefer an oven heated to 350°. Sometimes we first brown the roast, page 454. But usually we put a thermometer in it and simply place the meat, unbrowned, on a rack, in a pan directly in the preheated oven and forget about it until it is almost time to check for internal temperature. The method just described produces practically no fat or juice in the pan, and needs a gravy confected from precooked stocks, see (II, 138). In adopting either of the above methods, remember that if the roast is carved in the kitchen rather than at the table, the juices which run into the carving dish can and should be quickly defatted and incorporated into any gravy previously prepared—to give it a final authentic flavor. Meanwhile, keep the already sliced meat warm on a hot platter.

➧ Sometimes very low, slow roasting is suggested. ➧ It is important not to have the oven under 275°, for unwanted micro-organisms may not be destroyed below this temperature, no matter how long the cooking. ➧ The insertion of metal pins in a roast cuts down cooking time somewhat and the meat will be juicier but not quite as tender.

ABOUT BASTING MEAT

In roasting and broiling, everything is done to preserve the dry quality of the heat. If roasts are Prime grade, they are so heavy in fat that basting is not necessary. In fact, with prime meats, fat losses run as high as 40% of weight. Just brush a small amount of fat in the base of the pan to tide over until some from the meat is rendered. An exception is tenderloin, which may be simply rubbed with fat or oil or be larded or barded, page 453.

The leaner cuts profit by basting ➧ with melted fat. But the moment you baste with stocks or water, excess steam is created which lessens the dry heat quality that makes a roast so delicious. ➧ Baste preferably with fatty pan drippings by using a bulb-type baster, as sketched on the left, or with a spoon as shown on the right.

There are also 2 types of self-basting. One is with fat, in barding, page 454. The other is with steam, which takes place in a covered pan—when the steam rising from the food falls back from the lid onto the braising meat or stew. This kind of basting never goes on in roasting—where, to achieve the essential dry heat ➧ no cover is used.

ABOUT TIMING IN COOKING MEAT

Timing is given in each recipe, but it is most difficult to advise about this accurately without knowing the thickness of the meat, its quality, its shape and how much bone it contains. Ovens and broilers should always be preheated. All meat, we repeat, should be at about 70° throughout before roasting or broiling begins. If meat is chemically tenderized, the papain derivatives used in the household, see page 452, begin to take effect during cooking and greatly shorten its cooking period.

If meats have been ✻ frozen, bring them to 70° and time as for fresh meat. Thawing before cooking keeps to a minimum the amount of juices released. But there are times—occasional emergencies—when one must cook meat before thawing it.

In roasting unthawed frozen meat, preheat the oven to about 25° less than indicated in the recipes and allow about ½ again as much time for the cooking period.

In broiling unthawed meat, regardless of its thickness, place it at least 5 to 6 inches below the heat source. Again allow at least ½ again as much time as normally indicated. For further comments on timing, see page 97. ➧ To test for doneness, see below.

▲ In high altitudes, roasted and baked meats require no adjustment up to 7000 ft. After

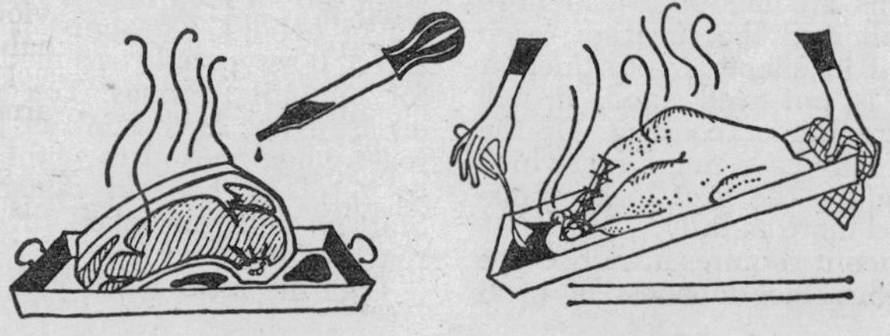

that a longer cooking period may be needed. We recommend the pressure cooking of meats only in cases of emergency. Tests show that these have less shrinkage and more flavor if cooked at 10 rather than at 15 pounds pressure.

ABOUT DONENESS IN MEAT

Rare, medium, or well done—these are such personal preferences that set rules become difficult to prescribe. What you should realize is that ➧ in cooking any meats, heat should at some point be high enough to destroy unwanted and harmful organisms. We give these necessary internal temperatures for various meats in our individual recipes and elsewhere in this chapter. But we ask you to realize that meat roasted for as long as 12 hours and to as high a temperature as 200° may still be insufficiently cooked to ensure safety—since roasting is merely a reflected heat; whereas stewing at a simmering temperature of 180° over a comparably long period will be sufficient—this heat being moist, and a more penetrating one. ➧ Reaching the proper temperature is especially vital for safety in cooking pork, page 484. We suggest in recipes for roasts, steaks and stews a certain timing—usually minutes to the pound at a given temperature. But with this rough and ready formula you may not get the result you expected. The reasons are many: if you have not allowed the meat to reach 70°, if its shape is very thick or if it is not well aged, it will require longer cooking. Or the meat may have much fat, which will allow the heat to be transmitted more rapidly.

Since it requires a trained eye to judge the doneness of meat from its external appearance ➧ use a meat thermometer for accurate results. Before broiling meat over 3 inches thick or before roasting it, insert the thermometer in the center and fleshy portion of the meat, away from bony or fatty sections. Unless the glass of the thermometer is metal-shielded, make a gash with a pointed sharp knife to ease the insertion of the thermometer. Place the top so that it is as far away from the source of heat as possible.

If you have no thermometer, there are two ways to judge doneness. In the touch method, firm meat is well done. If it responds as a cake does (II, 336) —is soft yet resilient—the meat is medium rare. You can also detect the degree of doneness by pricking roasted or broiled meats, but when you do you lose valuable juices. If the juice runs red, the meat is rare; pink, medium rare; colorless, well done.

➧ Pork and fowl with light meat must be cooked until the juice is colorless. Most other meats are overdone at this point.

To test for braised meats, use a sharply pointed knife near the bone. The juice should run clear.

ABOUT COOKING MEAT EN CROÛTE

Meat in a crust, or en croûte, lends itself particularly to buffet service. If served hot, the meat remains "à point," page 72, for at least half an hour. Hot or cold, the finished dish is beautiful to behold. The crust is not eaten. It serves only as a medium for retaining aromas. You may encase ham, fowl, lamb or beef roast when cooked to within ½ to ¾ of an hour of doneness. Starting with uncooked fowl or roast is described later.

Cool the meat while you prepare the following crust, heavy in egg, which lends the tensile strength necessary to keep large or heavy meats covered. Have all ingredients at 70°. Mix together, to the consistency of coarse corn meal:

4 cups all-purpose flour
1 cup shortening
1½ teaspoons salt

Make a well (II, 301) of these ingredients and work in one at a time:

3 to 4 eggs
½ cup water

Knead the dough until well bound. Roll into a ball and rest covered for several hours at 70°. Preheat the oven to 450°. Roll the dough into a large sheet, about 3/16 inch thick. Place the meat you want to cover so that the top surface is down on the dough. Then fold the dough over it, as neatly as possible, pressing it to take the form of the meat. Be careful to keep the covering intact. Then turn the covered meat right side up. Brush any excess flour off the dough with a dry brush.

Now the fun begins. From the pastry scraps that remain, cut rounds, flowers and leaves or any decorations that suit your mood. If you like, score them with a fork to give their surfaces a variation that will show up markedly after baking. You may even use Puff Paste (II, 300) for such trimmings. Space them out on the dough up to three thicknesses by applying French Egg Wash (II, 433) to each, as a glue. When you are satisfied with your design—and don't make it too cluttered—brush the surfaces with egg wash again. Cut a series of decorative gashes in the dough casing, as for a covered pie, to let the steam escape and to keep the crust from buckling. Put the covered meat in the hot oven, and ➧ reduce the heat at once to 350°. Allow the crust to bake until it is delicately browned. Repeat the egg glazing at the end of baking, for an even effect. You may also brush the crust with butter on removal from the oven.

Another way to bake en croûte is to use, instead of the dough indicated above, a stiff bread dough. Punch it down once before rolling it out and cover as previously described.

➧ To cook uncooked meat en croûte, prepare the dough described previously. Coat the meat to be covered with Egg Wash (II, 433). Fold the pastry around the meat and decorate as described above.

Bake the meat in a preheated 280° to 300° oven, 2 to 3 hours, depending on size. Hams and legs of lamb may be boned and stuffed before wrapping. If a stuffing is used, be sure the food it is made of is precooked, as the heat may not penetrate it sufficiently otherwise to cook it through.

ABOUT STORING COOKED MEAT

It is much safer to ➧ put meat into the refrigerator while still fairly hot and this is only a slightly more expensive way to refrigerate. ➧ Cover it.

If you prefer, you may also leave meat that has been cooked to cool ➧ covered for 2 hours before refrigerating.

Do not store ➧ meat in hot gravy in quantities larger than 1 quart. Drain off the gravy and allow it to cool separately if the amounts are larger. If meats are ➧ stuffed, unstuff them and store the stuffing separately.

ABOUT REHEATING MEAT

It is a great temptation to try to prepare large joints of meat in advance and reheat them just before serving. This is not good practice. For the heat to penetrate on reheating, a very long period is necessary and the meat tends to dry out.

With hash or sauced meats, be sure the sauce is ➧ just to the point of boiling before the meat is added. ➧ Reduce the heat at once and allow the meat to heat thoroughly. Serve at once. An even better way to reheat thin sliced meats is described on page 98.

ABOUT CARVING MEAT

The convenient ready-to-serve platter, or so-called Russian service, has almost displaced carving. Fortunately, a few hosts still delight in practicing this gracious skill. And, given a very sharp knife, a large platter and the most rudimentary knowledge of animal anatomy, almost anyone can learn to carve.

Illustrations throughout this chapter show the general direction taken in approaching major cuts. Most meats are cut against the grain, although a leg of lamb or mutton may also be cut with it. If you are trying out in the kitchen, use a board until you become worthy of the art and can carve on a platter without scratching it. Ply the knife with a long, light, pulling and pushing, sawlike action. Always try to keep your fork-hand behind, not in front of, the blade. Protect yourself further by using a fork with a thumb piece.

Slicing knives for ham, roast beef, big turkeys and pot roasts have a very flexible 10-inch blade, about 1¼ inches wide. Carving knives for game, loin of pork, rack of lamb or lobster are about a foot in length. Their 8½-inch pointed, rigidly firm blades, about 1¾ inches wide, are so shaped that at the blade edge they come to a fine V. ➧ Keeping the knife blade sharp and under easy control is important. But of equal importance to the successful carver is keeping the V-edge true by the use of a steel. And the following procedure should precede the use of the knife before each carving period. The steel, which must be kept magnetized, realigns the molecular structure of the blade.

➧ To true a blade, hold the steel firmly in the left hand, thumb on top of handle. Hold the knife in the right hand, point upward, and the hand slightly away from the body. Place the heel of the blade against the far side of the tip of the steel, as

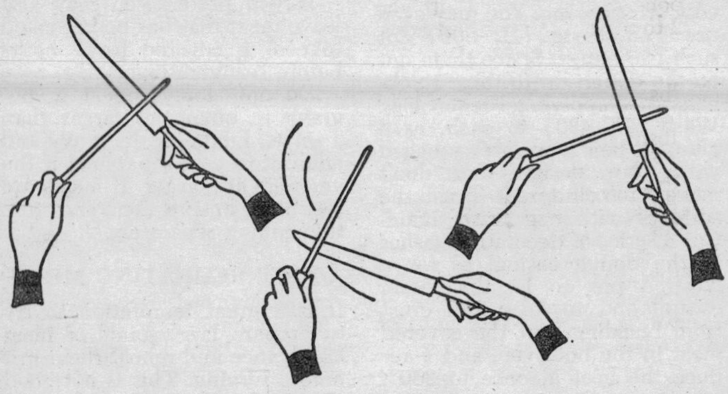

illustrated. The steel and blade should meet at about a 15° to 25° angle.

➧ Draw the blade across the steel, bringing it down toward the left hand, with a quick swinging motion of the right wrist. ➧ The entire blade should pass lightly over the steel. To start the second stroke, bring the knife into the same position as in the first, but this time the steel should lie behind the blade, away from you, as shown on the right. About twelve strokes are enough to true the edge.

Some carvers feel the results are better if they allow a roast to set—that is rest outside the oven on a hot platter. With very large joints which retain their heat well, this setting period may be from 30 to 45 minutes.

ABOUT ECONOMICAL USE OF LARGE CUTS OF MEAT

If shopping for a household of two, there are times when you may look longingly at the "weekly special" on meat. How tempting the standing rib roast of beef, the rump of beef, the leg of spring lamb, the loin of pork, the round of veal or the half or whole ham! But unless you are planning to have guests, it looks as if it is far more meat than you care to buy for two. But by taking advantage of special sales prices and planning ahead to freeze a part of the cut for future use, it is an economy to buy the larger piece. You can have your delicious roast for just two—or steaks from the ham or veal, chops from lamb or pork, short ribs from beef. Then the remainder may be used in many interesting leftover dishes.

2 RIBS OF BEEF—5 lbs.

Have butcher cut off:
Short Ribs, page 500; Roast Beef, page 463. The leftover beef can be reheated in: Cum-

GUIDE TO APPROXIMATE YIELD OR CUTS FROM 250 LB. SIDE OF BEEF, CUT FROM AN 800 LB. STEER

Please read About Steaks, page 472, and Fillet of Beef, page 472.

FROM 26 LBS. OF SHORTLOIN

You have a choice of club, sirloin and porterhouse steaks—which are a combination of T-bone, sirloin and fillet. But, if you want 5 lbs. of fillet from the shortloin, you must forego the porterhouse steaks, which will leave you 21 lbs. of shortloin for sirloin steaks, T-bone and club steaks. If you choose to have the fillet, see page 472 to utilize it to the best advantage.

FROM	CHOICE OF
21 lbs. of loin end	Butt steaks and roasts
2 lbs. of flank steak	Ground beef—flank steak
45 lbs. of boneless round	Top and bottom, Swiss steak, pot roasts, hamburger, cubed steak
23 lbs. of rib	7-rib roast, rolled roast, rib steaks
42 lbs. of boneless chuck	Ground beef, stew, pot roast
10 lbs. of boneless brisket	For braising, stewing, ground, corned beef
17 lbs. of plate	Ground beef, stew
10 lbs. of shank	Soup meat, marrow bones
49 lbs. of fat, bone and waste	Also, tripe, tongue, liver, heart, sweetbreads, brains, kidneys, oxtail and head
5 lbs. loss in trimming	

berland Sauce, page 372. Or used in Hot Roast Beef Sandwich with Olive Sauce, page 242; Shepherd's Pie, page 225; Leftover in Bacon, page 218; Peppers filled with Meat and Rice, page 308; Cold Roast Beef and Tomato Sauce, page 376; Acorn Squash Filled with Creamed Food, page 331.

RUMP OF BEEF—4 to 5 lbs.

Have butcher cut off a piece about 2 inches thick, dice into 1-inch cubes for:
Beef Stew with Wine, page 496. Or use in one piece for Pot Roast, page 498. Us the leftovers as Cold Roast Beef and Curry Sauce, page 363; or hot as beef reheated in Cumberland Sauce, page 372. Or use in Hot Roast Beef Sandwich, page 242; Turnovers filled with meat, page 210; or Leftover Timbales, page 202.

ROUND OF VEAL

Have butcher cut off 1 or 2 thin slices of veal for:

Veal Birds	Page 505
Veal Scallopini	479
Mexican Veal Steak	506
Wiener Schnitzel	480
Have another slice cut off to dice into 1-inch cubes for:	
Blanquette de Veau	504
Cubed Veal Baked in Sour Cream	506
Use the remainder for:	
Veal Roast	478
Use leftovers in:	
Curried Veal and Rice	217
Creamed Veal	217
Veal and Spinach	217
Veal Timbales	204
Meat Shortcakes	211

LEG OF LAMB—5 to 6 lbs.

Have butcher cut off:
4 chops for:

Broiled II	Page 483
Stuffed Lamb Chops	483
Also a slice about 2 inches thick, diced into 1-inch cubes for:	
Curried Lamb	509
Lamb Stew	508
Roast the remaining shank end	482
Leftovers may be used in:	
Veal or Lamb and Spinach Dish	217
Eggplant Filled with Leftover Food	291
Lamb Terrapin	318
Lamb Sandwich	246
Scotch Broth	116

LOIN OF PORK—9 to 10 lbs.

Have butcher cut off:
4 chops from center of loin for:

Pork Chops	Page 487
Deviled Pork Chops	512
Pork Chops Baked in Sour Cream	511
Use one end for:	
Pork Roast	485
Freeze the other end for:	
Pork Roast with Sauerkraut	487
Use leftovers in:	
Meat Pie Roll	211
Chop Suey	218
Shepherd's Pie	225
Pizza	213
Scrapple or Goetta	533

HALF HAM—4 to 7 lbs.

Have butcher cut off 1 or 2 slices to use for:

Broiled Ham	Page 491
Stuffed Ham Rolls, III	219
Ham with Fruit	490
Use remainder as:	
Baked Ham	488–490
Use leftovers for:	
Ham and Corn Croquettes	(II, 122)
Ham à la King	220
Ham Rolls with Asparagus	219
Jellied Ham Mousse	60
Split Pea or Lentil Soup	120

TO MAKE A FRILL FOR A SHANK BONE

To make a frill for a shank ham, a lamb bone or drumsticks, fold in half stiff paper dinner napkins, about 12 x 8 inches. Cut through fold at ½-inch intervals to within 1 inch of open edge. Reverse the fold, bringing the open edges together. Begin to roll the uncut portion of the newly folded paper, leaving an opening at the folded open edge big enough to slip over the bone. Fasten this roll with scotch tape and slide the frill over the bone.

ABOUT BEEF

Beef, its aging, grading and general characteristics are described in About Meats, page 449. With the exception of game, no meat profits more by proper aging. Few households are able to buy, not for lack of money, but for lack of supply, the kinds of beef purchased by hotels and clubs. The scarce superior grades are almost always reserved for these commercial establishments.

The American woman, through visual advertising, has been made to feel that bright red lean beef is the desirable grade, but actually beef for best flavor should be well aged to a purplish tone and show definite evidence of mottling, as well as heavy fat coverings.

ROAST BEEF

[3 to 4 Servings to the Pound]

Preheat oven to 550°.

When buying a standard rib of beef, be sure to have your butcher remove the spinal cord, the shoulder bone and the chine. Have him tie the chine back on—to keep the contour of the meat and to protect the eye of the roast during the cooking period. If the roast is made oven-ready in this way, the carving, illustrated, is very simple. Remove the roast from the refrigerator at least 3 hours before preparing for cooking. Trim off the excess fat and hard edges of:

A rib roast of beef

Place the roast, fat side up, on a rack in a pan in the oven. ➧ Reduce the heat immediately to 350° and cook 18 to 20 minutes to the pound for medium rare. To cook vegetables with roast, see page 258.

A rolled roast will require 5 to 10 minutes longer to the pound. To make gravy from pan drippings see page 258. Serve the roast with:

Macaroni Loaf, page 171
Yorkshire Pudding, page 182, or Tomato Pudding, page 335

To carve see below.

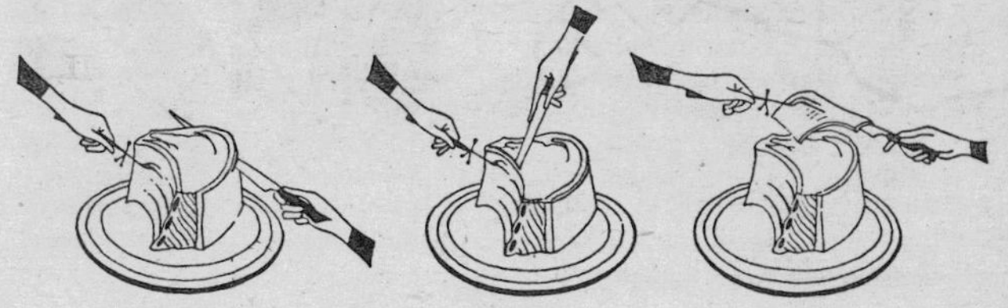

DIVISIONS OF COMMERCIAL CUTS AND RETAIL CUTS OF BEEF

BEEF

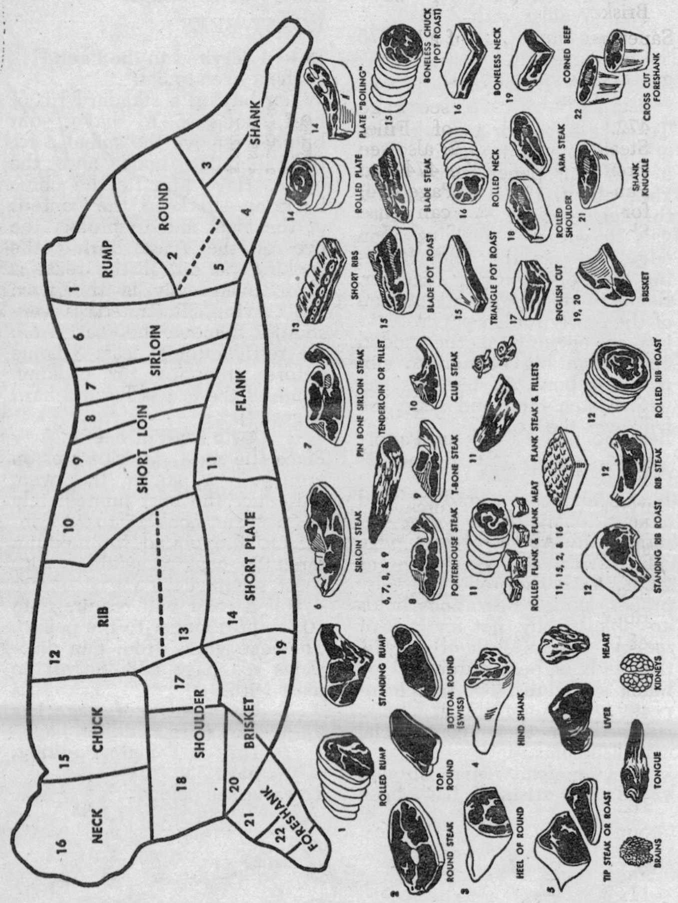

RECIPES KEYED TO CHART

Roast of Beef, Page 463; Rib 12; Sirloin 6–7; Short Loin 8–9–10.

Pot Roasts, Page 495; Shoulder 18; Chuck 15; Rump 1; or Brisket 19.

Sauerbraten, and Boeuf à la Mode, Page 497; Shoulder 18.

Steaks: For details of beef cuts bearing this name, see Page 472. For Chart of Fillet Steaks, see Page 472; also see Broiled Steaks, Page 474 and Pan-Broiled Steaks, Page 474, for which you can use Shoulder 18; Rib Steak 12; Tip Steak 5; Ground Round 2.

Boeuf Fondu Bourguignonne, Page 475: Fillet 6–9; Sirloin 6–7.

Beef Stroganoff, Page 476: Fillets 6–9.

Beef Kebabs, Page 476: Round 2; Sirloin 6–7; Fillets 6–9.

Beef Rolls, Roulades or Paupiettes, Page 502: Round 2; Flank 11.

Burgoo, Page 503; Chuck 15; Neck 16; Shoulder 18; Foreshank 21–22.

Sukiyaki, Page 477: Tenderloin 6–9; Sirloin Tip 6; Eye of Round 2.

Beef Goulash, Page 500: Round 2; Shinbone 21–22.

Flank Steak With Dressing, Page 499: Flank 11.

Oxtail Stew, Page 501: Tailbones.

Corned Beef, Page 493: Brisket 19.

Ground Beef and Meat Loaves, Page 522, and Hamburgers, Page 516: Chuck 15; Flank 11; Neck 16; Round 2.

Heart, Page 546, Tongue, Page 544, and Tripe, Page 548, are the favored beef variety meats.

BONE STRUCTURE AND COMMERCIAL CUTS FROM A CARCASS OF BEEF

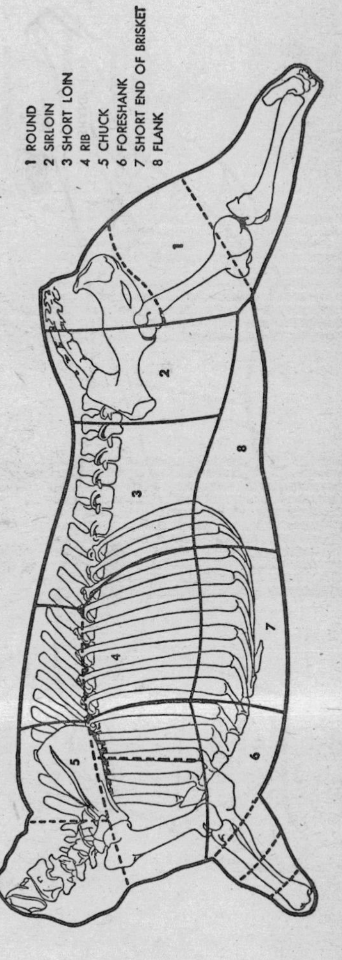

DIVISIONS OF COMMERCIAL CUTS AND RETAIL CUTS OF VEAL

VEAL

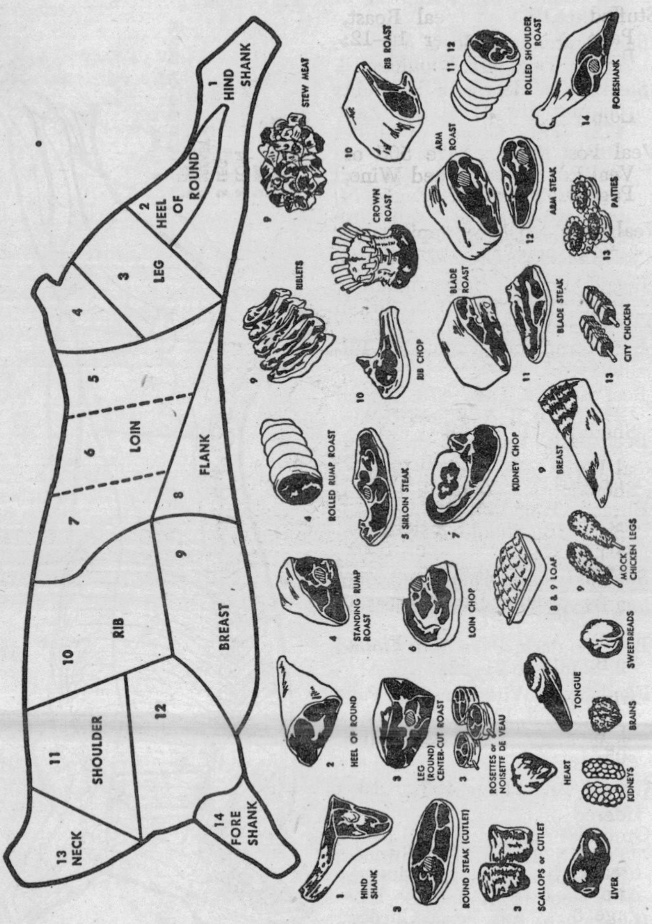

RECIPES KEYED TO CHART

Roast of Veal, Page 478: Rib 10.

Stuffed or Rolled Veal Roast, Page 478: Shoulder 11–12; Breast 9.

Veal Kidney Roast, Page 478: Loin 7.

Veal Post Roast, Page 505 or Veal Pot Roast In Red Wine, Page 503: Rump 4.

Veal Cutlet, Scaloppini or Schnitzel or Veal Parmigiana, Pages 479–481; Leg 3; Loin 5–6–7.

Veal Stew, or Veal Stew in Red Wine, Page 503: Breast 9; Neck 13.

Blanquette de Veau, Page 504: Shoulder 11–12.

Veal Porkolt, Page 500: Leg 3; Shoulder 11–12; Neck 13.

Mock Chicken Drumsticks or City Chicken, Page 505: Breast 9; Neck 13.

Osso Buco, Page 506: Shank 14.

Veal Patties, Page 518: Flank 8; Breast 9.

Terrine, Page 528: Leg 3.

Veal Birds or Paupiettes, Page 505: Leg 3.

All Veal Variety Meats are considered choice.

See Index for Liver, Sweetbreads, Brains, and Kidneys; Also Steak and Kidney Pie, Page 504, and Head Cheese and Brawn, Page 550.

BONE STRUCTURE AND COMMERCIAL CUTS FROM A CARCASS OF VEAL

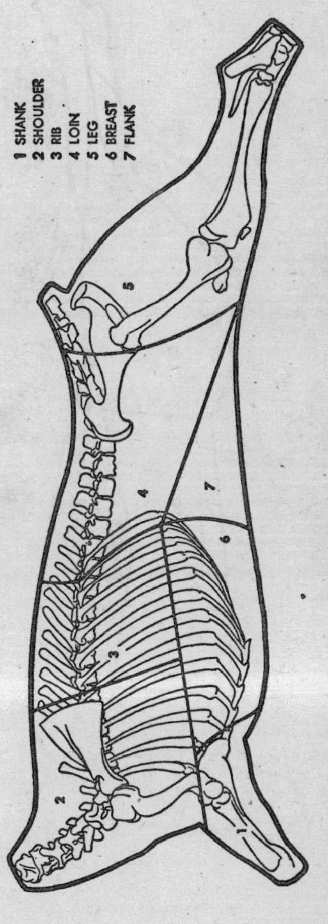

DIVISION OF COMMERCIAL CUTS AND RETAIL CUTS OF LAMB

LAMB

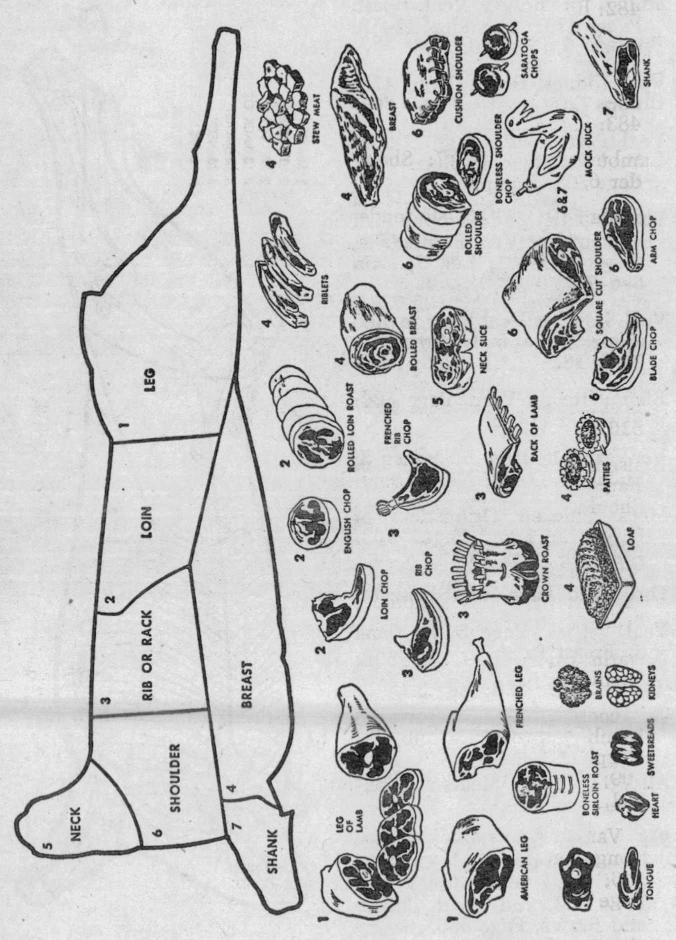

RECIPES KEYED TO CHART

Lamb or Mutton Roast, Page 482: Rib 3.

Broiled Lamb Chops, Page 483: Rib 3; Loin 2; Leg 1.

Broiled Lamb Kebabs, Page 483: Shoulder 6.

Lamburgers, Page 517: Shoulder 6.

Since lamb is a relatively tender meat, almost any cut, especially of young lamb, can be cooked by the dry heat methods above. Also see pages 482–483. Cuts from active areas where the muscle is firmer may be cooked according to the following moist heat methods on pages 506–510.

Braised Stuffed Shoulder or Farce of Lamb, Page 507: Shoulder 6.

Braised Lamb Shanks or Trotters, Page 508: Shank 7.

Irish Stew, Page 509: Shoulder 6; Breast 4.

Navarin Printanier, Page 508: Shoulder 6; Breast 4.

Try cooked lamb in Curry of Lamb, Page 501; Lamb and Eggplant Casserole, Page 509; Stuffed Eggplant, Page 291.

For Variety Meat Recipes, see Tongue in Creole Sauce, Page 546; Steak and Kidney Pie, Page 502.

BONE STRUCTURE AND COMMERCIAL CUTS FROM A CARCASS OF LAMB

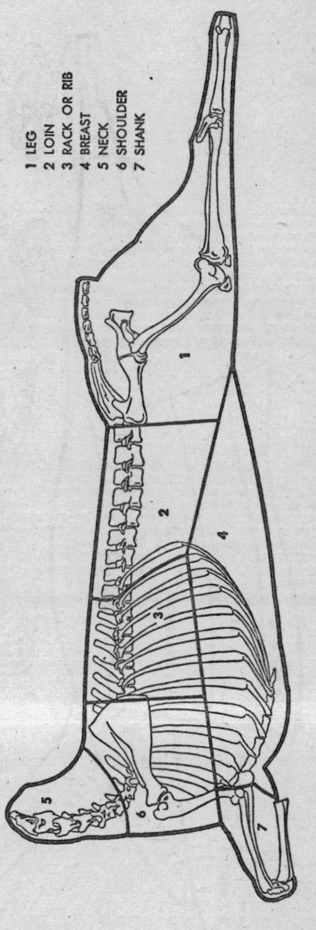

DIVISIONS OF COMMERCIAL CUTS AND RETAIL CUTS OF PORK

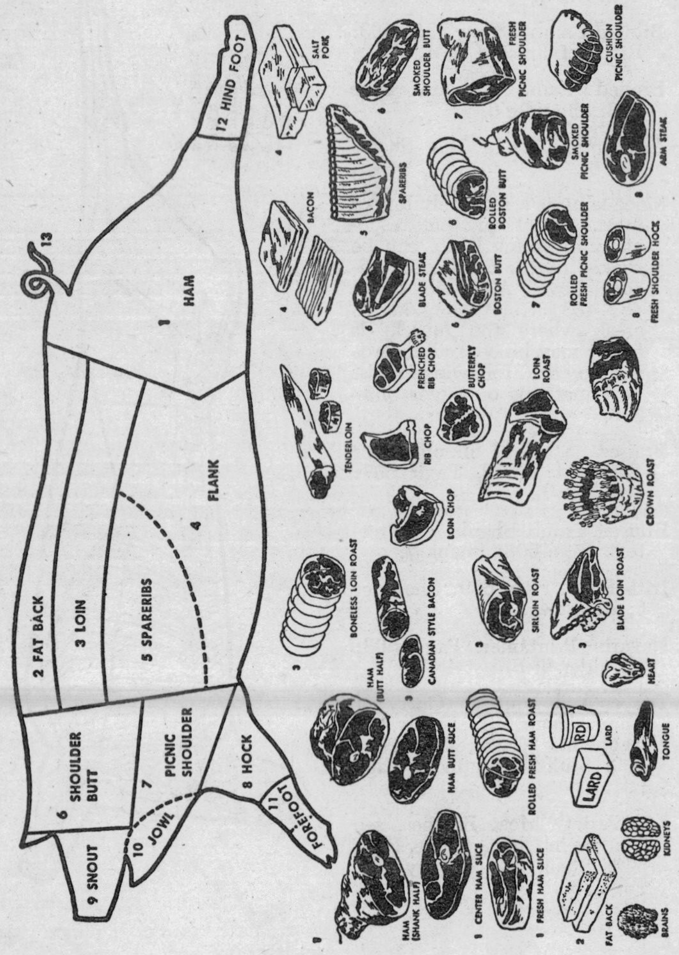

RECIPES KEYED TO CHART

Roast of Pork, Page 485: Loin 3.

Roast of Pork Stuffed with Sauerkraut, Page 487: Shoulder Butt 6.

Pork Tenderloin, Page 487: Loin 3.

Frenched Fruit Casserole, Page 487; Loin 3; with Mushrooms, Page 511: Loin 3.

Rib Pork Chops Broiled, Page 487: Loin 3.

Rib or Loin Chops, Page 511 or with Fruit, or Stuffed, Page 512: Loin 3.

Sweet and Sour Pork, Page 514: Boned Ribs 5.

Baked Spareribs, or Ribs With Sauerkraut, Page 514 or Barbecued Ribs, Page 97: Ribs 5.

Stewed Pork Hocks, Page 514: Hock 8.

Hams, Pages 489–491, or Ham En Croûte, Page 458, or Ham Slices Casseroled or with Fruit, Page 490: Ham 1.

Rolled Smoked Picnic Shoulder, Page 491: Picnic Shoulder 7.

Broiled or Sautéed Bacon, Page 491: Flank 4.

Broiled Sautéed or Baked Canadian Bacon, Page 492: Loin 3.

Parblanched Salt Pork, Page 551: Flank 4.

Pigs' Feet, Page 551: Forefoot 11.

Pork Scrapple or Goetta, Page 533: Shoulder Butt 6.

Pork Variety Meats are not choice with the exception of Suckling Pig's Livers, see Pâté En Croûte, Page 525; for Suckling Pig, see page 485.

BONE STRUCTURE AND COMMERCIAL CUTS FROM A CARCASS OF PORK

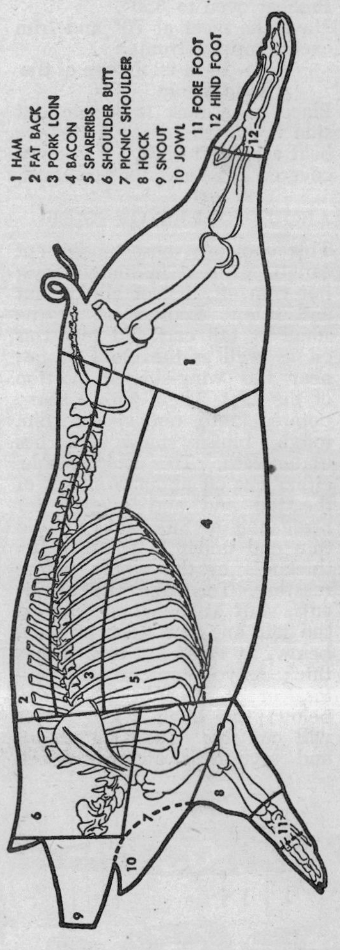

For ways to utilize leftover roasted meat, see Boeuf Miroton, page 217, and Luncheon Dishes, page 208.

ROAST STRIP SIRLOIN [24 to 30]

Preheat oven to 550°.
Have the meat at 70° and trim excess top fat from:

An 18 to 22 lb. eye of the strip sirloin

Place on a rack in a pan, fat side up, in the oven. ➧ Reduce heat at once to 350°. Roast uncovered 1½ hours for rare meat.

ABOUT FILLET OF BEEF

This choicest, most tender cut can be utilized in many ways; but trim off, first of all, the fat and sinew. Loosen fat at the small or tail end and tear this off as well as the clods of fat, near the wing-shaped portion of the fillet. Then, with a sharp pointed knife, remove the thin, tough, bluish sinew that lies underneath. To cook whole, either cut off about 6 inches of the tail end and save it for Stroganoff or Sukiyaki—or fold thin end under to equalize the thickness of the whole before roasting. To make the classic cuts, start at the upper end on the left and cut Filet Mignon, below, in slices 1½ to 2 inches thick. As you approach the center or Châteaubriand area, below, the small wing pieces will cut free. The Châteaubriand section is always cooked whole, either roasted or broiled, and is sliced at the table before serving. The narrower portion can be cut into 1-inch-thick slices called Tournedos, to within about 4 inches of the end. Use the tail again for Stroganoff, page 476, or Steak Tartare (II, 78).

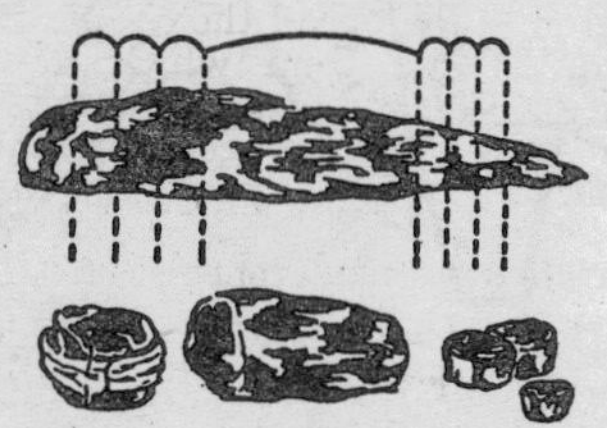

FILLET OR TENDERLOIN OF BEEF

[Allow ⅓ Pound per Serving]

Preheat oven to 500°.
Have the meat at room temperature. Remove the surplus fat and skin from:

At least a 5 lb. fillet of beef

You may lard, page 453, with narrow strips of:

(Salt pork or country bacon)

Fold over the thin ends of the fillet and secure them with string. If not larded, spread the meat generously with butter or tie strips of bacon over it. Do not cover or baste it. Place on a rack in a roasting pan in the oven. You may oil the pan. ➧ Reduce the heat immediately to 350° and bake from 18 to 30 minutes in all. A fillet is usually cooked rare when the internal temperature reaches 120°. Season when done. You may surround the fillet with:

Broiled Mushrooms, page 297

Garnish the platter with:

Sprigs of parsley
Soufflé Potatoes, page 316

Serve with:

Marchand de Vin Sauce, page 367
Bordelaise Sauce, page 366
Béarnaise Sauce, page 370

ABOUT STEAKS

When in doubt, the stock answer to the menu problem is, "Let's have steak!" Steak—from ⊟ charcoal grill to planked Châteaubriand, page 80—does duty for so many different occasions that we would like to discuss steak varieties below. Unless special recipes are given, they may all be broiled, page 455, or pan-broiled, page 455. The meat should of course ➧ be at least 70° and the ➧ grill should be hot and oiled ➧ the broiler preheated. ➧ Season at the end of cooking and not before.

Steak, hot or cold, is greatly enhanced by a sauce and the most usual accompaniments are one of the following:

Colbert Butter, page 384
Béarnaise Sauce, page 370
Bordelaise Sauce, page 366
Marchand de Vin Sauce, page 367
Sour Cream Horseradish Sauce, page 351
Mushroom Sauce, page 367

FLANK STEAK

This is considered the least choice cut, probably because so often poorly prepared. It is a treat if properly cooked, see London Broil, page 475.

HAMBURGER

This, too, can be a real treat, not just a stopgap, see page 516.

RUMP, SWISS AND ROUND STEAK

Made from the round, these are prized for their flavor but are never truly tender. Since they must be braised and do not respond to dry heat methods, they are steaks only in name, see Moist Heats, page 81. Scrape and serve raw for Steak Tartare (II, 78).

CUBE STEAKS

These are top butt or round and macerated to tenderize for grilling. They are usually tough.

RIB OR SPENCER STEAKS

These are comparable in price but varying in flavor and texture and cut from a choice area of the eye of the rib.

CLUB OR MINUTE STEAK

This is cut from the end of the shortloin and makes a good individual serving.

T-BONE STEAK

This also is cut from the shortloin but near the middle. It combines the tail of fillet and the tail of the sirloin.

PORTERHOUSE STEAK

Another shortloin cut. It is very like T-bone—but a larger version—and includes the choice fillet and choice sirloin.

SIRLOIN

Cut from the shortloin, it is comparable to a French entrecôte. Its flavor is the one associated most often with the word steak.

SIRLOIN STRIP STEAK

This is the eye of the sirloin—the choice cut most often met with in hotels. In serving large groups, the eye of the sirloin, 18 to 22 lbs., from which these strip steaks come, is often roasted whole, page 472, and sliced.

TENDERLOIN OR FILLET STEAKS

These include Filet Mignon, Châteaubriand, Tournedos,

Steak Tartare. They vary in name and size, depending on the portion of the fillet from which they are cut. For details, see the illustration on page 472. Prized for their tenderness, they are somewhat lacking in flavor and require an interesting sauce.

BROILED STEAK

Preheat broiler.
Prepare for cooking a 2-inch-thick:

Sirloin, T-bone, strip or porterhouse steak

Have the meat at room temperature. You may rub the steak with:

(A cut clove of garlic)

You may spread it an hour before it is cooked with:

(Olive oil)

Add:

(Grated onion and prepared mustard)

Or spread when ¾ cooked with:

French Dressing

A very thick steak may be browned on both sides, then cooked until done, 4 inches from the heat. When done, spread with:

Butter or the pan drippings, after removing most of the fat

Add:

Chopped parsley or chives

If the drippings are meager, you may add:

(1 to 2 tablespoons butter or wine)

Serve the steak garnished with:

Sautéed Mushrooms, page 296
French Fried Onions, page 303

Or serve with:

Bordelaise Sauce, page 366
Béarnaise Sauce, page 370
Maître d'Hôtel Butter, page 384
Marchand de Vin Sauce, page 367
Garlic Butter, page 385
Colbert Butter, page 384

PAN-BROILED STEAK

Prepare for cooking:

A beefsteak

Heat a heavy frying pan over lively heat until very hot. If the meat is not prime, rub the pan very lightly with:

A bit of beef fat

Put the steak in the pan and sear for 1 minute or until the blood rises on the uncooked surface. Turn and sear the other side.

➧ Reduce the heat and continue cooking the steak until done, about 10 minutes for a 1½-inch steak. Pour off any fat in the pan for, if it is allowed to remain, the steak will be "fried" and not "broiled." Season the steak with:

Salt and freshly ground pepper

Make with the drippings:

Pan Gravy, page 358

or use:

Maître d'Hôtel Butter, page 384

For suggestions for steak sauces, see Broiled Steak, above.
Serve with:

Franconia Potatoes, page 314

PAN-BROILED FILLET STEAK

Pan-broil, as above:

Four 1-inch fillet steaks

using, to prevent sticking, a small amount of:

Butter

When the meat is done—not more than 3 minutes to a side—deglaze the pan, page 358, with:

¼ cup dry red wine
2 tablespoons beef stock

1 teaspoon Meat Glaze (II, 145)

Serve with:

Artichoke hearts, stuffed with Creamed Spinach, page 326

BROILED TOURNEDOS OR FILET MIGNON STEAK

Preheat broiler.

Upon request a butcher usually will cut fillet steaks, shape them and surround them with a strip of bacon secured by a wooden pick. Otherwise follow instructions and sketch on page 472, to find from which portion of the fillet these cuts come. The thickness of the steaks may vary from ¾ to 1 inch or more.

Prepare for cooking:

Fillet steaks: 1 to 2 inches thick

Spread with:

Butter

Broil as for:

Broiled Steak, page 474

When done, remove the bacon.

Serve on:

A fried or toasted crouton, page 390

with:

Béarnaise Sauce, page 370
Lemon and parsley
Broiled Mushrooms, page 297
Potatoes Anna, page 315, or
Duchess Potatoes, page 319

STEAK AU POIVRE OR PEPPERED STEAK

Use:

Trimmed 1-inch-thick strip sirloin, club or filet mignon steaks

Crush:

1 to 2 tablespoons peppercorns

The pepper should not be ground but crushed coarsely on a board with a pressing, rolling movement, using the bottom of a pan. Press the steaks into the crushed pepper and work it into both sides of the meat with the heel of your palm or with the flat side of a cleaver. Sprinkle the bottom of a skillet with:

2 teaspoons salt

When it begins to brown, put the steaks into the pan and brown ➧ uncovered over high heat.

➧ Reduce to medium heat, turn the steaks and cook to desired degree of rareness. In a separate pan, prepare:

¼ cup butter
1 teaspoon Worcestershire sauce
2 tablespoons lemon juice

Remove the steaks from the pan in which they have been cooked and discard the pan drippings. Pour the butter mixture over steaks. Flambé steaks, page 80, with:

(2 oz. cognac)

LONDON BROIL OR FLANK STEAK

Preheat broiler.

Place on a greased broiler rack:

A 2 to 3 lb. flank steak

Broil within 2 inches of source of heat—the hotter the better—about 5 minutes on each side ➧ making sure the meat is kept rare. If a flank steak is cooked medium or well done, it becomes extremely tough. ➧ Carve by slicing against or across the grain to make it more tender.

Serve with:

Bearnaise Sauce, page 370
Bordelaise Sauce, page 366

BOEUF FONDU BOURGUIGNONNE

This dish is cooked at table in a special deep metal pot which narrows at the top to keep the butter from sputtering. It can be cooked in an electric skillet ➧ if the butter is sweet and clarified, which keeps it from popping. We love this dish inordinately. It gives the hostess an easy time, both from the cooking angle and from the entertaining one—as the guests quickly reveal their individual characteristics. They are all there—the hoarder, the cooperator, the kibitzer, the boss. ➧ Don't try to get more than 5 or 6 guests around one heat source. Allow for each person ⅓ to ½ lb. fillet of beef. Cut into ¾-inch dice:

About 3 lbs. fillet of beef

Have ready 2 to 4 sauces:

Mustard with capers
Thickened Tomato Sauce, page 376
Mayonnaise with garlic and herbs
Marchand de Vin with Mushrooms, page 367
A curry sauce
A chutney-based sauce
A sweet-sour sauce

Melt in an electric skillet:

1 cup clarified butter

When butter is brownish, announce the rules of the game. Allow to each guest only one to two pieces of meat at a time, so as to keep the cooking heat constant. Impale the beef on long forks, worry it around in the butter until it is done to your liking. If rare is your choice, the time is very short. Arrange the sauces on your plate like oils on a palette. The plate can be a compartmented one, but this is not necessary. Dip the hot browned meat in the sauce of your choice. Serve with the beef crusty French bread or rolls and a tossed salad—with green grapes or avocado slices.

BEEF STROGANOFF [4]

This dish ✱ freezes well and is economical when made with fillet ends. See chart, page 472.

I. Cut into ½-inch slices:

1½ lbs. fillet of beef

Pound them with a mallet until thin. Cut into strips about 1 inch wide. Melt in a pan:

1 tablespoon butter

Sauté in the butter for about 2 minutes:

¾ tablespoon grated onion

Sauté the beef quickly in the butter for about 5 minutes. Turn so that it will be browned evenly. Remove and keep it hot. Add to the pan:

2 tablespoons butter

Stir and sauté in the butter:

¾ lb. sliced mushrooms

Add the beef. Season with:

Salt and pepper
A grating of nutmeg
(½ teaspoon basil)

Add and heat, but do not boil:

¼ cup white wine
1 cup warm sweet or cultured sour cream

Serve with:

Green Noodles, page 149

II. Or have ready:

1¼ lbs. hot cooked fillet

Slice as described above, but omit the first sauté and add the grated onion to the mushrooms.

▤ BEEF KEBABS OR BEEF ON SKEWERS [4]

➧ Please read About Skewer Cooking, page 75, and About Marinades, page 380.

Preheat broiler or grill.

Use:

1½ lbs. better or good grade round

Cut the marinated beef, page 380, into about 1½-inch cubes. You may alternate the cubes on skewers with:

Parboiled onion slices
Firm tomato chunks
Mushrooms
Bacon, etc.

Or put the vegetables on separate skewers to cook more slowly at the side of the grill. Roll the filled skewers in:

Melted butter

Broil or grill about 3 inches from the source of heat. Brush while cooking with the melted butter. Turn to cook evenly, about 18 minutes for rare, 25 for well done.

Correct the seasoning

and serve hot. The meat may be presented flambé by igniting a brandy-soaked bit of cotton impaled on the sharp end of the skewer.

SUKIYAKI [4]

Known in Japan as a "friendship dish," this one-plate meal, which may be cooked in the kitchen in a heavy skillet, lends itself to pleasant preparation at table in an electric skillet. The cooking proceeds as an orderly ritual which lasts about 25 minutes, while the uniformly sliced ingredients are taken from a beautifully arranged platter. Have ready on the platter:

2 lbs. thinly sliced beef: sirloin tip, eye of the round or fillet of beef

The meat can be sliced most easily if put in the freezer about 20 minutes and then cut on a #5 slicer. When ready to cook, however, it should be ➧ at room temperature—as should all the other ingredients. Have ready:

2 strips beef suet, about 1 oz. each, or 3 tablespoons cooking oil

A small dish to hold:

½ cup thinly sliced onions
½ cup ¾-inch squares bean curd: Tofu

Arrange also on the platter in uniform diagonally cut sizes, see page 250:

6 scallions with 3 inches of green left on
6 ribs celery or Chinese cabbage
2 cups thinly sliced mushrooms
1 lb. spinach, cut in 1-inch strips after stem is removed, or water cress
2 cups bean sprouts or cooked, drained Shirataki

These last are spaghetti-shaped yam shreds. We find that if a single skillet is used for cooking, it is best to cook only half the amount on the platter at one time, sharing the first batch and then cooking the "seconds" later. Put the suet in the hot skillet over medium heat and, when it reaches the point of fragrance, remove the unmelted bits and add the thin beef slices. Cook ➧ without browning, turning frequently for about 3 minutes, then push the meat to one side of the skillet and sauté the vegetables. Add them in sequence, beginning with those that need longer cooking. First sauté the onions until almost golden, then as you incorporate the other vegetables, pour in a little at a time a mixture of:

½ cup soy sauce
½ cup stock

This procedure gives a quickly rising steam, but not enough moisture to waterlog the vegetables. Sprinkle over the vegetables while stirring them:

1 teaspoon sugar
½ teaspoon monosodium glutamate

From the sautéing of the onions through the rest of the vegetables cooking, count about 7 minutes. Then push the meat into the center of the skillet and combine with the sprouts or Shirataki, continuing to heat and stir for about 4 minutes more. The vegetables should retain their crispness and good color.

Correct the seasoning

Serve this mixture at once over:

Boiled Rice, page 158

As an authentic detail, you may have at room temperature a raw egg in a small dish into which bits of the Sukiyaki can be dipped before eating.

ABOUT VEAL

In America veal is a very misunderstood meat—and the milk-fed variety is hard to come by. Veal should be tender, succulent and white. If it is not, there are two ways to improve it. One is to blanch briefly, starting in cold water. The other is to soak refrigerated in milk overnight before using. Veal needs a careful cooking approach, as it is lacking in fat and may toughen quickly. Although abroad certain dishes—like Veal à la Meunière or à la Crème—are served both rosy and juicy, veal here is generally served after reaching an internal temperature of 175°. It is roasted 25 to 30 minutes per lb. until well done. Although a leg of veal may be roasted, most large pieces of veal are pot-roasted. The long round muscle of the leg, when cut across the grain, produces **scallops.**

VEAL ROAST STUFFED OR FARCI

The meat may be rubbed first with garlic or gashes may be cut in a shoulder roast, in which fine slivers of garlic, marjoram, peppercorns, anchovies or anchovy paste may be inserted.

Preheat oven to 450°.

Have a pocket cut in:

A breast or shoulder of veal

Remove the meat from the refrigerator at least ½ hour before preparing. Rub with:

Garlic

Dust the pocket lightly with:

Ginger

before filling with:

3 cups Dry Dressing, page 561, Bread Dressing, page 560, with 2 slices chopped salt pork added, Oyster Dressing, page 561, or Green Rice, page 159, the cheese omitted

Sew the pocket up with a coarse needle and thread. If the meat is not fat, rub with:

Butter

Dredge with:

Seasoned flour

Place in the oven in a greased roasting pan and ➧ reduce the heat to 300°. Bake ➧ uncovered about 20 to 30 minutes to the pound until done. You may place on the roast several strips of:

(Bacon)

Make:

Pan gravy, page 358

When the gravy is done, you may remove it from the heat and add:

(¼ cup cultured sour cream)
(1 or 2 tablespoons dry white wine)

Heat the gravy but ⚡ do not let it boil. To carve a stuffed veal shoulder, see illustration. For ways to utilize roasted meat, see Luncheon Dishes, page 208.

VEAL ROAST, KIDNEY, LOIN, ETC., OR ROLLED ROAST

Follow the preceding recipe for preparing and cooking breast or shoulder—but allow 35 to 40 minutes to the pound for rolled

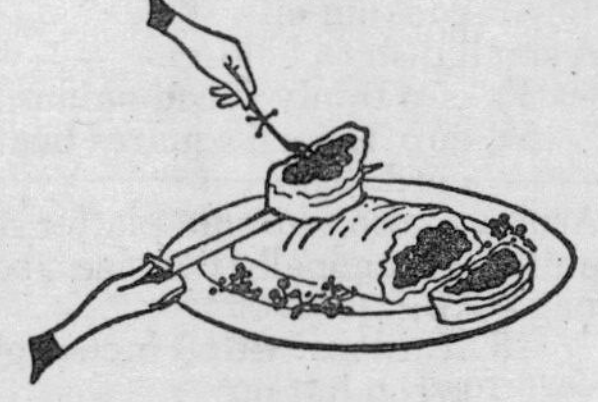

roast. Turn every ½ hour. You may add parboiled vegetables—potatoes, carrots, etc.—for the last ½ hour or so of cooking. If there are insufficient drippings, add a little fat to the pan. This roast is good served with:

Dumplings, page 178
Spatzen, page 179, and
Pickled Prunes (II, 108)

ABOUT VEAL CUTLETS

From these thin flattened pieces of meat come collops, scallops, scallopini and Schnitzels—all of which may be cooked with or without breading.

So-called "natural" cutlets, unflavored or very lightly so, are one of the easiest, quickest and most delightful of all.

For any of these dishes a white veal is best, sometimes hard to obtain. You may soak the veal in milk overnight, as suggested previously, or in lemon juice for 1 hour. Dry well before flouring or breading.

All these cutlets should be cut as thin as possible and may be pounded. The pounding gives a very different texture. Watch your thumb during this process. ➧ To pound, see illustration, page 452.

In the following recipes use about 1½ lbs. of veal that has been carefully trimmed and from which the bone has been removed. There is often a thin membrane that holds the meat taut as it cooks. Be sure it is slashed in a number of places before cooking. This should serve 3 to 4 persons. If you are serving more and have to repeat your sautéing, keep the already finished cutlets ➧ uncovered in a 250° oven until all the rest are ready.

VEAL CUTLET OR SCALLOPINI

Please read About Veal Cutlets, above. Dredge lightly with flour on one side only:

Thin pounded veal scallops

Sauté them, floured-side first in:

¼ cup butter

heated until fragrant. In about 3 minutes, when the juices begin to emerge on the upper side, turn the meat and continue to sauté for about 3 minutes more. Shake the skillet vigorously from time to time, until the meat is done. Veal is never served rare. Remove from the skillet and keep warm.

Deglaze the pan juices with:

½ cup veal or chicken stock or ¼ cup stock and ¼ cup Marsala or Madeira
Correct the seasoning

You may swirl in, at the end:

(1 tablespoon butter)

If you do not use the wine, you may add:

(1 tablespoon lemon juice)

Pour the sauce over the cutlets and serve at once.

VEAL SCALLOPINI WITH TOMATOES [3 to 4]

Preheat oven to 325°.

Cut into 1-inch squares:

1½ lbs. veal cut thin, trimmed, boned and pounded

Dredge with:

Flour

Brown in a mixture of:

1 tablespoon butter
1 tablespoon olive oil

Add:

½ lb. thinly sliced mushrooms
½ to 1 clove pressed garlic
2 tablespoons chopped parsley
2 tablespoons chopped fresh basil
½ cup peeled, seeded, diced, fresh tomatoes
½ cup Marsala
2 tablespoons Parmesan cheese

Cover and cook in a 325° oven for about 45 minutes.

VEAL PAPILLOTE

Veal lends itself very well to this method of cooking. See Papillote, page 87. Trim veal for cutlet. To season and cook, see Chicken Suprême Papillote, page 583.

VEAL PARMIGIANA

Slice a ¼-inch-thick:

Veal cutlet

into 2 x 2-inch slices. Pound thin until they reach about 3 x 3 inches. Dip into a:

Bound Breading (II, 160)

using equal parts bread crumbs and Parmesan cheese. Sauté the pieces until crisp in:

Clarified Butter, page 383

about 2 minutes on each side. Serve with:

Tomato Sauce, page 376

VEAL SCALLOP OR ESCALOPE DE VEAU ORLOFF

A good party dish, as it can be partially prepared in advance. Preheat oven to 350°.

Slice:

A ¼-inch-thick veal cutlet

into 2 x 2-inch slices. Pound them until they reach about 3 x 3 inches. Sauté until barely frizzled on both sides in:

Clarified Butter, page 383

Remove from pan and drain on absorbent paper. To make a **Soubise,** mix and grind in a food chopper:

½ cup cooked rice
½ cup white onions
½ cup mushrooms

Season with:

Salt and pepper

Cover each scallop of veal with:

1 tablespoon liver paste

Then press on firmly over each scallop the soubise mixture. Sprinkle over each:

1 teaspoon brandy or sherry

Dust generously with:

Grated Parmesan cheese

Place the scallop in an ovenproof serving platter and bake for about 15 minutes until the cheese is golden.

PAPRIKA SCHNITZEL OR CUTLET

➧ Please read About Veal Cutlets, page 479. Trim the edges and remove the bone from:

A ¼- to ½-inch-thick slice of veal from the round

Dredge one side only in:

Seasoned flour

Heat in a skillet:

¼ cup butter or bacon drippings

Sauté lightly in the fat:

(½ cup or more sliced onions)

Sauté the meat, first on the seasoned side, in the hot fat, until lightly browned. Turn, then add until the fat becomes red:

Paprika

Remove the pan from the heat and add:

1 cup boiling vegetable or chicken stock

Cover the skillet and cook the veal ➧ over very low heat until it is almost tender, about 15 minutes. Add:

½ cup cultured sour cream
Correct the seasoning

Serve garnished with:

Parsley, capers, sardelles
Applesauce (II, 95)
Creamed Spinach, page 326

WIENER SCHNITZEL OR BREADED VEAL CUTLET [3 to 4]

Viennese friends insist that the true Wiener Schnitzel is deep-fat fried—other authorities insist it is sautéed. But most typical Viennese recipes put up to ¾ cup of butter in the sauté pan which virtually gives a deep fat, rather than a sautéed result anyway, see page 79. Although there are many variations, we suggest the following. ➧ Please read About Veal Cutlets, page 479. Just before cooking, bread (II, 160):

1½ lbs. veal cutlet

Sauté over low heat for 2 minutes on one side in:

½ to ¾ cup butter

Turn and cook 2 minutes on the other side. Turn again and cook until done—about 10 to 15 minutes in all. Garnish with:

Lemon slices and rolled anchovies

If you also cap the garnished cutlet above with a fried egg, you may call it **Holstein.**

VEAL SCALLOPS WITH HAM [4]

This recipe is also good using pounded chicken breasts.
Pound:

2 veal cutlets

and slice into about 12 three-inch squares. Sauté the pieces until barely frizzled on both sides in:

Clarified Butter, page 383

Remove from pan and drain on absorbent paper. Cut into 6 thin slices:

Prosciutto or smoked ham

Place the ham on 6 slices of veal. Top with a similar sized slice of:

Swiss cheese

Cover each piece with the remaining veal slices. Gently pat in:

Bound Breading (II, 160)

Sauté in:

Clarified Butter, page 383

until golden on each side, about 3 minutes. Or you may bake the meat on an ovenproof platter in a 350° oven about 15 minutes.

ABOUT LAMB AND MUTTON

Since lamb is shipped from different climates it is no longer referred to as spring lamb. When it is from 3 to 5 months old, lamb is now called baby or milk-finished lamb. From 5 months to a year and a half, it is simply called lamb, and from there on out—mutton. Mutton may be substituted for lamb, but the cooking time is usually increased from 5 to 10 minutes to the pound. Both lamb and mutton are covered with a whitish brittle fat, called the fell, which is usually removed before cooking, as it tends to make the flavor of the meat strong. Almost any cut of lamb may be cooked by the dry heat methods which follow. For ground lamb recipes, see page 514. For moist heat methods, see Braises and Pot Roasts, page 493, and for cooked meat recipes, see Luncheon Dishes, page 208.

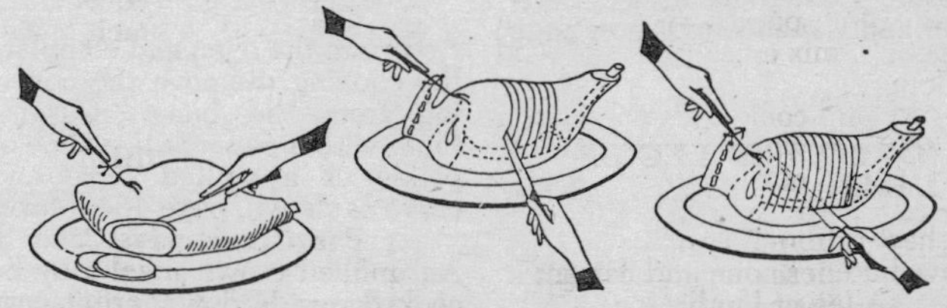

LAMB OR MUTTON ROAST

[About 8 Servings]
➧ Please see Economical Use of Large Cuts, page 461.
Preheat oven to 450°.
Remove from the refrigerator at least ½ hour before cooking:

A 5-lb. leg of lamb or mutton

Remove the fell or papery outer covering. Rub the meat with:

(Cut garlic or lemon and rosemary)

Insert under the skin, using a pointed knife:

(Slivers of garlic or herbs)

Place the meat fat side up on a rack in an uncovered pan. Immediately after putting it in the oven ➧ reduce the heat to 350°. Roast it 30 minutes to the pound if you want it well done or until the internal temperature is 175° to 180°. Most Europeans like lamb slightly rare or at an internal temperature of 160° to 165°. ➧ Do not cover or baste. Make:

Pan Gravy, page 358, using cultured sour cream or milk

Or serve the roast with:

Deglazed drippings, page 358

and:

Mint Sauce, page 371

If the mint sauce is not desired, see:

Cumberland Sauce, page 343

To carve a lamb roast, see the illustration, page 481, or carve it parallel to the bone. For ways of reusing roasted meat, see Leftover and Luncheon Dishes, page 208.

⊟ BARBECUED LEG OF LAMB

Preheat grill.
Have butcher bone and flatten:

A leg of lamb

At least 2 hours before cooking, cover the leg with:

Fresh mint

Rub with:

Dry mustard
Pepper
Onion juice

While the charcoal is burning down to embers, cook gently for about 5 minutes a sauce of:

¼ cup butter
½ clove garlic
1 tablespoon grated onion

Take out the garlic and add:

½ cup chopped fresh mint leaves
¼ cup butter

Put the lamb on the grill and brush often with the warm sauce. After about 20 minutes, salt and pepper and turn the meat. If you like lamb pink, it should be "à point" in 35 to 45 minutes, depending on the heat of the coals. Well-done lamb will take 15 minutes longer.

CROWN ROAST OF LAMB

[Allow 2 Ribs per Person]
Preheat oven to 450°.
Wipe with a cloth:

A crown roast of lamb

Protect the ends of the bones by covering with aluminum foil. Immediately after putting the meat in the oven ➧ reduce the heat to 350°. Process as directed for Lamb Roast, above, but remove the roast before the last hour of cooking. Fill the center with:

3 cups Bread Dressing, page 560, or Dressing for Cornish Hen, page 564

Return to the oven and complete the cooking. Remove the covering from the bones. Garnish them with a paper frill, a slice of pickle or a stuffed olive and carve as shown, page 484. Make:

Pan Gravy, page 358

An unfilled crown roast may be cooked upside down. Omit covering the bones. When done, fill the hollow of the roast with:

Green Peas, page 305

or with:

Baked Chestnuts, page 284

Garnish with:

Parsley

Serve with the gravy and:

Mint Sauce, page 371, or currant jelly

LAMB SHOULDER ROAST

[About 8 Servings]

Preheat oven to 450°.

Prepare or have prepared with one side left open for inserting dressing:

A 4- to 5-lb. cushion shoulder of lamb

Rub the meat with:

A cut clove of garlic

Fill the cavity with:

Bread or other dressing, page 560

Sew or skewer up the open side. Place the roast uncovered on a rack in a pan in the oven. ➧ Reduce the heat immediately to 350° until done, about 30 minutes to the pound. Serve with:

Pan Gravy, page 358

⊟ BROILED LAMB KEBABS [4]

Take:

1 lb. lamb shoulder

Cut the meat into 2-inch squares. Marinate if you like for 3 hours in Marinade I, page 380, turning several times.

Preheat broiler.

Place the meat on skewers, alternately with:

Pineapple slices
Blanched Bermuda onion slices
Tomatoes
Stuffed olives

Place 4 inches from the heat source and broil. Turn frequently. Baste while cooking with:

Butter or olive oil

and cook about 15 minutes or until done. Serve on a shallow bed of:

Cooked Green Rice, page 159

LAMB CHOPS

[2 Chops per Person]

➧ Trim the outer skin, which is strong in flavor, from:

Lamb chops

I. Pan-boiled

Sear the chops in a hot dry skillet. ➧ Reduce the heat and cook slowly until done. Allow for well-done 2-inch chops about 20 minutes, for 1½-inch chops about 16 minutes. Pour off the fat as it accumulates in the pan. Season the chops with:

Salt and freshly ground pepper

Serve very hot. Garnish with:

Parsley

II. Broiled

Follow directions for:

Broiled Steak, page 474

allowing a shorter time for cooking, according to the thickness of the chops.

STUFFED LAMB CHOPS [6]

I.

Preheat broiler.

To prepare for stuffing, see:

Braised Stuffed Pork Chops Cockaigne, page 512

Substitute:

6 double lamb chops

The chops may be wrapped before cooking with:

Strips of bacon

Use toothpicks to hold it in place.

II. Or cut out the bone from:

Lamb chops

Wrap the tail around:

1-inch balls of sausage meat

Secure them with a toothpick. Broil or pan-broil the chops.

GARNISHED ENGLISH MIXED GRILL [1 to 2]

While this is the classic serving for one, it does very well for 2 in our family.
Preheat broiler.
Grease the broiling rack. Arrange on it:

- **2 single lamb chops**
- **2 small link sausages**
- **2 chicken livers**
- **½ blanched veal kidney**
- **1 slice of bacon**
- **½ small tomato seasoned with salt, pepper and butter**
- **½ cup mushroom caps dipped in butter**
- **3 to 4 small whole blanched onions**

Place the broiler rack about 3 inches from the source of heat. During the cooking process, turn the meats and mushrooms. Baste if necessary with clarified butter. The cooking time is dependent on the thickness of the chops and the degree of doneness desired. Arrange ingredients on hot plates or a platter and serve with:

Sauce Béarnaise, page 370

ABOUT PORK

Someone has observed that a pig resembles a saint in that he is more honored after death than during his lifetime. Speaking further of his social standing, we have noticed that, when smoked, he is allowed to appear at quite fashionable functions; but that only one's best friends will confess to anything more than a bowing acquaintance with pork and sauerkraut or pickled pigs' feet.

High-grade pork is fine-grained and firm—the shoulder cuts finely marbled, the fat white. Because of the heavy fat content, all parts of pork can be roasted. Because of the pervasive fat, too, the meat is virtually self-basting. ➧ Pork demands thorough cooking. Otherwise the very harmful trichinae or parasites which often exist in it may be transmitted to the eater. Rules of thumb for judging doneness are to cook the meat until the juices run clear when the flesh is pricked and to make sure, when cut into, that the meat is white or greyish ➧ never pink. Slow cooking is desirable, allowing 30 to 45 minutes to the pound, 5 to 10 minutes longer per pound for rolled or stuffed roasts. Internal temperature should register 185°. The choice roasts are rib, loin and shoulder. The lower half of the foreleg—also called picnic—may be boned, rolled or flattened or rolled and stuffed. Fresh hams or legs of pork are good either roasted or braised. For details about cuts, consult the charts and compare them with the recipes listed. Also read Economical Use of Large Cuts, page 461.

For uses of cooked pork, see Luncheon Dishes, page 208.

ROAST OF PORK

Preheat oven to 450°.
Use for a fine, juicy roast:

A rib end of loin

Or roll or stuff a shoulder or loin, which will need about 10 minutes more cooking to the lb. than recommended here, even when the meat is at 70° before cooking. Rub the roast well with:

A cut clove of garlic, fresh sage, dried rosemary, tarragon or thyme

Dredge with:

Seasoned Flour (II, 160)

Place fat side up on a rack in a pan in the oven. ➧ Reduce the heat at once to 350°. Cook ➧ uncovered 30 to 35 minutes to the pound. The internal temperature should be 185°. Make:

Pan Gravy, page 358

You may roast alongside the meat for the last 35 minutes of cooking:

Peeled and parboiled sweet potatoes or parsnips

or on top of the roast:

Prunes and apricots

or serve the roast with:

Applesauce (II, 95), seasoned with 2 tablespoons horseradish and a grating of nutmeg
Sweet Potatoes and Apples, page 324
Apples with Sauerkraut (II, 95), or other sauerkraut variations
Apple and Onion Dish, page 304
Turnips and Apples, page 338
Puree of Lentils or Peas, page 306

➧ Please read about the Economical Use of Large Cuts, page 461; and for other ways of using leftover roasted meats, see Luncheon Dishes, page 208.

CROWN ROAST OF PORK

[Allow 2 Ribs per Person]
Preheat oven to 450°.
Wipe with a cloth:

A crown roast of pork

Protect the ends of the bones by covering with aluminum foil. Immediately after putting the roast in the oven ➧ reduce the heat to 350°, allowing 30 to 45 minutes to the pound. If the crown is not to be filled with dressing, omit covering the bones and cook the roast upside down. Serve filled with a cooked vegetable; or, if the roast is to be stuffed, remove it 1 hour before it is done and fill the center with:

Sausage Dressing, page 562
Apple and Onion Dressing, page 563
or fruit dressing

Return the roast to the oven and complete the cooking. Make

Pan Gravy, page 358

To garnish and to carve, see illustration, page 484. Serve with:

Glazed Onions, page 302
Cinnamon Apples (II, 94)
Water cress, or broiled canned apricots and crystallized ginger slices

ROAST SUCKLING PIG

We never think of suckling pig without thinking of our friend Amy, an American, long a resident of Mexico but determined to reconstruct in alien surroundings the traditional Christmas dinners of her youth. Describing the preparation of roast pig to her skilled Indian cook, she wound up with the announcement, "The pig is brought to table on plenty of greenery, with an apple in the mouth." The cook looked first baffled, then resentful and finally burst out with a succession of "no's." Her employer persisted patiently, but with increasing firmness. When the pig was served, she discovered that her cook could effect an entrée which surpassed her wildest expectations. There was plenty of greenery and a distinct air of martyrdom; but the apple was clenched, not in the pig's mouth, but in that of the desperate cook!

[10]

Preheat oven to 450°.

Dress, by drawing, scraping and cleaning:

A suckling pig

Remove eyeballs and lower the lids. The dressed pig should weigh about 12 pounds. Fill it with:

Onion Dressing, page 562, or
Forcemeat, page 564

It takes 2½ quarts of dressing to stuff a pig of this size. Multiply all your ingredients, but not the seasonings. Use these sparingly until the dressing is combined, then taste it and add what is lacking. Sew up the pig. Put a block of wood in its mouth to hold it open. Skewer the legs into position, pulling the forelegs forward and bending the hindlegs into a crouching stance. Rub the pig with:

Oil or soft butter
(A cut clove of garlic)

Dredge it with:

Flour

Cover the ears and the tail with aluminum foil. Place the pig in a pan ➧ uncovered, in the oven for 15 minutes. ➧ Reduce the heat to 325° and roast until tender, allowing 30 minutes to the pound. Baste every 15 minutes with:

About 2 cups boiling stock and the pan drippings

Remove the foil from ears and tail before serving. Place the pig on a platter. Remove the wood from the mouth. Replace it with a small:

Apple, lemon or carrot

Place in the eyes:

Raisins or cranberries

Drape around the neck a wreath of:

Small green leaves

or garnish the platter or board with:

Water cress

The pig may be surrounded with:

Cinnamon Apples (II, 94), Apples Stuffed with Sweet Potatoes, page 324, Apples Stuffed with Mincemeat (II, 315), Tomatoes Florentine, page 336, etc.

Make:

Pan Gravy, page 358

To carve, place head to left of carver. Remove forelegs and hams. Divide meat down center of back. Separate the ribs. Serve a section of crackling skin to each person.

FRESH HAM

I. You may place a fresh leg of pork called:

A fresh ham

in a marinade, page 380, and refrigerate covered for 24 to 48 hours.

Preheat oven to 450°.

Remove the ham from the marinade. Wipe dry. Cook as for:

Pork Roast, page 485

basting every ½ hour with part of the marinade or with the traditional:

(Beer)

Make:

Pan Gravy, page 358

Serve with any of the accompaniments suggested in Pork Roast.

II. Or cook a:

Boned fresh ham

as for:

Veal Pot Roast, page 505

PORK ROAST STUFFED WITH SAUERKRAUT

Preheat oven to 350°.
Have the butcher remove the bones from:

A pork shoulder

Fill it with:

Drained sauerkraut

Dredge with:

Flour

Prepare and cook as for:

Roast Shoulder of Lamb, page 483

PORK TENDERLOIN

Preheat oven to 350°.
Split lengthwise:

A pork tenderloin

Flatten it out. Rub lightly with:

Butter
(Garlic)

Spread with:

Bread Dressing, page 560, using 1/4 the amount given or with Apple and Sweet Potato Dressing, page 565, using about 1/3 the amount given, or with stewed, drained, pitted prunes

Sew or tie it up. Dredge with:

Seasoned flour

or brush with an unsalted fat. Place the tenderloin on a rack. Bake 30 to 45 minutes to the pound. Make:

Pan Gravy, page 358

You may add to the gravy:

(Cultured sour cream and cooked mushrooms or sweet cream and currant jelly)

FRENCHED PORK TENDERLOIN

Cut crosswise into 3/4-inch slices:

Pork tenderloin

Flatten the slices slightly with a cleaver, as shown on page 452. Dredge with:

(Flour)

Sauté as for:

Pork Chops, below

Add to the pan juices or the gravy you serve with the meat:

1/2 teaspoon grated lemon rind

PORK CHOPS

I. Sear in a hot pan:

Pork chops

in just enough cooking oil or rendered pork fat to keep them from sticking. Before searing, they may be rubbed with:

(Garlic or powdered rosemary)

After searing ➧ reduce the heat. Cook the chops slowly, covered or uncovered, until done. Pour off the excess grease as they cook. Season with:

Salt and pepper

Make:

Pan Gravy, page 358

II. Preheat oven to 350°.
A good way to do thick chops. After searing them as above, bake covered for about 1 hour:

4 pork chops

During the last half hour, you may add for seasoning:

3 tablespoons minced green pepper and celery
1 clove garlic
1 piece ginger root mashed in 1 tablespoon vinegar
3 slices orange
1/2 cup orange juice

PORK TENDERLOIN FRUIT CASSEROLE [6]

➧ Please read About Deep-Fat Frying, pages 75–79.
Preheat deep fryer to 375°.
Cut into 1/2-inch cubes:

1 lb. pork tenderloin

Dip the pieces into:

2 beaten eggs

then roll in:

2 tablespoons cornstarch

Deep fry for about 10 minutes. Drain. In a large, deep skillet, melt:

2 tablespoons cooking oil

Add the pork and:

2 tablespoons wine vinegar
2 tablespoons sugar
1 cup chicken stock
1 tablespoon catsup
1 cup canned pineapple pieces
1 chopped green pepper
½ cup thinly sliced carrots
1 teaspoon salt
A grating of fresh black pepper

Mix and cook over high heat for about 5 minutes, stirring constantly. Serve at once.

BREADED PORK CHOPS [4]

Rub with garlic:

4 half-inch-thick pork chops

Bread them (II, 160). Brown lightly, using a heavy hot pan, in:

2 to 3 tablespoons rendered pork fat or cooking oil

Reduce the heat. Cook uncovered for about 20 minutes longer or until done.

Make:

Pan Gravy, page 358

SWEET AND SOUR PORK [6]

➧ Please read About Deep-Fat Frying, pages 75–79.

Preheat deep fryer to 375°.

Cut into ½-inch squares:

2 lbs. boned pork loin

Toss with:

3 teaspoons soy sauce
3 tablespoons flour

Fry in deep fat until the squares come to the surface and float. When crisp and golden brown, drain on absorbent paper. Have ready and ➧ simmering the following sauce. Mix:

2 tablespoons water
1½ teaspoons cornstarch

Heat:

2 tablespoons lard

Sauté until golden:

1 very small chopped onion

Add:

6 tablespoons sugar
½ cup water
¼ finely chopped garlic clove
1 tablespoon soy sauce
¼ cup vinegar
½ cup chopped sweet and sour pickle
(6 pieces of red haw)

and the cornstarch mixture. Cook and stir for 1 minute. Add the meat and heat. Serve with:

Rice, page 158

ABOUT SALTED MEATS

Because of the prevalence of refrigeration, Ham (II, 543), Tongue, page 544, Corned Beef, page 492, and Salt Pork (II, 545), today are subjected to much weaker brining than formerly. Therefore a preliminary soaking or blanching in the kitchen, see Blanching II, page 88, can often be skipped. ➧ But all of these salted meats, of course, like brined vegetables, still are less valuable nutritionally than fresh meats. They are particularly enjoyed because of their "cured" flavors. If the meats were ➧ given heavy brines or aged like "old" hams, page 490, be sure to soak 12 hours—allowing 1 quart of water to 1 lb. of ham. Or ➧ parblanch them before cooking. After blanching, put the meat into rapidly boiling water, bring to a boil again and ➧ at once reduce the heat to a simmer. Salted meats are always cooked à blanc, see (II, 147). Cook ➧ uncovered until tender. Time indications are given in the recipes.

UNPROCESSED BAKED HAM

➧ Please read About Ham (II, 543).

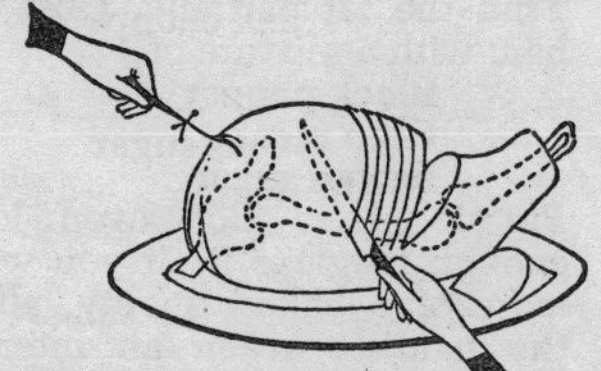

If it has not been processed, scrub well:

A smoked ham

Place it in a kettle of ▶ simmering:

Water, cider, beer or ginger ale

Add:

Vegetables suitable for soup
1 bay leaf
8 peppercorns
(6 allspice)

Simmer 20 to 30 minutes per lb. Allow a longer time per lb. for a small ham than for a large one. The thermometer will register 165° when the meat is done. This takes care of the actual cooking, but to make it look attractive at table proceed as follows.

Let it partially cool in the liquid in which it was cooked. Drain. Strip off skin.

Preheat oven to 425°.

Cover the top of the ham with:

Brown sugar
(A little dry mustard)

Stud with:

Whole cloves

Place in the oven and ▶ lower heat at once to 325° for about 20 minutes. Baste with a choice of:

1 cup cider, pineapple or orange juice, the juice of pickled peaches, cooked prunes or apricots, wine, ginger ale, molasses or beer

Cook for 30 minutes longer, without basting, after dredging with:

Brown sugar

sprinkling with:

Grated orange rind

and garnishing the top with:

Pineapple slices
Maraschino cherries

Serve with:

Raisin Cider Sauce, page 373, Sour Cream and Horseradish Sauce, page 362, Barbecue Sauce, page 374, Hot Cumberland Sauce, page 331, or horseradish

And:

Scalloped Potatoes, page 312, or a barquette of Puréed Chestnuts, page 283

To carve see sketch above.

PROCESSED BAKED HAM

▶ Please read About Ham (II, 543).

Preheat oven to 325°.

Unwrap and wipe with a damp cloth:

A processed ham

Bake on a rack, uncovered. Allow 30 minutes to the pound for ½ a ham, 25 minutes for a whole ham. The meat is done when the thermometer registers 160°. Take the ham from the oven about 1 hour before it is done. Remove the rind, all but a collar around the shank bone. Cut diagonal gashes across the fat side of the ham, in diamond shapes. Combine and glaze the top fat side of the ham with:

1⅓ cups brown sugar
2 teaspoons dry mustard

⅓ cup fine bread crumbs

Moisten these ingredients with:

3 tablespoons cider vinegar, prune juice, wine or ham drippings

Stud the fat at the intersections or center of each diamond with:

Whole cloves

Return the ham to the oven for about 45 minutes. ➧ Increase the heat to 425°. Bake 15 minutes longer. Place on a platter. Garnish with:

Cranberries and Orange Slices (II, 102), or Pineapple slices

heated in the pan for the last 15 minutes. Or with already cooked:

Apple Cups filled with sweet potatoes (II, 95)

The ham may be served with:

Marchand de Vin Sauce, page 367

or some other sauce for ham.

COUNTRY HAMS: VIRGINIA, SMITHFIELD, KENTUCKY, ETC.

It is the custom in some parts of the U.S. to hang hams, after special processing, for several years, after which time, of course, they develop a heavy exterior mold. ➧ To prepare one of these old hams, soak it in cold water to cover for 24 to 36 hours. Then scrub it well, using a brush and yellow soap, if necessary, to remove the mold. Rinse thoroughly and place in a kettle of simmering water, skin side down. Allow 20 minutes to the pound until the meat reaches an internal heat of 150°. Add to the water before last ¼ of cooking time:

1 quart cider

¼ cup brown sugar

Drain when the cooking time has elapsed. Remove the skin while the ham is still warm, being careful not to tear the fat. Trim the fat partially. Dust the ham with a mixture of:

Black pepper

Corn meal

Brown sugar

Put it in a 425° oven long enough to glaze it. If you want more of a baked quality, allow the ham to reach an internal heat of 160° to 165°. Serve hot or cold. Be sure to slice very, very thin.

CASSEROLED HAM SLICES [2 to 3]

Good dishes variously flavored are easily made from raw ham slices.

Preheat oven to 350°.

Place in a casserole:

A slice of smoked ham, about 1 inch thick

Pour over the ham:

Barbecue Sauce I or II, page 374 or Hot Cumberland Sauce, page 372

Bake ➧ covered, until tender, about 1 hour.

HAM BAKED WITH FRUIT [2 to 3]

Preheat oven to 325°.

Ham lends itself to combination with fruit—almost better than any other meat. You may arrange the fruit either between layers and on top of several ham slices or just on top of a single slice. If the ham is not fat, grease the bottom of a casserole lightly. Place in it:

A slice of ham, about 1 inch thick

Cover the ham with fruit seasoned to taste.

Sliced apples, oranges or cranberries

Sprinkled with:

Brown sugar or honey

Or cover with drained:

Slices of canned pineapple, apricots, peaches, red plums,

prunes, cherries or raisins

These may be sprinkled with:

Cinnamon, cloves or curry powder

➧ Cover the casserole with a lid. Baste several times with the pot juices or additional:

Fruit juice, sherry or cider

Bake about 45 minutes or until done. Uncover for the last 10 minutes of cooking.

HAM BAKED WITH TOMATOES AND CHEESE [2 to 3]

Preheat oven to 350°.

Place in a baking dish:

A slice of smoked ham, about 1 inch thick

Pour over it:

1 cup seeded, chopped, canned tomatoes

➧ Cover the dish. Bake the ham until tender, about ¾ hour. Uncover for the last 15 minutes of cooking. When you uncover, sprinkle over the ham:

¼ cup grated Parmesan cheese

BROILED HAM

[Allow ⅓ lb. per person]

Preheat broiler.

Slash in several places the fat edge of:

A piece of smoked ham, about 1 inch thick

Place it on a broiler rack, 3 inches below the heating unit. Broil 10 to 12 minutes to a side. A processed ham slice will require from 8 to 10 minutes to a side. You may brush the ham after cooking it on one side and turning it for final broiling with a mixture of:

1 teaspoon mustard
1 tablespoon lemon juice
¼ cup grape jelly

If you do not use the glaze, a traditional accompaniment is:

Corn Fritters, page 286
Tomato Slices, page 333

SAUTÉED HAM AND EGGS

Trim the edges of:

A thin slice of smoked ham

Rub a skillet with ham fat. Heat it. Brown the ham on one side, reverse it and brown on the other. Remove to a hot platter. Keep hot. Reduce the heat. Sauté gently in the tried-out ham fat:

Eggs, page 183

HAM BUTT, SHANK OR PICNIC HAM

Use these comparatively small cuts of ham as for:

New England Boiled Dinner, page 493

Cook the ham until nearly tender or until the internal temperature is 170°. Add the vegetables the last ½ hour of cooking.

SMOKED SHOULDER BUTT OR COTTAGE ROLL

This cut may be boned. You may cut slices from this piece for broiling or sautéing or you may roast or "boil" it.

ABOUT BACON

Crisp, thin, properly cured breakfast bacon is attainable, but sometimes the search is long. Bacon should have a good proportion of lean meat and not taste too salty. It cannot take much heat. Broil it or start it in a cold pan to keep it from curling. We have found this a better method than the use of pressure or of specialized gadgets. In pan-broiling, keep pouring off accumulated grease and watch carefully. Bacon burns in seconds and old bacon burns twice as fast as fresh.

Canadian bacon is from the eye of a pork loin, which accounts for its leanness and high cost. It should be treated more like ham. In England a side of salted smoked or dried bacon is called a gammon and a slice or portion is a rasher.

➧ Allow about 2 slices per person.

BROILED BACON

Preheat broiler.
Place on a fine wire broiler or rack in a dripping pan:

Strips of bacon

Keep the bacon about 5 inches from source of heat and broil until crisp. Drain on absorbent paper.

SAUTÉED BACON

➧ Please read About Bacon, page 491.
Place in a cold skillet:

Strips of bacon

Sauté slowly until done. You may pour off the drippings while cooking. Turn frequently. Place it between paper towels to drain.

CANADIAN BACON

If you are a twosome with a craving for ham but don't want leftovers, try this smoked substitute.

I. Place in boiling water to cover:

1 lb. or more Canadian bacon

➧ Simmer until tender, about 1 hour.

II. [8]

Preheat oven to 325°.
Combine and have ready:

½ cup brown sugar
½ teaspoon dry mustard
2 tablespoons fine bread crumbs
1 tablespoon cider vinegar

Bake uncovered for 1 hour. Baste every 15 minutes for 45 minutes with:

½ cup pineapple or other acid fruit juice, dry sherry, cider, ginger ale or a cola drink

Then spread the brown sugar mixture over it. Bake for about 15 minutes more or until the sugar has glazed.

III. Place in a heavy skillet:

⅛-to-¼-inch slices Canadian bacon

Cook them over low heat for 3 to 5 minutes. Turn frequently. When done, the lean part is a red brown and the fat a light golden brown. Serve with:

Hot Cumberland Sauce, page 372
Raisin Cider Sauce, page 373

ABOUT CORNED BEEF

At this printing, for want of a better substance the government still allows the use of sodium nitrate or saltpeter in commercial meat packing to prevent botulism. Packers also like the color it gives their meats.
To corn, combine:

4 quarts hot water
2 cups coarse salt
¼ cup sugar
2 tablespoons mixed whole spice
(1½ teaspoons saltpeter, for color)

When cool, pour over:

A 5 lb. piece of beef: brisket or tongue

which has been placed in a large enameled pot or stone jar. Add:

3 cloves garlic

Weight the meat to keep it submerged and cover the jar. Cure in the refrigerator for 3 weeks, turning the meat every 5 days.

➧ To cook corned beef, wash under running water to remove surface brine. Cover with boiling water and simmer 4 hours until a fork can penetrate to the center.
Serve hot with:

Horseradish Sauce, page 362

Boiled Potatoes, page 310
Gnocchi with Farina, page 157

Serve cold with:

Horseradish

➧ To press for slicing cold, when cool force into a deep pan. Cover and refrigerate weighted. The moisture pressed from the meat should form a jellied coating.

CORNED BEEF AND CABBAGE OR NEW ENGLAND BOILED DINNER

I. **[10 to 12]**

This is a delicious dinner using only corned beef, onions and cabbage, but it is customary to cook and serve separately:

10 to 12 beets

Skin and serve them with the rest of the dinner, garnished with:

Parsley

Prepare and cook:

Corned Beef, above

You may add about:

½ lb. salt pork

for the last 2 hours. Remove the meat from the pot. Peel, quarter and simmer in the stock for 30 minutes:

3 small parsnips
6 large carrots
3 large yellow turnips

Skin and add:

8 small onions

Peel, quarter and simmer in the stock for 15 minutes longer:

6 medium-sized potatoes

Cut into wedges, add and simmer until tender, for about 10 to 15 minutes:

A head of cabbage

Reheat the meat in the stock. Serve it on a platter, surrounded by the vegetables.

II. If using a ⊗ pressure cooker, use the ingredients above but cook for 10 minutes before adding the salt pork. Reduce heat. Add the salt pork. Bring up to pressure and cook 10 minutes more. Reduce pressure. Add the vegetables, except for beets. Bring up to pressure. Cook for 2 minutes more. Reduce pressure and serve at once, using the separately cooked beets as a garnish.

ABOUT BRAISING, POT-ROASTING AND STEWING

Escoffier believed that braising was a process which warranted the use of choice meats and the exercise of all his immense skill and patience. We concur. However, we wish to point out that quite inexpensive meat cuts can also be made to respond well not only to braising, but to other kinds of moist heat, like stewing and pot-roasting. Time, with most of them, is of the essence: relax and resign yourself to cooking ➧ very, very slowly and ➧ very, very long.

More exact directions will be given in each recipe. You can of course shortcut by using a ⊗ pressure cooker, but the necessarily high heat of this process will give you a less desirable result and a "canned" taste. Instead—and preferably—find yourself a ➧ heavy, covered pot or casserole, slightly bigger than the piece or quantity of meat you customarily cook. ➧ Do not use this process for a piece of meat over 4 to 5 pounds. If it is larger, cut it into pieces and make a stew of it, following the same method described for braising.

➧ If the meat is lean, you may want to lard it with seasoned Lardoons, page 453. If salt pork is called for and if it is very fat or salty, you may parblanch it, page 88, before rendering or before cooking it in a stew.

➧ Do not worry if the meat comes from an older animal. Maturity will add to its flavor. So will a good browning, page 494, in rendered fat of the same type, unless you are cooking veal or fowl. These are usually cooked "à blanc"—the term in this instance meaning that the meat is not seared before stewing. You may want to ➧ tenderize the meat by marinating, page 453; and you may dredge the meat with flour or not, as you like. ➧ If you do not dredge, be sure that the meat is wiped dry. When you have browned it on one side and are browning it on the other, you may add finely chopped onions. After it is seared, pour off all but 1 or 2 tablespoons of the fat which may have been rendered out of it. Then set the meat on a bed of about 1 cup Mirepoix (II, 221), on a rack, or on a rind of pork. Have ready enough ➧ boiling stock to cover the bottom of the pan, at least 1 to 2 inches. In any case, if you use more, barely cover the meat. ➧ Cover the pan tightly. As soon as the liquid reaches a boil, reduce the heat at once to ➧ maintain a simmer. Do not allow the liquid to get too low during the cooking. Replenish it with boiling stock or water, if necessary. Turn the meat over occasionally to keep it moist.

Vegetables may be cooked entirely in the pot-roasting pan. ➧ Allow about ¼ lb. vegetables to ¾ lb. meat. If cooking on top of the stove and if the vegetables are of medium size, add them during the last ¾ hour of cooking. But if they are very mature—especially carrots, onions, turnips, parsnips and the outer ribs of celery—they may profit by a brief blanching, see Blanching II, page 88. Or you may cook vegetables partially and separately before adding them toward the end of the pot-roasting. Should the stew or braise be cooked in the oven, the vegetables may need as long as 1½ hours. When the stew is served, the sauce will not be thick, but should have good body—what the French call "du corps."

➧ Always allow a stew to stand for at least 5 minutes off the heat so that grease rises and can be skimmed, page 109. To reheat leftover stews, see page 460. Also note recipes for cooked meats in Luncheon Dishes, page 208.

ABOUT MEAT PIES AND PIE TOPPING

To make meat pies taste and look well, be sure to have ➧ sufficient tastily seasoned gravy to almost cover the meat. There are several ways to top meat pies, but the trick in each instance is to assure the escape of steam, so that the under part of the crust will not be soggy. We find that unless the crusts are prebaked, it is difficult not to end up with some soggy surface. If you do not prebake, do brush the under surfaces exposed to moisture or steam with white of egg. ➧ Vent the crust well.

Prepare:

Any unsweetened Pie Dough (II, 293)

I. For a surefire method, cut and bake separately on a baking tin a piece, or pieces, of dough to cover the large or individual dishes in which you will serve the meat pie. To bake the dough, see (II, 295). Remember that pie dough shrinks in baking, so cut it slightly larger than the dish. Don't forget that this separate baking means you will have to cover your stew in some other way during the heating—such as with a tight-fitting lid. Just before serving, when the casserole has been heated through, place the prebaked crust on top and serve at once.

II. If you want to put the topping on before heating, preheat the oven to 350°. Fill the baking dish to be covered to within 1 inch of the top.
Place the dough on rather generously—to allow for shrinkage. Brush with Egg Wash (II, 433). Be sure to vent it well. Heat the dish for 45 minutes to 1 hour, when the stew should be thoroughly heated and the crust golden. You may brush the crust with butter before serving. When the stew is done, the sauce should not be thick, but should have good body.

BOILED BEEF OR BOEUF BOUILLI [4 to 6]

In his witty book about Viennese gourmandising, "Blue Trout and Black Truffles," Joseph Wechsberg describes no less than 24 different kinds of boiled beef specialties and announces categorically that in Imperial days only the best beef was "boiled." Viennese beef owes its special flavor to a special feed of sugar beet mash. Special feeding is the reason that the French, as well as the Viennese, consider this dish a treat rather than the boardinghouse stopgap it has come to be considered here. If you add Spaetzle, page 179, Noodles, page 172, or Dampfnudeln (II, 322), the result can become quite extraordinary.
Bring to a boil, in a heavy pot:

6 cups water

Put in:

3 lbs. lean, first cut brisket, bottom round or plate beef

Bring to a boil and skim the pot. Add:

1 onion stuck with 3 cloves
½ cup sliced carrots
½ cup sliced celery with leaves
1 teaspoon salt
(1 sliced turnip)

➧ Cover the pot closely and simmer the meat until tender, about 3 to 4 hours. Drain and reserve the stock. Melt:

¼ cup butter

Brown lightly in the butter:

¼ cup chopped onions

Stir until blended:

2 tablespoons flour

Stir in slowly 2 cups of the degreased stock. Season the sauce with:

2 tablespoons freshly grated horseradish
Salt
Vinegar or lemon juice
(Sugar)

Prepared horseradish contains vinegar and it is difficult to give exact proportions. So:

Correct the seasoning

Cut the meat into thin slices against the grain and reheat ➧ very briefly in the boiling gravy. Garnish with:

Chopped parsley

Serve with:

Boiled New Potatoes in their jackets, page 310
Sauerkraut, page 278
Dumplings, page 147

BEEF POT ROAST [6]

Please read About Pot Roasts, Braises and Stews, page 493.
Preheat oven to 300°.
Prepare for cooking:

3 to 4 lbs. beef shoulder, chuck, blade, boneless neck, rump or brisket

If the meat is lean, you may lard it, page 453. Rub the meat with:

(Garlic)

Dredge it in:

(Flour)

Heat in a heavy pan over lively heat:

2 tablespoons rendered suet or cooking oil

Brown the meat on all sides in the fat. ➧ Do not let it scorch. Add to the pot when the meat is half browned:

1 chopped carrot
1 rib diced celery
(1 small diced white turnip)
(2 tablespoons chopped green pepper)

When the meat is browned, pour off excess fat. Add to the pot:

1 small onion stuck with 3 cloves
2 cups boiling meat or vegetable stock or part stock and part dry wine

Cover and bake 2 to 3 hours. During this time turn the meat several times and, if necessary, add additional:

Hot stock

When the meat is firm,

Correct the seasoning

Pour off excess fat and serve with the pot liquor as it is or slightly thickened with:

Kneaded Butter, page 357

You may, if you wish, add to the pot roast drained boiled vegetables. Serve with:

Potato Pancakes, page 316, Kasha, page 157, or Green Noodles, page 173
Blue Plum Compote (II, 88)

BEEF POT ROAST IN SOUR CREAM AND WINE

Prepare:

Beef Pot Roast, above

Add to the liquid for gravy:

1 cup dry wine, preferably red
½ cup water

Pour it around the roast and cook until done. Heat over hot water and stir in just before serving:

¾ cup warm cultured sour cream

GASTON BEEF STEW [6]

This one-dish meal seems to taste better when cooked a day ahead.

Cut into small pieces and, if very salty, parblanch, page 88, briefly:

½ lb. salt pork

Dry the pork and sauté it slowly in a large skillet. Cut into pieces suitable for stewing:

2 lbs. beef

Brown the beef in the hot drippings over high heat. Pour off most of the accumulated fat. Sprinkle the meat with:

Seasoned flour

Combine and heat until boiling:

1½ chopped cloves garlic
1 large chopped onion
1 cup bouillon
1 cup canned tomato sauce
12 peppercorns
3 whole cloves
¼ cup chopped parsley
⅓ bay leaf

Place the meat in a heavy saucepan. Pour the above ingredients over it. Simmer closely covered for about 2 to 3 hours or until the meat can be easily pierced with a fork. During the last hour of cooking, add:

½ cup dry sherry or dry white wine

Cook separately until nearly tender:

6 medium-sized pared quartered potatoes
6 pared quartered carrots
1 stalk chopped celery

Add these vegetables for the last 15 minutes of cooking.

BEEF STEW WITH WINE OR BOEUF BOURGUIGNONNE [4 to 6]

For an added bouquet, you may marinate the diced meat overnight in wine. Drain the wine for later use in cooking. Preheat oven to 300°.

Try out:

½ lb. thinly sliced salt pork

or use 3 tablespoons butter

Peel, add and sauté lightly:

12 small onions or 4 shallots

Remove pork and onions from the pan. Cut into 1-inch dice and sauté in the hot fat until light brown:

2 lbs. lean beef

Sprinkle the meat with:

(1½ tablespoons flour)

Place it in an ovenproof dish with:

1 teaspoon salt
4 peppercorns
½ bay leaf
(½ teaspoon thyme or marjoram)

Cover the meat with:

Dry red wine and water—¾ part wine to ¼ part water

Cook ◆ covered in oven for 1 hour. Place the pork and onions on top and continue to cook for another hour or until the beef is tender. Or simmer the beef covered on top of the stove for about 1½ hours in all. You may add:

(1 cup sautéed mushrooms)
Correct the seasoning

and serve the stew sprinkled with:

Chopped parsley

Flambé at the last minute with:

(¼ cup brandy)

BEEF BRISKET WITH SAUERKRAUT [6]

Tie into a compact shape:

3 lbs. beef brisket

Melt in a deep kettle:

3 tablespoons bacon or other fat

Add, stir about and brown lightly:

(¼ cup chopped onions)

Add the meat and place over it:

2 lbs. sauerkraut

which then acts as a marinade. We prefer to add the sauerkraut after the meat has cooked about an hour. Add:

2 cups boiling water

Simmer the meat covered for about 2½ hours or until tender. Season with:

Salt and pepper
Dry white wine
(Caraway seed)

Serve with:

Boiled Potatoes, page 319

Pour over them:

Cultured sour cream
Chopped parsley or chives

SOUP MEAT

Sometimes, for reasons of economy, soup meat is served at table, but by and large it has, by this time, been deprived of most nutrients and flavor. Therefore, it must be presented with a self-assertive sauce. Brisket or other soup meat may be taken from the kettle before the vegetables are added. Serve it with:

Horseradish Sauce, page 362
Mustard Sauce, page 363, Thickened Tomato Sauce, page 376, or Brown Onion Sauce, page 366

SAUERBRATEN [6]

Prepare for cooking:

3 lbs. beef shoulder

Lard it, page 453, with:

18 seasoned lardoons, ¼ inch thick

or choose a fat cut of meat. Rub with:

Pepper
(Garlic)

Place in a deep crock or glass bowl. Heat but do not boil:

Equal parts mild vinegar or dry wine and water

Use in all about:

1 quart of liquid
½ cup sliced onion
2 bay leaves
1 teaspoon peppercorns
¼ cup sugar

Pour this mixture while hot over

the beef, so that it is more than ½ covered. Place a lid over the crock and refrigerate 24 hours to a week. The longer you leave it, the sourer the meat will get. Drain it, saving the marinade, and cook like:

Pot Roast, page 496

Use the vinegar mixture in place of stock. When the meat is tender, remove from the pot. Thicken the stock with:

Flour, see Pan Gravy, page 358

Add:

1 cup sweet or cultured sour cream

We like the gravy "straight." Some cooks add:

(Raisins, catsup and gingersnaps)

Serve the roast with:

Potato Dumplings, page 179, or
Potato Pancakes, page 316

and you will have a treat. ➧ This dish does not freeze successfully.

BOEUF À LA MODE

A pot roast de luxe, because so elegantly presented. The meat is sliced very thin and even, covered with a sauce, and the platter garnished with beautifully arranged vegetables.

Prepare the beef as for:

Sauerbraten, above

larding it but marinating only for 4 to 5 hours in a mixture of:

1½ to 2 cups dry red wine
¼ cup brandy

When ready to cook, add:

2 boned blanched calf feet

Use Blanch II, page 88, simmering for 10 minutes. ➧ Simmer covered for 3½ to 4 hours. You may, toward the last hour of cooking, add to the degreased sauce and cook with the meat:

1 cup parboiled, lightly sautéed carrots
1 cup parboiled, lightly sautéed onions

Just before serving, heat with the dish:

1 cup sautéed mushrooms

Serve the meat cut as described above, garnished with the vegetables and with the calf feet cut in one-inch squares.

SPICED BEEF [8]

Good served hot. Fine for a cold meat platter. Cover:

4 to 5 lbs. chuck roast

with:

Cider vinegar, dry wine or cider
2 sliced onions
½ bay leaf
1 teaspoon each cinnamon, allspice and cloves
1½ teaspoons salt
1 teaspoon pepper

Let the roast stand refrigerated in this marinade for 12 hours or more. Drain it and reserve the liquor.

Preheat oven to 275°.

Place the meat in a roasting pan. Heat to the boiling point and pour over it ½ the vinegar and:

2 cups water

Cover closely and roast for about 3 hours. Put through a grinder or mince, then sauté in butter until a golden brown:

2 onions
4 large carrots
1 medium yellow turnip
1 stalk celery

Add these ingredients to the roast for the last ½ hour of cooking. Add, if needed:

Salt

The stock may be thickened with:

Flour, see Gravy, page 358

CHUCK ROAST IN FOIL [12]

Foil-cooked meats often have a pasty look about them, but the use in this recipe of dehydrated onion soup gives great vigor of

color and flavor, in spite of the fact that the meat is not browned first. Try this for informal company.
Preheat oven to 300°.
Have ready 2 or 3 large pieces of heavy-duty foil. You may wipe the top of a:

7 lb. chuck roast

with:

Cooking oil

Sprinkle with:

½ to 1 package dehydrated onion soup

Place the center of the foil over it and turn the meat and foil over. Sprinkle the other side with:

½ to 1 package dehydrated onion soup

Now wrap the roast very carefully with the pieces of foil, so that no juices can escape. Place the package in a pan and bake for 3½ to 4 hours. If your company is informal, do not cut the foil until you are at table and ready to carve. The sudden burst of fragrance adds to the anticipation. Serve with:

Spaetzle, page 179
A rice ring with mushrooms filled with Parslied Peas, page 306

SWISS STEAK [6]

Preheat oven to 300°.
Trim the edges of a ¾-inch-thick:

2-lb. round steak

Rub with:

½ clove garlic

Pound into both sides of the steak, with the edge of a heavy plate or a mallet:

As much seasoned flour as the steak will hold

Cut it into pieces or leave it whole. If left whole, gash the edges to prevent curling. Heat in a large heavy casserole:

¼ cup bacon or ham drippings

Sear the steak on one side until brown. After you turn it over, add:

½ cup finely chopped onions
1 cup mixed finely chopped carrots, peppers and celery

Do not allow them to brown.

Correct the seasoning

Add:

(½ cup strained boiling tomatoes)
1 cup stock

Cover the casserole closely and place in the oven for 2 hours or more. Remove the steak to a hot platter. Strain the drippings. Degrease the drippings and make:

Pan Gravy, page 358

Pour the gravy over the steak. Serve with:

Mashed Potatoes, page 311

FLANK STEAK WITH DRESSING [4]

If you use sharp seasonings this gives a deviled effect.
Have ready:

A 2-lb. flank steak, page 473

Trim the edges. Season with and pound in:

1 teaspoon salt
⅛ teaspoon paprika
¼ teaspoon mustard
(⅛ teaspoon ginger)
(1 teaspoon Worcestershire sauce)

Melt:

¼ cup butter or bacon drippings

Add and sauté until brown:

2 tablespoons chopped onion

Add:

1 cup bread crumbs
¼ teaspoon salt
A few grains paprika
2 tablespoons chopped parsley
3 tablespoons chopped celery
1 slightly beaten egg

Spread this dressing over the flank steak, roll it loosely and tie it. For variety, try Sausage Dressing and apples, page 562.
Heat in a skillet:

3 tablespoons cooking oil

Sear the steak in the hot oil on all sides.
Preheat oven to 325°.
Place the steak in a casserole or closely covered dish. Stir into the oil in the skillet:

2 tablespoons flour

Add:

1 cup water or stock
1 cup tomato juice or dry wine
¼ teaspoon salt

Pour this mixture over the steak. Bake closely covered for about 1½ hours. Add seasoning if required. Serve the steak with a:

Green vegetable

SHORT RIBS OF BEEF [2]

Cut into about 3-inch pieces:

2 lbs. lean short ribs of beef

Place in a heavy pot with a lid:

5 cups water
1 small sliced onion
1 small sliced carrot
4 or more ribs celery with leaves

Bring these ingredients to the boiling point. Add the short ribs. Simmer ◗ covered until nearly tender, about 2 hours. Take out the meat. Strain and degrease the stock. Make about 3 cups of thin gravy, page 358, using:

¼ cup fat
¼ cup flour
3 cups stock

Season the gravy mildly with:

Salt and pepper
A few drops brown coloring

Preheat oven to 325°.
Heat in a heavy skillet:

¼ cup fat

Slice, add and stir about until light brown:

1 small onion

Brown the meat in the hot fat. Pour over it ½ the gravy. Bake ◗ uncovered for about 45 minutes and let it get brown and crisp. It may be basted occasionally with the drippings. Reheat the remaining gravy. Add:

1 teaspoon fresh marjoram
Correct the seasoning

Place the meat on a hot platter. Garnish with:

Mashed potatoes

Serve piping hot with gravy.

ABOUT GOULASH, GULYAS OR PÖRKOLT

This Hungarian specialty is cooked in many ways, but its most distinguishing seasoning is usually sweet paprika (II, 214). In Beef Goulash, the meat is browned. In the variations that follow it is cooked à blanc—that is, without even browning at all. Beef, veal, and other meats are used separately and in combination. If lamb and pork are included in some of the following recipes, the dish may be called **Pörkolt.** Vegetables are sometimes added for the last hour of cooking. Goulash is always highly spiced. Some epicures insist that freshly ground peppercorns are a requisite, others prefer the imported Rosen paprika. Some cooks use water as the liquid, others prefer stock or dry red wine.

BEEF GOULASH [6]

Cut into 1-inch cubes:

2 lbs. beef: round steak, shinbone or 1 lb. beef and 1 lb. lean veal

Melt in a heavy pot:

¼ cup butter or cooking oil

Brown the meat on both sides in the hot oil. Add and sauté:

1½ cups chopped onion

Add:

1 cup boiling Stock (II, 141), or tomato juice
1 teaspoon salt

½ teaspoon paprika

Use just enough stock to keep the meat from scorching and add more gradually during the cooking, as necessary. Cover the pot closely and simmer the meat for 1½ hours. Six small peeled potatoes may be added for the last ½ hour of cooking, but they do soak up the gravy which is apt to be the best part of the goulash. Remove the meat from the pot and thicken the stock for:

Gravy, page 358

It may be necessary to add stock or tomato juice.

Correct the seasoning

If potatoes have not been made an ingredient, serve the goulash with:

Polenta, page 156,
Spaetzle, page 179, or
Noodles, page 172

LAMB OR PORK GOULASH AU BLANC

Sauté in:

¾ cup butter
1½ to 2 cups chopped onions

Mash in a mortar and add:

1 teaspoon caraway
2 teaspoons marjoram
A grating of lemon rind
1 clove garlic
1 tablespoon sweet paprika

Add and bring to a boil:

1 cup water or stock

Add:

2 lbs. pork or lamb in 1½-inch cubes

Simmer covered for 1½ hours.
Garnish with:

Slivered red or green peppers

VEAL AND PORK GOULASH [4]

Sauté until light brown:

6 tablespoons chopped onions

in:

2 tablespoons butter

Add:

½ lb. one-inch veal cubes
½ lb. one-inch lean pork cubes

Heat and add:

1 lb. sauerkraut
1 teaspoon caraway seed

Simmer these ingredients covered for about 1 hour. Heat and add:

1 cup cultured sour cream
A generous grating of freshly ground pepper

Serve at once.

BELGIAN BEEF STEW OR CARBONNADE FLAMANDE [4]

Cut into 1½-inch cubes and coat in seasoned flour:

2 lbs. boneless beef: chuck, etc.

Sauté lightly in:

1 tablespoon butter
¼ cup thinly sliced onions

Put them to one side. Add:

1 tablespoon butter

and brown the floured meat. Drain off any excess fat. Combine and bring to a boil:

1 cup dark beer
1 pressed clove garlic
½ teaspoon sugar

Pour over the meat and onion mixture. Cover and simmer 2 to 2½ hours. After straining the sauce, you may add:

(½ teaspoon vinegar)

To serve, garnish meat with:

Parsley or dill new potatoes

Use sauce as gravy.

OXTAIL STEW [6]

Preheat oven to 350°.
Brown, page 454, in a heavy-lidded pan:

3 oxtails with separated joints

in:

3 tablespoons beef fat

with:

¼ cup diced onion

Add:

¼ cup Mirepoix (II, 221)
4 cups hot stock or ½ stock and ½ tomato juice or water
1 teaspoon salt
2 peppercorns

Simmer 3½ to 4 hours. During the last 35 minutes of cooking you may add:

½ cup diced celery
½ cup diced carrots
(¼ cup tomato paste)

When the meat is tender the stew degreased, page 109

Correct the seasoning

Thicken the liquid with:

2 tablespoons of Beurre Manié, page 357

Add:

2 tablespoons chopped parsley

ABOUT BEEF ROLLS, ROULADES OR PAUPIETTES

Thin strips of meat or fish rolled around vegetables or other stuffing are known also as Roulades or Paupiettes. They may be further wrapped in salt pork or bacon.

To make them with beef, use:

Thin strips of round or flank steak, 3 x 4 inches

Season with:

Salt and pepper

You may pound the meat. Place on each strip about 2 tablespoons of one of the following fillings:

I. A well-seasoned smoked or cooked sausage, 1 teaspoon chopped parsley or 1 sliver of dill pickle.

II. A thick julienned carrot, a rib of celery, 2 teaspoons minced ham.

III. 2 tablespoons seasoned cooked rice, 2 chopped stuffed olives.

Roll the meat and tie with string near both ends or wrap as for cabbage leaves, sketched on page 86. Dredge in:

Flour

Brown in bacon grease or rendered salt pork. Place in a casserole and use for every 6 rolls:

1½ cups stock or dry red wine
1½ to 2 tablespoons tomato paste

➧ Cover and cook slowly in a preheated 325° oven or on direct low heat for about 1 hour and 15 minutes.

STEAK AND KIDNEY PIE [4]

Preheat oven to 350°.

Classic recipes for this dish often call for beef kidneys. If they are used, they must be blanched, page 88, and the cooking time must be increased to assure tenderness. If a crust lines and covers the baker—a process we do not recommend, see below—the top should be protected until the final browning with a foil lightly placed over it. Cut into small, ½-inch-thick slices:

1½ lbs. round or other beef steak

Wash, skin and slice thin:

¾ lb. veal or lamb kidneys

Melt in a skillet:

3 tablespoons butter or beef fat

Sauté the kidneys in this over high heat for 1 to 2 minutes. Shake constantly. Shake the beef in a bag of:

Seasoned flour

Lightly grease an ovenproof baker. Place in it a layer of meat, then a layer of kidneys. Or you may reserve the kidneys and add them the last 15 minutes before placing the pastry cover. Add:

2 cups Brown Stock (II, 141)
1 cup dry red wine or beer

Cover the dish and bake for 1½ to 2 hours. Cool slightly. Raise oven heat to 400°. Cover the meat with:

Pâte Brisée (II, 297)

Bake about 12 to 15 minutes.

⊟ BURGOO [10–12]

One of those mixtures not unlike Mulligan and Brunswick Stews—a combination of meats, fowl and gleanings from the garden patch. Addicts—and there are many in Kentucky—claim this stew is best if served the day after it is made. Put in a heavy-lidded kettle with:

3 qts. water or stock
¾ lb. lean inch-diced stewing beef
¾ lb. inch-diced pork shoulder

Bring slowly to a boil. ➧ Reduce heat at once and simmer about 2½ hours. In another heavy kettle put:

1 disjointed 3½ lb. chicken

with:

Enough water to just cover

Bring these ingredients to a boil. ➧ Reduce the heat at once and simmer about 1 hour or until the meat can easily be removed from the bones. Put the chicken meat and the water in which it was cooked into the first kettle with the other meat after it has simmered the 2½ hours as directed. At this time, also add:

2½ cups quartered ripe, peeled and seeded tomatoes
1 cup fresh Lima beans
½ diced red pepper
4 diced green peppers
¾ cup diced onions
1 cup diced carrots
2 cups diced potatoes
1 bay leaf
1 tablespoon Worcestershire sauce

Simmer this whole mixture ½ hour or more before adding:

2 cups corn, cut freshly from the cob

Cook about 15 minutes more or until all the vegetables are soft.

Correct the seasoning

Serve hot in deep bowls with:

Chunks of French bread

on the side, to be used—you know how! It's that kind of a dish.

VEAL STEW [4]

Select:

1½ lbs. veal with little bone or 2 lbs. neck or shanks

The meat may be cooked in one piece, cut into 3-inch pieces or into 1½-inch cubes. Melt in a heavy pot or saucepan over moderate heat:

3 tablespoons butter or drippings

Brown the meat in the hot drippings. Reduce the heat. Cover the bottom of the pot ½ inch with boiling:

Vegetable Stock (II, 145)

Cover the pot closely and ➧ simmer the meat until tender, 45 minutes or more. Remove it from the pot. Strain the stock. Thicken it with:

Flour, see Pan Gravy, page 358

The browning of the meat in the fat is optional. For a pleasant change drop it directly into boiling vegetable stock and cook as directed. Serve the stew with:

Chopped parsley
Noodles, page 172
Farina Balls, page 147, or Rice Ring, page 162, and Fried Apples (II, 94)

or serve it in:

A Hominy Grits Ring, page 155

Veal stew is also good with a baked top crust. Follow the recipe for Quick Chicken Pot Pie, page 212.

VEAL STEW WITH RED WINE [4]

Cut into 12 chunks:

1½ lbs. boneless veal or beef
Roll each piece in:
½ slice bacon: 6 slices in all
Dredge the meat lightly with:
Flour
Melt in a heavy skillet:
2 tablespoons bacon or other fat
Add the meat and:
12 small peeled onions
Stir these ingredients about and permit them to brown on all sides. Remove them from the pan. Pour off all but 1 tablespoon of fat. Stir in:
1 tablespoon flour
Add and stir until smooth:
1½ cups consommé or stock
½ cup dry red wine
Add the meat and onions. Simmer closely covered 1½ to 2 hours until the meat is very tender. Season and serve with some baked dish like:
Crusty or Soft-Centered Spoon Bread (II, 279)

BLANQUETTE DE VEAU OR ELABORATE VEAL STEW [6]

Cut into 1-inch pieces:
1½ lbs. veal shoulder
1½ lbs. veal breast
Parblanch, page 88, the pieces of veal about 2 minutes in salted water. Drain and wash well under cold running water, removing all the scum. Put the meat in a heavy pan and add:
5 cups chicken or veal stock
1 large onion studded with 1 clove
1 peeled carrot
1 stalk chopped white celery
A Bouquet Garni (II, 220)
Simmer uncovered for about 1¼ to 1½ hours until the veal is tender and may be pierced with a fork. Now skim out the vegetables and the bouquet. Add:
24 small blanched white onions
2 cups fresh button mushroom caps
Simmer for about 10 minutes. Combine:
¼ cup flour
¼ cup butter
Add this thickener to the veal and simmer for another 10 minutes. Remove pan from heat. Mix together:
3 beaten egg yolks
½ cup whipping cream
Stir about 2 tablespoons of the hot veal stock into the egg mixture and return it to the pan. Add:
2 to 3 tablespoons lemon juice
Correct the seasoning
Serve with:
Noodles or rice
Garnished with:
Chopped parsley

VEAL AND PORK PIE [4]

Cut into 1-inch pieces:
½ lb. veal
½ lb. lean pork
Stir and brown the meat lightly in:
2 tablespoons butter or cooking oil
Add and simmer covered for about 15 minutes:
3 cups boiling water
1 teaspoon salt
½ teaspoon paprika
½ bay leaf
2 whole cloves
Remove spices. Add:
¼ cup diced carrots
¾ cup diced celery
1 cup diced potatoes
Bring the stew to the boiling point ➧ reduce the heat and simmer covered until the meat is tender, about 30 minutes longer.
Correct the seasoning
Make:
Pan Gravy, page 358
Preheat oven to 450°.

Place the stew in a baking dish. Top it while hot with:

Pie Crust (II, 293)

Bake for about 20 minutes.

MOCK CHICKEN DRUMSTICKS OR CITY CHICKEN [6]

Preheat oven to 325°.
Cut into 1 x 1½-inch pieces:

1 lb. veal steak
1 lb. pork steak

Arrange the veal and pork cubes alternately on 6 skewers. Press the pieces close together into the shape of a drumstick. Roll the meat in:

Seasoned flour

Beat:

1 egg
2 tablespoons water

Dip the sticks in the diluted egg, then roll in:

Bread crumbs

Melt in a skillet:

¼ cup butter

Brown the meat partially in the fat. Add:

1 tablespoon grated onion

Continue to brown the meat. Cover the bottom of the skillet with:

Boiling Stock (II, 141)

Cover the skillet and place in oven, about 50 minutes or until the meat is tender.
Make:

Pan Gravy, page 358

VEAL BIRDS OR PAUPIETTES

For other stuffings, see About Beef Rolls, page 502.
Trim the edges from ⅓-inch-thick:

Slices of veal from the round

Pound the meat with a cleaver and cut into pieces about 2 x 4 inches. Make the following dressing. Chop the meat trimmings and combine them with an equal amount of chopped:

Salt pork

Measure the salt pork and trimmings and add to them ½ the amount of:

Bread crumbs

Add:

Chopped onion, chopped raisins or seedless grapes
Chopped celery
(A grating of lemon rind)

Moisten these ingredients with sufficient:

Cream or stock

to hold them together. Spread the meat lightly with the dressing and roll it. Secure with skewers or thread. Roll the birds in:

Flour

Sauté them in hot:

Butter or cooking oil

until golden in color. Reduce the heat and add:

Hot cream, milk, stock or dry wine

until the meat is half covered. ➧ Cover the pot closely and simmer until tender, about 20 minutes.

Correct the seasoning

Add:

(½ lb. Sautéed Mushrooms, page 296)

Make:

Pan Gravy, page 358

VEAL POT ROAST

Please read About Pot Roasts, page 493.
Prepare by boning and rolling:

A rump roast of veal

Cook as for any unbrowned Stew, see à blanc, page 494. Classically, veal is not browned —but we've eaten some mighty good browned veal pot roasts! Use:

½ cup water for every lb. of meat

Or prepare:

Pot Roast in Sour Cream and Wine, page 496

omitting the browning. Add to the finished gravy:

(Capers, basil or thyme)

MEXICAN VEAL STEAK WITH NOODLES [6]

Cut into small slices:

1 lb. thin veal steak

Dredge with:

¼ cup flour

Heat:

3 teaspoons butter or olive oil

Sauté the meat quickly on both sides until brown. ➧ Reduce the heat. Cover the meat with:

1½ cups sliced onions
6 tablespoons chili sauce
1¼ cups boiling stock

➧ Simmer closely covered about ½ hour.

Meanwhile, cook and drain:

2 cups Noodles, page 172

Toss them in:

¾ cup cream of chicken soup

Serve the noodles mounded, covered with:

¼ cup buttered crumbs
2 tablespoons grated Parmesan cheese

Surround the noodles with the steak. Garnish with:

(Parsley)

CUBED VEAL BAKED IN SOUR CREAM [4]

Preheat oven to 300°.

Cut into cubes:

1½ lbs. boneless veal

Brown lightly in:

1½ tablespoons butter

Remove the meat to an oven-proof baking dish. Add to the butter, stir and sauté lightly:

1 tablespoon chopped onion
½ lb. sliced mushrooms

Remove from the heat. Stir in slowly:

1 tablespoon flour
⅓ cup stock
¾ cup cultured sour cream
½ teaspoon salt
⅛ teaspoon pepper

Pour sauce over the meat. Cover the dish. Bake for about 1 hour.

BAKED MARROW BONES OR OSSO BUCO [3]

Preheat oven to 300°.

➧ To make this dish really delectable, the animal should not be more than 2 months old. Saw into 2½ to 3 inch pieces:

2 lbs. shin bone of veal

Dip the bones first in:

Olive oil

Then in:

Seasoned flour

Heat in the pan:

¼ cup olive oil

To keep the marrow intact, set the bones upright. To conserve stock, place them as close as possible on the base of a heavy pan just large enough to hold them. Brown the bones very slowly for about 15 minutes. Pour over them:

½ cup white wine
(½ cup skinned, diced, seeded, fresh tomatoes)
Seasoned stock—enough to come at least ⅓ up the bones

Cover and bake for 1 to 1½ hours until the meat falls from them. Before serving, sprinkle the tops with:

Gremolata (II, 222)

Serve garnished with:

Fried Chipolata sausage and Boiled Chestnuts, page 283, or Risotto, page 165

BRAISED SHOULDER OF LAMB [6]

Melt in a heavy pot:

¼ cup cooking oil or butter

Sear on all sides in the hot fat:

A rolled shoulder of lamb

Remove it from the pot. Cook slowly in the fat for 10 minutes:

½ cup chopped onion
¼ cup chopped carrots
¼ cup chopped turnips
½ cup chopped celery with leaves
(1 sliced clove garlic)

Return the meat to the pot. Add:

½ **bay leaf**
4 **whole peppercorns**
1 **teaspoon salt**
4 **cups boiling vegetable stock or 3 cups stock and 1 cup tomato pulp**

➧ Cover the pot closely. ➧ Simmer the meat until tender, about 2 hours. When the meat is done, degrease the stew and thicken the stock slightly with:

Kneaded Butter, page 357

Serve the roast surrounded by the vegetables.

BRAISED STUFFED SHOULDER OR FARCE OF LAMB [6]

This cut is hard to carve unless boned. Its flavor is highly prized.

Preheat oven to 325°.

Bone:

A shoulder of lamb

You may rub it with:

(Garlic)

or insert slivers of garlic under the skin.

Prepare about:

3 **cups Bread Dressing, page 561**

Spread it on the meat. Roll like a jelly roll. Secure with string, or fasten with spiral skewers, page 572. Brown in:

3 **tablespoons cooking oil or butter**

Place in a roasting pan:

1 **cup Vegetable Stock (II, 145)**

Put the browned roast in it and cook ➧ covered, allowing about 40 minutes to the pound. You may put some of the bones in the pan. Meanwhile, prepare for cooking:

3 **cups diced vegetables: celery, carrots, onions, potatoes**

After the meat has cooked about 45 minutes, place the vegetables in the pan with:

1 **cup vegetable stock**

Cover and continue to cook the meat about 1 hour after adding the vegetables or until the internal temperature of the meat is 175° to 180°. Pour off, but reserve most of the liquid and allow the meat and vegetables to glaze by cooking them ➧ uncovered for about 10 minutes longer. Meanwhile, to make the sauce, degrease the reserved liquid and reduce it somewhat.

Correct the seasoning

before serving.

LAMB FORESTIÈRE OR MOCK VENISON

Wipe with a damp cloth:

A leg of lamb or mutton

Cover it with:

Buttermilk

Soak it refrigerated for 24 hours or more.

Preheat oven to 450°.

Drain, wipe dry and lard the meat, page 453, with:

Salt pork or bacon

Dot it with:

Butter

Dredge with:

Flour

Put the roast on a rack in a pan in the oven and bake for 15 minutes. Add:

½ **cup hot Vegetable Stock (II, 145)**

Cover closely. ➧ Reduce heat at once to 325°. When the roast is nearly done, allowing 35 minutes to the pound, remove the cover and add:

1 **cup Sautéed Mushrooms, page 296**

Pour over the roast:

1 **cup cultured sour cream**

Cook ➧ uncovered for 10 minutes.

Correct the seasoning

Make:

Pan Gravy, page 358

Serve the roast surrounded by:

Browned Potatoes, page 314

Garnish with:

Parsley

BRAISED LEG OF MUTTON OR LAMB

[About 8 Servings]

If cooked this way, the flavor is almost like venison.

Remove the fell from:

A 5 lb. leg of mutton or lamb

You may place the meat for several hours in a marinade, page 380, or you may rub it all over with:

(A cut clove of garlic)

Rub the meat with:

Butter

Melt in a heavy pan:

¼ cup fat or drippings

Brown the meat in it on all sides. Add:

4 cups boiling stock

Cover the pot. ▶ Simmer the meat until tender, allowing 30 minutes to the pound. Add boiling water, if necessary. After the meat has cooked for 1 hour, add:

2 small whole onions
3 peppercorns
3 cloves
A sprig of thyme or ½ teaspoon dried thyme
½ bay leaf

When the meat is tender, remove from the pot. Season with:

Salt

Place the meat where it will remain hot.

Serve with:

Caper Sauce, page 263

and

Puréed Turnips, page 338

BRAISED LAMB SHANKS OR TROTTERS [4]

Rub:

4 lamb shanks: 3¾ to 4 lbs.

with:

Garlic

Roll in:

Seasoned flour

Melt until fragrant:

2 tablespoons cooking oil

Partially sear the shanks and add:

2 tablespoons diced onion

Continue to cook the meat until browned on all sides. Pour off the fat. Place the meat on a rack in a lidded pan. Add:

1½ cups boiling stock
⅓ teaspoon pepper
1½ teaspoons salt
½ bay leaf

Cover the pan closely. ▶ Simmer the meat or bake covered in a 325° oven for about 1½ hours or until tender. You may add for the last ½ hour of cooking:

3 cups diced vegetables
½ cup boiling stock or water

The vegetables may be onions, carrots, celery, peppers, turnips, tomatoes and/or potatoes—a matter of choice and expediency. Strain, degrease and reduce the stock. Serve as it is or make:

Pan Gravy, page 358

If you have not added the vegetables, you may serve the shanks with:

Creole Sauce, page 380

LAMB STEW OR NAVARIN PRINTANIER [8]

Cut into about 1½-inch pieces:

1 lb. shoulder of lamb
1 lb. breast of lamb

Brown the meat in a heavy skillet in:

2 tablespoons fat

Remove the meat to a casserole. Pour off the fat and deglaze the pan with:

2 cups light stock

to which you may add:

2 tablespoons tomato paste

Bring to a boil and pour over the meat. ♦ Simmer covered. Meanwhile, peel and shape into ovals about 1½ inches long:

2 cups new potatoes
6 carrots
3 white turnips

Add:

18 small onions: about 1 inch

After the lamb has cooked about 1 hour, skim off the fat, add the vegetables to the casserole and ♦ simmer covered for about 1 hour longer or until the vegetables are tender. Have ready to add:

1 cup cooked fresh peas
1 cup cooked fresh green beans, cut in 1-inch lengths

When the lamb and vegetables in the casserole are tender, skim any fat from the casserole and gently fold in the cooked peas and beans. Serve at once, sprinkled with ½ cup finely chopped parsley.

IRISH STEW [4 to 6]

This famous stew is not browned.

Cut into 1½-inch cubes:

1½ lbs. lamb or mutton

Peel and slice to ⅛-inch thickness:

¾ cup onions
2½ lbs. potatoes

Put in the bottom of a heavy pan a layer of potatoes, a layer of meat, a few slices of onion. Repeat this twice, ending with potatoes on top. Season each layer with:

Salt and pepper

Add to the pot:

1 bay leaf

Pour over the layers:

2 cups boiling water or stock
2 tablespoons finely chopped parsley

Bring to a boil. ♦ Cover closely. Simmer gently over very low heat for about 2½ hours or until done. Shake the pot periodically so that the potatoes do not stick. When done, all the moisture should have been absorbed by the potatoes.

CURRY OF LAMB WITH RICE [4]

Remove the gristle and fat from:

A 2 lb. lamb shoulder

Cut the meat into 1-inch cubes. Heat:

3 tablespoons fat or cooking oil

Brown the meat in the hot fat with:

1 tablespoon chopped onion
⅔ teaspoon curry powder

Add:

1 cup light Stock (II, 142)
¼ cup or more chopped celery
2 tablespoons chopped parsley
(1 tablespoon chopped pimiento)
(¼ cup peeled, seeded, diced cucumbers)

Cover the meat and simmer until done, about ½ hour. Stir frequently.

Correct the seasoning

Make:

Pan Gravy, page 358

Place on a platter a mound of:

Rice, page 158

Arrange the meat and gravy around it. Garnish the platter with:

Parsley

CASSOULET

[About 12 Servings]

With a thicker texture than a pot au feu, this controversial dish from the South of France has one solid pivot—white beans. They are cooked usually with fresh pork and sausage: but often with mutton and "confit d'oie"—potted goose, page 589—or with duck, partridge or bacon. Goose fat is a frequent component, also an onion stuck with cloves. Vegetables vary seasonally. Garlic is essential. For this recipe you almost need a routing sheet. The beans soak overnight and are cooked the next day with meat and other trimmings. The pork roasts for a while before the lamb joins it. Then the meats that have been cooking with the beans are taken from the bone and sliced before they are returned to the beans. This way the flavors unite in a single casserole and make a final triumphant appearance under a golden crust of crumbs.

Soak overnight in cold water:

1 lb. white beans: haricots, marrow-fat or broad beans

Roast in a 350° oven for about 2½ hours or until tender:

3 lbs. Loin of Pork, page 485

Blanch, page 88, by placing in cold water and just bringing to a boil:

1 ham shank
1 lb. salt pork

Drain the beans. Heat the water in which they soaked, adding:

Enough water to make 4 quarts

Bring to a boil and skim the pot. Add the drained, blanched ham shank and salt pork and:

A Bouquet Garni (II, 220)
3 cloves garlic

Simmer covered for about 1½ hours. Add:

6 small white onions
½ lb. hard Italian sausage, like Salcisetta

➧ Simmer about 1 hour longer, until the beans are tender but still intact. Brown, page 454, in a heavy skillet:

3 lbs. rolled lamb shoulder

in:

1 tablespoon butter

Drain off any excess fat. Roast the meat and the bones from the lamb with the pork ➧ uncovered. ➧ After about 1½ hours, pour over it:

Thickened Tomato Sauce, page 376

and roast for about ½ hour more. ➧ Lower oven heat to 300°, then drain off and reserve the sauce and drippings. Remove and slice the meat of both the lamb and the pork roast. Drain the beans, adding the juice to the drained tomato sauce. Trim and slice the ham, the sausage and the salt pork in bite-sized pieces. Layer these meats with the beans in a casserole and skim excess fat from the combined tomato and bean juices before adding them to the other ingredients. Top with:

1 cup buttered dry bread crumbs

Bake about 1 hour longer in the oven, when the crumbs should have turned a golden color.

COUSCOUS [6]

As with most basic native dishes, variations of this North African specialty abound. The following version comes from friends in Libya.

Soak overnight and cook the following day until about half tender:

1 cup Chick Peas, page 264

Drain them. Cut into about 10 pieces:

2 lbs. lamb, mutton or beef

Brown lightly in:

1 tablespoon olive oil
2 tablespoons butter

While browning slowly for about 10 minutes, add:

¾ cup minced onion

When the onion is translucent, add:

2 teaspoons salt
½ teaspoon freshly ground pepper
⅛ teaspoon red pepper
½ teaspoon turmeric
2 tablespoons tomato paste

➧ Reduce heat and barely simmer this thick mixture for about 10 minutes more. Place in a heavy pot with:

2 knuckle bones

and enough:

Water to cover

➧ Simmer covered until the meat can be pierced with a fork, but still offers slight resistance. Add:

3 cups potatoes, cut Parisienne, page 250
2 cups coarsely diced yellow or white squash
2 cups coarsely diced zucchini

and the drained cooked chick peas. Add, if necessary:

Stock (II, 141)

➧ Simmer covered until the meat and vegetables are tender, about ¾ of an hour longer. Remove from heat and reserve this meat and vegetable mixture. When the fat rises to the top, skim and reserve 2 tablespoons of it. Rinse briefly and place in the top of a perforated steamer or a couscous pot:

1 lb. semolina, cracked millet, cracked wheat or kasha

Steam the cereal ➧ uncovered for 15 minutes, timing after you see steam rising from the top. Meanwhile reheat the meat and vegetable mixture. Drain the liquid and reserve it. Now ➧ working quickly so everything stays warm, remove the cereal from the steamer and add:

2 tablespoons orange flower water
¼ teaspoon cinnamon
¼ teaspoon cloves

Toss the seasoned couscous lightly in the 2 tablespoons of fat, reserved from the meat mixture, and put it in a serving dish. Pour over it 1 cup of the drained liquid. Put the meat, vegetables and chick peas on top of the couscous. Use the remaining liquid as a separate sauce. Serve at once.

PORK TENDERLOIN WITH MUSHROOMS AND OLIVES [4]

Cut into 1-inch crosswise slices:

1 lb. or more pork tenderloin

Roll in:

Seasoned flour

Sauté until golden in:

2 tablespoons butter

with:

A sliced onion

Bring just to the boiling point:

½ cup dry white wine

Pour over the meat. Add at this time:

½ lb. sliced mushrooms
(⅛ teaspoon fresh rosemary)

Cover the skillet closely. ➧ Simmer the rounds until they are done, about 30 minutes. Add:

6 sliced green olives, stuffed with almonds
(2 tablespoons lemon juice)

Serve the pork garnished with:

2 tablespoons chopped parsley

PORK CHOPS BAKED IN SOUR CREAM [4]

Preheat oven to 350°.

Dredge:

4 loin pork chops: ½ inch thick

with:

Seasoned flour or bread crumbs

Insert in each chop:

1 clove

Brown lightly in a little hot pork fat or lard. Place in a baking dish. Combine, heat and pour over the meat:

½ cup water or stock
½ bay leaf
2 tablespoons vinegar
1 tablespoon sugar
½ cup cultured sour cream
(¼ teaspoon summer savory)

Bake the chops ♦ covered for about 1 hour.

BRAISED PORK CHOPS CREOLE [6]

Preheat oven to 350°.
Dredge:

6 pork chops, ½ inch or more thick

with:

Flour

Brown them in:

Hot fat or cooking oil

Place in a baking dish. Combine, heat and pour around them:

1 can condensed tomato soup: 10½ oz.
1 can water or stock
½ cup chopped celery
1 chopped green pepper—seeds and membrane removed
¾ cup minced onions
¾ teaspoon salt
¼ teaspoon paprika

Bake ♦ covered for about 1¼ hours. ♦ Remove the cover for the last 15 minutes. Cover the top for this last period with:

Crushed cornflakes

BRAISED DEVILED PORK CHOPS [4]

Preheat oven to 325°.
Place in a dish:

4 pork chops, 1 inch thick

Marinate them for 3 to 6 hours covered and refrigerated in:

Pork Marinade, page 382

Drain the chops, reserving the marinade. Wipe them dry. Brown in a hot greased skillet. Heat the marinade and:

½ cup water or stock

Pour it around the chops. Bake ♦ covered until tender, about 1 hour.

BRAISED PORK CHOPS WITH FRUIT

[Allow 1 Chop per Person]
Preheat oven to 350°.
Sear in a hot, lightly greased skillet:

Trimmed pork chops, ¾ inch thick or more

Season lightly. Place on the chops, skin side down:

Halved, cored apples, pitted apricots, prunes or pineapple slices

Fill the centers of the fruit with:

Brown sugar

Cover the bottom of the skillet to ½ inch with:

Chicken stock and/or some of the fruit juice

♦ Cover the pan closely. Bake for about 50 minutes. Remove the chops from the pan carefully, so as not to disturb the fruit. Keep warm. Partially degrease and add to the pan juices:

¾ to 1 cup sweet or cultured sour cream

Serve this sauce with the chops and fruit.

BRAISED STUFFED PORK CHOPS COCKAIGNE [6]

Preheat oven to 350°.
Cut from the bone:

6 rib pork chops, ¾ to 1 inch thick

Cut the bone from the meat. Trim off the excess fat and cut a large gash or pocket into the side of each chop. Prepare a dressing of:

1 cup bread crumbs
¼ cup chopped celery
¼ cup chopped onions
2 tablespoons chopped parsley
Milk to moisten the dressing
¼ teaspoon salt
⅛ teaspoon paprika

These proportions and ingredients may be varied. Fill the pockets with the dressing. Skewer them. Sear the chops in a hot skillet and place in a pan with a little:

Milk or stock

➧ Cover the pan and bake about 1 hour and 15 minutes or until tender. Make:

Pan Gravy, page 358

PORK BIRDS [6]

Pound to the thickness of ¼ inch:

2 lbs. pork steaks which have been cut from the shoulder

Cut them into 6 oblong pieces. Spread them with half the recipe for:

Apricot or Prune Dressing, page 565

Roll them. Secure the rolls with string or toothpicks. Dredge in:

2 tablespoons flour

Brown in:

2 tablespoons fat

Add:

1 cup boiling water or Stock (II, 141)

Simmer covered for about 50 minutes or until tender. Serve with the liquor in the pan, degreased and thickened as:

Pan Gravy, page 358

or just reduced.

⊟ ABOUT SPARERIBS

[➧ Allow at Least 1 lb. per Person]

These gloriously messy old favorites can simply be baked in a 325° oven about 1½ hours; but there are a good many more lively things to do with them. We find parboiling, page 88, the ribs for about 3 or 4 minutes not only removes unwanted fat, but makes the end result very palatable. After parboiling, try one of the following recipes or barbecue them, page 97.

BAKED SPARERIBS WITH DRESSING [4]

Preheat oven to 500°.

As there is much bone and little meat to spareribs—we love the self-explanatory name—it is well to allow 1 pound of them to a person. Parboil for 2 minutes.

4 lbs. spareribs

Cut into 2 pieces. Spread 1 piece with:

Apple Onion Dressing, page 563

Cover the dressing with the other piece of meat. Tie the 2 pieces together. Rub the outside of the meat with:

2 tablespoons flour
⅛ teaspoon salt
A few grains pepper

Place on a rack in an uncovered roasting pan and ➧ reduce the heat at once to 325°. Bake for about 1 hour. Baste the meat every 10 minutes with the fat in the pan.

BAKED SPARERIBS WITH SAUERKRAUT [4]

Preheat oven to 400°.

Place in a mound, in the center of a small roasting pan:

1½ quarts Sauerkraut, page 278

Season:

4 lbs. parboiled spareribs, see above

lightly with:

Salt and pepper

Fold the ribs in half. Place between them:

Slices of onion

Cover the kraut with the folded spareribs. Bake ➧ uncovered in a hot oven until nicely browned. Baste frequently with kraut juice. Turn the ribs and brown the other side. Add water, if necessary. ➧ Cover the pan. ➧ Reduce the temperature to 350°. Parboil until nearly tender:

6 peeled medium-sized potatoes

When the meat is nearly done, after about 1¼ hours' cooking in all, uncover it and place the whole potatoes around it, turning them frequently to permit them to brown. Serve the ribs and vegetables when the meat is tender.

BOILED SPARERIBS

Place:

Spareribs

in:

Boiling water to cover

Add:

Salt and pepper
Chopped onion, celery, parsley and carrots
(1 teaspoon caraway seed)

➧ Simmer the meat covered until tender, from 1½ to 2 hours. Drain and serve on a mound of hot:

Sauerkraut or Red Cabbage, page 278

surrounded by:

Mashed Potatoes, page 211

SWEET-SOUR SPARERIBS

Preheat oven to 350°.
Cut into 2-inch pieces:

2 lbs. spareribs

Parboil, page 88, 3 to 4 minutes. Drain and dry. Brush with:

Soy sauce

Bake ➧ uncovered on a rack in a pan in the oven for 1 hour. Have ready the following sauce. Boil briefly:

½ cup vinegar
½ cup sugar
¼ cup sherry
1 tablespoon soy sauce
1 teaspoon fresh ginger

Mix together and add:

2 teaspoons cornstarch
1 tablespoon water

Cook until cornstarch is transparent. Pour the sauce over the cooked spareribs and serve at once with:

Baked Green Rice, page 159

STEWED PORK NECK BONES

Partly cover with seasoned boiling water:

Pork neck bones

➧ Simmer covered until tender, about 1½ hours. Vegetables may be added to the stew for the last ½ hour or so of cooking.

STEWED PORK HOCKS

Cover with seasoned boiling water:

Pork hocks

Simmer covered from 1½ to 3 hours. You may add potatoes for the last ½ hour of cooking or greens or cabbage for the last 20 minutes.

SALT PORK AND MILK GRAVY [4]

Dip thin slices of:

1 lb. salt pork

in:

Boiling water

Drain and dip in:

Corn meal

Brown slowly in a skillet, turning frequently. Thicken:

2 tablespoons drippings

With:

2 tablespoons flour, see Gravy, page 358

Pour in slowly:

1 cup milk

Serve with:

Boiled or baked potatoes

ABOUT GROUND MEAT VARIATIONS

When emergencies demand all our ingenuity to make meat stretch graciously or otherwise, we have discovered the incontrovertible fact that by grinding meat it can be made to seem in much more ample supply than it really is. This does not mean that all the variations listed in this section are economical—although some are definitely so. But many provide interesting blends, seasoning and combinations that give a much-sought variety in menu building. No one needs an introduction to hamburger, although many people should be alerted to the best actual handling of the meat and the best ways to retain its tenderness, and flavor during cooking. Meat loaves, pâtés and galantines, meat balls, croquettes, timbales, farces and mousses—all have their own individuality, which we hope you will discover and exploit.

Many other dishes using already cooked, diced, slivered and minced meats—which are rather different in texture—will be found in Luncheon and Supper Dishes, page 208. While grinding does, of course, help with tough and old meats, remember that ➧ the distinctive succulence of pâtés and galantines depends on a base of moist young meat. ➧ Do not store any uncooked ground meat longer than 24 hours. ➧ Be sure the mass is not more than 2 inches thick, so the cold can penetrate it quickly and thoroughly.

ABOUT HAMBURGER

A mother we know has made the disheartening discovery that her children will eat nothing but hamburger. She calls it "The Daily Grind." At home and abroad, indoors and out, the dispensing and downing of these meat patties is so nearly universal that it is worth considering for a moment from just what beef the commercial variety is built. So all-embracing did some butchers find the term "hamburger" that the law saw fit to define any beef sold under this term as at least 70% meat, 30% fat. Federal statute further forbids the use of sodium sulphite, an additive which keeps the meat rosy. Recent surveys, however, indicate that the practice is far from dead. Should you find the color of ground meat too persistently red—expose a sample to bright sunlight. Untreated meat will darken.

If, as many people do, you have lean beef ground specially for hamburgers, use chuck, flank, shank, neck, heel, round or hanging tenderloin. ➧ Twice-ground meat will compact more than once-ground. You may be surprised at the apparently large amount of fat you didn't see go into the grinder. Grinders are so constructed that often as much as a fourth of every pound of meat that goes in stays in; and the unexpected fat may come from the grinding of the previous order.

❄ To freeze beef for hamburgers, see (II, 552 and 561).

Good quality beef, freshly ground and used at once, needs only ➧ light shaping. You may want to incorporate into it some onion juice or finely chopped chives. ➧ If the beef has to be kept ground for 12 to 18 hours, it profits by having worked into it with a fork about 2 tablespoons beef stock for each pound of meat. This is done before shaping.

➧ If beef is to be "stretched," you may add to each pound about ½ cup soft bread crumbs (II, 159), soaking them briefly in about ½ cup seasoned milk or stock. Or you may use ½ cup finely grated raw carrots, potatoes or ground and cooked soy beans, page 265, or 1 cup dry processed cereal. ➧ Incorporate these ingredients into the meat lightly with a fork and, with a light touch, shape the mixture into patties. Always decide before you put the meat into the pan how thick you want the finished hamburger. ➧ Never compact it in the pan by pressing down on it with a spatula.

➧ To cook hamburger, consider your grind. The degree of fattiness is important in helping determine how you will treat the pan for sautéing or whether you will brush the patties with butter during broiling.

If you use ➧ ready-ground hamburger, preheat an ungreased skillet slowly, to the point where a small sample of meat when added will sizzle, not hiss sharply. Drop the patties in the pan and leave them, cooking over medium heat ➧ uncovered, for 3 or 4 minutes. During this time sufficient fat should be available from the patty itself to permit the hamburger to be turned without sticking. Turn and cook on the other side another 3 minutes or even longer, depending on the thickness of the patty and the whims of your diners.

Another prevalent, if flavor-destroying, way of preparing a fat-free pan is to preheat it slowly and scatter over the surface of it about 1 teaspoon salt for each pound of meat. The salt will keep quite lean meat from sticking—and for a very good reason. It draws the juices from the meat, see (II, 195). Because of this, too, we prefer ➧ withholding seasoning from hamburgers until after at least one side of the meat is seared. If you use ➧ very lean beef, you will need at least 1 tablespoon butter or suet added to the preheated skillet. Heat the fat to the point of fragrance before you add the meat, and proceed to cook as for ready-ground hamburger.

SAUTÉED HAMBURGERS [4]

➧ Please read About Hamburger, page 515. Shape lightly into patties, allowing 2 for each serving:

1 lb. ground beef

You may mix in lightly with a fork any one of the following. To stretch, add:

½ cup soft bread crumbs (II, 159)

soaked briefly in:

⅓ to ½ cup milk or stock

or add:

½ cup finely grated raw carrots or potatoes

moistened with:

2 tablespoons beef stock, cream, tomato paste or lemon juice

To flavor, use:

2 teaspoons chili sauce, 1 teaspoon ground anchovy or anchovy paste, 3 tablespoons sautéed mushrooms, 1 tablespoon finely diced stuffed olives or 1 teaspoon capers

or:

¼ teaspoon thyme
1 squeeze garlic clove
1 teaspoon Worcestershire sauce

or:

2 tablespoons fresh chopped parsley and chives or 1 tablespoon sautéed chopped shallots or onions

After turning to complete the cooking, season with about:

1 teaspoon salt
⅛ teaspoon pepper
(1 teaspoon monosodium glutamate)

Defat the pan drippings. Deglaze them with:

Stock

Reduce the juices slightly and pour over the patties before serving. Or mix with the pan juices a little:

Barbecue, chili sauce, tomato catsup, horseradish, a few chopped olives or sautéed onions or mushrooms

Or spread over them:

Herb butters or mustard, page 383
A slice of Swiss cheese, crumbled blue cheese

or grated cheddar or Parmesan

Run the patties briefly under a broiler. You may garnish the tops with one of the following:

Very thin, sweet, raw or sautéed onion slice
A slice of tomato or cucumber

BROILED HAMBURGERS [4]

Preheat broiler.
➧ Please read About Hamburger, page 515. Shape lightly into ¾-inch-thick patties:

1 lb. ground beef

Place them on a broiler pan, 4 inches from the heat, or place them so they cover the untoasted side of:

A piece of bread toasted on one side only

If on the bread broil about 10 minutes. If not broil 6 minutes on one side, turn and broil about 4 minutes on the other. If the meat is very lean, you may brush it during broiling with:

Butter

⊟ GRILLED HAMBURGERS

We have watched with agony as good juices fed the flames of barbecues and the guests were dealt dry chips. If you must grill ground meat, please see page 89.
Prepare previous recipe for:

Hamburgers

To make the meat adhere well during handling, you may add to it:

1 beaten egg for each pound

Proceed as for:

Broiled Hamburgers, above

⊟ SLOPPY JOES

[8 Sandwiches]
Sauté in:

2 tablespoons butter
½ cup minced onions
½ cup chopped green pepper, seeds and membrane removed

When these are translucent, add:

1½ lbs. ground beef

Cook and stir until meat is slightly browned. Add:

½ cup chopped mushrooms
2 to 4 tablespoons chili sauce
Correct the seasoning

Cook, uncovered, over low heat until the mushrooms are done. Fill with this hot mixture:

8 slightly toasted sandwich buns

⊟ FILLED BEEF OR LAMBURGERS [6]

Preheat broiler.
Vary the fillings by using chopped celery, pickles, chili sauce, bread dressing, chopped leftover vegetables.
➧ Please read About Hamburger, page 515. Sauté lightly:

(6 slices bacon)

Divide into 12 portions:

1½ lbs. ground beef or lamb

Shape into flat cakes and fill with:

I.

6 tablespoons chopped nut meats
3 tablespoons chopped parsley
2 tablespoons grated onion

II.

Anchovy and a few capers for each patty

III.

Slice of Roquefort or cheddar cheese or liverwurst

Spread it on 6 of the cakes. Top them with those remaining. Bind the edges with the partially sautéed bacon strips and fasten with a toothpick. Broil for 10 to 15 minutes, turning them once.

LIVER PATTIES [6]

Preheat oven to 350°.
Combine:

- 1 lb. ground liver
- 1 slice chopped bacon
- ½ cup dry bread crumbs
- ¼ cup evaporated milk or cream
- ½ teaspoon salt
- ⅛ teaspoon pepper
- 2 teaspoons grated onion
- 2 tablespoons chopped parsley

Shape these ingredients into 6 flat cakes. Wrap around them:

- 6 slices bacon

Secure the bacon with toothpicks. Place the cakes in a lightly greased pan. Bake until well browned, about 6 minutes. Turn to insure even baking.

CHICKEN, VEAL OR LAMB PATTIES [12 to14]

Preheat broiler.
The French make many attractive dishes by grinding uncooked meat or fish, shaping it with other ingredients and poaching, broiling or sautéing the patties. Cut the meat from:

- A 4½ lb. chicken or use 3½ lbs. veal or lamb

Pick over the carcass for all edible bits of meat. Put the meat through a grinder, using a coarse knife. Save the juices, if any. Combine the ground meat, the juices and:

- ¾ cup whipping cream
- 1½ cups soft bread crumbs
- 1 teaspoon salt
- 1 teaspoon dried basel or 1 tablespoon chopped parsley
- A grating of lemon rind
- ¼ teaspoon paprika
- A grating of nutmeg

Shape the mixture into 10 patties. Roll them in a:

- Bound Breading (II, 160)

Place them in a ◆ shallow greased pan. Broil under moderate heat about 10 minutes to a side or until lightly browned. The patties may be left unbreaded and poached in a pan in the oven in a small amount of milk or stock, enough to cover the bottom of the skillet, until done. This means very low heat. Serve with:

- Béarnaise Sauce, page 370, or
- Soubise Sauce, page 363

GERMAN MEATBALLS OR KOENIGSBERGER KLOPS

[6 Servings—About Ten 2-Inch Balls]

A good buffet dish.
Soak in water, milk or stock to cover:

- 1 slice of bread, 1 inch thick

Put through a meat grinder twice:

- 1½ lbs. meat: ½ lb. beef, ½ lb. veal, ½ lb. pork or liver

Beat well and add:

- 2 eggs

Melt:

- 1 tablespoon butter

Sauté in it until golden:

- ¼ cup finely minced onion

Add them to the meat. Wring the liquid from the bread. Add the bread to the meat and:

- 3 tablespoons chopped parsley
- 1¼ teaspoons salt
- ¼ teaspoon paprika
- ½ teaspoon grated lemon rind
- 1 teaspoon lemon juice
- 1 teaspoon Worcestershire sauce or a grating of nutmeg

A few minced sardelles or ¼ herring may be added to the meatballs at this time or they may be added later to the gravy. Combine these ingredients well. Do this lightly with the hands—a better method than using a fork or spoon. Shape lightly in 2-inch balls. Drop into:

5 **cups boiling Vegetable Stock (II, 142)**

➧ Simmer covered for about 15 minutes. Remove from the stock. Measure the stock. Make Gravy of it, page 358, by using, for every cup stock:

2 **tablespoons butter**
2 **tablespoons flour**
Correct the seasoning

Cook and stir until smooth and hot. Add:

2 **tablespoons capers, or 2 tablespoons chopped pickles, lemon juice or cultured sour cream**
2 **tablespoons chopped parsley**

Reheat the meatballs in the gravy. Serve with a platter of:

Boiled Noodles, page 172, or
Spaetzle, page 179

Cover generously with:

Buttered Crumbs, page 389

ITALIAN MEATBALLS

Preheat oven to 350°.
Follow the preceding rule for:

German Meatballs

Omit the Worcestershire sauce. Add to the meat mixture:

½ **chopped clove garlic**
3 **tablespoons grated Parmesan cheese**
¼ **teaspoon orégano**

Mix and form into balls. Brown lightly in:

2 **tablespoons butter**

Place in a casserole. Half cover with:

Unthickened Tomato Sauce, page 376, or
Marinara Sauce, page 379

Bake covered for about 30 minutes.

SWEDISH MEATBALLS

[6 Servings of About Eighteen 1½-Inch Balls]

There are many recipes for this dish, all similar to and, in our opinion, none superior to:

German Meatballs, page 518

Shape the meat into 1½-inch balls. Brown in:

1 **tablespoon butter or drippings**

Simmer closely covered until done, about 15 minutes, in:

2 **cups consommé or other stock**

Make:

Pan Gravy, page 358

Season it with:

Sherry

Reheat the balls in the gravy. This is attractive served in a chafing dish, garnished with:

Potato Dumplings, page 180

CHINESE MEATBALLS [6]

Shape into 18 balls:

1½ **lbs. ground beef**

Season with:

1½ **teaspoons salt**
1 **teaspoon monosodium glutamate**
1 **tablespoon finely chopped parsley**

Coat the balls with:

Fritter Batter for Meat (II, 125)

Let them dry on a rack for 30 minutes. Deep-fat fry, pages 75–79, at 375°, until golden brown. Serve at once, covered with a:

Chinese Sweet-Sour Sauce, page 371

PORK BALLS IN TOMATO SAUCE [4]

Soak in water to cover:

A slice of bread, 1½ inches thick

Wring the water from it. Add to the bread:

1 **lb. ground pork**
⅓ **cup chopped onion**
1 **beaten egg**

¾ teaspoon salt
¼ teaspoon paprika

Combine these ingredients lightly with the hands until well blended. Shape into 2-inch balls. Combine the contents of:

1 can tomato soup: 10½ oz.
An equal amount of water

Bring the liquid to the boiling point. Drop the balls into it. ➧ Reduce the heat at once. Cover the pan and simmer until done, about ½ hour.

SAUERKRAUT BALLS

[4 Dozen 1¼-Inch Balls]

The sauerkraut helps tenderize as well as flavor these meatballs. ➧ Please read About Deep-Fat Frying, pages 75–79.

Preheat deep fryer to 375°.

Grind with a medium blade:

½ lb. each ham, corned beef and lean pork

Sauté the meat in:

3 tablespoons butter or fat

with:

⅓ cup finely chopped onion

Mix, stir in and ➧ simmer until thick, stirring constantly:

2 cups flour
½ to 1 teaspoon dry mustard
1 teaspoon salt
2 cups milk

When this mixture has cooked, combine it with:

2 lbs. cooked, drained sauerkraut

Then regrind the entire mixture. Form into 1¼-inch balls. Roll them in:

Bound Breading (II, 160)

Deep fry until golden brown. Drain on absorbent paper and serve at once.

CHILI CON CARNE [8]

Melt:

2 to 3 tablespoons bacon drippings or butter

Sauté in the fat:

½ cup chopped onion or
½ chopped clove garlic

Add:

1 to 2 lbs. ground beef or lamb

Stir and sauté the beef until well done.

Add:

1¼ cups canned tomatoes
4 cups canned kidney beans
¾ teaspoon or more salt
½ bay leaf
(1 teaspoon sugar)
2 teaspoons to 2 tablespoons chili powder

depending on your taste and the strength of the chili powder. Cover and cook slowly for about 1 hour. Serve with:

Tortillas or crackers

PORCUPINES [6]

Combine:

1 lb. ground beef
½ cup bread crumbs
1 egg
¾ teaspoon salt
¼ teaspoon paprika
(2 tablespoons chopped green peppers)

Roll these ingredients ➧ lightly into balls. Press into flat cakes. Roll in:

¼ cup raw rice

Heat in a heavy pot:

Thickened Tomato Sauce, page 376

Add:

(1 teaspoon chili powder)

Add the meat cakes. Cover the pot. Simmer the meat for about 45 minutes.

Correct the seasoning and serve.

SPANISH CASSEROLE WITH RICE [6]

This is a one-dish meal.

Preheat oven to 350°.

Steam:

⅔ cup rice

Prepare:

1 cup chopped celery

¼ cup chopped green pepper

Melt in a saucepan:

2 tablespoons butter or other fat

Peel, chop and sauté in the butter until golden:

1 medium-sized onion

Add and sear:

1 lb. ground round steak

Season with:

¾ teaspoon salt
¼ teaspoon paprika

Place in a greased baking dish ⅓ of the rice and ½ of the meat. Sprinkle over it ½ of the celery and pepper. Repeat this process. Place the last of the rice on top. Pour over these ingredients:

1 can condensed tomato soup: 10½ oz.
Seasonings

Cover the dish and bake about ½ hour.

LAMB AND EGGPLANT CASSEROLE [4]

Preheat oven to 350°.

Pare and chop until fine:

1 medium-sized eggplant

Combine with:

2 cups ground lamb: 1 lb.
½ cup chopped onion
3 tablespoons chopped parsley
1 teaspoon salt
¼ teaspoon paprika
(½ teaspoon curry powder)
1 cup canned chopped tomatoes

Butter a casserole. Fill it with the lamb mixture. Bake covered for about ¾ hour. Remove the cover and let the top brown.

HAMBURGER CASSEROLE [4]

Preheat oven to 400°.

Melt in a skillet:

¼ cup butter

Sauté in it until the meat loses its ruddiness:

1 lb. ground steak or veal
1 cup minced celery
1 medium-sized cubed onion
½ lb. mushrooms

Add:

1 teaspoon salt

Place the ingredients in a casserole. Cover with:

1 cup condensed tomato soup

Bake for about 45 minutes. Serve with:

Fried Noodles, page 172

STUFFED CABBAGE OR GEFUELLTER KRAUTKOPF [6]

Separate and prepare by blanching for about 5 minutes, page 88:

The leaves from a head of cabbage

Reserve the liquor. Place the leaves at once on towels to drain. Prepare one of the following meat dressings.

I.

Soak in water for 2 minutes:

1 slice of bread, 1 inch thick

Press the water from it. Combine the bread with:

½ lb. ground pork
½ lb. ground beef
½ lb. ground veal
3 beaten eggs
¾ teaspoon salt
¼ teaspoon paprika

II.

Or use a filling of:

1 lb. fresh pork sausage meat
3 half-inch slices of bread
1 beaten egg

Line a bowl with a large napkin or cloth and fill it with alternate layers of the leaves and the meat dressing. Cover the top with 1 or 2 large leaves, gather up the cloth and tie it with a string. Place the bag in boiling water—the water in which the cabbage was boiled and as much fresh boiling water as needed to cover well. ➧ Simmer the cabbage gently for 2 hours if you are old-fashioned, but 45 minutes should be ample time. Drain it in a colander, untie the bag and place the cabbage in a hot serving dish. Serve with the following onion sauce. Brown in the top of a double boiler:

¼ **cup butter**

Add and stir until brown:

2 **tablespoons flour**

Have ready:

2 **cups Stock (II, 141) or cabbage water**

Stir ½ cup of this into the butter mixture. Add:

½ **cup or more chopped onion**

If required,

Correct the seasoning

Cook the onions covered ➧ over—not in—hot water, until they are very tender. Add the remainder of the stock gradually. The gravy is best when it is thick with onions.

GROUND BEEF IN CABBAGE LEAVES [4]

Preheat oven to 375°.
Wash and parblanch, page 88:

8 **large cabbage leaves**

Drain and dry them on a towel. Combine:

1 **lb. ground beef or a mixture of beef, veal, pork and liver**
3 **tablespoons finely chopped onions**
2 **tablespoons finely chopped parsley**
¾ **teaspoon salt**
½ **teaspoon thyme**
½ **mashed clove garlic**
A few grains cayenne

If you want a sweet-sour effect, add:

2 **tablespoons vinegar**
3 **tablespoons brown sugar**
1 **teaspoon capers**

Divide the meat mixture into 8 parts. Put one part on each cabbage leaf. Roll the leaves, as shown on page 86. Tie or secure them with toothpicks. Place them close together in a buttered baking dish. Dot each roll with:

½ **teaspoon butter**

Pour into the dish:

½ **cup boiling Stock (II, 141)**

or you may use:

½ **cup water, tomato juice or cultured sour cream and paprika**

Bake the rolls, covered, until the cabbage leaves are very tender, about 50 minutes.

STUFFED GRAPE LEAVES OR DOLMAS

[30 Dolmas or 9 to 10 Portions]

Prepare for stuffing:

30 **tender Grape Leaves, page 86**

Fill each one with a tablespoon of the following mixture:

2 **cups finely chopped onions**
½ **cup rice**
⅓ **cup olive oil**
2 **tablespoons finely chopped parsley**
2 **tablespoons finely chopped dill**
¼ **cup pine nuts**
¼ **cup currants**
(1 cup finely minced lamb)

Do not roll the leaves too tightly, as the rice will swell. Cook as directed, page 86, weighted, over low heat about 1½ hours. Serve chilled.

ABOUT MEAT LOAF

Although proportions of beef, veal and pork are specified in the following recipes, they may be varied, provided the total amount of meat remains the same. Be sure to ➧ cook thoroughly if pork is used. Handle ingredients for meat loaf ➧ lightly, mixing with a two-tined fork. To stretch, see About Hamburger, page 515.

Meat loaf may be mounded

on a flat greased pan or put into a greased ring mold or loaf pan. Also, it may be baked in 2 layers with a good stuffing between. You may pour about ½ cup of catsup in the bottom of the mold or pan before you fill it with the meat; or you may pour about 2 tablespoons of chili sauce over the meat loaf when it is half baked. This gives it a good flavor and a light crust.

For more rapid cooking, individual meat loaves take only about 15 minutes and—for attractive service—may be baked in greased muffin tins and glazed. Bake the loaf and baste it, as directed in the following recipes. You may cover it with a piece of foil. Remove the foil for the last ¼ hour of the baking period. If using chili sauce on top or covering the loaf with foil, do not baste it. Invert the mold.

Serve a ring hot, filled with green peas or some other vegetable and surrounded by browned potatoes. Or serve cold, filled with potato or some other vegetable salad.

MEAT LOAF [4]

I.

Preheat oven to 350°.
Combine and shape into a loaf:

1 lb. ground beef: ¼ this amount may be pork
(1 egg yolk)
2 tablespoons chopped parsley
1 tablespoon soft butter
1 tablespoon bread crumbs
1 teaspoon lemon juice
1 teaspoon salt
¼ teaspoon pepper
½ teaspoon onion juice

Place the loaf in a lightly greased pan. Bake it for 1 hour. Pour some over the top and baste at intervals with the remainder of:

¼ cup butter
1 cup Vegetable Stock (II, 142), or 1 cup boiling water plus ½ package dried soup mix

Serve the loaf with:

Sweet Potato Puffs, page 323

II. [4]

Preheat oven to 350°.
Place in a bowl:

1 lb. ground round steak
1 to 2 tablespoons horseradish
2 tablespoons catsup
1 teaspoon salt
¼ teaspoon pepper
½ cup cream

Grind in a food chopper then add:

6 slices bacon
2 medium-sized onions
1 cup broken-up crackers

Mix with a fork. Mold into a loaf. Roll it in:

¼ cup cracker crumbs

Place the loaf in a shallow baking pan. Pour into the pan:

½ cup stock

Bake the loaf for about 1½ hours. Baste occasionally, adding more liquid, if necessary. Make:

Pan Gravy, page 358

MEAT LOAF COCKAIGNE [6]

Preheat oven to 350°.
Mix lightly with:

1½ lbs. lean ground beef—be sure beef has only been ground once
1 can condensed cream of chicken or mushroom soup
¾ cup dry bread crumbs
¼ cup mixed fresh tarragon, parsley, basil or chives
1 teaspoon salt
1 pressed clove garlic
10 or more chopped stuffed olives or ¼ cup chopped water chestnuts

Place the mixture in a 4 x 8 x 4-inch pan. Bake about 45 minutes. Serve hot with:

(Thickened Tomato Sauce, page 376)

VEAL LOAF [8 to 10]

Preheat oven to 350°.
Grind:

2 lbs. veal
1 lb. smoked ham or sausage

Add and ◆ mix together very lightly:

1 tablespoon minced onion
¼ cup seeded chopped green pepper
2 beaten eggs
½ teaspoon salt
⅛ teaspoon paprika
¾ cup dry bread crumbs
1 cup condensed mushroom soup

Place ½ to ⅓ of this mixture in a 4 x 8 x 4-inch loaf pan. You may then press whole mushrooms or hard-cooked eggs, stuffed olives or pistachio nuts into the meat in a pattern. Cover with another third of meat and repeat the pattern or cover with half the meat. Bake for about 1 hour. Serve hot or cold.

LIVER LOAF [6 to 8]

This makes a most appetizing everyday liver spread.
Preheat oven to 350°.
Boil for 5 minutes:

1 cup water
1 medium-sized chopped onion
3 ribs celery with leaves

Prepare for cooking, page 535, slice, add and simmer for 2 minutes:

1 lb. liver: beef, lamb or pork

Drain, reserving liquid. Put liver and vegetables through a meat chopper with:

2 slices bacon or a 1½-inch cube salt pork

Add and blend well:

1 or 2 beaten eggs
¾ teaspoon salt
⅛ teaspoon pepper
1 cup cracker or dry bread crumbs
½ teaspoon dried marjoram or thyme
1 cup liquid: liver stock, milk, tomato juice, etc.

Pour into a greased loaf pan:

(½ cup catsup)

Place the meat in the pan. Bake for about 40 minutes.

RAW SMOKED HAM LOAF [4 to 6]

You may dress this up or down.
Preheat oven to 350°.
Try using:

½ cup crushed pineapple
½ teaspoon dry mustard

in the bottom of the pan or end up with the glazes suggested below. Grind:

1 lb. raw smoked ham
½ lb. lean pork
(½ onion)

Add and mix together with the hands:

2 well-beaten eggs
½ to 1 cup cracker or dry bread crumbs
An equal amount of milk
⅛ teaspoon pepper
3 tablespoons mixed fresh herbs

Shape into a loaf, place in a greased bread pan and bake for about 2 hours, basting frequently with:

Honey Glaze, page 387, or Spirit Glaze for Ham, page 387

ABOUT PÂTÉ DE FOIE

The famed foie gras of Europe is produced by the forced feeding of geese, which causes their livers to become marbled in appearance and so increase their bulk that they often account for ¼ the bird's weight. In this country the law forbids this practice, although unfatted goose liver is available. As a matter of fact, the liver of which American pâtés are usually composed—that of chickens

—makes a more than merely acceptable substitute.

⅄✻ PÂTÉ DE FOIE DE VOLAILLE OR CHICKEN LIVER PÂTÉ

I. [About Twenty ½-Inch Slices]

Divide into 3 parts:

1½ lbs. chicken livers

Blend one part with:

2 eggs

Blend the second part briefly with:

¼ cup whipping cream

Blend the third part with:

4 slices chopped bacon
1 egg
3 tablespoons cognac
2 tablespoons port wine
¼ cup flour

Mix these three blends together ➧ very lightly with:

1 teaspoon ginger
2 teaspoons salt
½ teaspoon black pepper
1 teaspoon allspice or nutmeg

Line a loaf pan with dough for a pâté, see this page.
Preheat oven to 325°.
Put ½ the above mixture in the loaf pan. You may add:

1 to 2 sliced truffles

Cover with the remaining mixture. Top with:

Thin-sliced salt pork

Cover tightly with foil. Bake the pâté in a pan of hot water for 1½ to 2 hours. Test for doneness, as for poultry.

II. ✻ [About 40 Slices, ½-Inch Thick]

Should the veal be red, as it is so often in our markets, marinate it overnight covered with milk and refrigerated.
➧ Please read About Pâté En Croûte below. Preheat oven to 325°.
Pound:

1 lb. white veal

Add to it and ➧ grind 3 times:

1½ lbs. chicken livers
¼ lb. salt pork
2 anchovy fillets

Mix in lightly until very smooth:

4 beaten eggs
½ cup whipping cream
3 tablespoons grated onion
2 tablespoons chopped parsley or chervil
⅛ teaspoon freshly ground black pepper
¼ cup cognac
1 tablespoon Madeira
2 tablespoons chopped truffles

You may put this mixture in a loaf pan lined with dough for pâté, page 527, or directly into a greased loaf pan. If you do not use the pastry liner on page 527, set the pan in a larger one of hot water. Bake for about 1½ hours or to an internal temperature of 180°. To test for doneness, see (II, 336). The pâté should still be pink in color when done. After cooling, you may glaze the pastry case with:

Aspic, page 387

if you do not plan freezing it.

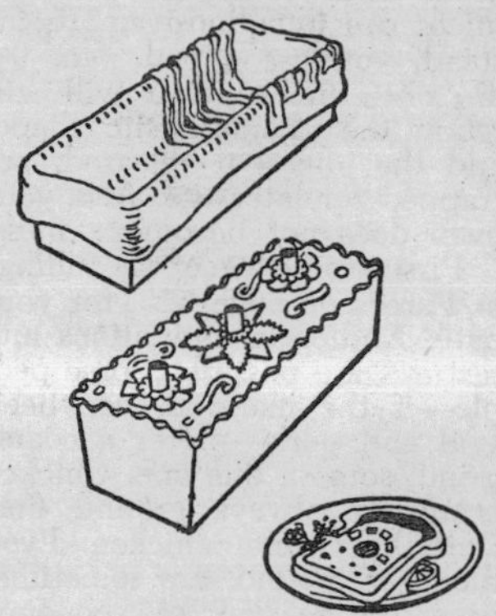

ABOUT PÂTÉ EN CROÛTE

The term alone evokes an instant image of glamorous dining. But for those of us who know pâtés only in canned form—

where the heat necessary to preserve them destroys their bloom —a good pâté maison is a revelation. And it makes us want at once to develop our own pâté ménagère. Basically this isn't any harder than making a meat pie. Pâté en croûte is beautiful to see in its glazed case. And it is even lovelier when sliced, revealing first the crusty edge and, within, the nugget-filled farce, with its clear gelatin top —see illustration. The novice does not realize that the crust is not really meant to be eaten, but is the protection the pâté needs to develop flavor to the fullest and to retain the juices.

Our friend, Chef Pierre Adrian, worried so about his American diners' insistence on consuming this tough protective coating that he now customarily uses a more appetizing, if harder to handle, pâte brisée (II, 297), to line his molds. He also suggests that the conventional hinged pâté molds nearly always leak and, should the pâté crust break in any way, the delicious juices run into the oven. If, instead, you use a loaf pan, 9 x 4½ x 4½ inches, you will still retain the characteristic shape, and the juices, if released, are trapped for later use. Also your oven does not become a mess.

First choose one of the Fillings or Farces on page 525, for your pâté. Endless combinations and textures are possible. Some people—if the materials are beef, veal and pork—prefer a coarse grind, some a fine one. Chicken is nearly always ground fine. Calf liver and chicken liver, diced or ground, are sometimes used for reasons of economy. Suckling pigs' livers are a real treat.

➧ Cut into dice only the tenderest, choicest parts of young meat—free from all connective tissue or sinew. Marinate these and any liver in white wine refrigerated for 24 hours. Foie gras is often marinated in cognac. Mix with at least ½, up to twice, as much fat as meat. Then grind both meat and fat together 3 times, with the finest meat grinder blade. You may be tempted to use a blender, but we find the texture that results is both stringy and pasty. The ground meat is then folded into the yolks, spices, cream and the other ingredients to form the pâté.

Now it's time to prepare the pâte or crust, which for easier handling should rest covered for several hours. Have ready the tenderloins, livers, truffles, tongue or other choice bits which will form the eventual mosaiclike pattern in cross section when the pâté is cut. Now, line the pâté mold with the crust. You may roll and fit it in by making a ⅛-inch-thick circular shape of ¾ of the dough. Reserve the other fourth for the lid. We find it easier to form ¾ of the dough into a thick oval approximately the size of the base of the mold and line the bottom. With the sides of the hands, used in chopping motions, gradually work the dough from the base so that it thins out and creeps up the sides. Then, with the fingers patting it thin, form the rest of the crust to lap over the top, page 525. Do not stretch the dough or tear it. Next, line the mold with thin strips of fat bacon in parallel U shapes, as sketched. Allow them to rest, temporarily, over the side. When the pâté is built up to the top, fold the bacon ends over to encase it completely. Now back to the lining. First spread on it a ¾-inch layer of farce. Begin then to imbed the choice solids called for in the recipe, separating and surrounding them with more of the farce, so that the pâté when cut shows a pattern in cross section, as sketched. When the mold is filled and the bacon placed over the top of the filling, crimp the edge of the dough and cut off the excess.

From the remaining ¼ amount of dough, roll a $\frac{3}{16}$-inch-thick section of crust for the lid. Brush the edges of the mold with Egg Wash (II, 433). In applying the top, pinch it onto the already crimped top edges. Do not stretch the dough, but leave it lax enough so that it will not crack or become distorted during baking. Cut from the scraps small geometric or floral shapes to ornament the top. Work your pattern around 2 or 3 circles which can hold pastry vents, as shown in the drawing. These will later form a guide for the funnel when the aspic is carefully poured between the pâté and the upper crust. Apply the ornaments with egg wash and brush the top with it before baking. Vent the top crust with a few fancy cuts, as you would for a pie. Preheat the oven to 400°. To avoid too rapid browning of the crust, you may have ready a piece of foil to put loosely over the top. This will protect it in the early stages of baking. As soon as you put the pâté in the oven ➧ lower the heat to 325°. Pâtés are usually cooked about 1½ hours. Test for doneness as for cake (II, 336).

Allow the pâté, still in the pan, to cool on a rack. When cold, fill the space which will have formed at the top between the filling and the crust by pouring through the vents enough flavorful aspic which—when it solidifies—will support the crust. Use a firm gelatin, allowing 1 tablespoon of gelatin for each cup of meat stock. Hold a funnel in one of the vents and pour the mixture—being careful not to moisten the crust on the outside. Allow the pâté to remain in the pan refrigerated until the aspic is set. To unmold the pâté, proceed as for unmolding a gelatin (II, 186). Use a rack, however, on which to reverse it—to facilitate turning the pâté right side up onto a serving platter.

Pâtés should, of course, be stored refrigerated and most pâtés profit by ➧ resting refrigerated for at least 48 hours before serving—so that the flavors blend and the contents are firm enough for even slicing.

When served, the whole pâté may be garnished with a border of chopped aspic jelly, parsley and lemon wedges. When serving, cut it with a warm knife. An individual serving should be at least ⅜ to ½ of an inch thick and garnished with parsley and a lemon wedge.

For the size described here, you can produce 40 servings this way: slice about ½ inch thick, then cut each slice in half on the diagonal.

CRUST OR PÂTE FOR PÂTÉ

Work together with your fingers until you have achieved the consistency of coarse corn meal:

6 cups sifted all-purpose flour
2 teaspoons salt
1½ cups lard or shortening

Make a well (II, 301) of these ingredients and break into the center, one at a time:

2 eggs

working them into the flour mixture from the inside and adding gradually:

About 3 cups water

You may need a little more water to make a dough that can be worked into a smooth mass and rolled into a ball. The mold is easier to form if you rest it covered at about 70° for several hours. To mold, see About Pâté en Croûte, page 525.

LIVER PÂTÉ

A less luxurious version of this dish may be made more quickly by omitting the gelatin and consommé.
Blend with a fork:
 1½ cups liver sausage
 ½ can condensed cream of tomato soup
Dissolve:
 1 tablespoon gelatin
in:
 ¼ cup cold water
Bring to a boil:
 1 can condensed consommé
and combine with the dissolved gelatin. Reserve ¾ cup of this mixture to line a pint mold. Add to the remainder:
 1 teaspoon Worcestershire sauce
 ¼ teaspoon salt
 (1 pressed clove garlic)
 (1 tablespoon finely chopped parsley)
and the blended liver mixture. Fold into the mold. Let set. Reverse to serve.

SOUFFLÉED LIVER PÂTÉ

Preheat oven to 350°.
I. Have ready two 9-inch bread pans, one rinsed in cold water, the other prepared as for a soufflé baker, page 196. Into the rinsed pan, pour ½ inch of the following gelatin mixture and place it in the refrigerator.
Soak for 3 minutes:
 2 teaspoons gelatin
in:
 ¼ cup cold water
Combine it with:
 2 cups well-seasoned Double Consommé, page 109
Reserve the rest of the gelatin mixture and keep it at room temperature. Grind:
 1 lb. raw chicken livers
➧ Or if you use ⅄ a blender put the liver and the following ingredients into it and blend briefly. Beat in:
 2 eggs
 2 egg yolks
 2 teaspoons onion juice
 2 tablespoons chopped parsley
Fold in:
 2 cups whipping cream
 2 stiffly beaten egg whites
Bake this mixture in the greased pan at 350° until set, about 1 hour. Before placing it in the oven, you may set the pan in a larger one of warm water. When the loaf is thoroughly cold, remove from the pan and place on top of the chilled and set gelatin. Pour the reserved gelatin over the reversed bottom of the loaf, letting it run down the sides so that it is entirely enclosed in the gelatin. Let the added gelatin set and the loaf become thoroughly chilled before serving. Unmold and decorate the top with:
 Thinly sliced limes
Garnish the platter with:
 Parsley

II. An alternate suggestion for glazing this loaf is to replace the consommé with a combination of 1 cup water or stock and 1 cup port wine. Jell and mold it in 2 steps, as described previously.

ABOUT TERRINES

Terrines are the poor relations of the pâté. They are often made from leftovers, game or rabbit. Like pâté, the meat must be succulent and is often in the form of medallions or scallops. ➧ There should be about ⅓ fresh veal to jelly the whole when it cools. Terrines are baked without a crust in lidded earthenware dishes. Set them in a pan of water. For an 11½ x 9 x 4½-inch size, allow about 2 hours of baking in a 300° oven. Use the following method or make up your own meat mixture which you may reinforce with liver. The meat may, if you like, be placed in a wine marinade before cooking.

✱ VEAL OR CHICKEN TERRINE

Line the bottom and sides of a mold with strips of bacon, overlapping them ever so slightly. Strew with:

1 tablespoon chopped parsley
1 tablespoon chopped onion

Pound very thin:

2 lbs. veal scallops, cut in ¼-inch-thick slices

In pounding veal, use your mallet with a glancing action, as sketched, page 452, and the meat will not stick to it. Have ready:

2 lbs. finely sliced ham, chicken or pork

Overlay the bacon with a layer of the thin pounded veal. Season it with:

A grind of pepper
A pinch of thyme
A pinch of powdered bay leaf

Put down a layer of the thin-sliced ham. Continue to build layers of parsley and onion and veal, seasoning and ham. Cover the top with overlapping bacon strips. Pour about:

A cup of white wine
A dash of brandy

over the meat layers until all the crevices are filled with liquid. Set the pan in a larger pan of hot water. Bake at 300° about 2 hours or until done. As soon as you remove the meat from the oven, cover with heavy aluminum foil and weight the layers with a brick. When the meat has cooled, a grease-covered jelly will have formed, which keeps the meat in prime condition. To serve, slice very thin. Use for hors d'oeuvre or as a main informal luncheon dish. Store refrigerated any that remains, covered with:

Clarified butter

ABOUT GALANTINES

When galantines appear in all their truffled chaud-froid splendor, it is hard to believe that they started out with the boning of a bird, page 570. Begin with a slit down the spine but it is vital that during the rest of the boning the skin be kept intact. If cut, as around the leg and wing joints, it must be patched by sewing.

GALANTINE OF TURKEY

[If Served Hot, 12 to 15 Servings —if Served Cold, 30 Servings]

Bone, page 570:

A 12- to 15-lb. turkey

Reserve the meat, including that cut from the drumsticks and the breast. Make a Stock (II, 143) of the bones. Reserve ½ the breast meat for decorations and cut it into ½-inch strips. Grind 3 times and put into a large bowl:

1 lb. lean white veal
1 lb. lean pork

as well as all the turkey meat, except the reserved portion. Season the mixture with:

¼ cup cognac, dry sherry or Madeira
1 teaspoon freshly grated nutmeg
Ground black pepper
2 teaspoons Worcestershire sauce
1 tablespoon salt
A dash hot pepper sauce
2 teaspoons monosodium glutamate

Add:

8 eggs
½ cup finely chopped parsley

Mix these ingredients into a smooth paste.

Correct the seasoning

Spread a large piece of clean linen or cheesecloth on the table. Place in the center of the cloth the turkey skin, outer side down, as shown in the center below. Carefully follow the instructions under Boned Chicken, page 585, about arranging the skin. Pat the meat mixture onto it in an even rectangular shape, extending it all the way to the edges. Arrange in neat alternating rows down the center, as shown:

Strips of cooked ham or tongue

and the reserved strips of turkey breast. Arrange a center row of:

Small whole truffles, page 300

Over the whole, sprinkle:

¾ cup pistachio nuts
¼ cup finely chopped parsley

Starting at the long side farthest away from you, pull the cloth toward you gently—rolling the filled turkey skin into a sausage-like shape. You do not want the cloth to be inside the turkey roll, but keep manipulating it until it forms an outside casing. You may need help. Tie the cloth securely at both ends. The roll should be smooth and even. Also tie it lengthwise, as sketched. Place it on a rack, seam side down, in a large poaching kettle. Add:

Mirepoix (II, 221)
Enough turkey or chicken Stock to cover (II, 142)

Cover the kettle and bring to a boil then ➧ reduce the heat and simmer very gently for 1½ to 2 hours until the roll is firm to the touch. Carefully remove it from the broth. You may serve it hot, sliced, with buttered toast. Or let it cool—wrapped—on a large platter. You may weight it if you wish. When it has reached at least room temperature, remove the outside wrapping and refrigerate thoroughly. To decorate, either use:

Chaud-Froid, page 388

or cover with a savory:

Aspic Glaze, page 388

made from the poaching broth. Serve thinly sliced with:

Buttered toast

as an hors d'oeuvre or an entrée.

ABOUT SAUSAGE

One of our early European memories was the rapt stance of the citizenry as they gazed at window displays of sausage. It made us aware for the first time of their wealth of choice and, on a considerably more limited scale, of our own. There is freshly ground sausage meat or Country Sausage, page 531, which must be used at once. There are smoked sausages: frankfurters, wieners or Vienna sausage, Bologna and Mettwurst

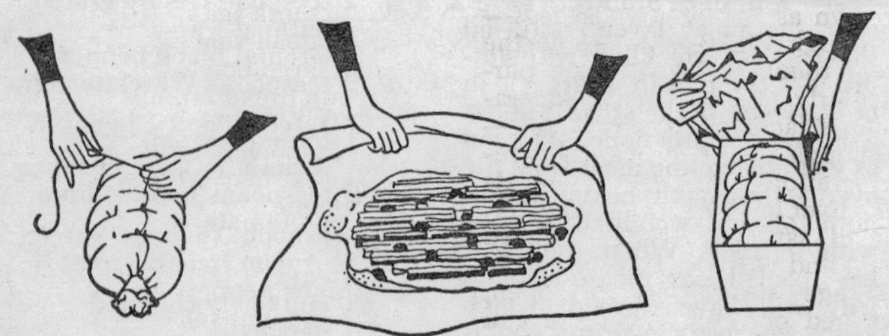

—all of which may be eaten as bought, but may also be simmered, baked or broiled for serving with pasta, hot vegetables and fruit garnish. See Stewed Fruits (II, 88). ➧ To make Smoked Sausages, see (II, 545).

If you broil or pan-fry these cased sausages ➧ prick them to keep the skins from bursting. This is not necessary if you have added a small quantity of water to the pan at the beginning of cooking or have first blanched, dried and floured them lightly before frying. Even then, if they swell quickly, prick them lightly before they burst, to give greater protection to the meat.

➧ For 4 servings, allow about 1 lb. of freshly ground sausage meat or the smoked types, slightly less for the more aged and drier types.

Dry sausages are also available: hard and soft cervelat, salami, saucison de Lyon, mortadella, pepperoni and chorizo. They are delicious as hors d'oeuvre, in sandwiches and for seasoning bland dishes.

Be sure that any kind of sausage you buy or make involves good quality meats. Cereal "stretchers" are almost certainly present in commercial sausages unless they are marked "pure" or "all meat." When properly made and if the casing is intact, dry sausages may be kept indefinitely in a cool place. For this reason, they have become known as "summer sausages"—although they are available the year round. Dry types are particularly prized when refrigeration is lacking. Available, too—although they need constant refrigeration—are spiced meats like liver loaf or Braunschweiger, blood sausage, deviled minced ham and veal loaves. ➧ Once the sausage casing is cut open, smoked or cooked sausage can be stored refrigerated about 1 week; semidry and dry types, 2 weeks or more.

COUNTRY SAUSAGE

At butchering time in our valley, the popular man is the one who knows how to flavor the sausage —not too much pepper or sage and just enough coriander. This process has to be played by ear, for ➧ uncooked meat cannot be tasted to correct the seasoning and the strength of spices is so variable. The best way to learn is to mix a small batch and cook up a sample for the always hungry helpers to test.

I. To each part:

Firm diced lard

Use:

2 parts lean ground pork

Season the lard with a mixture of:

Thyme
Summer savory
Coriander
Sweet marjoram
Pulverized bay leaf
Freshly ground pepper

➧ To cook fresh sausage patties, start them in a ➧ cold ungreased pan over moderate heat and cook until medium brown on both sides and done throughout.

II.

[6 Medium Patties]

If you have a sudden hankering for one of these small-scale recipes, grind ➧ twice with the finest grinder knives:

½ lb. lean pork
½ lb. pork fat
½ lb. lean veal

Mix in a large bowl:

1 cup bread crumbs
Grated rind of 1 lemon
¼ teaspoon each sage, sweet marjoram and thyme
⅛ teaspoon summer savory
½ teaspoon freshly ground black pepper
2 teaspoons salt

A grating of fresh nutmeg

Add the ground meat and form this mixture into a 1½-inch layer. Store overnight refrigerated and covered to blend the seasoning. ➧ To cook, see I, above.

SAUTÉED SAUSAGE MEAT PATTIES [4]

Combine:

1 lb. sausage meat
2 tablespoons flour
(¼ cup drained crushed pineapple or grated fresh apple)

Shape the meat into cakes ½ inch thick. Sprinkle with:

Flour

Heat a skillet. No fat is required. Brown the cakes quickly on both sides. Cover with a lid. ➧ Reduce the heat and cook about 10 minutes on one side. Pour off excess fat. Turn and cook 10 minutes on the other side or until done. Serve with:

Sautéed Onions, page 302
Applesauce (II, 95)

⊟ PAN-BROILED SAUSAGE [4]

➧ Please read About Sausage, page 530. Cut apart and place in a skillet:

8 sausages

Add:

½ cup boiling water

Cover the pan. Simmer gently, not over 190°, for 8 to 10 minutes or until almost done. Pour off the liquid. Return the sausages to the pan. Cook them over low heat, shaking the pan constantly until they are an even brown. Drain. Serve with:

Prepared mustard

For picnics, serve between:

Rolls

BROILED SAUSAGE PATTIES [2]

Preheat broiler.

Shape into 4 flat cakes:

½ lb. sausage meat

Roll the cakes in:

1 tablespoon flour

Broil under moderate heat for 8 to 10 minutes or until done. Arrange on a hot platter:

Apple Rings (II, 94)

Place the sausage cakes on them. Serve garnished with:

Parsley

BOILED SAUSAGE

Place in a kettle:

Smoked sausage

Cover with:

Boiling water

Simmer for about 10 minutes. Drain, skin, slice and serve with:

Sauerkraut, page 278

BAKED SAUSAGE MEAT RING [6]

Preheat oven to 350°.

Grease lightly a 7-inch ring mold. Press onto the bottom:

3 tablespoons cornflakes

Combine well:

1 lb. sausage meat
1 tablespoon minced onion
¾ cup fine bread crumbs
2 tablespoons chopped parsley
1 beaten egg

Place these ingredients in the mold. Bake the ring 15 minutes. Drain the fat from it. Bake 15 minutes longer or until done. Invert the ring onto a hot platter and fill the center with:

8 Scrambled Eggs, page 191

Garnish the top with:

Chopped parsley or paprika

BAKED SAUSAGE MEAT, SWEET POTATOES AND FRUIT [4]

Preheat oven to 350°.

This is a good dish for large groups.

Cook:

4 large sweet potatoes

Peel and cut them into thin slices. Grease a baking dish. Cover the bottom with ½ the sweet potatoes. Shape into 4 flat cakes:

1 lb. sausage meat

Brown the cakes lightly in a greased pan, to which you may add:

1 tablespoon minced bacon

Peel and cut into thick slices:

4 large apples or pineapple slices

Place the drained meat cakes on the sweet potatoes and cover with apple slices. Sprinkle lightly with:

Salt and brown sugar

Place the remaining sweet potatoes over the fruit. Brush the potatoes with:

Milk

and sprinkle with:

Brown sugar

Bake for about ¾ hour.

PORK SCRAPPLE OR GOETTA

[About 6 Servings]

If you use corn meal, call it scrapple. If you use oats, call it goetta. This may also be made with ¾ cup cooked pork. Use stock from the pork bones in cooking the cereal. Place in a pan:

2 lbs. pork neck bones or other bony pieces

Add:

1½ quarts boiling water
1 sliced onion
6 peppercorns
(1 small bay leaf)

Simmer the pork until the meat falls from the bones. Strain, reserving the liquor. There should be about 4 cups. Add water or light stock if necessary to make this amount. Prepare, using this liquid in place of boiling water:

Corn Meal Mush, page 157

You may substitute 1 cup oatmeal for the corn meal. In cooking oatmeal, you may want to reduce the liquid by one cup. Remove all meat from the pork bones and chop or grind it fine. Add it to the cooked mush. Season with:

Salt, if required
1 teaspoon or more grated onion
(½ teaspoon dried thyme or sage)
A grating of fresh nutmeg
A little cayenne

Pour the scrapple into a bread pan that has been rinsed with cold water. Let it stand until cold and firm. Slice it. To serve, sauté slowly in:

Melted butter or drippings

BLOOD SAUSAGE, BOUDIN NOIR OR BLACK PUDDING

Have the sausage casings ready. Cook gently without browning:

¾ cup finely chopped onions

in:

2 tablespoons lard

Dice into ½-inch cubes and half melt:

1 lb. fresh pork fat

Cool slightly and mix in a bowl with:

⅓ cup whipping cream
2 beaten eggs
A grind of fresh pepper
⅛ teaspoon fresh thyme
½ pulverized bay leaf

When these ingredients have been gently combined, mix in:

2 cups fresh pork blood

Fill casings about ⅘ full, as this mixture will swell during the poaching period. Without overcrowding, put the sealed casings into a wire basket. Plunge them into boiling water. ➧ Reduce heat at once to 200° to 203° and continue to cook at this temperature for about 20 minutes. Should any of the sausages rise to the surface of the simmering liquid, pierce them to release the air that might burst the skins. To serve, split and grill them very gently.

ABOUT VARIETY MEATS

Variety, we know, is the spice of life. And variety meats provide welcome relief from the weekly round of beef, pork, veal, chicken and fish. Variety meats include organ meats like sweetbreads, brains, liver and kidney; muscle meats like heart, tongue and tripe; and very bony-structured meats like tails, knucklebones and their delicious marrow centers. Time was when most of these tidbits were ours almost for the asking. Today, hospital authorities—aware of the special virtues of organ meats—purchase them in large quantity. And the remainder are increasingly used in meat processing. As a result, the American housewife is apt to find variety meats of all types scarcer and considerably more expensive than they were a decade ago. ➧ It is essential that these meats be very, very fresh. Even when they are, the pan drippings from kidney and liver may sometimes be strong, and some cooks prefer to discard them. If in doubt, taste the drippings before serving.

ABOUT LIVER

Chicken and calf livers are the tenderest and most desirable unless, of course, you can secure extra-fat goose livers—the kind which in Europe almost invariably find their way into Pâtés, page 524. Baby beef liver comes next for quality. It should be handled like that of lamb, sheep, pork and older beef livers—that is, soaked for about 30 minutes in a marinade, page 380, or in milk. Before cooking, all these stronger types of liver should be dried and the liquids in which they have been soaked discarded.

➧ To prepare any liver for cooking, wipe it first with a damp cloth, then remove the thin outer skin and veining. Except for the timing noted in individual recipes, the cooking method for liver generally is the same. ➧ Never toughen it by cooking it too long or over excessive heat. ➧ Never cook it beyond the point of tenderness. Sometimes the drippings in which liver has been cooked are bitter. Test them by tasting before you use them as sauce. Allow 1 pound liver for 4 servings.

CALF OR CHICKEN LIVER LYONNAISE [2]

➧ Please read About Liver, above.

Have sliced to a ⅓-inch even thickness:

½ lb. calf liver or 12 chicken livers cut in half

Season with:

Salt and pepper

Coat on both sides with:

Flour

➧ patting well between your hands to make the flour adhere and to remove the excess. Sauté until golden brown in:

2 tablespoons butter
¼ cup sliced onions
(¼ cup sliced mushrooms)

and set aside nearby. Now melt over high heat in a heavy skillet:

1 tablespoon butter

Heat it until it starts making slight crackling noises. Put the floured liver into the skillet, allowing 1 minute to each side. Remove the liver and discard the butter it was cooked in, which may be bitter. Put the liver on a hot plate, cover with the onion butter and:

Chopped parsley

Serve at once. We hate to add this, because we feel liver should be rare—but if you don't like it this way, cook it over medium heat 2 minutes to the side for medium doneness.

GOOSE LIVER

Goose liver is considered a great delicacy. Remove the gall bladder. Soak in cold salted water for 2 hours:

A goose liver

Dry it with a cloth.

I. Sprinkle it with:

1/8 teaspoon paprika
1/2 teaspoon sugar
1/8 teaspoon ginger

Sauté it in hot goose fat until it is tender. Excellent served with sautéed onions and apples and with a little dry sherry.

II. Prepare and soak as directed previously:

A goose liver

Place it in an ovenproof dish. Cover it with:

1 cup brown sugar
1/4 teaspoon salt
1 cup dry sherry

Broil it slowly for 1/2 hour. Watch it so that it does not burn. Baste it frequently to prevent a crust from forming. Cook sliced apples in a thick sirup until well glazed. Place them around the liver. Continue to baste with apple sirup until the liver is tender.

⊟ BROILED LIVER

➧ Please read About Liver, page 534.

I. Preheat broiler.

Some epicures have a preference for liver prepared in the following way—doctors have, too. We lean toward sautéed liver, but must acknowledge the good qualities of this recipe which accents liver—pure and simple.

Place on a broiler rack, about 3 inches from the source of heat:

Slices of calf liver, 1/3 inch thick

You may brush them with:

(Butter or cooking oil)

Leave the door of the broiling oven open. Broil the liver exactly 1 minute on each side.

Correct the seasoning

It is remarkably good as it is.

II. Preheat broiler.

Allowing 2 to 3 slices of bacon and onion for each slice of liver, broil:

Slices of lean thin bacon
Thin slices of Bermuda onion

Prepare:

Broiled Liver I, page 534

Serve the liver, bacon and onions on a hot platter garnished with:

Parsley
A lemon cut into quarters

BRAISED LIVER WITH VEGETABLES [6]

➧ Please read About Liver, page 534.

Cut into 1-inch slices:

1 1/2 lbs. beef or calf liver

If you substitute beef liver, you may lard it, page 453. Dredge with:

Seasoned flour

Brown the liver in:

1/4 cup hot bacon drippings

Combine and heap on the slices:

2 diced carrots
2 seeded chopped green peppers
6 small onions
1 cup sliced celery

Add to the pan:

1 cup boiling water or stock

Cover and simmer until the liver is tender. Add, if necessary, more boiling stock. Calf liver will be tender in about 15 minutes, beef liver in about 30.

BRAISED LIVER COCKAIGNE WITH WINE [8]

➧ Please read About Liver, page 534.

Place:

2½ lbs. calf liver in 1 piece

in the following marinade for 1 hour or more:

⅓ cup salad oil
1½ tablespoons lemon juice
¼ teaspoon salt
⅛ teaspoon paprika
¼ bay leaf

Turn it from time to time.

Preheat oven to 325°.

Melt in an ovenproof baking dish:

3 tablespoons butter

Add and stir about until lightly cooked:

1 small chopped onion or leek
1 diced carrot
2 or 3 diced ribs celery
2 or 3 sprigs minced parsley
1 tablespoon fresh basil or tarragon

Place the liver, marinade and all, in the ovenproof dish. Cover closely and bake until nearly tender, for about 50 minutes. Baste from time to time. If you wish to serve the liver without further additions, continue cooking it until very tender. The following ingredients are optional, but they complement the dish. While the liver is cooking, place in a heavy skillet:

4 slices diced bacon

Cook over very slow heat until the bacon is clear. Add and stir until well glazed:

18 small peeled shallots or onions
6 large or 8 small sliced carrots
3 ribs sliced celery

Add:

1 cup Stock (II, 141), or canned consommé

Cover the skillet and cook the vegetables over direct low heat for 15 minutes. Add them to the liver in the baking dish, cover and cook for 15 minutes longer. Drain the contents of the baking dish, reserving the liquor. Place the liver on a hot platter. Add to the liquor:

½ cup dry white wine, or
¼ cup dry sherry
(2 beaten egg yolks)

Cook and stir the sauce over low heat until hot. If you have added the eggs, do not permit it to boil. Pour the sauce over the liver. Serve with:

Small new browned potatoes

garnished with:

Parsley

BEEF LIVER CREOLE [4]

➧ Please read About Liver, page 534.

Cut into thin slices:

1 lb. beef liver

Dust the slices lightly with:

Flour

Melt, then brown the liver in:

3 tablespoons hot butter or drippings

Add:

1¼ cups sliced onions
1½ cups heated canned tomatoes
½ cup diced celery
1 thinly sliced green pepper
½ teaspoon salt
A few grains cayenne

Cover the pan and simmer these ingredients for about 20 minutes. Drain them. Thicken the liquid with:

Flour, see Pan Gravy, page 534

Add the liver and vegetables. Simmer 2 minutes longer. Serve with:

Boiled Rice, page 158, or Noodles, page 192

⊟ LIVER, PEPPER, ONIONS AND OLIVES ON SKEWERS [4]

Preheat broiler.

Simmer covered in a little boiling water until nearly tender:

¾ lb. calf liver

Drain the liver. Cut it into 1-inch cubes. Cut into quarters:

4 medium-sized onions

Place them in water to separate the sections. Cut into 1-inch pieces:

6 strips bacon

Cut into 1-inch pieces:

2 green peppers, seeds and membrane removed

Alternate on skewers pieces of liver, onion, green pepper, bacon and:

Stuffed olives

Heat in a skillet over low heat a few bacon scraps or butter. Add the filled skewers. Move them about and cook them for about 3 minutes. Place them under a broiler until the bacon is crisp and the liver is tender.

CHICKEN LIVERS À LA KING

Prepare:

1 cup or more Chicken Liver Lyonnaise, page 534

Serve in:

1 cup à la King Sauce, page 375

CHICKEN LIVERS IN BATTER

Preheat deep fryer to 375°.
Wipe with a cloth:

Chicken livers

Season them lightly with:

Salt and pepper

Dip them into:

Fritter Batter for Meat (II, 125)

Fry them in deep fat, pages 75–79, until well browned. Serve with:

Herb Omelet, page 187

or as a garnish for a hot vegetable plate.

ABOUT SWEETBREADS

To paraphrase Puck: "What foods these morsels be!" Veal sweetbreads are those most favored. But beef sweetbreads are sometimes incorporated into mixtures like meat pies, pâté and terrines. Sweetbreads, properly so-called, are the rounded more desirable "heart" or "kernel" types, the pancreas. Also sold as sweetbread is the less desirable "throat," which is the thymus gland of the animal.

➧ Like all organ meats, sweetbreads are highly perishable and should be prepared for use as soon as purchased. First soak them at least 1 hour in a large quantity of cold water to release any blood. You may change the water several times during this period. Next they must be blanched. This is done by putting them into cold acidulated water to cover (II, 148). Bring them slowly to a boil and simmer uncovered from 2 to 5 minutes depending on their size. Drain. Firm them by plunging them at once into cold water. When they have cooled, drain again and trim them by removing cartilage, tubes, connective tissue and tougher membrane. Weight them refrigerated for several hours if you plan using them whole. If you are not using them in one piece, break them into smaller sections with your hands, being careful not to disturb the very fine membrane that surrounds the smaller units. Allow 1 pair for 2 servings.

After these preliminary processes, to which all sweetbreads must be subjected, you may poach, braise, broil or sauce them.

SAUCED POACHED SWEETBREADS [2]

➧ Please read About Sweetbreads, above. Soak, blanch, firm, drain and trim:

1 pair calf sweetbreads

Bring to the boiling point:
Enough water to cover
to which you may add:
¼ cup chopped onions
3 ribs celery with yellow leaves
2 peppercorns
Drop the sweetbreads into the liquid and ➧ lower the heat at once. Simmer covered with a parchment paper, page 83, for about 15 to 20 minutes depending on size. ➧ Do not overcook. Serve in a delicate sauce flavored with:
1 tablespoon sherry, Madeira or brandy
Add a few:
Toasted English walnuts and/or almonds
Allow about:
1 cup Béchamel, Poulette, Mushroom or Wine Sauce for Light Meats
Sauced sweetbreads are often served on:
A thin slice of Virginia ham
or with a:
Spinach Ring, page 205, a Vegetable Soufflé, page 198, or Wild Rice, page 160.

SAUTÉED SWEETBREADS [2]

➧ Please read About Sweetbreads, page 537.
Blanch, firm, dry, trim and poach for about 25 minutes:
1 pair calf sweetbreads
Bread with a:
Seasoned Bound Breading (II, 160)
Sauté them in:
Hot butter
until they are a rich brown. Serve them with:
Cream sauce of sweetbread stock and cream
Season the stock with:
Sherry or lemon juice
Chopped parsley
Serve the sweetbreads with:
New potatoes and green peas
garnished with:
Watercress

BROILED SWEETBREADS [2]

➧ Please read About Sweetbreads, page 537.
Soak, blanch, firm, drain, trim and poach for about 25 minutes:
1 pair calf sweetbreads
Preheat broiler.
Place the broiling rack about 6 inches from the heat source. Break the sweetbreads into large pieces. Roll them in:
Seasoned flour
Surround them with:
Strips of bacon
Secure it with toothpicks. While broiling them, baste frequently with the juices that drip and, if they are rather dry, use additional:
Butter
Add to the drippings a small amount of:
(Sherry or lemon juice)
Serve with:
Madeira Sauce, Poulette Sauce or broiled tomatoes
or on a bed of:
Spinach

BRAISED SWEETBREADS [2]

Make this as simple or as fancy as you like. ➧ Please read About Sweetbreads, page 537.
Soak, blanch for 5 minutes, firm, drain and trim:
1 pair calf sweetbreads
You may press them between 2 plates under a weight if you want them to have uniform thickness and to mellow.
Preheat oven to 375°.
Break sweetbread into several large pieces. You may lard, page 453, the pieces or surround each one with:
(Strips of lean bacon,

very thin pieces of Virginia ham or smoked tongue)

Sauté in a casserole in:

2 tablespoons melted butter

for about 10 minutes or until the onions are transparent:

⅓ cup finely chopped onions
2 tablespoons finely minced carrot
⅓ cup chopped celery

Add:

½ cup dry white wine and ¾ cup light stock, or 1¼ cups stock
½ teaspoon salt
¼ teaspoon freshly ground white pepper

Arrange the sweetbreads on this bed of sautéed vegetables. ➧ Cover and bake for about 30 minutes.

This is an added touch, particularly good if you have used the ham or bacon. In a skillet, sauté for about 5 minutes:

(½ cup sliced mushrooms)
(¾ cup chopped cooked chestnuts, page 283)

in:

2 tablespoons butter

GLAZED SWEETBREADS [2]

➧ Please read About Sweetbreads, page 537.

Soak, blanch, firm, drain and trim:

1 pair calf sweetbreads

Melt in a casserole and sauté for about 10 minutes or until the onions are transparent:

3 tablespoons butter
2 tablespoons finely julienned carrots
2 tablespoons finely chopped shallots or onions

Add:

1½ cups veal stock

Simmer closely covered for about 20 minutes. ➧ Make sure that the vegetables do not brown. Add more stock, if necessary. When the sweetbreads are cooked, help to deglaze the pan by the addition of.

½ cup dry white wine
Correct the seasoning

Preheat oven to 400° for glazing.

Now, remove the sweetbreads from the pan, but keep warm in an ovenproof dish on which they can be served. Reduce the pan liquors to a demi-glaze. Cover the sweetbreads, allowing about 2 tablespoons of glaze for each one, and place the dish in the oven, basting often for about 10 minutes. Serve at once, garnished with:

Chervil or parsley

Serve with:

Fresh young peas
Soufflé Potatoes, page 316

RAGOÛT FIN [4]

A delicate and far-reaching dish. ➧ Please read About Sweetbreads, page 537.

Prepare and drain:

1 pair poached sweetbreads

Drain and cut in two:

2 cups cooked asparagus tips

Reserve the liquid. Melt in a heavy skillet:

¼ cup butter

Sauté in the butter for about 3 minutes:

½ lb. mushrooms
(¼ cup chopped shallots)

Remove them from the skillet. Add to the fat in it:

6 tablespoons butter

Add and stir until blended:

6 tablespoons flour

Stir in slowly:

3 cups liquid: milk or cream, asparagus water or Stock (II, 141)

When the sauce is smooth and boiling, add gradually the asparagus tips, the mushrooms and the sweetbreads. ➧ Reduce the heat. Put a small amount of sauce in a separate pan and beat in:

2 egg yolks

Combine the sauces and ➧ without letting them boil, stir for about 1 minute very gently, so as not to mash the asparagus. Season with:

Salt and paprika
Freshly grated nutmeg

Just before serving, add:

(2 tablespoons dry sherry or 1 teaspoon Worcestershire sauce)

Serve the ragoût at once in:

Hot patty shells, on hot buttered toast, in Bread Cases, page 208, in a baked Noodle Ring, page 173, or on hot Waffles (II, 119)

⊟ SWEETBREADS ON SKEWERS [2]

Preheat oven to 400°.

➧ Please read About Sweetbreads, page 537.

Soak, blanch for about 10 minutes, firm and trim:

1 pair calf sweetbreads

Break them into 1-inch chunks. Partially cook:

Thin slices of lean bacon

enough to surround the pieces of sweetbread. Spread:

Mushroom caps

lightly with:

Butter

Place the sweetbreads and the mushrooms alternately on skewers. Put them over the edge of a pan and bake for about 10 minutes or grill over charcoal until the bacon is crisp.

ABOUT BRAINS

Calf, sheep, lamb, pork and beef brains are listed in order of preference. Brains may be used in all recipes calling for sweetbreads but in both cases they must be very fresh.

➧ To prepare them, give them a preliminary soaking of about 3 hours in cold acidulated water (II, 148). After skinning, soak them in lukewarm water to free them from all traces of blood. Then, as they are rather mushy in texture, firm them by again blanching in acidulated water to cover for about 20 minutes for calf brains, 25 for the others. ➧ Be sure the water does not boil. Allow 1 pound of brains for 4 servings or 1 set for 2 servings.

Brains are often combined with eggs or in ragoût and soufflés with sweetbreads. Because they are bland, be sure to give the dish in which they are used a piquant flavoring, as suggested below.

SAUTÉED BRAINS [4]

➧ Please read About Brains, above.

Prepare:

2 sets cooked brains

Cut in two, lengthwise. Dry them between towels. Season them with:

Salt and paprika

Roll them in:

Corn meal or flour

Melt in a skillet rubbed with:

Garlic
⅓ cup butter or bacon grease

When the fat reaches the point of fragrance, cook the brains on each side for about 2 minutes. Cover them, reduce the heat and complete the cooking, about 10 minutes in all. Serve them with:

Lemon wedges
Thickened Tomato Sauce, page 376, or Worcestershire sauce
Beurre Noir, page 383

with a few:

Capers or black olives

BAKED BRAINS [3]

➧ Please read About Brains, page 540.
Preheat oven to 400°.
Chop coarsely:
  1 set cooked brains
Combine them with:
  ½ cup bread crumbs
  2 chopped hard-cooked eggs
  6 tablespoons cream
  1 tablespoon catsup
  2 peeled chopped green chilis
  ½ tablespoon lemon juice
  Correct the seasoning
Place in a greased baking dish or in individual dishes. Sprinkle the top with:
  Au Gratin II, page 389
Bake for about 15 minutes.

BAKED BRAINS AND EGGS [4]

➧ Please read About Brains, page 540.
Preheat oven to 350°.
Cut into 1-inch dice:
  2 sets cooked brains
Place them in 4 small greased casseroles.
Peel, seed and dice:
  4 tomatoes
Combine them with:
  1½ tablespoons hot olive oil
  1 teaspoon chopped parsley
  1 teaspoon chopped onion or chives
  Salt and paprika
  1 teaspoon brown sugar
Pour these ingredients into the casseroles.
Break into each one:
  1 egg
Bake for about 5 minutes until the eggs are firm. Melt and brown lightly:
  ¼ cup butter
Add:
  2 teaspoons lemon juice
Pour this over the eggs. Garnish with:
  Parsley
Serve at once.

BROILED BRAINS

➧ Please read About Brains, page 540.
Preheat broiler.
Brush:
  Cooked brains
with:
  Oil or melted butter
Dust with:
  Paprika
Place the broiler about 6 inches from the source of heat and broil the brains for about 8 minutes on each side or until done. Baste with oil or butter. Serve piping hot with:
  Broiled Bacon, page 492
  Chopped parsley and lemon wedges
or
  Grilled Tomato Slices, page 333
  Water Cress

ABOUT KIDNEYS

Veal kidneys are the most delicious. Those of lamb are somewhat soft and flat in flavor, but especially suitable for grilling. Large beef kidneys tend to be hard and strong in flavor. Soak them first for 2 hours in cold salted water. Off-flavors may be withdrawn either by blanching, page 88, in acidulated water or by drying after soaking and sautéing briefly over brisk heat, after which the kidneys are allowed to cool partially before cooking.

Beef, mutton and pork kidneys, which are prepared as for beef, are most often used in terrines, braises and stews where very slow cooking helps make them tender.

The white membrane should be snipped from all kidneys before they are washed. Curved scissors makes the job easier. Another way to remove the membrane conveniently is to sauté the kidneys first for about 1 minute in fat. Discard the fat.

➧ To prepare for broiling, almost halve them and keep from curling during cooking by skewering them open. Expose the cut side first to the heat.

Veal and lamb kidneys should be cooked for as short a time as possible over medium heat. ➧ Do not overcook. The center should be slightly pink. If kidneys are of the best quality, pan juices may be used. If not, discard the juices and use freshly melted butter or wine sauce. In any case, ➧ never allow kidneys to boil in a sauce, as this only hardens them. Pour the hot sauce over them or toss them in it for a moment or two.

Beef, mutton and pork kidneys need slow, moist cooking which is described in some of the following recipes. Allow 1 medium veal, 2 or 3 lamb, 1½ to 2 mutton, ½ beef or 1 small pork kidney per person. The veal kidney is surrounded by delicious delicate fat which you can use for seasoning or render for deep-fat frying, pages 75–79. If kidneys are to be ➧ flambéed, never do it for more than 1 minute. Longer exposure to this high heat will toughen them.

BAKED VEAL KIDNEYS

➧ Please read About Kidneys, page 541.
Preheat oven to 300°.
Note for the lone housekeeper: 1 kidney makes a fine little roast for 1 person. Prepare and bake kidneys, leaving the fat on.
Place in a pan, fat side up:

Veal kidneys

Bake them uncovered until tender, about 1 hour.

KIDNEY NUGGETS [2]

➧ Please read About Kidneys, page 541.
Preheat oven to 375°.
Prepare for cooking and slice in half:

4 lamb kidneys

Prepare:

Dressing for Stuffed Pork Chops, page 512

adding:

1 beaten egg

Spread the dressing on:

8 slices of thin lean bacon

Wrap the spread bacon around the kidney halves and fasten it with a toothpick. Bake about 20 minutes.

SAUTÉED KIDNEYS [3]

This could be called Kidneys Bercy because it has both shallots and dry white wine.
➧ Please read About Kidneys, page 541.
Remove some of the fat from:

3 veal kidneys

Cut them crosswise into slices, removing all the white tissue.
Rub a pan with:

(Garlic)

Melt in it:

¼ cup butter

Sauté in the butter until golden:

½ cup sliced onions or shallots

Remove the onions and keep hot. Then sauté the kidneys in the hot fat, a quick process, about 5 minutes. Add the onions and season with:

Salt and paprika
1 tablespoon lemon juice or ¼ cup dry white wine

You may serve this flambé, page 80, with:

Mushrooms on toast

SAUTÉED KIDNEYS WITH CELERY AND MUSHROOMS [4]

If you can get very young fresh kidneys and follow this recipe closely, you may imagine yourself—for a mealtime—in France.
➧ Please read About Kidneys, page 541.
Prepare:

8 lamb kidneys

Skin and quarter them. Sprinkle them with:

Lemon juice

Heat:

3 tablespoons butter or drippings

Sauté lightly in this:

1 cup chopped celery

¼ cup chopped onion

Add the kidneys. ➧ Simmer them covered for about 5 minutes. Stir in:

1 tablespoon flour

1 cup hot Stock (II, 141)

When these ingredients are blended, add:

½ lb. chopped mushrooms

Season the kidneys lightly with:

Paprika

Worcestershire sauce

Simmer them covered for about 15 minutes. Add:

2 tablespoons dry sherry

1 tablespoon chopped parsley

Correct the seasoning

and serve.

⊟ BROILED KIDNEYS

[Allow 1 Kidney per Person]

➧ Please read About Kidneys, page 541.

Preheat broiler.

Remove most of the fat from:

Veal kidneys

Cut them crosswise into slices. Broil them for about 5 minutes or until done. Turn them, baste with:

Melted butter

and broil for about 5 minutes longer. Season with:

Lemon juice

Salt and paprika

BROILED BEEF KIDNEYS, TOMATOES AND ONIONS [2]

➧ Please read About Kidneys, page 541.

Soak and blanch, page 88, in acidulated water for about 20 minutes or until tender:

A beef kidney

Cut it into ⅓-inch slices.

Preheat broiler.

Meanwhile, simmer until nearly tender:

Sliced onions

in:

Milk or water

Drain these ingredients. Dry them between towels. Grease an ovenproof dish. Arrange the kidneys and onions upon it with:

Thick slices tomato

Season the vegetables with:

Salt and pepper

Dot them and the meat with:

Butter

Place the broiler pan about 6 inches from the heat source and broil until the tomatoes are done. Dust with:

Finely chopped parsley

⊟ KIDNEYS EN BROCHETTE

[Individual Serving]

➧ Please read About Kidneys, page 541.

Prepare for cooking, allowing per serving:

1 veal or 3 lamb kidneys

Blanch in:

Milk or cold water and lemon juice

about 2 to 3 minutes or until tender. Dry. Cut in quarters. Wrap in:

Bacon

Arrange on skewers and broil 3 inches from the heat source, about 3 minutes. Turn and broil 3 minutes more. Serve at once.

VEAL KIDNEY CASSEROLE [4]

➧ Please read About Kidneys, page 541.

Preheat oven to 350°.

Wash and core:

4 veal kidneys

Skin and dice after heating them for about 1 minute in:

2 tablespoons fat

Discard the fat. Put the kidneys in a heated ovenproof dish. Then heat in a skillet:

1 tablespoon butter

Sauté in the butter:

¼ to ½ lb. sliced mushrooms
2 tablespoons minced onion or ¼ clove garlic
1 tablespoon minced parsley

Stir and cook these ingredients for about 2 minutes. Stir in:

3 tablespoons flour

Stir in:

1 cup boiling veal or light stock

Bring these ingredients to the boiling point.

Add:

¼ cup dry white wine or ½ cup orange juice
Correct the seasoning

Pour these ingredients into the casserole. Cover it closely. Bake for about 20 minutes or until tender. If you want to reduce the juices slightly, remove the kidneys and keep warm, then pour the thickened hot gravy over them. Have ready, by cutting into triangles:

4 thick slices bread

Sprinkle them with:

Grated cheese

Place them on top of the kidneys. Broil them until the cheese is melted.

KIDNEY STEW [4]

A favorite for Sunday breakfast. ➧ Please read About Kidneys, page 541.

Cut away all the white tissue from:

2 small beef kidneys

Drop them into acidulated water to cover and blanch, page 88, for 30 minutes or until tender. Remove the kidneys from the liquid and cool them. For easier slicing, you may place them in a covered dish in the refrigerator. When cold, cut the meat into wafer-thin slices. Melt:

1 or 2 tablespoons butter

Sauté the kidneys lightly in the hot butter. Remove the kidneys and keep them warm. Stir into the drippings:

1½ to 2 tablespoons flour

Pour in:

1 cup stock or ½ cup stock and ½ cup beer

Stir until the gravy is smooth and boiling. Flavor by adding:

1 slice lemon or 2 tablespoons tomato paste
Salt and paprika, as needed

Toss the kidneys in the hot sauce and serve on:

Noodles, page 192, toast or Corn Meal Waffles (II, 121)

Garnished with:

Chopped parsley

ABOUT TONGUE

No matter from which source—beef, calf, lamb or pork—the smaller-size tongues are usually preferable. The most commonly used and best flavored, whether fresh, smoked or pickled, is beef tongue. For prime texture, it should be under 3 pounds. ➧ Scrub the tongue well. If it is smoked or pickled, you may wish to blanch it first, page 88, simmering for about 10 minutes. Immerse the tongue in cold water. After draining, put it into seasoned boiling water to cover. ➧ Reduce the heat immediately and simmer uncovered 2 to 3 hours or until tender.

If the tongue is to be served hot, drain it from the hot water, plunge it into cold water for a moment so you can handle it, skin it and trim it by removing the roots, small bones and gristle and return it very briefly to the hot cooking water to reheat before serving.

If the tongue is to be served cold, take the pot from the heat when the tongue is tender, remove the tongue and allow it to cool just enough to handle comfortably. It skins easily at this point ➧ but not if you let it get cold. Trim it and return it to the pot to cool completely in the cooking liquor. It is attractive served with Chaud-Froid Sauce, page 388, or in the Aspic, page 546.

➧ To carve tongue, cut nearly through at the hump parallel to the base. But toward the tip, better-looking slices can be made if the cut is diagonal.

BOILED FRESH BEEF TONGUE [6 to 8]

➧ Please read About Tongue, page 544.
Place in a kettle:
A fresh beef or calf tongue: about 2 lbs.
Peel and add:
2 medium-sized onions
1 large carrot
3 or more ribs celery with leaves
6 sprigs parsley
8 peppercorns
Barely cover these ingredients with boiling water. Simmer the tongue uncovered until it is tender, about 3 hours for beef, about 2 hours for calf. Drain it. Skin and trim the tongue. Serve it with:
Mustard Sauce, page 363
Piquant Sauce, page 367
Hot Vinaigrette Sauce, page 341
Harvard Beets, page 270
Horseradish, capers or chopped pickle

BEEF TONGUE WITH RAISIN SAUCE

An undemanding dish to prepare while working on other things in the kitchen
➧ Please read About Tongue, page 544.
Cook, as in previous recipe:
A fresh beef tongue, boiled
After it has been skinned and trimmed, place it where it will keep hot.
Sauce:
Blanch, page 88, and split:
½ cup almonds
Place them in:
2 cups water
and simmer for 20 minutes. Add and simmer for ½ hour longer:
⅔ cup seedless raisins
Drain the sauce. Reserve the liquid. Melt:
6 tablespoons fat from the tongue stock or butter
Stir in until blended:
3 tablespoons flour
Stir in gradually:
The raisins, almond liquid and tongue stock to make 3 cups liquid in all
¼ cup crushed ginger snaps
(2 teaspoons Caramel II (II, 169))
Add the almonds, raisins and:
1 teaspoon grated lemond rind
Correct the seasoning
Serve the tongue with:
A Rice or Noodle Ring, pages 173, and 174, filled with green peas

BOILED CORNED OR PICKLED TONGUE

Keeps better in a refrigerator than ham and is a less usual emergency dish.
➧ Please read About Tongue, page 544. If the tongue is very salty, soak it or blanch it, page 88, in cold water to cover for several hours. Prepare as for Fresh Beef Tongue, Boiled, above, using:
A corned or pickled beef tongue

BOILED SMOKED TONGUE [6 to 8]

➧ Please read About Tongue, page 544.
Cover with cold water and soak in a cool place for 12 hours or blanch, page 88:

A 2-lb. smoked beef tongue

Drain, then cover the tongue with:

Fresh water

Add:

- **1 sliced or whole onion stuck with 3 cloves**
- **½ cup chopped celery with leaves**
- **3 bay leaves**
- **1 teaspoon peppercorns**

Simmer it uncovered until it is tender, from 2 to 4 hours. Skin and trim, as directed. Slice and serve hot with:

Creamed Spinach, page 326
Horseradish Sauce, page 362

or cold in:

Aspic, page 546

TONGUE BAKED IN CREOLE SAUCE [6]

➧ Please read About Tongue, page 544.
Cook:

A fresh or smoked tongue, about 1½ lbs., or 2 veal or 8 lamb tongues

Skin and trim as directed.
Preheat oven to 375°.
Prepare:

Creole Sauce, page 380

Place the drained tongue, sliced or unsliced, in a casserole. Pour the sauce over it. Bake it covered for ½ hour. Serve it with:

Chopped parsley

TONGUE IN ASPIC [8]

A fine-looking dish.
Cook:

A Smoked Beef Tongue, above

Leave it in the stock until it is cool, then prepare it as directed. Make the following aspic. Soak:

- **1½ tablespoons gelatin**

in:

- **½ cup cold beef stock**

Dissolve it in:

- **2½ cups boiling beef stock**
- **½ cup dry white wine or the juice of 2 lemons**
- **1 tablespoon sugar**
- **Salt, if required**
- **A few drops Caramel II (II, 169), or commercial coloring**
- **1 teaspoon Worcestershire sauce**

Chill the aspic and, when it is about to set, add:

- **½ cup chopped sweet-sour pickles**
- **1 cup chopped celery**
- **½ cup chopped green peppers**

Have ready a mold or bread pan moistened with cold water. Place a small amount of aspic in the bottom of the mold. If desired, mold into this carrots, cooked beets, canned mushrooms, etc. Put the tongue into the mold and pour the remaining aspic around and over it. When well chilled, unmold the aspic on a platter. Garnish it with:

Lettuce leaves
Deviled eggs
Parsley
Slices of lemon

Serve it with:

Mayonnaise or see Mayonnaise Collée, page 387

ABOUT HEART

Heart, which is firm and rather dry, is best prepared by slow cooking. In texture, it more nearly resembles muscle than organ meat and so may be used in many recipes calling for ground meat. An especially good way to prepare heart is to stuff it with a savory dressing. Before cooking, wash it well, removing fat, arteries, veins and blood and dry carefully. A 4- to 5-lb. beef heart will serve 6, a veal heart will serve 1.

BAKED STUFFED HEART [3]

➧ Please read About Heart, page 546.
Preheat oven to 325°.
Prepare:

A small beef heart or
3 veal hearts

Tie with a string to hold its shape if necessary. Place on a rack in an ovenproof dish and pour over it:

2 cups stock or diluted tomato soup

Place over the heart:

4 slices bacon

Cover the dish closely and bake until tender—if beef, a matter of 3 to 4 hours, if veal, about 2 hours. Remove the heart to a plate and cool it slightly. Heat in a double boiler, then fill the heart cavity with:

Apple and Onion Dressing, page 563, or
Olive and Celery Dressing, page 562

You will need about 1 cup for a veal heart, about 3 cups for a beef heart. ➧ To allow for expansion, do not pack the dressing tightly. Sprinkle the heart with:

Paprika

Return it to a 400° oven long enough to heat quickly before serving. The drippings may be thickened with:

Flour, see Pan Gravy, page 358

HEART EN PAPILLOTE [3]

Preheat oven to 400°.
Prepare:

Baked Stuffed Heart, this page

using a small beef heart. Before cooking wrap it in greased parchment paper, as shown on page 83. Put the wrapped heart on a rack in the oven. ➧ Reduce the heat at once to 300° and continue to bake for 2½ to 3 hours. About 15 minutes before serving, remove the paper and discard it. Baste the heart for about 10 minutes, allowing it to glaze in the drippings. Thicken the drippings with:

Flour, see Pan Gravy, page 358

and serve.

BRAISED HEART SLICES IN SOUR SAUCE [6]

A homey treat.
➧ Please read About Heart, page 546.
Prepare:

A 4 to 5 lb. beef heart or 6 veal hearts

If veal, you may halve the heart, if beef, cut it across the fiber into ¼-inch slices. Pour into a saucepan or ovenproof dish to the depth of ¾ inch:

Boiling water

Add:

¼ cup diced carrots
¼ cup chopped celery with leaves
¼ cup sliced onion
½ teaspoon salt
(¼ cup diced green pepper)

Place the heart slices on a rack in the pan, well above the water. Cover closely. Steam the meat until tender for about 1½ hours. Strain the stock. Chill and degrease it. Save the fat. Reserve the stock. Melt:

3 tablespoons butter or fat from the stock

Stir in:

3 tablespoons flour

Then add:

1½ cups stock

When it reaches a boil, add the meat and vegetables and ➧ reduce the heat. You may add:

2 tablespoons lemon juice or dry wine
½ teaspoon sweet marjoram or 2 tablespoons chopped parsley or olives
Correct the seasoning

Good with Spoon Bread (II, 279), rice or Potato Dumplings, page 180.

ABOUT TRIPE

If you start from scratch, cooking tripe is a long-drawn-out affair—as you will see by the following description. But today you will find almost everywhere that you can buy it partially precooked, so that your job is just the final seasoning and heating. Using the following recipes, you need only cook it about ½ hour, as in Spanish Tripe.

Tripe is the muscular lining of beef stomach. There are 4 kinds, all of which, as you will note, are used in at least one classic recipe. The fat part of the belly, called in France "gras double," usually comes already cooked. Then there are 3 different sections of honeycomb tripe which comes from the second stomach of beef—the extremity of the belly, which is only partially honeycombed, the dark and the light.

Fresh whole tripe calls for a minimum of 12 hours of cooking, some time-honored recipes demanding as much as 24. Sometimes tripe is pickled after cooking and served hot or cold in a marinade.

➧ To prepare fresh tripe, trim if necessary. ➧ Wash it thoroughly, soaking overnight, and blanch it, page 88, for ½ hour in salted water. Wash well again, drain and cut for cooking. When cooked, the texture of tripe should be like that of soft gristle. More often, alas, because the heat has not been kept low enough, it has the consistency of wet shoe leather.

COOKED TRIPE [4 to 5]

➧ Please read About Tripe, opposite.

Trim, wash, soak, blanch, wash again and drain:

2 lbs. fresh honeycomb tripe

Cut it into 1½- to 2-inch squares. Have ready a heavy pot that you can lid tightly later. Add to:

Enough water to cover
¼ teaspoon salt
¼ teaspoon sugar
1 clove garlic
⅔ cup chopped onion
1 cup chopped mixed celery and parsley
4 peppercorns

Bring to a boil and add the tripe. ➧ Reduce the heat at once. Seal the lid with a strip of pastry or tape (II, 293), and simmer for 12 hours. When the tripe is tender, you may serve it with:

Pan Gravy, page 358

seasoned with:

Salt
½ teaspoon mustard
1 teaspoon Worcestershire sauce

TRIPE À LA MODE DE CAEN [8]

This famous Normandy dish demands a deep earthenware casserole and the inclusion of all 4 types of beef tripe.

➧ Please read About Tripe, this page.

Preheat oven to 250°.

Trim, wash, soak, blanch, wash again, drain and cut into 1½-inch squares:

3 lbs. fresh tripe

Wash and blanch:

A split calf's foot

Peel and slice:

2 lbs. onions

Dice:

¼ lb. beef suet

Line the bottom of the casserole

with a layer of onions, then a layer of tripe and a sprinkling of the beef suet. Continue to build successive layers, topping with the split calf's foot and:

An onion stuck with
3 cloves
A bay leaf
A Bouquet Garni
(II, 220)

Pour over this:

¼ cup brandy

or, if you can get it:

¼ cup Calvados

and enough:

Cider or water

to cover all the ingredients. Bring just to a boil. Seal the casserole with a strip of Pastry Dough (II, 293). Bake in the oven at least 12 hours. When ready to serve, break the seal on the casserole, remove the bouquet garni, the bay leaf and the whole onion. Degrease the sauce and pick the meat from the calf's foot. Return the meat to the casserole to heat through and serve the tripe in individual hot covered casseroles, garnished with:

Boiled parsley potatoes

FRIED TRIPE

➧ Please read About Tripe, page 548.

Cut into squares or strips:

Cooked Tripe, page 548,
or precooked tripe

Sprinkle with:

Salt and paprika

Dip it into:

Fritter Batter for Meat
(II, 125)

Fry in deep fat, pages 75–79. Serve with:

Tartare Sauce, page 349

SPANISH TRIPE

➧ Please read About Tripe, page 548.

Wash partially precooked:

Tripe

Follow the directions for Cooked Tripe, page 548, and add to the vegetables:

1 cup more or less tomato purée
A few grains cayenne
1 teaspoon Worcestershire sauce

Simmer at least ½ hour and add for the last 15 minutes:

½ cup cooked minced ham
½ cup sliced mushrooms

Good served with:

Boiled Rice, page 158

LAMB FRIES [2]

Skin, cut into quarters:

4 medium lamb fries

You may marinate them for about 1 hour in:

(¼ cup olive oil)
(2 tablespoons lemon juice)

If you marinated them, dry them before rolling them in:

Bounding Bread
(II, 160)

Sauté until golden brown in:

¼ cup butter

Garnish with:

Fried Parsley, page 305

and serve with:

Tomato sauce

CALF OR LAMB HEAD

[4 Servings for a Calf Head—
2 Servings for Lamb]

It is always so easy to say, "Let the butcher prepare, etc." In this case, it is assumed that the head is skinned and the eyes removed. The head is split the long way, so the brains can be removed. We prefer to cook the Brains, page 540, and the Tongue, page 345, separately. Scrape away any clots. Soak overnight in salted cold water to cover:

1 calf or lamb head

Wash again in cold water. You may dry the head and brown it in butter or put in a large kettle and bring to a boil:

Enough water to cover the head

with:

1 carrot
1 onion
½ sliced lemon
1 bay leaf
4 cloves
1 tablespoon salt
¼ teaspoon pepper

In actuality you may also add, to keep the bones white:

(½ cup veal kidney fat or suet)

When this reaches a boil, add the head. ➧ Reduce the heat at once and simmer uncovered until the meat is tender, about 1 hour for lamb, about 2 hours for calf. If you have included the tongue, it may take a little longer. When the meat is tender, drain and remove it from the bones and dice it. Keep the meat warm. Skin, trim and slice the tongue. Meanwhile prepare a double portion of:

Rosemary Wine Sauce, page 369

using as stock the liquid in which the calf head was cooked.

Correct the seasoning

You may want to spice the sauce with:

Mild white wine vinegar, lemon juice or wine

Reheat the meat, the tongue and the cooked brains in the sauce. ➧ Do not boil. Serve this dish garnished with:

Chopped parsley

It is sometimes served with the addition at the last moment of:

½ cup scalded cream

Or part of the sauce is drained off into:

2 beaten egg yolks

Return this mixture to the pot. Heat, but do not boil, the sauce after adding the yolks. But ➧ if you add cream or egg yolks, to avoid curdling do not add lemon, vinegar or wine until the last moment.

HEAD CHEESE OR BRAWN [4]

A well-liked old-fashioned dish. Quarter:

A calf head

Clean teeth with a stiff brush, remove ears, brains, eyes, snout and most of the fat. Soak the quarters about 6 hours in cold water to extract the blood. Wash them. Cover with cold water, to which you may add:

2 onions
5 celery stalks

Simmer until the meat is ready to fall from the bones, about 2 to 3 hours. Drain but reserve stock. Chip the meat off the bones. Dice it. Cover it well with the stock. Reserve the brains. Now add:

Salt
Pepper
Herbs

Cook for ½ hour. Pour into a mold and cover with a cloth. Put a weight on top. Chill. Serve, cut into slices, with:

Vinaigrette Sauce, page 341

to which you have added the diced cooked brains.

CALF LUNGS OR LIGHTS [6]

Cut into julienne strips, wash well and simmer in stock until just tender, about 1½ hours:

3 lbs. calf lungs

Remove lungs and keep warm. Reduce the stock by ½, adding:

A Bouquet Garni (II, 220), of bayleaf, thyme and lemon rind

Brown in a heavy skillet:

½ cup flour
1 teaspoon sugar

Add:

½ cup butter

Stir until smooth and add:

½ cup finely minced onion

Strain the reduced stock and add it gradually to the flour mixture. Cook and stir until thickened.

Add:

1 tablespoon anchovy paste

Preheat oven to 325°.

Put the cooked lungs in a casserole. Cover with the sauce. Cover the whole tightly with a lid. Bake for about ½ hour. Before serving

Correct the seasoning

and stir in gently:

1 cup cream or cultured sour cream
1 tablespoon capers

Continue to bake until cream is heated through.

CHITTERLINGS [6 to 7]

We were well along in years before we discovered that the name of this dish had an "e," an "r," a "g"—and 3 syllables. Just after slaughtering, empty the large intestines of a young pig while still warm by turning them inside out and scraping as clean as possible. Soak 24 hours in cold salted water to cover. Then wash in 5 or 6 waters. Remove excess fat, but leave some for flavor. To:

10 lbs. chitterlings

allow:

1 garlic clove
½ sliced lemon
½ teaspoon salt
½ teaspoon pepper
½ teaspoon each thyme, clove, mace and allspice
1 bay leaf
¼ cup sliced onions
(3 red pepper pods)
2 tablespoons fresh parsley
2 tablespoons white wine vinegar
Enough cold water to cover

Add:

Chitterlings, cut up in 2-inch lengths

Bring slowly to a boil. ➧ Reduce the heat at once and simmer for about 3 hours. During the last 30 minutes of cooking, you may add:

(¼ cup tomato catsup)

Correct the seasoning

and serve with:

Corn Bread (II, 277)
Cole Slaw, page 36

SAUTÉED CHITTERLINGS

Prepare previous recipe for:

Chitterlings

omitting the vinegar and catsup. Drain and dry well. Dip in:

Seasoned flour

Sauté them gently in:

Butter

until a delicate brown.

STEWED PIGS' FEET [4]

Wash, leave whole or split in halves and blanch, page 88:

4 pigs' or calves' feet

You may wrap them in cheesecloth to retain their shape. Cover them with water. Bring just to a boil. ➧ Reduce the heat at once and simmer for about 4 hours uncovered. During the last 30 minutes of simmering, add:

1½ to 2 lbs. green beans, cabbage or sauerkraut

Cook the vegetables until they are tender.

Correct the seasoning

and serve hot.

JELLIED PIGS' OR CALVES' FEET [6]

Wash, leave whole or split in halves and blanch, page 88:

6 pigs' or calves' feet

You may wrap them in cheesecloth to retain their shape. Cover them with water. Add:

1 large sliced onion
1 cut clove garlic
1 sliced lemon
2 bay leaves
3 or 4 whole black peppercorns
6 or 8 whole cloves

Bring this mixture to the boiling point. ➧ Reduce the heat and simmer uncovered for about 4 hours. Add boiling water, if needed. Strain the stock through a sieve and reserve it. Remove the skin and the bones from the pigs' feet. Place the meat in the stock. Season to taste with:

White vinegar or dry wine

and

Correct the seasoning

Chop and add:

(1 pimiento, decorative but optional)

Pour the pigs' or calves' feet into a mold and chill until the stock is firm.

BAKED PIGS' FEET

Prepare:

Stewed Pigs' Feet, page 551

Preheat oven to 375°.
Cut the pigs' feet in two, lengthwise. Roll them in:

Melted butter

then in:

Corn meal or cracker crumbs

Bake them about 20 to 30 minutes or until tender. Serve with:

Sweet-sour Beets, page 270, or lemon wedges

BRAISED OXTAILS [5 to 6]

Preheat oven to 350°.
Cut into joints:

2 oxtails

Melt in a skillet:

¼ cup butter or beef drippings

Sauté the oxtail sections until they are browned. Season them with:

Salt and paprika

Add:

2 cups boiling Brown Stock I (II, 141), or tomato juice

Bring these ingredients to the boiling point. Place them in a casserole. Cover it closely. Bake until the oxtails are tender, 3 to 5 hours. Add additional stock, as needed. For the last 45 minutes of cooking, add:

8 small peeled onions
½ cup diced celery
¼ cup peeled diced carrots

When the oxtails are tender, strain the stock from them. Skim off most of the fat. Thicken the stock with:

Flour, see Pan Gravy, page 358
Correct the seasoning

Return the meat, the vegetables and the gravy to the casserole. Serve with a platter of:

Noodles, page 172

Cover the noodles with:

Au Gratin II, page 389

VARIETY MEAT PATTIES [4]

➧ Please read About Kidneys, page 541, About Liver, page 534, or About Brains, page 540. Prepare one of the following for cooking and then chop until fine:

2 pairs steamed brains, ½ lb. raw liver or 1 beef, 2 pork or veal or 5 lamb kidneys

Sprinkle them with:

1 tablespoon lemon juice

Rub a skillet with:

Garlic

Heat in it:

2 tablespoons butter

Sauté in this lightly:

1 chopped onion or leek
½ cup minced celery
2 tablespoons minced green pepper

Remove from heat. Add the chopped variety meat and:

¼ cup dry bread crumbs
¼ cup milk
1 egg
¼ teaspoon salt
¼ teaspoon freshly ground pepper
4 drops Worcestershire sauce
(¼ teaspoon caraway or dill seed)

Drop this mixture by the tablespoon into a hot pan, in which you have:

2 tablespoons hot bacon drippings

Brown the patties lightly on both sides. Serve them with:

Tomato sauce, slaw or Vegetables à la Grecque, page 257

CHICKEN GIBLETS

Dice, put in boiling water or stock, then ➧ reduce the heat at once and simmer until tender, about 1 hour:

Chicken giblets: gizzards and hearts

You may add, for the last 15 minutes of cooking:

Chopped green pepper
Chopped celery

Drain these ingredients, reserving the stock. Make:

Gravy, page 358

using:

2 tablespoons butter
2 tablespoons flour to 1 cup stock or stock and dry wine
Correct the seasoning

Add the giblets and vegetables and simmer ➧ but do not boil. Serve on:

Toast

COCKSCOMBS

These have been used since the time of Apicius as a garnish. Blanch:

Cockscombs

Peel off the outer skin. ➧ Steam, covered, on a:

Mirepoix (II, 221)

moistened with:

1 cup Mushroom Stock (II, 145)

until tender, about 45 to 50 minutes.

Preheat deep fryer to 375°. Drain well, cut an incision and stuff with:

Duxelles (II, 220)
Chicken Farce, page 564

Cover with:

Allemande Sauce, page 362

Dip in crumbs and deep-fat fry till crumbs color.

ABOUT MARROW

Spinal marrow, which is really a continuation of the brain, may be substituted in any of the recipes for brains. Bone marrow may be removed from split large bones. ➧ It must not be overcooked, as it is very fat and simply disintegrates under too high heat. Bone marrow may be cut into ½-inch slices and softened in the top of a double boiler or gently and briefly poached in a little stock, for about 1½ to 2 minutes. You may serve it this way for hors d'oeuvre. It may also be gently poached in the bone in water barely to cover or roasted in a 300° oven for about 1 hour. See also Marrow Balls, page 150, for soup and Osso Buco, page 506.

MARROW

I. Cut into ¼-inch rounds:

Marrow

Poach it gently in:

Stock (II, 141)

for a few minutes. Drain and serve at once on:

Toast rounds

II. Or use raw in a:

Sauce Bordelaise, page 366

GAME

ABOUT SMALL GAME

Small game such as rabbit, squirrel and muskrat may be substituted in most recipes calling for chicken. But following are some classic, and not so classic, recipes which take the special characteristics of these small animals into account. If you are a novice, the most important things to remember is ➧ never handle rabbit or any wild meat without using gloves, because of the danger of tularemia infection. ➧ Always make sure the meat of wild animals is sufficiently cooked. Be guided in your choice of recipe by the age of the animal. ➧ Use a moist heat process, page 81, for older animals.

ABOUT RABBITS AND HARES

When rabbit or hare is young and fresh, the cleft in the lip is narrow, the claws smooth and sharp. Test for the youth of the animal, also, by turning the claws sideways to see if they crack. The ears should be soft and bend easily. A young hare has a stumpy neck and long legs. To ensure tender meat, hang the animals by the feet from 1 to 4 days. They will, however, be tender without hanging if used before they have time to stiffen. Once stiffened, they are edible as long as the hind legs are rigid. Some of the most delicious game sauces use blood as a thickener. To trap and preserve the blood, see (II, 540). To incorporate it in a sauce, see page 357. Hares may weigh up to 10 to 14 pounds. European hare is all dark meat, while American domestic hare is all white.

➧ To dress rabbit or hare, sever the front legs at the joint, as shown (page 555) by the dotted line. Cut through the skin around the hind legs, as shown again by a dotted line. Tie the feet together securely. Hang the rabbit on a hook where tied. Pull the skin down off the legs, stripping it inside out like a glove, and over the body and forelegs. Sever the head and discard it with the skin. Slit the rabbit down the front. Remove the entrails and discard them, except for the heart and liver. Wash the carcass inside and out with acidulated water—water to which 1 or 2 tablespoons of vinegar are added. Rinse and dry carefully.

RABBIT OR HARE À LA MODE, HASENPFEFFER OR CIVET

Skin:

A rabbit

Cut into pieces by severing the legs at the joints and cutting the back in 3 sections. Place the pieces in a crock or jar. Marinate refrigerated for 24 to 48 hours in:

Cooked Marinade for Game, page 380

Drain and reserve the marinade. Dry the pieces of rabbit. Dip them in:

Flour

Brown until golden in:

3 tablespoons bacon drippings

Remove the browned rabbit to an ovenproof casserole.
Preheat oven to 350°.
Sauté in the pan the rabbit was browned in:

1 cup finely sliced onions
2 tablespoons butter

Add the sauté to the casserole with the warmed marinade and bring to a boil on top of the stove. ➧ Cover and remove to oven for about 1½ hours or until tender. Correct the seasoning. Place rabbit on a serving dish. Pour sauce over it. Serve with:

Noodles, page 172

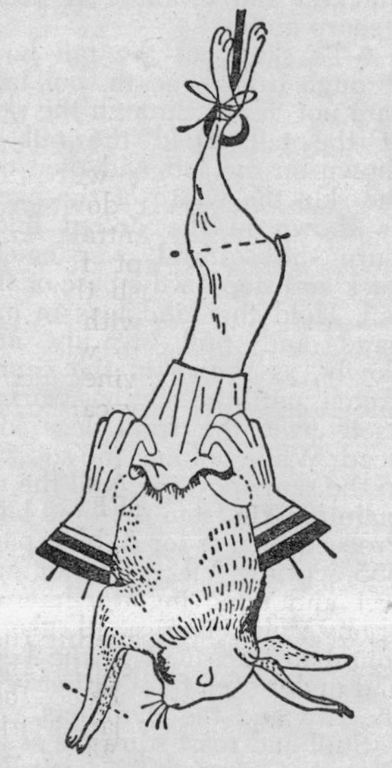

SAUTÉED RABBIT

If rabbit is very young, prepare as for:

Sautéed Chicken, page 577

Serve with:

Elderberry preserves

SMOTHERED RABBIT OR HARE WITH ONIONS

Skin, clean and cut into pieces:

A rabbit

Dredge with:

Seasoned flour

Melt in a pot or skillet:

3 tablespoons drippings or butter

Sauté the rabbit in the drippings until browned. Cover thickly with:

Sliced onions

Pour over them:

1 cup cultured sour cream

Cover the pot closely and simmer for 1 hour or place the pot in a slow oven—300°—and bake the rabbit until tender, 1 hour or more.

ROAST RABBIT OR HARE

Preheat oven to 450°.
Skin and clean:

A rabbit or hare

Stuff it with any recipe suitable for fowl, using the sautéed chopped liver. Close the opening and truss it. Brush the rabbit all over with:

Melted butter or cooking oil

Dredge with:

Seasoned flour

Place on a rack on its side in a roasting pan in the oven. ➧ Reduce the heat to 350°. Baste every 15 minutes with the drippings in the pan or, if necessary, with:

(Additional butter)

Turn the rabbit when cooking time is about ½ over. Cook until tender, about 1½ hours. Make:

Pan Gravy, page 358

FRICASSEE OF RABBIT OR HARE

Skin, clean and cut into pieces:

A rabbit

Dredge with:

Seasoned flour

Melt in a skillet:

¼ cup butter

or you may use:

(¼ lb. diced, lightly rendered salt pork—a wonderful substitution)

Add:

¼ cup chopped shallots or onions

(1 cup cut-up mushrooms)

Remove the shallots and mushrooms before sautéing the meat in the drippings until lightly browned. To flambé the rabbit pour over it:

(2 oz. brandy)

Add:

1½ cups stock or dry wine

and, in a cloth bag:

A piece of lemon rind
10 peppercorns
2 sprigs parsley
2 ribs celery with leaves

Cover the pot closely. Simmer the meat until done, 1 hour or more, or put it in a 300° oven covered for about 2 hours—but do not let it boil at any time. Ten minutes before you remove the rabbit from the pot, take out the seasoning bag and add the mushrooms and shallots. Place the rabbit on a hot serving dish. Remove the sauce from the heat and thicken with:

Beurre Manié, page 357

ABOUT SQUIRREL

Gray squirrels are the preferred ones; red squirrels are small and quite gamey in flavor. There are, proverbially, many ways to skin a squirrel, but some hunters claim the following one is the quickest and cleanest. It needs a sharp knife.

➧ To skin, cut the tail bone through from beneath, but take care not to cut through the skin of the tail. Hold the tail as shown on the left and then cut the skin the width of the back, as shown in the dotted lines. Turn the squirrel over on its back and step on the base of the tail. Hold the hind legs in one hand and pull steadily and slowly, as shown in the center sketch, until the skin has worked itself over the front legs and head. While holding the squirrel in the same position, pull the remaining skin from the hind legs. Proceed then as for Rabbit, page 555, cutting off the head and feet and removing the internal organs, plus two small glands found in the small of the back and under each foreleg, between the ribs and the shoulders.

Stuff and roast squirrels as for Pigeons, page 590, barding them, or use them in Brunswick Stew, page 582, or prepare as for Braised Chicken, page 578. Season the gravy with:

Walnut catsup

and serve with:

Polenta, page 157

OPOSSUM

If possible, trap 'possum and feed it on milk and cereals for 10 days before killing. Clean, but do not skin. Treat as for pig by immersing the unskinned animal in water just below the boiling point. Test frequently by plucking at the hair. When it slips out readily, remove the 'possum from the water and scrape. While scraping repeatedly, pour cool water over the surface of the animal. Remove small red glands in small of back and under each foreleg between the shoulder and rib. Parboil, page 88, 1 hour. Roast as for pork, page 485. Serve with:

Turnip greens

BEAR

Remove all fat from bear meat at once, as it turns rancid very quickly.

If marinated at least 24 hours in an oil-based marinade, all bear, except black bear, is edible. Cook after marination, as for any recipe for Beef Pot Roast or Stew, pages 493–505. Bear cub will need about 2½ hours' cooking; for an older animal, allow 3½ to 4 hours. Bear, like pork, can carry trichinosis, so be sure the meat is always well cooked through.

RACCOON

Skin, clean and soak overnight:

1 raccoon

in:

Salt water

Scrape off all fat inside and out. Blanch, page 88, for 45 minutes. Add:

2 tablespoons baking soda

and continue to cook uncovered for 5 minutes. Drain and wash in warm water. Put in cold water and bring to a boil. ➧ Reduce heat and simmer 15 minutes.

Preheat oven to 350°.

Stuff the raccoon with:

Bread Dressing, page 560

Bake covered, about 45 minutes ➧ uncover and bake 15 minutes longer before serving.

MUSKRAT [2]

Skin and remove all fat from hams of:

6 muskrats

Poach, page 83, for 45 minutes.

Sauté until golden:

½ cup minced onions

in:

2 tablespoons butter

Add the drained, dried muskrat hams and cook until brown. Serve with:

Creamed Celery, page 282

WOODCHUCK

Dress woodchuck as for rabbit, but watch for and remove 7 to 9 small sacs or kernels in the small of the back and under the forearm. Soak overnight in salted water. Drain and wipe dry. Cook by any recipe for rabbit or chicken.

BEAVER

Use young animals only.

Remove kernels in small of back and under forelegs, between rib and shoulder. Hang in the cold for several days. Poach in salted water for 1 hour. Braise as for beef, page 493, until tender.

BEAVER TAIL

Hold over open flame until rough skin blisters. Remove from heat. When cool, peel off skin. Roast over coals or simmer until tender.

PECCARY

Immediately after killing, remove the musk glands in the

middle of the back. This meat needs marinating before cooking. After this, you may prepare it as in any pork recipe in the section on Pot Roasts and Stews, page 493.

WILD BOAR

If very young, prepare as for:

Suckling Pig, page 486

If older, prepare by a moist heat process for:

Pork, page 512

ABOUT VENISON

This romantic word can cover any of the edible animals taken in the chase, but we are discussing here only antlered types. A famous sportsman called venison a gift of joy to some, a matter of secret interment to others.

Today, when hunters are so aware of the need to treat their booty with care from the moment it is shot, joy can prevail. No matter what the method of handling, certain preparations are basic. Game shot in an unsuspecting moment is more tender than game that is chased and will also deteriorate less quickly. Avoid buying any trapped animals for food. Immediate and careful gutting (II, 540), immediate removal of all hair near exposed flesh and prompt skinning are essential.

Some authorities recommend only a week of hanging, some as long as 4 weeks in 40° temperature in a cool, airy place, away from sun, screened against insects and protected from predators. Venison is lean and needs barding, page 454, or larding, page 453.

➧ Care must be taken, though, to remove all fat from any of these game animals themselves, as it grows rancid rapidly. ➧ Do not use it to grease pans or for sautéing or browning. The livers and heart are often eaten and should be marinated under refrigeration or soaked in salt water for 12 hours or longer. As with all game, the lushness of the season and the age of the animal contribute to the decision as to how to cook it.

Moose meat, which is relatively fat, calls for cooking like pork and can also have the same sweet and sweet-sour garnishes and sauces. Elk is more like beef than any other game. Calf elk sours rapidly. Cook it as for veal.

The choice cuts of very young deer or goat and fat old bucks can be roasted or broiled as for beef. Other cuts should be marinated, drained, dried and prepared as for any moist-processed beef, see pages 494–499.

For sauces for game, see page 366. Cabbage, turnips, chestnuts and mushrooms are often suggested as classic game accompaniments, as are brandied fruits.

SADDLE OF DEER, MOOSE OR ELK [8]

Preheat oven to 550°.

Lard, page 453.

A 6 to 7 lb. saddle of venison

Rub it with:

A cut clove of garlic

Butter

Place the roast, fat side up, uncovered on a rack in the oven. ➧ Reduce the heat to 350° and cook, allowing in all 20 minutes to the pound. Make:

Pan Gravy, page 358

Serve with:

Hot Cumberland Sauce, page 372

Wild Rice, page 160

ROAST LEG OF VENISON

Bard the roast. Cook as for Beef Roast, page 453.

VENISON STEAKS

I. Have ready:

½-inch young venison steaks

Before frying, rub with:

Garlic

To keep them crisp and brown on the outside, rare and juicy within, sauté them, page 79, in:

1 tablespoon butter
2 tablespoons cooking oil

5 to 6 minutes to the side. Serve with:

Hot Cumberland Sauce, page 372

or with:

Maître d'Hôtel Butter, page 384

or with:

Puréed celery with croutons and Sauce Poivrade, page 368

II. Soak for 24 hours refrigerated:

¾-inch venison steaks

in:

Lamb or Game Marinade, page 381

Drain and dry. Sauté and serve as for Venison Steaks I, above.

BRAISED VENISON

For this process, use the less tender cuts of meat either in 1 large piece or cut into small ones, but be sure to remove all fat. Place the meat in a marinade, page 380, from 12 to 48 hours in the refrigerator. Turn it from time to time. Dry it. Prepare as for Pot Roast, page 493. If you have marinated, use the marinade in the stock. Cook until tender—depending on the age of the animal.

VENISON HAMBURGER

To make this lean meat more interesting in ground form, combine:

2 parts ground venison

with:

1 part fresh sausage meat

Cook as for Hamburger, page 515, but allow extra time ▶ to be sure the meat is no longer pink.

VENISON MEAT LOAF

Prepare:

Meat Loaf I, page 523

using:

¾ lb. ground venison
¼ lb. ground sausage

STUFFINGS, DRESSINGS, FARCES OR FORCEMEAT

When you get that desperate feeling that you simply must find a new species of meat—try instead combining meats or variety meats with some unusual dressing or farce. Don't save stuffings just for heavy festive meals; make them part of your daily fare.

Many foreign and old-fashioned stuffing recipes call for bread soaked in a liquid and then pressed before using. We find that most American bakery breads are already so soft in texture that soaking produces too pasty a dressing.

The quality of the crumbs is very important, so check (II, 159) to differentiate between fresh or dry. ▶ Never grind bread, as the stuffing will be too compact. It is important ▶ to stuff food just before cooking; ▶ to handle stuffings lightly so as not to compact them; and ▶ to allow space when stuffing, so the mixture can swell and stay light. Should there be extra dressing that does not fit the cavity of fish, fowl or roast, cook it separately in a greased baking dish.

A useful rule of thumb in judging the amount of stuffing needed is ▶ to allow ½ cup of stuffing for each pound of bird or fish.

▶ Never use raw pork in dressings. Dressings are done when they reach an internal temperature of 165° to 170°.

For stuffings for vegetables, see individual stuffed vegetable recipes and page 256.

BREAD DRESSING WITH MUSHROOMS, OYSTERS, NUTS, GIBLETS, ETC.

[About 5 Cups]

There is no set rule for the proportions of ingredients in bread dressing. It should be palatable, light and slightly moist, well flavored but bland. Chopped green peppers, nut meats, sautéed mushrooms and drained or slightly sautéed oysters may be added to it. Stock or oyster liquor may be substituted for milk.

Chop:

Giblets

Melt:

¼ cup butter

Add and sauté for about 2 minutes:

(2 tablespoons or more chopped onion)

and the chopped giblets. Combine these ingredients with:

4 cups crustless day-old or slightly toasted, diced white, whole wheat or corn bread crumbs
¼ cup chopped parsley
¼ to 1 cup chopped celery
1 teaspoon dried tarragon or basil
¾ teaspoon salt
½ teaspoon paprika
⅛ teaspoon nutmeg
Milk, stock or melted butter to moisten the dressing very lightly
(2 or 3 eggs)

You may add:

1½ cups nut meats: Brazil, pine, pecans, walnuts

and one of the following:

1 cup browned sausage meat
1 cup or more sliced mushrooms, sautéed with onion
1 cup chopped or whole drained oysters
1 cup chopped or whole soft-shell clams
1 cup cooked chopped shrimp

DRY DRESSING

This name is given by our cook, Sarah Brown, to a dressing she frequently makes, which is by no means dry when served. Proportions seem to be of little importance here, as the ingredients are never measured and the dressing always turns out light and good. Chopped pecans, oysters, olives, etc., may be added to it.

Make of day-old white, graham or whole wheat bread:

Soft bread crumbs, as sketched on (II, 159)

Combine with:

Chopped celery
Chopped onion

Season with:

Salt and paprika

Partly fill chicken, quail or turkey with the dressing. Melt:

¾ to 1 cup butter

Pour ½ of it onto the dressing in the cavity. Fill it lightly with the remaining dressing and pour the remaining butter on it. Sew up the opening.

SHERRY BREAD DRESSING

[1½ Cups]

Soak for 10 minutes:

1 cup bread crumbs

in:

½ cup dry sherry

Wring the wine from the bread. Stir and sauté for 3 minutes:

¼ cup finely chopped green pepper
½ cup finely chopped onion

in:

3 tablespoons butter

Add the bread crumbs and:

2 teaspoons chili sauce
½ cup canned or Sautéed Mushrooms, page 296
2 tablespoons chopped parsley

OYSTER BREAD DRESSING

[2½ Cups]

Enough for a 4-lb. fish or the crop of a turkey.

Melt:

6 tablespoons butter

Sauté in the butter until brown:

¼ cup chopped onion

Add:

1 tablespoon chopped parsley
2 cups bread crumbs
1 cup drained whole or chopped oysters: ½ pint
¾ teaspoon salt
¼ teaspoon paprika
2 tablespoons capers
(½ cup drained chopped spinach)

BREAD DRESSING FOR FISH

[2 Cups]

A fine but plain, unsophisticated dressing. Combine:

1½ cups bread crumbs
2 tablespoons chopped onion
½ cup chopped celery
2 tablespoons chopped parsley
1 or 2 beaten eggs

Season these ingredients well with:

½ teaspoon salt
⅛ teaspoon paprika
½ teaspoon dried tarragon or dill seed
2 tablespoons capers
(¼ teaspoon nutmeg)

Use enough:

Milk, melted butter or soup stock
to make a loose dressing.

GREEN DRESSING FOR FISH OR FOWL

[About 1½ Cups]
This has a tempting pistachio green color. Sauté until transparent:
2 tablespoons chopped shallots
in:
2 tablespoons butter
Cool slightly. Place this in a blender and ⅄ blend to a paste with:
1 egg
½ cup tender celery with leaves
½ cup parsley tops
½ cup water cress tops
½ cup crumbled crustless bread
½ teaspoon salt
⅛ teaspoon dried basil
Blend in with a fork:
½ cup pulled crustless bread crumbs (II, 159)
¼ cup pistachio nuts or sliced water chestnuts

SAUSAGE DRESSING

[About 2½ Cups]
Heat and stir in a skillet:
½ cup sausage meat
Drain off the surplus fat. Add:
½ cup chopped celery
2 cups cracker crumbs
¼ teaspoon minced onion
¼ teaspoon salt
⅛ teaspoon paprika
(½ cup chopped tart apples)
Moisten the dressing with:
½ cup stock

CHESTNUT DRESSING FOR GAME

[About 4 Cups]
Rice:
2½ cups cooked chestnuts, page 283
Combine them with:
½ cup melted butter
1 teaspoon salt
⅛ teaspoon pepper
¼ cup cream
1 cup dry bread or cracker crumbs
2 tablespoons chopped parsley
½ cup chopped celery
(1 tablespoon grated onion or ¼ cup seedless raisins)
You may add, but remember this will increase the amount:
½ cup liver sausage, ¼ cup chopped Chipolata sausage or 2 cups raw or creamed oysters

ONION DRESSING

[About 4 Cups]
Prepare:
2 cups chopped onions
Drop them in:
4 cups boiling salted water
Simmer for 10 minutes. Drain. Mix the onions and:
3 cups dry bread crumbs
1 beaten egg
½ cup melted butter
¾ teaspoon salt
⅛ teaspoon paprika
½ teaspoon poultry seasoning
(1 cup chopped tart apple or ½ cup sliced olives)
Moisten the mixture slightly with:
Stock

FENNEL DRESSING

[About 1 Cup]
Brown:
1 cup bread crumbs
in:
1 tablespoon butter
1 teaspoon Meat Glaze (II, 145)
Cut into julienned strips:
1 carrot
1 white base of leek
2 stalks celery

Add the above to the butter mixture. Add:

2 drops garlic juice

and simmer until coated. Add:

A sprig of chopped fresh fennel
1 small pinch thyme and bay leaf
¼ teaspoon salt

Mix with the crumbs:

Freshly ground pepper

APPLE AND PRUNE DRESSING

[About 4½ Cups]

Combine lightly:

3 cups diced crustless bread
½ cup melted butter or drippings
1 cup cubed apples
¾ cup chopped cooked prunes
½ cup chopped nut meats
1 teaspoon salt
½ teaspoon paprika
1 tablespoon lemon juice

APPLE AND ONION DRESSING

[About 12 Cups]

Place in boiling water for 5 minutes:

1 cup raisins

Drain well. Add them to:

7 cups soft bread crumbs

Melt:

¾ cup butter

Sauté in it for 3 minutes:

1 cup chopped onion
1 chopped clove garlic
1 cup chopped celery

Add these ingredients to the bread crumbs with:

3 cups tart diced apples
¼ cup finely chopped parsley
1½ teaspoons salt
¼ teaspoon paprika

HAM DRESSING FOR TURKEY

[About 7 Cups]

Combine:

1 to 1½ cups ground cooked ham
4 cups soft bread crumbs (II, 159)
1 cup crushed pineapple
1 cup plumped white raisins
1 cup walnuts
¼ to ½ cup honey

LIVER DRESSING

[About 4 Cups]

Chop:

½ lb. calf or baby beef liver

Sauté it lightly in:

1½ tablespoons butter
(1 tablespoon grated onion)

Combine these ingredients with:

2 cups soft bread crumbs
¾ cup chopped nut meats
2 beaten eggs
½ cup rich milk or cream and stock
1 teaspoon salt
½ teaspoon paprika
1½ tablespoons mixed minced chives and parsley
1 teaspoon chopped fresh tarragon
½ teaspoon lemon juice
(2 tablespoons dry sherry)

RICE DRESSING

[About 5 Cups]

Mince:

6 slices bacon

Sauté lightly for 5 minutes with:

3 tablespoons chopped onion

Pour off all but 2 tablespoons of the fat. Combine the contents of the skillet with:

4 cups cooked rice
1 cup dry bread crumbs (II, 159)
1 cup chopped celery
¾ teaspoon salt
¼ teaspoon pepper
⅛ teaspoon sage or nutmeg
½ cup milk
½ cup cream

WILD RICE DRESSING FOR GAME

[About 3 Cups]

Chop:

Giblets

Bring to the boiling point:

4 cups water, stock or tomato juice
1 teaspoon salt

Drop the giblets into the water and simmer for about 15 minutes. Remove from the water, bring it to a rolling boil and stir into it:

1 cup wild rice, page 160

➧ Simmer until nearly tender, about 30 minutes. Melt in a skillet:

¼ cup butter

Sauté in it for about 3 minutes:

2 tablespoons chopped shallots
1 tablespoon chopped green pepper
¼ cup chopped celery

Add the hot drained rice and the chopped giblets. You may also use one or two of the following ingredients, but remember the quantity of dressing will be increased:

1 cup sautéed mushrooms
½ cup chopped ripe or green olives
¼ cup tomato paste
½ cup chopped nuts
½ cup sliced water chestnuts

DRESSING FOR CORNISH HEN OR PIGEON

Soak for 10 minutes:

½ cup white raisins

in:

¼ cup cognac

Sauté them in:

6 tablespoons butter

Add:

¼ cup chopped shallots

Combine with the above and toss lightly:

½ teaspoon salt
1½ cups Boiled Rice, page 158
¼ cup chopped pistachio nuts

CHICKEN FARCE OR FORCEMEAT

[Enough for 3 Six-Pound Chickens]

A gala stuffing for boned chicken, squabs or galantines. Grind 3 times:

About 3½ lbs. raw chicken meat
3 cups mushrooms

Add to this mixture:

2 cups pistachio nuts
1⅓ cups dry sherry
¼ cup sliced truffles
1 teaspoon grated onion
8 or 9 slightly beaten eggs
1½ cups butter, cut in small dice
1½ tablespoons salt
¼ teaspoon freshly ground pepper
Grating of fresh nutmeg

Moisten until just softened:

2 cups soft bread crumbs

in:

1½ to 2 cups milk

Add the bread crumbs to this mixture with:

¼ cup cognac, brandy, Madeira or lemon juice

SEAFOOD DRESSING

For filling fish or for use in Vegetable Cases, page 256.

Add to:

1 cup flaked crab meat, drained oysters or mussels
2 slightly beaten eggs

Melt:

2 tablespoons butter

Sauté in it:

½ cup chopped onion
¾ cup chopped celery
2 slices minced bacon
1 cup fresh bread crumbs

Combine with the seafood.

Correct the seasoning

Add:

(1 teaspoon Worcestershire sauce, 1 tablespoon dry

sherry, 1/8 teaspoon ginger or 1/2 teaspoon grated lemon rind)

TANGERINE OR PINEAPPLE RICE DRESSING

[2 Cups]
Try this for chicken and squab.
Combine:
- 6 ribs pascal celery, leaves and stems cut up
- 1/4 cup chopped parsley
- 1 cup dry cooked rice, lightly sautéed in chicken fat or butter
- Sections and julienned strips of 1 tangerine and its rind or 1 cup drained crushed pineapple
- 1/3 cup lightly sautéed shallots
- 1/3 cup lightly sautéed mushrooms
- (1/3 cup pine nuts)

APRICOT OR PRUNE DRESSING

[About 5 Cups]
Cut into strips:
- 1 1/2 cups cooked apricots or seeded prunes

Combine with:
- 4 cups dry bread crumbs or
- 3 cups Boiled Rice, page 158
- 1/4 cup melted butter
- 1/2 teaspoon salt
- 1/8 teaspoon pepper
- 1/2 cup chopped green pepper or celery

Moisten lightly with:
- Stock or apricot water

POTATO DRESSING

[About 6 Cups]
Beat:
- 2 eggs

Add:
- 2 cups milk

and pour over:
- 4 cups soft bread crumbs

Fold in:
- 1 1/2 cups freshly mashed potatoes

Sauté until golden:
- 1/2 cup finely chopped onion
- 1/2 cup finely chopped celery

in:
- 1/4 cup butter

Add:
- 2 tablespoons chopped parsley

Combine with the potato mixture.

SWEET POTATO AND SAUSAGE STUFFING

[About 7 Cups]
Sufficient for a 10 lb. turkey.
Prepare:
- 4 cups Mashed Sweet Potatoes, page 322

Sauté until light brown:
- 1/2 lb. sausage meat: 1 cup

Break it up with a fork. Remove it from the pan. Add to the pan and sauté for 3 minutes:
- 3 tablespoons chopped onion
- 1 cup chopped celery

Add the sausage meat, the sweet potatoes and:
- 2 cups dry bread crumbs
- (3 tablespoons chopped parsley)
- Correct the seasoning

Mix these ingredients well.

SWEET POTATO AND APPLE DRESSING

[About 5 Cups]
Prepare:
- Sweet Potatoes and Apples, page 324

replacing the apple water with light or dark stock.

APPLE DRESSING

[About 4 Cups]
Peel and slice:
- 6 cups tart cooking apples

Combine them with:
- 1 cup currants or raisins
- (2 tablespoons lemon juice)

You may steam the currants or

raisins in 2 tablespoons of water in the top of a double boiler for 15 minutes before combining with the apples.

SAUERKRAUT DRESSING FOR GAME

Mix:

1 quart chopped drained sauerkraut

with:

1 clove garlic
¼ cup chopped onion
1 tart peeled and chopped apple
(2 tablespoons brown sugar)
(¼ cup dried currants)
(1 cup chopped water chestnuts)
(⅛ teaspoon thyme)

Correct the seasoning

POULTRY AND GAME BIRDS

The chicken is a world-citizen; duck and geese cosmopolites. Along with a number of the game birds which migrate from continent to continent, they are international favorites. And each nation has learned to cook them in a manner distinctively its own. The worldly-wise cook will not be content with chicken dumplings, roast turkey or quail on toast. But he will welcome into the kitchen some of the specialties—chicken cacciatore, duck bigarade, turkey mole, pheasant smitane—all of which have enlivened a global cuisine.

The principles of cooking poultry and game birds are just sufficiently different to warrant separate treatment; wild fowl having its own peculiarities in handling before cooking. There is the length of hanging time and the method of determining age—the results of which, in turn, establish the specific method of cooking. ➧ Wild fowl also demands extra fat during the cooking process. Preliminaries are identical. Bleeding the bird, plucking, singeing, drawing, removing tendons, trussing, stuffing, cutting it up—even boning, if you need this information—these steps are alike for all fowl, wild or domestic, as described later.

Whether you shoot your bird, catch it or buy it, you will always have to assess its quality and potential, sizing it up for the application of those cooking techniques which will be most individually suitable and rewarding. ➧ See, for example, under the dry heat processes, page 73, ways to cook young birds. Consult the moist heat processes, page 81, for those of questionable age or cook them in milk or marinate to tenderize.

ABOUT POULTRY

Poultry cooks and tastes best if used within 8 to 24 hours after slaughter. Cut-up poultry is more perishable than whole birds and turkey more perishable than chicken. All poultry is difficult to keep well in home refrigerators and, if you have to hold it more than a day or two, cook it and reheat it in a sauce before serving. Should you have bought chicken in airtight wrappings, loosen the wrapping before refrigerating.

For amounts of bird to allow per serving, see individual recipes, but if a large number of people are to be fed, turkey meat is the least expensive and turkey breast yields the greatest amount of protein per pound—duck, the least. The net amount of edible meat, minus fat or skin, is about 46% for turkeys, 41% for chicken and 22% for duckling.

Although a federal inspection stamp for poultry is authorized, its use is voluntary and applies only to already slaughtered birds in interstate commerce. It is well worth looking for, as its presence insures certain sanitary and grading standards.

Young chickens of either sex are called broilers if they weigh about 2½ lbs. and fryers if they weigh 2½ to 3½ lbs. Roasters, also of either sex, are under 8 months old and weigh 3½ to 5 lbs. and are very good for rotisseries or for use in Suprêmes, page 583. Capons, or castrated males, weigh 6 to 8 lbs. "Fowl" is a broadly polite "nom de plume" for hens aged 10 months or more and "stag" and "cock" for males that are too old to roast, but are well-flavored adjuncts for the stock pot.

➧ To size up a chicken, look for moist skin, soft legs and feet, bright eyes, a red comb, a wing tip that yields readily if pressed back and, most importantly ➧ a flexible breastbone. If the tip of the bone bends easily, the bird is young; if it is stiff, the bird is past its prime. For prepackaged chicken, the last test is the only one applicable. ➧ Beware of skin which is dry, hard, purplish, broken, bruised or scaly or that has long hairs sprouting from it.

On any bird that is frozen, watch for brownish areas called freezer burn, which indicate dehydration or long and improper storage. ➧ Commercially frozen birds may have been watered before freezing and the loss of this water on thawing may make them more expensive and less flavorful than those freshly killed.

In some households, arguments rage every Thanksgiving as to whether a cock or a hen turkey is to grace the board. The butcher might settle most of these disputes, since he invariably charges more for the latter.

ABOUT PLUCKING AND SINGEING POULTRY

Poultry is usually plucked and drawn when purchased. Buy dry-picked poultry whenever possible. If it is not plucked, do so at once—except for those game birds which must hang and are easier to pluck later. It is much easier to pluck and draw a bird that is thoroughly chilled. ➧ To pluck, pick the feathers from a bird. Remove all pin feathers—use a pair of tweezers or grasp each pin feather between forefinger and the tip of a knife, then pull.

After removing the coarser feathers, if those remaining are downy or small, you may use the paraffin method. Make up a mixture of ⅜ lb. melted paraffin and 7 quarts boiling water. Brush enough of this mixture over the bird to cover. Allow it to harden. Pull against the paraffin coating and it will carry the feathers with it.

➧ TO SINGE A BIRD

Hold it by the legs and singe the pin feathers over a gas flame or a candle. Turn it, so that all parts of the skin are exposed to the heat. ➧ But do not singe a bird that is to be frozen until you are just ready to use it. The heat of singeing breaks down the fat and hastens rancidity.

ABOUT PREPARING AN UNDRAWN BIRD FOR SAUTÉ OR FRICASSEE

First remove the wings and legs as shown on page 569 and on left at the top of page 570. Then be careful in making the diagonal incision—shown in the center illustration, page 569, by a dotted line—not to cut so deeply as to pierce the innards. Now reach in with the palm down and loosen the entrails at the top of the cavity. Place the bird on its back as on the right and crack the backbone by bending it sharply. Cut around the vent and remove the entrails. Discard the lungs and kidneys and save the giblets. Remove the oil sac, as described on page 571.

ABOUT PREPARING GIBLETS

➧ Among the entrails of a fowl the most valuable are the giblets, the heart, the liver and the gizzard. Remove veins, arteries, thin membrane and blood from around the heart and discard them. Cut the green sac or gall bladder away from the liver very carefully. It is better to leave a small piece of liver attached to the sac than to cut the sac so close to the liver as to risk puncturing it, for the bitterness of its fluid will ruin whatever it touches. Discard the gall bladder. Cut away any portion of the liver which may be discolored. ➧ If the liver of a fryer is yellow, it should very definitely be discarded. However, it may be normal to find a yellow liver in a stewer. Sever the intestines from the gizzard and remove membrane and fat from it. Then cut a shallow slit along the indented curve of the gizzard, being careful not to cut so deeply as to pierce the lining of the inner sac. Push against the outside of the opened gizzard with the thumbs to force out the sac. Discard it. Wash and dry giblets. Keep them well refrigerated and use or cook them as soon as possible. See Variety Meats, page 552, for the many ways to use giblets as meat and for stuffing, as well as in Gravies and Sauces, page 358.

ABOUT CUTTING UP A DRAWN BIRD

If the bird has been drawn, hold it up by a wing, letting its weight tug against the skin at the wing joint, see below. Clip through the skin, flesh and joint, severing the wing from the body. Use the same method to sever the second wing. For easier eating, you may want to transform the wings into mock legs. Just cut off the wing tips and straighten the two remaining joints with the hands. You may have to cut through the skin to do this. Pull them into a straight line to look like a small double leg. Silly, but the wings seem to taste better this way.

To cut off the legs, press them outward and down. If the bird is young the joint will break easily under this pressure. You will have to make a longer gash into the skin of the legs and continue the cut until it nearly meets in the back. Now cut the body apart in two pieces, separating the breast from the back. Cut, as sketched —below—along the dotted line. With a young chicken, it is possible to make a gash toward the

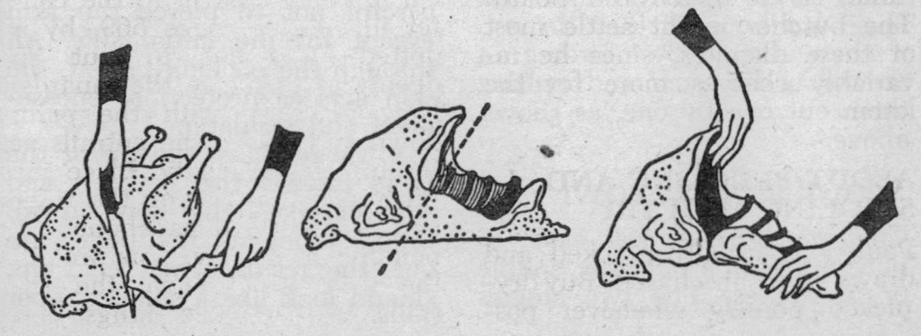

back on either side of the opening previously used to eviscerate the chicken and to pry the body apart until the back cracks, as shown on the right. Leave the breast in 1 piece or cut it into from 2 to 4 pieces.

➧ TO REMOVE TENDONS

In large domestic fowl and in game birds the leg tendons are apt to be tough and should be removed. Most butchers use a clever gadget that breaks the foot, holds the carcass securely and draws the tendons as the foot separates from the body. Amateurs have a somewhat harder time. It is easier to get the tendons out if the feet have not been cut off. Cut through the skin 1½ inches above the knee joint. Be careful not to cut the tendons. Lay the fowl down at the edge of a table or board, with the cut in the skin occurring just on the board and the rest of the leg projecting beyond it. Press the foot and ankle down, sharply, to snap the bone at the knee joint. Pull steadily. The tendons should come away with the foot and lower leg bone. If they do not, remove them by forcing a skewer under each and pulling them out one by one, as shown above.

ABOUT BONING FOWL

Chicken breasts are easy to bone either in a butterfly double or in singles. The two singles break down into a large upper and small lower fillet and are sometimes separated for quicker cooking. It is almost impossible to bone a bird that is already dressed and to restuff it to look like its original self. This is due to the careless way in which the cavity opening and neck are usually cut. A dressed fowl can, however, be made into a Galatine, page 529, but be sure to ➧ choose a bird in which the cavity opening is as small as possible.

In these instructions, we are assuming that the bird you are boning is not dressed. The procedure for boning a dressed one is very similar, except that you must provide protection against possible leakage from the entrails. Singe the bird, page 568. Cut off the feet and the first two joints of the wings. Cut off the head, so that the neck is as long as possible and at once catch and bind the two tubes that come from the craw, so that nothing from it can leak out. During the entire boning job—and it is not too difficult once you have tried it—➧ be careful not to pierce the skin except for the initial slits. All through the cooking period, the skin acts as protection, encasement and insulation.

➧ Always keep the tip of the knife toward the skeleton and stay close to the bone at all times. When all the bones are out, the result, when held up, should look like a small romper with wing and leg sleeves pulled into the lining.

Begin the boning by placing the bird breast down on the board. Make an incision the entire length of the spine, through both skin and flesh. Using a short, sharp-pointed boning knife, follow as close to the frame as you can cut, pushing the skin and flesh back as you cut. Work the skin of the neck down, so you can get the neck bone to extend way beyond it. Chop the neck off short, protecting the skin and being careful ➧ not to cut through the craw tubes. Work first toward the ball-and-socket joint of the shoulder, cutting it free and boning the shoulder blade. Pull the wing bone through from the inside, bringing the skin with it. Bone the meat from the wing and reserve it. Then strike for the ball-and-socket joint of the leg and pull the bone through. Reserve the meat. After you have freed and reserved both wings and legs, continue to work the meat free, first from one side of the body, then from the other, until the center front of the breast-bone is reached. ➧ Here great care is needed to free the skin without piercing it, as it is very thin at this point. You should now be able to get the whole skeleton out with its contents all in one piece. Leave the severing of the opening into the intestine to the last. When the skeleton is removed, wash the skin and flesh in cold running water and pat with a towel ➧ until it is very dry. For a farce for boned chicken, see page 564.

ABOUT PREPARING AN UNDRAWN BIRD FOR ROASTING

Cut off the head, so that the neck is as long as possible and at once catch hold of and bind the 2 tubes attached to the craw, to prevent leakage. Draw down the neck skin. Cut or twist off the neck, close to the body ➧ being careful not to tear or cut through the tubes or the neck skin. The skin should then be loose enough to allow you to reach in at the base of the neck and draw out the bound tubes and the crop.

Now make an incision through the skin below the breastbone, large enough to admit the hand, as sketched above. Insert the hand, palm down, into the cavity between the organs and the breast bone. Feel for the gizzard, which is firm and roundish and pull it out steadily. It will bring most of the other entrails with it. Keep giblets for gravies or stuffings. Remove the kidneys in the hollows near the base of the backbone and the spongy red lungs to either side of the spine between the ribs. Explore care-

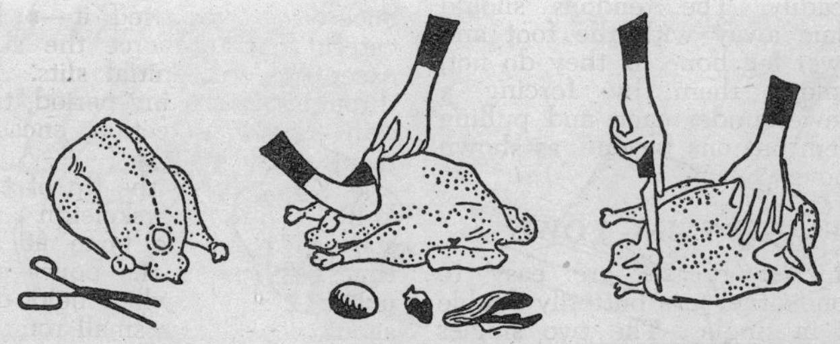

fully to ensure the removal of every bit of the viscera from the cavity, as well as surplus fat, as it may be too strong in flavor. Turn the chicken over and cut out the oil sac at the base of the tail, as shown on the right, by making a small oyster-shaped scoop above the heart-shaped area called the croupion or—by the irreverent—the pope's nose.

➧ Do not soak the bird in water at any time. Wipe it well with a damp cloth after drawing. Should it be necessary to wash the bird, hold it briefly under running water to cleanse the inside and ➧ dry it well with a cloth.

ABOUT STUFFING AND TRUSSING A BIRD

Always wait to stuff a bird until just before roasting. This may not be convenient, but it is much the safest procedure. Contamination is frequent in prestuffed fowl, for even when the dressing is refrigerated, the cold may not fully penetrate it.

Fill the bird only three-fourths full, as the dressing will expand. Stuff it loosely, as sketched below, left. Your task will be easier if you place the bird in a large pan. The crop cavity may be stuffed, too. You may also loosen the breast skin with a spoon and fill out the breast between the skin and the flesh. Close the openings with small skewers and a crisscrossed string. Or use a spiral skewer as shown in the center drawing, or sew them with the old-fashioned needle and thread. Fasten the legs so they will be close to the body by tying the ends of the drumsticks together, as shown in the center. Tie a piece of string around the skin of the neck. Leave two long ends. Turn the wings back, as shown on the right, and pass the string around them and secure it.

ABOUT ROASTING CHICKEN, CAPON, CORNISH HEN OR TURKEY

You may want to salt both the outside and inside of the poultry before roasting. We prefer to salt, if at all, after the browning and never salt the interior. If the bird is lean, rub it well with melted unsalted shortening. Place it on a greased rack ➧ uncovered, in a roasting pan, breast side up with the oven preheated to 450°. Reduce the heat immediately to 350°, baste frequently with pan drippings or additional fat and cook until tender. Some people like to use an even, slow heat throughout the cooking period, placing the bird in a preheated 325° oven and not basting at all. This method has gained popularity because it is carefree and because it was,

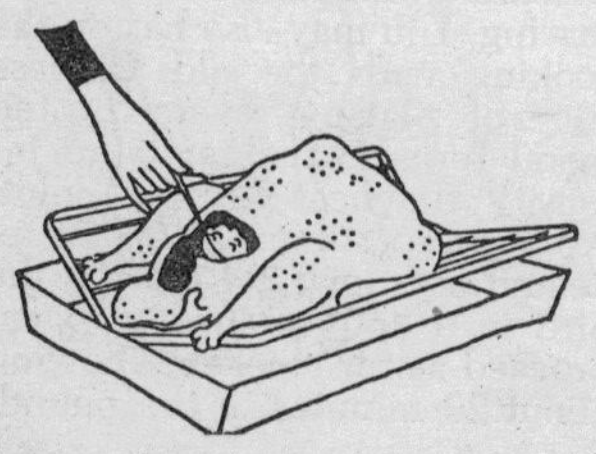

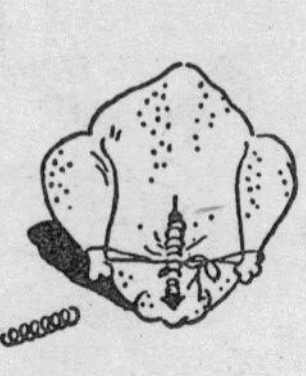

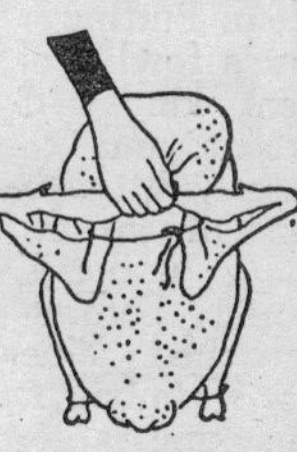

until recently, reputed to entail less meat shrinkage. It has now been conclusively proved that even-heat roasting does not reduce shrinkage. And we are quite convinced, on the basis of the old reliable taste-test, that the flavor of meat sealed at the onset of roasting by high heat is markedly superior.

➧ In timing meat, remember that many factors are involved: the age of the bird and its fat content, whether it was frozen or not and, of course, its size. If it is a large bird, the total cooking time required will be longer, but it will require less time per pound than a smaller one. ➧ Have fowl at 70° before putting it in the oven. If using a thermometer, insert it between the thigh and the body of the bird, taking care that the tip is not in contact with the bone. Cook to an internal temperature of 190°. If not using a thermometer, allow about 20 minutes to the pound for birds up to 6 pounds. For larger birds, allow about 15 minutes per pound. In either case, add about five minutes to the pound if the bird you are cooking is stuffed. Other popular tests for doneness are to prick the skin of the thigh to see if the juice runs clear or to jiggle the drumstick to see if the hip joint is loose. This latter response, we find, usually means that the bird is not done but overdone. As a matter of fact, in cooking any bird, you are faced with a real and built-in problem. Putting it simply, the flesh of a fowl is of two quite different kinds: the tender breast meat and the tougher, relatively fatty, legs. The breasts are usually just right—as the French say, "à point"—an appreciable time before the legs have reached doneness. To correct this imbalance, especially in cooking larger birds, cover the breast after the first hour of cooking with a cloth that has been dipped in melted unsalted shortening.

There are several ways to glaze a bird toward the end of cooking. You may remove the cloth and dust the bird with flour or coat it with a thin roux during the last half hour or so of cooking. When the flour or roux sets, baste frequently with pan drippings. If the flavor is compatible with your dressing, or if the bird is unstuffed, you may baste by brushing it with a combination of peach or apricot preserves or currant jelly mixed with melted butter.

ABOUT ROASTING DUCK OR GOOSE

Pluck, singe, draw and truss, as described on page 568. Since these birds are fat, it is wise, especially with mature ducks and geese, to ➧ preroast them for about 15 minutes before stuffing. We often prefer to prepare a separate stuffing in a baker, so that the dressing will not be overpowered by the flavor and slickness of the fat. But, whether these birds are preroasted or not ➧ they must be pricked frequently, if lightly, all over to allow excess fat to escape. If they are not stuffed, you can place a cored and peeled apple, a carrot, an onion, celery stalks or a potato in the body cavity to attract off-flavors. Discard these vegetables before serving. You may also hasten the cooking with the old Chinese trick of placing several heated metal forks in the cavity to intensify the heat at that point. After preroasting in a 400° preheated oven or after placing the bird in a 450° preheated oven, proceed as for chicken, allowing about 20 minutes to the pound.

ABOUT ROASTING FOWL IN FOIL

Today, "roasting" fowl in aluminum foil has become fashionable. But calling this process roasting is a misnomer, for true roasting can only go on under ventilation. The foil, which causes steam to form and entraps it, gives the bird a stewed taste. It also insulates against heat and when you cook in it you will need a hotter oven. A further caution: if you remove the foil during the last half hour or so of cooking in an attempt at browning, you will simply dry out the meat.

ABOUT CARVING FOWL

If a bird is to be carved at table ➧ be sure the heated platter is large enough and garnish it lightly with parsley or watercress. There is a subtle art to carving, which is not easily mastered. But a sharp, long-bladed knife and a two-tined fork with a guard are helpful for the amateur.

Place the bird, breast side up, on a platter. Insert the fork firmly into the knee joint, as sketched below. This will act as a lever to pull the leg away from the body of the bird. Slice the thigh flesh away from the body until the ball-and-socket hip joint is exposed. A twisting movement with the knife will disengage the tendons if the fork holds the tension against the knee. Have an extra platter close at hand, on which to place the leg. Cut the joint between the thigh and drumstick, as shown. Repeat the above, cutting off the other leg. Begin to arrange the pieces on the extra platter, so they will look attractive when it is passed. If a large bird is being carved, some slices of meat may be cut from the thigh and the drumstick at this time. Proceed to remove the wings in a similar manner and, if the bird is large, divide the wings at the major joint. To slice the breast, begin at the area nearest the neck and slice thinly across the grain—the entire length of the breast. If the bird is very large, such as a turkey, carve only one side, unless more is needed at the first serving. This way, the meat can be kept from drying out.

In carving a duck, you will find the leg joint is more difficult to sever because it is attached much farther under the bird and is somewhat recessed at the joint. Here, as in general, for the inexperienced carver or the impatient one, poultry shears are an inspired addition to his weaponry.

ROAST CHICKEN [6]

Preheat oven to 450°.

➧ Draw, singe, stuff and truss, pages 568–572:

A 4 to 5 lb. chicken or capon

Use for the stuffing ½ the recipe for:

Rice Dressing, page 563, Bread Dressing with Oysters, Nuts and Giblets, page 560, or Chestnut Dressing, page 562

or make:

2 cups Dry Dressing, page 561

replacing the onion with:

½ cup chopped leeks—white part only

and using:

French bread

Put the bird on a rack, uncovered, in the oven and ➧ reduce the heat at once to 350°. Roast about 20 minutes per pound. Serve with gravy, page 358.

ROAST STUFFED TURKEY [12]

Preheat oven to 450°.

➧ Draw, singe, stuff and truss, pages 568–572.

A 10 to 16 lb. turkey

5 cups of one of the following stuffings should fill a 10-lb. bird:

Dry Dressing, page 561
Potato Dressing, page 565, or ½ the recipe for Apple Onion Dressing, page 563

Or you may want to use two kinds of dressing, a richer one like:

Sausage or Oyster Dressing

in the crop and:

Celery or Bread Dressing

in the cavity. Put the bird on a rack, uncovered, in the oven and ➧ reduce the heat at once to 350°, allowing about 20 minutes to the pound for an unstuffed bird and 25 minutes for a stuffed one. Baste frequently or after first half hour cover the bird with a cloth soaked in melted butter. Baste frequently with pan drippings. Remove the cloth the last half hour of roasting so the bird may brown. If using a smaller turkey allow 20 to 25 minutes per lb. For a bird weighing 18 to 25 lbs., reduce the oven to 300° and allow 13 to 15 minutes per lb.

Make:

Pan Gravy, page 358

adding:

Sautéed Mushrooms, page 296

or flavoring it with the finely chopped giblets if they were not used in the stuffing.

CHICKEN AND TURKEY BAKED IN FOIL

Preheat oven to 450°.

If you don't have time to baste, an accepted way of cooking halves or parts of chicken or turkey is in a wrap of aluminum foil. But before roasting see Foil Cooking, page 86. Season it well, and add a little butter and fresh herbs, such as tarragon or rosemary. Or use one of the barbecue sauces on page 374.

Cook a 5 lb. stuffed chicken about 2½ to 3 hours; parts or halves about 45 minutes.

BROILED SPRING CHICKEN

[Allow ¾ Pound per Person]

Preheat broiler.

Clean and cut into halves:

Broilers

Rub them on both sides with:

Butter

Place them in a pan, skin side down. The skin side will brown quicker than the under side. Broil the chickens until brown, about 15 to 20 minutes, turning them occasionally. There are so many good basting sauces for broilers. We suggest that, during the cooking, you baste occasionally for excellent flavor with:

2 tablespoons butter to 1 tablespoon lemon juice
A grind of fresh pepper
(Fresh or dry herbs)

Or, for an accent on beautiful color:

2 tablespoons butter
¼ teaspoon paprika

Allow the above amounts for each ½ broiler. Or when the broilers are ready, flambé them, page 80, with:

1 oz. warmed brandy

for each broiler.
Or make:

A thickened Pan Gravy, page 358, using tarragon, or an unthickened one—deglazing with dry white wine

STUFFED BROILER

A convenient party dish, as all but the final heating may be done in advance. Broil each:

½ broiler, as above

until ¾ done. Remove from heat and cool. Stuff each broiler cavity with:

½ cup of any stuffing, page 560

Preheat oven to 350°.
Place the stuffed broilers on a baking tray and brush top of stuffing with:

Melted butter

Bake for 15 to 20 minutes or until both broiler and stuffing are heated through.

BROILED TURKEY

Prepare for cooking:

Turkeys weighing from 3 to 4 lbs.

Cut them into 4 pieces. Prepare as for:

Broiled Chicken, above

allowing about 45 minutes cooking time.

⊟ BARBECUED CHICKEN

➧ Please read About Outdoor Cooking, page 93. Prepare:

Broiled Chicken, above

placing the broiler 5 inches from the heat. Cook in all about 30 minutes, turning often and brushing the birds the last 10 minutes with:

A Barbecue Sauce, page 374

If preparing outdoors, place on a grill, cavity side down, for 15 minutes at moderate heat before turning and cooking until tender, about 10 minutes more.

OVEN-FRIED CHICKEN [2]

I.
Preheat oven to 350°.
Disjoint:

A broiler

Wipe dry. Dredge it in:

Seasoned flour

Heat to the point of fragrance in a heavy skillet:

¼ cup butter

Sauté the chicken lightly. Remove from the skillet to a rack in a baking pan. Baste with the skillet pan drippings. Let it bake until tender, about 30 to 35 minutes, basting with added fat if necessary and turning occasionally.

II. [2]
Preheat oven to 400°.
This is a simpler but not quite as tasty a version as I.
Disjoint:

A broiler

Use neck, wing tips for Stock (II, 142). Wipe the remaining pieces with a damp cloth and ➧ dry carefully. In a shallow 9 x 12 baking pan, melt in the preheated oven:

½ cup butter

Dredge the broiler in:

Seasoned flour

Remove the butter from the oven when melted and hot. Place the chicken in it ➧ skin side down. Baste the upper surface with melted butter from the pan. Put the uncovered pan back in the preheated oven and bake the chicken 20 to 30 minutes. Turn it skin side up. Put it back in the oven. ➧ Reduce the heat to 350° and bake until tender, about 30 to 35 minutes. ➧ Do not overcook or the chicken will be dry. While baking, baste the chicken several times with the drippings. You may also wish to remove the white meat portions and keep them warm, uncovered, while you continue to cook the dark meat slightly longer. Serve at once. For gravy and other suggestions, see page 358.

PAN-FRIED OR SAUTÉED CHICKEN

[Allow ¾ Pound per Person]
Please read About Sautéing, page 79.
Do not attempt to saute chicken in this way unless it is young and tender. Clean and cut into pieces:

Young chickens

Dredge them lightly with:

(Seasoned flour or corn meal)

Melt in a skillet:

A mixture of butter and oil

allowing for each half chicken 2 or more tablespoons of fat. When the fat has reached the point of fragrance, add the chicken. Cook and turn it in the hot fat until brown. Reduce the heat and continue cooking the chicken, turning frequently until done, from 20 to 30 minutes, according to size. ➧ Cook only until tender, as further cooking will dry and toughen the meat. Remove the chicken from the pan and make:

Pan Gravy, page 358

Add:

Cream or stock
Correct the seasoning

Serve at once, garnished with:

Parsley

CHICKEN IN BATTER [4]

I.
Preheat deep fryer to 350°.
➧ Please read About Deep-Fat Frying, pages 75–79.
Some cooks prepare this dish with raw chicken, as in the recipe. Others prefer to use a partially cooked fowl. Cut into pieces:

A young 3 lb. roasting chicken

Dip into:

Fritter Batter for Meat (II, 125)

Place the dipped pieces on a rack and let them dry for 15 to 30 minutes. Immerse them in the hot fat and cook for 15 to 17 minutes. Drain on paper towels. Serve hot or cold.

II.
[Allow ¾ Pound per Person]
Prepare:

A young 3 lb. roasting chicken

using the recipe for:

Chicken Stew, below

Remove the meat from the liquid. Cool thoroughly. Dry well. Preheat deep fryer to 375°.
Dip the chicken into:

Fritter Batter for Meat (II, 125)

and cook in deep fat until golden. Serve at once.

CHICKEN OR TURKEY STEW OR FRICASSEE [5]

I.
Clean and cut into pieces:

A 5 lb. stewing chicken

Place the chicken in a stewing pan and bring to the boiling point with:

3 cups water
1 sliced carrot
2 ribs celery with leaves
1 small sliced onion

Simmer the chicken about 15 minutes and remove scum. Continue to ➧ simmer uncovered until the chicken is tender, 2 hours or more. ➧ Do not boil at any time. At the end of the first hour of cooking, add:

3 or 4 peppercorns

Remove the chicken and strain the stock. If a very concentrated gravy is desired, boil the stock before thickening until it is reduced to 1½ cups. Thicken it with:

Flour, see Gravy, page 358

Pour the gravy over the chicken. Garnish it with:

Parsley

Serve it with:

Noodles, page 172
Dumplings, page 178 or
Boiled Rice, page 158

II. This can be a stew like Blanquette de Veau, page 504, cooking the meat for 45 minutes.

III. [4 to 5]

Have ready about:

1 dozen mushrooms
1 dozen small onions

cooked à Blanc, page 504, until tender. Cut into pieces:

A 5 lb. stewing chicken

reserving the neck and back for stock. Dust the meat with:

Flour

Melt in a heavy pan:

2 tablespoons butter

When the butter reaches the point of fragrance, add the floured chicken. Cook long enough so the flour crusts but does not color. Add just enough to cover:

Water or chicken stock
An onion stuck with 3 cloves
1 teaspoon salt

Bring the liquid to a boil. ➧ Reduce the heat at once. ➧ Simmer, uncovered, for about 45 minutes. Remove the meat and the clove-studded onion from the liquid. Discard the onion. Keep the meat warm. Melt in the top of a double boiler:

3 tablespoons butter

Add:

3 tablespoons all-purpose flour

Make a sauce by adding to above roux the liquid from the meat. Simmer, stirring, about 5 minutes. Have everything else ready to serve, because the sauce does not hold well once the eggs are added. Add ➧ off the heat:

3 beaten egg yolks
¾ cup cream

Place the sauce ➧ over—not in—hot water, stirring until the eggs thicken. Add the mushrooms and onions. Place the chicken on a hot platter, inside a:

Rice Ring, page 162

Pour the garnished sauce over the meat. You may decorate the platter with small bunches of:

Cooked carrots
Parsley

so arranged as to look like fresh carrots with tops.

BRAISED BROILERS

[Allow ¾ Pound per Person]

If you like your chicken falling from the bone, this is your recipe.

Preheat oven to 350°.

Clean and cut into quarters:

Young chickens

Heat in a skillet:

Butter

Add the chickens and sauté them until brown. Place in a baking dish. Pour over them, to the depth of 1 inch:

½ cup boiling Chicken Stock (II, 142), or milk

Before covering the dish, add:

(1 teaspoon sautéed chopped onions)
(1 teaspoon honey)

for each piece of chicken and for the pot a:

(Tiny pinch of rosemary)

Bake ➧ covered, about 40 minutes. When tender, remove them from the dish.

Make:

Pan Gravy, page 358

Add to the stock, if required:

Chicken Stock (II, 142)
Cream
Salt and pepper

MARYLAND CHICKEN [4 to 5]

Cut into pieces for serving:
A young frying chicken, about 3½ lbs.
Bread it by dipping each piece in:
Milk
and rolling it in:
Flour
Let dry for 1 hour. Heat in a heavy skillet:
½ to 1 inch fat, a combination of cooking oils or bacon drippings
Heat the fat until it reaches the point of fragrance. Add the chicken. Brown it on all sides.
Preheat oven to 375°.
Place the brown chicken in a fresh pan and bake, covered, until steamed through, about ½ hour. This Border dish is usually served with a cream gravy made from the drippings, that is, some of the fat thickened with:
Flour
to which milk is added, see Pan Gravy, page 358. You may further enrich the gravy with:
(Egg Yolks, page 356)
Serve with:
Ham and Corn Fritters (II, 128)

SMOTHERED CHICKEN [6 to 7]

Preheat oven to 350°.
Prepare for cooking:
A 4-lb. roasting chicken
Disjoint it. Place the chicken in a paper bag with:
¼ cup Seasoned Flour (II, 160)
Close the bag and shake vigorously.
Brown the chicken in:
¼ cup olive or salad oil
Place it in a casserole. Cook in the fat for 10 minutes:
1 small sliced onion
1 sliced clove garlic
3 or 4 chopped celery stalks
1 medium-sized carrot
Put the vegetables in the casserole. Pour over the mixture:
1½ cups hot chicken stock
Bake ♦ covered, for about 1½ hours or until tender. Add to the dish, 5 minutes before it is done:
(1 cup sliced sautéed mushrooms)
(12 stuffed sliced olives)

CHICKEN PAPRIKA [3]

Cut up as for frying:
A young chicken: about 2½ lbs.
Melt in a heavy pot:
1½ tablespoons butter
1½ tablespoons cooking oil
Add and simmer until golden:
1 cup chopped onions
2 teaspoons to 2 tablespoons mild paprika
Add:
½ teaspoon salt
2 cups well-seasoned stock
As soon as these ingredients have reached boiling point, add the chicken. ♦ Simmer it, covered, until tender, about 1 hour.
Stir:
1 teaspoon flour
into:
1 cup cultured sour cream
Stir it slowly into the pot. Heat the chicken 5 minutes longer but ♦ do not boil. Serve at once. Good with noodles or rice.

CHICKEN BRAISED IN WINE OR COQ AU VIN

We are often asked why this recipe turns out a rich medium brown rather than the very dark brown sometimes served in restaurants. Abroad, in country places where chickens are locally butchered, the blood is often kept and added to the gravy at the last minute as a thickener, see page 357. After this addition, it is not allowed to boil. Here in America, this effect is often imitated by adding caramel coloring. Recipe I is best with a youngish chicken.

If you have an old one, use II below.

I. [4]

Disjoint:

A broiler or roasting chicken

Use the back and neck for the stock pot. Melt:

3 tablespoons butter or olive oil

Add and brown lightly:

¼ lb. minced salt pork
¾ cup chopped mild onions or ½ cup pearl onions
1 sliced carrot
3 minced shallots
1 peeled clove garlic

Push the vegetables aside. Brown the chicken in the fat. Add and stir:

2 tablespoons flour
2 tablespoons minced parsley
1 tablespoon fresh chervil or marjoram
½ bay leaf
½ teaspoon thyme
1 teaspoon salt
⅛ teaspoon freshly ground pepper
(1 tablespoon brandy)

Stir in:

1½ cups dry red wine or sherry

Simmer the chicken over low heat until done, about 1 hour. Keep it covered. Add for the last 5 minutes of cooking:

½ lb. sliced mushrooms

Skim off excess fat.

Correct the seasoning

Serve the chicken on a hot platter, the sauce and vegetables poured over it.

II. To tenderize an old chicken before braising, place it in ➧ a closely lidded heavy casserole on a piece of bacon rind or a few strips of bacon. Put the casserole in a 250° oven for about 45 minutes or until the flesh of the bird becomes white and has a pleasant aroma. The chicken is then ready to use for braising, as in I above.

CHICKEN TARRAGON WITH WINE [4]

Disjoint:

2 broilers

Marinate the pieces for about 1 hour in:

¼ cup fresh or 2 tablespoons dried tarragon leaves
4 finely minced shallots
1 cup dry white wine

Preheat broiler.

Broil the chicken for about 20 minutes or until tender.

Baste it with:

Melted butter

and the strained marinade. Save some of the marinade to deglaze the broiler pan.

Correct the seasoning

and serve the chicken on a hot platter with the drippings poured over it.

HUNTER'S CHICKEN, CHICKEN CACCIATORE OR CHASSEUR [4]

Hunters always seem to have tomatoes and mushrooms handy. Cut into individual pieces:

A 4 lb. chicken

Dredge with:

2 to 3 tablespoons flour

Sauté until golden brown in:

¼ cup olive oil

with:

2 tablespoons chopped shallots
(1 minced clove garlic)

Add:

¼ cup Italian tomato paste
½ cup dry white wine
1 teaspoon salt
¼ teaspoon white pepper
¾ cup chicken stock
½ bay leaf
⅛ teaspoon thyme
⅛ teaspoon sweet marjoram
½ to 1 cup sliced mushrooms

(2 tablespoons brandy or
¼ cup Muscatel)

Simmer the chicken ◆ covered, for 1 hour or until tender. Serve with:

Boiled Spaghetti

CHICKEN MARENGO [8]

A good buffet casserole which profits by a day's aging, refrigerated.

Cut into quarters:

2 frying chickens

Sauté until delicately colored:

1 thinly sliced onion

in:

½ cup olive oil

then remove. Add the chicken pieces and brown on all sides. Add:

½ cup dry white wine
2 crushed cloves garlic
½ teaspoon thyme
1 bay leaf
Sprigs of parsley
1 cup chicken stock
2 cups Italian style tomatoes
Correct the seasoning

Cover the pot and simmer for about 1 hour, until tender. When meat is done, remove it to a platter. Strain the sauce and reduce it for about 5 minutes. Now sauté:

16 to 20 small white onions
1 lb. sliced mushrooms

in:

¼ cup butter
Juice of 1 lemon

Arrange chicken quarters, mushrooms, onions and:

1 cup pitted black olives

in a deep earthenware casserole. Sprinkle over all:

1 jigger cognac

Add the sauce and reheat in a 350° oven. Garnish with:

Chopped parsley

Serve with:

Rice

SPANISH CHICKEN [4]

Preheat oven to 350°.

Also see Paella, page 105.

Cut into pieces:

A 4 lb. frying chicken

Dredge them with:

Seasoned Flour (II, 160)

Heat in a skillet:

¼ cup olive oil

Brown the chicken in it. Place in a casserole. Sauté in the oil in the skillet:

¼ cup chopped onion
3 tablespoons chopped green pepper
1 minced clove garlic

Add:

½ cup chopped carrots
½ cup chopped celery
1 cup chopped, peeled, seeded tomatoes
¾ cup tomato juice

Pour these ingredients over the chicken in the casserole. Bake ◆ covered, for about 1 hour or until tender. Add, if needed:

Boiling stock

Five minutes before the chicken is done, add:

¾ cup Sautéed Mushrooms, page 296
⅓ cup sliced stuffed olives

Make:

Pan Gravy, page 358

FRENCH CASSEROLE CHICKEN [5]

Whenever we see one of our contemporaries trying to regain her youthful allure with gaudy sartorial trappings, we think of a dish we found in a collection of college alumnae recipes, called: "Suprême of Old Hen." We all know that "Suprême," in chef's parlance simply means a breast of fowl. But, in this case, it really lives up to its billing and makes such a good dish out of a poorish bird that the old girl is still an acceptable morsel.

Prepare for cooking and disjoint:

A 5 lb. fowl

Sear the pieces in:

¼ cup hot butter

Add:

¼ cup dry white wine

Remove the chicken from the pot. Place in the pot:

2 pared, cored, sliced tart apples
6 chopped celery ribs with leaves
1 minced or grated onion
3 sprigs parsley
½ teaspoon salt
¼ teaspoon paprika

Cover and cook these ingredients gently until tender. Stir in:

2½ tablespoons flour
2 cups Stock (II, 141)

Cook and stir the sauce until it boils. Add the chicken. Cover and simmer until it is tender, 1 hour or more. Remove the chicken to a hot ovenproof serving dish. Strain the sauce. Warm over hot water and add to the strained sauce:

⅓ cup sweet or cultured sour cream
Correct the seasoning

Add:

1 tablespoon fresh tarragon or basil

Pour the sauce over the chicken. Sprinkle it generously with:

Parmesan cheese

Place it under a broiler until the cheese is melted.

BRUNSWICK STEW [8]

Disjoint for cooking:

A 5 lb. chicken

Sauté it slowly until light brown in:

¼ cup butter or drippings

Remove from the pan. Brown in the fat:

½ cup chopped onions

Place in a large stewing pan the chicken, onions and:

1½ to 2 cups peeled, seeded, quartered tomatoes
3 cups fresh lima beans
1 cup boiling water
A few grains cayenne
(2 cloves)

➧ Simmer these ingredients, covered, until the chicken is nearly tender. Add:

3 cups corn, cut from the cob

Simmer the chicken and vegetable mixture, covered, until tender. The chicken meat may be removed from the bones.

Correct the seasoning

Add:

2 teaspoons Worcestershire sauce

Stir in:

(1 cup toasted bread crumbs)

CHICKEN KIEV [8]

Preheat deep fryer to 325°.
Bone, skin, page 570, cut in halves and pound, page 452, to a ¼-inch thickness:

4 chicken breasts

Form into 8 balls:

½ lb. butter

Roll butter balls lightly in a mixture of:

2 tablespoons chopped chives
2 tablespoons chopped parsley
(1 minced clove garlic)
¼ teaspoon white pepper

Place one of the seasoned butter balls in the center of each half breast and roll so that the butter is completely enclosed. Secure with a toothpick, if necessary. Dust with:

Flour

Brush with:

Beaten egg

Roll in:

Dry bread crumbs

Fry in deep fat, page 75, until golden brown, about 5 to 7 minutes.

BRANDIED CHICKEN BREASTS [4]

Remove the breasts from:

4 young chickens

Skin, bone and divide into halves, and rub with:

Brandy

Let them stand about 10 minutes. Season with:

Salt, pepper and marjoram

Heat to the point of fragrance:

6 tablespoons sweet butter

Sauté the fillets over medium heat, 6 to 8 minutes on each side. Remove to a heated ovenproof platter and keep warm. To the remaining butter in the pan, add:

½ cup dry sherry

Simmer over ♦ low heat until the liquid is reduced to half. Add, stirring constantly:

2 cups cream

beaten with:

4 egg yolks

Season with:

Salt, pepper and nutmeg

Stir and cook until slightly thickened. Pour the sauce over the chicken breasts. Sprinkle with:

Grated Swiss cheese

mixed with equal parts of:

Fine buttered crumbs

Glaze under the broiler.

BREAST OF CHICKEN COCKAIGNE

[Allow a Single Breast per Serving]

This delicate recipe does not work with frozen chicken. Cook up a flavorful stock (II, 142), from the skin and bones of the chicken you are using. Skin, bone, divide in halves:

Chicken breasts

When ready to cook, dust the chicken breasts, which should be 70°, lightly with:

Flour

For each breast, heat to the point of fragrance, in a heavy skillet:

½ tablespoon butter
½ tablespoon cooking oil

Put the floured pieces of chicken in the hot oil. Shake the pan constantly so the flour crusts but does not color. Cover and poach in the butter over very low heat, turning occasionally, for 10 to 15 minutes, depending on the thickness of the meat. Remove from heat and allow to stand covered for about 10 minutes more. This rather unorthodox procedure makes breasts puff up, so the meat is both tender and moist. Remove from the pan and keep warm. Make a gravy of the pan drippings and the stock made from the bones and skins.

CHICKEN SUPRÊME PAPILLOTE

Preheat oven to 400°.

Prepare:

Breast of Chicken Cockaigne

allowing it to cook until ½ done. Place it on a parchment heart for Papillote, page 88. Before folding, place:

1 tablespoon Colbert Butter, page 384

on each ½ breast. Seal the paper and bake on a baking sheet for about 15 minutes. Serve with:

Pilaf, page 166

STUFFED CHICKEN BREASTS

[Individual Serving]

These are quickly prepared in a chafing dish or electric skillet. Have ready:

A boned, skinned breast of chicken

beaten with a cleaver until very thin. Heat to the point of fragrance.

1½ to 2 tablespoons butter

Quickly move the chicken about in this hot fat until it is no longer pink, about 2 to 3 minutes in all. Fold this thin piece over once to hold:

1 thin slice Virginia ham
1 very thin small piece Swiss cheese

Remove the chicken from the

pan and keep it warm. Sauté with pan drippings:

1 tablespoon finely minced shallots
3 mushroom caps

When mushrooms have cooked for about 3 minutes, add:

¼ cup dry white wine
2 tablespoons freshly chopped, peeled, seeded tomato

Simmer about 3 minutes again. Add to this sauce:

2 tablespoons cream

Heat the chicken breasts in the sauce slowly, but ♦ do not let them boil. Turn them once or twice. When heated through, about 3 minutes, add:

1 tablespoon chopped parsley
Correct the seasoning

Serve at once, over:

Saffron rice or fine buttered noodles

CHICKEN BREASTS IN QUANTITY FOR CREAMING OR SALAD

This recipe is particularly useful in preparing large quantities of chicken meat for such dishes as Chicken à la King, page 226, or Chicken Pot Pies, page 212. Many knowledgeable cooks consider poaching an ideal approach, but we should like to suggest this method which we find more flavorful. After the chicken is baked, save the pan juices and make a stock of the skins and bones. Combine these two defatted by-products in making sauce if the chicken is to be served hot or in an aspic. Or use the juices and defatted stock for broth or other cooking if the chicken is served as salad.

Preheat oven to 300°.

Place on a rack in a large shallow pan, skin side up:

Chicken breasts

Brush them, allowing for each whole breast:

1½ tablespoons butter

Bake for about 1 hour. When slightly cooled, remove the skins and bone the breasts. Cover and refrigerate the meat until ready to use.

STUFFED CHICKEN LEGS

[Allow 1 or 2 Legs per Person]

I. Preheat oven to 350°.

Remove bone and tendons, page 570, from:

Large chicken legs

Stuff the cavities with:

Bread or other dressing, page 560

Close the opening with poultry pins. Brown the legs lightly in:

Butter or other fat

to which you may add:

A slice of onion

Place the stuffed legs in a casserole. Cover the bottom of the dish with:

⅓ inch boiling Chicken Stock (II, 142)

Bake the meat, covered, until tender, about 45 minutes. Make:

Pan Gravy, page 358

II. Bone:

4 chicken legs

Replace the bone with:

4 pineapple spears

Dredge the stuffed legs in:

A Bound Breading (II, 160)

Melt in a skillet, to the point of fragrance:

2 tablespoons butter
2 tablespoons cooking oil

Sauté the chicken legs, uncovered, until golden brown. Cover them with:

½ cup shredded fresh coconut

Cover the skillet and ♦ simmer the chicken until tender. Meanwhile, make up a mixture of:

½ cup pineapple sirup
½ cup chicken stock
2 slices fresh gingerroot
1 to 2 teaspoons cornstarch

and cook until the cornstarch is

clear. Pour this sauce over the chicken and heat through again. Serve with:

Rice and Orange and Avocado Salad

BONED CHICKEN

See About Boning Fowl, page 570.
This recipe, which we have enjoyed on many holiday occasions with Clara Kupferschmid, is one she has brought close to perfection over the years. Choose a very fresh, dry-picked, undressed:

6 lb. chicken

Be sure the skin is intact. Bone it, page 570. Allow for filling ⅓ of the recipe for:

Chicken Farce, page 564

Before stuffing the chicken, tie it off securely at the neck, wing ends and legs. Sew shut the vent under the tail. Be sure not to pack the farce or fill the skin too tightly or it may burst during the cooking as the stuffing swells. In filling, pretend you are a taxidermist or a frustrated sculptor and try to shape the stuffing so that, when you have sewed the seam down the back, the bird will resemble its former self. Preheat oven to 450°.

Bard, page 454, the chicken with:

⅛ inch thick salt pork

If you do not like a salt pork flavor, brush the bird generously all over with:

Clarified Butter, page 383

Allow, for this and for subsequent basting, about ½ lb. butter. Prick the chicken all over with a darning needle and repeat this operation after every basting. Place the bird on a rack in a pan in the hot oven and ➧ reduce the heat at once to 350°. If the chicken was not barded, baste it at 10-minute intervals after 40 minutes of cooking and continue until it is done, about 2 hours in all. If the bird was barded with salt pork, remove the barding about 20 minutes before the end of the cooking time in order to give the bird a better color. Boned stuffed chickens may be served hot, but are unusually delicious when chilled for at least 24 hours to allow the seasonings to develop.

Slice very thin with hot serrated knife when serving.

COUNTRY CAPTAIN OR EAST INDIA CHICKEN CURRY [4]

This dish has become a favorite in America, although it probably got its name not from the sea-captain who brought the recipe back to our shores, but from the Indian officer who first made him acquainted with it. So says Cecily Brownstone, a great friend; and this is her time-tested formula. For still another Oriental chicken curry, see Rijsttafel, page 166.

Preheat oven to 350°.

Cut into 10 pieces:

A fryer

Coat them with:

Seasoned Flour (II, 160)

Brown the chicken in:

¼ cup butter

Remove, drain and place in a casserole.

➧ Simmer gently in the pan drippings until golden:

¼ cup finely diced onions
½ cup finely diced green pepper
1 clove minced garlic
1½ teaspoons curry powder
½ teaspoon thyme

Add:

2 cups stewed tomatoes

and ➧ simmer until the pan is deglazed. Pour this sauce over the chicken and bake ➧ uncovered, for about 30 minutes or until the chicken is tender. During the last 5 minutes of cooking, add:

3 tablespoons currants

Serve with:

Steamed Rice

garnished with:

Toasted slivered almonds

CHICKEN OR TURKEY À LA CAMPAGNE [10 to 12]

Roast, uncovered, at 350° for 2 hours:

A 5-lb. chicken

Remove meat from bones. Use bones, skin and any vegetable parings in your stock pot. Sauté, page 296:

1 lb. small button mushrooms

Have ready:

1 cup cooked green peas
(3 cups canned artichoke hearts)

Prepare à la Parisienne, page 250:

1 cup each cooked carrots and white turnips

Arrange these ingredients in a 3-quart casserole, alternating layers of chicken and vegetables until all are used, with chicken on the top layer. Make the sauce by putting into a saucepan:

½ cup melted butter

Add and stir until smooth over low heat about:

½ cup flour

Continue to stir over low heat and add:

2 cups strong chicken stock
1 cup dry white wine
½ cup dry sherry
1 cup cream
½ cup chopped parsley

Season to taste with:

Salt
Monosodium glutamate
Freshly ground white pepper

Continue to cook over low heat for 10 minutes. Pour the sauce over the food in the casserole. Shake it well, so the sauce penetrates all layers. You may cover the top with:

Au Gratin, page 389

and heat for about 30 to 40 minutes.

If you ✻ freeze this mixture, cool uncovered before freezing. To reheat, remove from freezer 3 hours in advance. Bake, uncovered, at 350° for 1 to 1¼ hours.

TURKEY CASSEROLE MOLE

This Mexican recipe combines the native peppers and chocolate with a native bird. ➧ Please read About Deep-Fat Frying, pages 75–79.

Preheat deep fryer to 370°.

Cut up:

A 12- to 14-lb. turkey

Dip the pieces first in:

Milk

then in:

Flour

and put them on a rack to dry.

Prepare:

6 Chimayo peppers
6 broad peppers
3 chili peppers

If the chilies are dry, drop them into hot water for about 10 minutes before removing seeds and veins. Deep-fat fry all 3 kinds of peppers for about 5 minutes. Drain and reserve them.

Preheat oven to 325°.

When the turkey pieces have dried about 15 minutes, slide them gently into the 370° pepper-flavored fat and deep fry them for about 5 minutes. Drain the pieces and put them in a large casserole. Cover them with:

Turkey or game stock

➧ Cover the casserole and bake the turkey about 1 hour. Toast in a dry pan, over gentle heat:

1 tablespoon sesame seeds
½ cup pine nuts
½ cup blanched almonds

Grind together with the browned peppers:

2 tortillas
Cook:
3 minced cloves garlic
in
2 tablespoons oil
Add:
2 cups peeled, seeded tomatoes
1 bay leaf
½ teaspoon coriander
3 cloves
1 teaspoon cinnamon

Combine the above ingredients with the nuts and pepper mixture and ➧ simmer for 15 minutes. Put this thick sauce with about 2 cups of turkey stock over the cut up turkey and simmer, covered, for about 2½ hours more. This dish may be made a day or two before serving, but its most characteristic ingredient is reserved for the very last. Just before serving, add:
1 to 2 oz. grated chocolate
mixing it well into the heated sauce.

ROAST DOMESTIC DUCK [3]

Most duck on the American market is not descended from the wild native variety, but from a type bred in China where, of course, this bird is held in high esteem. As duck has both a heavy frame and a high fat content, allow 1⅓ to 1½ lbs. per serving.
Preheat oven to 450°.
Pick, clean and singe, page 568, if necessary:
A 5 to 6 lb. duckling
Rub it with:
(Garlic)
Place it on a rack in a roasting pan. Stuff with:
Celery stalks and sliced onions or a quartered apple, which you remove before serving, or with an apple stuffing, page 565

Put the bird in the oven and ➧ reduce the heat at once to 350°. Cook until tender, allowing about 20 minutes to the lb.
Make:
Pan Gravy, page 358
Serve with:
Polenta, page 156
or, if the duck has not been stuffed, with:
Crushed pineapple, Orange Sauce for Duck, page 365, Sauce Rouennaise, page 587, or any other suitable sauce

APRICOT HONEY GLAZED DUCK [2 to 3]

Preheat oven to 450°.
For those who like sweet with meat.
Prepare and roast as for Roast Duck:
3½ to 4 lb. domestic duck
Remove from oven just before done.
Make a thick glaze to pour over the duck. Combine and mix well:
1 cup apricot preserves
½ cup clover honey
1 tablespoon brandy
1 tablespoon cointreau or other orange-flavored liqueur
Coat the duck with this glaze and return to the oven for 10 to 15 minutes until the glaze caramelizes.

DUCKLING ROUENNAISE

Unless you choke your duck, pluck the down on its breast immediately afterward and cook it within 24 hours, you cannot lay claim to having produced an authentic Rouen duck. The first two steps assure the dark red flesh and the special flavor of this dish. If, as is likely, duck-strangling will bring you into local disrepute, you may waive the sturdy peasant preliminaries and serve a modified version, garnished with quotation marks. Clean:

A duckling

reserving the liver. Free it from the gall. Tuck the liver into the body cavity. Use a spit or rotisserie to roast the duck only 20 to 22 minutes in all. Only the breast and legs, if tender, are reserved and kept warm. The rest of the carcass is pressed, see About Salmi, page 592.
Meanwhile melt:

2 tablespoons butter

When the fat reaches the point of fragrance, add and simmer:

1 finely minced onion
¾ cup Burgundy

When the duckling is done, remove and crush the liver and add to the reduced wine mixture. Poach it gently in the wine with the drippings from the pressed carcass. Add several tablespoons of:

(Pâté de Foie, page 524)
Correct the seasoning

Slice the breast lengthwise into about 20 thin strips and put them in a chafing dish. Should you want to serve the legs, they must at this point be removed and grilled, as they are too raw without further cooking. We prefer to utilize them later in some other dish, so the breast can be served "à point."

➧ Cover the sliced meat quickly with the hot liver sauce, and serve ➧ immediately from the chafing dish at table.

ROAST DUCK BIGARADE

This famous recipe depends for its flavor on the Seville or bitter orange, known also as "bigarade."
Prepare:

Roast Duck, page 587

When it is done, remove it from the roasting pan and keep warm. Degrease the pan juices and deglaze the pan, as described in Orange Sauce for Duck or Goose, page 365, omitting the lemon juice. The curaçao is optional.

★ ROAST GOSLING OR GOOSE [6]

Economy-minded farmers raise geese because it takes only about ⅕ as much cereal feed to fatten them as it does for other fowl. Economy-minded housewives know that they get more protein value from turkey, page 567. There is, of course, the advantage of having goose liver, which is superior, page 524. Preroasting of goose or pricking to release fat is imperative, page 573. Unless goose is under ten months old, it is apt to be tough. Braise rather than roast any bird you suspect of being over this age limit.
Preheat oven to 450°.
Prepare for cooking, page 571:

An 8 lb. gosling or a
12 to 14 lb. goose

Fill the cavities with:

Apple, Prune, Chestnut or other dressing, page 560
(Sauerkraut made with wine)

Allow 1 cup dressing to each pound of bird. Place the goose on a rack in an uncovered pan, allowing 25 minutes to the pound. ➧ Reduce the heat at once to 350° and pour off the fat as it accumulates. Make:

Pan Gravy, page 358

Season it with:

Ginger and pearl onions

Or serve with:

Prunes in Wine (II, 108), Gooseberry Preserves (II, 581), Red Cabbage, page 277, Curried Fruit, or Chestnut Purée, page 283, and Cucumber Salad, page 43

BRAISED PARTS OF GOOSE OR GAENSEKLEIN

Rub with garlic:

Goose back, neck, gizzard, wings and heart

Let them stand for several hours. Place in a heavy pot. Add:

Mirepoix (II, 221)

Half cover with boiling water. Simmer ➧ closely covered, until nearly tender, about 1½ hours.

Correct the seasoning

and add:

(A pinch of ginger)

Cover and simmer the meat until tender, about ½ hour longer. Remove from the pot. Strain the stock, removing the grease. Make:

Pan Gravy, page 358

Pour it over the meat. Serve with:

Apples Stuffed with Sauerkraut

Also good with:

Chopped parsley
Dumplings and applesauce

POTTED GOOSE OR CONFIT D'OIE

Draw, pluck, singe, page 568, and cut as for fricassee:

A 10 lb. goose

Cut off, reserve and refrigerate the heavy fat. Salt the pieces of goose well on all sides. Place in an earthenware crock and weight with a nonresinous hardwood board. Cover and leave in a cool, dry place 6 to 8 days. When ready to cook, place the refrigerated fat in the bottom of a large heavy pan. Put on top of it:

A Bouquet Garni (II, 220)

Wipe the salt from the meat and put the pieces on the fat layer. ➧ Simmer slowly for about 2 to 4 hours. ➧ Be sure, as the fat melts, that there is enough to cover the meat completely. If not, add, as needed:

Lard

Use at once or store in a cool place, again, making sure that the meat is ➧ well covered with the fat. This dish will keep for months and can be served cold or reheated in the fat. If hot, a good accompaniment is:

Franconia Potatoes, page 314

which are cooked in the goose fat. Or use in:

Cassoulet, page 509

GUINEA FOWL, ROAST PIGEONS, SQUABS OR CORNISH HENS

[Allow 1 Small Bird Per Person]

Preheat oven to 450°.

Pick and draw:

Small guinea fowl, pigeons, squabs or Cornish hens

It is best to coat them with a Roux, page 355. They may be stuffed with:

Cooked Wild Rice, page 160, or Bread Dressing, etc., pages 560–566

or:

A Fruit Dressing, page 565

Bard, page 454, or brush with:

Melted butter

Dredge with flour. Place the birds, uncovered, in the oven. ➧ Reduce the heat at once to 350° and roast until tender, 45 minutes or more if stuffed, about 30 if not. They may be basted while cooking. If barded, remove the bacon and allow to brown. Make:

Pan Gravy, page 358 with mushrooms

or serve with:

Bar le Duc Jam (II, 576)

BREASTS OF GUINEA HEN

[Allow 1 Breast per Person]

Preheat oven to 425°.

Bard, page 454, each:

Breast of guinea hen

Put in oven and ➧ reduce the

heat at once to 350°. Baste the breasts frequently. Cook them for about 45 minutes or until they are tender. Serve "sous cloche," or under a glass bell, with:

Colbert Butter, page 384

POTTED PIGEONS OR SQUABS [6]

Preheat oven to 350°.
Cut into pieces or leave whole:
4 large pigeons or 6 squabs
Dredge them with:
Seasoned Flour (II, 160)
Melt:
¼ cup butter
Sauté the birds slowly in the butter until they are just seared. Place them in a casserole. Add to the fat in the pan:
¼ chopped onion
1 diced carrot
¼ cup chopped celery
Stir these ingredients for about 3 minutes. Add:
1 cup boiling chicken stock or water
Pour this over the birds. Cover them closely. Roast them until they are tender, about 45 to 60 minutes. You may add for the last ½ hour:
1 cup sliced mushrooms
Do not permit the birds to become dry. If they do, add more stock or water. Make:
Pan Gravy, page 358
to which you may add:
Cultured sour or sweet cream
(Chopped olives)
Serve the squabs in a border of:
Rice
Sprinkle them with:
Chopped parsley or chives

BROILED PIGEONS OR SQUABS

Preheat broiler.
Pick, then split down the back and remove entrails from:
Squabs
Flatten them. You may cut out the back bone with shears. Put them on a greased broiler, skin side up. Brush well with:
Melted butter
Place the birds 4 inches from the heat. Broil from 15 to 30 minutes, turning once. Season when you turn them with:
Salt and paprika
Serve on:
Buttered toast
Pour the drippings over them.
Good with:
Chopped parsley
Cranberry jelly
Crusty Spoon Bread (II, 279)

ABOUT WILD BIRDS

The opening of the season for grouse—that very British bird which dwells in and feeds on heather—stirs up a degree of knowledgeable excitement equalled only by a vendange in the Côte d'Or. All over Southern Europe, each autumn, small birds, spicy with berries, are netted by the hundreds. And along the shores of Chesapeake Bay, the canvasback duck—which in October feeds on the wild celery of the shoreline—is preferred above all others.

We lived for years under one of the major flyways of the world and looked forward to the days when the males in our family sought out the bird-blinds in the surrounding marshes and rich fields. On their return, dinner parties were held in profusion. The children usually clamored for the plump little quail, leaving the rare, well-hung ducks to their more sophisticated elders.

To a large extent, proper care, immediately after shooting, determines the ultimate excellence of flavor in wild birds. While the bird is still warm, the neck is split and the carcass bled. To keep the blood for use in sauces, see page 357. Check the neck for any undigested food and remove.

Some birds—snipe, woodcock and plover—are cooked with the trail still inside, see page 598. Quail and a few other smaller birds should be plucked, drawn and cooked within 24 hours of killing. But do not pluck or draw any wild fowl until you are ready to cook it, since the added surface exposure of the carcass to air will induce spoilage before the necessary tenderization can be accomplished.

To tenderize and improve flavor, it is necessary to hang many wild birds, specifically partridge, prairie fowl, ducks and plover, grouse and hazel hen—unless they are to be roasted. How long to hang depends first on age. Old birds can be held longer than young ones. A second consideration is the weather. In muggy periods ripening is accelerated. The third—and perhaps the most important—is personal preference. Some hunters go to extremes, holding a bird until the legs stiffen, even until head and body part company. A more moderate and acceptable state of maturity is reached when the feathers just above the tail can be drawn out easily or when a slight bluish green tinge appears on the thin skin of the abdomen. However long birds are to be hung ➧ suspend them, undrawn, by the feet ➧ in a cool, dry, airy place. If the weather is very warm, dust the feathers with charcoal. In any season, the birds should be protected with cheesecloth or screening.

➧ Dry pluck all fowl. Remember that this is easier to do if the bird is chilled. Scalding or soaking preparatory to plucking breaks down the fatty tissues in the skin too rapidly if they are subsequently to be held for even a short time or are to be frozen. ➧ To pluck, see page 588.

Before cooking, look the birds over carefully and remove any shot with a pointed utensil. Cut out meat that has discolored near the shot or any dog-damaged areas. Remove the oil sac, page 572. After plucking, wild fowl should never be washed before cooking, merely wiped with a damp cloth. Safe exceptions are fish-feeding ducks which, if they must be used, should be parblanched for ½ hour before cooking.

➧ Singe all fowl just before cooking, including those which have been frozen. ➧ All game should be at 70° before timing for cooking. The interior of the bird may first be salted or rinsed with 2 tablespoons of brandy or sherry. Should it be necessary to counteract a too gamey taste, we suggest cooking with sauerkraut or using a marinade. Never try to soak out the taste with water. If the bird is to be cooked unstuffed, the placement in it of an apple, an onion, a carrot, parsley, a few celery stalks or some juniper berries helps attract off-flavors. These fillers are, of course, discarded before serving.

➧ Age determines how wild fowl shall be cooked. To judge age refer to the individual recipes. If you are at all doubtful that a bird is young or prime, do not hesitate ➧ to use a moist heat method of cooking, page 81. Very old birds are fit only for the stock or soup pot or for making hash, forcemeat and sauces.

On many occasions only the breasts of wild fowl are served, as the legs are often tough and full of tendons. If you use the legs, remove the tendons, see page 570. Otherwise, simmer the legs with the wings, necks and giblets for game stock. This is most useful, for in no cooking is less gravy naturally produced as in that of game. Therefore, it is doubly important to increase the stock of the game you are cooking, in order to bring up the flavor of a sauce or aspic. If game stock is not available, veal is the most sympathetic substitute.

Before roasting or marinating wild fowl, break down the breast bone by a blow with the flat side of a cleaver. This not only makes carving easier, but reduces the amount of marinade needed. To prepare a wild fowl for broiling, split the back and spread the breasts flat, using poultry shears for small birds.

Whether roasted or broiled, wild birds are, without exception, leaner than domestic varieties and should usually be barded, page 454. Sometimes a flour and butter paste is used to coat them before the barding is applied. The barding may be removed halfway through the cooking process but, if so, basting with butter or pan drippings should continue until the bird is taken from the heat. If a paste has not been applied you may, after the removal of the barding, want to dust the bird with flour to hasten its browning.

➧ Most light-fleshed wild fowl is cooked well done and most dark fowl is cooked "vert-cuit" or "saignant," that is roasted brown on the outside under high heat, but still rare and running with juice and blood within. With these differences in mind, you can cook most wild fowl by the recipes suggested for chicken. pages 574 to 586, but suggestions are given in individual game recipes for those combinations which are classic with game.

Let us also recommend, as sympathetic accompaniments, a dressing of chestnuts or wild rice; a salad of chicory or cress; a dish of gooseberry or quince conserve; a sour cream or wine sauce—not too powerfully seasoned.

If you have more game than you can use immediately, you may consider freezing (II, 562), or smoking (II, 545). ➧ To cook smoked game, parsteam it (II, 545) a few minutes to remove excess salt. Then cook as for ham.

ABOUT SALMI OF WILD BIRDS

A true salmi has two major characteristics. The meat is roasted—barely so, if the game is dark. And the meat from the breasts and from the legs, if they are choice, is sliced and put to one side and kept warm. Preparation is concluded at table, much as in Duck Rouennaise, page 587, where the skin and the chopped carcass are pressed in a duck press. The pressed juices are combined with the flambéed livers, the sauce reduced with a Mirepoix and then strained. Reinforce the sauce by a Demi-glaze Sauce, page 365, or Sauce Espagnole, page 365, based on the same kind of game as that being served. If the game is a waterbird, the skin may be too oily to use. Salmis may also be enriched with mushrooms or truffles. The meat is just heated through at table in a chafing dish with this very rich sauce, given a swirl of butter, page 357, and served at once.

Obviously, a classic salmi, fully accoutered, is only for the skilled cook whose husband is a Nimrod and has presented her with more than a single bird. If she is less well endowed, she will have to base her sauce on the backs, wings and necks of the bird that is being presented and eke out her Espagnole Sauce with veal stock. Needless to say, the dish is rarely presented in its original form. And the salmis that appear on menus are usually made from reheated meat, with sauces which have been previously confected. They can still be delicious, especially if care is taken ➧ not to boil the sauce and thereby toughen the meat. Another simpler way to serve precooked game is to make up a mixture similar to Pheasant in Game Sauce, page 595, which lends itself even to ✻ freezing.

MARINATED WILD BIRDS [2]

➧ Please read About Wild Birds, page 590. Clean and disjoint a:

Pheasant, partridge or grouse

Place in a casserole and cover with a marinade of:

1 small quartered onion
1 small bay leaf
1 clove garlic
2 cups port wine
1½ teaspoons salt
½ teaspoon pepper

Be sure the wine covers the pieces. Let stand in the refrigerator for 3 days. Remove the bird from the marinade, dry with a towel. Save the marinade. Preheat oven to 375°.
Put:

2 tablespoons butter

in a casserole. Brown and roast the pieces for about 45 minutes, turning several times. Strain the marinade and pour it over the pieces. Return to the oven for another 30 minutes or until tender. Take the pieces from the casserole. Keep warm. Reduce the sauce and:

Correct the seasoning

Serve with:

Wild rice or noodles

ABOUT WILD DUCKS

Flavor depends so much on the way ducks have been feeding. The shallow water types may have been feeding in nearby grain fields and may be very succulent. These include mallard, black duck, pintail, baldpate, gadwall and teal. The deep-water or sea ducks thrive on aquatic vegetation. They include canvasback, redhead, the golden eyes, scaup and ring neck. The mergansers or fish eaters should be used only in emergencies.

Wild ducks are usually not stuffed, but their insides may be greased to help retain juices. If too gamey, they may be rubbed with ginger or lemon. Also celery, grapes or sliced apple in the cavity help minimize a too pronounced taste. Discard before serving.

Cooking times vary with types. They may be as long as 20 minutes for canvasback or just 12 minutes for teal.

ROAST WILD DUCK [4]

To draw, pluck, singe and truss ➧ please read About Wild Birds, page 590. This method seems to be the hunter's ideal. The juices are red and flow freely when the duck is carved.
Preheat oven to 500°.
Prepare:

2 wild ducks

Have them at room temperature. Dry them thoroughly inside and out. Rub the insides with:

Butter

Fill the cavities loosely with:

A few skinned onions or peeled, cored and chopped apples or drained sauerkraut

Bard, page 454. Place the ducks on a rack in a roasting pan. ➧

Reduce heat to 350° and roast, uncovered, for 18 to 20 minutes. Degrease the drippings, and add:

Wine and stock

Reduce, then remove from heat and add:

Cultured sour cream

Reheat, but ➧ do not boil. Serve at once with:

Braised Celery, page 282

▤ BROILED OR BARBECUED WILD DUCK

Preheat broiler.

A good way to cook wild duck and an easy fashion of serving it is to split it down the back, clean it well and wipe until dry. Rub with:

(Garlic)

Spread with:

Unsalted butter

Season with:

Paprika

Broil about 4 inches under the broiler or 4 inches above charcoal. Baste frequently with:

An unsalted fat or oil and wine

Cook until tender. Remove to a hot platter.

Correct the seasoning

Make a sauce with the drippings, page 358. Serve with:

Poached Oranges or Kumquats (II, 101)

Fried hominy is a well-known accompaniment to wild ducks. So are grilled sweet potatoes or apples stuffed with sweet potatoes.

BRAISED WILD DUCK

➧ To draw, pluck, singe and truss:

A wild duck

please read About Wild Birds, page 590. Melt in a heavy casserole:

4 tablespoons butter

When it reaches the point of fragrance, put in the duck and brown on all sides. Add, when browned:

1 leek—white part only or 6 button onions
4 tender turnips
1 Bouquet Garni (II, 220)

➧ Simmer, covered, 25 to 35 minutes or until the duck is tender. Degrease the drippings and garnish the casserole with:

Cooked tender green peas

Serve at once.

ABOUT PHEASANT

➧ Please read About Wild Birds, page 590. We hope your pheasant is young, with a flexible breast bone, grey legs and a pointed, large terminal feather in its wings. If it is a cock, it should have rounded, not sharp or long, spurs. Then you may roast or broil it even without hanging. Barding is advisable.

Otherwise, to give it both flavor and tenderness, about a 3 day hanging period is advised, during which the color of the breast will change somewhat and there will be a slight odor.

An old bird should be barded and either braised or used in a moist heat recipe, see page 81.

ROAST PHEASANT [3]

Preheat oven to 400°.

➧ Please read About Wild Birds, page 590, and About Pheasant, above.

Bard, page 454:

A young pheasant

You may stuff it with:

A Chestnut and Sausage Dressing

Place in oven. ➧ Reduce heat at once to 350°. Cook about 25 minutes to the lb. or until tender. If unstuffed, serve with:

Fried Croutons, page 390, Bread Sauce, page 364, Currant Jelly and

Braised Celery or Rice Pilaf, page 166, and Gooseberry Preserves (II, 581)

or, classically, with:

Sauce Smitane, page 364

BRAISED PHEASANT

This recipe comes from a hunting fan:

➧ Please read About Wild Birds, page 590, and About Pheasant, page 594.

Preheat oven to 400°.

Prepare:

A pheasant

Pound:

A thin slice salt pork

Separate the skin from the breast flesh of the pheasant and insert the salt pork. Place in the body cavity the pheasant liver and:

A small peeled tangerine

Lace the opening tightly. Truss the pheasant. Melt in a heavy pan:

¼ cup lard

Brown the pheasant, turning it and basting until it is golden all over. Place in a casserole. Add and turn in the fat:

12 sliced mushroom caps

Pour these over the pheasant. Melt in a saucepan:

¼ cup butter

Stir in, cook, but do not permit to brown:

3 shallots or 1 small minced onion
2 teaspoons flour

Stir in gradually:

¼ to ⅓ cup Marsala or Madeira
½ teaspoon salt and freshly ground pepper

Pour this into the casserole. Our correspondent adds a sprig of fresh fennel and 2 crushed juniper berries. ➧ Cover the casserole and bake the pheasant for about ½ hour. Serve it from the casserole with:

Fried hominy and currant jelly
A green salad

✱ PHEASANT IN GAME SAUCE [10 to 12]

Preheat oven to 400°.

Prepare for roasting:

5 or 6 pheasants

Bard, page 454, with:

Bacon or salt pork

Fill the cavity, if you wish to reduce the game taste, with:

Apple or onion slices

Discard them after birds are roasted. Roast at 400° for 20 minutes. Remove meat from bones. Keep the meat in as large pieces as possible. Cook for 2 hours or until reduced about ⅓, a stock made from the bones, skins, drippings and barding, using:

2 large chopped onions
2 cloves garlic
2 bay leaves
1 tablespoon black peppercorns
1 teaspoon thyme
1 small pinch rosemary
1 cup chopped parsley
(6 juniper berries)
¼ lb. ham trimmings
1 quart dry red wine
2 quarts water or chicken stock
Stems from 2 lbs. mushrooms
3 fresh tomatoes

Strain the stock and add it to:

¾ cup Cream Sauce, page 359

Add to this sauce:

Caps of 2 lbs. mushrooms
¾ cup red wine

Simmer about 25 minutes.

Correct the seasoning

Reduce by ⅓, strain and add:

¼ cup cognac

Simmer another 10 minutes. Arrange meat in 3-quart casserole. You may put it on a bed of:

(Cooked wild rice)

Pour sauce over it. To serve, reheat, uncovered, in a 350° oven, 45 to 55 minutes. If frozen, thaw and bring to room temperature before reheating.

PHEASANT SMITANE [3]

Bard, page 454:

A 3½ to 4 pound pheasant

with:

Sliced salt pork or bacon

Brown the pheasant in:

Butter

in a heavy pan. Then place in a deep casserole with the drippings. Cover tightly and let simmer over low heat until tender, about 45 minutes. Add:

4 cups diced tart apples
2 tablespoons cognac or Calvados
2 cups cultured sour cream
Correct the seasoning

and cook over low heat until the apples are tender. ➧ Do not boil. Serve with:

Wild rice, page 160

ABOUT PARTRIDGE

Beware of an old bird, which must be braised or marinated, even if it is hung to the maximum of seven days. You will recognize an old bird in its feathers—by a conspicuous red ring on the eye circle, its yellow beak, its dark legs and, in a restaurant, by the French term "perdrix." For, by some strange convention, old partridges—regardless of sex—are ungraciously designated as female. If a partridge is under six months old, it still has its pointed first-flight feather and, on the menu, is gallantly referred to as perdreau or male—sex discrimination again actually being ignored. The red-legged French partridges are larger and not considered as delicate as the English. There is some confusion in America about the very name of partridge. No true partridge is native, but the name is given in the north to the ruffed grouse and in the south to quail.

If the bird is fresh, it has a rigid vent. ➧ A true partridge can be cooked by any recipe for chicken if larded; or, if barded, as for pheasant. But, if it is old, a longer cooking period may be necessary. It may be served in a Salmi, page 592, as for duck. Some people like it braised with Sauerkraut, page 278, allowing 2 lbs. of the sauerkraut to three 3-lb. birds. Add the sauerkraut the last ½ hour of cooking. Others shudder at so strongly flavored an accompaniment. A more delicate one is Braised Endive, page 292—and stuff it before cooking with marrow. Or wrap the partridge in grape leaves, simmer it in wine and stock for 35 minutes. Then roast it in a 350° oven for 25 minutes. Allow 1 lb. per person. Make Pan Gravy, page 358, and serve the partridge with Boiled New Potatoes, page 310, and water cress.

GROUSE, PTARMIGAN OR PRAIRIE CHICKEN

[Allow 1 lb. per Person]

Preheat oven to 300°.

Young grouse which feeds on the tender shoots of the heather is one of the more coveted of all game. To test for youth, hold the bird aloft by the lower mandible. If this breaks, failing to support the weight of the bird, you have a young specimen. Roast or broil if young. Braise if old. The same treatments apply to Canadian Grouse or Black Game, also known as Black Grouse or Coq de Bruyère. Resinous in flavor, this is not quite as good as true grouse. However, it is cooked in the same way.

Prepare for cooking as you would a chicken:

Young grouse

You may lard the breast, page 453, with thin strips of:

Salt pork

or bard it, page 454. You may stuff it with:

A small apple, a skinned onion or ribs of celery

Grouse is served rare, to a pale pink tone. Allow about 30 to 45 minutes cooking in all. Baste it frequently with:

Melted butter or drippings

Remove the bacon. Brush the bird with:

Butter

Dredge it lightly with:

Flour

Place it in a hot 500° oven, until brown. Make:

Pan Gravy, page 358

Serve with:

Rowanberries or Cranberry Sauce

BROILED GROUSE

The bird must be young, see above. Bard, page 454, and broil only the:

Breast of young grouse

Prepare it by splitting down the back and flattening the breast without separating it. Brush with:

Cooking oil

Broil about 7 minutes to each side, heating the bony side first. It is classic to serve it with:

Bread Sauce, page 364, or Sauce Périgueux, page 367

WILD GOOSE AND WILD TURKEY

[1 lb. per Person]

If you talk to someone who has eaten only an old goose—and they do live to a great old age—he will claim it is abominable. Indeed, these birds are worth bothering with only if they are less than a year old. Hang from 24 hours to a week and cook with moist heat, page 81, whether the goose is old or young. Weights fluctuate, depending on variety and age, from about 4 to 9 lbs.

➧ To draw, pluck, singe and truss, see pages 568–572.

For young goose and wild turkey proceed as for turkey, page 574, or cut as for fricassee, page 568:

A 5 to 6 lb. wild goose

In a heavy casserole heat to the point of fragrance:

⅓ cup butter
1½ cups small, white, whole onions

Add:

¼ lb. finely diced salt pork

and continue to cook until onions are golden. Lift out onions and pork and discard. In the remaining fat, brown the cut up bird. Add:

Juice of ½ lemon
½ teaspoon allspice
(A few slivers gingerroot)

➧ Simmer, covered, about 30 minutes. Stir if necessary. Add:

2 cups dry red wine

➧ Simmer, covered, at least 45 minutes longer or until tender. Thicken the pan gravy slightly with:

Toasted dry bread crumbs

Serve with:

Noodles
Spiced apricots or crabapples

POTTED WILD FOWL

[Allow 1 lb. per Person]

A good way to preserve any extra wild fowl.

➧ Please read about Wild Goose, above.

Draw, pluck, singe and cut for fricassee:

A young wild goose or other wild fowl

Prepare as for:

Potted Goose, page 589

Serve either hot or cold.

HAZEL HEN

[Allow 1 lb. per Person]

Since this bird is quite resinous, it is best to poach it first in milk for 15 minutes. Bone and grill for about 12 minutes in all.

ABOUT SMALL GAME BIRDS

Birds here discussed are of many kinds: ortolans, figpickers, coot, doves, woodcock, snipe, rails, curlew, plover, quail, larks, reed birds, thrush, moorhen and gallinule. They are bracketed on the basis of similar treatment and the fact that they are served one or more to a person. ➧ Small birds are usually used as fresh as possible, although they remain edible as long as the legs are flexible. Quail, which is about the largest discussed here, should not be hung longer than 24 hours. ➧ All small birds should be dry plucked. In fact, some, like snipe, plover, ring dove and woodcock may be cooked undrawn, although the eyes and crop are discarded before roasting. To use the entrails after cooking, sieve or chop the intestines and flambé them, page 80, briefly, in cognac. Mix with pan drippings and spread on a crouton or over the bird as a glaze before serving. Or, if you draw the bird before cooking, reserve the intestines, chop them, sauté them briefly in butter, then proceed as above.

Small birds should be barded, page 88, or you may wrap them first in fig or grape leaves. All these birds lend themselves to roasting and skewering or broiling from 3 to 10 minutes. Blackbirds and crows, if eaten as a matter of necessity, must be parblanched first, page 88.

All these small birds produce very little pan dripping. Pour what there is on a Crouton, page 390, or a piece of crisp scrapple. Or combine the drippings with a Demiglaze Sauce and wine or lemon, page 365, with Smitane Sauce or Sauce Veneur or use any recipe for braised chicken—allowing in the timing for difference in size. Any peculiarities or classic combinations are listed in individual recipes.

ROASTED SMALL GAME BIRDS

➧ Please read About Small Birds, above.

Preheat oven to 450°.

Bard, page 454:

6 small birds

It is not necessary to stuff them, although a few peeled grapes or bits of celery or parsley may be tucked inside and discarded later. Place in the pan:

1 tablespoon butter

Bake the birds for about 5 minutes ➧ reduce the heat to 350° and bake them from 5 to 15 minutes longer, according to their size.

Quail—unstuffed 10 to 15 minutes

—stuffed 15 to 18 minutes

Woodcock 8 to 10 minutes

BROILED SMALL GAME BIRDS

Preheat broiler.

Bard, page 454:

6 small game birds

Place them on a broiler. Cook them from 12 to 20 minutes, according to size. Turn frequently. The barding may be removed toward the end of the cooking period and the birds browned briefly by further broiling. Add the juice of:

1 lemon

to:

Stock or wine

if there is an insufficient amount of drippings.

Correct the seasoning

Serve the birds on:

Fried toast

Pour the gravy over them. Garnish them with:

Parsley

Permit the sauce to soak into the toast.

BRAISED SMALL GAME BIRDS

➧ Please read About Small Game Birds, page 598.

Preheat oven to 350°.

Prepare for cooking:

6 birds

Melt in a saucepan:

2 tablespoons butter

Add and sauté for 1 minute:

A Mirepoix (II, 221)

Add the birds and sauté them until they are lightly browned. Add:

½ cup boiling stock or wine

Cover the birds with a poaching paper, page 83, and bake them for 15 to 20 minutes. Make:

Pan Gravy, page 358

Add to the gravy:

(2 tablespoons lemon juice or cultured sour cream or brandy)

Serve on:

Croutons, page 390

garnished with:

Parsley

⊟ SKEWERED SMALL BIRDS

➧ Please read About Small Game Birds, page 598.

Wrap in buttered grape or fig leaves:

Small birds

and then bard in very thin slices of:

Salt pork

Roast skewered over coals 10 to 15 minutes. To finish for serving, you may remove the barding, roll the birds in bread crumbs, baste with drippings and heat in a moderate oven 5 minutes longer.

DOVE OR WOOD PIGEONS [1 to 2]

➧ Please read About Small Game Birds, page 598.

A dark meat with a fine flavor. The brain may be mixed with the trail. To prepare these parts, see page 598. Unless the birds are very young, prepare as for:

Braised Small Game Birds, this page

Serve the sauce garnished with:

Almond stuffed olives

or with a compote of:

Red Sour Cherries (II, 88)

QUAIL

[1 per Person]

Sometimes called partridge in our deep South. ➧ Please read About Small Game Birds, page 598. This bird has a delicious white meat. If the fat of the bird is hard rather than firm before cooking, the flesh will be tough and must be prepared by a moist heat method. If the bird is young, roast or broil.

➧ Never overcook. Serve with:

Quince preserves and curried rice or water cress and lemon wedges

or serve with:

Sauce Smitane, page 364, and green grapes or a baked pear, the core stuffed with a pimiento

If you have broiled the quail, brush it with:

(Anchovy Butter, page 384)

SNIPE OR WOODCOCK

[Allow 1 to 2 Birds per Person]

Known in France as bécassine and bécasse, respectively, these birds are highly prized by some epicures, in the fall, when they are fat and meaty. But de Pomiane claims that it takes man's snobbishness to elevate to one of life's great moments the woodcock flambé, with its long beak, meager body and prominent eyes. He claims that even dogs scorn this status symbol and that the entrail-soaked crouton alone deserves attention.

◆ Please read About Small Game Birds, page 598.

Prepare and cook as for:

Small Game Birds, page 598

or use the recipe for Grouse, page 596. You may use the trail, see page 598. Skin the head, but leave it on. Remove the eyes and crop. Bring the long, curved beak down to pierce and hold the legs in place. Bard, page 454, and roast 10 to 15 minutes.

INDEX

"Knowledge," said Dr. Johnson, "is of two kinds. We know a subject as our own, or we know where we can find information on it." Below we put into your hands the second kind of knowledge—a kitchen-door key which will help to open up the first.

If you want information on a certain food you will find that the initial listing is often an "About"; giving characteristics, peculiarities of handling, tests for doneness, storage needs and serving quantities. The titles which follow usually indicate how that particular food may be cooked: Sweetbreads, braised, or Fish, broiled.

In using the Index look for a noun rather than an adjective: Torte, almond, not Almond Torte: unless the modifying term is a foreign one, in which case it will be listed and lead you to an explanation. Foreign terms are frequently translated in an alternate title, thus: Pickled Fish or Escabèche, revealing a process; or, as in Senegalese or Chicken Curry Soup, showing the ingredients mainly responsible for the term. Or the recipe itself will clear your doubts—for "à la mode" used with a savory food like beef will describe a stew, whereas with a sweet one, like pie or cake, it will indicate the expected scoop of ice cream. Since cooking terms, both foreign and domestic, are dealt with at the point of use, as described above, we have dispensed with a separate glossary.

Remember, too, that the book as a whole divides into three sections: The Foods We Eat, The Foods We Heat and the Foods We Keep, with Know Your Ingredients at the center of things. And that many "convenience" recipes are grouped under Lunch, Brunch and Supper Dishes. Within chapters, too, initial text or recipes often cover basic methods of preparation, and are followed, as in Fruits, Fish and Vegetables by alphabetical listings of varieties—from Apples to Rhubarb, Carp to Whale, Artichokes to Water Chestnuts. Under Meats you will find in the Index general comments and processes, with further references to Beef, Veal, Lamb, Pork, Ham, Ground and Variety Meats and Game. In this chapter a further differentiation is made between those cuts cooked by dry heat—often a quick process—and those cooked by moist heat which, to be effective, is always slower. Note, too, that in the listings below, illustrations can be found immediately by looking up the boldfaced numerals.

As you familiarize yourself with the "Joy" you will need the Index less and less and will become, in Dr. Johnson's fullest sense, a know-it-all. Meanwhile, happy hunting!